THE SWEEP OF AMERICAN HISTORY

CHAPTER 1

THE EUROPEAN BACKGROUND

Two of the most common questions that the historian asks of the past are: How did an event happen? Why did an event happen? Of these two questions the "How" of the past is generally the easier to answer. If H. Trevor Roper had set out to answer the question "How was the New World discovered?" he would have given us an account of the southern voyages of the Portuguese as they pushed back the frontiers of geographic knowledge; he would have followed this with the epic of Columbus's several voyages, and perhaps would have concluded with a description of Magellan's voyage around the world. This account would be rich in detail, stirring in excitement, and historically complex when dealing with the values and motives involved in the decision-making procedures of the several courts.

As enjoyable to read and as valuable to know as this might be, it is not what the author set about doing. Hugh Trevor-Roper, instead, has asked the question: "Why did Europe turn West?" This different question creates a different kind of history. We now are led into a series of complex variables such as the nature of public health, the conditions of land tenure, the economic systems of the several countries, the political institutions of the time, and a host of other factors. Moreover, these factors are not only more complicated in and of themselves but also

1

interact with each other in varying degrees. It is not surprising that the most serious historical controversies involve "Why" questions.

In reading this essay, bear in mind the continuing relationship of Europe to the New World. Also ask: If the New World was discovered by the Norsemen in the eleventh century, why did the discovery not "take" until Columbus rediscovered it in the fifteenth century? Is the answer to this question to be found in the changes in the nature of European society? Or is there another explanation?

For more detailed descriptions of Western Europe on the eve of discovery, see Edward P. Cheyney, *The Dawn of a New Era, 1250–1453** (1936), and Myron P. Gilmore, *The World of Humanism, 1453–1517** (1952). For a comprehensive discussion of probable Norse discoveries, R. A. Skelton, Thomas E. Marston, and George D. Painter's book, *The Vinland Map and the Tartar Relation* (1965), is indispensable. *The Vinland Map* and several other works on the same topic are critically reviewed by J. H. Parry in *Perspectives in American History,** Vol. I (1967).

* Available in a paperback edition.

EUROPE TURNS WEST
HUGH TREVOR-ROPER

If we were to take a date to represent the highest point of the European Middle Ages, I suppose that date would be about 1250. Up to that date we see—from about 1050 onwards—only advance. There is growth of population, agricultural revolution, technological advance. The frontiers of Christendom are pushed forward in all directions; new worlds are discovered, and also old; there is a sophistication of manners, a revival of letters. New institutions are founded, both lay and spiritual: on the one hand towns and universities, on the other new orders of improving monks and missionary friars. And meanwhile, within Europe, art and literature are reviving: barbarian Europe has been captured by its more cultivated victims, just as barbarian Rome had been fourteen centuries ago.

However, as history constantly reminds us,

> 'everything that grows
> holds in perfection but a little moment',

and from about 1300 the decline is obvious. Already in the middle of the thirteenth century the territorial expansion had been halted. In 1242 the eastward advance of the Teutonic Knights had been held up by the ruler of the Russian Slavs, Alexander Nevsky. . . . Directly or indirectly, feudalism was yielding to finance. In 1311, nine years after the feudal knights of France had gone down before the Flemish townsmen at Courtrai, a generation before they would go down before the English bowmen at Crécy, the Frankish chivalry of Greece was mown down on the banks of the river Cephisus by the plebian foot-soldiers of the Catalan company. . . .

But if the fourteenth century saw the downfall of European chivalry, it was not easy going for the bankers either. Indeed, in the years from 1300 to 1350 the heavyweight horsemen of the financial world suffered

SOURCE. From *The Rise of Christian Europe* by Hugh Trevor-Roper, pp. 161–164, 166, 168–170, and 172–191. Copyright 1965 by Thames and Hudson. Reprinted by permission of Harcourt, Brace & World, Inc., Thames and Hudson International, Ltd., and the author.

their Courtrai, their Cephisus, their Crécy too. It was half a century of successive bankruptcies. . . .

The financial crisis of the fourteenth century, like that of the early seventeenth century, or that of the nineteen-twenties, was not self-contained. It was part of a general crisis, a crisis of society, and—like those later crises—it marked the end of an age: the great divide between the age of expansion and the age of contraction, the earlier and the later Middle Ages. Moreover, it was accompanied by another, even greater disaster. The year after the collapse of its feudal and financial pillars, Europe, already weakened by a series of famines, was visited by a more general calamity: the Black Death.

The Black Death was bubonic plague, carried by black rats—or rather, by a flea parasitic on black rats—and spread, in favourable circumstances, in crowded, dirty, medieval towns. Once before it had come to Europe. In the sixth century, in the reign of Justinian, corn-ships had brought it to Constantinople, causing, in Gibbon's words, 'a visible decrease of the human species, which has never been repaired in some of the fairest countries of the globe'. In the words of one great authority on the subject, this terrible plague of Justinian's time and the Black Death of the fourteenth century 'are the two greatest pestilences in recorded history; each has no parallel except in the other'. At least they had no parallel when those words were written, in 1890. The earlier plague had come from Egypt, from Pelusium, the great port of entry for the goods of Asia. Perhaps the plague had been brought from Asia too. The Black Death came from Crimean Tartary, and it was from the Genoese station of Caffa in the Crimea, which had suffered a three years' siege by the Tartars, that Genoese ships brought it to Genoa in the spring of 1347. It also came indirectly through Constantinople, which was similarly infected from the Crimea. . . .

The Black Death raged at its worst for three years; but even when the worst was over it still lingered in the soil of Europe. There were five severe secondary outbreaks before 1400. Nor did they end with the century. Though it gradually contracted into the great cities, the plague was domesticated in Europe till the mid-seventeenth century. The Great Plague of London in 1665 was its last English, the plague of Marseilles in 1720 its last European, eruption. After that, conditions changed. In 1727 came a new invasion from the Russian steppes. Brown rats swarmed over the Volga, displacing the black rat, with its parasites and its plague.

The immediate consequences of this terrible mortality, which carried off in some places half, in general perhaps a third, of the population, were enormous. Everywhere there was a shortage of labour. Everywhere the established classes, the beneficiaries of past expansion, sought to conserve their now threatened gains by a policy of artificial reaction. To do so they devised new legislation, new machinery, even new myths. And everywhere, equally, there was resistance. In the expanding world of the twelfth and thirteenth centuries there had been room for all and a certain unity of social classes could be preserved. Landlords had granted freedom to their serfs because the serfs had acquired money from agriculture and could buy it, or because, if it were not granted, they might run away to the freedom of the new cities. In the cities, society had been fluid: apprentices had risen to be masters and the city offices had passed from old families to new. But in the contracting world of the fourteenth and fifteenth centuries there was less room; and the lord and peasant in the country, great merchant and small—or merchant and craftsman—in the town fought, the one to retain, the other to acquire his share of the dwindling stock of wealth or power.

The struggles did not all go the same way. In England, immediately after the Black Death, the landlords passed the Statute of Labourers, designed to peg agricultural wages at or near the rates obtaining before the plague. In France, a royal ordinance did the same. In Spain, similar regulations were issued by the *cortes* or Estates for the various regions. But ultimately, in most of these western countries, the shortage of labour gave advantages to labour, and peasants were able to buy their freedom. In eastern Europe, on the other hand, the landlords enforced their will. In the face of Slav pressure, they found means, little by little, to reimpose serfdom, so that by the sixteenth century, when the free peasantry of England boasted of their superiority to the wooden shoes and canvas breeches of the less free peasants of France, the French peasants could look with equal disdain at the serfs of Germany, sent out to gather snails and strawberries for their despotic masters. In each country the same causes led to the same 'landlord reaction'; but the outcome was different. Even in Spain there were differences between Catalonia, where the new legislation was afterwards revoked, and Castile where it was not. The same causes do not necessarily produce the same results in history; or at least, to do so, they require the same social context. Failing that context, the results may even be opposite.

Meanwhile, the towns too were in crisis. In the late fourteenth and the fifteenth centuries nearly all the established towns of Europe suffered eclipse. With the decline of population and of trade, their wealth and confidence sagged, and within them there were new struggles for privilege and power. To resolve these struggles, different factions sometimes appealed to neighbouring princes, and so the civil struggles of the towns became involved—often disastrously involved—in the foreign wars of kings. Sometimes, in their despair, the towns cannibalized their neighbours, as Florence strengthened itself by swallowing up Arezzo and Pisa, and Augsburg by squeezing out Memmingen and Ulm. And many towns, in the precariousness of trade, turned themselves into landlords. Land might bring its troubles but they were often less than the troubles of foreign trade. So the towns too became investors in the 'landlord reaction'. We see it happening in Barcelona where the city merchants switch their capital from overseas commerce to agricultural improvement at home. We see it most clearly in Venice. While the great Venetian merchants clung to their dwindling commercial empire in the Aegean sea, the lesser, weaker merchants supported a policy of conquering a *terra firma* on the mainland. In 1381 there was a general economic collapse of the merchant houses in Barcelona, followed, in the fifteenth century, by civil war. In the same fifteenth century Venice, which had hitherto looked seawards, to the gorgeous East, turned round and fought war after war to secure territory in Italy: territory in which, in the next century, Palladio would build and Veronese decorate the majestic villas of a once mercantile aristocracy which had gradually turned from commerce to office and from office to land.

Finally, what of the Church? In these years of depression it too turned in on itself. I have already remarked that any genuine, living counter-reformation, as distinct from mere reaction, must spring out of the same forces which have produced the original reformation. The friars had begun as revolutionary, not reactionary forces: they had canalized, in defence of the Church, some of the new radicalism of the twelfth-century heretics—the ideas of apostolic poverty and missionary evangelism. But in the fourteenth century this radicalism was effectively crushed out of the Church. The friars became an extra buttress of a bureaucratic property-owning Church deprived of spiritual authority first by the 'Babylonish captivity'—the migration of the papacy from Rome to Avignon—then by the 'Great Schism', when pope and antipope, from Rome and Avignon, hurled at each other their sizzling but ineffectual spiritual thunderbolts. In 1322 Pope John XXII, the risen cobbler's son who savoured the pleasures of wealth among the delicious, specially planted papal vineyards of Avignon, condemned as heretical the doctrine of the poverty of Christ and thereafter the early lives of St Francis were re-written to tone down the unfortunate views of the founder on that subject. The popular fame of the friars of the fourteenth and fifteenth centuries was less for their poverty and their preaching than for their wealth and the interesting new ways in which they built it up. The Franciscans were famous as the inventors or improvers of those 'mechanical' aids to religion which would provoke the Reformation: indulgences, fancy new devotions, new dogmas like the Immaculate Conception. The Dominicans built up their power as the formulators of orthodoxy, and as the manipulators of the Inquisition which would defend orthodoxy by crushing out every new idea.

As for the monks, if the new mendicant orders, which professed poverty, could boast so openly of their wealth, why should the old monasteries hold back? Everywhere the monasteries had extended their landed property. They too had invested in the 'landlord reaction'. The Black Death, in this respect, had been a positive benefit to them. In the years of desolation men had turned to religion and left their lands to the Church. And with land the monks also swallowed up the tithes of the parish churches. . . .

For of course this 'landlord reaction', this dull, reinforced, conservatism of the established classes, did not go unchallenged. It was challenged in the country: the fourteenth century was punctuated by desperate, sometimes terrible, peasant revolts. The peasants revolted in western Flanders from 1323 to 1328. In 1357 they revolted in France: it was the famous Jacquerie, which gave its name to all other purely peasant risings. In 1381 they revolted in England: it was the great Peasants' Revolt of Wat Tyler and Jack Straw whose names remained bogeys to alarm the gentry in the seventeenth century. In the towns, too, there were risings against the closed merchant oligarchies which controlled all economic life. Between 1348 and 1400 there were numerous 'strikes'—in Paris, in Speyer, in Siena, in Strassburg, in Constance. There were also some full-scale revolts. . . . It was called the rebellion of the Ciompi. 'It would be no exaggeration to say', wrote Henri Pirenne, that in those years 'on the banks of the Scheldt, as on those of the Arno, the revolutionaries sought to impose upon their adversaries the dictatorship of the proletariat.' And to sanction their revolt, peasants and craftsmen alike armed themselves against the Church of the rich with radical, heretical doctrines. In France and England the peasants attacked the great landowning abbeys and burnt their archives, the record of their own subjection; they listened to anarchical preachers of human equality like John Ball; and even unrevolutionary enemies of the Church, like Wyclif, found their doctrines turned into revolutionary slogans. Wyclif's heresies were preserved in England, especially by communities of weavers, and would survive to give substance to the Protestant Reformation of the sixteenth century. . . .

Finally, the fourteenth century saw another form of popular revolt: anti-semitism. Indebted peasants in the country, starving craftsmen in the towns, looked for scapegoats in their midst and found the Jews. The Jews were expelled from England in 1292. At the same time there were pogroms in the kingdom of Naples. In 1348–9, on the approach of the Black Death, the Jews were massacred throughout Switzerland and Germany. Popes, princes, bishops, great landlords, sought to protect them, for they found them useful; but in vain: in city after city the Jews were rounded up and burnt alive, until, as a German chronicler wrote, 'I would have believed that the last end of Jewry had come if the time prophesied by Elijah and Enoch had been completed; but since that is not so, some must survive, that the Scriptures may be fulfilled.' . . .

What was the cause of this general decline of the fourteenth century, this collapse of the vitality which had sustained Christendom in the two centuries of expansion? It was not only the Black Death. Population had already begun to fall before the plague had come, and it did not recover momentum until well after it was over. The abandonment of villages beyond the Elbe had also begun well before the Black Death; so had the agrarian and urban discontent in the West. In general a healthy society soon recovers from decimation by an epidemic. London would shrug off the terrible plagues of 1625 and 1665. It is feeble societies which are fatally damaged—and which then ascribe their weakness to that cause. We cannot therefore put all the blame on the Black Death. We have to ask why European society was already so enfeebled in the fourteenth century that the impact of the Black Death was so formidable. For one reason we must look once again outside Europe, to the source whence the Black Death and so much else had come: the East.

For these years of European reaction were years of spectacular change outside Europe; and once again, as in the days of the Huns and the Avars, the immediate cause of the change was one of those sudden, great confederations of the nomads of the steppe. This time it was the greatest of all such confederations: the Mongol confederation of Genghis Khan who, in the early thirteenth century, from his capital of Karakorum in Outer Mongolia, had created an empire of heathen conquest from the Pacific to the Volga. Under his sons and grandsons this empire was extended still farther. . . .

To the rulers of western Europe these convulsions of Islam were not unwelcome. Here was a powerful second front against Mamelukes and Turks; here also was a huge free-trade area from Budapest to Canton; and both could be exploited. Franciscan missionaries were sent to convert the heathen khans to Christianity and Italian merchants found their way, through Central Asia, into China, 'the head of the world and the beginning of the earth'. . . .These missionary efforts were a failure. . . .But the merchantile expeditions were more successful. The heathen khans needed foreign experts and preferred, in their immediate entourage, not to use either Moslems or Chinese. Genghis Khan liked Uighurs, those fascinating Turks of Sinkiang, who had once been Manichaeans and who now served their conquerors by reducing the Mongol language to writing. Under him the Uighurs became the court aristocracy of Karakorum, and he appointed an Uighur as tutor to his sons. But there were also Christians. Guillaume de Rubrouck found numbers of them in Karakorum in 1254; and when Kublai Khan established his power they began to flow to his courts at Cambalu and Peking. The first to come from Europe were two Venetian merchants, Niccòlo and Maffeo Polo, who set out from the Crimea via Bokhara to Peking. Ten years later Marco Polo, the son of Niccolò, would begin his fifteen years as a favoured officer of Kublai Khan, and by his famous book would inspire numerous other Italian merchants to find their way to China in the years 1300–50.

Thus, when the crusaders' way of imperialist colonization had failed, the alternative way of 'pure and friendly correspondence' succeeded, and in the century after the failure of the Crusades, Europe was still living, successfully, on the East. Indeed, it was living more successfully than ever. The great, orderly, tolerant Mongol Empire, crossed and re-crossed by continual caravans, provided one of the most effective means for the diffusion of culture and technology. It was in those years that some of the great Chinese inventions came to Europe. Gunpowder was first mentioned in Europe by Roger Bacon, the friend of that Guillaume de Rubrouck who had visited Karakorum. It was first used in the West, by both Christians and Moslems, in the early fourteenth century. Printing also reached Europe from China during the period of the Mongol peace. The first printed document in Europe is perhaps the stamped signature of the reply of Kayuk Khan to the pope, written in Uighur script, which Giovanni da Piano Carpini brought from Karakorum and which, long unknown, was discovered in the Vatican archives in 1920.

Such was the beneficent *Pax Mongolica* which coincided with the European prosperity of the thirteenth century, and brought Christendom, as never before, into touch with the great, old civilizations of the East. But in the middle of the fourteenth century, this Mongol peace came to an end in anarchy and civil war. In the Far East, a national revolt in China ultimately brought the native Ming dynasty to power, and Karakorum itself was burnt. In the Middle East, Mongol rule collapsed in

Persia; the great irrigation system of Mesopotamia, preserved for centuries, fell into ruin, and the anarchy was exploited by a new, temporary, destructive conqueror, Timur or Tamerlane. In the West, a new Turkish tribe, the Ottomans, displaced by the Mongol conquests, pushed into Europe, made their capital at Adrianople, and reduced the Greek emperor to vassalage. Thus the collapse of the Mongol Empire shook the fabric of society alike in China, in Islam, and in Europe. It was out of the anarchy in China, before the triumph of the Ming, that the Black Death came to Europe; it was during the anarchy of Islam that Ibn Khaldoun, in North Africa, elaborated his defeatist philosophy of history; and the convulsion of the Middle East, together with the collapse of the Mongol peace, dislocated the delicate mechanism of Europe's trade with the East. Indeed, the great caravan-route across Central Asia was finally broken: two centuries later, even its existence had been forgotten.

If the century from 1150 to 1250 can be seen as the highest point of medieval Europe, the century from 1350 to 1450 was, I suppose, the lowest. The old institutions had stiffened and a devitalized society could create no new, elastic institutions to replace them. In that period of contraction and reaction, of deadening clericalism and vain social revolt, intellectual life sank into formalism or took refuge from reality in satire, mysticism or myth. We have the good-humoured satire of Boccaccio and Chaucer, the bitter satire of *Piers Plowman*. We have the great medieval mystics, Suso and Tauler, Richard Rolle and Thomas à Kempis. Above all, we have the archaic myth of chivalry. Never was the spirit of feudalism so elaborate in literature as when it was dead in fact: when feudal bonds were rotted and feudal obligations ignored. . . .

If a philosopher, trained in modern theories of cyclical history, were to place himself in the early fifteenth century, what, I wonder, would he conclude? At that time, it must have seemed that the future was not with Europe, frozen in archaic postures and privileges, not with Islam, helpless before successive invaders, but with China. China had provided almost all the technical innovations of Europe, and now, under its new Ming dynasty, it seemed set on a new policy of expansion. In the years 1405–33 the Chinese court-eunuch Chêng-Ho—one of the really great eunuchs of history (Justinian's general Narses is the other)—led or sent a series of naval expeditions which brought the whole Indian Ocean under Chinese control. Thanks to his enterprise, the rulers of India and Ceylon, the commercial centres of Malacca and Calicut paid their tribute or sent their exotic wares to China. Chinese fleets visited the Red Sea and the coast of East Africa. Only a little continuity was necessary and perhaps Chinese fleets, half a century later, would have arrived in Lisbon and

London. Who would have supposed, at that time, that the reverse would happen: that instead, Portuguese fleets would arrive in Malacca and Calicut to divert the tribute of India and Ceylon westwards to Lisbon and Antwerp, and thereby initiate the new, half-millennial supremacy of Europe?

For this indeed is one of the apparent miracles of history. To explain it, Portuguese historians have discovered an almost fabulous character, Prince Henry of Portugal, 'the Navigator', the Chêng-Ho of the West (except that Prince Henry himself never went to sea), the solitary pioneer of European expansion, the founder of that trans-oceanic Portuguese Empire which was the first, and threatens to be the last, of European empires overseas. For some forty years, from about 1420 till his death in 1460, Prince Henry, we are told, sat at Sagres, on the Atlantic tip of southern Portugal, surrounded by his cartographers and scientists, devising ever new and longer journeys. What inspired him? A crusading zeal against the Moslems of Africa? A dream of India? An image of the legendary Christian king in the East, Prester John? We do not know. We only know that in those years fleet after fleet sailed out from Portugal into the Atlantic, down the coast of Africa, preparing the way for the great sudden voyages, at the end of the century, of Bartholomew Dias and Vasco da Gama, and for the new empire of Asia and Brazil.

The legend of Prince Henry reads well; but let us not be bowled over by it. True history is not made by single heroes. At most, such figures are catalysts, or leaders of forces already there, and the question we must ask is not who inspired those new Portuguese voyages, or with what motive, but why, in the fifteenth century, when the rest of Europe was apparently fixed in social sclerosis and economic decline, one corner of it was able to break the spell and set this new example. For it was an example of great importance. Thanks to the free competition between the monarchies of Europe, all the other maritime powers of Europe would soon turn aside to follow it; that imitation, and that competition, would give to Europe its long ascendancy over the rest of the world.

What was the particular character of Portuguese society in the fifteenth century? This is a large, factual question, to which nevertheless I shall offer a short general answer: an answer drawn not only from these particular circumstances but also from other comparable turning-points in history, when the centre of power has moved from one part to another of a continent or of the world.

For if history is to be seen, as I believe it should be seen, as a continuous process, then certain general conclusions always emerge. We find, for instance, that just as old institutions, unless they are continually adapted, will not serve new purposes, so new problems are rarely solved,

in the first instance, by old societies. The reason can easily be guessed.
Any society, so long as it is, or feels itself to be, a working society, tends
to invest in itself: a military society tends to become more military, a
bureaucratic society more bureaucratic, a commercial society more commercial, as the status and profits of war or office or commerce are enhanced by success, and institutions are framed to forward it. Therefore,
when such a society is hit by a general crisis, it finds itself partly paralysed
by the structural weight of increased social investment. The dominant
military or official or commercial classes cannot easily change their orientation; and their social dominance, and the institutions through which it
is exercised, prevent other classes from securing power or changing policy.
If policy is to be changed to meet new circumstances we are more likely
to find such a change, in the first instance, either in a complex elastic
society—what today we would call a liberal society—in which different
interests have separate, competing institutions, or in a less mature society:
a society whose institutions have not been hardened and whose vested
interests have not been deepened by past commitment. This general social
truth, it seems to me, explains why it was not Ming China but fifteenth-
century Europe, for all its temporary decline, which captured the next
stage of history, and why, within fifteenth-century Europe, it was not Italy
or Flanders or even France or England which showed the way, but a
minuscule kingdom at the back end of eastward-looking Europe, Portugal.

We have seen, in the century from 1350, all Europe in crisis and the
mature societies of Europe unable to create new institutions whereby to
surmount that crisis. To say that they did nothing in that century would
be an exaggeration. In numerous ways they responded to the challenge.
Some new techniques were devised, some new forms of social organization
were evolved. There was agricultural improvement: the landlord reaction
had its brighter side. There was a revolution in cloth manufacture and in
mining which made the fortune of new merchant cities in Germany. There
was a development of gilds which, for a time, preserved a social balance
in older cities. Princes, by extending their jurisdiction and absorbing
new areas, sometimes increased their free-trade area and learned mercantile policies from the cities which they subjected. But, in general,
what we see is over-emphasis on old forms; modification of old forms,
perhaps, but not discovery of new. Landlords seek to preserve their power
by reaction, not innovation. Capitalists, frustrated in trade, turn to banking or to land, or invest in taxes and offices. Even the gilds soon become
restrictive and crush production in the cities in which they triumph: the
economic decline of many a Swiss or German city was caused by this
'socialism' of the fifteenth century. In general, we may say that the existing structure of Europe, the structure acquired in the years of expansion,

and strengthened by the passage of time and growth of interests, continues to absorb its energies, and by absorbing them, to use them up. Even the artistic Renaissance of the fifteenth century is not necessarily a sign of progress. Lavish patronage of the arts is perfectly compatible—as in the Baroque age—with economic decline. The new princes and their couriers are often merchants who have switched their investment from trade to politics. Instead of increasing wealth by industry or commerce, they are accumulating it by taxation and dissipating it, through lack of other outlet, in conspicuous waste.

In Ming China it is the same. For centuries the Chinese Empire had lived on its bureaucracy of scholar-gentry, with which no dynasty could dispense. Foreign rulers might conquer central power, but always, in the end, they had turned to the Chinese bureaucracy in order to rule. Even the Mongols, in the end, had succumbed to it. They might prefer Uighurs or Christians at court; but there were not enough of them to go round the empire. So Kublai Khan ended by restoring the old bureaucracy, recruited by examination. When the nationalist Ming replaced the Mongols, they naturally returned with enthusiasm to the national system. Outwardly it might appear that Chêng-Ho was dished by a court intrigue; fundamentally, Chinese society was absorbed by its ancient structure, its ancient institutions.

But if China was a uniform, centralized empire, Europe's good fortune had always lain in its variety. If all Europe, like all China, had been centrally ruled, how different our history would have been! But in fact it was not so. In fact, in 1400, while the economic life of older Europe was being brought under princely control, there were some countries in which feudal institutions had taken but slender root, and one of those countries, happily placed for the new age, was Portugal.

The kingdom of Portugal, we have seen, had only been founded during the Second Crusade. It was a creation of northern Europe, like the kingdom of Jerusalem; and its very narrowness—a mere strip along the Atlantic coast—had protected it from the general fate of other societies in the fourteenth century. If Portugal, like Andalusia, had been reconquered from Islam by Castile, and governed from Burgos or Toledo, much of its economic life would no doubt have been drained away into the Spanish monarchy—as indeed was to happen after it was united with Spain in 1580. But because of its independence, and its smallness, it was forced to live by its own economy; and that economy lay on the sea. Portugal in the fifteenth century was like Genoa or Venice in the twelfth century, or Holland in the seventeenth: a small state forced by geography to look outwards to the sea. In the narrow space allowed to it there was no Portuguese feudalism powerful enough to absorb the mercantile life of its

Atlantic coast; and in the great depression of the fourteenth century, when the mercantile cities of the Mediterranean turned away from commerce to land or banking—when Venice became a land-power and Genoa a finance-capital, and when Barcelona was swallowed up by the kingdom of Aragon—Lisbon retained its old character. It was still a capital of merchants and seamen, carrying salt to northern Europe, entering the internal markets of northern Europe, fishing and whaling in the Atlantic Ocean. It was now also a main port of the route from north to south Europe—the sea-route which was becoming more popular as the land-route suffered from the crisis of the times and the exactions of its rulers.

To Lisbon therefore, the new Venice, the new Genoa of the Atlantic, the heirs of the old Venice, the old Genoa of the Mediterranean would now turn. In the middle of the fourteenth century Italian merchants, squeezed out of Italy—the Bardi of Florence, the Lomellini of Genoa— converged on Lisbon, just as the *émigré* capitalists of Counter-Reformation Europe would converge on seventeenth-century Amsterdam. In 1391, when the Jews were slaughtered throughout Spain, the Jewish cartographers of Majorca—the best in Europe, the makers of the great medieval 'portulans' or sea-maps—fled to Portugal. The mercantile and scientific expertise of Italy, Flanders and of Catalonia was united, in Portugal, with the native shipbuilding industry; and the result was to make Portugal an economic and maritime force, as Venice and Genoa had been, as Amsterdam would be.

As such, Portugal was brought into the wars of Europe. In the Hundred Years' War, that struggle of feudal princes for land in France, it was enlisted as the essential sea ally of England. It was to celebrate the Anglo-Portuguese victory of Aljubarrota that the great abbey of Batalha, the Battle Abbey of Portugal, was built. But the effect of the war, and the victory, was far more decisive for Portugal than for England. For Portugal, those years of war, 1383–5, were also years of internal revolution, a revolution which in form was dynastic, but which in substance went far deeper. It was a political and economic revolution which was the reverse of the other revolutions in Europe at that time. For whereas in the rest of Europe, in those years of crisis, feudal or bureaucratic princes were absorbing the once free cities—the Medici would become despots of Florence and the Visconti of Milan and the Dukes of Burgundy would absorb the cities of Flanders—the city of Lisbon was, in effect, to absorb the new Anglo-Portuguese dynasty of Aviz. In Portugal, and only in Portugal, the 'feudal' nobility, with their 'feudal' fighting tastes, would accept, through the house of Aviz, the leadership of those maritime, mercantile forces which in the Mediterranean would be turning, under the seduction of a hardening social structure, from the sea to the land, from commerce to finance. The arts in Italy and Flanders would be bent to glorify the new princely state, and the myths of the Church which sustained it; but in Portugal even solid stone would soon be made to re-create, with its fantastic imagery of twisted cables and symbolic anchors, coral and shells and waves, the spirit of maritime journeys, commerce, and the distant seas.

The result was spectacular. With new leadership, new financial resources, new technical developments, the Portuguese mercantile state would send ever stouter ships out into the Atlantic in search of that African gold which, for so long, had been the motor of European commerce with the East. With the new growth of population in the fifteenth century, a new movement of expansion would be launched, comparable with that movement of which the Crusades had been a part; and this time it would be launched from Portugal. The pioneers were not necessarily Portuguese. Prince Henry's explorers who first reached the equator, Alvise de Cadamosto and Antoniotto Usodimare were, respectively, a Venetian and a Genoese. The techniques of colonization were not necessarily Portuguese: the wine- and the sugar-industries which the Portuguese and Spaniards would plant in the islands of the Atlantic were those which the Venetians and Genoese had first established in the islands of the Mediterranean. Chios and Crete were the models for Madeira and the Canaries: the wine of Madeira is Malmsey from Greece. But Portugal accepted the legacy of Italy, and passed it on. Columbus was a Genoese in the service of Spain; Magellan, a Portuguese, was also in the service of Spain; but the voyages of both, no less than those of Bartholomew Dias and Vasco da Gama, were technically prepared by Portugal. From that little corner of Europe, from that solitary revolution of 1383, in the period of European recession, Europe found the way to America, to India, and round the world.

With the discovery of those new worlds, the medieval history of Europe can be said to have come to an end. Thanks to those discoveries, and to the institutions which could exploit them (for once again, let me repeat, contact alone is nothing: it is the power to grasp and learn from contact which counts), as well as to the continued fragmentation and competition of the European states, Europe since 1500 has in fact dominated and transformed the world. Slowly, with difficulty, other powers followed the Portuguese lead. The 'feudal' monarchies of the West adapted themselves to the new opportunities; the 'feudal' chivalry which had wasted itself in European anarchy was turned once again, as in the eleventh century, outward; and a new age began.

CHAPTER 2

THE SPANISH AND FRENCH IN AMERICA

In the beginning the New World was explored and partially settled by the Spanish, with the French not far behind. In it both nationalities discovered sources of potential wealth—the Spanish finding gold, silver, and staple crops and the French, furs. In the Caribbean and in Central and South America the Spanish colonized an area very suitable for large-scale farming and mining. The French, in that part of Canada along the St. Lawrence River, found a society of woodland Indians who would supply cheaply the furs in demand in European markets. French settlers engaged in subsistence farming, with furs as their major cash product, while the Spanish relied primarily on the products of mining and on crops such as tobacco and sugar. Ultimately, of course, the manner in which the French and Spanish sought to exploit the resources they found helped to shape, as did their European backgrounds, their respective patterns of settlement in the New World.

It is with these patterns of settlement that Professors Parry and Sutter are concerned in the two essays following. Both authors are particularly interested in the impact of settlement on the native Indian cultures. This is a subject that must be approached with extreme caution. All the European colonial groups exploited the Indians, but recent scholarship suggests that the nature and degree of exploitation were determined not so much by the national origins of the settlers as by national purposes and the objectives of the colonists themselves. It should be kept in mind that the 1500's and 1600's constituted, by our standards, a cruel age, and the Spanish, French, and English colonists were products of their age.

As you read these essays, you should try to determine how and why French and Spanish settlement patterns in the New World differed from each other. Are there any ways in which these differing patterns helped to shape the histories of the various nations that emerged from French and Spanish colonial settlements in the New World? What were the differences between French and Spanish attitudes toward, and treatment of, the Indians? How do the differing patterns of settlement help to explain these differences? As you read further in this volume, you should pose similar questions about the patterns of settlement in British North America.

There are a number of excellent works dealing with the French and Spanish nations in the New World. Among the best on the Spanish are Clarence H. Haring, *The Spanish Empire in America** (1947), and a more recent synthesis, Charles Gibson, *Spain in America** (1966). For an excellent treatment of Spanish Indian policy, see Lewis Hanke, *The Spanish Struggle for Justice in the Conquest of America** (1944). The Spanish and French explorers are ably discussed in John Bartlet Brebner, *The Explorers of North America, 1492–1806** (1964). For an excellent recent account of life in New France, see W. J. Eccles, *Canadian Society During the French Regime* (1968).

* Available in a paperback edition.

THE SILVER EMPIRE
J. H. PARRY

THE SPANISH CONQUEST

If the first two decades of the sixteenth century may be called the age of the professional explorer, the next three decades from 1520 to 1550, were the age of the *conquistadore*—the professional conqueror. In those years a few thousand down-at-heel swordsmen, themselves the product of the tradition of the Moorish wars, possessed themselves of most of the settled areas of both Americas and established the first great European land empire overseas.

Before 1520 most of the larger islands of the West Indies had been explored and a considerable number of Spaniards had settled, especially in Hispaniola and Cuba. These settlers imported cattle and horses, and negroes to replace the dwindling native Arawaks, and set up as slave-owning ranchers. Their settlements were turbulent and unstable. Many of the settlers were soldiers who had served in Moorish or Italian campaigns; there was no congenial work for them in Spain, nor did they propose to work in the Indies. They would settle for a short time, and then desert their holdings to investigate a rumoured gold strike, or simply through boredom and restlessness.

Balboa's glimpse of the Pacific in 1513 encouraged some of these adventurers to join in the general search for a sea passage through Central America; at various points on the Gulf coast these explorers found gold and silver ornaments in use among the natives, and heard rumours of civilized city-dwellers living in the mountains inland. Scattered through tropical America, mainly in highland areas, there were in fact a number of distinct peoples, who, though lacking wheeled vehicles and beasts of burden, and using tools of wood or stone, had nevertheless achieved a remarkable skill in some of the arts, in sculpture and building, in agriculture and in handicraft industries, including the working of soft metals. Their principal settlements, adorned with stone or

SOURCE. J. H. Parry, "The Silver Empire," *The Establishment of the European Hegemony*, London: Hutchinson and Co., Ltd., 1949, pp. 60–75. Copyright 1949. Reprinted by permission of Hutchinson and Co., Ltd., and the author.

adobe temples and community-houses, were large enough to be called cities. In two centres at least—in Mexico and the central plateau of the Andes—warlike tribes had established themselves as overlords, exacting tribute and forced labour from subject peoples over a wide area; and had set up political organizations bearing a superficial resemblance to empires or kingdoms in the Old World sense. Among Spaniards, the wealth and power of these peoples lost nothing in the telling; and for pious Christians their religions had a horrible fascination, combining, as in some cases they did, messianic legends of strange beauty with revolting rites of human sacrifice and ritual cannibalism.

The speed with which the Spanish *conquistadores* seized the chief centres of American civilization compares with the speed of Portuguese commercial expansion in the East; but the Spanish conquest achieved far more enduring results and its success is even harder to explain satisfactorily. The possession of firearms was an important but probably not a decisive factor. A ship carries its armament wherever it goes; but on land cannon had to be dragged over mountains and through swamps by human strength. The army with which Cortés invaded Mexico possessed only a few small cannon and thirteen muskets. Horses were perhaps more important than guns; but the Indians soon lost their fear of horses and even learned to ride them. Cortés had sixteen horses when he landed. For the most part his men fought on foot with sword, pike and crossbow. They had the advantage of steel over stone; but they were not a well-equipped European army fighting a horde of helpless savages.

The Spaniards had unbounded courage and the discipline of necessity. . . . They were able to exploit some of the legends and superstitions of their adversaries in such a way as to paralyse opposition, at least temporarily. They had the help of large numbers of Indian allies who—having never heard of King Log and King Stork—gleefully attacked their former overlords or rivals. Finally the Spaniards had the advantage of their truculent missionary faith: the Indian believed that his religion required him to fight and if need be to die bravely; the Spaniard believed that his religion enabled him to win.

The expedition destined for the conquest of Mexico, promoted by the Governor of Cuba and commanded by Cortés, consisted of about six hundred men. Cortés landed near what is now Vera Cruz in 1519 and began operations by two symbolic acts: the burning of the ships which had brought him from Cuba, and the ceremonious founding of a municipality. To the magistrates of the 'town' of Vera Cruz Cortés resigned the commission he had received in Cuba; from them, as representatives of the Spanish Crown in Mexico, he received a new commission, and having thus legalized as best he could his assumption of an independent command, he led his army up the rugged climb from the steamy jungles of Vera Cruz to the high plateau of central Mexico. The outlying towns of the plateau, after some fighting, agreed to help him with food, with porters, and with fighting men; and by playing adroitly upon the superstitions of Montezuma, the Aztec war-chief, Cortés effected the peaceful entry of his army into Tenochtitlán, the capital city, built upon islands in the lake of Mexico. His peaceful occupation was short-lived; the zeal of the Spaniards in destroying heathen temples caused a rising in which Montezuma was killed, and Cortés had to fight his way out of the city along the causeways by night, losing in that one night a third of his men and most of his baggage. The auxiliary tribes remained loyal to the Spanish alliance, however, and Cortés was reinforced by another expedition from Cuba. He had boats built for fighting on the lake, and laid formal siege to the city, systematically looting and destroying it building by building as he advanced towards the centre, until in 1521 the surviving Aztecs surrendered. In the beautiful Spanish city which Cortés began to build on the site, there is hardly a trace of the former Indian buildings: the place was built over as completely as the Roman cities of Europe.

Cortés showed genius, not only in holding his own men together, but in securing at least the passive loyalty of the conquered Indians. He worked so wisely that there was never afterwards any serious trouble with the natives of the plateau region. His imitators in Central and South America were less fortunate or less adroit. The Maya territories in Central America were subdued with great brutality by Cortés's lieutenants. The Inca Empire, with its centre at Cuzco on the high plateau of the Peruvian Andes, was not discovered by Spaniards until 1530, after eight years of exploration, by land from Cartagena, by sea from Panama. The conquest of Peru was organized by a syndicate whose principal member was an obscure adventurer named Francisco Pizarro. Pizarro entered Peru with a smaller following even than that of Cortés. He was fortunate in finding a usurper on the Inca throne. In imitation of Cortés he contrived to seize the person of this reigning chief, Atahualpa, whom he afterwards executed. Like Cortés, also, Pizarro organized his conquests by founding municipalities with due legal pomp. Like Cortés, he sent his lieutenants exploring, south into Chile, and north to Quito and New Granada. But though he had all Cortés' generalship, Pizarro had little of the diplomacy and charm which Cortés displayed. His appointment as governor of the best part of the Inca dominions provoked fierce personal quarrels and eventually civil war among the conquerors. Francisco Pizarro, his brother Gonzalo, his partner and rival Almagro, and hundreds of their followers were killed. Their factions raged intermittently for nearly twenty years, and peace was restored with great difficulty by the intervention of the home government.

Naturally the surviving Indian rulers tried to turn the situation to their own advantage; but too late. Only in southern Chile did Indian arms prevail against the Spaniards. A major rebellion in western Mexico was crushed by the first viceroy, Antonio de Mendoza, in 1542. By 1550 all the chief centres of settled population in tropical America were in Spanish hands—but not in the hands of the great *conquistadores*. Private commanders like Cortés, Pizarro, Belalcázar and Nuño de Guzmán, who depended for their power upon their personal following, if they escaped the knives of their rivals, were displaced by royal nominees. Exploration and conquests went on in frontier regions, in northern Mexico and east of the Andes; and in the fifteen-sixties a well-planned, ably-led, and almost bloodless conquest added the Philippines to the Spanish empire. In most parts of the Americas, however, the great age of the *conquistadores* ended when the principal settled areas were secure. Forests and empty prairies were not to their taste. Cortés spent his last years in bored and litigious retirement. There was little left for him to conquer.

THE THEORY OF EMPIRE

The Spanish conquest in America was a genuine crusade, appealing alike to the missionary's zeal for souls and the soldier's desire for military glory and for plunder. Unlike earlier crusades, however, it brought in its train an immense task of imperial government. The *conquistadores* had gone to America at their own expense, endured great hardships, risked their lives and fortunes—such as they were—without help from the Spanish state. Most of them looked forward to a pensioned retirement; some living in Spain upon the proceeds of their plunder, but many more living in the Indies upon the labour and the tribute of the conquered races as the Incas and the Aztecs had done before them. Left to themselves, they would probably have settled in loose communities, employing the feudal forms which already were anachronisms in Spain, exploiting the Indians as the needs of the moment dictated, and according verbal homage but little else to the Spanish Crown. Many of the rebel leaders in Peru—in particular, Gonzalo Pizarro—contemplated just such a society, extravagantly loyal in sentiment but in practice virtually independent.

The rulers of Spain never for a moment thought of allowing such a state of affairs to persist. In the late fifteenth and early sixteenth centuries the Crown, with considerable bloodshed and expense, had successfully cut the claws of the great feudal houses, of the knightly orders and of the privileged local corporations. A growing royal absolutism could not tolerate the emergence of a new feudal aristocracy overseas. At the same time royal government was by no means a lawless or unbridled absolutism. The Church and the legal profession were its honoured partners and its most useful servants. The conquest of America touched not only the royal authority, but the royal conscience and the tradition of royal justice.

Discussion of the nature and duties of kingship, in both legal and theological terms, was a commonplace in sixteenth-century Spain. It was an age of vigorous and outspoken political thought, thought which was, for the most part, resolutely opposed to despotism and which placed the law of God and the laws and customs of free peoples above the will of kings. The conquest of a great and semi-barbarous empire obviously presented a difficult problem to the apologists for constitutional kingship. They all admitted—no Catholic could deny—that the bulls issued by Alexander VI in 1493 had given to the Spanish Crown the duty and the sole right of converting the American natives to the Christian faith. If the Indians resisted the preaching of the Gospel, they might lawfully be subdued by force of arms. The duty of civilizing a barbarous people and the fact that the Spaniards were the first Europeans to discover America were valid, though secondary reasons for the conquest. But if the Indians should be reduced by a just conquest, what legal and political rights remained to them? Should their rulers be deposed—if indeed they had legitimate rulers? Should they be 'converted' by force? Might they be enslaved, or deprived of land or property? Were they to be subject to Spanish courts of law, civil and ecclesiastical? What claims had the Spanish settlers upon the tribute and labour of the Indians?

Spanish writers differed profoundly in their answers to these questions, and the main ground of difference was the nature of the Indians themselves. The colonists naturally emphasized the apparent idleness of people accustomed to subsistence farming, and the treacherous resentment of a conquered race. They claimed unfettered local lordship based on forced labour and maintained, not without some plausibility, that a paternal feudalism would best serve the interests of the Indians themselves. Many missionaries, on the other hand—in particular the famous Dominican preacher Las Casas—insisted on the purely spiritual nature of the Spanish enterprise. Las Casas's theory of empire rested upon the belief that the Indians, equally with the Spaniards, were the natural subjects of the Spanish Crown, and enjoyed from the moment of entering into the Spanish obedience all the guarantees of liberty and justice provided by the laws of Castille. He maintained that they were capable intellectually of discharging the duties of Spanish subjects and of receiving the faith. He contemplated an ideal empire in which the Indians would live under their own headmen but subject to the authority of benevolent royal officials who would instruct them in European customs and persuade them to abandon barbarous practices. The Church would proceed peacefully with its work of conversion and spiritual ministration. If other Europeans, as private persons, were allowed to reside in the Indies, they would live apart from the Indians and support themselves by their own labour.

Las Casas was no mere theorist, but a devoted missionary who had himself pacified a large and savage tract of country in Central America. In Spain he was a powerful and respected personality. He represented, of course, an extreme view. The opposite view, that of the colonists, also had its defenders, notably Juan Ginés de Sepúlveda, the distinguished scholar and humanist and friend of Erasmus, one of the ablest apologists of European imperialism. Between Sepúlveda and Las Casas, and between the schools and interests which they represented, there was fierce and acrimonious debate. The importance of such controversies lay in the public interest which they aroused, and in their effect on royal policy. Spanish methods of government, as distinct from methods of conquest, were cautious, legalistic, slow, above all conscientious. They were influenced both by reports of practical experience and by considerations of abstract right. By the middle of the sixteenth century there emerged from the dust of controversy an official policy and an official theory of empire which, despite constant vacillations in matters of detail, were maintained with very fair consistency for over two hundred years.

The Indies were kingdoms of the Crown of Castille, separate from the kingdoms of Spain, and administered through a separate royal council. The Indians were the direct subjects of the crown, not of the Spanish state or of any individual Spaniards. They were free men, and might not be enslaved unless taken in armed rebellion. Their land and property were their own, and might not be taken from them. Their headmen were to be confirmed in office and employed as minor officials. They were to be subject to Spanish courts of law, and might sue Spaniards and be sued by them; but their own laws were to be respected except where they were clearly barbarous or repugnant to the Spanish laws of the Indies.

The Indians were, of course, to be converted to Christianity as soon as possible and were to be admitted to all the sacraments of the Church. Their conversion was to be free and not forced, and their lapses into heresy were to be dealt with by the ordinary jurisdiction of the bishops, not by the Inquisition.

To meet the claims of the colonists, the Crown granted to deserving conquerors and settlers the right to draw the assessed tributes of speci-fied villages, by way of pension. These grants of *encomienda* involved no jurisdiction or territorial lordship; nor, after the middle of the century, forced labour. They did involve, for the *encomendero,* the obligation of military service and the duty of paying the salaries of the parish clergy. Forced labour was permitted—was indeed found to be indis-pensable; but under the *mita* or *repartimiento* system, the compulsion was applied by public, not private authority, and official wage-rates were laid down for labour so recruited.

Of course, the decrees enjoining this policy were often obstructed and sometimes openly defied; but that does not detract from the merits of the policy, as a product of sixteenth-century thought and experience. The enforcement of the policy, moreover, though incomplete, was by no means as incompetent as the enemies of Spain pretended.

SOLDIERS, MISSIONARIES AND LAWYERS

The Spaniards who went to the New World were not settlers seeking an empty land, but soldiers, missionaries, administrators—a ruling class. They sought not to displace the native population, but to organize it, educate it, and live by its labour. They took over as a going concern the systems of tribute collection formerly organized by the dominant tribes in Mexico and Peru. Within a few years they created a number of deeply-rooted vested interests, which made the enforcement of a uni-form official policy extremely difficult.

The most powerful group of interests was naturally that represented by the 'old conquerors' and their descendants. They formed a quarrel-some and disorderly society, whose good behaviour had to be bought with *encomiendas,* grants of land, and minor salaried offices. The one attempt made by the Crown to give legislative force to the proposals of Las Casas and to abolish the *encomienda,* in the 'new laws' of 1542, caused an armed revolt of the settlers of Peru, in which the viceroy was killed. The 'new laws' had to be amended; and the settlers constantly pressed for further concessions, in particular for the right to turn their *encomiendas* from terminable grants into entailed estates. There were never enough *encomiendas* or offices to go round, and almost from the beginning a 'poor white' class made its appearance, living among the Indians and giving endless trouble to the missionaries. Many settlers, rich and poor, took Indian wives, and so added a *mestizo* class to an already complex society. These people of mixed blood came in time to outnumber both pure Indians and pure Spaniards; and many of the Latin American peoples to-day are predominantly *mestizo*.

The Spanish settlers found their chief organs of expression in the town-councils, powerful and jealous of their privileges in the Indies as in Spain. There was nothing democratic about these bodies; they were local oligarchies. Councillors in the early days were appointed by military commanders or provincial governors, but in the second half of the sixteenth century the practice grew whereby they purchased their offices from the Crown for life. The councils elected municipal magistrates, and exercised wide administrative powers, not only within the town area, but over considerable tracts of surrounding country. They corresponded directly with the Crown and were always determined upholders of local Spanish interests. They rarely displayed much constructive vigour, however. They were neither responsible, nor in any exact sense representative institutions; and in the seventeenth century, as the power of the *corregidores* increased and the sale of offices became more nearly universal, the councils sank into decline.

The Spanish conquest, however, was a spiritual as well as a military conquest, and the principal local opposition to the rule of swordsmen came from the soldiers of the Church—the friars of the missionary Orders. All three Orders, but especially the Franciscans, in the early days sent picked men to the Indies, and the conversion they sought to achieve was more than a mere ourward conformity. The friars taught and preached, as soon as they were able, in the Indian languages. They established mission communities and made the mission Church the centre of the lives of many thousands of Indians. They made at least a beginning in the provision of both primary and secondary religious and literary education for the Indians—an ambitious undertaking designed, ultimately, to prepare selected Indians for the priesthood. It is true that this last undertaking was, in the main, a failure. The Church in the Indies never produced a numerous native priesthood, and its spiritual strength and hold upon its converts ultimately suffered as a consequence. The reasons for that failure are too complex for analysis here; what is certain, is that the policy of the Orders in the sixteenth century interfered with the lord-and-vassal relation which the settlers sought to establish with the Indians. The difference in attitude was not merely one of humanitarian sentiment; for the *encomienda* and *repartimiento* were not inherently cruel institutions, though they led to many abuses. The important differences were legal and spiritual.

On the whole, the Crown endorsed the views of the missionary Orders, but dared not enforce them in full. The friars also differed among themselves, and they, too, could be rebellious and impatient of control; not, of course, to the extent of armed revolt, but in many lesser acts of indiscipline. They challenged the power of the Crown indirectly on many occasions, by flouting the authority of the bishops whom the Crown appointed.

The differences among Spaniards were reflected by differences among the Indians themselves. For the most part the Indians showed a surprising docility and resignation. Their acquiescent nature, under the shock of conquest, often sank into apathetic melancholy, broken only by religious festivals and their accompanying drunken orgies. The settled Indians lost the material and spiritual culture of their ancestors, without fully acquiring that of the Spanish conquerors. They became strangers in their own land. Many tribes, however, remained unsubdued and dangerous throughout the colonial period, and even among the settled peoples wide differences persisted. Some Indian chiefs received *encomienda*s or became great landowners. Many others, if official reports are to be believed, willingly exploited their own people on behalf of the Spanish colonists. From the beginning, a considerable class of skilled workmen, household servants, and the like, threw in their lot with the Spanish community. In many parts of the Indies the old village life soon began to disintegrate, though not without protest. The Crown repeatedly insisted that Indian complaints should be freely heard, not only by the courts, but by the administrative authorities. The government even retained salaried advocates to present Indian pleas.

The royal insistence that all parties should have a hearing helps to explain one of the leading characteristics of Spanish colonial government —the great power and prestige of the professional judiciary. Ten *audiencias*—courts of appeal—were established in the Indies in the sixteenth century. The *audiencia* judges were always school-trained lawyers and always peninsular Spaniards. They were the only branch of the colonial service whom the Crown really trusted. Professional lawyers were the ideal agents of centralized government. They had no excessive family pride and no ambition, as a rule, for military glory. Their training gave them a deep respect for authority and a habit of careful attention to detail, while it discouraged any tendency towards rash or unauthorized action. Judges, moreover, representing the jurisdiction of the monarch, preserved a certain impersonality which helped them to control *conquistadores* who would have resented the authority of one of their own caste.

Every province had its governor and the governors of the two greatest provinces—Mexico and Peru—enjoyed the title and dignity of viceroys. Some of these governors were churchmen or lawyers; more were aristocratic soldiers; but under the suspicious Hapsburg kings, soldiers without armies. They were never trusted with the powers and temptations of independent command. Even a great administrator like Francisco de Toledo received inadequate support from home, and small thanks from Philip II for thirteen years of empire-building in Peru. Most viceroys served for much shorter terms, and all were carefully watched by their *audiencias*. The *audiencias* were much more than courts of appeal. They were cabinet councils empowered to advise the viceroys and governors in all administrative matters, to report on their conduct, and to hear appeals against their decisions. A viceroy might override his *audiencia* temporarily, but on appeal to Spain the judges were likely to be upheld; for the Council of the Indies was itself a predominantly legal body, to which colonial judges might hope to be promoted in due course of seniority.

This cumbrous system of checks and balances might make for impartiality and respect for law—respect, at least, for the forms of law. It certainly did not make for administrative efficiency or speed of action. All important decisions, and many unimportant ones, were made in Spain. In the Indies, there was no decision which could not be reversed and no jurisdiction which could not be inhibited. Appeals and counter-appeals might hold up essential action for years, until the occasion for it were forgotten. 'Obey but not enforce' became the administrative watchword of an empire whose legislation and basic policy were, in many respects, models of enlightment for their time.

ATLANTIC TRADE AND THE SILVER FLEETS

The characteristic occupation of the New World Spaniard was stock-farming. It was an occupation peculiarly well suited to the temperament of the *conquistadores,* an open-air life covering great areas of country, offering considerable excitement, calling for great skill in horsemanship and periodic outbursts of great energy, but for the most part requiring no steady or sustained effort. In Spain, the owners of flocks and herds were favoured socially and economically at the expense of the arable farmer; grazing rights tended to override all other kinds of land rights.

A similar situation soon arose in the temperate parts of Spanish America, where the work of arable farming was left mainly in the hands of the Indians. Horses, cattle and sheep were imported in great numbers and multiplied rapidly. As in all the economic activities of the Spaniards in the New World, the methods used were slovenly and wasteful. Leather commanded a high price in Europe in those turbulent times; for an ox-hide jerkin would turn a knife-thrust. Often the beasts were slaughtered for their hides alone, the carcases being left to rot on the ground. Nevertheless, the industry prospered. Great estates grew round the ranch-houses, where the Spanish ranchers lived in patriarchal state, surrounded by their poorer Spanish and *mestizo* dependents and their Indian *peones*.

In the tropical coast lands, where cattle could not thrive, the principal Spanish product was sugar, which had been introduced into the West Indies by Columbus and into Mexico by Cortés. Sugar was a crop which lent itself to large-scale production, since fairly elaborate equipment was needed for crushing the cane, extracting and refining the syrup, and crystallizing the final product. Sugar plantations were started by many Spaniards, particularly near the Caribbean and Gulf coasts. There was a steady demand for sugar—then an expensive luxury—in Europe, and the industry prospered reasonably in spite of wasteful methods and government interference. Both sugar and tobacco—a crop of great economic importance in the seventeenth century—were largely produced by slave labour, African negroes being imported for the purpose. Since negroes were the subjects of barbarous African kings and not of the king of Spain, there was no legal and little, if any, humanitarian objection to their purchase as slaves. They had to be obtained through Portuguese middlemen, and were extremely expensive in the Indies.

The animal and vegetable products of the Indies were almost insignificant to many Spaniards in comparison with the mineral products —the precious metals. Gold and silver mining in the early days of the conquest was a simple affair of prospecting and washing in likely streams; but about the middle of the sixteenth century, immensely productive silver veins were discovered at Zacatecas and Guanajuato in Mexico and Potosí in what is now Bolivia. Various forms of crude mass-production quickly took the place of the primitive washing process, and extensive plant—extensive for those days—was set up for extracting the silver from the ore, usually by a mercury amalgamation process. These developments produced lawless and exciting silver rushes, and special courts were hastily set up in the mining camps to register claims and settle disputes. Probably some Spaniards worked small claims by hand; but the typical silver miner was a capitalist and an employer of native labour, skilled and unskilled, on a fairly large scale.

The Crown claimed a share, usually one-fifth, of all metal produced. This was the income which aroused the envy and suspicion of all the other monarchs in Europe. In actual fact in most years it was probably not much more than ten or fifteen per cent of the total revenue of the Spanish Crown, and was pledged to German bankers long before it left America. The constant import of silver had disastrous effects on prices and on the economic structure of Spain as a whole—effects which contemporaries attributed to almost any cause but the right one. The economic theories of the time treated bullion as the most important and most valuable product of the Indies; the government sought by all possible means to encourage gold and silver mining, and to enforce payment of the bullion tax. A considerable body of officials was employed to weigh, test and stamp the silver ingots as they issued from the mines and to take out the royal share. Still further officials at the ports watched for attempts to smuggle unstamped silver. About the middle of the sixteenth century, a convoy system was devised for protecting the bullion cargoes on the Atlantic crossing. From 1564 two armed fleets were dispatched from Spain every year, one to Mexico and the Gulf ports, the other to the isthmus of Panama. Both fleets wintered in America and reassembled at Havana the following Spring for the return voyage. Each fleet consisted of from twenty to sixty sail, usually escorted by from two to six warships. It was forbidden for any ship to cross the Atlantic except in one of these convoys, unless special license had been granted. The sailings were sufficiently regular for privateers to lie in wait for them, and one or two ships were lost almost every year. The whole plan illustrated Philip II's excessive confidence in the power of combination and weight, and his inability to see the value of maneuvering and speed —the very mistake which led to the Armada disaster of 1588. Still, on the whole the convoys served their purpose; they maintained regular sailings for a century-and-a-half, and only three times during that period was a whole fleet intercepted and defeated, once by the English and twice by the Dutch. The cost of the convoys was borne by a heavy and complicated series of duties on all goods carried from or to America; so the safety of the fleets was dearly bought, and the whole arrangement added greatly to the delays in obtaining goods in the colonies, and to the price of the goods when they eventually arrived.

The trade to the colonies was a monopoly throughout most of the sixteenth and seventeenth centuries. The monopolist was not the Crown (as in Portugal), but the *consulado*—the merchant guild—of Seville, with its subsidiary organization at Cadiz. By an elaborate series of fictions, merchant houses all over Spain became members by proxy of the Seville guild, consigning their cargoes in the name of resident Seville merchants. Even foreign commercial firms, German, English and Flemish, adopted this device, so that the genuine members of the guild performed a vast commission business which came to over-shadow their own legitimate trade. Seville was the bottleneck of the Indies trade; a bottleneck still further narrowed by the licensing regulations of the royal House of Trade —licensing of emigrants, to prevent the emigration of Jews and heretics; licensing of ships, to ensure their sea-worthiness; of navigators, to ensure their competence. Some commodities might only be exported with special license—fire-arms and negro slaves, for instance. This regulation is understandable, since the Crown was always afraid of the possibility of a slave mutiny; but the whole system constituted a formidable obstacle to trade.

Apart from monopoly and regulation, there was a rigidity in the economic structure of Spain as a whole, which made a rapid expansion of export trade extremely difficult. Among the causes of this rigidity were the contempt widely felt for humdrum employment; the decline of handicrafts and agriculture, due to the Moorish wars and the expulsions of Jews and Moriscos; the privileges accorded to pastoral farming and the consequent damage to arable interests; the large proportion of people in unproductive occupations, especially the Church; heavy taxation and constant European war. Furthermore, the most flourishing commercial centres of Spain, in Cataluña and Aragon, were committed to their Mediterranean connections, and had no great interest in entering the Indies trade.

The whole of the Indies was an eager market for cloth, weapons, tools and hardware of all sorts, books, paper, wine, oil and slaves. Spanish producers could not, or would not, export these goods in sufficient quantities or at competitive prices. The Indies trade therefore was a standing temptation, not only to pirates and privateers, but to slavers, smugglers and illicit traders of all nations.

THE NEXT PLACE YOU COME TO
RUTH SUTTER

Spain's discovery of ready riches attracted people to the port at Sevilla, but not to it alone. Seamen from all parts of Europe and around the Mediterranean made their way to share—illegally—in the Spanish take. Beginning in 1522, when a collection of Aztecan treasures was captured by a French corsair, French pirates were a threat to Spanish claims. Their most permanent settlements were perhaps on board ship, for they did little to develop the harbors and coasts where they camped or lay in wait for Spanish ships, but their activities might have served to warn the Spaniards that the Americas would not forever be Spanish property.

Also attractive to the French and to other Europeans was fishing in the North Atlantic. The fishermen's communities were built no more solidly than those of the pirates, but over time fishing did have an effect on colonization. Fishing trips helped to build knowledge of western routes and areas not controlled by Spain, and in some instances fishing provided an economic base for settlement. Moreover, it was among the fishermen that the fur trade began, which attracted others to the North Atlantic lands in the seventeenth century.

There are records, vague enough to puzzle over but not so vague as to discount out of hand, of settlement attempts early in the sixteenth century: sandy and inhospitable Sable Island, for example, where cattle were taken about 1518 to supply the fishermen, and Cape Breton a couple of years later. An expedition to the St. Lawrence in 1541 is interesting because those who backed it expected to act out a dream of a northern Mexico replete with metal wealth. Jacques Cartier had gone "to the New lands to discover certain islands and countries where it is said that he should find great quantity of gold and other valuable things." Two Huron princes whom he took back to France with him, to learn the language for purposes of interpreting, spoke of kingdoms: their own, Hochelaga, in the environs of the island of Montreal; Saguenay, on a river that descends from Lake St. John to the St. Lawrence; and Canada, around the island of Orleans, with a village called Stadacona. On the next trip, however, the Huron seemed reluctant to take Cartier to Hochelaga; the village might not meet his expectations. The king-

SOURCE.   Ruth E. Sutter, *The Next Place You Come to: A Historical Introduction to Communities in North America,* © 1973, pp. 65–73. Reprinted by Permission of Prentice-Hall, Inc. Englewood Cliffs, N. J.

dom of Saguenay then became the goal—an equally elusive one. Theoretically, the territory was Spain's. But the French monarch, Francis I, said of
the Papal Bulls of 1493 and the Treaty of Tordesillas of 1494, which had in
effect divided the world between Spain and Portugal: "The sun shines for
me as well as for others. I should very much like to see the clause in Adam's
will that excludes me from a share of the world." He decided to help outfit
ten ships, provisioned for two years, to conquer Saguenay and settle the
area. In charge were Cartier in a military position and the Sieur de Roberval
in a governmental position. Roberval had some trouble locating volunteer
colonists, and the crew of soldiers, sailors, well-born adventurers, and craftsmen was supplemented with convicts released for the purpose and a few
women, it is said, of ill repute. Cartier set out ahead of them in 1541. He
fortified a place up-river from Stadacona, which he hoped was on the way to
Saguenay, and put some men to work planting a garden. They stayed the
winter, found some pretty but worthless metals and rocks, and then started
back to France, meeting Roberval on the way. Cartier displayed the treasures to him and then, according to Roberval, crept away in the middle of
the night in order to have all the glory, leaving him to stay for a winter in
turn without finding anything to keep him longer. Roberval's chief pilot later
insisted that the northern kingdoms were connected both to Peru and to the
Orient, but by then no one was listening.

It was not until the end of the century that further colonization attempts
were made. The compromises built into the Edict of Nantes provided an
opening, though a temporary one, for Huguenot commercial ventures. By
this time it was clear that profits could be made from furs, especially beaver
skins, obtained in North America. It was individual merchants and explorers who were at first most interested in French expansion in North America,
for Henry IV was concerned with reconstruction in France and his chief
minister, the Duc de Sully, thought the French character was not suited to
overseas colonization. He also disapproved of the means to finance it that
were being tried. A partnership or company would request a charter for a
monopoly of the fur trade, agreeing in return to various conditions, including taking a certain number of colonists per year to the New World. They
had trouble fulfilling the conditions, and traders who had been excluded
complained. Without government support colonization did not, in fact, proceed well. The first settler to come to the St. Lawrence valley with his family
for the purpose of clearing land and farming, Louis Hébert, a retired phar-
macist from Paris, arrived as late as 1617. In 1627, the year the Company
of One Hundred Associates was created by Louis XIII's chief minister,
Cardinal Richelieu, and the Huguenots were barred from New France, there
were fewer than 100 French settlers in northeastern North America, and in
1663, when colonial organization became royal business, there were about
2,000.

Samuel de Champlain, a Catholic associate of some Huguenots who had monopoly trading rights, was responsible for the first lasting settlements in Canada. He went to North America as a geographer, not particularly interested in either trade or colonization. The expeditions he accompanied in 1603 and 1604 were aimed at exploration and established Port Royal (1605) on the western coast of Nova Scotia mainly as a base of operations. There were forty-five settlers, however, who built their houses around a square, planted crops, and even organized a social club, The Order of Good Cheer. One wonders what their last meeting was like, for within two years the grantee, the Sieur de Monts, had lost his charter and most of the settlers returned to France. In 1608, De Monts obtained a new grant of a one-year monopoly of the fur trade, and Champlain turned toward the St. Lawrence valley. This time he decided that a securely based settlement would be advantageous both for trade and for further exploration. He began building his "Habitation" on the old site of Stadacona, which had by then been abandoned by the Indians. The river narrowed here—the Indians called the place Quebec, "the closed-up place"—and a bend in the river where the island of Orleans is situated helped to form a deep and protected harbor. Toward the end of the first year, before help arrived, Champlain noted that only eight were left of the twenty-eight who had begun the settlement, "and half of these were ailing." Yet Quebec was to become the capital of a new province for France. In the 1620's, when Richelieu was thinking that colonial development would increase French power in Europe, most of the French in North America were using Quebec as a home base, but only two families could be considered to have settled there permanently when English privateers attacked the town in 1629; the others—officials, traders, monks—were temporary or transient residents. Nor was the town to grow much in the next thirty years, though the number of missionaries increased. Champlain had gained the enmity of the Iroquois while attempting to maintain the friendship of fur-supplying Hurons, and Iroquois-Huron wars kept the area in turmoil. Moreover, settlers would clear the woodlands, and the fur trade depended on the original ecological conditions.

Government was a matter of company rule until 1647, when a colonial council was established to assist an appointed governor. Then, in 1663, the colony was turned into a royal province by Louis XIV and his finance minister, Colbert. Its form was similar to that of the centrally administered provinces in old France. Three main officials were appointed: governor, bishop, and *intendant*. The governorship was primarily a military position, though some who held it assumed or tried to assume wider authority. With the first governor, the Sieur de Courcelles, who arrived in 1665, came the Carignan-Salières regiment, the colony's first regular troops, who pushed the Iroquois back from French settlements (and destroyed a number of Iroquois settlements). As for the bishop, François de Laval had already been appointed (in 1658), though a separate diocese was not formally set up until 1674. It might also be noted that its area corresponded to that of the administrative district, a departure from the practice in France. Laval's personality and beliefs are said to have been at the heart of the development of the Catholic Church in Canada. He was appointed through the influence of Jesuits, and he represented the ultra-montane view of church-state relations, holding to the absolute supremacy of the Pope and insisting on church participation in state affairs. One of his earliest acts was to institute a seminary for training clergy locally. The position of *intendant* was perhaps the most important in breadth of powers, involving supervision of the administration of justice, law enforcement, provisioning of military forces, income and expenditures in the colony, and allocations of land. The first *intendant* was Jean Talon, who arrived in the colony in 1665 and returned to France in 1672 after a brief but intensive period of encouragement of immigration, exploration, new settlements, and diversification of the economy. Governor, bishop, and *intendant* headed a Sovereign Council that included from five to twelve citizens appointed on a yearly basis, an attorney general, and a registrar. This Council acted mainly as a court, though executive, administrative, and judicial functions were not differentiated. The king could, of course, act independently of his colonial officials. It was under him that the Ministry of the Marine had responsibility for colonial affairs. The king's will and Roman law were basic in colonial justice, although that body of law known as the Custom of Paris was also introduced (in 1637, and officially established in 1663), and a kind of common law developed out of the decisions of the Sovereign Council.

It is often emphasized that French Canadian law had its sources in feudal, rural society, and retained its older characteristics even when law more amenable to commercial activity had developed in France. Certainly the seigneurial system of land tenure provided a basic organizing principle for French Canadian society, at least in theory. However, French feudalism could not be exactly transplanted, for in Canada there was plenty of land and a royal administrative system to perform legal tasks that otherwise might have been the *seigneurs'* to do. It was, of course suited to providing for local government and defense in the wilderness. According to the feudal system, the *seigneur* owed judicial and military duties to his tenants and they, in turn, obedience and armed support to him.

Because the Canadian Indian population was not large and could not be organized for the French government's purposes as it was for Spain's in parts of Mexico and South America, the persons and religious orders with grants of land were required to bring settlers from France. They did not do so consistently or persistently, but with royal encouragement the population did increase. Talon's census of 1666 gave a total of 3,215, nearly two-thirds of which were males. One of his measures, therefore, for increasing the pop-

ulation was to have shiploads of girls—*filles du roi* ("king's daughters")—
sent out for wives for the colony's bachelors. Many of them came from Normandy, and people were also recruited from the rural districts around Paris,
Rouen, and La Rochelle. Other measures included bounties for families of
more than ten children; payments for marriage before sixteen years of age
for girls and twenty for boys; and fines for fathers whose children were still
single when they reached these ages. The population did more than double
during Talon's intendancy, and the census of 1681 showed a total of 9,677.
Then immigration fell off again and most of the later increase was the result
of a high birth rate.

The grants made to *seigneurs* fronted the rivers and extended inland.
Grants to their *habitants,* the tenant settlers, also began with river frontage
and ran in strips back through meadows and often to wooded slopes. The
settlement pattern that resulted was one of fairly close-set farmhouses along
the "road" of the river with fields and forest behind. With growth, a new
rang, or row, of holdings would be established in back of the first, with a road
parallel to the river and farmers' strips of land perpendicular to it. A parish
came into being when a church could be built and included the people who
supported it. At first a seigneury constituted a parish, but those in which
population increased greatly were eventually divided into several parishes.
"Parishes always tend to be convenience areas and, therefore, to be limited
topographically," Horace Miner says in his study of the parish of St. Denis.
"People at an inconvenient distance from the church will try to separate
themselves as a new parish. To do this they must be sufficiently numerous to
support a new church; therefore population distribution is an obvious factor" in parish building.

The information Miner gives on the settlement of the area where the
Rivière Ouelle empties into the St. Lawrence is interesting as background to
the development of the community of *rang* and parish. In 1672 Jean-Bap-
tiste Deschamps, a young officer in the Carignan-Salières regiment, married
a Canadian-born girl and was granted a seigneurial fief by the *intendant*
Talon. It had two leagues of frontage on the St. Lawrence and was one and
a half leagues in depth. Deschamps brought two carpenters, two masons,
and four laborers from France, and other settlers from around Quebec
joined them; nine years later eleven families had settled on this land and the
population had reached sixty-two. Whatever special skills the settlers had,
they also farmed and fished in these early years. By way of evidence for
there having been little social distinction between *seigneur* and *habitants,*
Miner notes that the *seigneur* had one servant boy, twelve head of cattle, fifteen *arpents* of land, and three guns, while one of the *habitants* had three
servants, sixteen head of cattle, fifty *arpents* of land, and fourteen guns.
(The average household had a 12-*arpent* frontage, or about 500 acres.)
When other seigneurial grants had been made in the area, a country *curé*
was appointed to make the rounds of the new settlements, covering a dis-

tance of seventy miles. The *seigneur's* house was used for masses and prayers at first, both during and between the *curé's* visits. If the *seigneur* was not resident in the community, as was the case in the St. Denis grant, the house of one of the *habitants* was used. In 1685 the *seigneur* of Rivière Ouelle donated land for a chapel. A Recollet missionary from France was the first to settle there; in 1690 a Canadian-trained priest was sent to the parish. During the eighteenth century the *habitants* of St. Denis went either to this church or to the one in the parish on the other side of them. Not until the 1830's was their settlement designated a parish. The new parish appears to have made topographical sense, since there was a natural barrier to travel and "no continuum of habitation from one parish to the next along the main road."

Once established as a religious unit, the parish would become a civil unit as well. Frontenac, during his first governorship (1672–1682), instituted the office of *captaine de milice,* to see that parish men and boys were trained in musketry. The appointed (and unpaid) captains of militia gradually took on other local tasks and roles—superintendent of roads, official host to guests, recorder—and became the main liaison between parish and central government. The parish church itself had functions that today would be called civil: maintaining records of births, marriages, and deaths, and conveying public proclamations to the community. *Curés* were early given the right to tithe parishioners to one twenty-sixth of their grain harvest, and for a time the tithes were the only taxes paid by the *habitants.* The church was thus the focus of a community that was at once territorial, religious, civil, and social in its nature. The *curé* would necessarily have a great effect on the community. He was present at the most important occasions in community members' lives, those that represented the cherished beliefs. Baptism, first communion, marriage, death—these were also occasions for gatherings and for discussion of community problems, and the priest often took a crucial part in proposing solutions. He had control over education and was influential in public opinion.

The *seigneur's* role was also important, representing prestige and social status, and perhaps reminding the new Canadians of traditional social organization. The role did not necessarily represent wealth. Many *seigneurs* were not materially better off than their *habitants. Seigneurs'* duties to tenants in the wilderness were, in fact, real burdens to some of them, such as when they had to feed them on their work days. Mostly, relations between *seigneur* and *habitant* were closer than in old France. One way in which some of them showed special status was, as in the Spanish colonies, by living in town (Montreal, Quebec, or Trois Rivières) part of the time. This alone would set them apart in the eyes of their *habitants,* although they were then faced with the problem of establishing and maintaining a position in town society.

The closest relationships were those of the *rang,* of *habitants* living near each other along a road. One road of a parish might provide easy access to one trading center, another to another center. The parish would not thereby be divided, but, as might be expected, there would be various degrees of familiarity within it. Trading centers were simply the location of those who became in time nonfarming specialists—tradesmen, craftsmen, and the like. By the time Miner was studying St. Denis (the 1930's), its center was a close cluster of houses, without farmlands, at an intersection. Early land divisions for inheritance brought residents even closer than they had been at first settlement (and intermarriage within a parish and between contiguous parishes kept families in contact). The Canadian historian Lower cites a story of a great elm tree that supposedly came to shade the frontages of three farms.

A general equality and ease of life was often remarked by Canadians and by visitors in the seventeenth and eighteenth centuries. In 1684 the Baron de Lahontan, who had just come to Canada as an officer of the Marines, wrote back to France:

As soon as we landed last year, Mr. *de la Barre* lodg'd our three Companies in some Cantons or Quarters in the Neighborhood of Quebec. The Planters call these places *Cotes,* which in *France* signifies no more than the Sea-Coast; tho' in this Country where the names of *Town* and *Village* are unknown, that word is made use of to express a Seignory or Manour, the Houses of which lie at the distance of two or three hundred Paces from one another, and are seated on the brink of the River of St. *Lawrence.* In earnest, Sir, the Boors of those Manors live with more ease and conveniency, than an infinity of the Gentlemen in *France.* . . . The poorest of them have four *Arpents* of Ground in front, and thirty or forty in depth. . . .

Most of the inhabitants are a free sort of People that remov'd hither from *France,* and brought with 'em but little Money to set up withal: The rest are those who were Soldiers . . . and they exchang'd a Military Post, for the Trade of *Agriculture.* . . .

In this Country everyone lives in a good and a well furnish'd House; and most of the Houses are of Wood, and two Stories high.

French-Canadian agriculture was mostly of the subsistence sort, with wheat the main crop, and evidently the farmers did not extend themselves to produce a surplus for export. Yet visitors kept being impressed with how much better off the Canadian was than his counterpart in Europe. He was never hungry, they said, and if winters were long and cold he had plenty of fuel. From a picture of *habitant* life first published in 1810:

The Habitans have almost every resource within their own families. . . . They build their own houses, barns, stables, and ovens; make their own carts, wheels, ploughs, harrows, and canoes. In short, their ingenuity, prompted as much by parsimony as the isolated situation in which they live, has provided them with every article of utility and every necessary of life. A Canadian will seldom or never purchase that which he can make himself; and I am of opinion that it is this saving spirit of frugality alone, which has induced them to follow the footsteps of their fathers, and which has prevented them from profiting by the modern improvements in husbandry, and the new implements of agriculture introduced by the English Settlers. . . .

They live on good terms with each other; parents and children to the third generation residing frequently in one house. The farm is divided as long as there is an acre to divide; and their desire of living together is a proof that they live happily, otherwise they would be anxious to part.

CHARTERS AND COVENANTS

The French settled along the St. Lawrence until by the mid-eighteenth century English invaders thought the river looked like one continuous village street. They developed Montreal and Quebec into lively administrative centers. They traveled the major waterways of North America, stopping over in Indian villages, building fur-trading posts and forts at key junctions, until they were scattered through the continent up to the Spanish borders. La Salle's expeditions toward the end of the seventeenth century worried Spain into new fort-building and town-building projects on its northern frontier. But in 1699 the Sieur d'Iberville, who had been sent to found a buffer colony on the Gulf Coast, wrote of another threat, one deriving from "the spirit of colonization." The English would finally chase all other nations out of America, he said, for "however much they enrich themselves [they] do not return to England but stay and will flourish by their riches and their great efforts; while the French abandon them and retire as soon as they have gained a little wealth."

"The spirit of colonization"—it would be hard to define it. What d'Iberville saw was a steady expansion of English settlements along the Atlantic seaboard and of trade with Indians inland. First colonial efforts were superficially alike for Spain, France, and England: abortive post building, wide-ranging exploration including feats with no practical outcome, infighting among the earliest settlers, searches for mineral wealth and then for profitable staple crops or other exports, and large land grants to proprietary persons who expected to have their lands worked by farmers in a position of dependency.

CHAPTER 3

ENGLAND ON THE
EVE OF COLONIZATION

American civilization is an outgrowth of European civilization, modified by the New World environment and experience. The United States,
of course, is in particular a product of the English heritage. The thirteen
original colonies were English before they were American, and because
they were English their colonial experience, their institutions, and their
patterns of life differed from those of the colonies of other European countries. Hence, if the student of United States history is to understand his
country's colonial experience, he must begin by examining the mother
country, England, in the period of European expansion and colonization.

In the next essay, the colonial historians, Max Savelle, of the University
of Washington, and Robert Middlekauff, of the University of California
at Berkeley, give a summary view of England on the eve of the English
colonization of America—a view based solidly on recent scholarship on
Elizabethan England. These authors perform two functions for the student
of American history. First, they examine English economic, political, and
religious institutions—institutions that were to play major roles in the establishment of the English colonies, and that were to be transferred to
America and modified by the American experience. Secondly, they focus
specifically on the factors and motives precipitating the migration of Englishmen to Virginia, New England, and the other English colonies.

In reading this and subsequent selections, explore the relationship between the political, economic, and religious conditions in England and the English colonial system that emerged in the New World. Did English institutions contribute to the success of the English colonial experiment? In light of the evidence presented by Professors Savelle and Middlekauff that the vast majority of English colonists were Anglicans who did *not* come to the colonies seeking "religious freedom," what were the motives that led thousands of Englishmen to pour into colonial America? Are these motives different from the motivations for Spanish settlement, examined in the previous selection?

Wallace Notestein, *The English People on the Eve of Colonization, 1603–1630** (1954), and Alfred L. Rowse, *The Elizabethans and America** (1959), are excellent studies of Elizabethan and Stuart England at the beginning of English colonization. William Haller, *The Rise of Puritanism** (1938), is indispensable.

* Available in a paperback edition.

ENGLAND ON THE EVE OF COLONIZATION
MAX SAVELLE AND ROBERT MIDDLEKAUFF

ENGLISH COMMERCIAL EXPANSION

Although most men in sixteenth-century England earned their living on the land, cultivating the soil or raising sheep and cattle, trade at home and abroad was growing. The wool trade with Flanders was the most important activity; the capital it provided financed other ventures organized and controlled by English merchants. Such control was a relatively new thing. Prior to the sixteenth century the English carrying trade had been monopolized by the Venetians on the one side and the Hanseatic League on the other. England was then the commercial outpost of Europe. But with the "discovery" of the Atlantic Ocean and the New World beyond, "the outpost of the Old World became the emporium for the new." For of all the modern nations of western Europe, England is the one most dependent upon commerce for progress, the one which is most clearly the result of, and the one whose history is most clearly determined by, the insularity of the country and its position at the crossroads of world trade. Englishmen were aware of the sudden expansion of British commerce and gloried in it. Richard Hakluyt gives expression to this enthusiasm for overseas commerce when he says:

Which of the kings of this land before her majesty [Elizabeth], had their banners ever seen in the Caspian Sea? Which of them hath ever dealt with the Emperor of Persia, as her Majesty hath done, and attained for her merchants large and loving privileges? Who ever saw, before this regiment, an English Ligier in the stately porch of the Grand Signor at Constantinople? Who ever found English consuls and agents at Tripolis in Syria, at Aleppo, at Babylon, at Balsara, and, which is more, who ever heard of Englishmen at Goa before now? What English ships did heretofore ever anchor in the mighty river of Plate?

SOURCE. From *A History of Colonial America*, Revised Edition, by Max Savelle and Robert Middlekauff, pp. 48–57. Copyright 1942, © 1964 by Holt, Rinehart and Winston, Inc. Reprinted by permission of Holt, Rinehart and Winston, Inc. and the authors.

An important element in this budding commercial adolescence of the Elizabethans that the patriot Hakluyt overlooked, however, was the fact that many of these vigorous English merchants were, to all intents and purposes, pirates. It is quite possible that he had Sir John Hawkins in mind when he wrote of the English ships that were anchoring "in the mighty river of Plate," and Hawkins had, indeed, carried British trade into distant places. But Hawkins had gone to the slave coasts of Africa in defiance of the Portuguese, and he had taken his cargoes of human freight, in 1562–1563 and 1568, to the Spanish colonies in defiance of Spanish regulations excluding foreign traders, and he had sold his Negroes to the Spanish planters—at the point of a gun when they were slow to buy. Spain had protested, but to no avail.

Quite the contrary, indeed; for Hawkins was only one of the best-known of the daredevil, swashbuckling English sailors, the "Elizabethan sea dogs," who drew no sharp distinction between piracy and legitimate trade, and who drew a certain unctuous satisfaction from hoodwinking, robbing, or even murdering Spaniards—after all, were not the Spaniards Catholics, the disciples of the papal "anti-christ," and the sworn enemies of England? No faith need be kept with Spaniards.

The greatest of the Elizabethan sea dogs was Francis Drake, who became "Sir" Francis Drake after he had "singed the king of Spain's beard" on both sides of the Atlantic. Drake was with Hawkins at San Juan de Ulloa, in 1568, when the expedition was trapped in the harbor by the great Spanish admiral Pedro Mendez de Aviles. Mendez violated the truce arranged between them, with the result that Hawkins lost all but two of his ships, his own and the one commanded by Drake. From that time on Drake became a terror to Spanish shipping and the Spanish colonies. His depredations reached their culmination in 1577–1581 when he sailed boldly into the Pacific and robbed ship after ship of its gold and silver treasure, failed to find a passage back to England north of California (New Albion), and returned round the world in his own small ship, renamed the *Golden Hind,* having enriched himself and his queen with Spanish gold.

This was the more adventurous, more irresponsible side of Elizabethan expansion, and it was not without its significance for the founding of a British empire in America, for Humphrey Gilbert and Walter Raleigh were no less "Elizabethan sea dogs" than Hawkins and Drake, and these were the men who first colonized Newfoundland and Virginia for England.

But Elizabethan expansion had its more conservative, more methodical and businesslike side in the rapid and substantial growth of Britain's world-wide trade. In the course of this expansion of British commerce the merchants, in the interest of greater capital strength, devised several forms of commercial organization that had considerable effect upon the later establishment of the colonies. The first of these types was the so-called "regulated company." Such a company would customarily be organized for the purpose of exploiting some commercial market or undertaking some commercial enterprise, and it would be composed of members who operated independently of each other under their own capital but who cooperated to the extent of obeying such regulations as were laid down by the company. The second general type of trading company was the so-called "semi-joint-stock company" that was customarily organized for a short period of time and usually for the purposes of one enterprise only. Under this type of organization a group of merchants would contribute a certain amount of capital each for the conduct of one trading expedition, say, to the coast of Africa, and that expedition would be conducted as a unit by the company; but the company would dissolve after the return of the expedition and the division of the profits. The third type, which is the more important of the three, was the permanent joint-stock company. Ordinarily such a company was composed of a permanent group of stockholders and was governed by a president or "treasurer," a board of directors called "assistants," and an assembly of the stockholders meeting periodically, usually every three months. There were other types of commercial companies, but it is this third type which is most important for the history of the British colonies in America; for this was the form eventually adopted by the Virginia Company and this commercial way of government was taken over in large measure by certain of the colonies for political purposes.

The first great overseas company in England was the Muscovy Company, founded in 1553 and chartered in 1555 with a capital of six thousand pounds, for a monopoly of the trade with Russia. While it was of the regulated type, it was governed democratically by a governor, an elected council of twenty-eight, and an assembly of all the investors. In 1577 the Cathay Company was organized along similar lines to exploit the trade of China. This was the company whose object was to discover the northwest passage and which sent Martin Frobisher out to do so. In 1581, the Levant Company was organized to exploit the trade of Turkey and the eastern Mediterranean, and in 1588 another company called the African Company was organized to exploit the British trade on the coast of Guinea.

The classic example of these British trading and colonizing companies was the British East India Company, founded in the year 1600 to exploit the trade of the East Indies. The seizure of Portugal by Philip II of Spain in 1580 drove the English and Dutch merchants, who had hitherto bought

Far-Eastern goods at Lisbon or Cadiz, into a direct trade with the East. And the first English expedition to the East Indies sailed under the command of Sir James Lancaster in 1591. This trade proved to be so profitable that companies were formed both in Holland and in England to promote it. The English company was formed under the leadership of Sir Thomas Smythe, perhaps the greatest capitalist of his day. Under its charter, this great company was both a corporation and a body politic, for it was given not only a monopoly of all the English trade in the lands between the Cape of Good Hope and the Straits of Magellan, but it was also empowered to license others to trade in this area, to buy land for the establishment of posts, and to make laws for the government of its trade and its lands. It could even fine and imprison offenders against the law and could maintain soldiers and armed fleets for its own protection. Not only was it empowered to carry on commerce, but it was practically sovereign within the areas defined by its charter. This company was governed by a president, a council of twenty-four assistants, and a general assembly of all the stockholders meeting annually. Within a very short time of its organization the East India Company began to pay fabulous profits and it served as both the inspiration and the model for the men who were responsible for the establishment of the colony of Virginia. It is to be noted also that the government of this company was democratic, in the sense that each stockholder in it was considered to have the same voice in its affairs as all the others.

These were the men, and such were the companies, who furnished the capital and the original impulse toward the founding of English colonies in America in the seventeenth century. Had it not been for the accumulation of capital in the hands of these merchant princes, surplus wealth which they were willing to risk in colonial enterprise, the settlement of British America probably could not have taken place at that time.

ENGLISH POLITICAL INSTITUTIONS

Englishmen who came to America left behind a complex structure of government. Heading it was the monarch in whose name all laws were made, justice was given, and officials chosen. The monarch's formal authority and prestige were immense but knowledge and wisdom and character were essential if he was to exercise his power effectively. Elizabeth, though a woman in a society long accustomed to male dominance, usually got her way in most matters on her charm and brilliance. Her councillors and her Parliaments soon came to sense that in her the nation had a leader with unsurpassed gifts. Her subjects respected her and soon loved her, and Elizabeth loved them. Like her father Henry VIII, the queen made policy and saw to it that her councillors worked in Parliament to secure the laws she considered desirable.

Her successors, James I and his son Charles I, allowed the royal power to decline. In political skill they were inferior leaders; moreover they lacked both the respect of the English people and Elizabeth's understanding of English institutions. Their failure was not simply political; personally James was mean-spirited and Charles, though pious and well-meaning, was dull and stupid.

Though the monarch had much hard work to do—especially if he was to keep himself informed of the activities of his government—most of the administrative supervision of government was carried on by the Privy Council. This body of great officials and advisers varied in size from twelve to twenty under Elizabeth. The early Stuarts, James I and Charles I, increased its members to over forty. The Privy Council's functions ranged from making decisions on large questions of policy and administration to the consideration of the smallest details of government. It helped conduct foreign affairs; it instructed ambassadors; it prepared legislation for Parliament's consideration; it supervised business; it supervised justices of the peace. Poor relief was a matter of concern to it, as were, also, the number of alehouses in a country village and a thousand other petty local problems.

Not the least of the Privy Council's concerns was Parliament. As the legislative body in England, Parliament was composed of two houses, the House of Lords and the House of Commons. The landed aristocracy and the high church officials—"lords temporal and spiritual"—sat in the House of Lords. On the surface, as the seventeenth century opened, the House of Lords still appeared to be the more powerful of the two houses. After all, it sometimes, when consulted, advised the king on important matters of state. Its members were the privileged class; they could be tried only by juries of their peers; and they had the privilege of direct, personal audience with the sovereign. Moreover, the House of Lords constituted a high court for the trial of impeachments and a final court of appeal from the lower courts of the realm. These were formidable powers, but the House of Lords had begun to decline in importance—most seriously in the reign of Elizabeth's father, Henry VIII. Henry, in the interests of his reformation of the church, had changed its composition by creating more temporal peers. The spiritual peers of Henry's creation and the recently created lay peers lacked independence and the House of Lords consequently lost force.

Equally important in the decline of the Lords was the rise of the House of Commons. Though the Tudors were masters at leading Parliament and getting what they wanted while conceding only what they desired in return, the House of Commons was maturing. Composed of the country gentry, government officials and lawyers, who sat as representatives of counties and boroughs, the House of Commons attracted some of the ablest men in the nation. By Elizabeth's day it had become a self-conscious, proud, and powerful body. Elizabeth, by careful management, had held it in check, but under James I Commons broke the old bonds. It developed an elaborate committee system and began staking out the limits of royal authority. Before the end of James' reign it had won the right to initiate legislation; the king's failure to keep privy councillors in the House of Commons advanced the process. Thus organized, the Commons legislated on its own initiative; furthermore, it began to assume certain executive functions; for example, it forced James to cancel a large number of patents, as licenses to do exclusive business were called.

On the local level, officials remained agents of the Crown and not of the Commons. In the county, the most important unit of local government, justices of the peace conducted the government. They were of course judicial officers. Cases of serious crimes were referred to a higher court, but the justices kept busy trying misdemeanors. Drunkenness, gambling, idleness, and a host of other small crimes concerned the justices, who could order whippings or impose fines. Their most important duties were administrative rather than judicial. Often the justices received directions from the Privy Council; more often they decided for themselves what had to be done—a bridge built, constables supervised, roads mended, the poor housed and fed, and so on.

The sheriff, also a royal appointee, helped them though he had his own duties to perform. Selected for one year, the sheriff was the king's representative in the county. He called together the county court; he supervised elections; he arrested criminals; he collected dues owed the king; and at times when the king passed through the sheriff entertained him and his court. The sheriff's job was an unpopular one—expensive and arduous— but indispensable to the welfare of the county.

There were other local officers of course; in the village the constable performed many tasks. He enforced the law and collected taxes, the most difficult of all his jobs. He was not alone in his responsibilities; church wardens, elected by the parish (a governmental and ecclesiastical unit) managed church property, kept up the church building, and collected the parish rates, among other tasks.

THE ENGLISH PROTESTANTS

Long before the Jamestown expedition of 1607 the lines of religious conflict in England had been drawn. Henry VIII had achieved the separation of the English Catholic Church from Rome by about 1540, and the two decades following that date were in large measure taken up with a struggle to decide whether England was to be Catholic or Protestant. Gradually Lutheran and Calvinistic ideas crept into English religious life, and at the time of the accession of Queen Elizabeth in 1558 England had become predominantly Protestant. The adoption of the Thirty-nine Articles in 1563 established Anglican Protestantism in England, and this core of Anglican doctrine was reinforced by the adoption of a new prayer book, the re-enactment of the Act of Supremacy, and the passage of the Act of Uniformity, all between 1559 and 1563.

Anglican Protestantism, as established in England by the "Elizabethan settlement," was governed by a hierarchy of archbishops, bishops, priests, and deacons. The monarch was the supreme head of the church, but its active leader was the archbishop of Canterbury, who was appointed by the king. It preserved a large portion of the Roman Catholic ritual, retaining a belief in the apostolic succession, the wearing of vestments by the clergy, the use of holy water, the sign of the cross, and other ritualistic practices.

But there were many men in England who were not satisfied with what they considered only a partial reformation of the English church by the Elizabethan settlement. They continued to agitate for a further purification, and for dispensing with the hierarchial organization of the church, the use of holy water, the sign of the cross, and other vestiges of the "papish" ritual. These men had no quarrel with the doctrines of the church, but sought only to purify it of "popery." For this reason they were called "Puritans." The Puritans themselves, however, split into various groups; one group of the Puritans favored a central, presbyterian form of church government, and were called "Presbyterians." Another group rejected all hierarchial or coercive church government and insisted upon the independence or autonomy of every congregation of believers; they were the "Congregationalists." Two types of congregationalism developed: the "Separatists" version that rejected all ties to the Church of England, and nonseparating congregationalism that held that the Church of England was the true church although corrupt and polluted. The Separatists founded Plymouth Colony in New England; the nonseparating Congregationalists settled the Massachusetts Bay Colony.

As time went on, the Puritans came to differ more and more widely from the Anglicans in matters other than church practice. As a reaction against the gaiety and the worldliness of Elizabethan England, for example, and as a part of their effort to live the sort of life prescribed by the Bible, they followed a rigorous code of morals, and Puritanism came also to mean a moral domination of one's self. Similarly, whereas Anglicanism allowed for a wide play of human reason in interpreting the Bible and other expressions of God's interest in men, the Puritans considered the Bible to be the literal word of God, the only clear and definite expression of the divine mind with regard to men. Puritanism thus came to be marked by its literalism and its disciplinarianism, whereas Anglicanism, while placing more emphasis upon ritual, was much more latitudinarian with regard to individual believers. Both these bodies of belief were of profound importance in the formation of an American colonial culture.

By the time of the accession of James I there were three major groups of religious believers in England: there were still some Roman Catholics, following their religion more or less surreptitiously; there was the great body of Anglican believers; and there were the Puritans, united in a desire to purify the Church of England, though differing in their ideas of the scriptural ecclesiastical organization. In 1604 about one thousand pastors of the Puritan persuasion presented the so-called "millenary petition" to King James I asking that they be allowed to worship in their churches according to their own Puritan way instead of according to the way laid down by the Elizabethan settlement. James is said to have heard their arguments until his patience was exhausted, and then, putting on his hat as though to leave, to have said "they will conform themselves or I will harry them out of the land."

That was the beginning of a new wave of official and semi-official persecution of the Puritans and Separatists. Those persecutions were not severe under King James I but became increasingly troublesome after the accession of Charles I and after Bishop William Laud of London became Archbishop of Canterbury in 1633. Laud attempted to force the Puritans to conform to the Anglican way. He even leaned somewhat toward Catholicism. But he probably made more Puritans by his reforms that he saved to the Anglican church. Thus, beginning about 1625 or a little earlier, there took place an era of religious persecution that brought sincere Puritans face to face with the necessity for deciding whether they would give up their Puritanism in Anglican conformity or seek for a haven of religious freedom elsewhere. To the motives for emigration springing from economic and political conditions, then, was added the desire to escape from religious persecution. All three of these sets of motives were important in the movement of men and women out of England into America in the first four decades of the seventeenth century.

THE MOVE TO AMERICA

Popular interest in emigration was spurred in a number of ways. The exploits of Hawkins, Drake, and other Elizabethan adventurers interested people; moreover such colonial promoters as Humphrey Gilbert, Walter Raleigh, and Richard Hakluyt "advertised" the New World. Elizabethan literature, indeed, is shot through with reflections of a widespread popular interest in the New World and the adventures to be had there. "The world's mine oyster, which I with sword will open!" exclaims one of the characters in *The Merry Wives of Windsor,* and Shakespeare's plays are full of the jargon of the sea and tales of far-off countries. *The Tempest* is said to have been inspired by the shipwreck of the Somers expedition on Bermuda in 1610. One of the most popular plays of the time was *Eastward Ho,* a play upon the popular craze for sailing, commerce, and exploration.

It took more, however, than a merely literary interest in adventures overseas to send thousands of common men away from their native land into the dangers and uncertainties of colonization in a distant wilderness. By the end of the sixteenth century England seemed to be overrun by beggars, vagrants, criminals, and the indigent poor. England seemed to be overpopulated. This condition was probably due to the social maladjustment brought about by the practice of enclosing agricultural land for sheep-raising purposes, which forced many agricultural workers off the land. England's total population, as a matter of fact, was hardly more than three million persons—considerably less than half the present population of the City of London—but near the end of Elizabeth's reign English leaders began to look toward colonies in the New World as a possible receptacle for the overflow of the burdensome "surplus" of population in England itself.

The flow of Englishmen overseas began with the founding of Virginia in 1607, and the first two decades of the seventeenth century constituted a period of English experimentation in colonization, not only in Virginia, but also in Newfoundland, along the shores of New England, in the islands of the West Indies, and on the mainland of South America. By 1620, however, the feasibility of colonies had been demonstrated, and in the next two decades, that is to say, between 1620 and 1640, the stream of emigration from England to America reached its flood.

During this twenty-year period some 70,000 people left England for the New World. Of the total, some 12,000 went to Virginia, Bermuda, and the new colony of Maryland. About 18,000 went to New England, 14,000 of whom stopped in Massachusetts Bay, and about 37,000 went to the West Indies, where some 18,000 settled in Barbados, 4000 in Nevis, 12,000 in St. Christopher's, and some 3000 in the smaller English islands.

These people came for a variety of reasons. Most seemed to desire a new start, either at getting a living or in realizing their own vision of a religious society. The Puritans who settled in Massachusetts Bay, for example, were filled with a desire to create "a city upon a hill"—a holy society that would serve as a model for the still unreformed Europe. Of course, many plain people came to New England and the other colonies with the hope that earning a living might be easier in the New World. Others simply looked forward to political and religious tranquility. It must be remembered, of course, that the vast majority of the Englishmen who came to the colonies as settlers were Anglicans, who had no quarrel with the established church or with the crown. Whatever their reasons, these people poured into America, in the first of many such hopeful movements.

CHAPTER 4

THE ORIGINAL AMERICANS

Like the Afro-American and the Chicano, the Indian American has been an invisible man to majority white Americans. In our literature and historiography he has generally been ignored, maligned, or stereotyped. Even when writers dealing with Indian subjects have been sympathetic, their treatments have usually been superficial and uninformed. Indians have been variously pictured as cruel, vicious, and rapacious savages, or as noble, war-bonneted, horse-riding children of nature; in many histories they have been treated as one of the natural factors, like weather and wild animals, impeding the westward march of civilization. Rarely have historians recognized the variety and complexity that characterized Indian society and culture. The Iroquois, for example, were as different from the Cheyenne as they were from the English, the Pueblos as different from the Cherokee as they were from the Spanish. Yet all of the diverse Indian cultures and people left their marks on the European colonists and on the land that they settled.

Professor Wilbur Jacobs is well aware of the cultural differences that existed among the original Americans, and he has carefully limited the essay that follows to a consideration of the woodland Indians of the Northeast, which was one of the major Indian cultural areas of North America. Similar essays could be written about the other major Indian cultural regions of the United States. Professor Jacobs' main emphasis in the essay is on the contributions made by the woodland Indians to European settlement and to the development of the American way of life; ultimately, he is most concerned with identifying what *all* Americans really owe the woodland Indians. In the course of his discussion, Jacobs of necessity deals with the patterns of life of these Indians, and he gives due consideration to the relations between them and the white newcomers. Of particular interest today is Jacobs' presentation of the woodland Indians' attitudes toward their environment and his suggestion that Americans of the 1970's can learn a great deal about ecology from the original inhabitants of our land.

In reading this selection, the student should try to dispel any stereotyped images of the Indian that he may have acquired and should view Indians as ordinary, flesh-and-blood, real people. What contributions did the woodland Indians make to European settlement and to the subsequent history of the American people? What have we learned from them, and what more might we learn from them? How should our treatment of the woodland Indians be evaluated? Finally, what do we owe them?

Perhaps Professor Jacobs' essay does not answer thoroughly all of the questions posed above. These questions, however, are significant, and the student is encouraged to look further for their answers. Some of the more comprehensive works on the subject are Wilbur Jacobs, *Dispossessing the American Indian** (1972), and William T. Hagan, *American Indians** (1961). A classic treatment of the original Americans is Clark Wissler, *Indians of the Plains** (1940). White attitudes toward the Indians are explored in Roy Harvey Pearce, *The Savages of America** (1963). Robert H. Lowie, *Indians of the Plains** (1954), discusses the archetypical Indian of tepee and feathered warbonnet.

* Available in a paperback edition.

WHAT WE OWE THE WOODLAND INDIANS
WILBUR JACOBS

The fatal confrontation between whites and Indians was not seen in colonial times as the clear-cut moral issue that it sometimes appears to us today. Along the white frontier, adjacent to the Indian country, there was an almost quiet desperation in the eager plowing up of virgin farmland. In the eighteenth century a great wave of settlement swept through the colonies, particularly in Pennsylvania where there was a peaceful invasion of the "Pennsylvania Dutch," or Germans. Close after these farmers came a flood of poverty-stricken Scotch-Irish who with axes and plows forced back the wall of forests. These restless, enterprising immigrants, led by a bevy of flinty Presbyterian ministers, inevitably collided with woodland Indians who fought to keep their ancestral lands in the interior valleys of the Susquehanna River and its tributaries.

Indian savagery in counterattacking caused unspeakable suffering for the Scotch-Irish during the last phases of the French and Indian War. One estimate is that by the time of Pontiac's War of Indian Independence about two thousand whites had been killed or had vanished as prisoners of raiding parties. Further south, settlements of Virginia pioneers penetrated the beautiful green valleys beyond the Blue Ridge. At intervals these farmers hurriedly enclosed cabins with crude stockades for refuge in time of attack. The frontier Virginia farmers were, in many respects, the historical ancestors of *Leatherstocking,* woodsmen and marksmen schooled in Indian warfare. . . .

The numerous war parties that ravaged the borders carved a path of total destruction. Whole districts were depopulated after having suffered the ordeal of the tomahawk and the firebrand. The thinly settled valleys of Appalachia were practically devoid of whites after widespread Indian attacks left slaughtered cattle, blazing dwellings, and the remains of clay-built chimneys. There were instances of torture, and the bodies of men and women remained lashed to trees, where they had died a fiery death.

Certainly the moral question is not a simple one. It deserves our attention because throughout history men have had to decide between what they believe is necessary or moral. If we make conclusive moral judgments on the confrontation between settlers and Indians, we may find ourselves eclipsed by righteous indignation. Most of us share, I think, a feeling of sympathy for the Indian because of the injustices he has suffered at the hands of the white man. There is, however, a danger of being locked into a sympathetic position so that one's indignation spills over against all those who had anything to do with Indians. One can rant equally against colonists, governments, missionaries, individual officials, military men, pioneers, and even against the Indians themselves who were corrupted by the whites who lavished gifts on them as a bribe for lands.

Nowhere is found the irreducible truth. But we can make an assessment of the human wreckage left in the debris of violence if we stand back from the details of the conflict. . . . In the case of the long conflict between the whites and woodland Indians, one may view the whole story as part of a process that transformed provincial America into the modern American nation of today. If we step away from the series of events to look at the trends behind them we can more clearly see the historical processes at work.

For instance, it is not difficult to see that harsh living conditions, contact with Indians both in peace and war, and remoteness from central authority, all influenced the emergence of a tough new American breed among the white settlers. The early frontier (as well as later frontiers) was a powerful force from the beginning in molding the national character and in promoting rugged democratic ideals. Frederick Jackson Turner talked little about the Indians or blacks because his was primarily an interpretation of history that concerned itself with white people. If we look at the same historical process to understand what happened to the Indian, we come to the inevitable conclusion that in early American history we are watching the expansion of one people into the territory occupied by another.

As the chapters in this book show us, native peoples have shared a somewhat common experience in their struggle to survive in a world once dominated by Euro-American civilization. The Indians who occupied the territories claimed by France in North America seem to have fared better than almost any other native people. Certainly the French were ingenious managers of Indians and adept at dominating their chiefs with special types of gifts. Essentially the history of New France tells us that Indian policy was channeled toward peaceful exploitation of the fur trade because the economy of Canada was never based primarily upon agriculture, but on fishing and trapping. Yet, despite their plan of coexistence with the Indians, the French could not prevent the involvement of Indians in a whole series of border wars with the English. It must nevertheless be said that the French, more than any other great European power seizing possession of a large area of North America, and despite the diffusion of trading goods, minimized the displacement of Indians and left native society relatively undisturbed.

Spain, though not dealt with in the foregoing chapters, deserves mention here because her actions differed from those of the French and other European powers. Spanish policy seems to have been very much to the point: develop and exploit the surface of the land and send riches back home. Indians were to be conquered, converted, and used. As in the case of French policy, the Indian had a place in the overall imperial scheme of empire.

British policy . . . allowed no particular place for the Indian. In a sense, he was a nonperson. British and colonials tended to use the Indians and then eliminate them or shove them aside. In the end, there was no real home left for the American Indian. Here again is a historical process that one can observe by scanning hundreds of treaties with exchanges of gifts, promises, and wampum belts.

It was the woodland Indians who had the longest series of contacts with Americans during the formative period of the American nation. They were the tribesmen who generously gave corn to the fledgling settlements at Jamestown and Plymouth. Indeed, they may have saved these small outposts of Europe from disappearing in the shadows of early American history that close off details of first attempts at colonization. Once the colonies were going concerns, the colonists saturated their public records with matters concerning the Indians. Their archives as we know them today are punctuated with accounts of treaties, wars, messages from headmen, chiefs and sachems, and news about enemy Indians who allowed themselves to become allies of the Spaniards or French. As the roots of settlement reached into the coastal river valleys, the fur traders, squatters, and land speculators fill records with controversies about their activities. The niagara of paperwork regarding them in the colonial archives leaves no doubt that there was continual border contact between whites and natives as the frontier moved westward. Although the daily contact was there, a kind of no-man's zone, or neutral belt of land, seems to have always separated Indian territory from the zigzagging white cutting edge of settlement. It was in this tinder box zone where, more often than not, friction so easily sparked a conflagration of violence.

One singular aspect of the tragic historical process that finally eliminated the woodland Indian's way of life was that he fought back. He had a stubborn resiliency. Furthermore, native Americans produced brilliant leadership that on occasion brought the whole westward movement to a halt. The Delaware Prophet and Pontiac are examples of Indian leaders who distinctly perceived the irreversible harm that Euro-American influences had had upon Indian societies. Pontiac became such an outstanding leader because he clearly diagnosed the permanent damage his people had suffered as they bore the brunt of fierce white competition for rich midwestern lands.

Fortunately for the Indians who fought under Pontiac and collaborated with him, the colonials were handicapped in carrying out their traditional

scorched-earth campaigns in which stored surpluses of food as well as orchards and grain fields were put to the torch. Pontiac and his tribesmen on
the woodland fringe were partly free from such danger because they were
mobile and flexible in their attacks and because their old hunting ethos allowed them to live off the animal life of the forest. The great wilderness
gave them shelter and provided a sanctuary when retreat became necessary.
But even with this significant advantage, the Indians could not win. Pontiac
and his confederates were doomed because in the long run all the advantages were on the side of the Anglo-Americans. What left its mark on the
Indian as well as the white man was the very bitterness of the struggle. If, in
the ordeal of Indian war, the whites developed stereotypes of a lowly savage, they also retained the image of a gallant warrior who fought for freedom to live his own life on his own land.

The retreat of the woodland tribes before the relentless advance of the
Anglo-American agricultural frontier is dramatically illustrated in the fate of
the Delawares. After the peace settlements of the Delaware War of
1756–57, these once loyal, peaceful allies of William Penn were promised
lands of the Wyoming Valley in the upper Susquehanna. But friction developed during the latter part of the eighteenth century after squatters moved
into the area. In a bloody confrontation the Indians counterattacked, but
were finally beaten off. The Delawares were later scattered in the removal,
some as far west as Texas. Francis Parkman in 1846 saw remnants of a
once proud people near Fort Leavenworth on the edge of the Great Plains
where he described them as a dying tribe, "worn and dingy" but nevertheless dangerous scavengers who lived by preying on other tribes.

What happened to the Iroquois league, composed of the most powerful of
the woodland tribes? A large proportion of the league members finally decided to maintain their alliances and fight on the side of England during the
Revolution. Their severe attacks on border outposts resulted in the Continental Congress sending a punitive military force under General John Sullivan that in 1779 left the main Iroquois towns, fields, and orchards in flames.
Sullivan's thoroughness in making a wasteland of the Iroquois strongholds at
last and forever broke their power.

Joseph Brant, the daring Mohawk chief who led his people against the
Americans, had been a student at Eleazar Wheelock's academy at Lebanon,
Connecticut (where Indian and white youths were given Christian missionary training). Combining the role of a British gentleman-officer and an Iroquois warrior-diplomat, Brant led his "civilized Indians" in hard-fought
campaigns that won the respect of his enemies. Brant's forces, well aware of
European ideas of superiority, waged a war that seldom violated European
standards of conduct. Butcheries committed by some of his Indian allies,
reminiscent of the seventeenth-century cruelties of the Iroquois, were the
work of roving bands eager for plunder and revenge against the Americans.

. . . Since the 1783 treaty of peace after the Revolution made no provision for the Iroquois, those that remained in the new United States were at the mercy of a government that classified them as "dependent nations." Soon they were engulfed in a sea of white population that flooded all around them. The Cayugas were quickly swept before the tide, and the once proud Senecas, desperately clinging to a small portion of their lands, were victimized by a hungry speculative group known as the Ogden Land Company that used rum and promises to win its concessions. As Lewis H. Morgan wrote disgustedly, protesting the exploitation of the Iroquois, "It is no small crime against humanity to seize the fireside and property of a whole community, without an equivalent against their will; and then to drive them, beggared and outraged into a wild and inhospitable wilderness."

Fortunately the Iroquois, after their revitalization movement under Handsome Lake, with some white help, were able to ward off those who would take all their land. The Iroquois emerged from a horticultural and hunting culture to an agricultural way of life by adding domestic animals and the plow about 1800. Individual Iroquois later took up skills as blacksmiths and as other types of artisans so that in the next generation they worked for wages at a number of trades. Then came schools and literacy. Though the Iroquois are "civilized" and some live in American cities, they still cannot be regarded as an urban people. Troubled by factionalism, a gradual erosion of their rich ceremonialism, and the loss of their lands, they survive in the midst of their conquerors. . . . In the words of the prophesy of Deganawidah:

> Hail, my grandsires!
> . . . the Great League which you established has grown old . . .
> You have said that
> Sad will be the fate of those who come in later times.

Today, still battling utility companies, they control minuscule reservations in New York. . . . Their Longhouse religion still prospers. Its main rivals are the Mormon and various Protestant religions. Some of the Iroquois, it will be recalled, were converted by Jesuit missionaries and later by Protestants, but Mormon proselytizing is recent. Despite the sullen tone of resentment among a few of the Indians (some of the Longhouse people I met objected to sending their children to the white man's schools), they still have a lively sense of humor, they still love their dances, their championship lacrosse teams, and their games. . . .

The removal of the Cherokees and other tribes of the Old South is surely one of the darkest chapters in American history. Today most of their descendants live in Arkansas and Oklahoma, sometimes as prosperous farmers and businessmen, although poverty haunts most of them as they, like the Iroquois, are slowly blended into the mainstream of American society. Still, the shock of being completely uprooted from their homes and removed during the age of Andrew Jackson will always be recalled by modern Cherokees, the Creeks, the Choctaws, and other descendants of Indian tribes. Jackson's implementation of the removal, with all the callousness of his military tactics in herding Cherokees and other Indians into compounds where they suffered from hunger and disease, will forever be associated with his name. Actually and surprisingly, the demand for removal of the Indians was President Thomas Jefferson's most significant and all-important innovation in the development of federal policy toward the Indians. Jefferson's ideas implied a kind of "human cattle drive" in which the whites pushed the woodland Indians ahead of them as range after range of new states were created up to and beyond the Mississippi. The whites would advance "compactly," Jefferson wrote, "as we multiply."

As Jefferson predicted, the Indians on the woodland fringe, belting the shores of the Mississippi, were also pushed westward during the 1830s. The swift retaliation against Blackhawk, who led Sauks and Foxes back across the Mississippi to their ancient homelands, brought about the so-called Blackhawk War. In his autobiography Blackhawk eloquently described his feeling for the land that had been lost by his people:

My reason teaches me that the land cannot be sold. The Great Spirit gave it to his children to live upon, and cultivate, as far as is necessary for their subsistence, they have the right to the soil. . . . Nothing can be sold, but such things as can be carried away.

. . .

Do we really owe the Indians anything? Have they made any singular contribution to our culture other than the mystical notion about husbanding the land and the natural environment? Is it possible that their special attitudes toward wildlife will ever help to cure our myopia about the natural balance that allows the wholesale poisoning and killing of eagles, bears, mountain lions (as well as a host of small animals), disrupting the food chain and affecting the populations of dependent species? Will we ever get away from the idea that the animals in their natural state are not there for "harvesting" by men?

Perhaps the study of Indians, particularly the woodland Indians, will show us the advantages of hunting with restraint and the importance of cultivating an attitude of respect toward animals and the ecological balance wheel. What seems likely, however, is that the white man will never understand Indian attitudes of reverence toward wildlife (just as he has not understood Indian attitudes toward the land). The bear could not be killed without an apology and ceremony of atonement by woodland Indians. How different the white man is. We permit extractive or exploitative industries to wipe out whole populations of animals without a whisper of protest. Lumber companies, for example, have concocted an ingenious kind of cyanide bomb, attractively baited but triggered to explode in any inquisitive bear's mouth if he is so foolish as to enter the domain of privately owned forests. Even our own government foresters have developed a competitive system announcing proudly the number of porcupine killed in their "green" sheet newsletters. Indeed, it almost seems as though our national policy is to exterminate any animal that is not deemed useful to business or bureaucrats. But, fortunately, there are voices of protest, and among those are representatives of the increasing population of the Indians themselves. As Vine Deloria, a Standing Rock Sioux, has phrased it:

. . . American society could save itself by listening to tribal people. While this would take a radical reorientation of concepts and values, it would be well worth the effort. The land-use philosophy of Indians is so utterly simple that it seems stupid to repeat it: man must live with other forms of life and not destroy it. . . . Reorientation would mean that public interest, indeed the interest in the survival of humanity as a species, must take precedent over special economic interests. . . . All of this must change drastically so that the life cycle will be restored.

. . .

We may come to appreciate the importance of the Indian's message to us if we pay more attention to the outright gifts the Indian made that have contributed to the prosperous, unique side of our life. The woodland Indians, for example, gave us their accumulated wisdom stored in experience gained by generations of native people. The settlers in all the early colonies learned quickly about the value of Indian maize (corn), squash, and pumpkins and soon adopted native planting and cooking techniques. Tobacco, regarded by the Indians as sacred with particular medicinal properties, was of course also readily planted by the first pioneers, although we may now question how beneficial a gift it was.

Of all the bounties the Indian turned over to the first European settlers, corn was perhaps the most significant contribution to the colonial boom in prosperity. Of those plants domesticated by the Indians corn is only less important than the potato (domesticated by Meso-American and South American Indians and brought to Europe by the Spaniards in the 1570s, eventually reaching Ireland about 1606) in feeding the modern world. Records for production of world staple crops in 1966 show that two from the Indians of the western hemisphere, maize and potatoes (531,641,000 metric tons), are second only to two crops from the Old World, wheat and rice (562,185,000 metric tons). There is more maize raised in North America than on any other continent, though most of it is used for cattle and hog feed. In the American South, corn bread, Johnny cake, and hominy are longtime favorites, as is "corn on the cob" in the American Midwest.

Besides items of food, the settlers borrowed Indian buckskin clothing and Indian canoes (the Chippewa birch-bark style is still reflected in modern canoes), snowshoes, and toboggans. Iroquois-style moccasins survive today. Woodland Indians, as one would expect, were expert craftsmen who had long experience in developing techniques of bending wood without splitting it for basket handles, frames for snowshoes, canoe ribs, and lacrosse rackets. They surely and swiftly tempered the wood with hot water or, in the case of dugout canoes, with burning. The Iroquois were among the best Indian carpenters, easily felling huge trees and fashioning beams and boards from a wide variety of woods. White pioneers and explorers survived in the wilderness because they mastered Indian techniques of building shelters in the woods or making utensils, weapons, or tools fashioned from wood. For example, those whites who knew how to make a strong rope from the inner bark of the willow, or how to build a good canoe in the woods, had prepared themselves for living alone beyond the limits of civilization.

Indian medical cures and skills, many of them lost with the passage of time, have also been of considerable value to those colonials who knew how to use them effectively. Indians had an almost astonishing number of remedies for toothaches, gangrene, ulcers, backaches, headaches, rheumatism, weak or sore eyes, and other complaints. They were also able to perform primitive surgery when required, and their medicine men, sometimes called conjurers, were not far behind modern physicians as successful practitioners in certain areas of psychiatry. The Iroquois, for example, were masters at interpreting the unconscious as it expressed itself in dreams.

To be sure, some of the Indian drugs were given in huge doses (enough for a horse), and some are known to be overrated or valueless. For instance, Seneca snakeroot *(Polygala senega L.)* was valued as a cure for coughs and other ailments as well as for snakebites. Though not recommended for snakebites, the *Pharmacopeia of the United States of America* reports its use today as an expectorant, cough remedy, emetic, and a stimulant. A particular favorite among the woodland Indians was the hemlock tree *(Tusuga canadenssis Carr.,* and other species), which is thought to have been used by Indians to cure scurvy among Cartier's men in 1535. A seventeenth-century New England writer, John Josselyn, reported that the natives healed sores and swellings from the inner bark of a young hemlock. The Ojibwas are said to have pulverized the bark and swallowed it to treat diarrhea. The Pottawatomis combined it with other materials for "flux," or diarrhea, and made tea from its leaves to bring on perspiration as a cure for colds. Other woodland tribes used the bark to stop bleeding and to heal cuts; they made hot tea with the leaves for sweat baths. Even the twigs were boiled by the Penobscots to make a tea for curing colds. About 170 drugs still listed in the *Pharmacopeia of the United States of America* and the *National Formulary* were known to the Indians north of Mexico.

Robert Beverley, an able writer on the early Virginia aborigines, had a high opinion of the curative powers of Indian medicine. Their medicine men, he wrote, were "very knowing in the hidden qualities of Plants and other Natural things." In an age when whites were more apt to dodge a bath than take one, Beverley noted the Indians "take great delight in Sweating, and therefore in every Town they have a Sweating House." Moreover, most Indians culminated the sweat bath with a dive into a nearby stream, a most exhilarating physical shock that some modern anthropologists believe is beneficial for nervous anxiety and illnesses that are today classified as psychosomatic.

Very significant for modern Americans are Indian contributions to what we now call obstetrics, gynecology, and pediatrics. The Indians were more rational than their white neighbors about relieving pain, especially in connection with labor, which some whites felt was a form of punishment justified by the original sin. Europeans, not always aware that the Indians aided childbirth by herbal medicines, often expressed amazement at the ease with which Indian babies were born. Ezra Stiles, a president of Yale College, was almost typical in his comment on the subject when he wrote: "I have often been told that a pregnant Squaw will turn aside & deliver herself, & take up the infant and wash it in a Brook and walk off."

Since woodland Indian women suckled their babies for as long as three years, few Indian children, reared on mother's milk, were deformed because of malnutrition. Furthermore, the arrival of babies was spaced. John Lawson, writing in the eighteenth century about Sioux woodland tribes on the Virginia frontier, argued that Indian women controlled family population because they had "an art to destroy Conception," an art that modern writers feel was based upon the use of certain herbs.

What is especially fascinating about Indian medicine is that some techniques that were employed are difficult if not impossible for the modern physician to duplicate. For instance, the enthusiastic participation of a whole aboriginal tribe in a healing rite with religious overtones combines to bring about hidden psychotherapeutic results. How could we ever hope to do as well as the Indian community cheering a sick person on to recovery? Medical science may yet still benefit by study of medicine men's techniques.

Indian medicine shows that the historical arrogance white Americans have had toward the Indian is misplaced. It is misplaced because clearly the Indians, in this case the woodland people, were, in certain areas of medical science, far in advance of their European contemporaries. Some of the colonial doctors, often part-time barbers or apothecaries, with standard remedies of calomel, bleeding, or opium, were superstitious rustics compared to the woodland Indian medicine man with his vast store of herbal medicines and his understanding of the psychological needs of his patients. Even Benjamin Rush, no doubt the leading physician of the Revolutionary generation, showed that he misunderstood Indian medicine when he said in 1774 that native remedies "were few in number," though he did acknowledge them to be "simple . . . full of strength." Whatever merit the Indian health remedies had, Rush correctly concluded, they were no match for the white man's plagues of smallpox and venereal disease.

If it has taken Americans centuries to come to appreciate the genius of Indian health remedies, a more self-evident contribution from the tribesmen is the thousands of Indian names and words that have enriched our vocabulary and made our language more euphonious. A number of our states have Indian names, and most place-names of those in the Midwest and East are taken from the woodland tribes: Milwaukee, Massachusetts, Illinois, Wisconsin, Michigan, Ontario, Mississippi, Alabama, Arkansas, Minnesota, and Pontiac are examples. One investigator identified some five thousand Indian place-names for New England alone! Many specific names and phrases reveal the historic influence of the woodland tribes and their brethren upon our society: "wampum," "wigwam," "mugwump," "caucus," "powwow," "papoose," "achem," "tepee," "succotash," together with such phrases as "bury the hatchet," "take up the hatchet," "smoke the peacepipe," "run the gauntlet." Scholars have found that Indians all over North America have modified our language, and that the number of Indian place-names in the one state of California numbers in the thousands.

Woodland Indians (as well as all other Indians) have over the centuries left a clear imprint on American culture, not only in language but in literature and in art. Take, for example, the colorful cycles of pioneer history and Indian-white relations that form the backdrop of James Fenimore Cooper's *Leatherstocking Tales.* The hero, a scout as we see him in the *Deerslayer,* has the spunk to resist worldly temptations. In the *Pathfinder* he marries himself to the wilderness after giving up his girl to another. Natty Bumppo's portrait, as it unfolds in later novels, *The Last of the Mohicans, The Pathfinder, The Pioneers,* and *The Prairie* reveals a character whose virtues are those of the woodland Indians and pioneers. He is courageous, reverent of nature, and just. Above all, he is a woodsman-hunter par excellence. By contrast, the pride and disillusionment of the Delaware Chingachgook shows another dimension of Indian character. Similarly, Henry Wadsworth Longfellow, poetically inaccurate in historical details, nevertheless immortalizes a symbolic but heroic figure of woodland Indian traits in *Hiawatha.* Out of this kind of tradition the Indian guide, or scout, the frontier ranger, the plainsman, the mountain man, and finally the cowboy emerge as character types combining traits of both white and Indian to become heroes of American history, literature, and drama.

· · ·

With spears, arrows, hatchets, bullets, and war paint, the woodland Indians held their own against the finest troops that Europe had. They went down in defeat not because they were beaten by better warriors or strategists, but because they could not fight off the overwhelming number of the enemy and his two-horned devil: disease and liquor. Even today we imitate him. There is no higher calling in the military service than that of the commando-ranger who gallantly fights our battles the world over. And no modern military ranger commander has better solved the problem of food logistics than the Iroquois raiding war chief whose men carried, in skin bags, parched maize flour, pulverized and mixed with dried berries and maple sugar. When water was added to this curious mixture, a handful could sustain a warrior for a day. In fact, he could sustain himself for months at a time while laying siege to the mission settlements of Canada and almost bringing the entire colony to its knees.

Yet even the formidable Iroquois were known as peacemakers and peacekeepers. It is probable that the Five Nations, having established "the Great Peace" between themselves with their historic constitution before the time of the first invasion by the white man, might never have embarked upon the long Huron war had their country not been depleted of furs by the Dutch fur trade. The sachems, drawing on their long cane pipes over the Onondaga council fires, could easily argue that despite the border wars over beaver, they wished to extend the Great Peace to Canada. As their representatives told the Jesuits, "If you love, as you say you do, our souls, love our bodies also, and let us henceforth be but one nation." They proposed peace with the French under the "Great Tree" many times. Fierce Iroquois warriors hidden behind a screen of forest looked on to see if their negotiators could ever persuade the French to share the Canadian beaver pelts so they could leave their deadly work undone. Finally the Iroquois war parties had to carve out their own destiny by physically opening up the Great Lakes beaver country. And in doing so, they all but killed off the Hurons. Later, during the Anglo-French wars of the eighteenth century, they preserved a policy of neutrality that was constantly attacked by the machinations of Sir William Johnson who plied their sachems and war chiefs with gaudy clothes, rum, and other gifts.

A recent book of documents dealing with the Indians of the southern colonial frontier, shows that the Cherokees and their allies were likewise eager to stop the bloody conflict in which they found themselves engulfed. We have in these documents, or "Indian Books," an expression of the Indian point of view as found in long communications from chiefs and headmen (and occasionally headwomen) among the Creeks, the Choctaws, the Catawbas, the Chickasaws, and the Cherokees. These lengthy "talks," as they were called, set forth a clear argument that the Indians, above all, wanted a fair deal in trade and honest clarity in treaty terms and negotiations. Time and again we find the Indians pleading that their "hearts is [sic] streight" and that they wanted "to live in Peace and Friendship." When the Cherokees in 1759 declared to the English, "we desire to keep free from any Disturbance or Blood," they spoke for most of the woodland tribes of the Old South. Is it possible that the American penchant for peace has an anchor chain deep in the historical past that ties us to the Indian?

It has often been said that the woodland people were so generous with their food and other possessions that when one starved, they all starved. Much of the present-giving took place because the Indians shared whatever they had with each other, with white colonists, and even with prisoners taken in war. Is it possible that the American proclivity for sharing, for philanthropy, for generous gifts, is related to the magnificent tradition of generosity among the woodland tribes? There was even a joyful element of play and ceremony around native giving. If Americans have similar feelings about sharing today, who is to say that the Indian was not at least partly responsible in making that subtle contribution to the American character? Indeed, gift-giving seems to have had profound implications for the American way of life.

The fact that the Colonial Indians refused to be drafted into slavery by their white conquerors, is the subject of much comment among the colonists. Except for some individual cases, Indians, praised for their fine physiques and intelligence by leading colonials, nevertheless resisted all colonial efforts to convert them into a labor force of field hands. True, there were sporadic efforts among the Carolinians to force native tribesmen removed from Apalachee Spanish missions into slavery, but even this effort was doomed to failure.

Why would the average woodland tribesman choose death as an alternate to being the white man's slave? Freedom was the Indian's element: freedom of movement, freedom of speech, freedom of action, freedom to do what he pleased to do whenever he chose to do it. Travelers among the Indians often spoke about mild parental discipline used to control Indian children who seemingly were only swayed by affectionate counseling. In the tribal relationships existing between adults, few leaders had any real semblance of authority. Sachems, subchiefs (or sagamores), medicine men, and conjurers had little personal dominance over their fellow-tribesmen except as they exerted it by sheer force of leadership and personality. White colonials, eager to identify Indian leaders who would authorize bargaining over lands and trade looked in vain for actual Indian "kings." Whites, however, did contribute to the prestige of particular chiefs by rewarding favored "treaty chiefs" with special medals, gorgets, and elaborate gifts, and this practice may well have had an influence in strengthening the posture of Indian leaders such as Teedyuscung of the Delawares and Pontiac in the late colonial period. Yet neither of these chiefs were despotic leaders who commanded underling tribesmen. In fact it is difficult, if not impossible, to find in the woodland Indian languages words that convey the full meaning of despotism, authoritarianism, or dictatorship, so far removed are such concepts from Indian thinking.

The religion of the woodland Indians, varying in rites and details from tribe to tribe in various linguistic families, was not forced upon those Indians who were adopted, nor did particular medicine men, conjurers, or prophets, attempt to stamp out religious beliefs of neighboring tribes. Of course the Indians did not attempt to force their beliefs on the white man. Despite the white man's arrogant assumption that his was the only religion, the Indian from the beginning believed in freedom of choice, a concept that eventually became one of the highly treasured "freedoms" of Americans today. Freedom of choice, of course, also meant freedom of religion. American ideals, in a host of different kinds of freedom, may not be entirely of European origin. Is it possible that we owe the Indian more of our heritage of freedom than we have heretofore acknowledged? Nowhere do we see Indian ideals more admired than among America's young people today. Indian lifestyles involving movement from place to place, communal democracy, reverence for nature, and dialogues on peace, are imitated everywhere by a new generation of Americans. Modern, youthful, concerned citizens have gone a long way in attempting to teach their elders about values of the old Indian way of life. Such instruction, as one would expect, has not always been received with gratitude. Nor have the Indians always admired their long-haired imitators, even when they talk about ecology. But at least there is talk and debate.

Academics still argue about whether the Indian confederations of colonial times had a tangible influence upon the fathers of the Constitution. The case for the Indians is not so far-fetched as one might think. Franklin, an admirer of the Iroquois league, had good reason to know its virtues for he had been an Indian commissioner at treaties, and at the Albany Conference of 1754 he and his fellow delegates had a whole series of scoldings from Old Hendrick of the Mohawks who praised the league and told them their disorganized, womanlike method of defense against the French was to be deplored. It is known that other framers of the Constitution had knowledge of Indian confederation systems and the ideals of Indian democracy. Moreover, these statesmen were avid readers of the French *philosophes* whose writings were partly influenced by descriptions of North American Indians set forth in the writings of French Jesuit missionaries. The noble savage idea, hammered into the writings of Michel de Montaigne and later French writers, including Rousseau, was embellished with the ideas of natural rights, of the equality of man, and with democratic tribal traditions of North

American Indians. Because the great Inca and Aztec regimes were swept so quickly out of existence by invading Spaniards and their societies were shrouded in mystery, the politics of the Iroquois league and other confederations among the woodland tribes became so significant to European observers.

As the French writers were fascinated by the Six Nations Iroquois, so Lewis H. Morgan, the father of American anthropology, a century later was also attracted to them. Their grand council, he said, was "the germ of modern parliament, congress, and legislature." William Fenton, the modern Iroquois scholar, went so far as to argue that the confederacy was a germ of the modern state that united tribes with adjacent territories and a common language for defense under a single political system.

With all their contributions and achievements in government, politics, language, medicine, agriculture, and ecology, it is nevertheless true that the woodland tribes, as well as most other Indians of North America, were concerned with the daily business of *living,* whereas the whites, especially those settlers of the British North American colonies, were largely concerned with *getting.* The Puritan ethic, so clearly spelled out in the writings of Benjamin Franklin and Thomas Jefferson as well as the Puritans themselves, stressed thrift and industry. By contrast, there was something almost sacrilegious about the lifestyle of the woodland Indians. From John Smith to Thomas Jefferson we find a whole series of Anglo-American writers who want to put these "indolent" natives to work tilling fields. The Indian, exposed to the marketplace economy and technology of the white man, could no longer continue his way of simple living. He had to be more concerned with getting in order to survive. The resulting degradation of the woodland tribes and finally the preaching of Handsome Lake's *gaiwiyoh,* "the good news," helped some of them to rise out of their demoralized state, as did the Iroquois. Other tribes had their leaders, too, such as the great Sequoia among the Cherokees, and John Ross, the Cherokee leader who helped his people to live after removal to a harsh new land.

Unfortunately whites still tend to associate "Indian" with dances, feathers, "arts and crafts," and bad whiskey. Such associations, part of the historic stereotype of the Indian, have prevented us from appreciating the tremendous potentialities of Indian wisdom. It is even feasible that Indian tribalism could have a successful impact upon the modern world in the sense that it gives self-respect to the individual as well as the group. Furthermore, it is closely identified with the land because tribal groups have been rooted in specific land areas for thousands of years. It may be that the way of life of the Indian (as well as other "savage" tribes, in the language of older evolutionism), with its web of significance in which man obtains an acceptable relationship with the world at large, the universe, and the ecology surrounding him, may have true meaning for America today.

In the tribe, competition and individual initiative are subordinated to the idea of the harmonious whole. Thus people are able to adjust more easily to each other. The tribal way of judging a man by what he accomplishes is also significant because of its simplicity. If a man's I.Q. is not computed, his potential becomes an object of possible praise, and if his wealth is not hoarded to be compared with that of others, he may be judged simply by what he does. Even more important, the tribal man never is, or was, historically so conservative and unchangeable that he did not adapt to new situations. Certainly the story of humanity would have been vastly different if mankind had not adjusted to necessary changes. Can modern America actually benefit from Indian tribalism as part of the American heritage? Is it possible that our huge bureaucracies and polluted, overgrown cities—unmanageable and seemingly uncontrollable—are our only alternatives?

From the historical perspective, we can see flaws in the tribal way of life that made it difficult, at times almost impossible, for the Indians to seek the best accommodation with whites. Perhaps the greatest weakness of Indian society was its own hubris. The singleminded pride of the woodland tribes may have proved to be their undoing because it tended to make them more susceptible to easy conquest by the white man's entrepreneurial economy, which, in turn, greatly weakened Indian self-sufficiency. It is undoubtedly true that the woodland tribes at first had no real concept of what an "Indian" actually was. For instance, to a Choctaw, whites, Chickasaws, or Catawbas, though human beings, were regarded as three types of outsiders. It was not until the eighteenth century that the woodland tribes of the interior began to realize that they had something in common with each other as opposed to the Europeans. We see this in speeches at Indian treaties when chiefs comment on Indian lifestyles and loss of hunting territories. By the time Pontiac appeared upon the scene many woodland tribes were willing to cooperate to ally themselves and pit their strength against this white outsider whose presence blighted their manner of living.

Through study and renewed appreciation of Indian history we may, perhaps, recapture and preserve much of that rich Indian inheritance for all Americans. Is it not possible that the Indian wisdom of our heritage may help us to turn more and more toward nature, to succor the richness of the earth and the spirit of mankind?

We know that the Judeo-Christian traditions of man's dominion over nature have been at least partly responsible for the spread of the white American style of technology. Somehow we seem to have built a value structure out of this heritage which supports technological advance in the belief that this kind of progress coincides with God's will. The monotheism of early Christianity "liberated" mankind from the religions of antiquity which tended to view a universe with all things having a certain spiritual essence. Although Christianity had its spirits, none were contained in animals, plants, or sacred rocks or waterfalls. As a distinguished historian of science has argued, "To a Christian a tree can be no more than a physical fact. The whole concept of the sacred grove is alien to Christianity and to the ethos of the West." Despite such an interpretation, it is hard to prove by close examination of Genesis, for example, that there is biblical justification for the ravaging of the earth, that we have divine license to dig, chop, crush, and kill as we wish. And the teachings of St. Francis set forth the idea that it is the duty of all men to show respect for animal life, domestic animals and birds, as well as wildlife. Americans seem, however, to have persuaded themselves that in exploitation for immediate wealth they can do as they please without accounting for their actions. Now, perhaps, we may reconsider difficult questions that the American Indian heritage poses for us: should we have a concern, even a moral obligation, for a bear, a grove of redwoods, a sacred lake, or even a wolf, a coyote, or an alligator? From a practical standpoint, should we not regard the land as a depreciable resource in only finite supply? If we are able to reassess our values, surely the American Indian concept of Mother Earth will help us on the way to comprehending ecological righteousness in the modern world.

CHAPTER 5

THE INFLUENCE OF THE
FRONTIER ENVIRONMENT

More than 75 years ago, in July 1893, Frederick Jackson Turner, a young assistant professor at the University of Wisconsin, delivered a paper to the American Historical Association, meeting on the grounds of the Chicago World's Fair. The paper "The Significance of the Frontier in American History" is the best-known and probably the most important essay ever written in the field of American history. Turner argued that American historians, in interpreting the American past, tended to overemphasize European factors and to ignore American factors. "The true point of view in the history of this nation," he said, "is not the Atlantic coast, it is the Great West." The development of American institutions and of the American character could be explained, Turner suggested, by the "existence of an area of free land, its continuous recession, and the advance of American settlement westward. . . ."

The Turner thesis, or frontier hypothesis, was put forward as one of the possible explanations of American development. Unfortunately, until Turner's death in 1932, his views enjoyed overenthusiastic and uncritical acceptance; then, in the 1930's and 1940's his thesis was violently and unreasonably attacked by critics in history and other disciplines. In the 1950's and 1960's a "third generation" of the frontier hypothesis emerged.

In *America's Frontier Heritage,* Professor Ray Allen Billington, once a student of Turner's, seeks to summarize the findings of the "third generation" and to reappraise the entire hypothesis in the light of modern research. To accomplish these tasks, he has utilized several hundred eighteenth- and nineteenth-century travel accounts and recent studies of sociologists, anthropologists, social psychologists, and demographers.

In the next selection, Professor Billington examines the influence of both environment and heredity on man's social behavior, evaluates the role of the physical environment and the social environment in determining cultural patterns, and applies these findings to the development of American institutions and American character traits on the frontier. He suggests that the end products were determined not by the European heritage alone nor by the physical wilderness frontier alone, but primarily by the clash of traditional controls and values with a changing and innovative social environment on the frontier.

In seeking to appraise the influence of the frontier on American civilization, Professor Billington raises this fundamental question: Can a culture be basically altered by transplantation to a different physical environment? What is his answer? Does he see the development of a distinctive national character in colonial and nineteenth-century America? If so, in explaining this development, what weight does Professor Billington give to the various forces operating on the Americans—their European heritage, the wilderness frontier, and what he identifies as the social environment?

With a plethora of excellent material on this subject, students can begin with Frederick Jackson Turner, "The Significance of the Frontier in American History" (reprinted in numerous places). A provocative two-part article is Stanley Elkins and Eric McKitrick, "A Meaning for Turner's Frontier," *Political Science Quarterly,* LXIX (July 1954) and (December 1954). Billington's *America's Frontier Heritage** is a thorough and penetrating treatment of the subject.

* Available in a paperback edition.

THE FRONTIER AND THE AMERICAN CHARACTER

RAY A. BILLINGTON

Let us indulge in a thoroughly unhistorical speculation. Suppose that in the year A.D. 752 the emperor Hsiian Tsung, wearying of the brilliant scholars in his Academy of Letters and moved by the plight of his overcrowded peasantry, decided to dispatch his most experienced navigator, Bo Ko Lum, to search for a route to thinly settled Europe. Assume that Bo Ko Lum, sailing eastward with three sturdy ships, made his landfall in a gentle country that he mistook for a remote outpost of the Frankish kingdom where he was welcomed by friendly natives, called by the Chinese, Red Franks. Pretend that this newly discovered continent, later called Frankland, was occupied over the next century by hundreds of thousands of settlers from China's overpopulated mainland. They would fashion rice paddies, build their pagodas to worship at the shrine of Buddha, and slowly advance their Asiatic civilization eastward, led by venturesome fur trappers in flowing silken robes. As they moved ever onward toward the rising sun until they reached the distant Atlantic they would leave behind a new Orient, transplanted across the seas, and modeled after the Orient they had left behind.

But would this civilization be an exact replica of the old? It would not. Chinese pioneers would discover that silken robes were less resistant to wilderness wear than jackets and pantaloons of hides, that corn and wheat were more easily produced than rice, and that decrees of a distant emperor were easily ignored by a people whose unique problems demanded unique local solutions. They would, over the course of years, change in appearance, in dietary habits, and in social values as the wilderness of Frankland altered their customs and institutions. A future Chinese historian might write that they had been Franklandized by the New World environment. Yet would this transformation convert the colonists into replicas of the pioneers who actually settled the Wests? Certainly not. Trans-

SOURCE. From Chapter Three (pp. 47–61) of *America's Frontier Heritage* by Ray Allen Billington. Copyright © 1966 by Ray Allen Billington. Reprinted by permission of Holt, Rinehart and Winston, Inc. and the author.

planted cultural patterns would be too powerful to be completely submerged. The imaginary Frankland as an outpost of China would have
borne little resemblance to the actual America as an outpost of England.
But it would also show little similarity to the China from which the settlers
had come.

This imagined situation brings into focus the basic question that must
be answered if we are to appraise the influence of the frontier on American
civilization. Can a culture be basically altered by transplantation to a different physical environment? And, if it can, how is this accomplished?
To solve these problems we must weigh the relative influence of traditional
cultural forces and the physical environment in shaping group cultures.

Geneticists have learned a great deal about the hereditary process. They
know that traits are transmitted from parents to children through the
forty-six chromosomes present in every fertilized ovum, that these chromosomes are made up of complex molecules called "genes," and that these
genes are reshuffled from generation to generation, giving rise to the endless new combinations that relieve us of the unpleasant necessity of all
looking alike. They also know that hereditary traits are rigidly restrained
(save in the rare case of mutations) and that they are passed along by
the genes from generation to generation utterly unchanged by life experiences. This means that *learned* skills or experiences cannot be inherited;
we inherit only a certain physical-chemical organization observable in the
form of the physical structure, intelligence, temperament, and innate
drives.

Environment plays an equally important role in shaping our behavior.
Actually we are influenced by two interacting environments, the "primary"
or *physical* environment that comprises the world of nature about us, and
the "secondary" or *social* environment provided by the human group in
which we find ourselves. Of these two, the latter is more immediately
important, for the social group serves as a medium through which primary
environmental forces reach the individual; its influence operates within
limits set by the physical environment but within these limits it plays a
transcendent role. Each group has its own patterns of behavior known as
a *culture,* which include the shared knowledge, beliefs, customs, and habits
that have been acquired by living together over the course of generations.
These "cultures" vary from group to group and account for many of the
differences that distinguish peoples; they determine the nature of the skills
that we acquire, the knowledge that we accumulate, the basic assumptions
that we hold, and the conscious or unconscious values that govern our
behavior. This means that each group has its own social environment
that affects the behavior of those within the group.

The culture of any people tends to change constantly as traditional practices are eliminated and adjustments made to meet new situations. In a forming social order these changes occur frequently as the group adjusts itself to its physical environment, accustoms itself to surrounding peoples, and experiments with behavior patterns. Once established, however, these patterns tend to perpetuate themselves; although change continues, the rate of change slows as each society tends to regard its culture as proper and to resist further alteration. At this point in social evolution the group is a victim of ethnocentrism.

Thus man's social behavior is influenced by both heredity and environment. Inherited characteristics are passed from generation to generation and change so slowly as the evolutionary process operates that differences are not observable within historical periods; they are unaffected by experience, although modes of expression may be altered by cultural change. Environment is both physical and social, with the latter more determinative of social behavior within limits set by the former. Central to the social environment is the "culture" of each group. This emerges in the early stages of social organization and while changing constantly to adapt to changing conditions—in the physical environment, technology, ethnic variation, and the like—tends to solidify and to be increasingly resistant to change as ethnocentrism becomes a factor. Such changes as do occur after this point result from continuing alterations in the physical environment and from interaction with adjacent cultures that mutually influence each other.

Against this background of established theory, we can ask three questions essential to understanding the frontier process: Is the behavior pattern of the individual altered by changes in the physical environment? Is it changed by deviations in the social environment? And does an alteration in the social environment affect group behavior? Experiments conducted by anthropologists, sociologists, and social psychologists shed some light on these problems.

Social scientists are now unanimous in their belief that the physical environment is not solely determinative of human behavior. Two obvious examples will demonstrate this point. First, several different cultures have been shown to exist within one physical environment: the Hopi and Navajo Indians of the southwestern United States lived during the early nineteenth century in the same geographic province, yet the Hopi were monogamous, adept in ceramic arts, skilled weavers, and capable farmers, while the Navajo were polygamous, produced no ceramics, confined weaving to women, and supported themselves by herding livestock. Second, intruding cultures adapt differently to identical physical environments. Southern

California was occupied successively by Indians, Spaniards, Mexicans, and Anglo-Americans. The Indians developed a culture based on food gathering, the Spanish-Mexicans one resting on herding, and the Anglo-Americans one built on farming and industry. Obviously the reaction of any culture to the physical environment depends not only on the environment but on the nature of the transplanted culture.

If the geographic setting does not determine cultural patterns, are they altered by the changing social environment? Two seemingly unrelated experiments show this to be the case. In one a young ape, reared in the identical environment of a human child of his own age, learned eating and toilet habits and even the meaning of some words but could never speak, for no amount of training could offset the limitations imposed by heredity. In another a young girl who had been neglected by her parents and allowed to rear herself in a dark closet was given the best training possible when discovered, but was never able to catch up with her age group in skills, language, or mental ability. Environment blocked the mental and social growth of the girl, just as heredity blocked the mental and social growth of the ape.

Further evidence indicating the ability of the social environment to alter human behavior is provided by numerous experiments with identical twins. Having the same genetic origin, and thus the same heredity influence, any differences between such twins must depend on the different social and physical environments in which they have been reared. Studies in such cases suggest that the intelligence level as measured by IQ tests is directly proportional to the amount of education; two sisters separated at the age of eighteen months and subjected to different educational experiences showed a difference of twenty-four points on the intelligence-quotient scale at the age of thirty-five years. Similar experiments indicate that in both intelligence and personality the deviation between identical twins reared apart is as great as between nonrelated persons. These results are substantiated by studies of Negro children transplanted from the inferior schools of the segregated South to the better schools of the North; they reveal a steady improvement in intelligence and social behavior as the inherited abilities of the Negroes are altered by an improved environment. The child of a steelworker in Birmingham, England, suddenly shifted to the home of a steelworker in Birmingham, Alabama, would act and talk and think differently than if he had been raised at home. Yet the physical environment would be about the same in each instance; the principal change would be in the social environment.

Studies also suggest that social environment changes group behavior. Japanese living in Hawaii develop mannerisms different from those of their homeland, revealed especially by more individualistic and assertive attitudes. Similarly Chinese transplanted to Hawaii and to the mainland of the United States behave differently; those in Hawaii are more outward in their emotional expressions than those on the mainland, who feel restrained by the presence of unsympathetic Occidentals. The inscrutable Oriental of California's discriminatory past became a gay, laughing extrovert in Honolulu, where he felt accepted and free of social disapproval. That group traits can be modified is also shown by studies of ability in different classes in the United States; these reveal that children on high socioeconomic levels are more intelligent than those from lower classes. Research such as this, fragmentary though it may be, indicates that both individuals and groups respond to social-environmental forces.

Yet such changes when they do occur are accomplished only by overcoming a vast inertia of tradition that varies its influence with each situation. A few examples will make this clear. New Englanders originally built two-story barns on hillsides where hay wagons could drive directly into lofts on the second floor; their descendants in the flat Middle West continued to build barns in this fashion even though they had to construct an earthen runway to the second floor. Londoners in the seventeenth century adjusted to the narrow streets by building overhanging second floors; these same Londoners built identical homes in Boston where space was no problem. Roads were laid out along sectional lines in the Midwest; pioneers in mountainous country continued to follow surveyors' range lines even though highways following hill contours would have been easier to construct. Summer vacations for schoolchildren originated in farm areas where help was needed in planting and harvesting, but persist in the schools of urban America. Clearly cultural patterns, once established, can be changed only with difficulty, despite alterations in the social environment.

These conclusions can be substantiated—but by no means proved— by observations of modern groups brought face to face with conditions comparable to those that existed on the American frontier. During the 1930s the Farm Security Administration established seven communities where families from a variety of backgrounds were abruptly brought together. Their behavior in this unfamiliar situation, not unlike that of a pioneer settlement, suggests that the social environment altered behavior patterns very much as it did in the successive Wests. Social relationships tended to disintegrate, as men and women associated with others of comparable economic status or whose personalities complemented their own. The new friendships were formed with those living nearby, for a more extended time was needed to develop relations with persons of like interests living far away. Particularly marked was the tendency of families that had been most mobile in the past to leave the communities, explaining that their golden dreams had not materialized. These behavior patterns were a product of the unfamiliar social environment; notable, however, is the fact that they only slightly modified established habits.

On the basis of these modern-day studies by behavioral scientists we can advance certain hypotheses that can be applied to frontier societies:

The "primary" or physical environment did not directly determine such cultural deviations as existed on the frontier, although it laid the basis for such deviations by offering individuals a unique man-land ratio that stimulated an urge for self-advancement.

The differing *social* environment of frontier communities fostered the growth of unique folk cultures, based on but distinguishable from those of the successive Easts. This was because:

(a) The diversity of ethnic and social types attracted to pioneer settlements contributed to creating a fluid social order where ethnocentrism was lacking.

(b) Social controls and traditionalism were diminished by isolation and the dispersion of settlement, with a corresponding impetus to innovation.

(c) The absence of a solidified social order with established in-groups and out-groups allowed opportunity for greater vertical mobility.

In essence, then, the principal effect of the frontier social environment was to weaken traditional controls and values. The pioneer found himself in a fluid, ever-changing, unstabilized society, where accustomed behavior did not bring predictable results and where experimentation seemed more essential than in established cultures. Change, not tradition, was the order of life.

Just as important was the fact that the pioneers realized that in moving westward they severed their ties with tradition. The act of migration disrupted the social relationships that had assisted them in patterning their behavior in their old homes. In their new homes the sense of nonbelonging was accentuated, for most frontier communities were settled by men and women from a variety of places and social backgrounds; Yankees and Yorkers, Southerners and Northerners, natives and immigrants, all met and mingled on a common ground. Language barriers and differing social customs made cohesion difficult, for a Vermonter in Illinois might not be able to communicate with the German who lived nearby, or might feel superior to the Tennessee uplander who had taken out the next farm. Distances between neighbors, growing steadily greater as the frontier moved westward across the prairies and plains of mid-America, also heightened the feeling of removal from the group, as did the economic uncertainty of life in an untested new region. The typical frontiersman was oppressed by a sense of social weightlessness (to borrow a term from the space age), which generated a feeling of not belonging fatal to cultural cohesiveness.

The result was a mild form of mass anomie everywhere on the frontier. To some degree all pioneers, even those who succeeded most rapidly, felt a sense of social deprivation, based on their failure to establish comforting social relationships with their neighbors, the absense of defined social norms, and the failure of the new land to meet their unrealistic expectations. This was reflected in the lawlessness and dis-order usual in most frontier communities, by the emotional religious practices common there, and by continuing mobility. It was revealed also by the greater degree of political participation in frontier areas as individuals sought to gain status and economic benefits by assuming leadership roles in the unstructured society. These attitudes and desires marked frontier communities as different from those with tightly struc-tured cultures. Rarely had society been so disrupted, so fluid, and so susceptible to forces inviting change. Here was a new social environment, powerful enough to alter men and institutions.

Let no one, however, be misled into believing that the frontier could affect *major* changes in either the personalities or the behavioral patterns of frontiersmen. As in human behavior today, the bulk of the customs and beliefs of the pioneers were transmitted, and were only slightly modified by the changing culture in which they lived. This can be demonstrated by contrasting the civilizations that emerged in Spanish and English America. True, the physical environment of these two areas varied greatly. North America, with its well-watered woodlands, its fertile prairies, and its vast resources in forest and mineral wealth, offered far greater opportunity for the relatively propertyless individual than less-favored South America. There rugged mountains, semiarid plateaus, and dense jungles restricted the areas where small farmers or herdsmen could utilize nature. Only on the Argentine pampas and the Brazilian plains did a temperate climate, navigable rivers, and good soil beckon exploiters, and even there government largess rather than individual initiative gov-erned the settlement process. Yet men, not geography, explain the differences between the Anglo-American and Latin-American frontiers, for individuals of different backgrounds will respond in different ways to identical physical environments.

The ferment of the Anglo-American frontier was partly a product of the ferment of the democratic, commercial, and industrial societies in which it originated. These produced settlers who, by training and tradition, were capable of unleashing the energies of individual initiative to extract the frontier's natural resources. On the other hand, the Latin-American pioneers were governed by traditions that ill-equipped them to exploit the New World's riches, for they had been reared in a culture where the individual's freedom—politically, religiously, and economically—was rigidly restrained.

For this difference the chronology of settlement was partly responsible. Spain's New World frontier was founded, and its culture solidified, in the fifteenth and sixteenth centuries when Europe was entering its modern age. An absolute monarchy had just been imposed on the feudal nobles, middle-class capitalism was in its infancy, church and state were united under the dictates of the crown, and explosive nationalism prevailed in the wake of the expulsion of the Moors. The resulting combination of royal absolutism, a militant national church, and a martial spirit created a colonial society in which the small-propertied individual was allowed scant freedom to exploit frontier resources. He was restricted politically by all-powerful viceroys, commercially by an inflexible mercantile system, and economically by the operation of the semimanorial *mita* and *encomienda*. Moreover, a humane church policy that sought conversion rather than extermination for the Indians helped create a native labor force to monopolize jobs that might otherwise have attracted immigrants from Spain. The result was a transplanted European culture, administered by a centralized bureaucracy, and designed to enrich the monarch and his favorites rather than the individual pioneer.

England, on the other hand, entered the race for colonies in the seventeenth century, with institutions far more modern than those Spain transplanted to America. The political theories of the Stuart monarch were still those of divine right and royal absolutism, but both the promoters of England's colonies and the "adventurers" who peopled them were generally foes of this official theory and active proponents of parliamentary constitutionalism. Thus inclined, they were ready to accord the colonists a degree of self-rule, as they did when Virginia established its House of Burgesses and Massachusetts its General Court—steps that established a precedent for representative government. Political liberty was strengthened by the constitutional controversies that troubled England during the remainder of the seventeenth century. The Puritan rebellion and the Glorious Revolution were shattering blows against absolutism. That the colonists would have followed the path toward democracy, with or without a frontier environment, seems doubtful had the way not been pointed by these events.

Economic institutions emerging in England also favored the rise of a colonial spirit of individual initiative. The prevailing theories of commercial capitalism, combined with a lack of effective centralized authority at home, allowed the English colonies to be established as quasi-public enterprises founded in the hope of gain. This, in turn, permitted the colony planters to slough away the restrictive controls that shackled the economy of less developed nations—feudal land tenure, medieval guilds, and monopolistic trading concepts. Instead, private land ownership, individual handicraft trades, the wage system, indentured servitude, and private contracts became the hallmarks of the American economy, all offering opportunity to farmers, planters, merchants, and craftsmen to better themselves. The English pioneer came from a culture where he had been trained emotionally to exploit the resources of the frontier. He was equipped, as his Latin-American counterpart was not, to move whenever opportunity beckoned, and to profit by each move.

This was demonstrated as the Anglo-American frontier crept westward, for the ethnic groups that it attracted responded in different ways to the physical environment. Most who migrated directly from Europe to the West integrated rapidly into pioneer communities, thus falling at once into the social environment of the frontier. These men and women soon learned the customs and language of those about them, and within a generation or two were almost indistinguishable from their neighbors. Other Europeans, however, settled in ethnic communities where they spoke their native language and remained isolated from the practices of American pioneers. The persistence with which Old World customs and thought patterns were retained in these pockets of settlement demonstrated that the *physical* environment of the frontier did not alter newcomers. This was the function of the *social* environment alone.

The French who occupied a number of town sites in the Mississippi Valley during the seventeenth and eighteenth centuries clearly illustrate this fact. There they remained until the nineteenth century when American pioneers engulfed the lands about them, living and working as had their ancestors and revealing few of the traits of the stereotyped pioneer. By contrast with their new neighbors, the French were indolent and lazy, lacking the bustle and energy usual among small-propertied frontiersmen. They enjoyed dancing and music, and shocked the sober

Americans with their gaiety. Mobility was uncommon; they preferred to stay near their churches and families rather than seek opportunity elsewhere. Their farming habits were similarly inherited, for they tilled long fields modeled after those of manorial France, even though the landscape of the midwest was ill-suited to this division. Their farm implements were those of their ancestors rather than those developed in America.

Germans who fled the Rhenish Palatinate in the seventeenth and eighteenth centuries to establish themselves in the Pennsylvania back country, and their countrymen who filled pockets of settlements in the Middle West a hundred years later, similarly remained stubbornly resistant to the process of "Americanization" that was supposed to take place on the frontier. Their dream was of a good barn and security, not speculative profits. So they showed no tendency to move about as did the usual pioneers; the "Pennsylvania Dutch" of today offer convincing proof of their willingness to stay in one place. Because they had permanence in mind, they cleared the land thoroughly, shunning the slovenly habits of their American neighbors, and preserved its fertility by manuring and by rotating crops. Knowing that well-cared-for animals ate less, they built sturdy stone barns with overhanging eaves, even though they and their families lived for a time in hovels. While Americans were inclined to plant cash crops that would bring the greatest return, the Germans used their fields for a variety of crops to protect against the disaster that might fall through blight or a glutting of the market. This same frugal spirit compelled them to consume the produce that was less in demand, and sell the choice or most expensive products. They lived, in other words, much as their peasant ancestors had lived in Germany. The speculative, exploitive, wasteful habits of frontier America affected them not.

While Germans and French best illustrated the different responses of ethnic groups to the physical environments of the frontier, all nationalities responded in predictable ways. Contemporaries sometimes amused themselves by ranking newcomers according to their skills in pioneering. Germans and Scots were rated "the most industrious, prudent, and successful." The Irish were labeled inadequate for wilderness tasks because of indolence and love of village life, the French because they reverted to hunting, and the English because they clung so tenaciously to British customs. Tales were told of newcomers from England whose cattle died when their owners insisted that barns were as unnecessary in Pennsylvania as in Cornwall, who laboriously dug wells when sparkling water could be dipped from streams, and who insisted on migrating with all their belongings when their needs could have been supplied from the countryside. John Bull, wrote one visitor to the West, would carry with him not only every possession "but even the fast-anchored isle itself, could he but cut it from its moorings." Clearly the physical environment of the frontier did not recast newcomers into a common mold.

This was to be expected. Men instinctively resist change; traditional patterns of behavior create a comforting sense of security that is lost with innovation. Too, imitation requires far less effort than invention. Pittsburgh's founding fathers based the first municipal code of the village on the codes of other eastern cities with which they were familiar. When Louisville founded its school system a delegate was sent east to "examine the most respectable of their monitorial establishments." The first school was modeled on one in New York with modifications adapted from Philadelphia and a faculty recruited from Columbia, Yale, and London. Nostalgia also played a role in perpetuating traditional practices on frontiers, for homes that had been forsaken in the East were endowed with warmth and glamor in the imagination of homesick pioneers. Even the half-savage mountain men thought longingly of the civilized life they had forsaken. One told of riding into a grove of cottonwoods where birds sang merrily. "I laied down in the shade and enjoyed their twittering for some hours," he wrote that night. "It reminded me of home & civilisation." Added a traveler much among the pioneers of the Far West: "The thought of home is ever rolled, like a sweet morsel, under the tongues of their souls." Resistance to the corroding influence of a frontier environment was heightened by such sentiments.

No physical environment could have weakened such allegiance to traditionalism, but not even established custom could withstand the corroding impact of the frontier *social* environment. Behavioral patterns, value scales, and modes of thought that emerged in early pioneer communities and that were carried from community to community by successive waves of advancing frontiersmen proved too powerful to be resisted. Even the "ethnic pockets" that clung most doggedly to Old World habits were affected as American neighbors demonstrated the practicality of frontier-tested practices. A German traveler in the West, after noting that one of his newly arrived countrymen looked completely out of place, went on: "Visit him on his thriving farm ten years hence, and, except in the single point of language, you will find him (unless he has settled among a nest of his countrymen) at home among his neighbors, and happily conforming to their usages." Even the most hidebound Englishman learned, as one of them observed, "that he has got to a place where it answers to spend land to save labour; the reverse of his experience in England; and he soon becomes as slovenly a farmer as the American, and begins immediately to grow rich." Conformity to a unique social environment was easier than resistance. The frontier did alter individuals and institutions.

For the spatial frontier, to the visitor or new settler, was a different world. Those who crossed the borderline and recorded their impressions spoke of a cultural fault as observable as a geological fault. Beyond they found a people who behaved and thought and lived in a manner distinctly different from Easterners. Here was "a state of society wholly differing from any that we had seen before," wrote one traveler, and another felt that he was suddenly "a stranger among a people, whose modes of existence and ways of thinking are of a widely different character from those, in the midst of which he has been reared." Americans were as conscious of the division between East and West as travelers from overseas. "Language, ideas, manners, customs—all are new," observed a pioneer newly arrived in backwoods Michigan; "yes, even language; for to the instructed person from one of our great Eastern cities, the talk of the true back-woods-man is scarcely intelligible." Added another from the Ohio Valley frontier of the 1830s: "The people of the west, viewed as individuals, resemble the inhabitants of almost every clime; but taken as a whole, they are unlike every people under heaven. They have come hither from the four quarters of the globe, with manners and habits and genius and temperament, as different as the nations from which they have severally sprung. Every thing is new, just coming into existence." These observers, and others like them, were acutely aware that the social environment of the frontier was distinct from that of the East.

These differences, moreover, were altering the whole national character and converting the Americans into a people strangely unlike the Europeans from whom they sprang. "If I were to draw a comparison between the English and Americans," one English traveler decided, "I should say that there is almost as much difference between the two nations . . . as there has long been between the English and the Dutch"; another judged them to be "as unlike the English as any people can well be." Significantly, the features that most clearly marked the Americans as unique were frontier characteristics, and were found most deeply etched in the West. Travelers observed there the "slight, but perceptible peculiarities of national character which our peculiar circumstances and condition have imposed upon us"; those same traits were "least observable where the population is most mixed, and are scarcely perceptible in our larger commercial towns and cities." Lord Bryce, one of the most penetrating observers of nineteenth-century America, believed that the West was the most distinctively American part of America, precisely because the points in which it differed from the East were the points in which America as a whole differed from Europe.

Observers differed widely on the exact traits that were emerging in the American character as a result of the pioneering experience, but agreed on certain basic characteristics. One Westerner, who pondered much on the West's influence during the 1850s, believed that the frontier spawned a desire for individual self-improvement even at the expense of society, a supreme confidence that refused to recognize error, and a restlessness that led men to change their habits as often as they did their abodes. Three decades later a visitor to the Far West concluded that a capacity for self-help, a willingness to aid others in distress, a dislike of hypocrisy and pretence, and a manliness exhibited in respect to women were basic frontier traits. To Lord Bryce the Westerner was unique in his veneration of democracy, his unwavering nationalism, and his belief that the world could be reformed with his help; he was also unusual in his practicality, his materialistic philosophy, his aggressive optimism, and his go-getter attitude.

Few observers of the Western scene were capable of such penetrating observations, but many contributed their mite to the picture of the American frontiersman. To polished travelers from London or Boston he was an uncouth savage, degraded by his wilderness environment, and a traitor to the civilization in which he was reared. "As man civilizes the wilderness," wrote a visitor from Britain, "the wilderness more or less brutalizes him. In thus elevating nature he degrades himself." Indolence, profligacy, and bad manners were as truly a product of the frontier as deer hides or beaver pelts to the majority of observers. Few recognized that refinements could not flourish in a new country, and that this regression toward the primitive was only temporary.

To those who could see the true man beneath his uncouth manners, the pioneer was distinguished by a variety of traits, good and bad. He was notable for his openness, the easy manner in which he adjusted to new situations, and his attachment to freedom. Some visitors branded him as hopelessly utilitarian and dourly taciturn; nearly all marked his restless energy, his eager perseverance, and his willingness to support "every species of improvement, both public and private." Scarcely an observer but commented on his lack of attachment to place, and his tendency to roam constantly. "A restless temper seems to me one of the distinctive traits of this people," noted Alexis de Tocqueville. ". . . We have been told that the same man has often tried ten estates. He has appeared successively as merchant, lawyer, doctor, minister of the gospel. He has lived in twenty different places and nowhere found ties to detain him." Incomplete though this catalogue may be, it suggests that those who knew nineteenth-century America best recognized that a national character was developing, and that it was rooted in the frontiering background of the people.

CHAPTER 6

THE VIRGINIANS

William Byrd said "In the beginning, all America was Virginia." Yet, too often the Virginia colonial experience is slighted in courses in American history, since emphasis is focused on the New England Puritans, whose dramatic story has become part of American popular culture. Puritan contributions to the development of American institutions are usually stressed. The unfortunate aspect of the neglect of the Virginians is not that there is intrinsically great significance in the fact that Virginia was established in 1607 as the first successful English colony. More regretable is the neglect of the significance of the Virginia colonial experience and the positive contributions of Virginia to American historical development.

In this selection, Professor Daniel J. Boorstin gives meaning to the Virginia colonial experience. His emphasis in these excerpts from *The Americans: The Colonial Experience,* * is on the government and the politics of colonial Virginia. The Virginia story, Boorstin suggests, is quite different from that of New England, of Pennsylvania, or of Georgia, where colonists attempted, at least partly, to escape from some aspects of the English background. The Virginians were not theorists, visionaries, or reformers; they were practical realists and men of affairs who sought to realize English ideals in the New World, and who, after a bad start, succeeded remarkably well.

Professor Boorstin does not suggest that colonial Virginia was the ideal American society, and the student reader should try to identify the weaknesses of eighteenth-century Virginia as well as its strengths. Virginia produced more of the great men of the Revolutionary generation than any other colony, and the contributions of these and other Virginians in the critical early years of the Republic were indispensable to the development of the nation. How does Boorstin explain this extraordinary achievement of Virginia during her Golden Age? How does he account for the decline of Virginian leadership in the nation after the end of the early national period?

D. Alan Williams, "Colonial Virginia: Aristocratic Self-Government," in *Main Problems in American History** (1964), edited by Howard H. Quint, Dean Albertson, and Milton Cantor, is a brief but penetrating analysis of colonial Virginia. Louis B. Wright, *First Gentlement of Virginia** (1940), and Charles S. Sydnor, *Gentleman Freeholders** (1952), are delightful as well as informative works.

* Available in a paperback edition.

TRANSPLANTERS: THE VIRGINIANS
DANIEL J. BOORSTIN

> "Thus, in the beginning, all the world was America, and more so than it is now. . . ."
>
> JOHN LOCKE

> "In the beginning, All America was Virginia."
>
> WILLIAM BYRD

Virginia is a different story. Here we see no grandiose scheme, no attempt to rule by an idea, but an earthy effort to transplant institutions. If other colonies sought escape from English vices, Virginians wished to fulfill English virtues. Let other colonies dazzle the world with a City upon a Hill, inspire by a commonwealth of brotherly love, or encourage with a vast humanitarian experiment. The model in Virginians' heads was compounded of the actual features of a going community: the England, especially the rural England, of the 17th and 18th century. If Virginia was to be in any way better than England, it was not because Virginians pursued ideals which Englishmen did not have; rather that here were novel opportunities to realize the English ideals. A middle-class Englishman was to find space in Virginia to become a new kind of English country gentleman. An unpredictable alchemy transformed the ways of the English manor-house into the habits of a New World republic. Squire Westerns and Horace Walpoles underwent an Atlantic sea-change which made them into Edmund Pendletons, Thomas Jeffersons, and George Washingtons. What made them American was not what they sought but what they accomplished. . . .

GOVERNMENT BY GENTRY

It would be a great mistake to assume that the cozy, aristocratic character of Virginia society had nothing to do with its civic virtues. Only a

SOURCE. Daniel J. Boorstin, *The Americans: The Colonial Experience,* New York: Random House, 1958, pp. 97–98, 110–123, 139–141, 143. Copyright 1958 by Daniel J. Boorstin. Reprinted by permission of Random House, Inc. and the author.

perverse hindsight has made the political institutions of colonial Virginia a leveling democracy in embryo. When George Washington feared for the preservation of self-government and the rights of Englishmen, it was the political customs of mid-18th century Virginia that he must have had in mind, for he knew no others. Those customs were the representative institutions of a Virginia-bred aristocracy, whose peculiarly aristocratic virtues nourished American representative government at its roots. And those roots reached back to Virginia's Golden Day.

Never did a governing class take its political duties more seriously: power carried with it the duty to govern. Thus, while Virginia had a restrictive suffrage throughout the colonial period, it also had a law of compulsory voting. In a few other colonies occasional statutes punished the qualified voter who did not appear at the polls, and it is uncertain how strenuously the Virginia law was enforced, but the continuous course of such legislation in Virginia from the early days till after the Revolution testifies to the persistent belief that government was a duty. If the ordinary voter was required to cast his ballot, men of greater substance were expected to carry heavier burdens. When Jefferson, under particularly unhappy circumstances in 1781, yearned for "the independance of private life," he was describing the relief for which many men of prominent Virginia families must have longed.

Just as the owner of a large plantation had thrust on him tasks of management which he could not escape—he had to lay out orchards, decide on the time to plant and to cut the tobacco, find raw materials for shoes and clothing, and look after the health of the slaves—so he had political duties which he could not shirk. The successful planter developed perforce the habit of command. He came to manage the affairs of the colony with the same self-assurance he showed in managing his private estate. If the plantation was a little colony in itself, which had to be governed with tact, authority, and prudence, the colony of Virginia was in turn ruled like a large plantation. The major dignities and decisions rested on those who held the largest stake.

The roster of the House of Burgesses is a list of leading planters. The upward political path from the seat of the vestryman or justice of the peace to the Governor's Council was guarded all along the way by the local gentry. Seeking a political career without their approval was hopeless. And the House of Burgesses, which increased in power during the colonial period until it dominated the Governor and Council, was hardly more than the political workshop of a ruling aristocracy. Here were made the major decisions about the price and quality of tobacco, taxation, education, Indian relations, and religion. It was here that men were trained and scrutinized before advancement to higher office. Freeholders elected the Burgesses, but only the Burgesses themselves had the power to advance Virginians to higher honors, and the Burgesses conscientiously sifted upper-class Virginians for the tasks of government. Although there were less than a hundred seats in the House of Burgesses in the mid-18th century, nearly all prominent Virginians of the century had served an apprenticeship in the House.

Members disagreed much less than we might suppose, and their discussions little resembled the debate of a modern legislature. Although outspoken conflict marked the years of the Stamp Act, the politics of the House did not harden into party lines. Virginians were not prepared for the idea of political parties in the early years of the new government. As the 18th century wore on, the ruling Burgesses seemed to become more harmonious and singleminded, willing to recognize leadership among men of quite different political complexions. Thus when the House, sitting as the Virginia Convention of 1774, chose its delegates to the first Continental Congress, it elected Peyton Randolph, Richard Bland, and Edmund Pendleton, who had been conservatives in the recent Stamp Act controversy, as well as their opponents, Richard Henry Lee and Patrick Henry.

Perhaps never in recent times has a ruling group taken a more proprietary attitude towards public office. During the years of the Revolution and the first decades of independence, the Burgesses selected (almost exclusively from their own membership) the Virginia governors, councilmembers, judges, military officers, and delegates to Federal conventions. Their personal knowledge of each member of the Virginia ruling class qualified them to distribute public dignities and burdens with an impressive, if not quite infallible, wisdom.

This snugness of the ruling Virginians did, of course, have its less attractive side, which was displayed in the notorious Robinson Affair. No modern journalist could have concocted anything more sensational than these sober facts. When John Robinson, Speaker of the House of Burgesses and Treasurer of the colony, died, Purdie's *Virginia Gazette* (May 16, 1766) with unintended irony declared it "a calamity to be lamented by the unfortunate and indigent who were wont to be relieved and cherished by his humanity and liberality." The embarrassing dimensions of Robinson's generosity, through long suspected, were not confirmed until the administrators of his estate began to cast up their accounts. They then discovered that Robinson, while Treasurer of the colony, had drawn on the public funds to the extent of £100,761:7:5, which he had lent out to scores of his friends. These amounts varied from

£14,921 lent to William Byrd III (who had failed to inherit his ancestors' business acumen and was unlucky at cards to boot), Lewis Burwell's £6274, Carter Braxton's £3848, and Archibald Cary's £3975, down to Richard Henry Lee's £12 and Patrick Henry's £11. Members of the Governor's Council owed Robinson nearly £16,000; those of the House of Burgesses over £37,000. Edmund Pendleton, administrator of the estate, who spent twelve of the best years of his life trying to settle it, had himself been favored with £1020. As the accounts of the estate unfolded, it appeared that there was hardly a Virginia family of prominence that had not been helped in distress by Robinson's generosity with the public funds. This vast network of indebtedness explains the reluctance of the Burgesses over so many years to separate the offices of Speaker and Treasurer or to make a thorough audit of the colony's accounts. The affable Robinson had made the public treasury a relief chest for the ruling clique.

Two peculiar facts about this affair give us valuable clues to the morals and customs of the rulers of Virginia. First, Robinson had never used any of the funds for his personal benefit—except insofar as he was benefited by the gratitude of his friends. Second, when the facts were revealed the leading Burgesses hardly reproached Robinson for misappropriating public money; they came near praising him for his excess of virtue. When Robert Carter Nicholas (Robinson's successor as Treasurer) hinted at some impropriety, he was denounced for the suggestion; he found it politic to deny the innuendo and declared the loans "more owing to a mistaken kind of Humanity and Compassion for Persons in Distress." Governor Fauquier expressed the general sentiment when, after hearing Pendleton's report on the Robinson estate, he said, "Such was the Sensibility of his too benevolent Heart." Whatever we may think of Robinson himself, his career revealed a community where public power belonged to a privileged few.

This power did carry with it corresponding and sometimes burdensome duties. Almost from the beginning the House of Burgesses strictly required all members to be present at the opening of each session. A Burgess who failed to attend the convening of the House was, according to an Act of 1659–60 and repeated reënactments, fined three hundred pounds of tobacco for every twenty-four hours of unexcused absence. At the opening sitting, the Speaker would read letters from members explaining their absence, and their reasons would be approved or rejected. It was not unknown—as in the case of James Bray in 1691—for the House to be so offended by an explanation that the Speaker issued a warrant for the member's arrest, holding him in custody until he offered suitable apology. Special tasks, such as the election of the Speaker, made attendance at the opening session important, but the House was only slightly indulgent toward Burgesses who missed any regular session. Before the end of the 17th century the fine of two shillings and sixpence was increased to one hogshead of tobacco for each absence from a sitting. When, during the session of 1684, five members failed to answer a roll-call and were found to have gone home without consent of the House, a resolution ordered the sheriffs of their counties to collect from each negligent Burgess a fine of one thousand pounds of tobacco. They were not readmitted to the House until they had apologized.

The House of Burgesses very early (in 1666) disclaimed the right to relieve any duly elected member of his duty of attending, even when his constituents formally requested it. This doctrine survived the 18th century to plague the unhappy Jefferson in May 1782 when, just after his retirement under a cloud of censure as Governor of Virginia, the people of Albemarle County elected him delegate to the House. Weary of office and smarting from the public ingratitude, Jefferson wished to decline the office. When he sent his refusal to John Tyler, Speaker of the House, the ominous reply informed him that "the Constitution in the Opinion of the Members will not warrant the acceptance of your resignation." Tyler warned Jefferson "that good and able Men had better govern than be govern'd, since 'tis possible, indeed highly probable, that if the able and good withdraw themselves from Society, the venal and ignorant will succeed." Finally Jefferson was urged "to give attendance without incuring the Censure of being seized."

The Virginia Burgesses were, of course, "elected." Their election, if less corrupt and more open to talent, much resembled the English "election" of members of Parliament in the same period. It was nothing like a free-for-all in which any ambitious young man could seek his political fortune; the election was a process in which freeholders made their choice from among the gentlemen. Technically the qualifications for a Burgess were no greater than those for a voter, but in practice the candidates for the House were members of the gentry.

Elections took place in an intimate atmosphere which emphasized both the munificence of the candidates and the power of the freeholders, a strange combination of protocol and conviviality. Campaign oratory seems to have counted for very little; only an unusually pompous and obtuse gentleman would orate to neighbors who had known him since childhood. Seldom was there a public debate on the "issues," but even the best known candidate could not hope for success unless he had taken the trouble to mingle with his constituents. Convention forbade a candidate's soliciting votes, or even voting for himself, and there was no party organization. A candidate was, however, expected to use indirect (usually gastronomic) means of persuasion; no one could hope for election without "treating" the voters. Large quantities of rum punch, ginger cakes, and barbecued beef or pork persuaded prudent voters that their candidate possessed the liberality and the substance to represent them properly in the Assembly. Such entertainment was expensive. Samuel Overton of Hanover County estimated his cost for two elections at £75; George Washington's expenditures when he stood for Burgess were never less than £25 and on one occasion about £50. Such a sum was several times what it would have cost a man to buy the house and land required to qualify him as a voter. A Virginia statute did, of course, prohibit anyone "directly or indirectly" giving "money, meat, drink . . . present, gift, reward, or entertainment. . . . in order to be elected, or for being elected to serve in the General Assembly," but this law seems to have been seldom enforced. A general reputation for hospitality was actually the best defense against suspicions of bribery at election time.

Voting took place in the county courthouse or, in good weather, on the courthouse green. It differed from a modern American election mainly in the publicity given to every voter's choice and in the resulting opportunity for gratitude or resentment between the candidate and his constituents. By an almost unbroken custom, candidates were expected to be present at the voting-place. At a table sat the sheriff, the candidates, and the clerks (including one for each candidate). The voters came up one at a time to announce their choices, which were recorded publicly like a box-score. Since anyone present could always see the latest count, a candidate could at the last minute send supporters to bring in additional needed votes. As each voter declared his preference, shouts of approval would come from one side and hoots from another, while the betting-odds changed and new wagers were laid. The favored candidate would rise, bow, and express thanks to the voter: "Mr. Buchanan, I shall treasure that vote in my memory. It will be regarded as a feather in my cap forever." This personal acknowledgment of the voter's confidence was so customary that in the rare case when the candidate could not be present he delegated a friend to make his obeisances for him. When George Washington's command of the Frederick militia kept him at Fort Cumberland during the 1758 election, his friend James Wood, the most influential man in the county, sat at the poll and thanked each voter individually for his compliment to the absent colonel. A less common method of voting was by a show of hands, acclamation, or some other informal expression.

The control of the gentry over elections was by no means confined to their ability to earn the favorable opinion of the voters. For the gentry chose the sheriff from among themselves, and the sheriff managed the elections. He decided whether any individual was qualified to vote; he set the date of the election; he fixed the hour for opening and closing the polls; there was no appeal from his decisions except to the House of Burgesses, which was always reluctant to override local officials.

"Gentlemen freeholders," the sheriff would finally proclaim from the courthouse door, "come into court and give your votes or the poll will be closed." Sometimes the election would be ended by two o'clock in the afternoon, but if the sheriff found that many voters had been kept away "by rain or rise of watercourses," he might prolong the election into another day. What modern candidate would not envy the Virginia gentleman his power to keep the polls open until the winning votes had been rounded up!

Virginia law permitted a gentleman freeholder to vote in every county where he possessed the property qualification. If he was qualified in three counties he could vote for three sets of Burgesses. Since a man could represent in the House of Burgesses any district where he could vote, this further widened the political opportunities of the larger planters. They could choose to run where their chances seemed best. Many great Virginians, including George Washington, Patrick Henry, John Marshall, and Benjamin Harrison, used their extensive and dispersed landholdings to advance their political fortunes.

A REPUBLIC OF NEIGHBORS

The aristocratic character of Virginia republicanism helps explain why Virginians like Jefferson and Washington had more confidence in representative government than had many of their thoughtful contemporaries from other parts of the country. John Adams, Alexander Hamilton, and Gouverneur Morris came from colonies where "The people" were a volatile city crowd: "a great beast." For Virginians a "republican" government was an intricately balanced traditional arrangement.

If a modern historian had invented an allegory to tell this story he could hardly have done better than *The Candidates; or, the Humours of a Virginia Election,* a comedy in three acts written by Robert Munford of Mecklenburg in 1770. This little play is perhaps the first to express the American talent for making sport of politics. In it a small group of voters plays an affable and passive, but by no means foolish, role. Everyone, including the candidates, is confident that these voters can judge human quality and that they will see through a designing, ambitious, or dishonest candidate.

> WOU' DBE: Well, I've felt the pulse of all the leading men, and find they beat still for Worthy, and myself. Strutabout and Smallhopes fawn and cringe in so abject a manner, for the few votes they get, that I'm in hopes they'll be soon heartily despised.
>
>> The prudent candidate who hopes to rise,
>> Ne'er deigns to hide it, in a mean disguise.
>> Will, to his place, with moderation slide,
>> And win his way, or not resist the tide.
>> The fool, aspiring to bright honour's post,
>> In noise, in shouts, and tumults oft, is lost.

The gentlemen freeholders naturally come to despise Strutabout and Smallhopes and the wealthy toper Sir John Tody, while they learn to respect Wou'dbe and Worthy.

> WORTHY: I have little inclination to the service; you know my aversion to public life, Wou'dbe, and how little I have ever courted the people for the troublesome office they have hitherto imposed upon me.
>
> WOU' DBE: I believe you enjoy as much domestic happiness as any person, and that your aversion to a public life proceeds from the pleasure you find at home. But, sir, it surely is the duty of every man who has abilities to serve his country, to take up the burden, and bear it with patience.

The well-oiled machinery of aristocracy, far from thwarting the will of the people, simply saves the people from mistakes: the sheriff is always there to close the polls at the appropriate moment. The sensible neighbors finally elect the two able candidates by acclamation. This is happy evidence, Wou'dbe rejoices, of "a spirit of independence becoming Virginians."

These customs of the Virginia countryside bred a similar independence among the Burgesses themselves. Everything that made Virginia's elections aristocratic—the tendency to inherit posts in the House of Burgesses, the self-assurance and security of the large planters—encouraged Burgesses to be reasonable and independent in their judgment. Once in the legislature they seldom glanced over their shoulders for the smile or frown of their constituency, a habit which often makes a modern representative the fragile mirror of those who elect him.

It was generally accepted in Virginia in those days that the ruling planters of good family had a prescriptive right to become ruling Burgesses, always, of course, provided they had earned the good opinion of their less substantial neighbors. "There is a greater distinction supported between the different classes of life here," observed John F. D. Smyth as late as the Revolution, "than perhaps in any of the rest of the colonies; nor does the spirit of equality, and levelling principle, which pervades the greatest part of America, prevail to such as extent in Virginia." The large planter, busy with his own affairs, was deterred from standing for Burgess less by the risk of defeat than by the certainty of victory.

This security of social position bred a wholesome vigor of judgment which made the Virginia House of Burgesses a place for deliberation and discussion rarely found among modern legislatures. Burgesses came close to Edmund Burke's ideal of the representative who owed allegiance not to the whim of his constituency but only to his private judgment. The voters in colonial Virginia had just enough power to prevent the irresponsibility of their representatives, but not enough to secure their servility. This was a delicate balance, but it had a great deal to do with the effectiveness of the legislature. In Munford's *Candidates* the virtuous Wou'dbe scrupulously avoided promising to do whatever the people wished, since the people would not have chosen him unless they had preferred his judgment to theirs. The most famous example of this Burkean independence comes from a later day: in 1788, in the Virginia Convention called to ratify the new Federal Constitution, at least eight delegates voted for the new government against the wishes of their electors.

The contrast between the atmosphere in the Virginia Burgesses and in a modern state legislature is only partly explained by the talents of the representatives. The seriousness, wisdom, honesty, and eloquence in the deliberations of the Burgesses during the crucial years of the Stamp Act—the "most bloody" debates which Jefferson, then a student at the College, heard from the door of the chamber—was not due only to the greatness of the men and the issues. These men were not satisfied to be spokesmen of their voters' whims. Their speeches were serious and sometimes subtle arguments directed to fellow-legislators. Their debate lacked that meandering and miscellaneous, if amusing, irrelevance of the modern Congressional Record and its local counterparts. In those days it was still customary for a legislator (at least in Virginia) to give more time to the deliberations of his House than to answering mail from his constituents, to making "news" in legislative committees, or to seeking jobs for faithful supporters. American folklore has only a little exaggerated: the Virginia House of Burgesses was a meeting of gods on Olympus compared to a modern state legislature.

These men were talking to each other; none of them was much impressed by the flowery phrase. With the conspicuous exception of a few like Patrick Henry, Virginia's representatives talked in sober and conversational style; there has seldom been an age of representative government when the power to orate was less important. Within the intimacy of the House of Burgesses, which any visitor to Colonial Williamsburg can sense today, persuasive argument was of first importance; demagoguery was useless. Jefferson was not an eloquent speaker, a fact which led him later to send his annual messages to Congress rather than deliver them in person; Washington and Madison were hardly better. And the leading figures in the Burgesses in the 18th century—men like Richard Bland, Peyton Randolph, and John Robinson—were all ungraceful speakers. The House of Burgesses (like its English counterpart, the House of Commons) was an exclusive club where gentlemen seriously discussed public problems.

Virginia was governed by its men of property. There was no family of substance without members in the Governor's Council, the House of Burgesses, the county court or other governing bodies; and there was no governing body of the colony that was not dominated by the men of substance. These men presumably, and usually in fact, possessed the best knowledge of the large economic and political problems of the community: the price of tobacco and the cost of producing it, the quality of essential imports, the location of indispensable markets, the character of necessary shipping, the routes of primary roads, the places of the most useful ferries.

Land—land to use, to waste, to divide among one's children—was the foundation of all the governing families and the fortunes of Virginia. The power to give or to deny land, those vast virgin tracts expected to appreciate most in the next decades, rested in the hands of the government, especially in the House of Burgesses and the Governor's Council.

The Burgesses also possessed important routine powers over already-settled land, powers which in England were held by the courts. In England if a landholder inherited entailed land which he wanted to deal with as full owner, he followed certain complicated but routine court procedures which ingenious lawyers had developed. Not so in Virginia. There any heir who wanted to get rid of such restrictions had to secure in his own name, and for that particular piece of land, a private Act of the House of Burgesses. Between 1711 and 1774 a total of one hundred and twenty-five such Acts were passed; nearly three-fourths of them for members of such leading families as the Armisteads, Beverleys, Braxtons, Burwells, Carters, Dandridges, Eppes, Pages, Tazewells, Wormeleys, Washingtons, and Yeates. All these, either in their own person or through relatives, would have been represented in the House which acted on their petition. Such private Acts of the House were a necessity for the substantial planter: without them he was not free to deal with his land, to move his labor force, or to dispose of worn-out parcels in order to acquire lands farther west.

Still more important was the power of the Burgesses and the Governor's Council over that treasure-house of the West to which they held the legal keys. There was nothing secret or underhanded about any of this. Under the prevailing system of soil-exhaustion, with fluctuating tobacco prices and the exorbitant demands of London merchants, simple prudence had made tobacco planters into land speculators. George Washington, though shrewd and ambitious, was no gambler, but he seized opportunities to enlarge his holdings. He saw that a westward-pushing population would raise the value of the fertile piedmont; it was important to be alert and acquire good land early. In June 1767 Washington advised his friend, the unfortunate Captain John Posey who had been sinking deeper and deeper into debt, to "look to Frederick, and see what fortunes were made by the Hites and the first takers up of those lands: Nay, how the greatest estates we have in this Colony were made. Was it not by taking up and purchasing at very low rates the rich back lands which were thought nothing of in those days, but are now the most valuable lands that we possess?" In the middle years of the century, after his stint with Braddock and before his Revolutionary command, Washington like many of his fellow Virginia aristocrats, was in Douglas Freeman's accurate phrase, a "land hunter."

To satisfy land-hunger in Virginia one needed not only a strong body but a shrewd political sense. The pathway to landed wealth lay, not only through uncharted tracts in the wilderness, but also through the corridors of government buildings in Williamsburg. This was the "inside track," well-worn by leading Virginians, to the fertile expanses of the unsettled south and west. There was hardly a fortune in Virginia which had not been sought out in this fashion. When William Byrd was appointed by the government to survey the dividing line between Virginia and North Carolina in 1728, he saw the wealth of the fertile bottom-land and christened it the "Land of Eden." He seized the morally dubious opportunity to buy 20,000 acres from the North Carolina commissioners to whom it had been given for their services. In 1742, he secured the again "lucky" chance to patent another 105,000 acres, which he had hoped to get free but for which he actually paid the bargain price of £525. At his death this man owned 179,440 acres of the richest land in the colony —the fruit of his "public services" as much as of his business enterprise.

In none of the "public business" which engaged Washington's interest during his early years in the House of Burgesses was he more active than in trying to secure parcels of land for himself and his fellow-veterans of 1754. Governor Dinwiddie's emergency Proclamation of February 1754 had supposedly rewarded these veterans with "200,000 acres of his majesty's lands on the Ohio," but it was Washington's activity—which included the promotion of bills in the House of Burgesses, letters to the Governor, and addresses to the Governor's Council—that eighteen years later secured the actual allotment of thousands of acres. Washington took the initiative in securing the grant, in locating the land, and in allotting the acreage among different claimants in proportion to rank. His own reward was 24,100 acres. Of this 18,500 was his personal allotment, which he himself apportioned, and 5600 came from allotments of others which his special position had enabled him to buy cheap. He also had the advantage of knowing first-hand precisely the land which would be divided; and hence he could be sure that the tracts rewarding his patriotism were not unworthy of him. Under the circumstances Washington had no reason to feel that he had unduly favored himself. "I might add without much arrogance," he wrote, "that if it had not been for my unremitted attention to every favorable circumstance, not a single acre of land would ever have been obtained." With no more immodesty Washington might have claimed credit for the thousands of acres which he and other leading Virginians were to secure through the Great Dismal Swamp Company and the Mississippi Company; in every case the help of government agencies was essential.

The weaknesses of representative government in Virginia's Golden Age were on the side of realism, practicality, and a too nice equivalence of economic and political power. These were the mistakes of men of affairs rather than of visionaries, reformers, or revolutionaries. While Virginians of great landed wealth could grow wealthier, white men at the bottom of the ladder sometimes found it impossible to reach the next-to-the-bottom rung, and the Negro had no chance to rise above servitude. It was, however, also true that their aristocracy showed as high a talent for government as that of any other community before or since. And once a man was on his way up the ladder, there was little to stop him.

How irrelevant to look to the bookish prospectuses of English or French political theorists—of Locke, Montesquieu, or Rousseau—to explain Virginia's political enthusiasms! Americans who knew the reality did not need the dream. Virginians who would fight to preserve representative government and would offer "their Lives, their Fortunes, and their sacred Honor" on the altar of the British Constitution had not produced a single important treatise on political theory. Knowing what representative government was, why should they speculate about what it ought to be? The great Virginians were in the closest touch with the world of conflicting interests. They possessed a sense of full-bodied economic and political reality, but no particular genius for the abstractions of closet-philosophy. This was to prove one of their greatest strengths.

Why should Burgesses disparage the common people—or declaim in favor of government by "the rich and the well-born"? They actually lived where the people acquiesced in government by the rich and well-born; and where the rich and well-born did not overbear the people. Those Virginians who came to show an uncritical faith in the will of the people had founded it on a solid but narrow experience: their experience of rural neighbors who trusted the political talents of their extraordinarily able aristocracy. Business, the opportunity to get rich and to get poor, had vitalized and added mobility to that aristocracy. One could move into it and, if incompetent, one would almost surely drop out of it, or at least be denied the avenue to political power.

During the 18th century there was little evidence of dissatisfaction with the way of government described here. Since the people acquiesced, the ruling Burgesses had no reason to think ill of their way of life. Although there were some minor political and economic reforms in Virginia during the latter half of the century, these were all very much within the established framework of Virginia's Golden Age. In the eyes of the more influential (and even the more Revolutionary) Virginians, the American Revolution was itself an attempt to preserve the moderate ways of that age.

As the ruling Virginians admired the ideal of the English gentleman, the genteel canon they most scrupulously followed was Moderation. Unlike some of their English gentlemen-contemporaries, they did not despise trade or labor, nor did they admire an idle aristocracy. Nor, unlike some later Jacksonian Americans or European leveling democrats, did they particularly idealize the horny-handed laborer. In Brathwait's *English Gentleman,* Virginians could read that Moderation had a threefold aspect, and must be exercised equally in matters of Mind, Body, and Fortune.

"Moderation," they learned, was "a vertue so necessary, and well deserving the acquaintance of a Gentleman, (who is to be imagined as one new come to his lands, and therefore stands in great need of so discreet an Attendant) as there is no one vertue better sorting ranke." This ancient virtue, needed for governing a community, was no less desirable in those matters of religion, over which Europeans had tortured one another for centuries. . . .

CITIZENS OF VIRGINIA

Nothing could be more misleading than to think of Virginians as "Citizens of the World." In common with American leaders since their day, they preferred to start from their own problems. Their point of departure was their location in time and space.

If George Washington seems colorless to us today it is partly because our latter-day democratic prejudices have blinded us to the colors of his Virginia. It is hard to bring ourselves to believe that the great Virginia fathers of the Republic were nourished in the soil of aristocracy, slavery, and an established church. Modern American democracy, we are told, must have had its roots in some 18th-century "democracy"; so we have looked for its seeds in the New England Town Meeting (supposed to be a microcosm of democracy) rather than in the Virginia tobacco aristocracy. But the ways of history are obscure and even self-contradictory. May not the proudly independent spirit of the Virginia planting aristocrats have been rooted in their vast plantations, in their sense of aristocratic responsibility? May not the value they placed on their individual liberties have been increased by the sharp contrast with the slavery they saw about them? May not their aristocratic habit of mind—their "habit of command" and their belief that they could make judgments on behalf of their community—have helped make them leaders of an American Revolution? Perhaps revolutions are always led by people who build, in Justice Holmes' phrase, "upon an aristocratic assumption that you know what is good for them better than they—which no doubt you do." Perhaps a reliable toleration has its roots in the quiet catholicity of a not-too-passionate established church, rather than in the explicit liberalism of rationalists and anti-religionists.

The Virginians had indeed inoculated themselves against all strong viruses; they, least of all people, sought to grasp the truths—whether of religion, of government, or of society—suddenly and as a whole. Their empirical, and even their reforming, spirit was grown in the tobacco-soil of Virginia, and not in the corrosive absolutes which poured out of Europe in their century. Traditionalism—their loyalty to the working ways of ancient England—rooted them in time; localism—their loyalty to the habits of their parish and county and to their friends and neighbors—rooted them in space. The strength of both these sentiments (and, to be precise, we should call them sentiments rather than philosophies) accounts for much of what they made of Virginia, and of what Virginia in the critical early years of the Republic gave to America. The strength of their traditionalism was before long to be expressed in the American Revolution in defense of the rights of Englishmen. The strength of their localism was expressed in the autonomy of the parish and in the federal spirit, in the Constitution and in the devotion to States' rights. The fact that their tradition was loosely stated—their model was the life of the English country gentleman—made their tie to tradition no less real. There was no part of life which an ideal so vague and so real did not touch. Their narrower, more legal traditionalism was also to have its day: in the Revolution, when they would be required to state in precise legal language how their rights as Englishmen had been violated. But the traditionalism of Virginia in the Golden Age was lived out with a quiet and pervasive intensity. Their very strength as transplanters came from their willingness to transform as they transplanted, to flavor the distant past with the local present.

Their localism has been given far too little attention and too little credit. In these days, when States' rights are out of fashion, we are too often told that a man's preoccupation with the habits of the place where he lives can only drag the national progress. We are fortunate that 18th-century Virginians thought differently. Their concern with the special requirements of their own particular place on earth not only flavored their political life and expectations; it gave all their thinking the aroma of the specific and kept all their social ideals within finite bounds. It was the seed of Federalism, without which the nation could not have lived and liberal institutions could not have flourished. . . .

The supreme irony in the story of Virginia was the last act in the colonial drama. That act occurred in the Revolution itself, in the framing of the Federal Constitution and in the rule of the Virginia Dynasty (Washington-Jefferson-Madison-Monroe) within the Federal government. The leaders of that age were the last flower of the aristocracy of mid-18th century Virginia, not the first flower of a national spirit. The Revolution which the Virginia aristocracy did so much to make and "win" was in fact the suicide of the Virginia aristocracy. The turmoil of the War, the destruction wrought in Virginia by British troops, the disestablishment of the Church, the disruption of commerce, and the decline of tobacco-culture all spelled the decline of the aristocracy and its institutions.

The Federal Constitution was a national road on which there was no return. The leadership of Virginians in Federal life continued only so long as the national government was an aristocratic camaraderie like that of Virginia. When the United States ceased to be a greater Virginia, Virginians ceased to govern the United States. The virtues of 18th-century Virginia, when writ large, would seem to be vices. Localism would become sectionalism; the special interests of where a man lived would come to seem petty and disruptive.

CHAPTER 7

THE PURITANS

With the exceptions of the Indians and the blacks, probably no group in colonial North America has been more misunderstood than the Puritans. Every college student knows what the terms puritanical and Puritan mean in the twentieth century, but many do not know what these terms mean when they are applied to seventeenth-century New England. The conclusion that the Puritans were religious is unquestioned, but the assumption that they were prudes is not based on historical facts or on a knowledge of either the period or of the people. What is clear about the first generation of Puritans in New England is that they were intensely dedicated to their faith and to what the late Professor Perry Miller referred to as their "errand." The early Puritans were convinced that it was God's work that they performed as they labored in the wilderness to establish their Zion, and they were bitterly disappointed when their experiment in the wilderness was not adopted by the mother country as a model for social and governmental reform.

They succeeded in establishing their Zion, but they did not do what many of them had set out to accomplish. They did not influence, by their example, the rulers of England to change English government to a government modeled after the Puritan experiment in New England. Thus they were not brought back to England in triumph; indeed, most remained in the New World. The life they made for themselves in New England is the subject of Professor Lockridge's essay.

This essay raises some important questions. First, how did life in the New World differ from life in the Old? Was there in reality an abundance of free land, and if so, how did this factor modify social patterns and structure? How closely do the people described in this essay fit your preconceived image of the Puritans? Finally, and perhaps most important, how have Americans been influenced by the Puritans?

As might be expected, the literature on the Puritans is voluminous. Among the best of the monographs is Kenneth A. Lockridge, *A New England Town: The First Hundred Years** (1970). Perry Miller, the first historian of the twentieth century to examine the Puritans on their own terms, explores the many facets of those fascinating people in *Errand In the Wilderness** (1956), and *The New England Mind,** 2 vols. (1939, 1953). Samuel Eliot Morison's *Builders of the Bay Colony** (1930) contains a series of engaging biographies. Edmund S. Morgan analyzes John Winthrop's historical role in *The Puritan Dilemma** (1958), discusses daily life in *The Puritan Family** (1966), and in "The Puritans and Sex," *New England Quarterly, XV* (1942), destroys the idea of Puritan prudery.

* Available in a paperback edition.

A NEW ENGLAND TOWN
KENNETH A. LOCKRIDGE

It has become fashionable to view the settlers of Massachusetts Bay as men more pulled to America by the opportunity to found a new society than pushed there by the persecutions of Anglican England. Michael Metcalf, one of the founders of Dedham and for a time its schoolmaster, would have disagreed violently. On abandoning his homeland and his career as a master weaver in provincial Norwich, Metcalf had written a long letter "to all true professors of Christ's gospel" within that city. Trying to justify his sudden departure from the Puritan community, he spoke of "the great trouble I sustained in the Arch-Deacon's and Bishop's court at the hands of my enemies concerning the matter of bowing as well as for other matters of like consequence." When hauled before the ecclesiastical court he had expertly quoted against the judges their own theologians and the Bible itself, but to his disgust "their learned and invincible arguments to refute my assertions were these: 'Blockhead, old heretic, the devil made you, I will send you to the devil.' " Frustration gave way to fear when "enemies conspired against me to take away my life, and sometimes, to avoid their hands, my wife did hide me in the roof of the house, covering me with straw." Having become a marked man, he had no choice but to flee to America. He counseled his less notorious fellow Puritans to remain in Norwich if they possibly could, advising them to "be not discouraged, . . . be chearly . . . have patience . . . abide the will of God, who worketh all things for the best for you." A "loving brother in exile persecuted for Christ's verity," Michael Metcalf would go out alone and unwilling to the savage land of Massachusetts. He went with his eyes on England, not on America: "O Norwich! The beauty of my native country—what shall I say unto thee."

Lives of other early settlers offer other glancing insights into the society of early Dedham. William Bearstow (alias Barstow, Beerstowe, Barstawe), for example, was neither as upright nor as articulate as Metcalf. The Assistants of the colony ordered him "to be whipped for drunkenness" in 1636. By the next year he was admitted to Dedham, where he was assigned a small bachelor's lot. Never a member of the church or a freeman of the col-

SOURCE. Reprinted from *A New England Town, The First Hundred Years* by Kenneth A. Lockridge. By permission of W. W. Norton & Company, Inc. Copyright © 1970 by W. W. Norton & Company, Inc.

ony, his subsequent land grants were below the average while his public responsibilities were limited to duties about the hog-yard in 1637 and menial
labor on a boundary commission of 1641. At one point the town accused
Bearstow of illegally felling timber. He and another defendant pleaded that
it was all a "misunderstanding," but the town found them guilty, concluding
that, "being poor and confessing their fault," the men should lose only the
wood and their labor. The term "poor" was reserved to describe persons
truly destitute, so it is likely that Bearstow had fallen on hard times. By
1639 he had a wife and child to support, and by 1643 two more children.
As if to compound his problems, the soil of his eight-acre home lot was
found to be stony and he had to ask compensation from the town in the
form of additional land elsewhere. Sometime after 1643 he removed to Scituate, Massachusetts, selling his land in Dedham shortly thereafter. At this
point he disappears from the record. Perhaps he became a solid citizen of
Scituate, for he did leave some sort of estate at his death in 1668. It can
only be said that for the brief time he was in Dedham William Bearstow was
not a model Puritan and was not finding the New World a land of milk and
honey.

Robert Hinsdell left facts in a trail that will be familiar to Americans as
that of the classic pioneer. A pillar of the Dedham church, he was also a
member of the first panel of selectmen. He had no trouble in supporting a
family which included a wife and six children. In 1651, when an outlying
region of the original Dedham grant became the town of Medfield, he
moved there and there continued as a respected, prosperous man. Then
Hinsdell's life changed abruptly. His attempt to become a merchant went
awry, ending in 1663 with the surrender of his ninety-acre farm to the attorney of one Jeremiah Tawke, a London clothier to whom he owed 153
pounds. By this time others of his lands in Medfield had been mortgaged,
and in 1671 he sold them all to the wealthy Samuel Shrimpton of Boston.
Leaving the scene of his failure, Hinsdell moved out to the frontier town of
Hadley, thence to a still more exposed settlement which later became the
town of Deerfield. Here he and his family settled; he became a deacon in the
church and set about clearing his new lands for agriculture. Four years later,
when the Indians rose against the colony, Boston raised an expedition to defend the frontier, but at a place since named Bloody Brook the Indians en-
circled and overwhelmed the small force. In the massacre Robert Hinsdell
and all his sons fell. The long series of moves beginning in England ended
there at Bloody Brook in a death that was to become a more usual end for
later Americans likewise seeking to begin life anew in the West.

Not everyone who moved from Dedham moved west; Henry Phillips got
fed up and moved back to the city. He had done well enough since his arrival in 1637, for by 1656 he was a member of the church, an officer of the mi-

litia company, and was receiving better-than-average dividends of public land. But the village did not offer him scope for his talents. Angry over the battle for larger proprietary shares in which he had led a group of dissatisfied settlers, Phillips moved to Boston without waiting for the compromise which ultimately restored harmony. In Boston he showed himself to be a versatile man, becoming a deacon of the First Church, a deputy to the General Court, and an enterprising butcher who built a successful business by catering to the colony's leaders. He died in 1685, after thirty years of urban life, wealthy and sufficiently well known to merit mention in Samuel Sewall's famous diary.

Death as well as disappearance from the records might remove a man from Dedham's history. Edward Alleyn—"Mr." Alleyn, a title usually reserved for university graduates—began what might have been a career of considerable distinction. A pillar of the local church and one of the first panel of selectmen, he was the town's regular deputy to the General Court following 1638. After numerous services to the community he acquired the honorary title of "gent." More tangible recognition took the form of a farm of 350 acres given him by the town. While active and widely employed in the government of the colony, Alleyn found time to dabble in schemes for establishing an iron industry. But in 1642 Edward Alleyn was killed while in Boston on public business, so a career which might have revealed the heights to which a townsman could reach from a base in a rural community was terminated before it had properly begun. Not all the settlers lived to ripe old ages from which they could reflect upon the meaning of their emigration to the New World.

Still, some of them did become virtual patriarchs, relics of the exodus surviving into the days of the third generation. John Gay died in 1688 after half a century in Dedham. His experience described a long descending curve from the respectability of wealth and service into old age and relative poverty. The richest man in town in 1661 and variously a selectman, constable, and member of a county Grand Jury, Gay eased out of public life while his estate slowly tapered down to a mere ninety pounds at his death. Much of the wealth must have gone to his sons, yet other men gave property to their sons while still alive without making themselves near-paupers. And Gay's son, Nathaniel, could not have received too much from his father, since he too died possessed of a small estate. Whatever the reason, it was possible to live so long in the New World and come to so little—not to real poverty, to be sure, but not much above bare subsistence either.

The departures and sad deaths just chronicled may give the impression that Dedham was possessed by a malevolent spirit. Not so. Success was possible, provided vast riches were not the expectation. John Dwight was able to give his son a house and land and still have an estate worth more than

500 pounds on his death in 1660. The usual landmarks of local service and church membership distinguished his career, but more relevant were the large grants of land that went with the distinction of sixteen terms as selectman. Together with judicious purchases, these grants made Dwight one of the richest townsmen in the years between 1649 and 1660. He passed both his comfortable estate and his prestige on to his son, Timothy, thereby initiating a family line marked by both distinctions.

Eleazer Lusher was the one settler who could have made a fortune had he wished. Within the town his political influence was unmatched, while within the colony he was one of a handful of men who made the vital decisions. His position as deputy and as Assistant brought him into contact with enterprising men from all over New England. Yet Lusher never became overwhelmingly wealthy. His estate of some 500 pounds was less than the estates of several of his village neighbors and only grants of land from town and colony in recognition of his services brought his estate up to this moderate level. He died less wealthy than almost any of his fellow Assistants, never having become a land speculator or merchant as did so many who moved in the higher spheres of power. Whether because of his ignorance or, more likely, because of his restraint, at the end he bequeathed to the distant relatives who survived him only the possessions of a solid local farmer.

These are the outlines of eight lives, the lives of eight Englishmen who came to Dedham early in the seventeenth century. They are varied lives and the possibilities they raise are fascinating. Yet they have limitations. Because the record is meager, their outlines lack many of the meanings which might have been garnered. Only an exceptional life left testimony enough for a full biography and the most exceptional of men often left no clue to their inner thoughts. Moreover, even the sparse details that survive concerning these plain men reveal how difficult it is to base generalizations on the peculiarities of individual lives. For every model Puritan there was a ne'er-do-well; for every pioneer, a butcher; for every patriarch, a man who died prematurely. The very variety which lends fascination also frustrates any attempt to characterize the whole society through individual histories. Ultimately the underlying patterns of society in Dedham can emerge only from a consideration of the dull samenesses which have ever dominated human existence. And what the common features of all lives portray is an isolated, small, stable, homogeneous agricultural community which resembled the rural society of seventeenth-century Europe as much as it resembled the "land of opportunity" dear to the hearts of generations of American students and scholars.

. . .

The overwhelming majority of the settlers came to Dedham to stay. They neither ranged restlessly west nor sought wealth in the developing metropolis of Boston. Most put up temporarily in a nearby town while they looked things over, then moved to Dedham and there initiated a sequence of generations which would intertwine their names with the history of the town for several centuries to come. Because of the stability of the settlers and their posterity, the town became a self-contained social unit, almost hermetically sealed off from the rest of the world. Less than one percent of the adult males in town in a given year would be newcomers, while less than one percent of the adult males would emigrate in a given year. Some of the rare immigrants settled permanently in the town, but others were drifters who did not stay more than a few years and whose departure merely served to raise a little the low level of emigration. Most of the remaining emigrants moved no farther than an adjoining town or "moved" only in the eyes of the law when the distant part of Dedham in which they had always lived was incorporated as a new town. A scattering of officials and servants came and went; young women from nearby towns married into local families while young ladies of Dedham married in turn into the families of those towns; and some young men left town before reaching the age at which they appeared in the records. Otherwise, hardly anyone stirred in or out. By way of comparison, the only contemporary English villages whose level of mobility is known were consistently more mobile than this American village.

In fact, the society of the village was quite narrow and self-centered. The number of family names actually declined from sixty-three in 1648 to fifty-seven in 1688, and an increasing majority of the population belonged to a group of thirty-odd enduring clans who could trace their roots back beyond 1648. Collectively and individually the members of the commune had little to do with outside authorities. They obeyed the law of the colony, but not always. They paid their colony taxes, but the taxes paid for local purposes were usually twice as great. As the town sought to avoid involvement in the courts of the colony, so did each man. The average inhabitant was a plaintiff or defendant in civil proceedings no more than once in his life-time and involvements in criminal proceedings were virtually nonexistent. Nearly all land transactions were small exchanges between Dedham men. Two or three speculators excepted, the seventeenth-century farmer dealt with his neighbors, or with farmers of adjoining towns on those few occasions on which the land he sought was just over the town line.

Seventeenth-century Dedham was a small place, including on the average about 500 souls. It was a little larger than the usual English village and a little smaller than most French villages, but was of a size common to many rural communities in the Atlantic civilization of the time. Yet the town grew steadily throughout the century. The population in 1648 was approximately 400; by 1700, it had risen to nearly 750. Natural increase accounted for the growth, since net immigration was negligible. The significance of the healthy rate of natural increase can only be appreciated in the light of the stagnation which characterized the level of population in the villages of seventeenth-century England and France. If Dedham was growing steadily while its counterparts in Europe were growing little if at all, then the fundamental conditions of life in Dedham must have been better than in Europe.

Better in what way? The obvious explanation that springs to mind is that the birth rate must have been higher in Dedham than in seventeenth-century European villages. Surely these young settlers in a new land were prolific in a way impossible in the crowded, marginal villages of the Old World? But it was not so, for the birth rate was about forty births per 1000 population per year—a rate significantly but not remarkably higher than the birth rates of the villages of Clayworth and Cogenhoe in England and Crulai in France. Other figures support this judgment. The average intervals between births, the average number of births per marriage and the average number of marriages per 1000 population were substantially the same in Dedham as in these Old World villages. The devastating statistic which confirms this conclusion is the average age at marriage, which in Europe ranged around twenty-five years for women and twenty-seven years for men and in Dedham was twenty-three for women and twenty-five for men. The difference in female marriage ages argues for a slightly higher birth rate in Dedham—since the younger woman marry, the longer they are "eligible" to have children and the shorter the part of their fertile span that is wasted—but similarity is the main point. And, whether twenty-five or twenty-seven, the middle twenties are a late time for a man to begin married life. In a patronizing assumption of New World superiority, American demographers have commented sadly on the unfortunate conditions that kept European men from acquiring the wherewithal to support a family until they were nearly thirty. Their assumption was wrong, because in Dedham just as in Crulai or Clayworth a man did not find opportunity so plentiful that he could marry as young as he chose.

A great part of Dedham's steady growth and corresponding natural advantages over European villages must be explained through a lower death rate. At most, there were twenty-seven deaths per 1000 per year as against rates of thirty to forty and higher in Europe. Much of the difference can probably be ascribed to such long-range causes as better diet or better housing, conditions which acted year in and year out to prolong the lives of older persons and to ensure that more infants survived the critical days following birth. A more readily identifiable difference lay in the relative absence of short-range demographic "crises" in Dedham. In Europe, particularly in France, famines and plagues struck repeatedly. Often coming in clusters within a ten or twenty-year period, these disasters could wipe out a tenth, a quarter, a half or more of the population of a village. Crises were so severe in some French villages that they created "echoes," periods of low births a generation apart reflecting the initial crisis period of deaths and delayed marriages: fewer children were born or survived birth during a crisis; on reaching maturity their generation had fewer persons available for mariage; a generation with fewer marriages had fewer children; and so it went until circumstances smoothed out the echoing flaw over a period of three or four generations. Dedham went through well over a half century without experiencing a single crisis which removed as much as ten percent of its population within a two-year span. For some reason this New World village was spared at least the worst ravages of disease, famine, and climate, effects all too familiar to rural Europeans of the time. It would be foolish to launch out in Jeffersonian praises of the benefits of benevolent nature in a new land free from the depravities of Europe, yet it is clear that the new land had some material gifts to offer and freedoms to bestow other than the freedom from Anglican persecution.

The town's insulation from the forces of nature had other results. Dedham paralleled Crulai in its seasons of birth, conceptions reaching a peak in the spring and descending to a low in the autumn. But in the New World town the difference between the month of highest conceptions and the month of lowest conceptions was lower than in Crulai. Children were being conceived throughout the year with distinctly less regard for the natural forces—climate, food, labor, whatever—which tended to impose a cyclic yearly pattern of conception on all the rural societies of the world.

Yet in other ways nature did impose itself on human life in Dedham in just the same way and often as severely as in Europe. The similarities in birth rates and marriage ages bear witness to this truth, as does the parallel timing of the yearly cycle of conception. Then too, this town had its severe years; 1675–76 saw twenty-five deaths occur in Dedham. Several of the twenty-five were killed fighting in the same Indian war (King Philip's War) that had resulted in Robert Hinsdell's death, but most died of age and disease in the long season of alarms and excursions that accompanied the war. And year in and year out the seasons of death in Dedham were the same as in the European villages. In all, deaths occured most frequently in the winter months, when cold, poor diet, and confinement combined to weaken the strong and kill the weak. No insulation from nature blessed Dedham with a reduction in the toll of deaths that mounted to a peak every December, January, February.

The economy was agricultural. Men called themselves "yeoman" or "husbandman" as any farmer called himself in England. There was always a miller or two, a blacksmith, a cordwainer or other artisan in the town to supply the specialized needs of the economy, but easily eighty-five percent of the male inhabitants characterized themselves as farmers and most of the rest derived the greater part of their support from the land. It was an unspecialized agriculture which they practiced, devoted largely to mere subsistence, and was very like the agriculture practiced in many sections of rural England. The same oaken tubs full of the same crops (peas, barley, wheat, rye, oats, hay, fruit) from fields of similar sizes rested in identical rooms in matching houses of farmers who achieved equal if modest prosperity and participated in like rural offices (poundkeeper, fenceviewer, hogreeve) in Dedham as in England.

What exactly might a farmer possess? His land aside, he would own essentially the possessions of an English yeoman farmer: within his house of two to eight rooms were a few beds, chests and chairs, a little pewter or silver, perhaps two changes of clothing and a good suit and cloak, a Bible, sometimes with commentaries thereon; outside was a barn or lean-to containing agricultural tools, a cart, bins, bowls, pots and pans, a few bushels of each of the staple crops, and finally a horse or two, several cattle and five or six each of sheep and swine. His whole estate would come to between 200 and 400 pounds Massachusetts currency.

No crop became a cash crop grown in quantity at the expense of others. The agricultural surpluses listed in the inventories varied with the season but were always small and distributed among three or four crops. This held for livestock as well. John Allin died in possession of twenty-eight sheep in 1671, John Bacon of twenty-four cattle in 1683, but these relatively modest herds were the height of acquisition in an economy in which specialized entrepreneurial farming was unknown. The farmers doubtless traded small quantities of grain, wood, beef and hides in nearby Boston in order to obtain the few manufactured necessities that were beyond their means to produce. Still, the message of the inventories of their estates is unmistakable: no single crop or animal dominated the village economy, and the farmers died without leaving the multiplicity of debts or credits with Boston merchants which would have resulted from a more developed commercial relationship.

Yet this simple subsistence economy was also an economy of abundance, for there was an incomparable abundance of land. To be sure, soil was often poor; even free public land grants had to be surveyed at some expense; a man's grant might be distant from his home; and if land was cheap to buy that was in part because it was wilderness land that would take years of backbreaking labor to clear. Yet there was land. Privately owned land cost shillings an acre instead of pounds an acre as in England, and most townships were giving it away free. In Dedham, the conservatism of the town's early land policy did not last forever. No more than 3000 acres had been allotted in the first twenty years, but in the next twelve years over 15,000 acres were divided among the proprietors. A man who lived in the town for any twenty-five year span between 1636 and 1686 received between fifty and 500 acres from the town, 150 acres on the average. This was by no means a farmstead beyond the wildest dreams of a successful English yeoman, but it meant security for the whole society of the village since it made every man a potential yeoman, a status enjoyed by only a fortunate minority of the English rural populace. It was a promise to every man's posterity, guaranteeing that the next generation would inherit the raw material of self-support. Even a younger son of a less than distinguished settler could expect a patrimony which would keep him from having to rent land or work for another man or beg in the streets.

The leaders of the colony reflected a general awareness of the unique abundance of the New World in the novel inheritance law they created. In England, the lands of a man who left no will would go to his eldest son under the law of primogeniture, whose aim was to prevent the fragmentation of holdings which would follow from a division among all the sons. This law arose from a mentality of scarcity. It left the landless younger sons to fend for themselves. In New England the law provided for the division of the whole estate among all the children of the deceased. Why turn younger sons out on the society without land or perhaps daughters without a decent dowry, why invite social disorder, when there was enough to provide for all? The plentitude of land, the novel intestacy law, and the benevolent practices of those yeomen who did leave wills combined in New England to offer the entire second generation the promise of prosperity within the familiar social framework of the village in which their fathers had settled. It was a deeply satisfying prospect to men whose homeland had contained a fair share of wandering laborers, struggling apprentices, and paupers.

As might be expected, the society of the town was rather homogeneous. The circumstances of the emigration had fostered a certain homogeneity from the very beginning, for no noblemen or true English gentlemen settled in Dedham, while the few servants among the founders soon became independent yeomen. Though the social policy of the founders had embraced a degree of social differentiation by recognizing "rank and quality" earned in England as the basis for larger allotments of land in the New World, in fact the settlers of appreciable "rank and quality" were few, they did not receive extremely large bonuses of land as a result of their distinction, and they had to compete for allotments with men who met the more practical standards for extra land—such as skill in farming or large families. Above all, the abundance of land and the simplicity of the economy mitigated against the rapid evolution of radical social differences among the middle-class Englishmen who settled the town. Impoverished "laborers" hardly existed in this society of abundant land. Servants amounted to less than five percent of the population and were nearly all either captive Indians, Negro slaves (of whom there were very few), or young children serving in another family as part of their upbringing. The occasional "poor" individual was usually a sick widow or an orphan, or an improvident half-wit. On the other hand men who came to be known as "gentleman" were even more rare and had earned their titles through long and distinguished public service. The more wealthy farmers—even those of families with original pretensions to a little "rank and quality" and who were called on to serve as selectmen not infrequently —continued to refer to themselves as yeomen, which they were. They might have had a little more wealth and distinction than the average farmer, but their estates were identical in structure to those of men with half as much wealth and their style of life was correspondingly similar—a style in which every man toiled on his own lands. While they no doubt expected and certainly were given respect, they retained a good measure of Puritan honesty about their social position and refused to take titles of gentility.

The distribution of taxable wealth reflected the *de facto* homogeneity of the economy and the society. The five percent of men who paid the highest taxes controlled but fifteen percent of the taxable wealth in Dedham. This degree of concentration implied a certain hierarchy of wealth within the town, but was far more equitable than the concentration of wealth in the hands of the few which came to prevail in seventeenth-century Boston. In this developing commercial center the richest five percent of men controlled twenty-five percent of the wealth. At the bottom of the social spectrum, the lowest twenty percent of men owned eight percent of the taxable wealth in Dedham as against three percent of the wealth in Boston.

So the cheapness of land and the low level of the subsistence economy had done much to keep the distribution of wealth relatively even and the spectrum of social rank narrow, thereby making it easier for the town's leaders to maintain a social harmony predicated on a judicious blending of collective interest with a moderate degree of hierarchy. If anything, it had been necessary to emphasize the latter just a little here and there, to prevent its being swallowed in the former. The founders of Boston faced an opposite problem, as its distribution of wealth indicates, and the brief history of utopian impulse in that city showed the deadly effects of excessive concentration of wealth resulting from rapid economic development.

In sum, what kind of life did such a society offer? It certainly offered a man the opportunity to live a long life on his own land among a group of equals or near-equals. But this appealing prospect was tempered by the inherent conservatism of the social environment. To follow the fortunes of a young man from year to year is to perceive the bonds which knit him to his society and his society to the special world of all peasant villages. He could expect to be a farmer, like his father. He would stay in the village, for his father's death held out the promise of land. It would take time, for almost any farmer who passed forty would live to be sixty before dying. A son might be given lands while the patriarch was still alive, but woe unto him who angered his father! (There was the story of one father who cut his second son out of his will because he dared to disobey his father's order to grow barley on the five acres given him to test his sense of the land.) Of course a youth could strike out on his own within the town . . . if he could find a way to earn money, that is, and if his father would let him, since a man was not really free of paternal discipline until he reached the voting age of twenty-four. But at last the day would come when his inheritance finally cleared the courts. Even if his father had been well off, it might not be much, by the time the older brothers got their shares and part of the estate was set aside for the use of the widow. Still, it would do for a start, and now, at the age of twenty-five or twenty-six, he could marry and begin a family. The land would take some clearing and it was sometimes thin soil such as could drive a man to other employment if other were to be had, but it was his land and better than nothing. Twenty or thirty years of hard work aided by the labor of his own sons might enable the farmer to save enough to buy a little extra land, and dividends of public land would further swell his holdings. By now in his late forties himself, he might have earned enough respect to be elected selectman. But by now he was nearly an old man, left to husband his estate for the sons who were in their turn anticipating their father's will. At least he had had the satisfaction of progressing as well as most: no one had passed him by on the way to fabulous riches, nor would any catastrophe be likely to wipe out his holdings. He depended on no city man or foreigner for his income, and, although his home could be easily destroyed by fire, it could as easily be rebuilt out of local materials with the help of his neighbors. It would have been a good enough life, though rather hard and lonely since his wife and youngest child had died.

. . .

So on the one hand it was unmistakably an "American" society. The seemingly unending potentialities of the virgin lands which surrounded Dedham had their due effects on the life of every man, helping to prolong that life and opening to it possibilities unthinkable for the Everyman of England. The absence of a privileged aristocracy and of the masses of the poor left the community free of the drastic human inequalities which plagued European society. Life was indeed better than in England and far removed from the sometimes appalling conditions of France under the old regime.

But the America of social diversity and ideological pluralism was never more distant. If the society was one of opportunity, it was the continually present opportunity to take up land and become another subsistence farmer. No social or industrial revolution was taking place, increasing social opportunity by altering its distribution in the society or by opening new avenues of upward mobility. And the equality of the society was nothing less than the equality of economic interests which lies at the heart, not of modern plural-istic democracy, but of Marxist-Leninist democracy. One class, one interest, one mind—how can there help but be voluntary unanimity within such a so-ciety? As it was to have been yet never was and never could be with Marx's hopelessly idealized industrial proletariat, so to a remarkable degree, it real-ly was with the farmers of the Dedham commune.

Furthermore, an awareness of the diverse possibilities of rural society in seventeenth-century Europe can serve as a needed corrective for the evi-dence of uniquely American opportunity in Dedham. Europe included many nations, each with many regions. Here and there in the interstices of Old World society can be found villages whose way of life resembled that of "American" Dedham. The English village of Wilston Magna is one exam-ple. By the seventeenth century there were no lords of the manor in this vil-lage, all having sold out to peasant proprietors. Many families owned land, farming areas of twenty to forty acres for the most part, areas comparable to those actually under cultivation in early Dedham. It was "a solid community of middling size farmers, . . . with no overshadowing family at the top, ..." Not an isolated case, the English village was "representative of a considerable number of midland villages where a substantial body of peas-ant proprietors still kept their hold on the land."

If some Old World villages offered many of the beneficial conditions found in New World Dedham, it is even more true that New World Dedham embodied many of the traditional conditions found in most Old World vil-lages. Dedham, Clayworth, and Crulai were three small agricultural villages which existed in an age long before modern medicine, scientific farming, and industrial productivity. Winter was to be feared in each of them, har-vests were a gamble that kept men aware of Providence, diseases arose and subsided outside of all human control and infants died in numbers that would shock us today. A man ready to marry did not just go out and get a job; he prepared a farm of his own or else made sure he could expect to in-herit the family home and acres. A person who lived to seventy, a normal life-span in our century, found that he was one of the few survivors of his gen-eration. Collectively, a town was likely to retain its customs and peculiarities for a long time. The few newcomers admitted each year soon adopted the ways found comfortable by the clansmen of the town for generations past. Few left town, for the ways of the community were reassuringly familiar. Most men showed the typical peasant's satisfaction with the *status quo:* It worked for his father and for his father before him, why tinker with success? Why, especially when it could be dangerous? Some of Dedham's customs may have been unique, but chances are they soon became as unthinkingly rigid as any in Europe. It could hardly have been otherwise in a society that in so many ways still followed the ancient, universal patterns of rural life.

CHAPTER 8

THE COLONIAL
WAY OF LIFE

Our concern with the early development of American institutions and traditions, such as democracy, nationalism, and religious freedom, sometimes causes us to overlook the people who molded these institutions, and who created the American republic. Most students of American history are familiar with some of the figures who founded the English colonies, such as Captain John Smith and William Penn, and with a few others who struggled for American independence, such as Benjamin Franklin and George Washington. But what about the people who lived between the era of Smith and the era of Franklin—the pioneers who actually settled and, in so doing, shaped America?

In this selection, John R. Alden focuses on the colonial Americans. As he suggests, it was not clear to the casual observer (even on the eve of the Revolution) that the inhabitants of the English colonies were an important people. Indeed, there was so much diversity and division among the colonial Americans that any but the most astute observer might well have despaired of an attempt to find a basic unity that would have justified calling the colonists "a people." The different patterns of life in the Southern, the New England, and the Middle colonies provide the basic format for Alden's essay. He concentrates on the styles of living in the three colonial sections, examining the economic pursuits, the

119

class structure, the education, the arts, the religion, and the ethnic strains of the population.

In reading this selection, concentrate on two areas of concern. First, how did the colonial Americans differ from the Americans of today? Were they sturdier, more virtuous, and more deeply committed to American ideals? Or were they much like us, motivated by the same basic concerns? Second, in seeking to grasp the essence of the different patterns of life in colonial America, try to identify those forces or factors that tended to fuse the colonists into a common and distinct people. Professor Alden clearly asserts that from 1607 onward the colonists were growing together and, also, were growing apart from their European kin. Is this argument persuasive in light of the evidence of diversity and division presented in his essay?

Students interested in pursuing this subject will delight in John C. Miller, *The First Frontier; Life in Colonial America** (1966). D. J. Boorstin, *The Americans: The Colonial Experience** (1958), L. B. Wright, *The Cultural Life of the American Colonies** (1957), and Clarence L. Ver Steeg, *The Formative Years, 1607–1763* (1964), explore certain aspects of this subject.

* Available in a paperback edition.

THE COLONIAL AMERICANS
JOHN R. ALDEN

When the French withdrew from North America, it was not obvious to every casual observer that the Americans were an important people. Nevertheless, it is clear enough in retrospect that their condition, except for that of the Negro slaves, was nearly as comfortable, commodious, and secure as might be in a brutal and most uncertain world. So long as the British navy continued to dominate the Atlantic—and it seemed likely to maintain its sway for decades—they did not need to fear invasion by Bourbon armies. Nor must they be fundamentally concerned about an Indian threat, even though the red-skinned warriors, with or without European allies, could create havoc and agony on the western frontiers. They were not only as safe as a people might be from alien enemies in the North Atlantic world but were endowed by the Treaty of Paris with a vast prospect of expansion, even to the shores of California. The astute Benjamin Franklin, and with him John Adams, considering the maturity, the numbers, and the wealth of the Americans, and observing their rapid and continuing increase in both population and riches, had already discerned that they would become truly powerful in the British Empire, or conceivably as citizens of an independent nation. Less penetrating eyes saw the Americans as mere colonists, thinly scattered along the edge of a vast continent; divided from one another by clashing economic interests; set apart by antagonistic social structures; linguistically and culturally diverse; provincially jealous and hostile because of quarrels over boundaries, lands, and commerce; and kept apart by distance and bad roads. It was doubted they were even a people. Were they not Yankees, Pennsylvanians, and Carolinians, rather than Americans? Unquestionably there was remarkable variety among them, and one may readily distinguish among three regions, the Southern colonies, New England, and the Middle colonies. Divergence and conflict between East and West—between Tidewater and interior—also existed. But the Americans, though heterogeneous, had much in common. Indicative of their true unity is the fact that

SOURCE. From *Pioneer America*, by John R. Alden. Copyright 1966 by John R. Alden, pp. 47–61. Reprinted by permission of Alfred Knopf, Inc.

they had come to be called "Americans." That name was in part applied to them for convenience. More important, it recognized that they were a people not basically different from one another, and that they were not merely Englishmen who happened to reside in North America.

To say that the Southern colonies, Maryland, Virginia, the Carolinas, and Georgia, differed economically and socially from the others is not to offer a novel or dramatic insight. The long growing season and plentiful rainfall in those regions made possible, even relatively easy, the production of tobacco in Virginia and Maryland, and of rice and indigo in the Low Country of the Carolinas and Georgia centering upon Charleston. Tobacco and rice could profitably be sold abroad; and England after 1748 paid a bounty on and supplied a market for indigo, used in the making of dyes. All three could be raised in quantity by unskilled labor, under direction. Hence the bringing in of large numbers of Negro slaves, the very cheapest of workers, at least in the short run. Hence also, in great part, the rise of plantations. After 1700, sanguinely hoping for big crops obtained at low cost and sold at high prices, many Marylanders and Virginians grew more and more of the "yellow weed," acquired more land upon which to grow it and more slaves to care for it. In the Low Country rice and indigo planters similarly dreamed of easy wealth and expanded their land and slaveholdings. The plantation owners prospered, although their debts often mounted almost as swiftly as their assets. Thus agriculture in the South acquired a special cast, and there was frequently, alas, one plantation where several homestead farmers and their families could have lived in freedom and comfort. Trade did not thrive in that region as it did elsewhere in the colonies. Charleston, colonial capital of South Carolina and busy port of the Low Country, grew into a small city. It was the only one in the entire Southern region.

The social order in the South, principally based upon its special economy, was also distinctive. It was peculiar in that its bottom was composed of a mass of Negroes, who were, with few exceptions, slaves. Nine out of every ten American Negroes lived, or at least existed, in the Southern colonies. About one third of the people in the entire South were Negro. Some of the blacks were household servants and mechanics; most of them were valued because they cared for crops and produced progeny. Above the Negroes were all the whites, among whom the English element was principal, although Scotch-Irish, Germans, and Scots were also numerous. Above all the other whites was a gentry, an untitled American aristocracy, composed almost exclusively of plantation owners. It was a relatively new aristocracy, membership in it being founded on the possession of wealth rather than patrician ancestors. The worthy person, even the unworthy one, was not barred from it because his father had engaged in commerce; a man who belonged to it might himself be occupied in trade as well as agriculture. At the end of the colonial era, gentry included George Washington, whose father was not quite of it; Edmund Pendleton, who was descended from a bond servant; and Benjamin Powell, in youth a wheelwright, a carpenter, who had earned himself the title of "Gent" by merit. Below that gentry, and often confused with it, were many not-so-rich planters and substantial homestead farmers. These, along with shopkeepers and a few professional folk, composed a middle class. This middle class has escaped the attention it deserves because it lacks the glamor of aristocracy, the brutal charm of slavery. Beneath the middle class were the bond servants, numerous only in Virginia and Maryland, whose status was, of course, temporary. Above the slaves were the "poor white trash," not yet known by that name but real enough. The "trash" should be distinguished from the many whites who were poor only in possessions. Ignorant, lazy, quarrelsome, lawless, and fecund, those degraded people were more numerous than the Southern gentry. It should be added that white men of all classes contributed to the blood stock of the Negroes, who were moving biologically toward their masters and mistresses.

Fascinating as life in the country may be, rural lanes are not the smoothest or broadest highways to learning and the arts. Roads in the Southern colonies were bad, and the region lagged in terms of educational and intellectual advance. Education largely remained a private affair, and elementary schools supported by churches and individual benevolence were available only to a minority of children. The offspring of the slaves were seldom taught more than the performance of physical tasks. The young, male and female, of plain farmers often learned only to write their names. The sons of the aristocracy were commonly instructed by tutors—their sisters learned but to read and write, to play a musical instrument, to dance, and to pursue the domestic arts. Not infrequently a young gentleman continued his studies at the College of William and Mary, founded in 1693, for several generations the only institution of higher learning in the South, or at a college to the north, or at an English private school or university. One finds some of them studying Latin at Westminster School, law at the Inns of Court in London, medicine in Edinburgh and Leyden. However, formal education at the higher levels was not easily available to the middle class, and it was not sought by the majority of young gentlemen. It could not be secured in Charleston, for there was no college there during the colonial time. Nor was Charleston remarkable as a city that nourished literary and artistic talent, although her richer residents wrote essays and verse.

Something more should be said about the males of the Southern aristocracy, for it contributed great men to America and to the world. From it came Thomas Jefferson and James Madison, who were college men, scholars, and cultivated gentlemen as well as philosophers and statesmen. However, the usual man of the gentry was less given to intellectual pursuits. He was comparable to an English squire. He belonged to the Anglican Church, which was established in all the Southern colonies, but he was not devout. He managed his lands and his slaves, hunted, danced, watched cockfights, gambled, and frequently visited his neighbors. Most important, he engaged in politics. The gentry dominated local government in parish and county, and usually both houses of the Southern colonial legislatures—not so thoroughly in North Carolina as elsewhere, for that "valley of humility between two mountains of conceit" contained fewer aristocrats and more homestead farmers than did her neighbors. The aristocrats were splendidly schooled in public affairs, read and wrote about them, acquired breadth of view in statecraft, and gained the polish of men of the world. Of such was the Virginian, George Washington. He and his like offered both sturdy and informed leadership.

In his time New England produced no heroic figure equal to Washington, but many worthy men sprang from its thin soil and stony hillsides. The Yankees, as the inhabitants of the region north of Long Island Sound and east of the Hudson River were commonly designated after the middle of the eighteenth century, varied from the Southerners in both appearance and reality. If New England was not lavishly endowed with natural resources, its people were energetic, thrifty, and ingenious, like those of the Dutch provinces and the Swiss cantons. Moreover, the Yankees commanded more good land than the Dutch, far more generous forests than the Swiss. Most of them were tillers of the soil, farmers who owned their fields, wood lots, and orchards. Many, however, were carpenters, masons, mechanics of all sorts, and traders. The same man might engage in two or more pursuits, farming and fishing, lumbering and shipbuilding, trading and tavern-keeping. Cramped by the lack of fertile soil, the Yankees made ships and went to sea. They gathered abundant crops of fish off their own coasts and on the Grand Banks of Newfoundland; and they turned to maritime commerce with singular success. It is often said that the increasingly evident affluence of Massachusetts rested upon the carcasses of codfish; underneath it also were the trunks of pines and oaks, potent rum, and the bodies of slaves carried from Africa. Merchants grew wealthy in Massachusetts, and in New England, from oceanic traffic as well as fishing.

There were few slaves in New England; few citizens equivalent to the "poor white trash"; few bond servants; and an aristocracy less conspicuous, less powerful, and less glamorous than that of the Southern colonies. Upon the stable and diversified economy of the Yankee country was based a large middle class. Its members usually had the right to vote, and their will was potent in public affairs. Aristocrats did not dominate in Massachusetts or Connecticut as they did in Virginia and South Carolina. A distinction made in the seventeenth century between the "gentleman" and the "goodman" had softened. Moreover, the Congregationalist clergy had lost prestige and influence. The men of the cloth had been, to a degree, displaced by men of money. Nevertheless, New England had its first families of wealthy merchants, landowners, officeholders, lawyers, and clergy. With strong support from the middle class, they were the leaders in that region. So firm was their grasp upon the body politic in Connecticut that they formed a "standing order" which endured for generations. Even so, Hutchinsons, Saltonstalls, Trumbulls, and Griswolds did not have the social and political stature of the Southern Lees, Carters, and Pinckneys. New England society was semi-democratic.

Before the end of the colonial time the prosperous New Englanders offered outward evidence of their wealth in their clothes, coaches, carriages, and homes. The well-to-do wore garb like that of English gentlemen and ladies, like that of Southern aristocrats. They had their wines as well as their rum, and their big houses. More impressive than their mansions were the New England churches in austere elegance; more pleasing to the generous-minded observer than those mansions were the neat, attractive homes of tens of thousands of villagers and farmers. The New England village had acquired a charm and beauty which long endured. New England also had cities—Newport, which would afterward cease to grow rapidly; and Boston, which was the second largest American city and would retain importance in commerce, in banking, in education, and in the sight of its citizens. English travelers visiting the Yankee country in the eighteenth century, and later, remarked that it bore a greater resemblance to Old England than other parts of America. Its people continued to be almost entirely of English descent until the nineteenth century was well under way.

The Yankees were also the best educated of the colonists. Elementary instruction was quite readily available to them, often at public expense. As the American Revolution approached, the New Englander was usually literate. Moreover, there were many men among the Yankees who were college graduates. Harvard was the only college in New England until

Yale was founded in 1701. Nevertheless, the two colleges sent forth hundreds of informed and thoughtful men in the eighteenth century. After 1764 the College of Rhode Island (Brown University) and after 1769 Dartmouth contributed to the supply of well-educated men in the colonies. It was further increased by private study and reading, for those who earnestly sought to learn often had access to books.

Instruction of the young, even in New England, was interrupted by the tasks of transplanting from Old England, and learning and the arts did not flourish steadily from the beginning of settlement. There was, to be sure, a transit of European civilization, at least the English variety of it. However, all of that civilization did not promptly pass over the ocean, and things physical during many decades occupied minds and energies at the expense of things intellectual and artistic in New England. So it was everywhere in America as people flooded into wild new territories. Included among those who went to New England in the second quarter of the seventeenth century were many scholars, both clerical and lay. Moreover, Harvard produced gifted and learned men even in its first years. Nevertheless, there was a cultural sag in New England; it could not and did not keep pace with the Mother Country.

Nevertheless, New England spawned scholars, writers, and even a distinguished artist in the colonial time. In the South, William Byrd II of Westover, author of charming sketches of life in Virginia and North Carolina, stands out because so few men in that region distinguished themselves in letters before the onset of the American Revolution. He would have had more literary company among the Yankees. But let us not make too much of New Englanders who studied, wrote, or dabbled in the arts. We should not praise highly men—or women—who would in no way have been remarkable on the eastern side of the Atlantic. Eschewing ancestor worship, no American will classify the New England poet Edward Taylor, who was born in Old England, with John Milton, or match Cotton Mather of Massachusetts against John Locke. Mather was only a bright star in a sequestered corner of America. If he presciently declared that disease was caused by tiny invisible animals, he also believed that witches were both real and visible. His intellect was chaotic as well as brilliant. Of the Reverend Jonathan Edwards, who has been sufficiently admired by later American generations, it may be said that he was a gifted theologian and an acute philosopher, that he put the case for freedom of the human will in the face of an omniscient God as well as the logician may do it. In the London of his day Edwards would not have been a man of small repute. Another New Englander, John Singleton Copley, of a later generation than Edwards, actually did win fame in

England. Copley went abroad to study painting, was acclaimed in London for his artistry, remained in England, and fathered a lord chancellor. His best work, however, was done before he left his native country. Portraits that he painted of various Americans are remarkable for their realism and craftsmanship. However, he is not usually ranked with his English contemporaries Sir Joshua Reynolds and Thomas Gainsborough.

Material, educational, and intellectual advances, so important in themselves, also profoundly affected the Congregational establishment in New England. Almost united with the state, except in Rhode Island, the Puritan church wielded vast power in seventeenth-century New England. The will of the orthodox Puritan clergy and laymen was dominant alike in public and personal affairs. Punishing heresy, even Anglican deviations, they most earnestly strove to preserve the true church and the Puritan way. Congregations vied with legislatures in the curbing of the unfaithful, the heedless, the willful, and the wicked. Idolatry and blasphemy were at one time capital crimes in Massachusetts, and persons who denied belief in the resurrection of the body or in the validity of infant baptism, even persons who withdrew from communion, could be banished. On the other hand, Puritan congregations formally inquired into the behavior of their members and excommunicated men and women of heretical belief and unpleasing conduct; in 1640 Captain John Underhill was driven from communion in Boston because he had committed and had tried to commit adultery—and would not offer a suitable confession. Far less heinous offenses were similarly punished. Without the confession and repentance of the parents, a child conceived before their marriage might be denied baptism. It was widely believed among the Puritans that a child born on Sunday was conceived on a Sunday and so was especially burdened with sin. The true New England Puritan feared that even he, the seemingly anointed, might at last be disappointed, and he kept both his own and his brother's conscience. It ought to be added that, to his credit, he was not a prohibitionist. Congregational clergymen drank rum, and Harvard students were daily served beer with bread and beef. The "steady habits" for which the men of Connecticut have long been famous included toping. It is claimed, in fact, that some New England towns required by law the maintenance of an ordinary, or tavern, conveniently near the village place of worship. It is notorious that the Puritans of eastern Massachusetts hanged nineteen persons found guilty of witchcraft after 1688. They were not the first to suffer for that crime in Massachusetts. One ought not exaggerate the significance of the hysteria about witches that convulsed Salem—and Boston—toward the close of the seventeenth century. Belief in witchcraft was not confined to the Puritans—nor were barbarous punishments. In England in 1765 a woman convicted of poisoning her husband was burned at the stake. The execution of innocent victims accused of witchcraft is evidence of a sort that Puritanism was in decline.

So it was, but in slow descent. The New Englanders, as their lives on earth became longer and more pleasant, worried less about their existence beyond the grave. Doubtless they became more tolerant in their beliefs as they voyaged distantly and conversed with men subscribing to creeds other than their own. Deism, which obtained many converts in Europe subsequent to the discoveries of Isaac Newton, spread to America. Even Puritan clergymen increasingly preached about the God of love, saying less about the God of justice, before whom even well-educated Puritans had bowed in utter fear. Some of the ministers slipped toward Unitarianism. Weakened by assults from worldly prosperity and secular learning, orthodox Puritanism lost communicants, especially those with social pretensions, to newly founded Anglican churches. It suffered further from schism. It was hit hard in the 1740s by a wave of pietistic and emotional revivalism, the "Great Awakening." The ravings, the rantings, and the frenzies of the "Great Awakening," which Jonathan Edwards, who ought to have known better, helped to stimulate, grievously offended the Congregationalists who clung to traditional Puritan emphasis upon religious law and logic. As the American Revolution approached, the Congregational establishment was not what it had been. In 1755 at Marblehead, Massachusetts, Mrs. John Glover confessed in open church that she had engaged in sexual intercourse with her husband before their marriage. But there is no record that Glover, later a valiant and most useful officer who served under General Washington, humbled himself in church before he defied his King.

Let it not be thought that the New Englanders internally led dark, dismal, and desperate lives. Their religious notions and moral codes were their own and hence were not utterly unsuited to them. One may not say that they were an unhappy people. Were the Spartans, with their rigid rules? Or the Samurai, because of their Bushido? If not gay or frivolous, the Yankee could nevertheless be contented, even joyful. Consider the radiant and touching lines addressed by the Puritan poet Mrs. Anne Broadstreet "To my Dear and Loving Husband."

> My love is such that Rivers cannot quench,
> Nor ought but love from thee give recompence.
> Thy love is such I can no way repay;
> The heavens reward thee manifold I pray.
> Then while we live, in love let's so persever,
> That when we live no more, we may live ever.

Between the colonial extremes were the Middle colonies, New York, New Jersey, Pennsylvania, and Delaware, moderate in climate, immoderately furnished with good soil, great rivers, and splendid harbors. They were the "bread colonies," sending grain and flour to distant places. But their lands bounteously gave forth iron as well as wheat and corn, and manufacturers of the black metal in the Middle colonies offered dangerous competition to those of Sheffield and other English cities before 1750. Water-borne craft in large numbers plowed the Hudson and the Delaware. Philadelphia and New York were centers of both river and oceanic traffic. As the era of the Revolution drew near, Philadelphia, with more than 20,000 citizens, was the largest American city, and New York threatened to pass Boston in population. Had they been located in England, the two cities would have been important there. Their well-to-do merchants, such as John Watts of Manhattan and Israel Pemberton of Philadelphia, together with country magnates, gladly supplied a gentry in the region between Connecticut and Maryland. That aristocracy was a trifle closer to the Southern aristocracy than was the patrician class of New England. Some of its members, such as the Philipses, Livingstons, and Van Rensselaers of New York, owned wide estates and dictated to numerous tenants and white servants. In Delaware the masters and mistresses of Negro slaves lived much like their counterparts in Virginia. The Middle colonies had their sharp social gradations but also a middle class almost as large proportionately as that of New England. Plain farmers who owned their good land were numerous, and artisans and traders thrived in cities, towns, and villages.

Remarkable in that early Middle America was the variety of its people, for it was the home of large non-English minorities, notably German, Scotch-Irish, and Dutch. The ancestors of the Pennsylvanians were as much German as they were English; and the Scotch-Irish settled thickly in the interior of William Penn's colony. Preachers exhorted their congregations in Dutch in several communities of New York and New Jersey until the end of the eighteenth century; and the use of German, at least of a sort, persisted in German enclaves of Pennsylvania into the twentieth century. Equally various were the churches, none of them established, except that the Anglican Church was officially recognized in three New York counties. The followers of Calvin, English, Scotch-Irish, German, and Dutch, were numerous; Lutherans, Moravians, Anglicans, Quakers, and Jews worshiped the Creator in their several ways. These were all the more diverse because the "Great Awakening" and its emotional Christianity disturbed and divided several of the sects. That Christianity of enthusiasm, of hell-fire and brimstone, indeed, spread throughout the colonies, and waves of it were to assail the American people again and again.

The "Great Awakening" does not offer testimony to educational and intellectual advance. Men and women who lost their self-control in eagerness to save their souls might speak in "strange tongues" but not in Latin. Their religious frolicking might lead them to read the Holy Scriptures but hardly the plays of Shakespeare. However, there were other awakenings in the Middle colonies. Schools maintained at public expense were less common than in New England, but many privately managed ones, often maintained by clergymen and churches, purveyed elementary instruction. That devotion to learning so characteristic of the Scots was displayed by Scottish and Scotch-Irish Presbyterians in America; the Dutch and many of the Germans also set high value upon knowledge. The task of civilizing the young was not neglected in the Middle colonies. In that region no fewer than four universities were born before the Revolution: Princeton, founded in 1746; the University of Pennsylvania, established as an academy at Philadelphia in 1751; Columbia, appearing three years later as King's College; and Rutgers, which began as Queen's College in 1766.

Those central colonies had their full colonial share of talented and learned men in the eighteenth century. In New York the Scottish-born official, Cadwallader Colden, wrote a worthy history of the Iroquois and more than dabbled in medicine and physics. He erroneously believed that he had made discoveries correcting mistakes of Newton. William Livingston of New York and New Jersey was a poet, essayist, polemicist, and politician. In Pennsylvania the Bartrams, John and William, father and son, distinguished themselves as botanists; the charming *Travels* of the younger Bartram would supply imagery for Samuel Coleridge's "Kubla Khan." By far the most distinguished man in all the colonies before the Revolution was, of course, Benjamin Franklin, Boston-born but a Philadelphian during most of his long and busy life. One may not properly describe in a brief space his many-faceted genius, his diverse achievements. Born the son of an artisan, he became a printer, philosopher, essayist, postal official, superb propagandist, inventor, politician, and diplomat. He contributed importantly to knowledge about electricity, and he wrote his classic autobiography. His education was largely informal, his donations to mankind cardinal and profuse. Not without faults—there was a strain of grating smugness in him—he was the very model of the self-made and well-made man in the American "land of opportunity."

It is apparent enough that variety and contrariety were characteristics of the American scene after the middle of the eighteenth century. Nor have all the colonial divergencies and clashes been mentioned, for they existed between East and West as well as North and South. Indeed, division between East and West, in one form or another, like that between North and South, was to endure into the twentieth century. It appeared as soon as the colonists moved inland, from the coastal plain to the Piedmont above it, into the so-called Old West. The people of the Old West, especially those from Pennsylvania southward, were poorer, less educated, less European, and more American than those of the Atlantic Tidewater. The Tidewater leaned toward the aristocratic, the Old West toward the democratic. The interior folk were often indebted to their more prosperous fellows of the coastal plain. The Tidewater did not always exert itself to help defend the Old West against the Indians; it was reluctant to give the newly settled areas representation in the colonial assemblies in proportion to numbers; and it sometimes discriminated against the people of the interior with respect to taxation. In the Southern colonies the homestead farmer of the interior, owning few or no slaves, was set against the wealthy planter to the east. Hence came political collisions, and even unsuccessful rebellions by the people of the interior. They took up arms under Nathaniel Bacon in Virginia in 1676. In Pennsylvania they marched against Philadelphia in 1764; soon afterward, as Regulators, they created uproar in the Carolinas. Bacon's Rebellion was not put down without bloodshed, and an uprising of the Regulators in North Carolina continued until they were crushed by Governor William Tryon and provincial militia in the pitched battle of the Alamance in 1771.

One may be tempted to magnify the cleavages among the colonial Americans. For they had much in common from the beginning, and they became more alike. One may think too much about their varied ancestral roots in Europe and Africa, English, Welsh, Scottish Lowland and Scottish Highland, Scotch-Irish, Irish, Dutch, Flemish, German, Swedish, Finnish, French, Swiss, Jewish, and Negro. It should be observed that virtually all of the European forebears of the colonists lived on the lands and islands north of the Pyrenees and west of the Elbe River. They were west Europeans, and both they and their descendants in America were overwhelmingly Protestant, if of many sects. Moreover, the English element in America was easily principal in the colonial bloodstock, and the English language, modified somewhat in the American environment, prevailed without serious contest over other European, and African, ones. English ways of thought, English institutions retained an easy ascendancy. Karl Schmidt became Charles Smith, and Hans Fuchs became John Fox, and the Smiths and Foxes gradually learned to think like their English-speaking neighbors. Besides, although German, Dutch, and French elements persisted, there was much intermarriage between the

English and European parts of the colonial population before the beginning of the Revolution—it would accelerate.

Tending to fuse, even with the Negroes, the colonists also became less and less like the English at home.

> Leaving the old, both worlds at once they view
> That stand upon the threshold of the new.

Not too different from one another when they emigrated to the New World, the settlers were brought closer together by common experiences and interests in America, these being other than those influencing their brethren in the Old World. From 1607 onward they encountered similar troubles in subduing Nature. They had the same enemies, the Indians, the Spanish, and the French. They had a common experience of contest with English authority. Hence they grew together, and at the same time apart from their kin on the European continent and in the British Isles. That they had become like one another and unlike their blood relatives beyond the Atlantic was recognized by the observant and assumed by the less perceptive among them well before the Americans and the English exchanged shots at Lexington. It is significant that the terms "America" and "American," to indicate Britain's colonies on the mainland of North America and one of their inhabitants, had come into everyday use by the 1760s. While it is clear that these names were increasingly employed because of convenience—there were no brief equivalent terms—they were also used because they were needed to identify a distinct area and people. Thus the question posed by J. Hector St. John de Crèvecoeur and so often quoted, "What then is this American, this new man?" To be sure, the wide and growing gap between the American and the Englishman was not yet seen by all in America or England. An American in the 1760s might still refer to the Mother Country as "home"; and an Englishman might assume that a citizen of New London, Connecticut, if not the equal of one of Old London, if only a "poor relation," was nevertheless English. But that gap between the Englishman and the American became ever greater after the collapse of the French empire in North America. After 1783, when England recognized the independence of the United States, there would be no serious question that its citizens, an incomplete compound of old breeds, had become a distinct and new one.

CHAPTER 9

COLONIAL GOVERNMENT AND POLITICS

In this section from *The First American Revolution* (1958),* a revision of his *Seedtime of the Republic* (1953), Clinton Rossiter is concerned not with the mechanics or methods of colonial politics but, instead, with the institutions through which and around which colonial politics developed. In short, he is interested in the *political culture* of the colonies.

Much has been written about the nature of colonial politics. It has been described as a great wave of the future with political freedom as the eventual goal. It has been discussed by "Progressive" historians such as Carl L. Becker, Charles A. Beard, and Vernon L. Parrington as a radical versus conservative struggle over who "should rule at home." The "Imperial" school of historians has inferred that it was a political struggle waged in a framework of general ignorance of the problems of governing a vast empire. But in all of these interpretations only a few scholars have examined the nature of the offices and political institutions over which these struggles were waged, as does Professor Rossiter in this section.

Does the nature of political institutions alter the type of politics that take place? How? Can differences between English and Spanish colonial political and revolutionary struggles be traced to different institutions?

133

In addition to the various schools of studies mentioned above, the student might well consult studies such as Charles M. Andrews' magnificent, although slightly dated, *Colonial Background of the American Revolution** (1924) and Leonard W. Labaree, *Royal Government in America* (1930). More recent studies are Charles S. Sydnor, *Gentlemen Freeholders: Political Practices in Washington's Virginia** (1952), and Jack P. Greene, *The Quest for Power* (1963). For an excellent discussion of the importance of the *political culture* and the problems of this period as well as the literature on the subject, see Jack P. Greene, "Changing Interpretations of Early American Politics," Ray Allen Billington (ed.), *The Reinterpretation of Early American History** (1966).

* Available in a paperback edition.

SELF-GOVERNMENT BEFORE DEMOCRACY: THE PATTERN OF COLONIAL POLITICS
CLINTON ROSSITER

The bisection of early American history into the years before and after the Glorious Revolution, a favorite device of colonial historians, has special application to colonial government. The first period of political development, which lasted from the Jamestown settlement (1607) to the withdrawal, alteration, and restoration of the Massachusetts charter (1684–1691), was one of "alarum and excursion" in the mother country and self-determination in the colonies. The second, which began with the creation of the Board of Trade (1696) and ended with the outburst of resistance to the Stamp Act (1765), was one of fast-growing imperial concern in England and even faster-growing political maturity in America. The influence of the first period upon the second, of the century of neglect upon the century of oversight, was great if not indeed decisive. Habits of self-government were implanted in New England and Virginia that no new policy of empire, no matter how autocratic in conception and efficient in execution, could ever have rooted out.

Except for short terms, in isolated localities, and among small groups of pioneers, there was little political democracy in the colonial period. Generations of well-meaning historians and patriots have done the colonists no service by insisting that they and their institutions were democratic. There was a good deal of practical content injected into the ancient phrase "liberty of the subject"; there were unusual opportunities for self-government at all levels; and there was thinking and talking about democracy that outran actual performance. Yet for the most part government in the colonies was simply a less corrupt and oppressive, more popular and easygoing version of government at home, and thus was characterized by limited suffrage, aristocratic leadership, and both deference and indifference among the mass of men. The governments

SOURCE. Clinton Rossiter, *The First American Revolution; The American Colonies on the Eve of Independence,* New York: Harcourt, Brace & World, Inc., 1953, pp. 100–124. Copyright 1953, 1956 by Clinton Rossiter. Reprinted by permission of Harcourt, Brace & World, Inc., and the author.

of the continental colonies were a stage in the development of American democracy rather than democracy itself. The thoughts of good colonists were thoughts of liberty and self-government rather than of equality and mass participation. The course of political freedom was halting, full of starts and stops and discouraging retreats, yet over the generations it went slowly and painfully upward to ultimate triumph.

I

The pattern of government in each colony was determined by its "constitution," leading elements of which were the original charter, grant, or patent and its renewals, commissions, and instructions to the governor, orders-in-council and other directions from the mother country, codes of laws, and local custom and practice. The charter, grant, or patent was the basic document; there were three kinds of charter and thus three types of colony in early America:

The royal colony was, from a constitutional point of view, a political entity in which the Crown was immediately supreme and sovereign. In theory, all officials and institutions existed at the pleasure of the King; in practice, the colonists shared heavily in determining their political destinies, especially through the assembly and institutions of local government. The royal colony was easily the most satisfactory type in terms of English interests. Had the early imperialists had their way, royal government would have been installed without delay throughout the empire. Even though it was not, the trend toward centralization of power in the Crown went on apace, and by the middle of the eighteenth century eight of thirteen colonies were royal in constitution: Virginia, New York, New Hampshire, Massachusetts, New Jersey, North Carolina, South Carolina, and Georgia.

The proprietary was a colony in which political power and ownership of the land were placed in the hands of one or more private individuals. The model of such proprietaries as Maryland and the Carolinas was the county palatine of Durham, a feudal principality in which the Bishop of Durham, for reasons of state, had been granted the powers of a virtually absolute king. Because of weaknesses inherent in its constitutional structure, which took little time coming to the surface in the wilderness, the proprietary was pretty much a failure in colonial America. Some proprietorships were converted into royal colonies; others made such heavy concessions to imperial demands from above and popular urges from below as to be scarcely distinguishable from royal colonies. Although nine colonies were originally constituted as proprietorships under royal favor, only three—Pennsylvania, Delaware, and Maryland—were in existence in 1765.

Connecticut and Rhode Island, both founded without authority from the Crown, were granted royal charters of incorporation at the time of the Restoration. Despite repeated threats of judicial or legislative revocation, they clung to their corporate charters and unique status of independence throughout the eighteenth century. In these two colonies the pattern of self-government was most firmly established. Although the Crown retained considerable authority over their military, diplomatic, and commercial affairs, the extent of supervision was spotty and discontinuous. An especially sour Tory, John Mein of Boston, was not too far from the truth when he wrote of Connecticut and Rhode Island: "The people in those Colonies chuse their Governors, Judges, Assemblymen, Counsellors, and all the rest of their Officers; and the King and Parliament have as much influence there as in the wilds of Tartary." In the commonwealth period (1630–1684) Massachusetts was an extraordinary type of corporate colony—extraordinary alike in origin, form, and pretensions to independence. Although the charter of 1691 established Massachusetts as a royal colony, the corporate features were never entirely eradicated.

The governor—in the royal colonies a viceroy appointed by the King, in the proprietaries an agent selected by the proprietors, in Connecticut and Rhode Island a local gentleman chosen by the assembly—was the key official in each of the colonies. In the royal and proprietary colonies he was the focus of internal politics and external relations. As representative of the sponsoring agency in England, especially of the Crown, he exercised most of the ancient executive prerogatives: command of the forces; the summoning, proroguing, and dissolution of the assembly; an absolute veto over legislation; appointment to subordinate offices; leadership of the church wherever established; the royal prerogative of mercy; oversight, at least by instruction, in financial affairs; and often, with the council, the responsibility of serving as the colony's court of last resort. In short, he was the symbol and fact of imperial authority—a dignified chief of state, a powerful political and military official, a direct participant in legislative and judicial affairs, and the linchpin of empire.

Over against the governor, representative of England and monarchy, was set the assembly, representative of colony and people. The political and constitutional history of colonial America appears often to have been nothing so much as a huge, ill-tempered tug-of-war between governors and assemblies, and it was the latter that grew steadily more robust in the struggle for power. Some assemblies were established under royal, proprietary, or trading-company favor; others were spontaneous creations of the men on the spot. Grounded firmly in representative and electoral systems that were the direct ancestors of present American practice, converted sooner or later by circumstance into a bicameral structure (everywhere except Pennsylvania), persuaded through experience that they could wield all the traditional powers and privileges of a legislature, the assemblies were the most important instruments of popular government in colonial America. The growth of such techniques of representation as residence requirements, constituency payments, annual elections, instructions, voting by ballot, and bans on place-holding by assemblymen is evidence that the assemblies were far more advanced toward the idea of a popular legislature than was the House of Commons.

In each colony there was also a conciliar body, generally made up of twelve gentlemen of property and prestige, which exercised important functions of an executive, legislative, and judicial character. The council acted for the governor as advisory cabinet, with the assembly as upper house of a bicameral legislature, and again with the governor as highest provincial court of appeals in civil cases (and in Virginia in criminal cases as well). It was often as powerful an agent of royal authority as the governor. The normal method of appointment of councilors was by the Crown, on recommendation of the governor. The principal instance of deviation from this scheme was to be found in Massachusetts. The charter of 1691, which could not ignore the years of republican independence, provided for a council of twenty-eight to be chosen annually by the general court subject to the veto of the governor.

In its origins and early development the judicial system of colonial America paid scant attention to English precedents. In the seventeenth century the differences between the courts of one colony and the next were so pronounced that it is impossible to make any general statement about them. What existed in most colonies was a practical system of law and courts in which there was much emphasis on the colonists' own rude notions of justice and little on uniform practice or a trained bench and bar. In Massachusetts lawyers were forbidden to practice, and in all colonies the prejudice against them was surprisingly strong. In part this could be traced to English antecedents; the Fundamental Constitutions of Carolina labeled it "a base and vile thing to plead for money or reward." In part it was the natural reaction of a frontier society to a profession identified with the complexities of civilization.

In the eighteenth century, chiefly at the behest of the Crown and under the pressures of a maturing society, the trend was everywhere toward uniformity in organization and improvement in professional standards. By 1765 the judicial system in most colonies was regularized and independent, and the chief agents of the system, the lawyers, were climbing into the political saddle. The remarkably fair trial of Captain John Preston and his men for the Boston Massacre and the overwhelming resistance of the judiciary to general writs of assistance are proof of the vitality of the court system inherited by the Revolutionary generation.

II

No account of government in colonial America would be complete without some mention of the complexity of officials active in England and the colonies as agents of the Crown's belated attempt to prosecute a consistent imperial policy. The word "complexity" is used advisedly, for in the eighteenth century there were so many officials and committees engaged in overseeing the colonies that it is almost impossible to fix with exactness their powers, functions, and relations to one another. Several features of imperial administration, however, are beyond dispute. Control of the colonies was exercised in the name of the King and thus as an extraordinary assertion of the royal prerogative, which by this time had lost most of its meaning in the mother country. Parliament, which was preoccupied with weightier affairs, was quite unsure of its right to legislate in support or restraint of this last significant manifestation of the prerogative. Neither Crown nor Parliament created much in the way of special machinery for colonial affairs, and for the most part regular executive agencies expanded their activities to include the colonies. Final authority over the colonies resided in the Privy Council, but the actual task of supervision was carried on by committees of the Council, regular agencies, and one specially constituted board. The most important of these varied instruments were:

The Board of Trade, or "Lords Commissioners of Trade and Plantations," was a staff and advisory agency independent of the Privy Council. The Board was charged with drafting instructions for the governors, hearing colonial complaints, suggesting appointments, collecting information for purposes of more effective oversight and direction, and reviewing colonial laws. Although the Board was inferior in legal status and had no sanctions at its command, it wielded much influence through its correspondence with governors and through reports and recommendations to the Crown. Rarely did the Privy Council disregard its advisory verdict on the wisdom or legality of colonial legislation.

The Committee of the Privy Council, often known as "the Lords of the Committee of Council for hearing appeals and complaints from the plantations," was an agency whose functions are clear in its title. This committee provided, for those colonists able and willing to make use of its machinery, a reasonably impartial and efficient high court of appeals. Its chief purpose was not to do justice or develop an imperial common law, but to protect prerogative and mercantilism against colonial interference. . . .

Last in order, but in many ways first in importance, was the Secretary of State for the Southern Department, the chief official for colonial affairs in the developing cabinet system. The first concern of the Secretary of State was war and diplomacy with France and Spain; his conduct of office thus bore directly upon problems of security for the colonies. The makings of a unified system of colonial control were present in this office, but for several reasons—the lack of interest in colonial affairs of most incumbents, the preoccupation of the Secretary with the over-all pattern of war and diplomacy, and the rapid turnover in personnel— these potentialities were never realized.

The result of this conjunction of too much organization for detail and too little concern for unity—especially when intensified by distance, slowness of communication, inferiority of personnel, corruption, bribery, and colonial obstinacy—was a large measure of self-government for the colonies. Each of the chief weapons of imperial control—the viceregal authority of the governor, appeals to the Privy Council, and royal disallowance of colonial legislation—proved defective or inadequate in action. The governor was one thing in the instructions of the Board of Trade, quite another in Williamsburg, Boston, or New York. The system of appeals to the Privy Council was workable enough, but was confined to cases in which a sizable sum was at stake. In the entire colonial period less than two hundred cases from the American colonies were prosecuted before the Council. Whatever it was to become in later years, it was not in the eighteenth century a supreme court of empire. The extent of imperial control exercised through the technique of royal disallowance may be judged from the figures: From 1691 to the end of the colonial period roughly 8,500 laws were submitted for approval. Of these some 470, or 5.5 per cent, were disallowed. The practice of submission and examination was loose and was particularly hampered by the fact of distance. Considerable success was achieved by English authorities in blocking laws that encroached on the prerogative, affected England's commercial interests, interfered with the established church, tampered with the currency, and altered the laws of inheritance; yet for the most part the threat of royal disallowance had surprisingly little effect on the course of colonial self-government. . . .

III

If the pattern of colonial politics was marked by a growing measure of self-government and home rule, then the question arises: Who were the "selves" who did the governing? Who ruled at home? An answer can be found by considering three related problems: the nature of the suffrage in the various colonies; the extent to which the suffrage was actually exercised; the intensity of popular interest and participation in affairs of town and colony.

The history of the colonial suffrage, like the history of almost all early American institutions, was one of primitive diversity in the seventeenth century and maturing uniformity in the eighteenth. A wide variety of practice prevailed before 1690, ranging from the narrow limitation of church membership in Massachusetts to something quite close to white manhood suffrage during the first years in Virginia, Rhode Island, West Jersey, and several other localities. As the settlements developed into more stable societies, demands arose for a broader suffrage in the auto-cratic colonies and a narrower one in the popular. By the turn of the century, some sort of property qualification for voting had been estab-lished in every colony, and this feature of American politics continued in force until well after the winning of independence. In part the require-ment of property holding was fostered by English authorities, who had begun to insist in charters and instructions that

> You shall take care that the members of the assembly be elected only by *ffreeholders,* as being more agreeable to the custome of England, to which you are as nigh as conveniently you can to conforme yourselfe.

In part it could be traced to the fact that the colonists, too, were Englishmen and therefore felt, consciously or unconsciously, the urge to conform to ancient ways. It was inevitable that men of their blood and traditions should be impelled by the rise of a propertied class to restrict the suffrage to those who were in it.

The details of these property requirements furnish yet another instance of English practice adapted to American conditions. In most colonies the basic qualification was the famous "forty-shilling freehold." Seven of them —New Hampshire, Rhode Island, New York, New Jersey, Virginia, North Carolina, and Georgia—made the possession of land an absolute re-quirement; the others recognized property other than real estate. Every-where a "stake-in-society" was the door to political enfranchisement, and almost everywhere additional restrictions kept women, youths, Catholics, Jews, infidels, Negroes, Indians, mulattoes, indentured servants, and other "inferior" persons from the polls. A few, but only a very few, voices were lifted in protest against limited suffrage. Perhaps the clearest of these spoke through an advertisement in a Philadelphia newspaper in 1737:

> A PECUNIARY Gratification is offered to any of the learned or unlearned, who shall *Mathematically* prove, that a Man's having a property in a Tract of Land, more or less, is thereby entitled to any Advantage, *in point of understanding,* over another Fellow, who has no other Estate, than
> "THE AIR . . . *to breathe in,* THE EARTH . . . *to walk upon,* and ALL OF THE WORLD . . . *to drink of."*

Accurate figures of the voting potential in each colony are not easy to establish. The best estimate would be that something like one out of every four white males was eligible to vote for representatives in the assembly, perhaps one out of three for elective officers in towns and in boroughs with open charters of incorporation. There were many deviations, both upward and downward, from these averages, depending, for example, upon the local price and availability of land, proximity to the frontier, and the origins and attitudes of the inhabitants. It must be emphasized that these figures are estimates only, for reliable statistics are just not to be found.

If these figures are discouraging to those who think of the colonies as a Paradise Lost of American democracy, even more discouraging are estimates of exercise of the suffrage. Again the pattern is one of extreme variation from one time and locality to the next, but in general there existed what appears at first glance to have been an attitude of astounding apathy toward campaigns and elections. Not only was but one in four white males eligible to vote; in many places but one in four of those eligible even bothered to vote. Records of the late eighteenth century show that in several supposedly hotly contested elections in Massachusetts an average of one qualified voter in five took the trouble to vote. The figures are better, but not too much better, in Virginia and the middle colonies. Apathy toward elections was a widespread feature of colonial politics, and there were no campaigns to "get out the vote."

The third point of inquiry, the intensity of popular interest and participation in affairs of town and colony, has already been largely answered. What was true of voting was doubly true of office-holding: Restrictions were many and aspirants few. In an age when breadwinning consumed all a man's time and energy, when travel was difficult and political parties nonexistent, when government was severely limited in scope and touched many men not at all, and when the pace of life went slowly, political indifference—to elections, to office-holding, and to issues—was well-nigh inevitable. Despite eloquent references to "an aroused people" in certain memorable debates in the assemblies, politics in colonial America was the province of those with particular interests to defend or with a natural flair for public action. The number of such persons was never and nowhere very large. The political apathy of the colonial press, punctured only occasionally before 1765 by a thorough airing of some local squabble, is proof of the slow pace of political life. "Publick Lethargy" was under constant attack by colonial penmen.

This does not mean that the declarations and decisions of the attentive few or the experiences and instincts of the indifferent many were any the less important to the progress of American liberty. The few in their assemblies, town meetings, and polls held the democratic future in trust and acted out on a small stage the great drama of constitutional government that was in time to call millions into the supporting cast. The many, too, had their notion of liberty and self-government: to be left alone to pursue their own destinies. When government became important or oppressive enough, they found ways other than politics to express their wishes and to influence action. Sullen resistance, riots, and "going out west" are not generally recommended as effective techniques of political freedom, but in colonial times they served a very real purpose.

These are the facts of political participation in the American colonies: Only a fraction could participate and even a lesser fraction did; the colonies were still well ahead of practice in almost all other countries; and many men never cared one way or the other about political power. Nor should it be forgotten that in a society so amazingly fluid for the age, a society where people could "move on" and where land was cheap and plentiful, the privilege of the suffrage was something that almost any white man could win. The records prove that everywhere, even in aristocratic New York and South Carolina, men of mean birth and menial occupation could aspire to political power and prominence. And that a man in eighteenth-century Virginia or New England had neither opportunity nor desire to vote or hold office did not mean that he considered himself a slave. In an age when politics was one of the least of man's worries, the poll lists were one of the lesser criteria of the progress of liberty.

IV

Seeds of contention between governor and assembly were sown with profusion in the constitutions of the eleven royal or proprietary colonies. The inherent contradiction between the interests and attitudes of the mother country and those of the distant colonies was especially apparent in this instance. On one hand stood the royal or proprietary governor—in four cases out of five an Englishman, in the fifth a loyal colonial, in any case an agent of the prerogative with a commission and instructions that made him an autocrat not beholden to colonial direction. On the other stood the provincial assembly—the articulate organ of a breed of men who were more English than the English in their obstinacy, pride, and hypersensitivity in matters of self-government. From the outset the system gaped at the middle, and the final triumph of the assembly was almost foreordained. Although the governor occupied a position of overwhelming constitutional superiority, it was undercut repeatedly by circumstances in colony and empire.

The governors got far more verbal than practical support from the authorities at home. The remoteness of colonial capitals and the lack of either an imperial policy or the will to execute it created a situation in which the governor was left pretty much on his own. It was he, not the Board of Trade, who had to live with the colonists; it was his estimate of the expedient, not the Board's demand of the impossible, that controlled decisions taken on the spot. The governor was too often left defenseless against what Governor Clinton of New York labeled the assembly's "continued Grasping at Power."

The colonists fell naturally into an opinion of their governors best summed up in Franklin's remark about "men of vicious characters and broken fortunes, sent by a Minister to get them out of the way." We know today that this was rarely the case, that the governors were neither better nor worse than the officials who carried on the public business of England. There were men as bad as Cornbury and Fletcher, but there were also men as good as Dinwiddie, the Wentworths, Spotswood, Hunter, Pownall, Burnet, Shirley, Glen, and Dobbs. No matter who the governors were, however, most colonists agreed with the New York Assembly of 1749 that they were

generally entire Strangers to the People they are sent to govern . . . their Interest is entirely distinct . . . they seldom regard the Welfare of the People, otherwise than as they can make it subservient to their own particular Interest.

In this instance the myth was more telling than the fact, and the myth was one of "men of broken fortunes, dissolute and ignorant, too vile to be employed near home," a calumny that the English press printed and the colonial press reprinted with glee. Recognition of the alien purposes of the royal governors and misrepresentation of their personal traits did much to strengthen the morale and ambitions of the colonial assemblies, not that they needed it.

Colonial legislators were persistent, clever, and vigilant, and over the years they advanced a surprisingly coherent policy in constitutional matters. The struggle for power was not always so bitter and devisive as some history books would have it, for several colonies enjoyed extended periods of political quiescence and good will. Yet the trend of power moved almost always toward the assembly, which used this power to fight its way ever higher in the name of "the people" and "our ancient and undoubted rights and privileges as Englishmen."

The lack of real toughness in the imperialists in England permitted the colonists to exploit to the limit the fatal defect of the colonial constitutions: the location of the power of the purse in colonial hands, a defect compounded by the failure of the Crown to provide a permanent civil list in any of the colonies. No one was more aware than the governor himself that, in Governor Bernard's words, "the Want of a certain and adequate civil List to each Colony" was "the Root of the American Disorders." Far too many officials, institutions, and necessities of empire were left dependent upon the willingness of the assemblies to tax friends and neighbors and thus upon the natural desire to fix conditions upon any and all grants.

Occasionally in spectacular political warfare accompanied by newspaper attacks on the governors, but more often through unpublicized day-to-day encroachments, the assemblies grasped for privileges and powers like those of the House of Commons. Several of Parliament's hard-earned privileges—control over procedure, freedom of debate, determination of disputed elections—were secured by the assemblies. Others —the "Speaker's Petition," control over sessions, regulation of elections, creation of new electoral districts—were not, and over these the struggle raged in almost every colony. The Crown defended with tenacity the governor's power to prorogue and dissolve the assembly and the final weapons of gubernatorial veto and royal disallowance. Yet the area of assembly freedom grew ever wider, especially as it came home to more and more colonists that the fight for parliamentary privilege was at bottom a fight for the liberty of the subject.

The assemblies also used the purse to pry their way into executive affairs. For example, by designating a specific person to receive the salary of an office they usurped the power of appointment; by naming their own committees and even their own treasurer to verify expenditures they encroached substantially on the governor's command of the militia and control over military stores; and by the famous expedient of tampering with the governor's salary they brought more than one recalcitrant to heel in such matters as personnel and jurisdiction of colonial courts. The governors of Georgia and Virginia were the only viceroys whose salaries were not dependent on the pleasure of the assembly or, as in the case of the North Carolina quit rents, on an unsatisfactory substitute arrangement. Especially acrimonious battles were fought in New York and Massachusetts over the assembly's calculated practice of annual grants to the governor—with the assembly emerging victorious. The provision in the Constitution of 1787 forbidding the raising or lowering of the President's compensation attests the respect in which eighteenth-century Americans held this technique.

By 1765 the assembly was dominant in almost every colony in continental America. The royal power of disallowance was still strong enough to prevent a complete overriding of the governor and other imperial officials, but shrewd observers were beginning to realize that only the full power of Parliament was now equal to the centrifugal practices of the assemblies. Most discouraging to proponents of empire was the inability of English authorities to secure positive accomplishments. The record of colonial co-operation, or rather non-co-operation, in time of war must have been hard to swallow. The assemblies recorded their most spectacular gains, especially in their campaign to control the public purse, in the French and Indian War. More than one governor must have felt that he rather than the French was the enemy to be reduced to a plea for mercy.

The struggles of the colonial assemblies provide an instructive example of the way in which men distrustful of democracy in one century can, by fighting for their own privileges and opinions, open the way to democracy in the next. Indeed, "distrustful of democracy" is the very best that can be said of cliques that controlled assemblies in New Hampshire, Pennsylvania, the Carolinas, and Virginia. The records show up many colonial parliamentarians as illtempered, petty, self-seeking, tiresome little men more often than not committed to the intolerant side of questions of religious and social freedom. Yet the assemblies also counted an unusual range of strong and able men, many of whom were genuinely progressive in their opinions. The Whigs in the colonial legislatures had a limited popularism as their goal, but in driving toward it they unloosed forces that would not be halted short of total political democracy. And their arguments proved in time to be fully convertible to democratic currency.

The colonial assemblies, like the dissenting churches, were influential schools of American political thought. The system under which delegates were chosen was one as representative of "the people" as could be erected in those days of concern for Whig ideals of liberty. The proceedings of the assemblies were open to public inspection and criticism, their journals were printed and distributed, and their exchanges with the governors, especially those of a pungent nature, got thorough coverage in the colonial press. Just about all that the people of South Carolina knew of Massachusetts was that there, too, the assembly hacked away resolutely at the governor's position and powers. There can be no argument with Charles M. Andrews's conclusion: "In the development of American political ideas and social practices, the influence of the popular assembly . . . is the most potent single factor underlying our American system of government."

CHAPTER 10

IMPERIAL POLICY: MERCANTILISM AND THE NAVIGATION ACTS

In the seventeenth and eighteenth centuries, Great Britain was one of the major imperial powers. By 1763 she had reached the zenith of her power and domination; yet, twenty years later she was forced to sign a peace treaty that stripped her of her thirteen mainland colonies in America. What brought about this sudden reversal of British fortune? The answer of American patriots of the Revolutionary era—a view long since rejected by historians but surprisingly prevalent still—was that British tyranny had prompted America's struggle for independence. What constituted this so-called tyranny? Primarily, the taxation (without representation) levied by Parliament in the 1760's and 1770's, but also the sometimes oppressive Navigation Acts and the other mercantilist regulations imposed on the colonists by the British from 1650 on.

The way in which Great Britain governed and managed her empire is clearly of major importance in explaining the coming of the American Revolution. Hence, the next two readings are devoted to considerations of British imperial policy and its implementation. In the selection below, from *Origins of the American Revolution,** Professor John C. Miller concentrates on imperial policies and practices up to 1763. Professor Miller suggests that the principles of mercantilism were largely responsible for shaping the British Empire and for determining the role and the function of the British colonies. Mercantilism found its most important expression in the Navigation Acts of the seventeenth century, which formed the basis of British colonial policy. In the following pages, Professor Miller is primarily concerned with the effects of British mercantilism—in particular with the effects of the Navigation Acts—on the American colonies, and with the reactions and attitudes of the colonists to imperial policy. In conclusion, Miller seeks to determine precisely what part the Navigation Acts and the system of mercantilism played in the coming of the Revolution.

In reading this selection, the student should determine the essential nature of the British imperial system. What principles shaped this system, and how did these principles affect the English conception of the relationship between the mother country and the colonies? To what extent did this conception work toward or against the preservation of a healthy and enduring empire? The reader should also be concerned with the specific effects of mercantilist policy on the economy and the thought of the several sections of the British mainland colonies. A careful reading of the impact of mercantilism not only tells us something about the causes of the Revolutionary War but also something of the mind of the colonial American.

Carl Ubbelohde, *The American Colonies and the British Empire, 1607-1763** (1968), Oliver M. Dickerson, *The Navigation Acts and the American Revolution** (1951), Lawrence A. Harper, "Mercantilism and the American Revolution," *The Canadian Historical Review,* XXIII (March, 1942), and Curtis P. Nettles, "British Mercantilism and the Economic Development of the Thirteen Colonies," *The Journal of Economic History,* XII (Spring, 1952), offer additional treatments of this subject.

* Available in a paperback edition.

THE ECONOMIC BACKGROUND
JOHN C. MILLER

In 1763, Great Britain attained a height of power and dominion which led many Englishmen to conclude that a new Roman Empire had been brought into being through the genius of William Pitt and the valor of British arms. France and Spain, united by the Family Compact, had been decisively defeated and a large part of North America and India had been brought under British control. A period of "prosperity and glory unknown to any former age" seemed to be opening for Great Britain and her colonies. Yet those Englishmen who in 1763 regarded themselves as the heirs of Rome soon perceived a new and highly disquieting resemblance between Britain and Rome: the British Empire seemed about to go the way of the Roman Empire. It appeared probable that the same generation of Englishmen which saw the empire reach its highest point of grandeur would be the witness of its decline and fall. So swiftly did fortune turn that William Pitt, who had brought Great Britain to the zenith, died in the House of Lords fifteen years later in one of England's darkest hours.

The Englishmen who lost the American colonies were not solely responsible for the catastrophe which overtook the empire, although George III and his ministers must bear a large share of the blame. Because Americans were such good Englishmen—in the seventeenth-century mold—and held fast to the liberal traditions of English history, they made uncommonly troublesome subjects from the point of view of British imperialists. Eighteenth-century Englishmen found Americans "of a disposition haughty and insolent, impatient of rule, disdaining subjection, and by all means affecting independence"—in sharp contrast to "the remarkably pliant and submissive disposition" of the inhabitants of Bengal. As a result, the British Empire was at best, in Benjamin Franklin's words, a fragile Chinese vase which required far more delicate handling than George III and his baggage-smashing ministers gave it. Yet it is true that if the Englishmen of George III's reign blundered and muddled,

SOURCE. John C. Miller, *Origins of the American Revolution*, Boston: Little, Brown & Co., 1943, pp. 3–25. Copyright 1943 by John C. Miller. Reprinted by permission of the author.

their failure was partly owing to the fact that they had inherited a traditional conception of the relationship between mother country and colonies which proved, in the crisis, an utterly false set of rules for preserving a great empire. Many of the seeds of the American Revolution existed in the British Empire almost from its beginning. George III and his advisers ripened them and planted a new crop of grievances of their own in the colonies. They harvested the bitter fruit in 1776.

The British Empire of which George III became sovereign in 1760 was shaped largely by the principles of mercantilism. The goal of mercantilism—today it would be called economic nationalism—was the creation of a self-sufficient empire from which foreign trade and commerce were excluded; the domination of vital trade routes; and the acquisition of abundant stores of gold and silver by the mother country. Mercantilism was designed to gird a nation for war by recruiting its economic strength and crippling that of its rivals. Inevitably, mercantilism itself bred war: as the nations sought to bring vital trade routes under their control and to seize choice spots of the earth's surface and then bolt the door against foreigners, national rivalries were brought to white heat. George III's empire had not been created by the exercise of the virtues of faith, hope, and charity. Sterner stuff was required of empire-builders and the English had it in abundance. They struck down the Dutch in a series of bitterly fought naval wars; and in 1763 they succeeded in attaining a hard-won, "true, national felicity upon the ruins of the House of Bourbon."

The Laws of Trade and Navigation or Navigation Acts enacted by the English Parliament during the seventeenth century were mercantilism translated into statute law. Although these acts were only a part of English mercantilism, they were its most important expression and formed the basis of British colonial policy long after the American Revolution had demonstrated their inadequacy. By mercantilist theory, the function of the colonies was to produce raw materals for the use of the mother country, to consume its manufactures and to foster its shipping; and the purpose of the Laws of Trade and Navigation was to ensure that the English colonies fulfilled these ends. This implied, as mercantilists readily admitted, that the colonies were to remain dependent agricultural regions, closely tied to the economy of an industrialized mother country. No mercantilist saw any impropriety in consigning the Western Hemisphere to a position of perpetual economic inferiority.

In a larger sense, the purpose of the Navigation Acts was to enable England, by augmenting her national strength, to triumph over France, Spain, and Holland in the struggle for world power. In the seventeenth and eighteenth centuries, a self-sufficient mercantilist empire was thought essential to national greatness and to victory over aggrandizing rival states. The Act of 1651—the first of the Navigation Acts—was directed mainly against the Dutch who by dint of sharpness in trade, financial resources which permitted them to give more liberal credit than the English, and the quality of the merchandise they purveyed, had been able to get the better of English merchants not merely in world trade but in the English colonies themselves. To cripple Dutch competition and lay the menace of the Dutch state to England's maritime supremacy, the English Parliament declared in 1651 that no goods the growth of Asia, Africa, and America could be carried to England, Ireland, the English colonies, except in English, Irish, or colonial ships, manned by sailors "for the most part" subjects of the Commonwealth. Dutch shipping was further discriminated against by the provision that goods from Europe could enter England, Ireland, and the colonies only if they were transported in the ships of the country "in which the said goods are the growth, production, or manufacture."

But the Navigation Act of 1651, however successful in barring Dutch and other foreign ships from trade with the English colonies, fell far short of erecting a mercantilist empire. Under its provisions, the colonists were able to send their products to any foreign market and to buy manufactured goods wherever they pleased—and Americans took full advantage of this privilege. After the restoration of Charles II in 1660, the English Parliament quickly set about closing the breaches in the mercantilist walls which remained after the Act of 1651. The Navigation Act of 1660—the so-called "great Palladium" or Magna Carta of English commerce—went far towards making the English Empire truly mercantilistic. This measure prescribed that no foreign ships could engage in trade with the English colonies or import any of their products into England—a re-enactment of the Act of 1651. To guard further against the intrusion of foreign competition, all foreign merchants were excluded from the colonies. At the same time, England made clear its intention of concentrating control of the resources of her colonies in her own hands. It was ordered that certain commodities were to be "enumerated"—that is, that they could be sent only to England, Ireland and Wales, and—after the Act of Union—to Scotland. Despite the fact that it was greatly to the convenience and profit of the colonists to ship these products directly to the European market, the English government insisted that they must first pass through England, Ireland, or Wales, although from thence they might be re-exported to the European continent.

The commodities thus singled out for the mother country's monopolization were those generally regarded as essential to the wealth and power of the state which were not produced in the British Isles themselves:

sugar, tobacco, cotton, indigo, and dye woods—the oil, rubber, and steel of modern imperialism. No country could hope to attain self-sufficiency without an ample supply of these semitropical products; and by enumerating them England hoped to relieve herself of dependence upon France and Holland and, ultimately, to oblige those powers to buy from her.

Although many important products of the American colonies were not enumerated—fish, hides, and flour, for example, were never monopolized by Great Britain—and might, therefore, be carried directly to European markets, this latitude permitted colonial trade was steadily narrowed during the eighteenth century. Great Britain adopted the practice of enumerating whatever commodities strengthened her trading position in world markets, benefited British manufacturers and merchants, or added revenue to the customs. This policy led to the enumeration of rice, molasses, naval stores, and furs prior to 1764. In that year, George Grenville, the British Chancellor of the Exchequer, in his efforts to raise a colonial revenue and strengthen the mercantile system added more colonial commodities to the list than had been enumerated during the entire period since the passage of the Navigation Act of 1660.

In 1663, the structure of English mercantilism was completed with the passage by Parliament of the so-called Staple Act. This law prohibited the importation of goods direct from Europe to England's American colonies: with few exceptions, notably wine from Madeira and the Azores, European goods were required to be first carried to England, where, after payment of duties, they might be reshipped to the colonies —if Americans were still willing to pay the cost, now greatly enhanced by duties and handling charges. Thus, in their completed form, the Navigation Acts required the colonists to send many of their most important raw products to Britain and to purchase almost all their manufactured goods in the same market. As a result, British merchants and manufacturers were placed in a position to determine the prices of what Americans bought and sold. Although the sharp edge of this pincers aimed at colonial producers was blunted by the fact that British capitalism was becoming increasingly competitive and, in consequence, probably few price-fixing agreements were entered into by British merchants or manufacturers, we shall see that many colonists raised the cry that they were being cruelly exploited by the system erected by the Laws of Trade.

In this manner, British colonial policy came to be dominated by the mercantilist principle that "all plantations endamage their mother kingdom, where the trades of such plantations are not confined to the mother kingdom by good laws and severe execution of them." For the remainder of the colonial period, the British government sought to tighten the screws of commercial monopoly upon the colonists and to devise means of more strictly enforcing the Laws of Trade. Even after 1764 when the British government turned its attention to raising a revenue in the provinces, it did not lose sight of the necessity of maintaining control of colonial commerce and trade. The Acts of Trade and Navigation were upheld to the last, and even the staunchest defenders of colonial liberty in England, including William Pitt, insisted upon keeping the colonies in economic leading-strings. The monopolization of colonial trade was held to be the *raison d'être* of the empire: "If we allow France and Holland to supply them with fabric," an Englishmen said, "we may just as well give up all ideas of having colonies at all." During the revolutionary period, English propagandists learned that nothing succeeded in incensing Englishmen against the colonists as did the charge that Americans were seeking to throw off the restraints of the Navigation Acts and to establish free trade with the world.

Because British imperialism was primarily commercial, the British merchants and manufacturers regarded the empire as very nearly the best of all possible empires. Until 1764, at least, the government carefully consulted the interests of British businessmen in formulating its colonial policy. During this period, British merchants and manufacturers found the American colonists rapidly becoming their best customers. Trade with the colonies grew steadily: in 1772, the exports of Great Britain to the colonies alone almost equaled her entire exports in 1704. On the eve of the American Revolution, one third of the shipping of the British Empire was engaged in the colonial trade. "The vast cities along the coast of England and Scotland," it was said, ". . . are sprung from contemptible villages only by the American trade." "The American," observed an Englishman, "is apparelled from head to foot in our manufactures . . . he scarcely drinks, sits, moves, labours or recreates himself, without contributing to the emolument of the mother country." In 1774, it was estimated that in the province of New York eleven out of twelve inhabitants wore clothing of British manufacture.

The spice to this feast was the fact that, thanks to the Navigation Acts, the expanding colonial market was protected from the competition of Dutch, French, Spaniards, and all other interlopers. As a result, the colonies helped cushion Great Britain against postwar depressions: when peace brought a revival of European manufacturing—with consequent loss to British businessmen who had profited hugely from the destruction of European industry—the colonies offered a market relatively free from competition. Here the merchants and manufacturers might charge what the traffic would bear, although their monopoly was tempered by American smuggling and by the reluctance of Americans to pay their debts to their British creditors. Nevertheless, British businessmen had their hands deep in Americans' pockets, and as long as the mercantilist system should endure, they looked forward to engrossing "all the money our colonists should ever possess."

This trade was financed in large part by credit advanced by British merchants to their colonial customers, whether Northern merchants or Southern planters. "Credit," observed an Englishman early in the eighteenth century, "is a profitable plant that yields more fruit to our trade than the whole specie of the kingdom." Indeed, trade between Great Britain and the colonies could scarcely have been carried on without credit, for the operating capital of American planters and merchants came mainly from this source. Northern merchants in turn were enabled to extend credit to colonial farmers and thereby push forward the area of settlement; but throughout the colonial period the base of the pyramid of debt rested upon the shoulders of British merchants and manufacturers. In consequence, the capitalists of the mother country soon acquired a huge financial stake in the American colonies. By 1760, the value of British exports to the colonies was estimated to total £2,000,000 a year; but British merchants carried over £4,000,000 of American debts on their ledgers. In the case of Southern planters, they depended largely upon the sale of future crops for repayment; as regards Northern merchants, British creditors relied upon the colonists' ability to gather enough cash from the African slave trade, the fisheries, and the West Indies to pay their debts. In both cases, the merchants could ill afford to see colonial prosperity undermined by unwise restrictions, but on the other hand they felt obliged to maintain close watch over American affairs lest the colonies evade the laws upon which the monopoly of the mother country rested or seek to make themselves unwelcome competitors of British merchants in the markets of the empire.

The imposition of the mercantilist system exacted heavy sacrifices from the American colonists during the seventeenth century. Instead of the freedom of trade with the world which they had largely enjoyed prior to 1651, they were now confined for the most part to the markets of the mother country and other parts of the empire; and the colonial consumer was delivered over to the English merchant and manufacturer. From a free-trade area, the British Empire was transformed into a highly protected market closed to foreign competition. The losses in liberty and material prosperity attendant upon this economic reorganization of the empire were borne chiefly by the colonists; from the beginning, whether mercantilism appeared beneficent or oppressive depended largely from what side of the Atlantic it was viewed.

But as the mercantilists frequently pointed out, Americans were compensated for the restrictions imposed by the mother country upon their trade and commerce. Mercantilists did not advocate the exploitation by the mother country of the colonies: their ideal was rather an empire in which every part contributed to the best of its ability toward the goal of self-sufficiency; and they insisted that the good of the whole be made the guiding principle of the mother country's colonial policy. Accordingly, in exchange for the monopoly enjoyed by the mother country in the colonies, a virtual monopoly of the English market was given the producers of certain colonial commodities. All foreign tobacco, for example, was excluded from England (although this restriction was later modified to permit the importation of some Portuguese and Spanish tobacco) and Englishmen were forbidden to plant tobacco in England—a law which was consistently violated until at the end of the seventeenth century the price of tobacco became so low that it was no longer profitable to grow it there. Moreover, tariff protection was given by the mother country to sugar, cotton, and indigo grown in the British colonies—thus placing a burden on the English consumer who, in an open market, undoubtedly could have bought cheaper. At the same time, bounties were given upon the production of naval stores, pitch, silk, and wine in the colonies—in the hope that the empire would become self-sufficient in these commodities and that Americans, if encouraged to produce raw materials, would be diverted from manufacturing for themselves.

Yet despite the benefits of mercantilism, Americans surrendered their economic liberties grudgingly. They lamented that the Dutch traders who in the seventeenth century sold goods at one-third the price charged by English merchants came among them no longer and that in their stead appeared Englishmen who, as the governor of Virginia said, would "faine bring us to the same poverty, wherein the Dutch found and relieved us." Bacon's Rebellion was caused in part by the depression that struck Virginia in the wake of the Acts of Trade. The Massachusetts General Court declared in the seventeenth century that it would not obey the Navigation Acts because the people of Massachusetts were not represented in the English Parliament and because "the lawes of England are bounded within the fower seas, and do not reach America"—a more sweeping assertion of colonial rights than was made by Americans until 1776.

As Great Britain became increasingly industrialized during the eighteenth century, the chorus of complaint in the colonies against high-priced

British goods subsided, although the Southern planters remained unreconciled to British monopoly. In general, the price of British manufactures declined and the quality improved to such a degree that it is doubtful if the colonists could have bought cheaper from their old friends the Dutch. This was not true, however, of India goods, of which large quantities were purchased by Americans, a substantial part being smuggled from Holland. But even so there was considerable foundation for the claim made by Englishmen in the eighteenth century that the Acts of Trade could not justly be regarded as a hardship by Americans inasmuch as they procured cheaper and better goods in England than could have been bought in France or Holland. Later, after the United States had achieved its independence, Lord Sheffield was to elaborate this argument into the theory— and win the British government to his view—that the young republic was so inextricably bound to English economy that it could not break its bonds regardless of how inconsiderately it was treated by Great Britain.

New England did not readily fit into the mercantilists' scheme of a rightly ordered empire. Instead of busying themselves at home producing necessities for the mother country and exchanging them for English manufactures, the Puritans took to the sea with such vigor that it was said their commerce smelled as strongly of fish as their theology did of brimstone. Except for timber and masts, New England lacked valuable staples required by the mother country. And so New Englanders derived little advantage, in contrast to the Southern colonists, from English bounties: "A Cargo of any of them [bountied commodities] will be returned to us in a few Trunks of Fripperies," they said, "and we should be Bankrupt to Great Britain every Ten Years."

The Puritans found that their salvation lay in manufacturing on their own and in pursuing that "coy mistress, trade" over a large part of the world in order to scrape together enough cash to pay for the goods they imported from Great Britain. During the colonial period, the exports of the Northern colonies to Great Britain were far less than their imports from her; but the merchants prospered despite this adverse balance of trade. By engaging in the slave trade, making rum, exploiting the fisheries, manufacturing for the Middle and Southern colonies as well as for their own use, and acting as middlemen between land-bound colonists and English businessmen, they found profitable outlet for their energy and capital. The freightage, commissions, and charges for services and credits paid by the colonial consumer helped build the American seaports and laid the foundations for many of the early American fortunes. Herein the colonial merchants came into collision with the British merchants, who, by virtue of their vast financial resources, enjoyed a considerable advantage over their American rivals. But the colonists were by no means outclassed: ships could be built cheaper in New England than elsewhere in the British Empire; New Englanders possessed a canniness in trade that staggered even the Scotch; and they were masters of the art of slipping a cargo of contraband past the inefficient and undermanned colonial customhouse.

Under these circumstances, the American merchants found little quarrel with the Laws of Trade as they were actually enforced; they grew up under the system and—except for restrictions upon their trade with the foreign West Indies—were not unduly hampered by British commercial laws. The British Empire, they learned, was, in the main, big enough to hold both themselves and the British merchants, and so long as the mother country did not begrudge them a profit or too strictly enforce its laws they were in general well content. Given the lax enforcement of the Acts of Trade—by which the door was left ajar for highly profitable smuggling—and the advantages of carrying on business within the British Empire—one of the greatest trading areas in the world—it is not probable that the Navigation Acts alone would have produced a revolutionary spirit among American businessmen. On the contrary, the conviction was strongly established among many colonists that their economic well-being depended upon remaining within the empire and enjoying the benefits of its highly protected markets.

In the Middle colonies, where a far more even balance prevailed between agriculture and commerce than in New England, the Acts of Trade inflicted little appreciable hardship. These provinces exported large quantities of cereals and lumber to the European continent and the West Indies. It is important to observe in this connection that their trade with the West Indies, like that of the New England colonies, was not restricted to the British West Indies; the most profitable branch of their commerce was with the French, Dutch, and Spanish islands. Although this trade was not prohibited by the Navigation Acts, it ran counter to every principle of mercantilism and in 1733 was virtually prohibited by an act of Parliament which, as will be seen, proved unenforceable. In studying the origins of the American Revolution, it ought to be borne in mind that the prosperity of New England and the Middle colonies depended in a large measure upon a trade which had been built up outside the walls which mercantilists sought to erect around the empire.

Neither New England nor the Middle colonies were as intimately tied to the British market as were the staple colonies of the North American continent and the West Indies. Whereas the Northern colonies failed to produce vital raw materials required by the mother country and so fell short of the mercantilists' ideal, the Southern colonies fulfilled their highest expectations. These provinces constituted a rich agricultural area which supplied the mother country with such valuable products as tobacco, naval stores, rice, indigo, cotton, and sugar—the chief staples of commerce—and received in exchange British-manufactured goods. These commodities were enumerated and the planters themselves had little opportunity to supplement their incomes by smuggling. Moreover, they were excellent customers of British merchants and manufacturers. While it is true that all the American colonies depended largely upon imports of manufactured articles from Great Britain to maintain a European living standard in the New World, the Southern staple colonies were so lacking in local industries that they were compelled to look to the mother country for virtually all their manufactured goods.

Mercantilists rejoiced in the Southern staple colonies as the jewels of the empire; but many planters found that the shoe of mercantilism pinched acutely. The tightness of the squeeze differed considerably, however, among the various kinds of planters. Although they were all more or less at the mercy of the British merchants and manufacturers who sold them goods and advanced them credit, some planters had secured preferential treatment from the mother country. In 1730, for example, the British government partially met the demands of the Carolina rice growers by permitting them to export rice—which had been enumerated by the British government in 1704—to southern Europe, although they were still forbidden to import manufactures except through Great Britain. In 1739, the sugar planters of the West Indies were likewise given the privilege of exporting sugar directly to Europe although they produced barely enough to supply the needs of the British Empire alone. This concession was won largely because of the presence in the British Parliament of a powerful bloc of absentee West India planters aided by a lobby of West India merchants. As a result, during the eighteenth century, the sugar colonies were in little danger of finding their interests sacrificed to those of the mother country or of the Northern colonies; on the contrary, the Northern colonists and the British consumer were in dire danger of being made the victims of West Indian cupidity.

No such advantages were enjoyed by the tobacco growers of Virginia and Maryland. Certainly as regards tobacco, Great Britain was not in any sense "the natural entrepôt for the American trade with the continent" which the Laws of Trade sought to make it—rather, it was a bottleneck through which the British government attempted to force colonial trade. Of the 96,000 hogsheads of tobacco sent by Maryland

and Virginia to England each year, 82,000 were re-exported to the continent, competing there with Spanish tobacco; and this re-exported tobacco paid double freight, insurance, commissions, and handling charges. Daniel Dulany of Maryland estimated that the Southern tobacco growers would have received £3 more for every hogshead they sent abroad had they been permitted to ship direct to the continent instead of through England. In addition, the British government insisted upon its pound of flesh from the planters. A heavy duty was imposed upon all tobacco imported into Great Britain; and from this source the government drew a revenue of almost £400,000 a year. The planters complained that this duty was levied upon them rather than upon the British consumer and that they were thereby more heavily taxed than even the British squires.

The reason why the planters, more than other Americans, found their lot galling under British mercantilism was partly owing to their practice of pledging future crops in exchange for credits advanced them by British businessmen. In order to protect themselves against loss, the British merchants charged the planters high prices and high interest rates. Of the £4,000,000 owing British merchants by Americans in 1760, over half had been incurred by Southern planters. It is not surprising, therefore, that from the point of view of the tobacco growers, the Acts of Trade seemed designed chiefly for the better exploitation of American producers. . . .

It became increasingly clear to Americans during the eighteenth century that the British Empire was not, as the mercantilists envisaged, a government of King, Lords, and Commons in which the welfare of the whole empire was the chief concern of imperial legislation, but a government of British merchants and manufacturers who pursued their own interests even at the expense of the colonists. . . .

By 1763, it had been made painfully evident to Americans that whenever a colonial commodity became important it was enumerated; and whenever colonial enterprise competed with powerful British interest it was struck down by an act of Parliament. To protect the monopoly of British manufacturers, Parliament forbade Americans to export colonial wool, woolens, and hats from one colony to another on pain of seizure of ship and cargo; and in 1750 the erection of plating or slitting mills was prohibited. These acts were not part of the Laws of Trade but they were a significant manifestation of mercantilism. They were the work of British manufacturers who believed that colonial manufacturing was responsible for the hard times that had befallen these industries in Old England. Mercantilists warmly espoused the cause of the distressed

English manufacturers: the colonists, they contended, must be prevented from rivaling the mother country since the very reason for their existence was to increase her wealth, not to compete with her industries. . . .

It cannot be denied that there was widespread discontent among the colonists, particularly among the Southern planters, with the workings of British mercantilism. Certainly, they regarded a larger measure of economic freedom as one of the most desirable results of the revolutionary agitation of 1765–1776. The closing of certain channels of trade essential to the well-being of the Northern colonies and the efforts of the mother country to enforce the Acts of Trade after 1764 brought Northern merchants to see British mercantilism eye to eye with the Southern tobacco growers. In the correspondence of colonial merchants and planters there is a growing volume of complaint that they were risking their capital and expending their energy for the enrichment of British merchants and manufacturers. They chafed under a system which bottled up initiative and confined trade to channels prescribed by the British government, which, as was well known, frequently acted at the behest of powerful British commercial and manufacturing interests. We shall find that as Americans progressively enlarged their demands for liberty after 1765, the Acts of Trade and the entire system of British mercantilism came to be included within their definition of tyranny. Without doubt, underlying the resounding phrases and ideals of the American Revolution, there was a solid foundation of economic grievances which played an important part in determining the course taken by both the Northern merchants and the Southern planters.

Yet it cannot be said that Americans were driven to rebellion by intolerable economic oppression. In general, after the postwar depression of 1763–1765, the revolutionary period was an era of growth and prosperity for the colonies. The British "tyranny" against which Americans rebelled did little to impede their material development; on the contrary, the population continued to double every generation by natural means and the demand for British manufactures increased apace. In many New England towns it was difficult to find a man not in easy circumstances. The colonial seaports continued to hum with business: in 1762 New York had 477 vessels; by 1772, the number had increased to 709.

CHAPTER 11

THE NEW
IMPERIAL POLICY

Of the several schools of historical thought as to why the American Revolution came, one of the more important is the "Imperial" school, whose most distinguished member is Lawrence Henry Gipson. This group of historians derives its name from its insistence that the only way to understand properly the problems of the North American colonies is to view them in the broadest perspective as members of the British Empire. When this is done, they contend, we can see that the American situation was neither onerous nor oppressive.

In this essay, Professor Gipson examines the effects on relations between the North American colonies and the mother country of the Great War for Empire (more commonly but less accurately known as the French and Indian War). In this examination, Gipson raises several questions.

The most important question is whether the American Revolution was inevitable. If so, why? Given the modified situation that victory over the French produced, could the British administrators have done anything to prevent the revolution? If so, what?

Of almost equal importance is the problem involving the time and the meaning of the revolution. Did the actual revolution occur between the years 1776–1783, during the period of combat? Or did the real revolution come about in the minds of the people earlier, perhaps from 1763 to 1776, with the war years being merely the necessarily violent demonstration to the English of the realities of the new situation?

As might be expected, the literature on this subject is enormous. Professor Gipson has conveniently summarized the results of a lifetime of study in his *The Coming of the Revolution** (1954). For a point of view different from that of the "Imperial" school, see Edmund S. Morgan, *The Birth of the Republic** (1956). For a very convenient summary of the positions and writings of the various schools, along with an up-to-date bibliography, see Esmond Wright, *Causes and Consequences of the American Revolution** (1966). An excellent short essay on the meaning of the revolution is Jack Greene, *The Reappraisal of the American Revolution in Recent Historical Literature** (1967).

* Available in a paperback edition.

THE AMERICAN REVOLUTION AS AN AFTERMATH OF THE GREAT WAR FOR THE EMPIRE, 1754–1763

LAWRENCE HENRY GIPSON

Great wars in modern times have too frequently been the breeders of revolution. The exhausting armed struggles in which France became engaged in the latter half of the eighteenth century led as directly to the French Revolution as did the First World War to the Russian Revolution; it may be said as truly that the American Revolution was an aftermath of the Anglo-French conflict in the New World carried on between 1754 and 1763. This is by no means to deny that other factors were involved in the launching of these revolutionary movements. Before proceeding with an analysis of the theme of this paper, however, it would be well to consider the wording of the title given to it. . . .

A struggle of such proportions, involving tremendous stakes, deserves a name accurately descriptive of its place in the history of the English-speaking people, and the title "the French and Indian War", as suggested, in no way fulfills this need. For the war was not, as the name would seem to imply, a conflict largely between English and French New World colonials and their Indian allies, nor was it localized in North America to the extent that the name would appear to indicate. In contrast, it was waged both before and after an open declaration of war by the British and French nations with all their resources for nine years on three oceans, and much of the land washed by the waters of them, and it ultimately brought in both Spain, allied to France, and Portugal, allied to Great Britain. While it involved, it is true, as the name would connote, wilderness fighting, yet of equal, if not greater, importance in assessing its final outcome was the pouring forth of Britain's financial resources in a vast program of shipbuilding, in the equipment and sup-

SOURCE. Lawrence Henry Gipson, "The American Revolution as an Aftermath of the Great War for the Empire, 1754–1763," *The Political Science Quarterly*, LXV, March 1950, pp. 86–104. Copyright 1950 by the editors of *The Political Science Quarterly*. Reprinted with permission of *The Political Science Quarterly* and the author.

port of the British and colonial armies and the royal navy, and in the subsidization both of allies on the European continent and of the colonies in America. . . .

The development of the war into one for the military mastery of the North American continent came with the growing conviction on the part of the British ministers that nothing short of this drastic step would realize the primary aims of the government in arriving at the determination, as the result of appeals from the colonies for assistance, to challenge the right of French troops to be planted well within the borders of the Nova Scotia peninsula and at the forks of the Ohio. One may go as far as to state that the acquisition of Canada—as an objective sought by mercantilists to contribute to the wealth of Great Britain—would have seemed fantastic to any contemporary who had the slightest knowledge of the tremendous financial drain that that great possession had been on the treasury of the French King for over a century before 1754. Moreover, the motives that ultimately led, after much searching of heart, to its retention after its conquest by Great Britain were not commercial but strategic and had primarily in view the security and welfare of the older American colonies.

In view of these facts, not to be confused with surmises, the name *"the Great War for the Empire"* seems to the writer not only not inappropriate but among all the names heretofore applied to the war in question by far the most suitable that can be used by one concerned with the history of the old British Empire, who seeks earnestly to maintain that standard of exactness in terminology, as well as in other respects, which the public has a right to demand of him. . . .

But to return to the last phases of the Great War for the Empire. The British customs officials—spurred into unusual activity in the face of Pitt's demand for the strict enforcement of the Trade and Navigation Acts in order to break up the pernicious practice of bringing aid and comfort to the enemy—were led to employ writs of assistance for the purpose of laying their hands upon goods landed in American ports and secured in exchange for American provisions sent for the most part either directly or indirectly to the French West Indies. Although in the midst of hostilities, most of the merchants in Boston showed bitter opposition to the writs and equally ardent support of James Otis' declaration made in open court in 1761 that Parliament, acting within the limits of the constitution, was powerless to extend the use of these writs to America, whatever its authority might be in Great Britain. The importance of this declaration lies not so much in its immediate effect but rather in the fact that it was indicative of the line of attack that not only Otis would subsequently follow but also the Adamses, Hawley, Hancock, and other popular leaders in the Bay colony during the developing crisis, in the laying down of constitutional restrictions upon the power of Parliament to legislate for America. Further, it is clear that, even before the Great War for the Empire had been terminated, there were those in the province who had begun to view Great Britain as the real enemy rather than France.

Just as definitely as was the issue over writs of assistance related to the war under consideration was that growing out of the twopenny acts of the Virginia Assembly. In search of funds for maintaining the frontier defensive forces under the command of Colonel George Washington, the Assembly was led to pass in 1755 and 1758 those highly questionable laws as favorable to the tobacco planters as they were indefensively unjust to the clergy. Even assuming the fact that these laws were war measures, and therefore in a sense emergency measures, it was inconceivable that the Privy Council would permit so palpable a violation of contractural relations as they involved. The royal disallowance of the laws in question opened the way for Patrick Henry, the year that hostilities were terminated by the Peace of Paris, not only to challenge in the Louisa County courthouse the right of the King in Council to refuse to approve any law that a colony might pass that in its judgment was a good law, but to affirm that such refusal was nothing less than an act of tyranny on the part of the King. It was thus resentment at the overturning of Virginia war legislation that led to this attack upon the judicial authority of review by the Crown—an authority exercised previously without serious protest for over a century. It should also be noted that the Henry thesis helped to lay the foundation for the theory of equality of colonial laws with those passed by Parliament, a theory of the constitution of the empire that most American leaders in 1774 had come to accept in arguing that if the King could no longer exercise a veto over the acts of the legislature of Great Britain, it was unjust that he should do so over those of the colonial assemblies.

But the most fateful aftermath of the Great War for the Empire, with respect to the maintenance of the historic connection between the mother country and the colonies, grew out of the problem of the control and support not only of the vast trans-Appalachian interior, the right to which was now confirmed by treaty to Great Britain, but of the new acquisitions in North America secured from France and Spain. Under the terms of the royal Proclamation of 1763, French Canada to the east of the Great Lakes was organized as the Province of Quebec; most of old Spanish Florida became the Province of East Florida; and those areas, previously held by Spain as well as by France to the west of the Apalachicola and to the east of New Orleans and its immediate environs, became the Province of West Florida. The Proclamations indicated that proper inducements would be offered British and other Protestants to establish themselves in these new provinces. With respect to the trans-Appalachian region, however, it created there a temporary but vast Indian reserve by laying down as a barrier the crest of the mountains beyond which there should be no white settlement except by specific permission of the Crown.

The Proclamation has been represented not only as a blunder, the result largely of carelessness and ignorance on the part of those responsible for it, but also as a cynical attempt by the British ministry to embody mercantilistic principles in an American land policy that in itself ran counter to the charter limits of many of the colonies and the interests in general of the colonials. Nevertheless, this view of the Proclamation fails to take into account the fact that it was the offspring of war and that the trans-Appalachian aspects of it were an almost inevitable result of promises made during the progress of hostilities. For both in the Treaty of Easton in 1758 with the Ohio Valley Indians, a treaty ratified by the Crown, and in the asserverations of such military leaders as Colonel Bouquet, these Indians were assured that they would be secure in their trans-Appalachian lands as a reward for deserting their allies, the French. As a sign of good faith, the lands lying within the bounds of Pennsylvania to the west of the mountains, purchased by the Proprietors from the Six Nations in 1754, were solemnly released. Thus committed in honor in the course of the war, what could the Cabinet Council at its termination do other than it finally did in the Proclamation of 1763? But this step not only was in opposition to the interests of such groups of land speculators as, for example, the Patrick Henry group in Virginia and the Richard Henderson group in North Carolina, both of whom boldly ignored the Proclamation in negotiating with the Cherokee Indians for land grants, but also led to open defiance of this imperial regulation by frontiersmen who, moving beyond the mountains by the thousands, proceeded to settle within the Indian reserve—some on lands previously occupied before the beginning of the late war or before the great Indian revolt in 1763, and others on new lands.

The Proclamation line of 1763 might have become an issue, indeed a most formidable one, between the government of Great Britain and the colonials, had not the former acquiesced in the inevitable and confirmed certain Indian treaties that provided for the transfer of much of the land which had been the particular object of quest on the part of speculators and of those moving westward from the settled areas to establish new homes. Such were the treaties of Hard Labor, Fort Stanwix, Lochaber, and the modification of the last-named by the Donelson agreement with the Cherokees in 1771. Nor did the regulation of the trans-Appalachian Indian trade create serious colonial irritation, especially in view of the failure of the government to implement the elaborate Board of Trade plan drawn up in 1764. The same, however, cannot be said of the program put forward by the ministry and accepted by Parliament for securing the means to maintain order and provide protection for this vast area and the new acquisitions to the north and south of it.

Theoretically, it would have been possible for the government of Great Britain to have dropped onto the lap of the old continental colonies the entire responsibility for maintaining garrisons at various strategic points in North America—in Canada, about the Great Lakes, in the Ohio and Mississippi valleys, and in East and West Florida. In spite, however, of assertions made by some prominent colonials, such as Franklin, in 1765 and 1766, that the colonies would be able and were willing to take up the burden of providing for the defense of America, this, under the circumstances, was utterly chimerical, involving, as it would have, not only a vast expenditure of funds but highly complicated inter-colonial arrangements, even in the face of the most serious inter-colonial rivalry such as that between Pennsylvania and Virginia respecting the control of the upper Ohio Valley. The very proportions of the task were an insuperable obstacle to leaving it to the colonies; and the colonies, moreover, would have been faced by another impediment almost as difficult to surmount—the utter aversion of Americans of the eighteenth century, by and large, to the dull routine of garrison duty. This was emphasized by the Massachusetts Bay Assembly in 1755 in its appeal to the government of Great Britain after Braddock's defeat to send regulars to man the frontier forts of that province; the dispatches of Colonel George Washington in 1756 and in 1757 respecting the shameful desertion of militiamen, ordered to hold the chain of posts on the western frontier of Virginia in order to check the frightful French and Indian raids, support this position, as does the testimony in 1757 of Governor Lyttleton of South Carolina, who made clear that the inhabitants of that colony were not at all adapted to this type of work. The post-war task of garrison duty was clearly one to be assumed by regulars held to their duty under firm discipline and capable of being shifted from one strategic point to another as circumstances might require. Further, to be effective, any plan for the defense of the new possessions and the trans-Appalachian region demanded unity of command, something the colonies could not provide. Manifestly this could be done only through the instrumentalities of the mother country.

The British ministry, thus confronted with the problem of guaranteeing the necessary security for the extended empire in North America, which it was estimated would involve the annual expenditure of from three to four hundred thousand pounds for the maintenance of ten thousand troops—according to various estimates made by General Amherst and others in 1764 and to be found among the Shelburne Papers—was impelled to raise the question: Should not the colonials be expected to assume some definite part of the cost of this? In view of the fact that it was felt not only that they were in a position to do so but that the stability of these outlying possessions was a matter of greater concern and importance generally to them, by reason of their proximity, than to the people of the mother country three thousand miles away, the answer was in the affirmative. The reason for this is not hard to fathom. The nine years of war had involved Britons in tremendous expenditures. In spite of very heavy taxation during these years, the people were left saddled at the termination of hostilities with a national debt of unprecedented proportions for that day and age of over *one hundred and forty million pounds*. It was necessary not only to service and to retire this debt, in so far as was possible, but also to meet the ordinary demands of the civil government and to maintain the navy at a point of strength that would offer some assurance that France and Spain would have no desire in the future to plan a war to recover their territorial losses. In addition to all this, there was now the problem of meeting the charges necessary for keeping the new possessions in North America under firm military control for their internal good order and for protection from outside interference.

It may be noted that before the war the British budget had called for average annual expenditures of six and a half million pounds; between the years 1756 and 1766 these expenditures mounted to fourteen and a half million pounds a year on the average and from the latter date to 1775 ranged close to ten million pounds. As a result, the annual per capita tax in Great Britain, from 1763 to 1775, without considering local rates, was many times the average annual per capita tax in even those American colonies that made the greatest contribution to the Great War for the Empire, such as Massachusetts Bay and Connecticut—without reference to those colonies that had done little or nothing in this conflict, and therefore had accumulated little in the way of a war debt, such as Maryland and Georgia. The student of the history of the old British Empire, in fact, should accept with great reserve statements to the contrary—some of them quite irresponsible in nature —made by Americans during the heat of the controversy, with respect to the nature of the public burdens they were obliged to carry in the years preceding the outbreak of the Revolutionary War. In this connection a study of parliamentary reimbursement of colonial war expenses from 1756 to 1763 in its relation to public debts in America between the years 1763 and 1775 is most revealing. As to American public finances, all that space will here permit is to state that there is abundant evidence to indicate that, during the five-year period preceding the outbreak of the Revolutionary War, had the inhabitants of any of the thirteen colonies, which therefore included those of Massachusetts Bay and Virginia, been taxed in one of these years at the average high per capita rate that the British people were taxed from 1760 to 1775, the proceeds of that one year's tax not only would have taken care of the ordinary expenditures of the colony in question for that year but also would have quite liquidated its war debt, so little of which remained in any of the colonies by 1770. Well may John Adams have admitted in 1780 what was equally true in 1770: "America is not used to great taxes, and the people there are not yet disciplined to such enormous taxation as in England."

Assuming, as did the Grenville ministry in 1764, the justice of expecting the Americans to share in the cost of policing the new possessions in North America, the simplest and most obvious way, it might appear, to secure this contribution to a common end so important to both Americans and Britons was to request the colonial governments to make definite grants of funds. This was the requisition or quota system that had been employed in the course of the recent war. But the most obvious objections to it were voiced that same year by Benjamin Franklin, who, incidentally, was to reverse himself the following year in conferring with Grenville as the Pennsylvania London agent. In expressing confidentially his personal, rather than any official, views to his friend Richard Jackson on June 25, 1764 he declared: "Quota's would be difficult to settle at first with Equality, and would, if they could be made equal at first, soon become unequal, and never would be satisfactory." Indeed, experience with this system in practice, as a settled method of guaranteeing even the minimum essential resources for the end in view, had shown its weakness and utter unfairness. If it could not work equitably even in war time, could it be expected to work in peace? It is, therefore, not surprising that this method of securing even a portion of the funds required for North American security should have been rejected in favor of some plan that presented better prospects of a definite American revenue.

The plan of last resort to the ministry was therefore to ask Parliament to act. That Grenville, however, was aware that serious objections might be raised against any direct taxation of the colonials by the government of Great Britain is indicated by the caution with which he approached the solution of the problem of securing from America about a third of the total cost of its defense. The so-called Sugar Act first of all was passed at his request. This provided for import duties on certain West Indian and other products. Colonial import duties imposed by Parliament, at least since 1733, were no innovation. But the anticipated yield of these duties fell far short of the desired one hundred thousand pounds. He therefore, in introducing the bill for the above Act, raised the question of a stamp duty but requested postponement of parliamentary action until the colonial governments had been consulted. The latter were thereupon requested to make any suggestions for ways of raising an American fund that might seem more proper to the people than such a tax. Further, it would appear—at least, according to various London advices published in Franklin and Hall's *Pennsylvania Gazette*—that proposals were seriously considered by the Cabinet Council during the fall of 1764 for extending to the colonies representation in Parliament through the election of members to the House of Commons by various colonial assemblies. However, it is quite clear that by the beginning of 1765 any such proposals, as seem to have been under deliberation by the ministry, had been put aside when Grenville at length had become convinced that representation in Parliament was neither actively sought nor even desired by Americans. For the South Carolina Commons House of Assembly went strongly on record against this idea in September 1764 and was followed by the Virginia House of Burgesses in December. In fact, when in the presence of the London colonial agents the minister had outlined the objections raised by Americans to the idea of such representation, no one of them, including Franklin, was prepared to deny the validity of these objections. That he was not mistaken in the opposition of Americans at large to sending members to Parliament, in spite of the advocacy of this by James Otis, is clear in the resolutions passed both by other colonial assemblies than the ones to which reference has been made and by the Stamp Act Congress in 1765. Indeed, in 1768 the House of Representatives of Massachusetts Bay went so far in its famous Circular Letter framed in opposition to the Townshend duties as to make clear that the people of that colony actually preferred taxation by Parliament without representation to such taxation with representation.

When—in view of the failure of the colonial governments to suggest any practicable, alternate plan for making some contribution to the post-war defensive program in North America—Grenville finally urged in Parliament the passage of an American stamp bill, he acted on an un-warranted assumption. This assumption was—in paraphrasing the min-ister's remarks to the colonial agents in 1765—that opposition to stamp taxes, for the specific purpose in mind, would disappear in America both in light of the benefits such provision would bring to colonials in general and by reason of the plain justice of the measure itself; and that, in place of opposition, an atmosphere of mutual goodwill would be gen-erated by a growing recognition on the part of Americans that they could trust the benevolence of the mother country to act with fairness to all within the empire. Instead, with the news of the passage of the act, cries of British tyranny and impending slavery soon resounded throughout the entire eastern Atlantic American seaboard. What would have been the fate of the empire had Grenville remained in office to *attempt to enforce the act, no one can say.* But as members of the opposition to the Rockingham ministry, he and his brother, Earl Temple, raised their voices—one as a commoner, the other as a peer—in warning that the American colonies would inevitably be lost to the empire should Parlia-ment be led to repeal the act in face of colonial resistance and the pressure of British merchants. Had Parliament determined, in spite of violence and threats of violence, to enforce the act, it might have meant open rebellion and civil war, ten years before it actually occurred. In-stead, this body decided to yield and, in spite of the passing of the so-called Declaratory Act setting forth its fundamental powers to legis-late on all matters relating to the empire, suffered a loss of prestige in the New World that was never to be regained.

But the Stamp Act was not the sole object of attack by colonials. To many of them not only the Sugar Act of 1764 but the whole English pre-war trade and navigation system was equally, if not actually more, obnoxious. Indeed, the unusual energy displayed by the navy and the customs officials, spurred into action by Pitt during the latter years of the war—bringing with it the condemnation in courts of vice-admiralty of many American vessels whose owners were guilty of serious trade vio-lations, if not greater crimes—generated a degree of antagonism against the whole body of late seventeenth- and early eighteenth-century restric-tions on commercial intercourse such as never had previously existed. It is not without significance that the greatest acts of terrorism and destruction during the great riot of August 1765 in Boston were directed not against the Massachusetts Bay stamp distributor but against those officials responsible for encouraging and supporting the enforcement, during the late war, of the various trade acts passed long before its beginning in 1754. The hatred also of the Rhode Island merchants, as a group, against the restrictions of the navigation system as well as against the Sugar Act of 1764, remained constant. Moreover, in December 1766 most of the New York merchants, over two hundred in number, showed their repugnance to the way that this system was functioning by a strongly worded petition to the House of Commons in which they enumerated an impressive list of grievances that they asked to be redressed. Even Chatham, the great friend of America, regarded their petition "highly improper: in point of time most absurd, in the extent of their pretensions, most excessive; and in the reasoning, most grossly fallacious and offensive." In fact, all the leading men in Great Britain supported the system of trade restrictions.

Nevertheless, the determination of the government—in view especially of the great financial burdens that the late war had placed upon the mother country—to enforce it now much more effectively than had been done before 1754, and to that end in 1767 to pass appropriate legislation in order to secure funds from the colonies by way of import duties so that public officials in America might be held to greater accountability when paid their salaries by the Crown, could have only one result: the combined resistance of those, on the one hand, opposed to any type of taxation that Parliament might apply to America and of those, on the other, desiring to free the colonies of hampering trade restrictions.

The suggestion on the part of the Continental Congress in 1774 that Americans would uphold the British navigation system, if exempted from Parliamentary taxation, while a shrewd gesture to win support in England, had really, it would seem, no other significance. For it is utterly inconceivable that the Congress itself, or the individual colonial governments, could have set up machinery capable of preventing violations of the system at will on the part of those whose financial interests were adversely affected by its operation. Moreover, it is obvious that, by the time the news had reached America that Lord North's ministry had secured the passage of the coercive acts—for the most part directed against Massachusetts Bay and the defiant destruction of the East India Company's tea—leading colonials, among them Franklin, had arrived at the conclusion that Parliament possessed powers so very limited with respect to the empire that without the consent of the local assemblies it could pass neither constitutional nor fiscal legislation that affected Americans and the framework of their governments. It is equally obvious that this represented a most revolutionary position when contrasted with that held by Franklin and the other delegates to the Albany Congress twenty years earlier. For it was in 1754 that the famous Plan of Union was drawn up there and approved by the Congress—a plan based upon the view that Parliament, and not the Crown, had supreme authority within the empire, an authority that alone was adequate in view of framers of the Plan to bring about fundamental changes in the constitutions of the colonies in order legally to clothe the proposed union government with adequate fiscal as well as other powers.

In accounting for the radical change in attitude of many leading colonials between the years 1754 and 1774 respecting the nature of the constitution of the empire, surely among the factors that must be weighed was the truly overwhelming victory achieved in the Great War for the Empire. This victory not only freed colonials for the first time in the history of the English-speaking people in the New World from dread of the French, their Indian allies, and the Spaniards, but, what is of equal significance, opened up to them the prospect, if given freedom of action, of a vast growth of power and wealth with an amazing westward expansion. Indeed, it is abundantly clear that a continued subordination of the colonies to the government of Great Britain was no longer considered an asset in the eyes of many Americans by 1774, as it had been so judged by them to be in 1754, but rather an onerous liability. What, pray tell, had the debt-ridden mother country to offer in 1774 to the now geographically secure, politically mature, prosperous, dynamic, and self-reliant offspring along the Atlantic seaboard, except the dubious opportunity of accepting new, as well as retaining old, burdens? And these burdens would have to be borne in order to lighten somewhat the great financial load that the taxpayers of Great Britain were forced to carry by reason of obligations the nation had assumed both in the course of the late war and at its termination. If many Americans thought they had a perfect right to profit personally by trading with the enemy in time of war, how much more deeply must they have resented in time of peace the serious efforts made by the home government to enforce the elaborate restrictions on commercial intercourse? Again, if, even after the defeat of Colonel Washington at Great Meadows in 1754, colonials such as Franklin were opposed to paying any tax levied by Parliament for establishing a fund for the defense of North America, how much more must they have been inclined to oppose such taxation to that end with the passing in 1763 of the great international crisis?

At this point the question must be frankly faced: If France had won the war decisively and thereby consolidated her position and perfected her claims in Nova Scotia, as well as to the southward of the St. Lawrence, in the Great Lakes region, and in the Ohio and Mississippi valleys, is it at all likely that colonials would have made so fundamental a constitutional issue of the extension to them of the principle of the British stamp tax? Would they have resisted such a tax had Parliament imposed it in order to provide on a equitable basis the maximum resources for guaranteeing their safety, at a time when they were faced on their highly restricted borders by a militant, victorious enemy having at its command thousands of ferocious redskins? Again, accepting the fact of Britain's victory, is it not reasonable to believe that, had Great Britain at the close of the triumphant war left Canada to France and carefully limited her territorial demands in North America to those comparatively modest objectives that she had in mind at its beginning, there would have been no very powerful movement within the foreseeable future toward complete colonial autonomy—not to mention American independence? Would not Americans have continued to feel the need as in the past to rely for their safety and welfare upon British sea power and British land power, as well as upon British resources generally? In other words, was Governor Thomas Hutchinson of Massachusetts Bay far mistaken when, in analyzing the American situation late in 1773, he affirmed in writing to the Earl of Dartmouth:

Before the peace [of 1763] I thought nothing so much to be desired as the cession of Canada. I am now convinced that if it had remained to the French none of the spirit of opposition to the Mother Country would have yet appeared & I think the effects of it [that is, the cession of Canada] worse than all we had to fear from the French or Indians.

In conclusion, it may be said that it would be idle to deny that most colonials in the eighteenth century at one time or another felt strongly the desire for freedom of action in a wider variety of ways than was legally permitted before 1754. Indeed, one can readily uncover these strong impulses even in the early part of the seventeenth century. Yet Americans were, by and large, realists, as were the British, and under the functioning of the imperial system from, let us say, 1650 to 1750 great mutual advantages were enjoyed, with a fair division, taking everything into consideration, of the financial burdens necessary to support the system. However, the mounting Anglo-French rivalry in North America from 1750 onward, the outbreak of hostilities in 1754, and the subsequent nine years of fighting destroyed the old equilibrium, leaving the colonials after 1760 in a highly favored position in comparison with the taxpayers of Great Britain. Attempts on the part of the Crown and Parliament to restore by statute the old balance led directly to the American constitutional crisis, out of which came the Revolutionary War and the establishment of American independence. Such, ironically, was the aftermath of the Great War for the Empire, a war that Britons believed, as the Earl of Shelburne affirmed in 1762 in Parliament, was begun for the "security of the British colonies in N. America. . . ."

CHAPTER 12

THE GENESIS OF
AMERICAN NATIONALISM

The coming of the American Revolution too often is described in negative terms as primarily the response of the colonists to the imperial legislation of the 1760's and 1770's. This view tends either to ignore or to de-emphasize significant internal developments in the colonies that also must be considered if one is to understand fully the American Revolution.

Professor Max Savelle's analysis of these internal developments in *Seeds of Liberty: The Genesis of the American Mind** explores the early origins and patterns of American culture, thought, and way of life. In the following selection, he concentrates on the genesis and early development of an American nationalism. He suggests that, even before 1750, Americans exhibited a common loyalty to shared American purposes and ideals. The roots of this new American self-consciousness lay deep in the colonial past; but, in the resistance to imperial control, the American sense of identity was most clearly expressed and resulted in relatively unified political action. Numerous forces—economic, social, intellectual and cultural, military, and political—operated to draw the thirteen colonies together into a distinctively American entity. Professor Savelle discusses these forces, the nature of the nascent American nationalism, and the influence of American self-consciousness on the coming of the American Revolution.

The question of American unity in the colonial period is raised in a previous selection by Professor John R. Alden. Although Alden and Professor Savelle focus on different aspects of colonial history—Alden on the varied patterns of colonial life and Savelle on the genesis of American nationalism—do they basically agree about the colonial development of American distinctiveness and self-consciousness? What factors does Savelle emphasize as contributing significantly to the development of American nationalism, and how do these compare with the ones identified by Alden? More important, what was the nature and the extent of American nationalism? What was the ideal toward which the Americans were driven by their concept of American distinctiveness and unity? Finally, what was the influence of developing nationalism on the coming of the American Revolution?

Carl Degler, *Out of Our Past: The Forces that Shaped Modern America,** (1958), has an outstanding chapter on the awakening of American nationalism. Clinton Rossiter, *Seedtime of the Republic** [Part I: *The First American Revolution*] (1956), and Daniel J. Boorstin, *The Americans: The Colonial Experience** (1958), are also rewarding reading on this subject.

* Available in a paperback edition.

THE GENESIS OF AN "AMERICAN" NATIONALISM
MAX SAVELLE

A common loyalty to a common American purpose and ideal was beginning to emerge among the Americans even before 1750. And it was this new American self-consciousness in all things, this new loyalty to America, that was to give the Americans an intellectual and emotional sense of unity of purpose and ideal. It was the conflict with the mother country over the question of taxation, to be sure, that galvanized this American self-consciousness into dramatic literary expression and political action; but its beginnings lie farther back than that: its roots are deeply embedded in the earliest American experience.

The people of the British colonies in America did not yet, in the year 1750, constitute a homogeneous social entity. For the British Empire in this hemisphere was composed of a congeries of disparate settlements and societies from the primitive trading posts on the shores of Hudson Bay and British Guiana to the highly sophisticated societies of New York, Virginia, or Jamaica. Yet thirteen of the twenty-odd colonies were passing, more or less consciously, through a process that was at once drawing them together toward homogeneity and distinguishing them, as a single unit, from all the others. For these thirteen, located along the eastern seaboard of the continent, were being subtly fused by a number of forces that were daily becoming more powerful.

Among these forces were the influences exerted by increased commercial, social, and intellectual intercourse between colonies. As roads from one colony to another appeared, finally binding them together on one long string from Portsmouth to Savannah, the spreading consciousness of a common cultural tradition could not fail to grow. This development seems to have been an almost inevitable consequence of the expansion of populations that brought the people of one colony to rubbing elbows with the people of the next. As the means of communication were expanded and

SOURCE. Max Savelle, *Seeds of Liberty: The Genesis of the American Mind,* Seattle: University of Washington Press, 1948, pp. 564–582. Copyright 1948. Reprinted with permission of the author.

improved, travel increased; and the traveler from Boston in Charleston, for example, found that the citizens of the two places had much in common. Travel and writing led to intercolonial marriages; and as the number of colleges increased and their fame spread, more and more young men crossed intercolonial boundaries in quest of education. These intellectual and social and economic forces making for closer association were well under way by the middle of the century.

One of the most obvious of these forces was the binding effect of intercolonial trade. And the continued growth of intercolonial economic relations gave impetus to the already well-developed consciousness of the differentness of American economic interests from those of the mother country. The appearance of an American self-consciousness in the realm of economic affairs, in fact, had had its beginning very early in the history of the colonies, and had sprung originally from the realization that their economic interests diverged, at many important points, from those of the mother country. The Navigation Acts and the Acts of Trade had been efforts to force American economic life into the imperial pattern, but they had been only partially successful; and many Americans such as Franklin had begun to question, as early as about 1750, the validity of the entire system. But the formulation of a positive feeling of economic nationalism did not really appear until the conflict with the mother country over the program, initiated about 1764, to make the old imperial system really effective. The colonies, thrown on the defensive, were forced to elaborate reasons for their opposition to the mother country, and some Americans went on beyond their economic philosophy in defense of their liberties to emotional glorifications of the economic grandeur and destiny of America as a whole or of one's own province as a separate unit. Such, for example, was the sentiment of Daniel Dulany, writing in Virginia in. 1765:

Let the manufacture of *America* be the symbol of dignity, the badge of virtue, and it will soon break the fetters of distress. A garment of linsey-woolsey, when made the distinction of real patriotism, is more honourable and attractive of respect and veneration, than all the pageantry, and the robes, and the plumes, and the diadem of an emperor without it. Let the emulation be not in the richness and variety of foreign productions, but in the improvement and perfection of our own. . . . I have in my younger days seen fine sights, and been captivated by their dazzling pomp and glittering splendor; but the sight of our representatives, all adorned in compleat dresses of their own leather, and flax, and wool, manufactured by the art and industry of the inhabitants of *Virginia*, would excite, not the gaze of admiration, the flutter of an agitated imagination, or the momentary amusement of a transient scene, but a calm, solid, heart-felt delight. Such a sigh would give me more pleasure than the most splendid and magnificent spectacle the most exquisite taste ever painted, the richest fancy ever imagined, realized to the view . . . as much more pleasure as a good mind would receive from the contemplation of virtue, than of elegance; of the spirit of patriotism, than the ostentation of opulence.

The solid intellectual bases for an American national feeling were being laid in the 1740's and 1750's. One of the greatest of the agencies for such a development was the post-office, of which, significantly enough, Benjamin Franklin became the head in 1753. Franklin had actively sought the office of Deputy Postmaster-General for America, partly because he thought it might be remunerative, but also, as he said in his letter to Peter Collinson, because he felt sure the post-office could be made an effective agency for the development of an active intercolonial intellectual exchange. He believed the work of the Philosophical Society would be extended by it, and that Philadelphia might well become the cultural capital of America.

There were probably not many men in America who saw the intellectual maturity of America as Franklin saw it in 1743, or believed that the colonies were culturally so mature. Yet the organization and the success and permanence of the American Philosophical Society may be taken, perhaps, as evidence that in 1743 and the years following there was enough and sufficiently widespread intercolonial interest in intellectual matters to permit of this year being used as the marker of the birth of an American cultural self-consciousness. For the exchange of ideas and associations that resulted must have given considerable impetus to the growth of a sense of a common American intellectual life.

Even if Franklin had been alone in his effort to draw the colonies together culturally, as he was not, his own sponsoring of an intercolonial cultural development was a significant manifestation of his early "Americanism"; and if in 1743 he was giving form to an American cultural life, twenty years later he was beginning to see in America the very heart and center of the culture of western civilization.

Meanwhile, a cultural self-consciousness was also appearing in other lines of literary production, one of the most notable of which was history. It is probably not without significance, and highly symptomatic of the dawning self-consciousness of the Americans, that Dr. William Douglass's *Summary, Historical and Political, of the British Settlements in North-America,* which was intended to cover the entire Anglo-American colonial area on the continent of North America, appeared between the years 1747 and 1752. The fact that it was not completed does not diminish the significance of the author's conception; for he gave the first important literary and documentary expression to an American continental self-consciousness.

One of the most important manifestations of the awakening cultural self-consciousness of the Americans was the deliberate effort of William Smith and his circle of young littérateurs and artists in Philadelphia to make for America a place in the cultural sun. All of the magazines that were launched between 1740 and 1760 show this cultural objective, in one way or another; and the *American Magazine,* published by Smith and his circle, is full of literary and historical expressions of it.

The Americans, indeed, were slowly but surely awakening to a realization of their own traditions and a sense of their own glorious future as a distinct people, in all the realms of their thinking. Already, for example, American patriots were beginning to extol the humanitarianism of America as a refuge for the poor and the oppressed, and the virtues of "The American, this new man," as the product of the melting-pot. Poor Richard expressed this popular sentiment in 1752 when he sang the praises of this country as a place

> Where the sick Stranger joys to find a Home,
> Where casual Ill, maim'd Labour, freely come;
> Those worn with Age, Infirmity or Care,
> Find Rest, Relief, and Health returning fair.
> There too the Walls of rising Schools ascend,
> For Publick Spirit still is Learning's Friend,
> Where Science, Virtue, sown with liberal Hand,
> In future Patriots shall inspire the Land.

But the love of one's country inspired by its humanitarian welcome to the poor and suffering of the world was looked upon with a jaundiced eye by those hundred-per-cent .patriots who feared the possible un-American activities and influence of the foreigners on our soil. This was the sort of fear which, mixed with religious distrust, led to the passage of the Connecticut "Act Providing Relief against the evil and dangerous Designs of Foreigners and Suspected Persons"; this was the fear, also, that led William Smith to write his diatribes against the Pennsylvania Germans, and William Douglass to pour out the vials of his wrath against the Quakers in his bitter exclamation that "the pusilanimous Doctrine of not defending themselves by force against an invading Enemy is very absurd: PRO PATRIA *is not only a Law of Nations, but of Nature."*

Even Franklin, in almost the same moment when with the popular voice of Poor Richard he was extolling the national melting-pot, could privately express his fear that the Germans might prove to be too un-American in their influence to be absorbed:

This will in a few Years become a *German* Colony: Instead of their Learning our Language, we must learn their's, or live as in a foreign country. Already the *English* begin to quit particular Neighbourhoods surrounded by *Dutch* [Germans], being made uneasy by the Disagreeableness of disonant Manners; and in Time, Numbers will probably quit the Province for the same Reason. Besides, the *Dutch* under-live, and are thereby enabled to under-work and under-sell the *English;* who are thereby extremely incommoded, and consequently disgusted, so that there can be no cordial Affection or Unity between the two Nations.

The split in nationalistic pride between those who glorify the melting-pot and those who fear the un-American activities of foreigners whose ideals do not exactly coincide with their own is no new thing; it has apparently been one of the dialectical strains within American nationalistic feeling almost from the beginning. . . .

Franklin believed strongly in the educational value of history, not merely for the promotion of the social ideal and the virtues of citizenship, but also for inculcation in the student of the peculiar virtues and advantages of his own people: "If the new *Universal History* were also read, it would give a connected idea of human affairs, so far as it goes, which should be followed by the best Modern histories, particularly of our mother country; then of these colonies; which should be accompanied with observations on their rise, increase, use to Great Britain, encouragements and discouragements, the means to make them flourishing, and secure their liberties."

This was written in 1749. Yet there is unquestionably present in this recommendation a consciousness of the peculiar differentness of the colonies, of their common problems, and the preciousness of their liberties. It is this idealization of the abstract qualities of one's own people that is the essence of nationalism. If this was not nationalism itself, then it was surely the psychological germ from which an American nationalism was to grow.

But it was in the face of a common enemy that the nationalistic feelings of the Americans found the freest and most intense expression in the 1750's. For at this point "Tory" feelings and "American" feelings could merge; and the approach of the Seven Years' War was unquestionably the great catalyst that precipitated the most eloquent expressions of America's nascent nationalism. This strong anti-Gallican animosity had been vocal, in fact, since the War of the Austrian Succession (King George's War) and the thrill of general exultation that ran through all the colonies over the capture of Louisbourg in 1745 by a little band of New Englanders. . . .

This deep and intense fear and hatred of a common enemy, the sentiment that might be called a sense of the "Gallic peril," was expressed in many places and in many ways. It appears again and again in the newspapers and in the pamphlets, especially in the mid-century armed truce between 1748 and 1754. The French were the great enemy of all the colonies except the small, coast-bound provinces like Rhode Island, Connecticut, New Jersey, and Delaware; and as population had expanded even farther and farther westward, the inevitability of eventual conflict had become increasingly apparent to everybody, including the French themselves. The governors of New France repeatedly warned their mother country, especially the Marquis de la Galissonnière, of the irrepressible expansiveness of the British Americans. But the French forts built along the frontier from Crown Point in the north to Fort Toulouse in the south appeared to the British colonists only the visible evidence of an aggressive French determination at least to hem them in along the seaboard. The alarmists, however, saw a greater threat than that and warned their readers that the French would reach out to the coast itself and, it might be, one day drive the British from the Atlantic coastal plain altogether, or, worse still, reduce all the Americans to slavery. One of the easiest ways, obviously, for the French to do this, would be by alienating the "foreigners" along the frontier. The French had lately been active along the Ohio, building forts and establishing control over the Indians; since the Quakers of Pennsylvania were pacifists, it seemed to William Smith that it would be extremely easy, even what the French actually designed, to make, by way of Pennsylvania, a breach in the solid front of the English colonies.

Many Americans were in a state of deathly fear of the French and their iniquitous designs, and the sermons of the period sought to whip their audiences into a fervor of patriotic defense of American soil and liberties. Here is an example from Jonathan Mayhew:

And what horrid scene is this, which restless, roving fancy, or something of an higher nature, presents to me, and so chills my blood! Do I behold these territories of freedom, become the prey of arbitrary power? . . . Do I see the slaves of Lewis with their Indian allies, dispossessing the free-born [American] subjects of King George, of the inheritance received from their forefathers, and purchased by them at the expense of their ease, their treasure, their blood! . . . Do I see protestant, there, stealing a look at his bible, and being tak[en] in the fact, punished like a felon! . . . Do I see all liberty, property, religion, happiness, changed, or rather transubstantiated, into slavery, poverty, superstition, wretchedness!

Freedom of property, freedom to work, freedom of worship, the free pursuit of happiness; these American freedoms were threatened by Louis XV of France, monstrous symbol of dictatorial government menacing the liberty of the world, and especially American freedom! This was an ideological war; and the forces of nationalistic emotion were called upon to defend the American-English ideal of liberty against the rapacious Juggernaut of popish authoritarianism. If there ever was a war of Anglo-American aggressive expansionism, the Seven Years' War in America was that war. Yet that did not prevent the intellectual leaders from preaching, in all sincerity of conviction, and the people from believing, that it was a holy war in the name of an ideal, the ideal of "British" (American) liberty and self-government. Samuel Davies, in Virginia, could pull out all the stops on the organ of his eloquence to stir the Virginians to patriotic self-sacrifice:

and shall these Ravages go on uncheck'd? Shall *Virginia* incur the Guilt, and the everlasting Shame of tamely exchanging her Liberty, her Religion, and her All, for arbitrary *Gallic* Power, and for Popish Slavery, Tyranny, and Massacre? Alas! are there none of her Children, that enjoyed all the Blessings of her Peace, that will espouse her Cause, and befriend her now in the Time of her Danger? Are *Britons* utterly degenerated by so short a Remove from their Mother-Country? Is the Spirit of Patriotism entirely extinguished among us? And must I give thee up for lost, O my Country! and all that is included in that important Word? . . .

Many of the Americans, if not all, were being drawn swiftly and deeply into the continental mood of nationalistic self-defense. The Albany Congress, with its plan for intercolonial union, was more a practical effort at defense than a sounding-board of psychological nationalism; yet its members were moved by the same patriotic sentiments that were moving the souls of so many other Americans; and William Livingston reported that "The speakers [at the conference] . . . were not many; but of those who spoke, some delivered themselves with singular energy and eloquence. All were inflamed with a patriot spirit, and the debates were nervous and pathetic [fervent]. This assembly . . . might very properly be compared to one of the ancient Greek conventions, for supporting their expiring liberty against the power of the Persian empire, or that Lewis of Greece, Philip of Macedon."

Samuel Davies probably expressed the common mood of most Americans when he said, in 1756: "Now what can be more important, what more interesting, than our country! Our country is a word of the highest and most endearing import: it includes our friends and relatives, our liberty, our property, our religion: in short, it includes our earthly all. And when the fate of our country and all that it includes, is dreadfully doubt-full . . . every mind that has the least thought, must be agitated with many eager, dubious expectations. This is the present situation of our country. . . ." . . .

The final climax of American nationalistic conviction eventually came in the realm of political thought, which epitomized the whole struggle of the Americans and their culture-complex for self-expression. And this trend toward a political nationalism looked two ways; for while it was expressing itself positively along the lines of the struggle for political self-direction, it was also expressing itself negatively in the increasing resistance to control by the mother country.

Thus in the same years in which the colonists were beginning to sense the reality of their common cause and purpose toward their French and Indian enemies, they were also awakening to a consciousness of the common nature of their problems toward the mother country. Hitherto, of course, and even now, the American's highest loyalty was to England and to his King. But these years marked the moment of his awakening, in the course of his struggle over the prerogative, over the regulation of commerce, and over taxation, to the fact of his differentness from Englishmen: the fact that, somehow, the American and the Englishman, though ruled by the same King, were not the same men, that England and America were not the same society; and that for the American, though he might still be supremely loyal to his King, the society in which he breathed and had his being was American, not English; and his loyalty to his King was really a symbol of his loyalty to his colony, and through it, eventually, to "America." Jonathan Mayhew's sermon on unlimited submission was a clear warning to the English crown to govern the colonies according to the social compact between them, delivered without for a moment contemplating a reduction of American loyalty. With the same candor within the bounds of "British" loyalty Franklin was criticizing the mother country for her shortsightedness in insisting upon the Navigation Acts. A wise mother he said, would not do it; and he was speaking for all the colonies, not just one or several.

That some such feeling of differentness was taking shape in Franklin's mind between 1750 and 1755, despite his enthusiastic expansionist imperialism, is clear from his writing during this period touching upon the relations of the colonies to the mother country, economic as well as political. For he not only criticized the unwisdom of Parliamentary restraints upon colonial trade, but, more positively, suggested a greater imperial union, with the colonies enjoying a much more important place in imperial deliberations, representation in an imperial parliament, and greater recognition of the uniqueness of the way of life of the colonies as a distinct unit in the Empire. In his eighteenth-century quest for a natural order in human affairs corollary to the order in the physical universe, he was discovering, or thought he was, the natural processes by which societies are formed. The American society had been formed by the natural process; it was different from the society from which it sprang; and it must be respected as being so. There began to be implicit in Franklin's criticisms of England a principle, the nationalistic counterpart of his sociological and economic thinking, of the naturalistic origins and peculiarities of nations. This principle, gradually becoming clearer in his own mind as it found expression in his political thoughts on the nature of the British Empire between 1765 and 1775, did not, as yet, conflict with the principle of loyalty to the King. Franklin was an ardent and patriotic Briton; but he was also a patriotic American, fired with a sense of the future greatness of his native land.

The growing feeling of criticism of England and the nebular beginning of an intercolonial solidarity were not confined to the struggle of the assemblies against the prerogative, nor even to politics. The manifold activities of the colonial agents in England also reflect the increasing complexity of the problem of forestalling interference in colonial affairs; and the agents were now finding it increasingly to their advantage to present a common front. A very significant case of this sort of co-operative action took place between 1750 and 1753, when the northern colonial agents in London found themselves lined up in a solid front against the sugar-planters of the British West Indies and their agents for the preservation of the trade of the northern colonies with the French West Indies. The proposed restrictions upon that trade, said the northern agents, would paralyze the northern colonies economically; moreover, the restrictions would constitute a violation of the American's rights as Englishmen. Significantly, their protest was based upon the economic differentness of the colonies from England.

This united effort of the agents was successful. The passage of the Sugar Act in 1764 brought the agents together again, and from then on they were regularly instructed to co-operate on questions of common interest; after the Stamp Act of 1765 they met together regularly to formulate joint policies. The significant development here was, of course, the emergence of a united, co-operative front toward the mother country among the colonies through their agents in England. The common front represented in the colonial mind the idea of common interests and a common cause.

During the Seven Years' War in America the feeling of difference between "Americans" and "Englishmen" was heightened by their relationships in military operations. The British soldiers and officers looked down upon their cruder American cousins and infuriated them by their own discrimination and patronizing attitude. This is well illustrated at the time of Braddock's defeat, when, though everybody deplored the disaster itself, there was more than a little grim satisfaction in American commentaries which pointed to it as a lesson to teach the supercilious British that the Americans knew more about warfare in America and claimed that British honor was saved, after all, by the Americans, without whom the disaster would have been far greater than it was.

This mood of American importance in imperial affairs was no passing fancy, either. For there were numerous Americans who felt that it was to the colonials that victory was due, and that the mother country actually owed them a debt of gratitude for making possible so great an expansion of the Empire. . . .

The ideas and sentiments in this curious "Who won the war?" argument are clearly the impulses of a young and bumptious nationalism, the more clearly so because they were the feelings of not just one American, but probably most of them. The Americans were thinking of themselves now as different from their English cousins and as entitled to the respect due to a people that has arrived at political and cultural maturity. As Franklin put it in a letter to Lord Kames in 1767:

Every man in England seems to consider himself a piece of a sovereign over America; seems to jostle himself into the throne with the King, and talks of *our subjects in the colonies.* . . . But America, an immense Territory, favored by nature with all the advantages of climate, soils, great navigable rivers, lakes, &c., must become a great country, populous and mighty; and will, in a less time than is generally conceived, be able to shake off any shackles that may be imposed upon her, and perhaps place them on the imposers. . . . And yet there remains among that people so much respect, veneration, and affection for Britain, that, if cultivated prudently, with a kind usage and tenderness for their privileges, they might be easily governed still for ages, without force or any considerable expense. But I do not see here a sufficient quantity of the wisdom, that is necessary to produce such a conduct, and I lament the want of it.

Franklin was warning England of the psychological facts. But a subtle and significant change had now taken place in his mind. He no longer spoke of Americans as identical with Britons, or of the colonies as part of England. They were separate; they had only respect and reverence for the great traditions and ideals of the British way of life and all that that could mean; but they were now a separate people, among the other British peoples.

The loyalties of the Americans were becoming more and more sharply divided. The American mentality was growing conscious of this divergence, thinking of itself as a distinct, "American" entity within the Empire, and of England and its people as alien to itself. This was a psychological phenomenon, a factor of profound importance for the future of the Empire and for America. From Franklin's position of 1767 it was but a short step to Jefferson's position of 1774, which spoke of Englishmen as foreigners to America, and to the eloquent Patrick Henry's "I am an American." Or to that of John Randolph, who warned the mother country, on the eve of the Revolution:

The Histories of dependent States put it beyond a Doubt that America, when she is able to protect herself, will acknowledge no Superiority in another. That she will be capable, some Time or other, to establish an Independence, must appear evident to every One, who is acquainted with her present Situation and growing Strength. But although it must be apparent to everyone that *America* will, in short Period, attain to a State of Maturity, yet, if *Great Britain* could be prevailed on to govern her Colonies to their Satisfaction, from the force of Habit, and the good Impressions which a pleasing Intercourse must occasion, I am persuaded that she would procrastinate our Separation from her, and carry on an exclusive Trade with us, so long as she is able to maintain her Weight in the political scale of *Europe;* but, on the contrary, if she persevere in her Rigour, and the Colonies will not relax on their Part, the Parent will probably soon be without a Child, and the Offspring become unable to support itself.

What the Americans were driving for was a recognition, by the mother country, of the now self-confident American national personality. The child had grown up and become a man. Psychologically, the American Revolution was a war to force the mother country to admit this basic fact. The Americans were perfectly willing, even anxious, given the mother country's admission of their national maturity, to remain members of the imperial family. But that was just the tragic point at which British nationalism found itself in conflict with British-American nationalism, and since neither one could accept the ideal and the point of view of the other, the British-American mind became the American mind, simply.

Thus the ardent national feeling that burst into flame in the Revolution was but the culmination of a long development, the explosion that marked the climax of a long smoldering fire of increasing intensity. It had had its birth within the folds of "British" patriotism; but, beginning as a loyalty to one's province, it had grown into a consciousness of problems and ideals common to all the provinces, first in matters of defense, then in cultural relationships, and finally in the problems of relationship with the mother country. Had Britain been wise enough to understand this aspect of the American mind and to accommodate British colonial policy to it, as it did a century later in the case of Canada, there is every reason to suppose that the colonies might have become the first associated nation in a new British Commonwealth of Nations. But, as Franklin sadly lamented, there wasn't enough of that sort of wisdom in Britain.

The American consciousness of national selfhood that was beginning to show its rudimentary forms by about 1750 was thus not merely allowed to grow naturally, but was actually forced into a flaming patriotic growth by the policies of the mother country. As it existed in its primitive form in 1750 it was a still nebular consciousness of, and loyalty to, the more heroic aspects of American life: the military exploits at Louisburg; the common fear of the common enemies, French and Indian, to the westward; a sense of the glorious manifest destiny of America beyond the mountains and as the future seat of the arts and sciences on this continent. As yet in 1750 and 1760 it was a glorification of Britain in America; by the end of the Seven Years' War loyalty to America was sharply distinguished, by some at least, from loyalty to Britain. As the sixties wore on into the seventies American patriots began to see that there were actually two nationalities involved, with their respective nationalisms.

It was this sense of the ineffable beauty and splendor of America and its promise to the world that inspired Philip Freneau to mark the culmination of American nationalistic feeling in his *Poem on the Rising Glory of America* in 1771. Freneau was no rebel; he had no more thought of throwing off British allegiance in 1771 than most other Americans. But he envisioned his America as a nation within a British family of nations. His poem assumed the sort of British Empire that Benjamin Franklin was at that moment beginning to define as a federation of quasi-independent or autonomous states; his patriotism was the prototype of the intra-imperial patriotism of a Canada or an Australia of a later day:

> To mighty nations shall the people grow
> Which cultivate the banks of many a flood,
> In chrystal currents poured from the hills
> Apalachia nam'd, to lave the sands
> Of Carolina, Georgia, and the plains
> Stretch'd out from thence far to the burning Line,
> St. Johns or Clarendon or Albemarle. . . .

> And here fair freedom shall forever reign.
> I see a train, a glorious train appear,
> Of Patriots plac'd in equal fame with those
> Who nobly fell for Athens or for Rome.

It should be emphasized that this American nationalism of 1770 was not a nationalism of independence. It was a nationalism that expected to find self-expression within the framework of the Empire. For conflicts of economic interest and ideologies alone were not necessarily and inevitably productive of civil war; neither, indeed, was conflict in religion, or in culture, or even politics. All these things might be adjusted peaceably; but when pride was pitted against pride, emotion against emotion; ideal of American "liberty" against ideal of an imperial unity to be imposed by force, if necessary, then, and then only, civil war was, in the nature of men and things, inevitable. This germinal American nationalism was nationalism in its best sense—national self-realization, pride in national tradition and achievement, and a sense of the greatness of the national destiny—a sort of national self-respect or pride that made it impossible to submit to the benighted stubbornness of George III and his ministers. Given the men, their convictions, and their mood, given, that is, the self-consciousness and the self-confidence of the American national mind, the outcome could hardly have been otherwise. For these thirteen of the British colonies in America had become a nation. And Patrick Henry, like so many other Americans fired by the discovery of his own America and driven to desperation by the utter inability of Britain to comprehend the nationhood of America, burst out with his famous cry: "The distinction between Virginians, Pennsylvanians, New Yorkers, and New Englanders, are no more. I am not a Virginian, but an American."

CHAPTER 13

THE WAR OF INDEPENDENCE: THE INTERNAL "REVOLUTION"

As Professor Alden points out, there is more to winning independence than winning a war. If, in addition, the country is embarking on a social revolution, then the problem becomes even more complex. Not only must order be restored but also the basic nature of society must be modified. The old rulers must be displaced and the new ones must be phased in without destroying the good order of society any more than necessary. This transfer of power and authority must often be made at a time when interior disunity and confusion are at their maximum and exterior pressure, or its imminent threat, is also intense. This was the situation that faced the colonists during the period covered by this selection.

It is hardly surprising that the colonists, under these conditions, borrowed from their old charters, did not submit their new governing documents to the voters, and exhibited the conservatism mentioned by Alden. The fact that any innovations appeared under these conditions is more surprising. But, as Alden points out, important reforms and innovations took place at the state level during the war.

This dichotomy of important change and temporary patchwork has led historians of this period to pose this question: Exactly how revolutionary was the Revolution? This question, in turn, raises another one: Were these revolutionary changes consciously revolutionary, or were the colonists merely removing the vestiges of British rule without contemplating the consequences?

The best description of the processes by which the new governments were formed is Elisha Douglass, *Rebels and Democrats: The Struggle for Equal Political Rights and Majority Rule During the American Revolution** (1955). Although older, Allan Nevins, *The American States During and After Revolution, 1775–1789,* is still valuable. The classic statement on the revolutionary nature of the change is found in J. Franklin Jameson, *The American Revolution Considered As A Social Movement** (1926). This study has been closely examined by Fredrick B. Tolles in "The American Revolution Considered as a Social Movement: A Re-Evaluation," *American Historical Review,* LX (1954), and found to be basically sound but overstated. Louis B. Hartz, *The Liberal Tradition in America** (1954), and Daniel J. Boorstin, *The Genius of American Politics** (1953), do not agree with Jameson or Tolles. See also Jackson Turner Main, *The Upper House in Revolutionary America* (1968), which complements Jameson's study of social forces from a political perspective.

* Available in a paperback edition.

REFORMATION IN THE STATES
JOHN R. ALDEN

While the Continentals and militia fought against Britain, other patriots, assuming ultimate victory, remolded their political and social institutions. They created written constitutions both for the several states and for the United States; made careful provision for the protection of personal liberties; struck at religious privilege; assailed barbarous punishments for crime; moved haltingly in the direction of political democracy; redistributed land; and even ventured to attack the institution of Negro slavery. They initiated an "Internal Revolution" which continued beyond the war and exercised an enduring influence.

The War of Independence was hardly begun when the patriots began to try to form legal and permanent governments in the colony-states. Overturning regimes sanctioned by Britain, they were often forced for a time to govern through revolutionary and extralegal—if not illegal—conventions and committees. But they desired political institutions more stable, more ordered, and better calculated to preserve and enhance their own liberties, if not those of the Tories. Very generally, in part because of their long acquaintance with colonial charters, they looked upon the written constitution as indispensable. In the fall of 1775 John Adams developed a model constitution; early in 1776 Tom Paine proposed another. Even before Paine's model appeared, the New Hampshire patriots adopted for temporary use a written constitution which endured until 1784. The South Carolina patriots adopted a temporary constitution in March, 1776, one intended to be permanent in 1778. Two such documents designed for long use were actually promulgated before the Declaration of Independence, in Virginia and New Jersey, and six others before the close of 1777. Rhode Island and Connecticut continued in effect their colonial charters with minor revisions. Massachusetts similarly, but temporarily, operated its charter until 1780, when a carefully drawn basic document was put into effect.

SOURCE. John Richard Alden, *The American Revolution, 1775–1783*, New York: Harper & Row, Publishers, 1954, pp. 150–163. Copyright 1954 by Harper & Brothers. Reprinted by permission of Harper & Row, Publishers, and the author.

It is a striking fact that the early state constitutions were neither prepared by conventions especially elected for the purpose nor submitted
to the voters for approval. In a few instances they were drawn up and
declared in operation by legislative bodies chosen in elections in which
constitution-making was not an issue. More commonly, they were conceived and declared in effect by legislators to whom the voters had entrusted the tasks of fashioning statutory and fundamental law. Thus even
those who enjoyed the privilege of the ballot had little or no opportunity
to voice their desires. This fact was a matter of concern to many patriots,
including Jefferson, who insisted that any constitution intended to be
more than temporary should be sanctioned by the voters.

That the basic law guaranteeing the rights of the individual and establishing the framework of state government might be adopted without ratification aroused the citizens of Massachusetts. When, in September, 1776,
the towns of that state were asked whether they would permit the General
Court to draft a constitution, Concord as well as other towns vigorously
replied in the negative. Concord insisted that a prime purpose of such
a document was "to secure the subject in the possession and enjoyment
of their rights and privileges, against any encroachments of the governing
part." If a General Court could mold a basic document, then another
such assemblage could later alter it at will. Of what avail then a fundamental law? Accordingly Concord urged that a convention be specially
elected to draw up a constitution and that the citizens of the state be
given an opportunity to inspect and comment upon the result before it
should be put into practice. A mass meeting at Pittsfield proposed that a
constitution should become valid only when approved by a majority of
the voters. The General Court decided to draft such a document, which
it submitted to referendum, but its handiwork was overwhelmingly defeated at the polls. In consequence the legislature called a state constitutional convention, which met in 1779–80 and which at least pretended to
submit its product to the voters. More than a year earlier the first such
convention had met in New Hampshire, but its work had been disapproved
by the towns of that state. In 1783 another New Hampshire convention
produced a document which received their consent. Massachusetts and
her neighbor thus inaugurated the familiar and exceedingly important
devices of the constitutional convention and the constitutional referendum.
Further, since their method of constitution-making implied the supremacy
of constitutions over legislative acts, the road was opened for the development of judicial review.

The Revolutionary state constitutions were often hurriedly drafted in
the midst of other business, even by legislatures in flight before advancing

British troops. In some cases there was little quarreling regarding their provisions, in others heated controversy. Nevertheless, on the whole, the work was amazingly well done, since the majority of the constitutions intended for permanent use remained in force for a generation or more.

On the surface, the new basic state laws were much alike. As a general rule, they contained a Bill of Rights; all provided for an elected legislature, usually consisting of two houses; all arranged for a governor (or president) elected either by the voters or by the legislature; all granted the suffrage only to property owners or taxpayers; and most of them gave at least lip service to the principle of separation of powers. But if the governments set up by these documents differed little in form, there were important variations in substance. In some instances these constitutions were devised by patriots who wanted little or no change beyond separation from Britain —by Conservatives; in others, they were composed by patriots who desired independence and alterations in the direction of political democracy and social equality—by Radicals; in still others, neither the influence of the Conservatives nor that of the Radicals was decisive.

In the main, the forms of government under the new state constitutions were patterned after those in vogue in the colonies before 1775, with elected governors and senates replacing governors and councils chosen by the crown or the proprietors. The substance was largely derived from the colonial experience of 150 years and from the doctrines of natural rights and compact so splendidly asserted in the Declaration of Independence, and again in the Massachusetts constitution of 1780. In the latter document it is declared that "The body politic is formed by a voluntary association of individuals; it is a social compact, by which the whole people covenants with each citizen, and each with the whole people that all shall be governed by certain laws for the common good"; and also, that "The people alone have an incontestible unalienable, and indefensible right to institute government, and to reform, alter, or totally change the same when their protection, safety, prosperity, and happiness require it." These ideas were derived from study of the writings of a galaxy of British and European political theorists, especially those of John Locke. From Locke, and perhaps more particularly from Montesquieu, came another concept of great importance, separation of powers among the branches of government in order to prevent any one of them from becoming dominant and tyrannical.

Although the makers of the first state constitutions quite uniformly subscribed to Lockeian principles, they did not agree with respect to their meaning and their application. The drafters quarreled little about statements inserted in the Bills of Rights guaranteeing trial by jury, the right of petition, freedom from self-incrimination, and other rights familiar to English law. They fought, and often bitterly, over provisions regarding religion, the suffrage, qualifications for office-holding, the powers of the governor as against those of the legislature, and other crucial issues. In fact, the Conservatives and the Radicals were seriously at odds regarding the political and social goals of the Revolution.

In essence, the Conservatives, though devoted to the ideal of independence, feared excessive change. In the seats of authority formerly occupied by royal appointees, they now wished to place the propertied, the educated, and the socially qualified. They despised and dreaded majority rule because they conceived the humbler and less learned patriots to be incapable and even depraved. They opposed "mob rule" as leading to anarchy or dictatorship. Not a few of them defended established churches, feudal arrangements of primogeniture and entail, and privilege generally for the select and the superior. Had they been able to impose their will, the great planters, the wealthy merchants, and a portion of the clergy—the upper middle class—would have formed an American aristocracy and an American oligarchy. The Conservatives read their Locke as the British landed aristocracy and the British merchants read him after the Glorious Revolution of 1688. In the compact mechanics, small farmers, and slaves were not full and equal partners.

The Radicals refused to concede that the only great purpose of the patriots was separation from Britain. They would not admit that their rights—the rights of mankind—would be secured by the mere disappearance of royal and proprietary officials. To them Lockeian philosophy was a system of thought which sanctified neither rule by Britain nor domination by privileged Americans. They argued that all citizens were equal participants in compact. They were likely to look upon government as at best a necessary evil and to seek to limit its powers. They insisted that the suffrage should be generously granted, even that it should not be denied to any adult white male. They demanded just apportionment of legislative seats, so that the vote of the farmer and the frontiersman in the interior would have equal weight with that of the seaboard merchant and planter—tidewater areas were then frequently over-represented. The Radicals would place power in the legislature rather than in the executive or the judiciary, since the legislature would be most responsive to popular will. Conceding that the wishes of a minority should be given thoughtful consideration, they were prone to insist upon majority rule.

Nor was Radical thought confined to things political. Enlightened "leftists" of the War of Independence demanded complete religious freedom; they inveighed against hereditary aristocracy and legal and customary arrangements which favored the eldest son at the expense of his brothers and sisters. They asked at least a modicum of free public education for the sons and daughters of all free men. They urged reform of civil and criminal law to prevent injustice and cruel punishments, and they assailed brutal treatment of prisoners. Some even attacked the institution of Negro slavery as inhumane and unwarranted either by Locke or by God. In short, many Radical leaders, and at least a portion of their followers, entertained views which may be described as liberal or progressive and as logical.

To be sure, all the Radicals were not occupied with altruistic designs for present and future improvement—they were not all Jeffersons. Some were shiftless, irresponsible, and unprincipled folk who found in the Revolution opportunity to evade payment of taxes and debts, to pull down to their own level envied neighbors, and to exalt themselves without resort to toil. Nor were all the Conservatives mere crass devotees of personal and class interests. A number, among them Henry Laurens of South Carolina, were troubled because they were fighting for the rights of man while continuing to hold Negroes in bondage. Many of them desired religious freedom. Indeed, many Conservatives were moderate men hardly to be distinguished from the milder Radicals. In fact, no hard and fast line can be drawn between Conservatives and Radicals. Within both groups there were infinite variations, and some individuals shifted from one camp to the other.

In the struggle between the Conservatives and Radicals the latter group possessed important advantages. The Tories, who in the main would have been natural allies of the Conservatives, were commonly excluded from public life and even from the ballot. Moreover, many men who had not been permitted to vote before the war had been allowed to help choose Revolutionary conventions and legislatures. These clung to the ballot as more permanent regimes appeared. The Second Continental Congress itself advised "a full and free representation of the people" in constitution-making; and the influence of the new voters is to be discerned in the basic state documents. Inevitably, the majority of these suddenly enfranchised men joined the Radicals. In addition, the Conservatives, crying out against Britain, had come forth in defense of the rights of man and against taxation without representation, and had thus supplied their fellow patriots with ammunition which could be used against themselves. They could hardly deny the logic of the demands by the Radicals that the franchise be given to many of those voteless in colonial days; nor could they easily counter Radical arguments for redistricting of seats in the legislatures. The interior regions, "the Old West," had long been so patently underrepresented in the colony-states, especially in Pennsylvania, Virginia, and South Carolina, that the justice of those arguments was obvious. Yet in giving way to the Radicals on these points the Conservatives suffered serious diminution of their influence, not only because the new voters were inclined toward the Radicals, but also because "the Old West" was their stronghold. In sum, the Conservatives found it impossible to control the patriots as a whole and to insist that the only great goal of the war was severance from Britain.

Among the patriots were divisions along socio-economic lines. The small and tenant farmers, the frontier folk, and unpropertied people of the seacoast towns and cities tended to oppose the planters and merchants in the camp of the Conservatives. Class lines were not always clearly drawn, however. Jarring concepts were debated rather than settled by force; conflicting interests were compromised rather than decided by blows; and the Radicals found their most effective leaders among planters and certain merchants, lawyers, and other men of wealth, such as Jefferson, Richard Henry Lee, George Mason, George Wythe, Franklin, George Bryan, Thomas McKean, and Elbridge Gerry.

The influence of the Radicals may readily be discerned in the provisions of the new state constitutions concerning the ballot and qualifications for office-holding. Under these any taxpayer in Pennsylvania, Delaware, North Carolina, Georgia, and Vermont could vote. Any Virginian owning twenty-five acres of improved soil or five hundred acres of undeveloped land possessed the ballot. In the other states the suffrage was less generously offered to men who possessed either land or personal property in some quantity, or paid fairly substantial amounts in taxes. Very commonly, higher qualifications in the way of property or payment of taxes were required for members of the lower house of the legislature, still higher ones for membership in the upper house, and occasionally even higher ones for persons serving as governors. Office-holding was thus frequently reserved for men of means; no state conceded manhood suffrage; and plural voting on the basis of ownership of land was still possible in several states. But if political democracy had not been achieved, it is nevertheless true that the voting population was larger than it was in colonial days. Land was cheap, and the privilege of the ballot was often easily within the reach even of the poor. Since the Tories were usually disfranchised and since many sought safety in exile, there came a more or less permanent swing to the left in American politics.

The influence of the Radicals is also to be observed in the provisions of the early constitutions concerning the powers of the respective branches of government. While expressions of respect for the principle of separation of powers were freely offered, authority was usually centered in the legislature, and especially in the lower house. The Radicals feared strong executives and distrusted independent judiciaries. As a result the governor was given an effective veto only in Massachusetts, and he was in some states a mere figurehead. In several states judges were chosen by the legislature, and for very short terms. The Radicals believed, and not without reason, that the legislatures would be more responsive to the public will, particularly since they were also able in a number of states to require frequent elections. The political systems set up in states where Radicals were dominant—for example, Pennsylvania, Virginia, and North Carolina—were accordingly ill balanced and not too efficient. They were, however, far more democratic than those established in states under Conservative domination—for example, Maryland.

Much redistricting in the direction of political justice and democracy is also to be found in these constitutions. In Pennsylvania the southeastern counties, almost absurdly overrepresented before 1775, lost their special and privileged position. In Virginia the Piedmont and Shenandoah regions received for the first time representation in accordance with their numerous population. Sectional favoritism was also eliminated in North Carolina. Concessions were made to interior folk in South Carolina and Massachusetts, although the Lowlands about Charleston continued for some years to hold a favored position. Frontier democracy was given larger opportunity to express itself, an opportunity which was not wasted.

The makers of fundamental law in the Revolutionary period also took long strides toward religious freedom. Before the war there was a relatively large measure of toleration everywhere in the Thirteen Colonies, but complete religious freedom nowhere except in Rhode Island. In no fewer than nine colonies there were established tax-supported churches, enjoying privileges varying greatly from place to place. In New England, except for Rhode Island, the Congregational Church had the support of the state, while the Anglican Church was official in a few counties of New York and in all the colonies from Maryland to Georgia. It was usually difficult and sometimes impossible for a member of a dissenting sect to escape taxation for the support of the established church in his colony; and he who was attached to no religious organization could not evade it. Universally, save in Rhode Island (which in the eighteenth century restricted the political activities of Catholics and Jews), there were discriminations of one sort or another, relatively mild in Pennsylvania and Delaware, onerous in Congregational New England and Episcopalian Maryland and Virginia. Connecticut law still required church attendance; Roman Catholics could not hold office in Maryland.

The movement for disestablishment was facilitated by the fact that in no state were the Anglicans in a numerical majority. Except in Virginia, it was easy to reduce the Church of England to the level of other churches, for Presbyterians, Lutherans, Baptists, Roman Catholics, its own laymen, and deists (numerous among the leaders of the patriots) joined in the attack upon it. In Virginia, where the Anglicans formed perhaps half of the churchgoing population and included the bulk of the planters, there was a bitter struggle. However, Anglican clergymen in the upper South were distinguished for neither piety nor learning, and they were frequently Tories. Finally, the Church was definitely disestablished in the Old Dominion. The Congregational state churches in New England were less vulnerable; they lost some of their privileges, but were not deprived of all vestige of official sanction until the nineteenth century was well under way.

Disestablishment was, of course, not the equivalent of complete religious freedom, which was not attained in most of the states for some years. Thus New Jersey and the Carolinas continued to require that officeholders be Protestants; Massachusetts insisted that they declare themselves to be Christians; and Delaware demanded from them, and also from members of the legislature, that they declare their belief in the Holy Trinity. These and similar restrictions were soon to disappear. The trend was toward total religious liberty, with Jefferson and James Madison pointing the way in Virginia. In the Old Dominion the principle of toleration was incorporated in the Declaration of Rights of 1776. In the following year statutes requiring church attendance and the use of public money to support the Episcopal Church were repealed. The Episcopal Church fought bitterly against disestablishment and received powerful assistance from other Protestant sects, which desired that public funds be devoted to the maintenance of all the major Christian churches. Although the Episcopalian Church was deprived of all official status two years later, Patrick Henry, young John Marshall, and apparently Washington joined the ranks of those who wished to compel all citizens to help finance the Christian sects. Henry was able to mobilize a large majority in the assembly in favor of the scheme, but Jefferson, James Madison, and George Mason fought it persistently and imaginatively. At length the proposal was dropped, and the Statute of Religious Liberty, drawn up by Jefferson and sponsored by his friends, became law in 1786. In a long, rhetorical, and yet moving preamble the act condemned utterly all efforts to employ the power of government in behalf of any species of religion and affirmed that "truth is great and will prevail if left to herself. . . ." It was accordingly enacted "that no man shall be compelled to frequent or support any religious worship, place or ministry whatsoever, nor shall be enforced, restrained, molested, or burthened in his body or goods, nor shall otherwise suffer on account of his religious opinions or beliefs; but that all men shall be free to profess, and by argument to maintain, their opinion in matters of religion, and that the same shall in no wise diminish, enlarge, or affect their civil capacities." Jefferson was justly proud of his contribution to religious freedom.

The Revolutionary generation, seeking to assert the natural rights of mankind, could not but be conscience-stricken when it considered the lot in America of some of the children of Nature's God, the Negroes, who composed one-fifth of the total population and half of that of South Carolina. Almost all of the Negroes were slaves. Generally they were held in mild subjection. Nevertheless, slavery then, as later, had its horrors, the worst of which was the traffic in human bodies between Africa and America. That brutal commerce had aroused indignation before the war, and the importation of slaves had been halted in Rhode Island, Connecticut, and Pennsylvania, but the British government and its representatives in the colonies had prevented the passage of similar laws in the royal colonies. When Britain and British officials could no longer interfere, American legislatures, with that of Delaware leading the way in 1776, undertook to put an end to the traffic. During and immediately after the war the introduction from foreign lands of enslaved blacks was forbidden in all the states, save for South Carolina and Georgia. Even in the far South there was much sentiment in favor of such action, and importation was temporarily forbidden in South Carolina in 1787 and again in 1788.

The patriots did not content themselves merely with endeavors to destroy the oceanic slave trade. In the spring of 1775 there was formed at Philadelphia the first antislavery society in America, and many patriots, Conservative and Radical, including Washington, Jefferson, Madison, Patrick Henry, and Horatio Gates, were soon afterward urging the outlawing of Negro bondage. Economic interest, ignorance, feelings of racial superiority, and fear of the consequences of emancipation usually postponed or prevented action. Nevertheless, a few Negroes received their freedom in return for honorable military service in the war; and many thousands obtained it by manumission, made relatively easy by law in Virginia in 1782 and also by other states in the South. Moreover, Pennsylvania provided for gradual emancipation by a law of 1780; and statements of the Massachusetts Bill of Rights of the same year, including one which declared that "All men are born free and equal," were construed three years later by the highest court of that state to mean that slavery was outlawed. Certain other Northern states soon followed the examples of Pennsylvania and Massachusetts. Others did not act until after the close

of the century. In the South, however, where there were both proportionately and absolutely many more slaves, sentiment began to swing after
the war toward protecting that institution.

If the patriots indirectly gave support to the concept of aristocracy by
their failure to abolish slavery, they struck hard at that concept nonetheless. Provisions that there should be neither a privileged class nor hereditary offices were inserted in several of the first state constitutions. Two
denied the legislature the power to create titles of nobility! Georgia even
refused the privileges of voting and office-holding to persons claiming
titles. Manorial rights and quitrents vanished. What was more important,
the patriots demolished those twin props of landed aristocracy, primogeniture and entail. At the beginning of the war entailment, though forbidden
in South Carolina, was more or less legal elsewhere. Primogeniture
flourished in New York and the Southern colonies; in Pennsylvania, Delaware, New Jersey, and New England the eldest son received a double
share in inheritance. With Jefferson and Virginia once again leading the
way, these arrangements so well calculated to preserve family estates collapsed before the assaults of the reformers. By 1786 entails had been
abolished or rendered innocuous in every state; by 1792 primogeniture
had disappeared; indeed, by that time equality in intestate succession was
universally established. The results of these wholesale changes are difficult
to measure, but in some areas they may have contributed to a more
equitable distribution of land. Whatever the actual results, the social structure had been altered in the direction of equality.

The importance of redistribution of land, as Jefferson fully appreciated,
can scarcely be overestimated. Ownership of soil brought relative economic independence, and with it advance in social and political status.
More owners meant more democracy, social and political. Happily, redistribution proceeded during and immediately after the War of Independence, not only through the eradication of laws forcing and permitting
concentration of ownership, but also through the abolition of British authority over the trans-Allegheny West and the confiscation of Tory property. The bars to westward settlement set up by the Proclamation of
October 7, 1763, and later British restrictive measures vanished. Moreover, the great speculators in lands beyond the mountains, highly favored
under the royal regime, found it somewhat more difficult to secure large
grants from the state and federal governments at the expense of the
small farmer. Thus the path of the humble to landownership in the eastern
part of the Mississippi Valley was made somewhat broader and smoother.
To be sure, this result was hardly discernible until the war had ended
and large-scale expansion beyond the mountains began.

The effects of confiscation of lands owned by Tories, however, appeared almost immediately. On November 27, 1777, the Continental Congress recommended that the states seize and sell the estates of Loyalists, the proceeds to be used to finance the war. The idea of paying for the war in part at the expense of the Tories was a popular one among the patriots. Indeed, some states had already begun the process of confiscation. Now it was greatly hastened, and every state without exception declared Tory lands forfeited or at least subject to forfeiture. The result was a spate of sales of those lands which continued even after the close of the conflict. Whatever may be said about the treatment thus meted out to the supporters of Britain and the widespread corruption attendant upon such sales, many large estates were broken up and dispersed in smaller holdings among the patriots. In New York the lands of Tory James De Lancey became the property of 275 different persons; those of Tory Roger Morris went to nearly 250; and large tracts owned by Tories in the central and northern parts of the state were sold to poor farmers in quantities from one hundred to five hundred acres. Since many of the Loyalists sooner or later went into exile (although some returned), it may be said that conservatism was permanently weakened both by their departure and by the fact that the less affluent were often enabled to acquire their properties and to move upward economically and socially.

If this analysis of change in the states accompanying and resulting from the war is already lengthy, it should nevertheless be recalled that the era of the Revolution brought increased pressure for more lenient treatment of debtors, for improvement in prison conditions, and for the revision and modernization of civil and criminal law. Certainly, education, in some part at least because of Revolutionary ferment, entered upon a new course. The concept of education at public expense received added impulse. In 1776 John Adams declared that "Laws for the liberal education of youth, especially of the lower class of people, are so extremely wise and useful, that, to a humane and generous mind, no expense for this purpose would be thought extravagant." Jefferson, who was equally convinced with Adams of the values of education and of the desirability of spreading widely its benefits, proposed three years later that Virginia establish public schools for elementary instruction and remold the College of William and Mary into something approaching a university. Five Revolutionary state constitutions urged that provision be made for schools, in some instances specifically for free schools. It was apparent to many patriot leaders that the new American society in process of formation required diffusion of education, if for no other reason to the end that the less affluent citizens who were wielding influence in public affairs should be sufficiently enlightened to carry their burdens. Although the war temporarily interfered with the operations of schools and colleges, and although the proposals of Jefferson, and others like him, were temporarily set aside, the concept of a freer and more democratic educational system gained converts. Indicative of the future was the action of the legislature of Georgia in 1783 giving one thousand acres of land to every county for the support of schools.

CHAPTER 14

THE NEW NATION
UNDER THE ARTICLES
OF CONFEDERATION

It can hardly be argued that the decade of the 1780's was not a critical period in the history of the United States. Yet there is considerable doubt that it was *the critical period of American history,* as claimed by John Fiske in his widely influential book of that title. The traditional, or Fiske interpretation of the 1780's held that an exceptionally weak and inept Articles of Confederation government was responsible for bringing the nation to the brink of disaster, from which it was rescued only by the magnificent efforts of the "founding fathers." Revisionists counter that the period was much more complex than the traditional view would indicate. They suggest that the major disruptive forces of the decade—post-war demobilization, economic dislocation, and fundamental political conflict—would have operated regardless of the government in power.

The strength and effectiveness of the government under the Articles is difficult to determine with any degree of exactitude. In this selection, Professor Merrill Jensen, a leading critic of the Fiske viewpoint, suggests that the government was not nearly so defective as earlier historians believed. Jensen argues persuasively that it was not the imminent collapse of the Confederation which led to the calling of the Constitutional

Convention of 1787 and the creation of a new Constitution. These developments represented instead the victory of one political group in the fundamental political conflict which Jensen sees as the essence of the period of the 1780's.

In reading this selection the student should consider carefully three basic matters. First, does Professor Jensen's terminology for the two opposing political groups help to clarify or to obscure the basic nature of the political conflict of the period? What characteristics does Jensen ascribe to the opposing groups? Which group represented the cause of democratic government? Second, what was the precise nature—particularly the central issue—of the disagreement between the two groups? Third, was the conflict finally settled in the 1780's, or anytime thereafter? If not, what has been the nature of the continuing disagreement? Has this disagreement always been, as Professor Jensen argues it was in the 1780's, over the issue of democracy as a way of government for the United States?

The student wishing more information on this topic should begin his reading in Jensen, *The Articles of Confederation** (1940), and *The New Nation** (1950), from which this selection is taken. Also he, at least, should sample John Fiske, *The Critical Period of American History* (1916, second edition), to get a taste of the other side of the debate. A modern analysis that disagrees with Jensen is found in Oscar and Mary Handlin, "Radicals and Conservatives in Massachusetts after Independence," *New England Quarterly,* XVII (1944). The standard biographies of men such as George Washington, John Adams, Thomas Jefferson, James Madison, and Alexander Hamilton can be read profitably for a knowledge of the period. See also the bibliography and selection for Chapter 16 of this volume.

* Available in a paperback edition.

THE SIGNIFICANCE OF THE CONFEDERATION PERIOD

MERRILL JENSEN

This book is an account of the first years of the new nation that was born of the American Revolution. Like every other segment of time, the history of the United States from 1781 to 1789 was an integral part of the past in which it was rooted and of the future into which it was growing. It was a time when men believed they could shape the future of the new nation, and since it was also a time in which they disagreed as to what that future should be, they discussed great issues with a forthrightness and realism seldom equalled in political debates. The history of the Confederation is therefore one of great inherent importance for the study of human society if for no other reason than that during it men debated publicly and even violently the question of whether or not people could govern themselves.

Aside from its inherent importance, the history of the Confederation has been of enormous significance to one generation of Americans after another in the years since then. Repeatedly Americans have turned to that history in the course of innumerable social and political struggles. They have done so because it was during those years that the Articles of Confederation were replaced by the Constitution of 1787. In order to explain their Constitution, Americans have appealed to the history of the period out of which it came. In the course of such appeals, sometimes honestly for light and guidance and sometimes only for support of partisan arguments, Americans have usually found what they sought. As a result the "history" has been obscured in a haze of ideas, quotations, and assumptions torn bodily from the context of fact that alone gives them meaning. Again and again political opponents have asserted that the founding fathers stood for this or that, while their writings have stood idly and helplessly in volumes on shelves or have lain buried in yellowed manuscripts and newspapers.

SOURCE. Merrill Jensen, *The New Nation: A History of the United States During the Confederation, 1781–1789*, New York: Alfred A. Knopf, Inc., 1950, pp. vii–xiv and 422–428. Copyright 1950 by Alfred A. Knopf, Inc. Reprinted by permission of A. A. Knopf, Inc. and the author.

Since the founding fathers themselves disagreed as to the nature of the history of the period and as to the best kind of government for the new nation, it is possible to find arguments to support almost any interpretation one chooses. It is not surprising therefore that conflicting interpretations have filled thousands of pages and that all this effort has never produced any final answers and probably never will, for men have ever interpreted the two constitutions of the United States in terms of their hopes, interests, and beliefs rather than in terms of knowable facts.

The conflict of interpretation has been continuous ever since the first debates over the Articles of Confederation in the summer of 1776. Men then differed as to the kind of government which should be created for the new nation. They continued to debate the issue during the 1780's. The members of the Convention of 1787 differed as to the need for and the amount of constitutional change. When the Constitution was submitted to the public in October 1787 the controversy rose to new heights. Men talked in public meetings and wrote private letters and public essays in an effort to explain, justify, or denounce what the Convention had done. They disagreed as to what had happened since the war. Some said there had been chaos; others said there had been peace and prosperity. Some said there would be chaos without the new Constitution; others that there would be chaos if it were adopted.

Once it was adopted Thomas Jefferson and Alexander Hamilton, with two opposed ideals of what the United States should be, laid down two classic and contradictory opinions of the nature of the Constitution. These two basic interpretations may be simply stated. Jefferson held that the central government was sharply limited by the letter of the Constitution; that in effect the states retained their sovereign powers except where they are specifically delegated. Hamilton argued in effect that the central government was a national government which could not be restrained by a strict interpretation of the Constitution or by ideas of state sovereignty. These rival interpretations did not originate with Hamilton and Jefferson, for they had been the very core of constitutional debate ever since the Declaration of Independence, and even before it, for that matter.

Jefferson and his followers used the states rights idea to oppose the plans of the Federalists when they passed the Alien and Sedition Acts in 1798. But when Jefferson became president and purchased Louisiana, he justified his actions by constitutional theories that even Hamilton hardly dared use. Meanwhile Jefferson's opponents seized upon his earlier theories in a vain attempt to block the expansion of the United States. They did so again during the War of 1812 when the Federalists of New England became out-and-out exponents of "states rights" and threatened secession because they were opposed to the war.

In the decades before the Civil War, Daniel Webster and John C. Calhoun carried on the dispute, each having changed sides since his youthful years in politics. Webster, who had been a states rights spokesman during the War of 1812, became the high priest of nationalism, while Calhoun, a leading nationalist in 1812, became the high priest of the states rights idea which he elaborated to defend the slave-owning aristocracy of the South.

The Civil War itself was the bloody climax of a social conflict in which the ultimate nature of the Constitution was argued again and again in seeking support for and arguments against antagonistic programs. But even the Civil War did not finally settle the constitutional issue. The stresses and strains that came with the rise of industrial and finance capitalism produced demands for social and regulatory legislation. The passage of such legislation by the states involved the interpretation of the nature of the Constitution, for business interests regulated by state governments denied their authority and appealed to the national courts. Those courts soon denied the power of regulation to state legislatures. Then, when regulatory laws were passed by the national government, the regulated interests evolved a "states rights" theory that limited the power of the central government, and the national courts once more agreed.

Throughout American history the courts have drawn boundary lines between state and national authority. The pose of judicial impartiality and finality assumed by the courts cannot hide the fact that they have shifted those boundary lines with the shifting winds of politics, and always with sufficient precedents, if not with adequate grace. As a result they had created by 1900 a legal and constitutional no man's land in which all sorts of activity could be carried on without effective regulation by either state or national governments.

The crash of American economy in 1929 once more posed in imperative terms the problem of the nature of the Constitution. How should it, how could it deal with the potentiality of chaos inherent in unemployment, starvation, and bankruptcy, and ultimately, the loss of faith in the utility of the economic and political foundation of the society itself?

As the national government began to act where, plainly, state and local governments had failed to or were unable to act, the question of constitutionality was raised. For a time the courts once more listened to and heeded states rights constitutional theories which were expounded by opponents of the New Deal. New Deal lawyers, in turn, adopted as weapons John Marshall's nationalistic interpretations of the Constitution for ends which Marshall himself would have fought to the death. President Roosevelt, in his fight on the Supreme Court, declared that the Constitution was not a lawyer's document; yet some of the ablest lawyers who ever lived in America wrote it. New Deal publicists wrote tracts in the guise of history to prove that there had been a "national sovereignty" in the United States from the beginning of the Revolution. Therefore, they argued, the courts could not stop the New Deal from doing what needed doing by following a strict interpretation of the Constitution. Both the New Dealers and the Republicans insisted that they were the sole heirs of the legacy of Thomas Jefferson, while Alexander Hamilton went into an eclipse from which he has not yet emerged.

The most recent appeal to the history of the Confederation Period has come from those who support some form of world government. Adequate arguments for such a government can be found in twentieth-century experience, but, like most men, its backers turn to history for analogies and lessons.

When the League of Nations was set up at the end of the First World War men turned to American history after the American Revolution as a parallel experience. At that time books were written to show the "chaos" of the Confederation Period and the happy solution that came with the Constitution of 1787. Among them was a book by a great authority on international law with the title *James Madison's Notes of Debates in the Federal Convention of 1787 and their Relation to a More Perfect Society of Nations*. The book was widely distributed by the Carnegie Endowment for International Peace. This and other books like it had little relation to the realities of world politics in the 1920's and 1930's, but despite this supporters of the United Nations and of various plans of world government have again turned to the history of the American states after the American Revolution. . . .

Even if it can be granted that most appeals to the history of the Confederation have been sincere, let it also be said that they have seldom been infused with any knowledge of the period or its problems. The result has been the drawing of lessons the past does not have to teach. This is a luxury too expensive in an age when men have discovered how to unhinge the very force that holds matter itself together but have advanced very little beyond cave men in their notions of how to live peacefully with one another.

Yet it is little wonder that such false lessons have been drawn in the twentieth century because most of them have come from John Fiske's

The Critical Period of American History, a book of vast influence but of no value as either history or example. Fiske, a philosopher and popular lecturer, wrote the book "without fear and without research," to use the words of Charles A. Beard. As long ago as 1905, Andrew C. Mc-Laughlin, an impeccably conservative historian of the Constitution who wrote a far better book on the same period, said that Fiske's book was "altogether without scientific standing, because it is little more than a remarkably skillful adaption of a very few secondary authorities show-ing almost no evidence of first hand acquaintance with the sources."

The story told by Fiske and repeated by publicists and scholars who have not worked in the field—and some who have, for that matter—is based on the assumption that this was *the* "critical period" of American history during which unselfish patriots rescued the new nation from impending anarchy, if not from chaos itself. The picture is one of stag-nation, ineptitude, bankruptcy, corruption, and disintegration. Such a pic-ture is at worst false and at best grossly distorted. It is therefore im-portant to attempt a history which makes an effort to examine the sources, which is concerned with the nature of political and economic problems rather than with proving that one side or another in the in-numerable political battles of the period was "right" or "wrong." Noth-ing is to be gained by following a "chaos and patriots to the rescue" interpretation. We have too long ignored the fact that thoroughly pa-triotic Americans during the 1780's did not believe there was chaos and emphatically denied that their supposed rescuers were patriotic. The point is that there were patriots on both sides of the issue, but that they differed as to desirable goals for the new nation. At the same time, of course, there were men as narrow and selfish on both sides as their political enemies said they were.

If one approaches the history of the Confederation in this way, if one tries to see it as men who lived in it saw it and to write of it in their terms, one may achieve some semblance of reality. It is not the task of the historian to defend or attack the various groups of men whose conflicts were the essence of the period, but to set forth what they believed and what they tried to achieve. This can be illustrated no bet-ter than in the definition of terms. Throughout this book the words "federalist" and "nationalist" are used to describe two opposed bodies of opinion as to the best kind of central government for the United States. In so doing I have followed the members of the Convention of 1787. Those men believed that the Articles of Confederation provided for a "federal" government and the majority of them wanted to replace it with a "national" government. The fact that the men who wanted a national government called themselves Federalists after their work was submitted to the public is relevant to the history of politics after 1787, not to the discussion of the nature of the central government prior to and during the Convention of 1787.

Whatever the confusion since then, there was none at the time. Gouverneur Morris stated the issue concisely in the Convention when he "explained the distinction between a federal and a national, supreme government; the former being a mere compact resting on the good faith of the parties; the latter having a complete and compulsive operation." This explanation was in answer to those members of the Convention who wanted to know what Edmund Randolph meant in his opening speech when he spoke of the "defects of the federal system, the necessity of transforming it into a national efficient government. . . ."

The issue was not, as has been argued from time to time, whether there was a "nation" before the adoption of the Constitution of 1787. That was not the question at all during the 1780's. There was a new nation, as the men of the time agreed: they disagreed as to whether the new nation should have a federal or a national government. They did so from the outset of the Revolution and men have continued to do so ever since. The Constitution of 1787 was, as Madison said, both national and federal. And while this fact has led to innumerable conflicts of interpretation, it has also been a source of strength; for as one political group after another has gotten control of the central government it has been able to shape the constitution to its needs and desires. Thus with the single exception of the Civil War, peaceful change has always been possible, and as long as Americans are willing to accept the decisions of ballot boxes, legislatures, and courts, the Constitution will continue to change with changing needs and pressures. . . .

The foregoing pages indicate that the Confederation Period was one of great significance, but not of the kind that tradition has led us to believe. The "critical period" idea was the result of an uncritical acceptance of the arguments of the victorious party in a long political battle, of a failure to face the fact that partisan propaganda is not history but only historical evidence. What emerges instead is a much more complex and important story in which several themes are interwoven. It was a period of what we would call post-war demobilization, of sudden economic change, dislocation, and expansion, and of fundamental conflict over the nature of the Constitution of the United States. Each of these themes is so interwoven with the others that any separation is arbitrary but, taken separately or together, they are better keys to an understanding of the period than the traditional one.

At the end of the war Americans faced innumerable problems arising from it. What should be done with war veterans? Should the Loyalists return to their homes? What should be our relations with foreign friends and foes? Should commerce be free or should there be discrimination, and if so, against whom and for whose benefit? How would peace affect the economy? How should the war debt be paid? What kind of taxes should be levied to pay it, and who should pay them? When the war-boom collapsed, why did it? What should the state or central governments, or both, do about it? Should government encourage one form of economic enterprise over another or should it keep hands off? What about discontented groups: should government ignore them, cater to them, or forcibly suppress those who might revolt?

Such questions or others like them have probably been asked after every great war in history. They were asked, debated, and given various solutions during the 1780's. The significance of those debates and solutions has often been misunderstood. This is no better illustrated than in the case of the national debt during the 1780's which is usually discussed only in terms of depreciation and nonpayment of interest. Actually much more was involved than this. The debt was fantastically low compared with the national debt of today—about twelve dollars per capita as compared with seventeen hundred—and the nation had vast untouched natural resources with which to pay it. Multitudes of accounts had to be reduced to simple forms so that they could be paid, and this the Confederation government managed to do. But even more important that the economics of the national debt was its politics: should it be paid by the states or the central government? A fundamental assumption of every political leader was that the political agency which paid the debt would hold the balance of power in the new nation. Hence, the supporters of a strong central government insisted that the national debt must be paid by Congress while their opponents insisted that it should be divided among the states and paid by them. The latter group was on the way to victory by the end of the 1780's, for they were supported by clamoring creditors. The result was that one state after another assumed portions of the national debt owing to its citizens. Thus the traditional story is so out of context as to be virtually meaningless. This is true of other traditions as well. Most of the ports of the world were open, not closed, to American citizens. Reciprocity and equal treatment of all United States citizens was the rule in the tonnage and tariff acts of the states, not trade barriers.

To say that many of the pessimistic traditions are false is not to say that all Americans were peaceful and satisfied. The holders of national and state debts wanted bigger payments than they got. The merchants wanted more government aid than was given them. The farmers, hit by high taxes and rigid collection of both taxes and private debts, demanded relief in the form of lower taxes and government loans from state legislatures. Such demands kept state politics in an uproar during the 1780's. However, the often violent expression of such discontents in politics should not blind us to the fact that the period was one of extraordinary economic growth. Merchants owned more ships at the end of the 1780's than they had at the beginning of the Revolution, and they carried a greater share of American produce. By 1790 the export of agricultural produce was double what it had been before the war. American cities grew rapidly, with the result that housing was scarce and building booms produced a labor shortage. Tens of thousands of farmers spread outwards to the frontiers. There can be no question but that freedom from the British Empire resulted in a surge of activity in all phases of American life. Of course not all the problems of the new nation were solved by 1789—all have not yet been solved—but there is no evidence of stagnation and decay in the 1780's. Instead the story is one of a newly free people who seized upon every means to improve and enrich themselves in a nation which they believed had a golden destiny.

Politically the dominating fact of the Confederation Period was the struggle between two groups of leaders to shape the character of the state and central governments. The revolutionary constitutions of the states placed final power in the legislatures and made the executive and judicial branches subservient to them. The members of the colonial aristocracy who became Patriots, and new men who gained economic power during the Revolution deplored this fact, but they were unable to alter the state constitutions during the 1780's. Meanwhile they tried persistently to strengthen the central government. These men were the nationalists of the 1780's.

On the other hand the men who were the true federalists believed that the greatest gain of the Revolution was the independence of the several states and the creation of a central government subservient to them. The leaders of this group from the Declaration of Independence to the Convention of 1787 were Samuel Adams, Patrick Henry, Richard Henry Lee, George Clinton, James Warren, Samuel Bryan, George Bryan, Elbridge Gerry, George Mason and a host of less well known but no less important men in each of the states. Most of these men believed, as a result of their experience with Great Britain before 1776 and of their reading of history, that the states could be best governed without the intervention of a powerful central government. Some of them had programs of political and social reform; others had none at all. Some had a vision of democracy; others had no desire except to control their states for whatever satisfaction such control might offer. Some were in fact as narrow and provincial as their opponents said they were. However, the best of them agreed that the central government needed more power, but they wanted that power given so as not to alter the basic character of the Articles of Confederation. Here is where they were in fundamental disagreement with the nationalists who wanted to remove the central government from the control of the state legislatures.

The nationalist leaders from the Declaration of Independence to the Philadelphia convention were men like Robert Morris, John Jay, Gouverneur Morris, James Wilson, Alexander Hamilton, Henry Knox, James Duane, George Washington, James Madison, and many lesser men. Most of these men were by temperament or economic interest believers in executive and judicial rather than legislative control of state and central governments, in the rigorous collection of taxes, and, as creditors, in strict payment of public and private debts. They declared that national honor and prestige could be maintained only by a powerful central government. Naturally, not all men who used such language used it sincerely, for some were as selfish and greedy as their opponents said they were. The nationalists frankly disliked the political heritage of the Revolution. They deplored the fact there was no check upon the actions of majorities in state legislatures; that there was no central government to which minorities could appeal from the decisions of such majorities, as they had done before the Revolution.

There were men who veered from side to side, but their number is relatively small and their veering is of little significance as compared with the fact that from the outset of the Revolution there were two consistently opposed bodies of opinion as to the nature of the central government. There was, of course, a wide variation of belief among adherents of both points of view. There were extremists who wanted no central government at all and others who wanted to wipe out the states entirely. There were some who wanted a monarchy and others who would have welcomed dictatorship. But such extremists are not representative of the two great bodies of men whose conflict was the essence of the years both before and after 1789.

While the federalist leaders gradually moved to a position where they were willing to add specific powers to the Articles of Confederation, the nationalist leaders campaigned steadily for the kind of government they wanted. During the war they argued that it could not be won without creating a powerful central government. After the war they insisted that such a government was necessary to do justice to public creditors, solve the problems of post-war trade, bring about recovery from depression, and win the respect of the world for the new nation. Meanwhile their experience with majorities in state legislatures merely intensified their desire. They became desperate as state after state in 1785 and 1786 adopted some form of paper money that could be loaned on farm mortgages and be used to pay taxes, and in some cases private debts as well. When they were able to hold off such demands and farmers revolted, as in Massachusetts, they were thoroughly frightened.

They looked upon such events as evidence of the horrors of unchecked democracy and they said so in poetry, private letters, newspaper essays, and public speeches. The problem, they said, was to find some refuge from democracy. They worked hard to control state legislatures and they were often successful, but such control was uncertain at best, for annual elections meant a constant threat of overturn and the threat was realized repeatedly.

We may not call it democracy, but they did. Edmund Randolph put their case bluntly in his opening speech in the Convention of 1787. He said, "our chief danger arises from the democratic parts of our constitutions . . . None of the [state] constitutions have provided a sufficient check against the democracy. The feeble senate of Virginia is a phantom. Maryland has a more powerful senate, but the late distractions in that state, have discovered that it is not powerful enough. The check established in the constitutions of New York and Massachusetts is yet a stronger barrier against democracy, but they all seem insufficient." Outside the Convention General Knox was saying that a "mad democracy sweeps away every moral trait from the human character" and that the Convention would "clip the wings of a mad democracy." James Madison in the *Federalist Papers* argued that the new Constitution should be adopted because a "republican" form of government was better than a "democracy."

The debate was white-hot and was carried on with utter frankness. It was white-hot because for a moment in history self-government by majorities within particular political boundaries was possible. Those majorities could do what they wanted, and some of them knew what they wanted. Democracy was no vague ideal, but a concrete program: it meant definite things in politics, economics, and religion. Whatever side of the controversy we take, whether we think the majorities in state legislatures governed badly or well—the fact to face is that men of the 1780's believed that the issue was democracy as a way of government for the United States of those days.

They faced the issue squarely. They thought hard and realistically about the problems of government. They understood that society is complex and that the truth about it is multifold rather than simple. James Madison summed it up as well as it has ever been done. There are, he said, many passions and interests in society and these will ever clash for control of government and will ever interpret their own desires as the good of the whole. Men like Madison and John Adams believed, as Madison said, that the "great desideratum which has not yet been found for Republican governments seems to be some disinterested and dispassionate umpire in disputes between different passions and interests in the state." In the tenth number of *The Federalist,* after citing various origins of political parties, Madison said that "the most durable source of factions [parties] has been the various and unequal distribution of property. Those who hold and those who are without property have ever formed distinct interests in society. Those who are creditors and those whose are debtors, fall under a like discrimination. A landed interest, a manufacturing interest, a mercantile interest, a monied interest, with many lesser interests, grow up of necessity in civilized nations, and divide them into different classes, actuated by different sentiments and views. The regulation of these various and interfering interests forms the principal task of modern legislation, and involves the spirit of party and faction in the necessary and ordinary operations of the government."

The constitutional debate of the 1780's was thus carried on by men with a realistic appreciation of the social forces lying behind constitutional forms and theories, by men who were aware of the relationship between economic and political power. This realistic approach was lost sight of in the nineteenth century by romantic democrats who believed that once every man had the right to vote the problems of society could be solved. It was lost sight of too by those who came to believe in an oversimplified economic interpretation of history. In a sense they were as romantic as the democrats, for they assumed a rationality in the historic process that is not always supported by the evidence.

If the history of the Confederation has anything to offer us it is the realistic approach to politics so widely held by the political leaders of the time, however much they might differ as to forms of government and desirable goals for the new nation. Throughout the Confederation men with rival goals pushed two programs simultaneously. The federalists tried to strengthen the Articles of Confederation; the nationalists tried to create a new constitution by means of a convention, and thus avoid the method of change prescribed by the Articles of Confederation. The movement to strengthen the Articles failed on the verge of success; the movement to call a convention succeeded on the verge of failure. The failure of one movement and the success of the other, however we may interpret them, is one of the dramatic stories in the history of politics.

CHAPTER 15

THE FRAMING OF
THE CONSTITUTION

One of the ancient truisms of American history is that the United States Constitution is a "bundle of compromises." In the literature on the subject it is easy to find authorities who wish otherwise, but it is easier to find those who see in the compromises the strengths of the document and, ultimately, of the nation. John P. Roche clearly belongs to this latter group. His article, however, does not so much exalt the compromises as it shows why they were a necessary part of the process—a necessity that was based on the dual requirement of writing a document the delegates could agree on and of preparing a document the people would accept as the foundation of their government. A document written under these circumstances is bound to be vague in some places and open to conflicting interpretation in others. The United States Constitution is no exception.

In explaining the processes by which these compromises were effected, Professor Roche concentrates primarily on the Constitutional Convention and the framing of the document itself. His chief interest is the political process that resulted in the framing of the Constitution and its subsequent ratification. He examines the role of ideas in the deliberations of the Convention, the political realities of the 1780's that influenced the work of the Convention, and, more briefly, the meaning of the document that was ultimately ratified as the Constitution of the United States. In this task Professor Roche comes as close as any student of the constitutional period to presenting the Founding Fathers on their own terms.

A number of questions should be kept in mind as you read this essay. First, what was the primary motivation driving the framers of the Constitution? Does Professor Roche see the Founding Fathers essentially as political ideologues or as practical and realistic politicians? If the latter, were they aristocratic elitists or majoritarians who were keenly interested in the possible reactions of their constituencies? How does Professor Roche rate the achievement of the Founding Fathers? Finally, what does Professor Roche say about the nature of the Constitution itself and its meaning for Americans then and now?

The literature on the Constitutional Convention and its offspring is monumental. For an understanding of both, one would do well to begin with Arthur Holcombe's *Our More Perfect Union* (1950). An excellent collection of the contemporary accounts of the convention is Max Farrand, *The Records of the Federal Convention of 1787,** 4 Vols. (1911), although the casual student is more likely to finish and enjoy Farrand's *The Framing of the Constitution of the United States** (1913). Charles A. Beard's epochal study, *An Economic Interpretation of the Constitution of the United States** (1913, 1935, 1962), has been subjected to detailed and telling criticism in Robert E. Brown, *Charles Beard and the Constitution** (1953), and Forrest McDonald, *We the People: The Economic Origins of the Constitution** (1958). However, Professor Beard is not without his defenders; see particularly Jackson Turner Main, *The Anti-Federalists: Critics of the Constitution, 1781–1788** (1962). For a readable, accurate, and popularized version of the Constitutional Convention see Clinton Rossiter, *1787: The Grand Convention** (1966).

* Available in a paperback edition.

THE MAKING OF THE CONSTITUTION
JOHN P. ROCHE

Over the last century and a half, the work of the Constitutional Convention and the motives of the Founding Fathers have been analyzed under a number of different ideological auspices. To one generation of historians, the hand of God was moving in the assembly; under a later dispensation, the dialectic (at various levels of philosophical sophistication) replaced the Deity: "relationships of production" moved into the niche previously reserved for Love of Country. Thus in counterpoint to the Zeitgeist, the Framers have undergone miraculous metamorphoses: at one time acclaimed as liberals and bold social engineers, today they appear in the guise of sound Burkean conservatives, men who in our time would subscribe to *Fortune,* look to Walter Lippmann for political theory, and chuckle patronizingly at the antics of Barry Goldwater. The implicit assumption is that if James Madison were among us, he would be President of the Ford Foundation, while Alexander Hamilton would chair the Committee for Economic Development.

The "Fathers" have thus been admitted to our best circles; the revolutionary ferocity which confiscated all Tory property in reach and populated New Brunswick with outlaws has been converted by the "Miltown School" of American historians into a benign dedication to "consensus" and "prescriptive rights." The Daughters of the American Revolution have, through the ministrations of Professors Boorstin, Hartz, and Rossiter, at last found ancestors worthy of their descendants. It is not my purpose here to argue that the "Fathers" were, in fact, radical revolutionaries; that proposition has been brilliantly demonstrated by Robert R. Palmer in his *Age of the Democratic Revolution.* My concern is with the further position that not only were they revolutionaries, but also they were democrats. Indeed, in my view, there is one fundamental truth about the Founding Fathers that *every* generation of Zeitgeisters has done its best to obscure: they were first and foremost superb democratic politicians. I suspect that in a contemporary setting, James Madison would be Speaker of the House of Representatives and Hamilton would be the *eminence grise* dominating *(pace* Theodore Sorenson or Sherman Adams) the Executive Office of the President. They were, with their colleagues, *political men*—not metaphysicians, disembodied con-

SOURCE. John P. Roche, "The Founding Fathers: A Reform Caucus in Action," *The American Political Science Review,* Vol. LV, December 1961, pp. 799–816.

servatives or Agents of History—and as recent research into the nature of American politics in the 1780s confirms, they were committed (perhaps willy-nilly) to working within the democratic framework, within a universe of public approval. Charles Beard *and* the filiopietists to the contrary notwithstanding, the Philadelphia Convention was not a College of Cardinals or a council of Platonic guardians working within a manipulative, predemocratic framework; it was a *nationalist* reform caucus which had to operate with great delicacy and skill in a political cosmos full of enemies to achieve the one definitive goal—popular approbation.

Perhaps the time has come, to borrow Walton Hamilton's fine phrase, to raise the Framers from immortality to mortality, to give them credit for their magnificent demonstration of the art of democratic politics. The point must be reemphasized; they *made* history and did it within the limits of consensus. . . . What inspiration they got came from their collective experience as professional politicians in a democratic society. As John Dickinson put it to his fellow delegates on August 13, "Experience must be our guide. Reason may mislead us."

In this context, let us examine the problems they confronted and the solutions they evolved. The convention has been described picturesquely as a counter-revolutionary junta and the Constitution as a *coup d'etat,* but this has been accomplished by withdrawing the whole history of the movement for constitutional reform from its true context. No doubt the goals of the constitutional elite were "subversive" to the existing political order, but it is overlooked that their subversion could only have succeeded if the people of the United States endorsed it by regularized procedures. Indubitably they were "plotting" to establish a much stronger central government than existed under the Articles, but only in the sense in which one could argue equally well that John F. Kennedy was, from 1956 to 1960, "plotting" to become President. In short, on the fundamental *procedural* level, the Constitutionalists had to work according to the prevailing rules of the game. . . .

I

When the Constitutionalists went forth to subvert the Confederation, they utilized the mechanisms of political legitimacy. And the roadblocks which confronted them were formidable. At the same time, they were endowed with certain potent political assets. The history of the United States from 1786 to 1790 was largely one of a masterful employment of political expertise by the Constitutionalists as against bumbling, erratic behavior by the opponents of reform. Effectively, the Constitutionalists had to induce the states, by democratic techniques of coercion, to emasculate themselves. To be specific, if New York had refused to join the new Union, the project was doomed; yet before New York was safely in, the reluctant state legislature had *sua sponte* to take the following steps: (1) agree to send delegates to the Philadelphia Convention; (2) provide maintenance for these delegates (these were distinct stages: New Hampshire was early in naming delegates, but did not provide for their maintenance until July); (3) set up the special *ad hoc* convention to decide on ratification; and (4) concede to the decision of the *ad hoc* convention that New York should participate. New York admittedly was a tricky state, with a strong interest in a *status quo* which permitted her to exploit New Jersey and Connecticut, but the same legal hurdles exised in every state. And at the risk of becoming boring, it must be reiterated that the *only* weapon in the Constitutionalist arsenal was an effective mobilization of public opinion.

The group which undertook this struggle was an interesting amalgam of a few dedicated nationalists with the self-interested spokesmen of various parochial bailiwicks. The Georgians, for example, wanted a strong central authority to provide military protection for their huge, underpopulated state against the Creek Confederacy; Jerseymen and Connecticuters wanted to escape from economic bondage to New York; the Virginians hoped to establish a system which would give that great state its rightful place in the councils of the republic. The dominant figures in the politics of these states therefore cooperated in the call for the Convention. In other states, the thrust towards national reform was taken up by opposition groups who added the "national interest" to their weapons system; in Pennsylvania, for instance, the group fighting to revise the Constitution of 1776 came out four-square behind the Constitutionalists, and in New York, Hamilton and the Schuyler *ambiance* took the same tack against George Clinton. There was, of course, a large element of personality in the affair: there is reason to suspect that Patrick Henry's opposition to the Convention and the Constitution was founded on his conviction that Jefferson was behind both, and a close study of local politics elsewhere would surely reveal that others supported the Constitution for the simple (and politically quite sufficient) reason that the "wrong" people were against it.

To say this is not to suggest that the Constitution rested on a foundation of impure or base motives. It is rather to argue that in politics there are no immaculate conceptions, and that in the drive for a stronger general government, motives of all sorts played a part. Few men in the history of mankind have espoused a view of the "common good" or "public interest" that militated against their private status; even Plato with all his reverence for disembodied reason managed to put philosophers on top of the pile. Thus it is not surprising that a number of diversified private interests joined to push the nationalist public interest; what would have been surprising was the absence of such a pragmatic united front. . . .

As Stanley Elkins and Eric McKitrick have suggested in a perceptive essay, what distinguished the leaders of the Constitutionalist caucus from their enemies was a "Continental" approach to political, economic and military issues. To the extent that they shared an institutional base of operations, it was the Continental Congress (thirty-nine of the delegates to the Federal Convention had served in Congress), and this was hardly a locale which inspired respect for the state governments. Robert de Jouvenal observed French politics half a century ago and noted that a revolutionary Deputy had more in common with a non-revolutionary Deputy than he had with a revolutionary non-Deputy; similarly one can surmise that membership in the Congress under the Articles of Confederation worked to establish a continental frame of reference, that a Congressman from Pennsylvania and one from South Carolina would share a universe of discourse which provided them with a conceptual common denominator *vis à vis* their respective state legislatures. This was particularly true with respect to external affairs: the average state legislator was probably about as concerned with foreign policy then as he is today, but Congressmen were constantly forced to take the broad view of American prestige, were compelled to listen to the reports of Secretary John Jay and to the dispatches and pleas from their frustrated envoys in Britain, France and Spain. From considerations such as these, a "Continental" ideology developed which seems to have demanded a revision of our domestic institutions primarily on the ground that only by invigorating our general government could we assume our rightful place in the international arena. Indeed, an argument with great force—particularly since Washington was its incarnation—urged that our very survival in the Hobbesian jungle of world politics depended upon a reordering and strengthening of our national sovereignty.

Note that I am not endorsing the "Critical Period" thesis; on the contrary, Merrill Jensen seems to me quite sound in his view that for most Americans, engaged as they were in self-sustaining agriculture, the "Critical Period" was not particularly critical. In fact, the great achievement of the Constitutionalists was their ultimate success in convincing the elected representatives of a majority of the white male population that change was imperative. A small group of political leaders with a Continental vision and essentially a consciousness of the United States' *international* impotence, provided the matrix of the movement. To their standard other leaders rallied with their own parallel ambitions. Their great assets were (1) the presence in their caucus of the one authentic American "father figure," George Washington, whose prestige was enormous; (2) the energy and talent of their leadership (in which one must include the towering intellectuals of the time, John Adams and Thomas Jefferson, despite their absence abroad), and their communications "network," which was far superior to anything on the opposition side; (3) the preemptive skill which made "their" issue The Issue and kept the locally oriented opposition permanently on the defensive; and (4) the subjective consideration that these men were spokesmen of a new and compelling credo: *American* nationalism, that ill-defined but nonetheless potent sense of collective purpose that emerged from the American Revolution.

Despite great institutional handicaps, the Constitutionalists managed in the mid-1780s to mount an offensive which gained momentum as years went by. Their greatest problem was lethargy, and paradoxically, the number of barriers in their path may have proved an advantage in the long run. Beginning with the initial battle to get the Constitutional Convention called and delegates appointed, they could never relax, never let up the pressure. In practical terms, this meant that the local "organizations" created by the Constitutionalists were perpetually in movement building up their cadres for the next fight. (The word organization has to be used with great caution: a political organization in the United States—as in contemporary England—generally consisted of a magnate and his following, or a coalition of magnates. This did not necessarily mean that it was "undemocratic" or "aristocratic," in the Aristotelian sense of the word: while a few magnates such as the Livingstons could draft their followings, most exercised their leadership without coercion on the basis of popular endorsement. . . .)

The Constitutionalists got the jump on the "opposition" (a collective noun: oppositions would be more correct) at the outset with the demand for a Convention. Their opponents were caught in an old political trap: they were not being asked to approve any specific program of reform, but only to endorse a meeting to discuss and recommend needed reforms. If they took a hard line at the first stage, they were put in the position of glorifying the *status quo* and of denying the need for *any* changes. Moreover, the Constitutionalists could go to the people with a persuasive argument for "fair play" —"How can you condemn reform before you know precisely what is involved?" Since the state legislatures obviously would have the final say on any proposals that might emerge from the Convention, the Constitutionalists were merely reasonable men asking for a chance. Besides, since they did not make any concrete proposals at that stage, they were in a position to capitalize on every sort of generalized discontent with the Confederation.

Perhaps because of their poor intelligence system, perhaps because of over-confidence generated by the failure of all previous efforts to alter the Articles, the opposition awoke too late to the dangers that confronted them in 1787. Not only did the Constitutionalists manage to get every state but Rhode Island . . . to appoint delegates to Philadelphia, but when the results were in, it appeared that they dominated the delegations. Given the apathy of the opposition, this was a natural phenomenon: in an ideologically non-

polarized political atmosphere those who get appointed to a special committee are likely to be the men who supported the movement for its creation.
Even George Clinton, who seems to have been the first opposition leader to
awake to the possibility of trouble, could not prevent the New York legislature from appointing Alexander Hamilton—though he did have the foresight to send two of his henchmen to dominate the delegation. Incidentally,
much has been made of the fact that the delegates to Philadelphia were not
elected by the people; some have adduced this fact as evidence of the "undemocratic" character of the gathering. But put in the context of the time,
this argument is wholly specious: the central goverment under the Articles
was considered a creature of the component states and in all the states but
Rhode Island, Connecticut and New Hampshire, members of the national
Congress were chosen by the state legislatures. . . .

II

With delegations safely named, the focus shifted to Philadelphia. While
waiting for a quorum to assemble, James Madison got busy and drafted the
so-called Randolph or Virginia Plan with the aid of the Virginia delegation.
This was a political master-stroke. Its consequence was that once business
got underway, the framework of discussion was established on Madison's
terms. There was no interminable argument over agenda; instead the delegates took the Virginia Resolutions—"just for purposes of discussion"—as
their point of departure. And along with Madison's proposals, many of
which were buried in the course of the summer, went his major premise: a
new start on a Constitution rather than piecemeal amendment. This was not
necessarily revolutionary—a little exegesis could demonstrate that a new
Constitution might be formulated as "amendments" to the Articles of Confederation—but Madison's proposal that this "lump sum" amendment go
into effect after approval by nine states (the Articles required unanimous
state approval for any amendment) was thoroughly subversive.

Standard treatments of the Convention divide the delegates into "nationalists" and "states'-righters" with various improvised shadings ("moderate
nationalists," etc.), but these are *a posteriori* categories which obfuscate
more than they clarify. What is striking to one who analyzes the Convention
as a case-study in democratic politics is the lack of clear-cut ideological divisions in the Convention. Indeed, I submit that the evidence—Madison's
Notes, the correspondence of the delegates, and debates on ratification—
indicates that this was a remarkably homogeneous body on the ideological
level. Yates and Lansing, Clinton's two chaperones for Hamilton, left in disgust on July 10. (Is there anything more tedious than sitting through endless
disputes on matters one deems fundamentally misconceived? It takes an iron

will to spend a hot summer as an ideological *agent provocateur.*) Luther Martin, Maryland's bibulous narcissist, left on September 4 in a huff when he discovered that others did not share his self-esteem; others went home for personal reasons. But the hard core of delegates accepted a grinding regimen throughout the attrition of a Philadelphia summer precisely because they shared the Constitutionalist goal.

Basic differences of opinion emerged, of course, but these were not ideological; they were *structural.* If the so-called "states'-rights" group had not accepted the fundamental purposes of the Convention, they could simply have pulled out and by doing so have aborted the whole enterprise. Instead of bolting, they returned day after day to argue and to compromise. An interesting symbol of this basic homogeneity was the initial agreement on secrecy: these professional politicians did not want to become prisoners of publicity; they wanted to retain that freedom of maneuver which is only possible when men are not forced to take public stands in the preliminary stages of negotiation. There was no legal means of binding the tongues of the delegates: at any stage in the game a delegate with basic principled objections to the emerging project could have taken the stump (as Luther Martin did after his exit) and denounced the convention to the skies. Yet Madison did not even inform Thomas Jefferson in Paris of the course of the deliberations and available correspondence indicates that the delegates generally observed the injunction. Secrecy is certainly uncharacteristic of any assembly marked by strong ideological polarization. . . .

Commentators on the Constitution who have read *The Federalist* in lieu of reading the actual debates have credited the Fathers with the invention of a sublime concept called "Federalism." Unfortunately *The Federalist* is probative evidence for only one proposition: that Hamilton and Madison were inspired propagandists with a genius for retrospective symmetry. Federalism, as the theory is generally defined, was an improvisation which was later promoted into a political theory. Experts on "federalism" should take to heart the advice of David Hume, who warned in his *Of the Rise and Progress of the Arts and Sciences* that " . . . there is no subject in which we must proceed with more caution than in [history], lest we assign causes which never existed and reduce what is merely contingent to stable and universal principles." In any event, the final balance in the Constitution between the states and the nation must have come as a great disappointment to Madison, while Hamilton's unitary views are too well known to need elucidation.

It is indeed astonishing how those who have glibly designated James Madison the "father" of Federalism have overlooked the solid body of fact which indicates that he shared Hamilton's quest for a unitary central government. To be specific, they have avoided examining the clear import of the Madison-Virginia Plan, and have disregarded Madison's dogged inch-by-inch retreat from the bastions of centralization. The Virginia Plan envisioned a unitary national government effectively freed from and dominant over the states. The lower house of the national legislature was to be elected directly by the people of the states with membership proportional to population. The upper house was to be selected by the lower and the two chambers would elect the executive and choose the judges. The national government would be thus cut completely loose from the states.

The structure of the general government was freed from state control in a truly radical fashion, but the scope of the authority of the national sovereign as Madison initially formulated it was breathtaking. . . . The national legislature was to be empowered to disallow the acts of state legislatures, and the central government was vested, in addition to the powers of the nation under the Articles of Confederation, with plenary authority wherever ". . . the separate States are incompetent or in which the harmony of the United States may be interrupted by the exercise of individual legislation." Finally, just to lock the door against state intrusion, the national Congress was to be given the power to use military force on recalcitrant states. This was Madison's "model" of an ideal national government, though it later received little publicity in *The Federalist.*

The interesting thing was the reaction of the Convention to this militant program for a strong autonomous central government. Some delegates were startled, some obviously leery of so comprehensive a project of reform, but nobody set off any fireworks and nobody walked out. Moreover, in the two weeks that followed, the Virginia Plan received substantial endorsement *en principe*; the initial temper of the gathering can be deduced from the approval "without debate or dissent," on May 31, of the Sixth Resolution which granted Congress the authority to disallow state legislation " . . . contravening *in its opinion* the Articles of Union." Indeed, an amendment was included to bar states from contravening national treaties.

The Virginia Plan may therefore be considered, in ideological terms, as the delegates' Utopia, but as the discussions continued and became more specific, many of those present began to have second thoughts. After all, they were not residents of Utopia or guardians in Plato's Republic who could simply impose a philosophical ideal on subordinate strata of the population. They were practical politicians in a democratic society, and no matter what their private dreams might be, they had to take home an acceptable package and defend it—and their own political futures—against predictable attack. On June 14 the breaking point between dream and reality took place. Apparently realizing that under the Virginia Plan, Massachusetts, Virginia and Pennsylvania could virtually dominate the national goverment —and probably appreciating that to sell this program to "the folks back home" would be impossible—the delegates from the small states dug in their heels and demanded time for a consideration of alternatives. . . .

The bare outline of the *Journal* entry for Tuesday, June 14, is suggestive to anyone with extensive experience in deliberative bodies. "It was moved by Mr. Patterson [*sic,* Paterson's name was one of those consistently misspelled by Madison and everybody else] seconded by Mr. Randolph that the further consideration of the report from the Committee of the whole House [endorsing the Virginia Plan] be postponed til tomorrow, and before the question for postponement was taken. It was moved by Mr. Randolph seconded by Mr. Patterson that the House adjourn." The House adjourned by obvious prearrangement of the two principals: since the preceding Saturday when Brearley and Paterson of New Jersey had announced their fundamental discontent with the representational features of the Virginia Plan, the informal pressure had certainly been building up to slow down the streamroller. Doubtless there were extended arguments at the Indian Queen between Madison and Paterson, the latter insisting that events were moving rapidly towards a probably disastrous conclusion, towards a political suicide pact. Now the process of accommodation was put into action smoothly— and wisely, given the character and strength of the doubters. Madison had the votes, but this was one of those situations where the enforcement of mechanical majoritarianism could easily have destroyed the objectives of the majority: the Constitutionalists were in quest of a qualitative as well as a quantitative consensus. . . .

III

According to the standard script, at this point the "states'-rights" group intervened in force behind the New Jersey Plan, which has been characteristically portrayed as a reversion to the *status quo* under the Articles of Confederation with but minor modifications. A careful examination of the evidence indicates that only in a marginal sense is this an accurate description. It is true that the New Jersey Plan put the states back into the institutional picture, but one could argue that to do so was a recognition of political reality rather than an affirmation of states'-rights. A serious case can be made that the advocates of the New Jersey Plan, far from being ideological addicts of states'-rights, intended to substitute for the Virginia Plan a system which would both retain strong national power and have a chance of adoption in the states. The leading spokesman for the project asserted quite clearly that his views were based more on counsels of expediency than on principle; said Paterson on June 16: "I came here not to speak my own sentiments, but the sentiments of those who sent me. Our object is not such a

Governmt. as may be best in itself, but such a one as our Constituents have authorized us to prepare, and as they will approve. . . ."

This was a defense of political acumen, not of states'-rights. In fact, Paterson's notes of his speech can easily be construed as an argument for attaining the substantive objectives of the Virginia Plan by a sound political route, *i.e.,* pouring the new wine in the old bottles. . . . In other words, the advocates of the New Jersey Plan concentrated their fire on what they held to be the *political liabilities* of the Virginia Plan—which were matters of institutional structure—rather than on the proposed scope of national authority. Indeed, the Supremacy Clause of the Constitution first saw the light of day in Paterson's Sixth Resolution; the New Jersey Plan contemplated the use of military force to secure compliance with national law; and finally Paterson made clear his view that under either the Virginia or the New Jersey systems, the general government would " . . . act on individuals and not on states." From the states'-rights viewpoint, this was heresy: the fundament of that doctrine was the proposition that any central government had as its constituents the states, not the people, and could only reach the people through the agency of the state government.

Paterson then reopened the agenda of the Convention, but he did so within a distinctly nationalist framework. Paterson's position was one of favoring a strong central government in principle, but opposing one which in fact *put the big states in the saddle.* (The Virginia Plan, for all its abstract merits, did very well by Virginia.) . . . This makes it sound as though Paterson was prepared to accept a strong unified central government along the lines of the Virginia Plan if the existing states were eliminated. He may have gotten the idea from his New Jersey colleague Judge David Brearley, who on June 9 had commented that the only remedy to the dilemma over representation was ". . . that a map of the U.S. be spread out, that all the existing boundaries be erased, and that a new partition of the whole be made into 13 equal parts." According to Yates, Brearley added at this point, ". . . then a government on the present [Virginia Plan] system will be just."

This proposition was never pushed—it was patently unrealistic—but one can appreciate its purpose: it would have separated the men from the boys in the large-state delegations. How attached would the Virginians have been to their reform principles if Virginia were to disappear as a component geographical unit (the largest) for representational purpose? Up to this point, the Virginians had been in the happy position of supporting high ideals with that inner confidence born of knowledge that the "public interest" they endorsed would nourish their private interest. Worse, they had shown little willingness to compromise. Now the delegates from the small states announced that they were unprepared to be offered up as sacrificial victims to a "national interest" which reflected Virginia's parochial ambition. . . .

Paterson spoke on Saturday, and one can surmise that over the weekend there was a good deal of consultation, argument, and caucusing among the delegates. One member at least prepared a full length address: on Monday Alexander Hamilton, previously mute, rose and delivered a six-hour oration. It was a remarkably apolitical speech; the gist of his position was that *both* the Virginia and New Jersey Plans were inadequately centralist, and he detailed a reform program which was reminiscent of the Protectorate under the Cromwellian *Instrument of Government* of 1653. It has been suggested that Hamilton did this in the best political tradition to emphasize the moderate character of the Virginia Plan, to give the cautious delegates something *really* to worry about, but this interpretation seems somehow too clever. Particularly since the sentiments Hamilton expressed happened to be completely consistent with those he privately—and sometimes publicly—expressed throughout his life. He wanted, to take a striking phrase from a letter to George Washington, a "strong well mounted government"; in essence, the Hamilton Plan contemplated an elected life monarch, virtually free of public control, on the Hobbesian ground that only in this fashion could strength and stability be achieved. The other alternatives, he argued, would put policy-making at the mercy of the passions of the mob; only if the sovereign was beyond the reach of selfish influence would it be possible to have government in the interests of the whole community.

From all accounts, this was a masterful and compelling speech, but (aside from furnishing John Lansing and Luther Martin with ammunition for later use against the Constitution) it made little impact. Hamilton was simply transmitting on a different wave-length from the rest of the delegates; the latter adjourned after his great effort, admired his rhetoric, and then returned to business. It was rather as if they had taken a day off to attend the opera. Hamilton, never a particularly patient man or much of a negotiator, stayed for another ten days and then left, in considerable disgust, for New York. Although he came back to Philadelphia sporadically and attended the last two weeks of the Convention, Hamilton played no part in the laborious task of hammering out the Constitution. His day came later when he led the New York Constitutionalists into the savage imbroglio over ratification—an arena in which his unmatched talent for dirty political infighting may well have won the day. For instance, in the New York Ratifying Convention, Lansing threw back into Hamilton's teeth the sentiments the latter had expressed in his June 18 oration in the Convention. However, having since retreated to the fine defensive positions immortalized in *The Federalist,* the Colonel flatly denied that he had ever been an enemy of the states, or had believed that conflict between states and nation was inexorable! As Madison's authoritative *Notes* did not appear until 1840, and there had been no press coverage, there was no way to verify his assertions, so in the words of the reporter, ". . . a warm personal altercation between [Lansing and Hamilton] engrossed the remainder of the day [June 28, 1788]."

IV

On Tuesday morning, June 19, the vacation was over. James Madison led off with a long, carefully reasoned speech analyzing the New Jersey Plan which, while intellectually vigorous in its criticisms, was quite conciliatory in mood. "The great difficulty," he observed, "lies in the affair of Representation; and if this could be adjusted, all others would be surmountable." (As events were to demonstrate, this diagnosis was correct.) When he finished, a vote was taken on whether to continue with the Virginia Plan as the nucleus for a new constitution: seven states voted "Yes"; New York, New Jersey, and Delaware voted "No"; and Maryland, whose position often depended on which delegates happened to be on the floor, divided. Paterson, it seems, lost decisively; yet in a fundamental sense he and his allies had achieved their purpose: from that day onward, it could never be forgotten that the state governments loomed ominously in the background and that no verbal incantations could exorcise their power. Moreover, nobody bolted the convention: Paterson and his colleagues took their defeat in stride and set to work to modify the Virginia Plan, particularly with respect to its provisions on representation in the national legislature. Indeed, they won an immediate rhetorical bonus; when Oliver Ellsworth of Connecticut rose to move that the word "national" be expunged from the Third Virginia Resolution ("Resolved that a *national* Government ought to be established consisting of a *supreme* Legislative, Executive and Judiciary"), Randolph agreed and the motion passed unanimously. The process of compromise had begun.

For the next two weeks, the delegates circled around the problem of legislative representation. The Connecticut delegation appears to have evolved a possible compromise quite early in the debates, but the Virginians and particularly Madison (unaware that he would later be acclaimed as the prophet of "federalism") fought obdurately against providing for equal representation of states in the second chamber. There was a good deal of acrimony and at one point Benjamin Franklin—of all people—proposed the institution of a daily prayer; practical politicians in the gathering, however, were meditating more on the merits of a good committee than on the utility of Divine intervention. On July 2, the ice began to break when through a number of fortuitous events—and one that seems deliberate—the majority against equality of representation was converted into a dead tie. The Convention had reached the stage where it was "ripe" for a solution (presumably all the therapeutic speeches had been made), and the South Carolinians proposed a committee. Madison and James Wilson wanted none of it, but with only Pennsylvania dissenting, the body voted to establish a working party on the problem of representation.

The members of this committee, one from each state, were elected by the delegates—and a very interesting committee it was. Despite the fact that the Virginia Plan had held majority support up to that date, neither Madison nor Randolph was selected (Mason was the Virginian) and Baldwin of Georgia, whose shift in position had resulted in the tie, was chosen. From the composition, it was clear that this was not to be a "fighting" committee: the emphasis in membership was on what might be described as "second-level political entrepreneurs." On the basis of the discussions up to that time, only Luther Martin of Maryland could be described as a "bitter-ender." Admittedly, some divination enters into this sort of analysis, but one does get a sense of the mood of the delegates from these choices—including the interesting selection of Benjamin Franklin, despite his age and intellectual wobbliness, over the brilliant and incisive Wilson or the sharp, polemical Gouverneur Morris, to represent Pennsylvania. His passion for conciliation was more valuable at this juncture than Wilson's logical genius, or Morris' acerbic wit.

There is a common rumor that the Framers divided their time between philosophical discussions of government and reading the classics in political theory. Perhaps this is as good a time as any to note that their concerns were highly practical, that they spent little time canvassing abstractions. A number of them had some acquaintance with the history of political theory . . . , and it was a poor rhetorician indeed who could not cite Locke, Montesquieu, or Harrington *in support* of a desired goal. Yet up to this point in the deliberations, no one had expounded a defense of states'-rights or the "separation of powers" on anything resembling a theoretical basis. It should be reiterated that the Madison model had no room either for the states or for the "separation of powers": effectively *all* governmental power was vested in the national legislature. The merits of Montesquieu did not turn up until *The Federalist;* and although a perverse argument could be made that Madison's ideal was truly in the tradition of John Locke's *Second Treatise of Government,* the Locke whom the American rebels treated as an honorary president was a pluralistic defender of vested rights, not of parliamentary supremacy.

It would be tedious to continue a blow-by-blow analysis of the work of the delegates; the critical fight was over representation of the states and once the Connecticut Compromise was adopted on July 17, the Convention was over the hump. Madison, James Wilson, and Gouverneur Morris of New York (who was there representing Pennsylvania!) fought the compromise all the way in a last-ditch effort to get a unitary state with parliamentary supremacy. But their allies deserted them and they demonstrated after their defeat the essentially opportunist character of their objections—using "opportunist" here in a non-pejorative sense, to indicate a willingness to swallow their objections and get on with the business. Moreover, once the compromise had carried (by five states to four, with one state divided), its advocates threw themselves vigorously into the job of strengthening the general government's substantive powers—as might have been predicted, indeed, from Paterson's early statements. It nourishes an increased respect for Madison's devotion to the art of politics, to realize that this dogged fighter could sit down six months later and prepare essays for *The Federalist* in contradiction to his basic convictions about the true course the Convention should have taken.

V

Two tricky issues will serve to illustrate the later process of accommodation. The first was the institutional position of the Executive. Madison argued for an executive chosen by the National Legislature and on May 29 this had been adopted with a provision that after his seven-year term was concluded, the chief magistrate should not be eligible for reelection. In late July this was reopened and for a week the matter was argued from several different points of view. A good deal of desultory speech-making ensued, but the gist of the problem was the opposition from two sources to election by the legislature. One group felt that the states should have a hand in the process; another small but influential circle urged direct election by the people. There were a number of proposals: election by the people, election by state governors, by electors chosen by state legislatures, by the National Legislature (James Wilson, perhaps ironically, proposed at one point that an Electoral College be chosen by lot from the National Legislature!), and there was some resemblance to three-dimensional chess in the dispute because of the presence of two other variables, length of tenure and reeligibility. Finally, after opening, reopening, and re-reopening the debate, the thorny problem was consigned to a committee for resolution.

The Brearley Committee on Postponed Matters was a superb aggregation of talent and its compromise on the Executive was a masterpiece of political improvisation. (The Electoral College, its creation, however, had little in its favor as an *institution*—as the delegates well appreciated.) The point of departure for all discussion about the presidency in the Convention was that in immediate terms, the problem was non-existent; in other words, everybody present knew that under any system devised, George Washington would be President. Thus they were dealing in the future tense and to a body of working politicians the merits of the Brearley proposal were obvious: everybody got a piece of cake. . . . First, the state legislatures had the right to determine the mode of selection of the electors; second, the small states received a bonus in the Electoral College in the form of a guaranteed minimum of three votes while the big states got acceptance of the principle of proportional power; third, if the state legislatures agreed (as six did in the first presidential election), the people could be involved directly in the choice of electors; and finally, if no candidate received a majority in the College, the right of decision passed to the National Legislature with each state exercising equal strength. (In the Brearley recommendation, the election went to the Senate, but a motion from the floor substituted the House; this was accepted on the ground that the Senate already had enough authority over the executive in its treaty and appointment powers.)

This compromise was almost too good to be true, and the Framers snapped it up with little debate or controversy. No one seemed to think well of the College as an *institution;* indeed, what evidence there is suggests that there was an assumption that once Washington had finished his tenure as President, the electors would cease to produce majorities and the chief executive would usually be chosen in the House. George Mason observed casually that the selection would be made in the House nineteen times in twenty and no one seriously disputed this point. The vital aspect of the Electoral College was that it got the Convention over the hurdle and protected everybody's interests. The future was left to cope with the problem of what to do with this Rube Goldbert mechanism.

In short, the Framers did not in their wisdom endow the United States with a College of Cardinals—the Electoral College was neither an exercise in applied Platonism nor an experiment in indirect government based on elitist distrust of the masses. It was merely a jerry-rigged improvisation which has subsequently been endowed with a high theoretical content. When an elector from Oklahoma in 1960 refused to cast his vote for Nixon (naming Byrd and Goldwater instead) on the ground that the Founding Fathers intended him to exercise his great independent wisdom, he was indulging in historical fantasy. If one were to indulge in counter-fantasy, he would be tempted to suggest that the Fathers would be startled to find the College still in operation—and perhaps even dismayed at their descendants' lack of judgment or inventiveness.

The second issue on which some substantial practical bargaining took place was slavery. The morality of slavery was, by design, not at issue; but in its other concrete aspects, slavery colored the arguments over taxation, commerce, and representation. The "Three-Fifths Compromise," that three-fifths of the slaves would be counted both for representation and for purposes of direct taxation (which was drawn from the past—it was a formula of Madison's utilized by Congress in 1783 to establish the basis of state contributions to the Confederation treasury) had allayed some Northern fears about Southern over-representation (no one then foresaw the trivial role that direct taxation would play in later federal financial policy), but doubts still remained. The Southerners, on the other hand, were afraid that Congressional control over commerce would lead to the exclusion of slaves or to their excessive taxation as imports. Moreover, the Southerners were disturbed over "navigation acts," *i.e.,* tariffs, or special legislation providing, for example, that exports be carried only in American ships; as a section depending upon exports, they wanted protection from the potential voracity of their commercial brethren of the Eastern states. To achieve this end, Mason and others urged that the Constitution include a proviso that navigation and commercial laws should require a two-thirds vote in Congress.

These problems came to a head in late August and, as usual, were handed to a committee in the hope that, in Gouverneur Morris' words, ". . . these things may form a bargain among the Northern and Southern states." The Committee reported its measures of reconciliation on August 25, and on August 29 the package was wrapped up and delivered. . . .

On the floor of the Convention there was a virtual love-feast on this happy occasion. Charles Pinckney of South Carolina attempted to overturn the committee's decision, when the compromise was reported to the Convention, by insisting that the South needed protection from the imperialism of the Northern states. But his Southern colleagues were not prepared to rock the boat. . . . Many Southern leaders were later—in the wake of the "Tariff of Abominations"—to rue this day of reconciliation; Calhoun's *Disquisition on Government* was little more than an extension of the argument in the Convention against permitting a congressional majority to enact navigation acts.

VI

Drawing on their vast collective political experience, utilizing every weapon in the politician's arsenal, looking constantly over their shoulders at their constituents, the delegates put together a Constitution. It was a make-shift affair; some sticky issues (for example, the qualification of voters) they ducked entirely; others they mastered with that ancient instrument of political sagacity, studied ambiguity (for example, citizenship), and some they just overlooked. In this last category, I suspect, fell the matter of the power of the federal courts to determine the constitutionality of acts of Congress. When the judicial article was formulated (Article III of the Constitution), deliberations were still in the stage where the legislature was endowed with broad power under the Randolph formulation, authority which by its own terms was scarcely amenable to judicial review. In essence, courts could hardly determine when ". . . the separate States are incompetent or . . . the harmony of the United States may be interrupted"; the National Legislature, as critics pointed out, was free to define its own jurisdiction. Later the definition of legislative authority was changed into the form we know, a series of stipulated powers, *but the delegates never seriously reexamined the jurisdiction of the judiciary under this new limited formulation.* All arguments on the intention of the Framers in this matter are thus deductive and *a posteriori,* though some obviously make more sense than others.

The Framers were busy and distinguished men, anxious to get back to their families, their positions, and their constituents, not members of the French Academy devoting a lifetime to a dictionary. They were trying to do an important job, and do it in such a fashion that their handiwork would be acceptable to very diverse constituencies. No one was rhapsodic about the final document, but it was a beginning, a move in the right direction, and one they had reason to believe the people would endorse. In addition, since they had modified the impossible amendment provisions of the Articles (the requirement of unanimity which could always be frustrated by "Rogues Island") to one demanding approval by only three-quarters of the states, they seemed confident that gaps in the fabric which experience would reveal could be rewoven without undue difficulty.

So with a neat phrase introduced by Benjamin Franklin (but devised by Gouverneur Morris) which made their decision sound unanimous, and an inspired benediction by the Old Doctor urging doubters to doubt their own infallibility, the Constitution was accepted and signed. Curiously, Edmund Randolph, who had played so vital a role throughout, refused to sign, as did his fellow Virginian George Mason and Elbridge Gerry of Massachusetts. Randolph's behavior was eccentric, to say the least—his excuses for refusing his signature have a factitious ring even at this late date; the best explanation seems to be that he was afraid that the Constitution would prove to be a liability in Virginia politics, where Patrick Henry was burning up the countryside with impassioned denunciations. Presumably, Randolph wanted to check the temper of the populace before he risked his reputation, and perhaps his job, in a fight with both Henry and Richard Henry Lee. Events lend some justification to this speculation: after much temporizing and use of the conditional subjunctive tense, Randolph endorsed ratification in Virginia and ended up getting the best of both worlds.

Madison, despite his reservations about the Constitution, was the campaign manager in ratification. His first task was to get the Congress in New York to light its own funeral pyre by approving the "amendments" to the Articles and sending them on to the state legislatures. Above all, momentum had to be maintained. The anti-Constitutionalists, now thoroughly alarmed and no novices in politics, realized that their best tactic was attrition rather than direct opposition. Thus they settled on a position expressing qualified approval but calling for a second Convention to remedy various defects (the one with the most demagogic appeal was the lack of a Bill of Rights). Madison knew that to accede to this demand would be equivalent to losing the battle, nor would he agree to conditional approval (despite wavering even by Hamilton). This was an all-or-nothing proposition: national salvation or national impotence with no intermediate positions possible. Unable to get congressional approval, he settled for second best: a unanimous resolution of Congress transmitting the Constitution to the states for whatever action they saw fit to take. The opponents then moved from New York and the Congress, where they had attempted to attach amendments and conditions, to the states for the final battle.

At first the campaign for ratification went beautifully: within eight months after the delegates set their names to the document, eight states had ratified. Only in Massachusetts had the result been close (187–168). Theoretically, a ratification by one more state convention would set the new government in motion, but in fact until Virginia and New York acceded to the new Union, the latter was a fiction. New Hampshire was the next to ratify; Rhode Island was involved in its characteristic political convulsions (the Legislature there sent the Constitution out to the towns for decision by popular vote and it got lost among a series of local issues); North Carolina's convention did not meet until July and then postponed a final decision. This is hardly the place for an extensive analysis of the conventions of New York and Virginia. Suffice it to say that the Constitutionalists clearly outmaneuvered their opponents, forced them into impossible political positions, and won both states narrowly. The Virginia Convention could serve as a classic study in effective floor management: Patrick Henry had to be contained, and a reading of the debates discloses a standard two-stage technique. Henry would give a four- or five-hour speech denouncing some section of the Constitution on every conceivable ground (the federal district, he averred at one point, would become a haven for convicts escaping from state authority!); when Henry subsided, "Mr. Lee of Westmoreland" would rise and literally poleaxe him with sardonic invective (when Henry complained about the militia power, "Lighthorse Harry" really punched below the belt: observing that while the former Governor had been sitting in Richmond during the Revolution, *he* had been out in the trenches with the troops and thus felt better qualified to discuss military affairs). Then the gentlemanly Constitutionalists (Madison, Pendleton and Marshall) would pick up the matters at issue and examine them in the light of reason.

Indeed, modern Americans who tend to think of James Madison as a rather dessicated character should spend some time with this transcript. Probably Madison put on his most spectacular demonstration of nimble rhetoric in what might be called "The Battle of the Absent Authorities." Patrick Henry in the course of one of his harangues alleged that Jefferson was known to be opposed to Virginia's approving the Constitution. This was clever: Henry hated Jefferson, but was prepared to use any weapon that came to hand. Madison's riposte was superb: First, he said that with all due respect to the great reputation of Jefferson, he was not in the country and therefore could not formulate an adequate judgment; second, no one should utilize the reputation of an out-sider—the Virginia Convention was there to think for itself; third, if there were to be recourse to outsiders, the opinions of George Washington should certainly be taken into consideration; and finally, he knew from privileged personal communications from Jefferson that in fact the latter *strongly favored* the Constitution. To devise an assault route into this rhetorical fortress was literally impossible.

VII

The fight was over; all that remained now was to establish the new frame of government in the spirit of its framers. And who were better qualified for this task than the Framers themselves? Thus victory for the Constitution meant simultaneous victory for the Constitutionalists; the anti-Constitutionalists either capitulated or vanished into limbo—soon Patrick Henry would be offered a seat on the Supreme Court and Luther Martin would be known as the Federalist "bull-dog." And irony of ironies, Alexander Hamilton and James Madison would shortly accumulate a reputation as the formulators of what is often alleged to be our political theory, the concept of "federalism." Also, on the other side of the ledger, the arguments would soon appear over what the Framers "really meant"; while these disputes have assumed the proportions of a big scholarly business in the last century, they began almost before the ink on the Constitution was dry. One of the best early ones featured Hamilton versus Madison on the scope of presidential power, and other Framers characteristically assumed positions in this and other disputes on the basis of their political convictions.

Probably our greatest difficulty is that we know so much more about what the Framers *should have meant* than they themselves did. We are intimately acquainted with the problems that their Constitution should have been designed to master; in short, we have read the mystery story backwards. If we are to get the right "feel" for their time and their circumstances, we must in Maitland's phrase, ". . . think ourselves back into a twilight." Obviously, no one can pretend completely to escape from the solipsistic web of his own environment, but if the effort is made, it is possible to appreciate the past roughly on its own terms. The first step in this process is to abandon the academic premise that because we can ask a question, there must be an answer.

Thus we can ask what the Framers meant when they gave Congress the power to regulate interstate and foreign commerce, and we emerge, reluctantly perhaps, with the reply that . . . they may not have known what they meant, that there may not have been any semantic consensus. The Convention was not a seminar in analytic philosophy or linguistic analysis. Commerce was *commerce*—and if different interpretations of the word arose, later generations could worry about the problem of definition. The delegates were in a hurry to get a new government established; when definitional arguments arose, they characteristically took refuge in ambiguity. If different men voted for the same proposition for varying reasons, that was politics (and still is); if later generations were unsettled by this lack of precision, that would be their problem.

There was a good deal of definitional pluralism with respect to the problems the delegates did discuss, but when we move to the question of extrapolated intentions, we enter the realm of spiritualism. When men in our time, for instance, launch into elaborate talmudic exegesis to demonstrate that federal aid to parochial schools is (or is not) in accord with the intentions of the men who established the Republic and endorsed the Bill of Rights, they are engaging in historical Extra-Sensory Perception. (If one were to join this E. S. P. contingent for a minute, he might suggest that the hard-boiled politicians who wrote the Constitution and Bill of Rights would chuckle scornfully at such an invocation of authority: obviously a politician would chart his course on the intentions of the living, not of the dead, and count the number of Catholics in his constituency.)

The Constitution, then, was not an apotheosis of "constitutionalism," a triumph of architectonic genius; it was a patch-work sewn together under the pressure of both time and events by a group of extremely talented democratic politicians. They refused to attempt the establishment of a strong, centralized sovereignty on the principle of legislative supremacy for the excellent reason that the people would not accept it. They risked their political fortunes by opposing the established doctrines of state sovereignty because they were convinced that the existing system was leading to national impotence and probably foreign domination. For two years, they worked to get a convention established. For over three months, in what must have seemed to the faithful participants an endless process of give-and-take, they reasoned, cajoled, threatened, and bargained amongst themselves. The result was a Constitution which the people, in fact, by democratic processes, did accept, and a new and far better national government was established.

Beginning with the inspired propaganda of Hamilton, Madison and Jay, the ideological build-up got under way. *The Federalist* had little impact on the ratification of the Constitution, except perhaps in New York, but this volume had enormous influence on the image of the Constitution in the minds of future generations, particularly on historians and political scientists who have an innate fondness for theoretical symmetry. Yet, while the shades of Locke and Montesquieu *may* have been hovering in the background, and the delegates *may* have been unconscious instruments of a transcendent *telos,* the careful observer of the day-to-day work of the Convention finds no over-arching principles. The "separation of powers" to him seems to be a by-product of suspicion, and "federalism" he views as a *pis aller,* as the farthest point the delegates felt they could go in the destruction of state power without themselves inviting repudiation.

To conclude, the Constitution was neither a victory for abstract theory nor a great practical success. Well over half a million men had to die on the battlefields of the Civil War before certain constitutional principles could be defined—a baleful consideration which is somehow overlooked in our customary tributes to the farsighted genius of the Framers and to the supposed American talent for "constitutionalism." The Constitution was, however, a vivid demonstration of effective democratic political action, and of the forging of a national elite which literally persuaded its countrymen to hoist themselves by their own boot straps. American pro-consuls would be wise not to translate the Constitution into Japanese, or Swahili, or treat it as a work of semi-Divine origin; but when students of comparative politics examine the process of nation-building in countries newly freed from colonial rule, they may find the American experience instructive as a classic example of the potentialities of a democratic elite.

CHAPTER 16

THE FOUNDING FATHERS

In the foregoing selection, we examined the framing of the Federal Constitution in light of the basic constitutional principles that emerged in that document. In Chapter 14, we considered national affairs under the Articles of Confederation and were introduced to the "revisionist" view of the founding fathers as self-interested conservatives who feared democracy and repudiated the political heritage of the Revolution. The nineteenth-century traditional image of the framers of the Constitution as an assemblage of all-wise, farsighted demigods who, in a single stroke, produced the world's greatest political document is still prevalent. A third generation of historians of the Revolutionary era accepts neither the traditionalist nor the revisionist point of view.

The next selection focuses directly on the founding fathers. Stanley Elkins and Eric McKitrick, members of the third generation of historians, are unsatisfied with the two older, symbolic images of the founding fathers—the traditional "father" image and the revisionist "conservative" image. In their article, "The Founding Fathers: Young Men of the Revolution," they point out that recent research and writing on the framers is still in progress, and that, as yet, no new, clear, and systematic point of view has emerged. Elkins and McKitrick suggest that the new work will not be complete nor satisfactory until a new, symbolic image of the Founding Fathers is created to replace the old tired ones. In this selection, these authors search for such an image.

247

The first question which the student should consider in reading this selection is why, in the opinion of the authors, a fresh *symbolic* image of the Founding Fathers is necessary to an understanding of the Revolutionary era of United States history. Do you agree with this basic contention of the authors? Second, in what aspects of the history of this period do the authors find the basis for a new image of the Federalist framers and supporters of the Constitution? Third, what constituted the real struggle between the Federalists and the Anti-Federalists? In seeking to identify the basic source of conflict over the Constitution, what do Elkins and McKitrick suggest about the revisionist argument that the fight was fundamentally one between the conservatives and the democrats, between the man of property and the propertyless, and between the nationalists and the champions of localism? Finally, do you believe that this selection tends to humanize the Founding Fathers, thus making them more understandable to us today?

Cecilia Kenyon, "Men of Little Faith: The Anti-Federalists on the Nature of Representative Government," *William and Mary Quarterly,* XII (January, 1955), and Merrill Jensen, *The New Nation** (1950), present ideas that Elkins and McKitrick find useful. Both can be read with profit by the interested student. Carl Degler has an excellent, broadly interpretive essay on the Revolutionary and Constitutional eras in *Out of Our Past: The Forces that Shaped Modern America** (1958).

* Available in a paperback edition.

THE FOUNDING FATHERS: YOUNG MEN OF THE REVOLUTION

STANLEY ELKINS AND ERIC McKITRICK

The intelligent American of today may know a great deal about his history, but the chances are that he feels none too secure about the Founding Fathers and the framing and ratification of the Federal Constitution. He is no longer certain what the "enlightened" version of that story is, or even whether there is one. This is because, in the century and three quarters since the Constitution was written, our best thinking on that subject has gone through two dramatically different phases and is at this moment about to enter a third.

Americans in the nineteenth century, whenever they reviewed the events of the founding, made reference to an Olympian gathering of wise and virtuous men who stood splendidly above all faction, ignored petty self-interest, and concerned themselves only with the freedom and well-being of their fellow-countrymen. This attitude toward the Fathers has actually never died out; it still tends to prevail in American history curricula right up through most of the secondary schools. But bright young people arriving at college have been regularly discovering, for nearly the last fifty years, that in the innermost circle this was regarded as an old-fashioned, immensely oversimplified, and rather dewy-eyed view of the Founding Fathers and their work. Ever since J. Allen Smith and Charles Beard wrote in the early years of the twentieth century, the "educated" picture of the Fathers has been that of a group not of disinterested patriots but of hard-fisted conservatives who were looking out for their own interests and those of their class. According to this worldlier view, the document which they wrote—and in which they embodied these interests—was hardly intended as a thrust toward popular and democratic government. On the contrary, its centralizing tendencies all reflected the Fathers' distrust of the local and popular rule which had been too little restrained under the Articles of Confederation. The authors

SOURCE. Stanley Elkins and Eric McKitrick, "The Founding Fathers: Young Men of the Revolution," *The Political Science Quarterly*, LXVII (June 1961), pp. 181–216. Reprinted by permission of the authors.

of the Constitution represented the privileged part of society. Naturally, then, their desire for a strong central government was, among other things, an effort to achieve solid national guarantees for the rights of property—rights not adequately protected under the Articles—and to obtain for the propertied class (their own) a favored position under the new government.

This "revisionist" point of view—that of the Founding Fathers as self-interested conservatives—has had immeasurable influence in the upper reaches of American historical thought. Much of what at first seemed audacious to the point of lèse majesté came ultimately to be taken as commonplace. The Tory-like, almost backward-turning quality which this approach has imparted to the picture of constitution-making even renders it plausible to think of the Philadelphia Convention of 1787 as a counter-revolutionary conspiracy, which is just the way a number of writers have actually described it. That is, since the Articles of Confederation were the product of the Revolution, to overthrow the Articles was—at least symbolically—to repudiate the Revolution. The Declaration of Independence and the Constitution represented two very different, and in some ways opposing, sets of aspirations; and (so the reasoning goes) the Philadelphia Convention was thus a significant turning-away from, rather than an adherence to, the spirit of the Declaration.

In very recent years, however, a whole new cycle of writing and thinking and research has been underway; the revisionists of the previous generation are themselves being revised. The economic ideas of the late Professor Beard, which dominated this field for so long, have been partially if not wholly discredited. And yet many of the old impressions, intermingled with still older ones, persist. Much of the new work, moreover, though excellent and systematic, is still in progress. Consequently the entire subject of the Constitution and its creation has become a little murky; new notions having the clarity and assuredness of the old have not as yet fully emerged; and meanwhile one is not altogether certain what to think.

Before the significance of all this new work can be justly assessed, and before consistent themes in it may be identified with any assurance, an effort should be made to retrace somewhat the psychology of previous conceptions. At the same time, it should be recognized that any amount of fresh writing on this subject will continue to lack something until it can present us with a clear new symbolic image of the Fathers themselves. The importance of this point lies in the function that symbols have for organizing the historical imagination, and the old ones are a little tired. The "father" image is well and good, and so also in certain respects is the "conservative" one. But we may suppose that these men saw them-selves at the time as playing other rôles too, rôles that did not partake so much of retrospection, age, and restraint as those which would come to be assigned to them in after years. The Republic is now very old, as republics go, yet it *was* young once, and so were its founders. With youth goes energy, and the "energy" principle may be more suggestive now, in reviewing the experience of the founding, than the principle of paternal conservatism. . . .

IV

The work of Merrill Jensen, done in the 1930's and 1940's, has suffered somewhat in reputation due to the sweep and vehemence of the anti-Beardian reaction. Yet that work contains perceptions which ought not to be written off in the general shuffle. They derive not so much from the over-all Beardian traditions and influences amid which Jensen wrote, as from that particular sector of the subject which he marked off and preëmpted for his own. Simply by committing himself —alone among Beardians and non-Beardians—to presenting the Con-federation era as a legitimate phase of American history, entitled to be taken seriously like any other and having a positive side as well as a negative one, he has forced upon us a peculiar point of view which, by the same token, yields its own special budget of insights. For example, Jensen has been profoundly impressed by the sheer force, determination, and drive of such nationalist leaders as Hamilton, Madison, Jay, Knox, and the Morrises. This energy, he feels, created the central problem of the Confederation and was the major cause of its collapse. He deplores this, seeing in the Confederation "democratic" virtues which it probably never had, finding in the Federalists an "aristocratic" character which in actual fact was as much or more to be found in the Anti-Federalists, smelling plots everywhere, and in general shaping his nomenclature to fit his own values and preferences. But if Professor Jensen seems to have called everything by the wrong name, it is well to remember that nomen-clature is not everything. The important thing—what does ring true— is that this driving "nationalist" energy was, in all probability, central to the movement that gave the United States a new government.

The other side of the picture, which does not seem to have engaged Jensen's mind half so much, was the peculiar sloth and inertia of the Anti-Federalists. Cecilia Kenyon, in a brilliant essay on these men,[1] has

---

[1] "Men of Little Faith: The Anti-Federalists on the Nature of Representative Gov-ernment," *William and Mary Quarterly*, XII, 3rd ser. (January 1955), pp. 3–43.

shown them as an amazingly reactionary lot. They were transfixed by
the specter of power. It was not the power of the aristocracy that they
feared, but power of any kind, democratic or otherwise, that they could
not control for themselves. Their chief concern was to keep governments
as limited and as closely tied to local interests as possible. Their minds
could not embrace the concept of a national interest which they themselves might share and which could transcend their own parochial concerns. Republican government that went beyond the compass of state
boundaries was something they could not imagine. Thus the chief difference between Federalists and Anti-Federalists had little to do with
"democracy" (George Clinton and Patrick Henry were no more willing
than Gouverneur Morris to trust the innate virtue of the people), but
rather in the Federalists' conviction that there was such a thing as
national interest and that a government could be established to care for
it which was fully in keeping with republican principles. To the Federalists this was not only possible but absolutely necessary, if the nation
was to avoid a future of political impotence, internal discord, and in the
end foreign intervention. So far so good. But still, exactly how did such
convictions get themselves generated?

Merrill Jensen has argued that the Federalists, by and large, were
reluctant revolutionaries who had feared the consequences of a break
with England and had joined the Revolution only when it was clear that
independence was inevitable. The argument is plausible; few of the
men most prominent later on as Federalists had been quite so hot for
revolution in the very beginning as Patrick Henry and Samuel Adams.
But this may not be altogether fair; Adams and Henry were already
veteran political campaigners at the outbreak of hostilities, while the
most vigorous of the future Federalists were still mere youngsters. The
argument, indeed, could be turned entirely around: the source of
Federalist, or nationalist, energy was not any "distaste" for the Revolution on these men's part, but rather their profound and growing involvement in it.

Much depends here on the way one pictures the Revolution. In the
beginning it simply consisted of a number of state revolts loosely directed
by the Continental Congress; and for many men, absorbed in their effort
to preserve the independence of their own states, it never progressed
much beyond that stage even in the face of invasion. But the Revolution
had another aspect, one which developed with time and left a deep
imprint on those connected with it, and this was its character as a
continental war effort. If there is any one feature that most unites the
future leading supporters of the Constitution, it was their close engage-

ment with this continental aspect of the Revolution. A remarkably large number of these someday Federalists were in the Continental Army, served as diplomats or key administrative officers of the Confederation government, or, as members of Congress, played leading rôles on those committees primarily responsible for the conduct of the war.

Merrill Jensen has compiled two lists, with nine names in each, of the men whom he considers to have been the leading spirits of the Federalists and Anti-Federalists respectively. It would be well to have a good look at this sample. The Federalists—Jensen calls them "nationalists"—were Robert Morris, John Jay, James Wilson, Alexander Hamilton, Henry Knox, James Duane, George Washington, James Madison, and Gouverneur Morris. Washington, Knox, and Hamilton were deeply involved in Continental military affairs; Robert Morris was Superintendent of Finance; Jay was president of the Continental Congress and minister plenipotentiary to Spain (he would later be appointed Secretary for Foreign Affairs); Wilson, Duane, and Gouverneur Morris were members of Congress, all three being active members of the war committees. The Anti-Federalist group presents a very different picture. It consisted of Samuel Adams, Patrick Henry, Richard Henry Lee, George Clinton, James Warren, Samuel Bryan, George Bryan, George Mason, and Elbridge Gerry. Only three of these—Gerry, Lee, and Adams—served in Congress, and the latter two fought consistently against any effort to give Congress executive powers. Their constant preoccupation was state sovereignty rather than national efficiency. Henry and Clinton were active war governors, concerned primarily with state rather than national problems, while Warren, Mason, and the two Bryans were essentially state politicians.

The age difference between these two groups is especially striking. The Federalists were on the average ten to twelve years younger than the Anti-Federalists. At the outbreak of the Revolution George Washington, at 44, was the oldest of the lot; six were under 35 and four were in their twenties. Of the Anti-Federalists, only three were under 40 in 1776, and one of these, Samuel Bryan, the son of George Bryan, was a boy of 16.

This age differential takes on a special significance when it is related to the career profiles of the men concerned. Nearly half of the Federalist group—Gouverneur Morris, Madison, Hamilton, and Knox—quite literally saw their careers launched in the Revolution. The remaining five—Washington, Jay, Duane, Wilson, and Robert Morris—though established in public affairs beforehand, became nationally known after 1776 and the wide public recognition which they subsequently achieved came first and foremost through their identification with the continental war effort. All of them had been united in an experience, and had formed commitments, which dissolved provincial boundaries; they had come to full public maturity in a setting which enabled ambition, public service, leadership, and self-fulfillment to be conceived, for each in his way, with a grandeur of scope unknown to any previous generation. The careers of the Anti-Federalists, on the other hand, were not only state-centered but—aside from those of Clinton, Gerry, and the young Bryan—rested heavily on events that preceded rather than followed 1776. . . .

The logic of these careers, then, was in large measure tied to a chronology which did not apply in the same way to all the men in public life during the two decades of the 1770's and 1780's. A significant proportion of relative newcomers, with prospects initially modest, happened to have their careers opened up at a particular time and in such a way that their very public personalities came to be staked upon the national quality of the experience which had formed them. In a number of outstanding cases energy, initiative, talent, and ambition had combined with a conception of affairs which had grown immense in scope and promise by the close of the Revolution. There is every reason to think that a contraction of this scope, in the years that immediately followed, operated as a powerful challenge.

V

The stages through which the constitutional movement proceeded in the 1780's add up to a fascinating story in political management, marked by no little élan and dash. That movement, viewed in the light of the Federalist leaders' commitment to the Revolution, raises some nice points as to who were the "conservatives" and who were the "radicals." The spirit of unity generated by the struggle for independence had, in the eyes of those most closely involved in coördinating the effort, lapsed; provincial factions were reverting to the old provincial ways. The impulse to arrest disorder and to revive the flame of revolutionary unity may be pictured in "conservative" terms, but this becomes quite awkward when we look for terms with which to picture the other impulse, so different in nature: the urge to rest, to drift, to turn back the clock.

Various writers have said that the activities of the Federalists during this period had in them a clear element of the conspiratorial. Insofar as this refers to a strong line of political strategy, it correctly locates a key element in the movement. Yet without a growing base of popular dissatisfaction with the status quo, the Federalists could have skulked and plotted forever without accomplishing anything. We now know, thanks to recent scholarship, that numerous elements of the public were only too ripe for change. But the work of organizing such a sentiment was quite another matter; it took an immense effort of will just to get it off the ground. Though it would be wrong to think of the Constitution as something that had to be carried in the face of deep and basic popular opposition, it certainly required a series of brilliant maneuvers to escape the deadening clutch of particularism and inertia. An Anti-Federalist "no" could register on exactly the same plane as a Federalist "yes" while requiring a fraction of the energy. It was for this reason that the Federalists, even though they cannot be said to have circumvented the popular will, did have to use techniques which in their sustained drive, tactical mobility, and risk-taking smacked more than a little of the revolutionary. . . .

Whether or not the years between 1783 and 1786 should be viewed as a "critical period" depends very much on whose angle they are viewed from. Although it was a time of economic depression, the depressed conditions were not felt in all areas of economic life with the same force, nor were they nearly as damaging in some localities as in others; the interdependence of economic enterprise was not then what it would become later on, and a depression in Massachusetts did not necessarily imply one in Virginia, or even in New York. Moreover, there were definite signs of improvement by 1786. Nor can it necessarily be said that government on the state level lacked vitality. Most of the states were addressing their problems with energy and decision. There were problems everywhere, of course, many of them very grave, and in some cases (those of New Jersey and Connecticut in particular) solutions seemed almost beyond the individual state's resources. Yet it would be wrong, as Merrill Jensen points out, to assume that no solutions were possible within the framework which then existed. It is especially important to remember that when most people thought of "the government" they were not thinking of Congress at all, but of their own state legislature. For them, therefore, it was by no means self-evident that the period through which they were living was one of drift and governmental impotence.

But through the eyes of men who had come to view the states collectively as a "country" and to think in continental terms, things looked altogether different. From their viewpoint the Confederation was fast approaching the point of ruin. Fewer and fewer states were meeting their requisition payments, and Congress could not even pay its bills. The states refused to accept any impost which they themselves could not control, and even if all the rest accepted, the continued refusal of New York (which was not likely to change) would render any impost all but valueless. Local fears and jealousies blocked all efforts to establish uniform regulation of commerce, even though some such regulation seemed indispensable. A number of the states, New York in particular, openly ignored the peace treaty with England and passed discriminatory legislation against former Loyalists; consequently England, using as a pretext Congress' inability to enforce the treaty, refused to surrender the northwest posts. Morale in Congress was very low as members complained that lack of a quorum prevented them most of the time from transacting any business; even when a quorum was present, a few negative votes could block important legislation indefinitely. Any significant change, or any substantial increase in the power of Congress, required unanimous approval by the states, and as things then stood this had become very remote. Finally, major states such as New York and Virginia were simply paying less and less attention to Congress. The danger was not so much that of a split with the Confederation—Congress lacked the strength that would make any such "split" seem very urgent—but rather a policy of neglect that would just allow Congress to wither away from inactivity.

These were the conditions that set the stage for a fresh effort—the Annapolis Convention of 1786—to strengthen the continental government. The year before, Madison had arranged a conference between Maryland and Virginia for the regulation of commerce on the Potomac, and its success had led John Tyler and Madison to propose a measure in the Virginia Assembly that would give Congress power to regulate commerce throughout the Confederation. Though nothing came of it, a plan was devised in its place whereby the several states would be invited to take part in a convention to be held at Annapolis in September, 1786, for the purpose of discussing commercial problems. The snapping-point came when delegates from only five states appeared. The rest either distrusted one another's intentions (the northeastern states doubted the southerners' interest in commerce) or else suspected a trick to strengthen the Confederation government at their expense. It was apparent that no serious action could be taken at that time. But the dozen delegates who did come (Hamilton and Madison being in their forefront) were by definition those most concerned over the state of the national government, and they soon concluded that their only hope of saving it lay in some audacious plenary gesture. It was at this meeting, amid the mortification of still another failure, that they planned the Philadelphia Convention.

The revolutionary character of this move—though some writers have correctly perceived it—has been obscured both by the stateliness of historical retrospection and by certain legal peculiarities which allowed the proceeding to appear a good deal less subversive than it actually was. The "report" of the Annapolis meeting was actually a call, drafted by

Hamilton and carefully edited by Madison, for delegates of all the states to meet in convention at Philadelphia the following May for the purpose of revising the Articles of Confederation. Congress itself transmitted the call, and in so doing was in effect being brought to by-pass its own constituted limits. On the one hand, any effort to change the government within the rules laid down by the Articles would have required a unanimous approval which could never be obtained. But on the other hand, the very helplessness which the several states had imposed upon the central government meant in practice that the states were sovereign and could do anything they pleased with it. It was precisely this that the nationalists now prepared to exploit: this legal paradox had hitherto prevented the growth of strong loyalty to the existing Confederation and could presently allow that same Confederation, through the action of the states, to be undermined in the deceptive odor of legitimacy. Thus the Beardian school of constitutional thought, for all its errors of economic analysis and its transposing of ideological semantics, has called attention to one element—the element of subversion—that is actually entitled to some consideration.

But if the movement had its plotters, balance requires us to add that the "plot" now had a considerable measure of potential support, and that the authority against which the plot was aimed had become little more than a husk. Up to this time every nationalist move, including the Annapolis Convention, had been easily blocked. But things were now happening in such a way as to tip the balance and to offer the nationalists for the first time a better-than-even chance of success. There had been a marked improvement in business, but shippers in Boston, New York, and Philadelphia were still in serious trouble. Retaliatory measures against Great Britain through state legislation had proved ineffective and useless; there was danger, at the same time, that local manufacturing interests might be successful in pushing through high state tariffs. In the second place, New York's refusal to reconsider a national impost, except on terms that would have removed its effectiveness, cut the ground from under the moderates who had argued that, given only a little time, everything could be worked out. This did not leave much alternative to a major revision of the national government. Then there were Rhode Island's difficulties with inflationary paper money. Although that state's financial schemes actually made a certain amount of sense, they provided the nationalists with wonderful propaganda and helped to create an image of parochial irresponsibility. . . .

We have already seen that nineteenth century habits of thought created a ponderous array of stereotypes around the historic Philadelphia conclave of 1787. Twentieth century thought and scholarship, on the other hand, had the task of breaking free from them, and to have done so is a noteworthy achievement. And yet one must return to the point that stereotypes themselves require some form of explanation. The legend of a transcendent effort of statesmanship, issuing forth in a miraculously perfect instrument of government, emerges again and again despite all efforts either to conjure it out of existence or to give it some sort of rational linkage with mortal affairs. Why should the legend be so extraordinarily durable, and was there anything so special about the circumstances that set it on its way so unerringly and so soon?

The circumstances *were,* in fact, special; given a set of delegates of well over average ability, the Philadelphia meeting provides a really classic study in the sociology of intellect. Divine accident, though in some measure present in men's doings always, is not required as a part of this particular equation. The key conditions were all present in a pattern that virtually guaranteed for the meeting an optimum of effectiveness. A sufficient number of states were represented so that the delegates could, without strain, realistically picture themselves as thinking, acting, and making decisions in the name of the entire nation. They themselves, moreover, represented interests throughout the country that were diverse enough, and they had enough personal prestige at home, that they could act in the assurance of having their decisions treated at least with respectful attention. There had also been at work a remarkably effective process of self-selection, as to both men and states. Rhode Island ignored the convention, and as a result its position was not even considered there. There were leading state particularists such as Patrick Henry and Richard Henry Lee who were elected as delegates but refused to serve. The Anti-Federalist position, indeed, was hardly represented at all, and the few men who did represent it had surprisingly little to say. Yates and Lansing simply left before the convention was over. Thus a group already predisposed in a national direction could proceed unhampered by the friction of basic opposition in its midst.

This made it possible for the delegates to "try on" various alternatives without having to remain accountable for everything they said. At the same time, being relieved from all outside pressures meant that the only way a man could expect to make a real difference in the convention's deliberations was to reach, through main persuasion, other men of considerable ability and experience. Participants and audience were therefore one, and this in itself imposed standards of debate which were quite exacting. In such a setting the best minds in the convention were accorded an authority which they would not have had in political debates aimed at an indiscriminate public.

Thus the elements of secrecy, the general inclination for a national government, and the process whereby the delegates came to terms with their colleagues—appreciating their requirements and adjusting to their interests—all combined to produce a growing esprit de corps. As initial agreements were worked out, it became exceedingly difficult for the Philadelphia delegates not to grow more and more committed to the product of their joint efforts. Indeed, this was in all likelihood the key mechanism, more important than any other in explaining not only the peculiar genius of the main compromises but also the general fitness of the document as a whole. That is, a group of two or more intelligent men who are subject to no cross-pressures and whose principal commitment is to the success of an idea, are perfectly capable—as in our scientific communities of today—of performing what appear to be prodigies of intellect. Moving, as it were, in the same direction with a specific purpose, they can function at maximum efficiency. It was this that the historians of the nineteenth century did in their way see, and celebrated with sweeping rhetorical flourishes, when they took for granted that if an occasion of this sort could not call forth the highest level of statesmanship available, then it was impossible to imagine another that could.

Once the Philadelphia Convention had been allowed to meet and the delegates had managed, after more than three months of work, to hammer out a document that the great majority of them could sign, the political position of the Federalists changed dramatically. Despite the major battles still impending, for practical purposes they now had the initiative. The principal weapon of the Anti-Federalists—inertia—had greatly declined in effectiveness, for with the new program in motion it was no longer enough simply to argue that a new federal government was unnecessary. They would have to take positive steps in blocking it; they would have to arouse the people and convince them that the Constitution represented a positive danger.

Moreover, the Federalists had set the terms of ratification in such a way as to give the maximum advantage to energy and purpose; the key choices, this time, had been so arranged that they would fall right. Only nine states had to ratify before the Constitution would go into effect. Not only would this rule out the possibility of one or two states holding up the entire effort, but it meant that the Confederation would be automatically destroyed as an alternative before the difficult battles in New York and Virginia had to be faced. (By then, Patrick Henry in Virginia would have nothing but a vague alliance with North Carolina to offer as a counter-choice.) Besides, there was good reason to believe that at least four or five states, and possibly as many as seven, could be counted as safe, which meant that serious fighting in the first phase would be limited to two or three states. And finally, conditions were so set that the "snowball" principle would at each successive point favor the Federalists.

As for the actual process of acceptance, ratification would be done through state conventions elected for the purpose. Not only would this circumvent the vested interests of the legislatures and the ruling coteries that frequented the state capitals, but it gave the Federalists two separate chances to make their case—once to the people and once to the conventions. If the elected delegates were not initially disposed to do the desired thing, there was still a chance, after the convention met, of persuading them. Due partly to the hampering factor of transportation and distance, delegates had to have considerable leeway of choice and what amounted to quasi-plenipotentiary powers. Thus there could be no such thing as a fully "instructed" delegation, and members might meanwhile remain susceptible to argument and conversion. The convention device, moreover, enabled the Federalists to run as delegates men who would not normally take part in state politics.

The revolutionary verve and ardor of the Federalists, their resources of will and energy, their willingness to scheme tirelessly, campaign everywhere, and sweat and agonize over every vote meant in effect that despite all the hairbreadth squeezes and rigors of the struggle, the Anti-Federalists would lose every crucial test. There was, to be sure, an Anti-Federalist effort. But with no program, no really viable commitments, and little purposeful organization, the Anti-Federalists somehow always managed to move too late and with too little. They would sit and watch their great stronghold, New York, being snatched away from them despite a two-to-one Anti-Federalist majority in a convention presided over by their own chief, George Clinton. To them, the New York Federalists must have seemed possessed of the devil. The Federalists' convention men included Alexander Hamilton, James Duane, John Jay, and Robert Livingston—who knew, as did everyone else, that the new government was doomed unless Virginia and New York joined it. They insisted on debating the Constitution section by section instead of as a whole, which meant that they could out-argue the Anti-Federalists on every substantive issue and meanwhile delay the vote until New Hampshire and Virginia had had a chance to ratify. (Madison and Hamilton had a horse relay system in readiness to rush the Virginia news northward as quickly as possible.) By the time the New York convention was ready to act, ten others had ratified, and at the final moment Hamilton and his allies spread the chilling rumor that New York City was about to secede from the state. The Anti-Federalists, who had had enough, directed a chosen number of their delegates to cross over, and solemnly capitulated.

In the end, of course, everyone "crossed over." The speed with which this occurred once the continental revolutionists had made their point, and the ease with which the Constitution so soon became an object of universal veneration, still stands as one of the minor marvels of American history. But the document did contain certain implications, of a quasi-philosophical nature, that make the reasons for this ready consensus not so very difficult to find. It established a national government whose basic outlines were sufficiently congenial to the underlying commitments of the whole culture—republicanism and capitalism—that the likelihood of its being the subject of a true ideological clash was never very real. That the Constitution should mount guard over the rights of property— "realty," "personalty," or any other kind—was questioned by nobody. There had certainly been a struggle, a long and exhausting one, but we should not be deceived as to its nature. It was not fought on economic grounds; it was not a matter of ideology; it was not, in the fullest and most fundamental sense, even a struggle between nationalism and lo-calism. The key struggle was between inertia and energy; with inertia overcome, everything changed.

There were, of course, lingering objections and misgivings; many of the problems involved had been genuinely puzzling and difficult; and there remained doubters who had to be converted. But then the perfect bridge whereby all could become Federalists within a year was the addi-tion of a Bill of Rights. After the French Revolution, anti-constitution-alism in France would be a burning issue for generations; in America, an anti-constitutional party was undreamed of after 1789. With the Bill of Rights, the remaining opponents of the new system could say that, ever watchful of tyranny, they had now got what they wanted. Moreover, the Young Men of the Revolution might at last imagine, after a dozen years of anxiety, that *their* Revolution had been a success.

CHAPTER 17

WASHINGTON:
THE FIRST PRESIDENT

He is "Freedom's myth" and "more than man," Virginia poet James Barron Hope wrote of Washington in 1858. Although not as well known as "Light-Horse Harry" Lee's eulogistic "first in war, first in peace and first in the hearts of his countrymen," Hope's words are more suggestive of Washington's apotheosis, the process by which, through the years, a mere mortal has become America's immortal Father-Hero. The Washington myth is so entrenched in the minds of Americans that Washington the man is virtually unknown, and his real greatness is generally unappreciated.

In this selection, J. A. Carroll seeks a more human Washington. Although Washington was well known to his contemporaries, and although his Administrations have been thoroughly researched by historians, the figure of Washington is still obscure. In particular, a persistent vagueness exists about his role as President. Professor Carroll suggests that an assessment of that role is not an easy task. Washington's character, he believes, is "better sensed than analyzed." Washington was a doer rather than a thinker, and he does not "emerge spontaneously in a pattern" but "appears gradually in a procession of events." Hence, Professor Carroll is concerned with the achievements of Washington's Administrations, concentrating on American avoidance of involvement in European wars. In the story of these achievements, a viable picture of Washington as a man as well as a President emerges.

In reading this essay, attempt to determine the kind of man Washington was and the kind of President he made. What were his major characteristics? To what extent was he his own President? Equally important, how can we explain the rise and the strength of the Washington myth? Here, the student should consider carefully Professor Carroll's suggestions about the relationship of reality to the creation and persistence of the legend.

Indispensible in a consideration of this topic is Bernard Mayo's delightful and penetrating essay on Washington in *Myths and Men: Patrick Henry, George Washington, Thomas Jefferson** (1959). Excellent interpretative essays on Washington and his administrations are found in Marcus Cunliffe, *The Nation Takes Shape: 1789–1837** (1959), and Esmond Wright, *The Fabric of Freedom: 1763–1800** (1961). Among the many useful biographies are Bernhard Knollenberg, *Washington and the Revolution* (1940), and D. S. Freeman, *George Washington,* 5 Vols. (1948-1952).

* Available in a paperback edition.

GEORGE WASHINGTON
JOHN A. CARROLL

Close to ten o'clock on the morning of April 16, 1789, a tall man in his fifty-seventh year, dressed for travel in blue broadcloth and black boots and holding a tricorn hat in his hand, stood for a very brief moment on the piazza at Mount Vernon. From here on a clear day he could see some distance down the several miles of river that bordered his plantation, and the broad and quiet Potomac always rested his spirit. But there was no time left to contemplate the view. Makers of history, unlike those who study it, seldom are allowed the pleasures of retrospection.

General George Washington, soldier of the Revolution and Virginia's foremost farmer, was ready to make a journey that would put him into a new career. Two days earlier he had received notice of his elevation, by the vote of every elector, to the office of President of the United States—and now his carriage was waiting. "I bade adieu to Mount Vernon, to private life, and to domestic felicity," he wrote that night in his diary, "and, with a mind oppressed with more anxious and painful sensations than I have words to express, set out for New York . . . with the best disposition to render service to my country in obedience to its call. . . ." A few miles up the road at Wise's Tavern, the citizens of Alexandria honored their neighbor with a farewell dinner. "Go," Mayor Ramsay exhorted the President-elect, "and make a grateful people happy."

As it soon proved, the people of the United States were grateful indeed in 1789 that General Washington had consented to serve as chief magistrate of their new republic. His eight-day journey to New York, the first capital city, was in the manner of a triumphal procession of a Roman conqueror. At Baltimore, at Wilmington, at Philadelphia, at every town and coach stop along the route he was fêted with the pealing of bells, gun salutes, toasts and huzzas, gratulatory speeches and odes, parades and public banquets, and pyrotechnics through the night. The people of Trenton, eager to excel in their demonstration, provided a caparisoned

SOURCE. J. A. Carroll, "George Washington," in Morton Borden, ed., *America's Ten Greatest Presidents,* Chicago: Rand McNally, 1961, pp. 5–30. Copyright 1961 by Rand McNally & Co. Reprinted by permission of Rand McNally & Co. and the editor.

white horse which Washington rode as ladies sung to him and children threw flowers in his path. Finally, after crossing Newark Bay in a festooned barge with a train of flag-flying small craft in his wake, the President-elect was met at the Battery by thousands of New Yorkers. The crowd was so dense, and so determined to applaud and admire, that it took Washington almost an hour to make his way from the wharf to the "Executive Mansion" nearby at No. 3 Cherry Street. If this was adulation in the extreme, if it was almost idolatry, it was something deeper also. Here, unmistakably, was a manifestation of the ebullient hopes of a people recently free and a nation freshly born.

Of the several presidents of the United States who have served their countrymen memorably in critical periods, none experienced so full a measure of public esteem in the hour of inauguration as George Washington. No chief executive has entered office better known to his contemporaries. From New England to Georgia in 1789 Washington was celebrated as the American Atlas, the American Fabius, the Cincinnatus of the Western Hemisphere; for almost a decade now he had heard references to himself as "Father of his Country." In 1783, upon retirement to his farm after eight years as Commander in Chief of the Continental Army, he was by all odds the most famous man in America. Even as proprietor of Mount Vernon he had been conspicuous, a kind of national host whose beautiful home on the Potomac became, as he said, a "well-resorted tavern" for unexpected and unannounced travelers of every type. His appearance at the Philadelphia Convention in 1787 brought him again into public view, and the architects and advertisers of the Constitution were quick to dramatize the fact that General Washington had presided at the rebuilding of the old Articles of Confederation into the "New Roof of Federalism." So familiar was his name by 1788 that no other could be mentioned seriously for the highest office in the new system of government. . . . The first presidential election was a formality in the strictest sense, and unanimity was inevitable. The soldier-farmer from Virginia was the one American that his fellow-citizens, be they Federalists or "anti-Feds," knew best of all.

It is curious, then, that perhaps no president has proven more mysterious to posterity than the first. Historians have found it reasonably easy to chronicle the events of Washington's two administrations because the records and literary remains of the years 1789-97 are abundant. They have been able to dissect and to understand the opposite philosophies, social and economic, of the dominant personalities of the period, Alexander Hamilton and Thomas Jefferson. In detailed monographs they have shown how the clashing concepts of these two men ignited a political fire which, despite Washington's avowed determination to "walk on a straight line" and to act as "President of all the people," quickly divided the nation into sectional parties—Federalists following Hamilton north-ward and eastward, Republican-Democrats following Jefferson southward and westward. Scholars have identified party strife in the United States with the revolutionary upheavals that convulsed Europe in the 1790's, and possibly some have gone too far in ascribing "Anglomania" to Feder-alist leaders and "Gallomania" to Republicans. Washington's administra-tions, in any case, have been much discussed by modern historians. Their specialized studies fill a long shelf, and their conclusions are distilled accurately in many textbooks. Yet, to Americans in the twentieth century, President Washington presents something of an enigma. Confi-dent as we may be that we understand the period, we do not always understand the man. . . .

Like a good poem, George Washington's character is perhaps better sensed than analyzed. It is better, in any case, to contemplate Washington in full size than to examine him by synthetic lens. Washington was not an architect in ideas; he was essentially a man of deeds. His thoughts do not array themselves in a convenient constellation that may be understood in outline; rather they form a massive milky way that must be considered from end to end. Washington does not emerge spontaneously in a pattern; he appears gradually in a procession of events. He is best portrayed not in composite overview, but by scrutiny of his thoughts and interpretation of his actions at climactic moments of his career. . . .

Reduced to enumeration, the achievements of Washington's administra-tions count to not less than ten. During his presidency the United States government gained its executive and legislative precedents, appended a bill of rights to the Constitution, established its credit at home and abroad, fostered manufacturing and encouraged commerce, survived a serious in-surrection in the mountains of Pennsylvania, secured the transmontane frontier against Indian depredations, effected the removal of British troops from the Old Northwest, checked Spanish encroachments in the Old Southwest and obtained transit rights on the Mississippi, forged a policy for the disposition of public lands, and avoided involvement in the vortex of European wars. Analysis will reveal that Washington's hand was large in many of these accomplishments, and that in several his role was decisive. Proud of their record, Federalists were quick to acknowl-edge this: Washington's leadership was never nebulous to them. "Such a Chief Magistrate," said Fisher Ames, "appears like the pole star in a clear sky. . . . His Presidency will form an epoch and be distinguished as the Age of Washington." Ames was an orator who arranged his words nicely, but he was also as intuitive and straight-speaking a Federalist as there was in the party. However reluctantly, Republicans came to the same conclusion. In 1796 Jefferson expressed it simply: "One man outweighs them all in influence over the people."

Yet, by the eyes of posterity, Washington's role has not been seen in so sharp a light. It has long been a fashion to regard President Washington's administrations not so much his as Alexander Hamilton's. Critical research in the twentieth century has established beyond question that the genius and energy of Hamilton were responsible for much that the Federal government did—and, indeed, for much of what happened in the United States—between 1789 and 1797. As Senator William Maclay, dour Republican of Pennsylvania, remarked testily, "Mr. Hamilton is all powerful and fails in nothing he attempts." No student of the period would deny Hamilton's significance, but it may be that emphasis on the brilliance of the "Young Lothario" of the Federalists has worked to the disadvantage of a deeper consideration of the President's own part in the affairs of the new republic. In its business, great and small, the President was always there. He was neither listless nor dull, as sometimes he has been portrayed, and neither too old nor too deaf to participate fully. "He was an Aegis," Hamilton admitted, "very essential to me."

Surely it is not incorrect to think of the Federalist era as the heyday of Hamiltonian ideals. But it is quite wrong to suppose that Washington loved the pomp and ceremony with which his aides surrounded him, that his attitudes were more English than American, or that he concurred readily with Hamilton's extreme and often-quoted remark on the necessity of rule by the "rich and well-born." And it is altogether wrong to imagine that the President responded automatically to Hamilton's every suggestion, that he permitted a Svengali-like control to be exercised over him, or that he turned to Hamilton in helpless frustration when the pressures of office became too great.

Washington did none of these things. Instead, as chief executive, he developed to a remarkable degree the science of deliberate and responsible consultation. While Hamilton served as secretary of the treasury and Jefferson as secretary of state, Washington solicited advice from them almost equally. In 1789 and 1790 he consulted the "heads of departments" individually on specific matters, and made his decision largely on one officer's specific advice. By the end of 1791, however, he was calling them together for discussion of larger problems. The Cabinet met several times in 1792, and many times during Washington's second term. Washington's closest friend in the Cabinet was neither Hamilton nor Jefferson but rather his old military comrade, General Henry Knox, the secretary of war. It may be argued reasonably that Knox, who served until 1795, was a convenient mirror for Hamilton's views; but in these same years the President's thinking over a wide range of major problems more nearly approximated that of Edmund Randolph than of any other member of the Cabinet. This gifted Virginian was in no way a Hamiltonian Federalist—and, according to Jefferson, not very much of a Republican. Jefferson thought Randolph "indecisive" and a "chameleon." Washington thought him impartial and sound. . . .

Of the ten enumerated achievements of Washington's administrations, the last in the list is perhaps the first in significance. Nothing that the Federalists did between 1789 and 1797 was of larger moment then, or deserves the larger gratitude of posterity, than their efforts to keep the United States out of the wars of the French Revolution. Whether their sympathies incline to the Federalists or to the Republicans, historians have been in general agreement that American participation in the wars which erupted in Europe in 1793 would have proven disastrous. The American Union, then just four years old, scarcely could have survived such an experience. No man in the United States saw this more clearly in 1793 than George Washington. And in no instance during his tenure as chief executive did Washington demonstrate his role in the government so abundantly, or his greatness in statecraft so dramatically, as in the decisions he made—and in the manner he made them—early in that year. The preservation of American neutrality was Washington's mightiest personal achievement as President of the United States. In February, March, and April of 1793 he forged the neutral rule in its fundamental form, and through the next four years his every policy was built on it. Of the several examples that might be used to indicate the active hand of Washington in the great affairs of government, this one has been chosen as much for its illustrative value as for its importance.

On March 4, 1793, in the Senate chamber at Philadelphia, Washington took the presidential oath for the second time. The first Federal administration, he could be sure, had accomplished much. Procedures had been established and many precedents set, the Constitution had been enlarged with the Bill of Rights, the stature of the central government had been assured, the machinery of national finance put into motion, and plans had been laid for a permanent capital city to be erected on the north bank of the Potomac. With these specifics and with the rapid rise of manufacturing and commerce that augured so well for the prosperity of the nation, Washington was immensely pleased. "A spirit of improvement displays itself in every quarter," he declared, "and principally in objects of the greatest public utility . . . things which seem eminently calculated to promote the advantage and accommodation of the people at large." The young republic had come far since 1789; further progress, the President felt, was certain if citizens would fix their minds and fasten their energies on such internal and immediate goals as inland navigation, road and bridge building, and settlement of the frontier. Then suddenly, in the opening weeks of his second term, the United States approached the precipice of war. The appeal of the French Revolution now threatened to draw the new American nation into a global conflict that would obliterate its fairest prospects.

Satisfied as he was with the results of his first administration, Washington entered his second term in a mood of apprehension. The national progress in which he took such pride had been gained, he knew, only at a very dear price. The bills on funding, assumption, residence, the excise, and the national bank—each one a device of Hamilton's to engross the prestige of the Federal government and multiply its powers under the Constitution—had loosened a torrent of opposition, criticism of Hamilton and Vice President Adams as "monocrats," and denunciation of all Federalists as "speculators" and "corruptionists." In Congress and in every city the Federalist followers of Hamilton and the Republican disciples of Jefferson were arguing vociferously, hurling epithets in their newspapers, and straining for advantage in what Fisher Ames now aptly styled "the pitched battle of parties." And, as political strife came to high tide in the vice-presidental contest of 1792 between the Federalist Adams and the candidate of the Republicans, Governor George Clinton of New York, Washington realized that the ebb of controversy soon would wash against his own door. No longer could he regard himself as "President of all the people," and he hardly could expect the same immunity in his second term that had shielded his office and his person from public censure in the first. "Convulsed as we are," Edmund Randolph warned him early in 1793, "I cannot but believe that there is scarcely a man in the Government whom party will not sooner or later destine for an attack."

Washington was past sixty, his health uncertain and his hearing impaired, and he longed for the shade of retirement at Mount Vernon more fervently now than ever. Still, because both Hamilton and Jefferson had urged him to do so—and because both Secretaries promised to remain in the Cabinet—he consented to a second term. "The motives which induced my acceptance," he wrote to a friend, "are the same which have ever ruled my decision, when the public desire (or, as my countrymen are pleased to denominate it, the *public good*) are placed in the scale against my personal enjoyment or private interest." But now, he might have added, Hamilton and Jefferson seemed farther than ever from agreement on just what constituted the "public good," and at this moment his countrymen were exhibiting a "public desire" that alarmed and dismayed him. The anxiety of Americans for news of the French Revolution was so intense as to be frightening. Did the people of the United States feel such communion with the cause of France that they might actually wish to plunge into the European conflagration? . . .

Washington scarcely would have denied that the good will of the French was precious to him. His personal gratitude to the soldiers of France for their unstinting aid in the war of American independence could never be dimmed. Without quibble he approved Jefferson's official reply to formal notification of the establishment of the French Republic: "The Government and the citizens of the United States . . . consider the union of principles and pursuits between our two countries as a link which binds still closer their interests and affections." But beyond this the President would not go. He did not agree with Jefferson that America's experiment in representative government was tied irrevocably to the French Revolution. As Washington walked alone in High Street, taking his exercise in the early mornings of March, he saw the tricolor on display in Philadelphia windows and knew that his nation was drifting into a storm of difficulties, a tempest of diplomatic problems blowing together with domestic ones, that would put to an ultimate test his wisdom and skill as national helmsman. If Washington was the "indispensable" leader, as his admirers had insisted in 1789 and again recently, this was the crisis that would show it. If his first term had been disfigured somewhat by conflicting attitudes in his Cabinet and the subsequent rise of parties, factionalism would now thicken and spread under new stimuli from abroad. The questions of policy would be large, complex, fraught with peril. Anticipating them, the President let the whole business filter through his mind time and again. Finally he was resolved on two points: Whatever developed in Europe, the United States must remain strictly neutral; whatever developed in the Cabinet or in the public temper, the President must remain impartial and dispassionate. The pilot must steer a safe and constant course. . . .

On April 4 [1793] the post to Mount Vernon brought a note from Jefferson, who expressed his feeling that recent stories of Anglo-French hostilities were exaggerated—and that it was more probable that England faced a civil war. Eight days later the President opened a letter from Hamilton which could leave "no room for doubt" that a global conflagration was raging. Marie Antoinette had been executed, Hamilton wrote, and on February 1 the French Republic had formally declared war against the British Empire, the Spanish Empire, and The Netherlands.

Hamilton's letter was sent on April 5; Jefferson wrote on the seventh that a general war was now "extremely probable" and the United States should "take every justifiable measure for preserving our neutrality" while providing France with "those necessaries for war which must be brought across the Atlantic." On the same day that he received Hamilton's communication, and before Jefferson's had arrived, the President penned his instructions. "It behooves the Government of this country," he wrote the Secretary of State, "to use every means in its power to prevent the citizens . . . from embroiling us with either [belligerent]"; would Jefferson, therefore, please give "mature consideration" to a plan which would insure "a strict neutrality"? In the same post he placed notes to Hamilton and Secretary of War Knox which made unmistakably clear the President's wish for "immediate precautionary measures." The next morning, April 13, his coach left for Philadelphia by the shortest possible route, and Washington was in High Street by late afternoon on the seventeenth.

When Jefferson appeared at the President's office early the next day, he had in hand four dispatches from Thomas Pinckney at London—each many weeks old and of trivial content. These the Secretary of State presented, but he had prepared no memorandum and could offer no plan to guarantee the nation a neutral role in the European war. If Washington's temper rose, he kept it in leash. Later the same day he saw Hamilton, and the Secretary of the Treasury spread before him the detailed draft of a program for "perfect" neutrality. Hamilton had a set of questions on paper, and the logic behind them in his mind; he even had ready a suggested "proclamation," the text of which Chief Justice John Jay had written hastily at his request. It was obvious that the Secretary of the Treasury had been feverishly occupied for some time in business that properly belonged to the Secretary of State; it was equally obvious that the two Cabinet officers had conferred not at all on the vital business in point. The President did not know the extent of Hamilton's dabbling in diplomatics; he was unaware of Hamilton's confidential assurances to the British envoy at Philadelphia, George Hammond, that the United States would maintain—as the Englishman reported to his superiors—"as strict a neutrality" as possible because "any event which might endanger the external tranquility . . . would be fatal to the systems he [Hamilton] has formed. . . ." Whatever the indiscretions of the Secretary of the Treasury, they would not blur the blueprint he advanced at this moment. The President had decided on neutrality. What he needed was a prescription for it. Hamilton had that in hand, and Jefferson did not.

No time was to be lost. Washington copied out Hamilton's interrogatories, labeled them "sundry questions . . . arising from the present posture of affairs in Europe," and sent identical lists to Jefferson, Knox, and Randolph with a request that the Cabinet meet at his house the next morning, April 19, at nine. The President's covering note did not indicate that Hamilton had originated the questions; but this is not to imply, as some historians have, that Washington was attempting to deceive his advisers. He could hardly have been able to conceal their authorship; nor would he have tried. . . .

The questions totaled to thirteen, but essentially the "doubts" were three. Should the President issue a proclamation to the American public, and should it include an explicit "declaration of neutrality"? Should Genêt, who would arrive soon as minister of the new French government, be formally accredited; and, if so, should his reception be "absolute" or "qualified"? Could and should the United States either disavow or suspend the Treaties of Alliance and Commerce made with France in 1778? The second and third points, Washington realized, would be highly antagonistic to Jefferson. They challenged the legitimacy of the Republic of France and suggested that the French Revolution ultimately would fail—as Hamilton plainly expected it would. Should the *de facto* government in France be recognized forthwith? Should the United States in 1793 be free to annul treaties concluded in 1778 with a monarchy that was now overturned, or were those treaties always to be valid because they existed between the *peoples* of nations rather than between the *governments* of nations? By their nature these considerations were central to the whole problem of erecting a permanent neutrality for the United States. Washington saw this and was grateful to Hamilton for raising pertinent points which soon would have to be discussed at length and in depth by the Cabinet. No precedent stood as a sure guide on the question of recognition, and likewise none on the validity of treaties. The President might anticipate long legalistic arguments and much heated opinion in his Cabinet before a decision could be wrought on either point.

There need be no delay, however, in adopting "immediate precautionary measures" against possible participation by Americans in the European war. To Washington this was the immediate issue, the paramount one. Questions of *de facto* recognition and the status of treaties could be, as they were, "postponed for further consideration" to "another day"; but the first question could not. What should the President do to prevent unneutral acts by Americans which might propel the United States into war? If American enthusiasm for the cause of the French Revolution was as intense as it appeared to be, a belligerent act might occur at any hour in any of a dozen seaports. The slightest unneutral gesture might be seized upon by the English, and America again might be fighting for her own freedom. It would be too late then to argue on the finer distinctions of international law, and Washington did not wish to debate them in detail until he had taken "immediate precautionary measures" to insure that no accident or irresponsible act would bring war to the shores of the American republic. This was the crisis of Friday, April 19, 1793—and George Washington did not mistake it.

Should the President, then, issue a public proclamation, and should it include a "declaration of neutrality"? Hamilton, Knox, and Randolph considered an immediate proclamation to be imperative. Jefferson acquiesced, but insisted that a "declaration of neutrality" would amount to "a declaration that there should be no war," and, he said, only Congress had the right to determine that question. "If on the one hand the Legislature have the right to declare war," Hamilton answered, "it is on the other the duty of the Executive to preserve peace till the declaration is made." But Jefferson had another argument, a compelling one, against any "premature declaration" that the United States would remain neutral. "It would be better," he reasoned, "to hold back the declaration of neutrality as a thing worth something" to each side. This was the same logic on which the Secretary of State had premised his opinion regarding Miranda's possible attack on Spanish Louisiana—that the United States must be "free to act" in pressing for diplomatic concessions—and now Jefferson wished to wring from the British "the broadest privileges" that American neutrality would buy. Redcoats of His Majesty's Canadian regiments still occupied seven forts on American soil in the Northwest; this might be a way to get them out. Washington liked the idea, and on his preference the decision of April 19 was made: the President would issue a proclamation immediately, but it would not contain an explicit "declaration of neutrality." It would serve as a positive warning to American citizens against "all acts and proceedings inconsistent with the duties of a friendly nation toward those at war," but it would avoid words and phrases that might negate the bargaining power of the United States in the market place of diplomacy.

The decision of April 19, 1793, established an important precedent in American history, but neither Hamilton nor Jefferson took particular satisfaction in the day's work. . . . Hamilton's friend, Senator Rufus King of New York, expressed the attitude of most Federalists in his reaction: "I could have wished to have seen in some part of it the word 'neutrality' which everyone would have understood and felt the force of. . . . We must not become entangled with this mad war." James Madison's response characterized that of ardent Republicans: "It wounds the popular feelings by a seeming indifference to the cause of liberty." And President Washington, a few hours after he had issued the proclamation, explained his decision in these words: "To administer justice and receive it from every power will, I hope, be always found the most prominent feature in the administration of this country; and I flatter myself that nothing short of imperious necessity can occasion a breach with any of them." It was, he said, "the sincere wish of the United States to . . . live in peace and amity with all the inhabitants of the earth."

The work of George Washington as a statesman has been obscured to posterity not only by Alexander Hamilton's ascendancy in the 1790's, but equally as much by the very legend that attaches to his name. That legend is essentially military, and has been so from its seeding. . . .

This fact does much to explain why his achievements as president are not as obvious to posterity as they should be. Washington was a statesman fully as long as he was a soldier, and his achievements in council were fully as significant as those in the field. But he was first a soldier, and primacy is vital in legend-making. So is drama, and so also is an undisputed leading role. The campaigns of the Revolution can be rendered infinitely more interesting than the problems of statecraft in the formative period. And, as a soldier, Washington occupied the center of the stage. . . .

Washington's popularity as a biographical subject is easily explained. He was America's first hero in war. John Adams, who was capable of descending to a certain level of bitterness during the years that he served inconspicuously as vice president in Washington's administrations, put it this way: "The history of our Revolution will be one continued lie from one end to the other. The essence of the whole will be that Dr. Franklin's electrical rod smote the earth and out sprang General Washington, that Franklin electrified him with his rod, and thence forward these two conducted all the policy, negotiations, legislatures, and war." Neither Benjamin Franklin's admirers nor Washington's have ever advanced this theory, but certainly the Commander in Chief of the Continental Army emerged from the war of independence with a major share of credit for its success. Then, as many Americans delighted in depicting it, the General followed the noble example of the Roman soldier Cincinnatus by retiring modestly to his farm and plow in the bright hour of victory—and this, above victory itself, emblazoned him with greatness in the eyes of the people. . . .

Like the flora of his Virginia, the legend of George Washington was early to blossom. Within a half dozen years of his death in 1799, American readers already had the choice of two biographies. One was a thin, simple book of eighty pages which presented the fiction of the cherry tree and the prayer in the snow at Valley Forge, and in the last paragraph ushered its subject through the Pearly Gates and into the Kingdom of the Angels. Few biographers of any hero have dared to go this far, but Mason Locke Weems was a self-styled clergyman and he was unfettered by footnotes. His *Life of General Washington* earned "Parson" Weems an emperor's ransom in royalties and a reputation as one of the most pleasant and plausible charlatans in American literature. Such success with Washington prompted Weems to consider the careers of other champions of the Revolution, and he did not lay down his prolific pen for many years. . . .

While the legend of Washington has been heavy with the laurels of the soldier, it nonetheless has communicated a valid impression. For all the ardor of their researches, modern historians have not turned up evidence that Washington in life was appreciably less than the great American patriot imaginatively painted in words by Weems. Catch-penny debunkers appear occasionally, to be sure, but they are compensated for their efforts as much in ridicule as in royalties. This is as it should be. Washington's life and times have been rigorously researched, his silhouette has been exposed to different light by different scholars, and we may be certain today that he is quite deserving of the halo that has been his. Weems, so fictitious in detail, was authentic in spirit: George Washington was a great and good man, great in the largest sense and good in the deepest. . . .

However deep the roots of any legend, it will die in poor ground. The legend of George Washington did not wither because its soil was uniquely rich. In an oration at St. Paul's Church in New York, Gouverneur Morris spoke a sentence that goes far to explain its endurance. "Born to high destinies," said Morris, Washington was "fashioned for them by the hand of nature." Had this not been so perfectly true, it is doubtful that this legend would have flowered as it did. More than any personage of his time and more perhaps than any American who followed him to the national stage, Washington presented an ideal subject for adulation. In him, physically and psychologically, were the elements of heroism. In seeing Washington, in meeting him, Americans and Europeans alike received the same spontaneous impression. Many described it, but none better than Jefferson who saw him daily for several years. As the first Secretary of State appraised the first President, "His person was fine, his stature exactly what one would wish," and more:

His mind was great and powerful, without being of the very first order; his penetration strong, though not so accurate as that of a Newton, Bacon, or Locke; and as far as he saw, no judgment was ever sounder. It was slow in operation, being little aided by invention or imagination, but sure in conclusion. . . . Perhaps the strongest feature in his character was prudence, never acting until every circumstance, every consideration, was maturely weighed; refraining when he saw a doubt, but, when once decided, going through with his purposes whatever obstacles opposed. His integrity was most pure, his justice the most inflexible I have ever known, no motives or interest or consanguinity of friendship or hatred being able to bias his decision. . . . On the whole, his character was in its mass perfect, in nothing bad, in few points indifferent; and it may truly be said that never did nature and fortune combine more perfectly to make a man great, and to place him in the same constellation with whatever worthies have merited from man an everlasting remembrance. . . .

CHAPTER 18

THE NEW NATION
AND THE WORLD

Historians have long recognized the importance of mercantilism in the economic and political development of Western Europe in the seventeenth and eighteenth centuries. Mercantilism, of course, provided the major impetus for the establishment of the Western European empires in the New World, and the authors of several previous selections in this volume discussed the role that British mercantilism played in the development of the American colonies and in the coming of the American Revolution. Most historians have assumed that the revolt against Great Britain was also a revolt against mercantilism, and they have set forth the proposition that the young American nation rejected an aggressive mercantilist foreign policy in favor of a passive neutrality which would insure that domestic development could occur safely and in relative isolation.

It is appropriate that a growing number of scholars of the last two decades, when the United States has been repeatedly characterized as an imperialistic power, should reexamine the underlying motivations that influenced the early leaders of the nation. In this selection, William A. Williams, one of the earliest and most respected of the New Left revisionist historians, reaches what will be for many readers a surprising conclusion. From the beginning of their national experience, Professor Williams suggests, Americans thought of their nation as an empire. According to Williams, Americans

279

continued even after independence to adhere to the tenets and principles of mercantilism, and this pattern of thought was of overriding significance in American domestic and foreign developments from the Revolutionary era to the age of Jackson. In the following selection, Professor Williams examines the impact of the mercantilist concept on the major events and personalities of the period.

How does Professor Williams' definition of mercantilism compare with the definitions put forth in previous selections? Is expansionism of greater significance in Professor Williams' definition of mercantilism than it is in those of other authors? What is unusual about Professor Williams' discussion of James Madison's ideas and activities? Do you agree with the author's characterization of Alexander Hamilton as only a halfhearted mercantilist? Finally, who is the historical hero of the essay? Why?

Anyone interested in Professor Williams' thesis should read his *Contours of American History** (1961) for the full exposition of his ideas. Walter LaFeber has elaborated on Williams' basic thesis in "Foreign Policies of a New Nation: Franklin, Madison, and the 'Dream of a New Land to Fulfill with People in Self-Control,' 1750–1804," in *From Colony To Empire: Essays in the History of American Foreign Relations* (1972), edited by William A. Williams. A modification of these views is to be found in Richard W. Van Alstyne, *The Rising American Empire** (1960). Samuel F. Bemis, the dean of traditional American diplomatic historians, has two excellent monographs, *Pinckney's Treaty** (1926) and *Jay's Treaty** (1923), which are basic to an understanding of the period. More recent studies in the traditional vein are Felix Gilbert, *The Beginnings of American Foreign Policy** (1961), and Paul A. Varg, *Foreign Policies of the Founding Fathers** (1963).

* Available in a paperback edition.

THE AGE OF MERCANTILISM
WILLIAM APPLEMAN WILLIAMS

Based upon the suggestion by Curtis P. Nettels that one of the consequences of British mercantilism was the creation "of a new mercantilist state on this side of the Atlantic," and upon recent re-evaluations of mercantilism by William D. Grampp, Gunnar Myrdal, Jacob Viner, Charles Wilson, and others, this essay advances the hypothesis that the central characteristic of American history from 1763 to 1828 was in fact the development and maturation of an American mercantilism. Let it be emphasized that the interpretation is offered as a hypothesis and no more—as an idea to be examined and tested, then accepted, modified, or rejected on the basis of its relevance and validity. There is no intention, furthermore, even to imply that the approach as here stated offers final answers to all the vexing problems connected with understanding early American society. It is merely proposed that a reexamination of the era from this angle may lead to new insights, and hence contribute to a broader interpretation of the period.

At the outset, for example, the use of the concept of mercantilism restores to its properly central place the fact that Americans thought of themselves as an empire at the very beginning of their national existence—as part of their assertive self-consciousness which culminated in the American Revolution. Though it may seem surprising, especially when contrasted with the image of isolationism which has been accepted so long, in reality this early predominance of a pattern of empire thought is neither strange nor very difficult to explain. Having matured in an age of empires as part of an empire, the colonists naturally saw themselves in the same light once they joined issue with the mother country.

Revolutionary leaders were confident of their ability "not only to take territory by the sword, but to hold and govern it under a colonial status." Long before the break with England, for example, Benjamin Franklin was a leader of those who entertained a "burning interest in westward expansion." At the threshold of the revolution he visualized an American Empire including Canada, the Spanish Floridas, the West Indies, and perhaps even Ireland. George Washington, John Adams, John Livingston, and Thomas Lee were

SOURCE. William A. Williams, "The Age of Mercantilism: An Interpretation of The American Political Economy 1763–1828," V. 15, October 1958, The William and Mary Quarterly. Reprinted by permission from William A. Williams.

among those who shared such conceptions of an American Empire. By the end of the war, such men as Silas Deane looked forward to the time when "Great Britain, America and Russia united will command not barely Europe, but the whole world united." And in 1789, after remarking that "it is well known that empire has been travelling from east to west," Congregational minister and geographer Jedidiah Morse concluded that "probably her last and broadest seat will be America . . . the largest empire that ever existed."

While the vigor, even cockiness, of such statements may be explained by the consciousness of having whipped the champion, the underlying emphasis on expansion and empire was an integral part of the general outlook of mercantilism, a conception of the world shared by most of the revolutionary generation. Though they revolted against British mercantilism, there is considerable evidence to suggest that early American leaders did not, as so often is assumed, rebel against the idea and practice of mercantilism itself. In stressing the role of natural-rights philosophy in the thinking of the leaders of the revolution, the traditional view of the American Revolution has slighted this key point.

An acceptance of natural law is not incompatible with mercantilism, as is indicated by John Locke's vigorous espousal of both systems. Much of the talk in America about natural rights, moreover, concerned what Thomas Paine called the "natural right" to one's own empire. And though they were willing to use Adam Smith's polemic in behalf of laissez faire as a weapon against British mercantilism (and against their domestic opponents), most Americans adhered firmly in their own practice to the principle that the state had to intervene in economic affairs. America's romance with Smith's laissez faire came later and was of relatively short duration. Hence it would appear that a better understanding of early American history depends in considerable measure upon a grasp of the nature and practice of American mercantilism as it developed between 1763 and 1825.

Traditionally thought of as little more than a narrow and selfish point of view held by the trading interest, mercantilism was in fact a broad definition and explanation of the world shared by most of Western Europe in the seventeenth and eighteenth centuries. In this sense it was the basic outlook of those who labored to build a dynamic balanced economy of agriculture and business organized on a capitalistic basis within a nationalistic framework. Depending upon their specific function and power at any given stage in the process, mercantilists argued among themselves over the best means to achieve and maintain such a system—and differed in their estimates of whether or not it had been established—but they agreed on the objective and upon the need to use the state as a tool.

Whether agrarian or urban, therefore, mercantilists were essentially nationalists who strove for self-sufficiency through increased domestic production and a favorable balance (and terms) of trade. Their emphasis on production and the control of export markets and sources of raw materials, rather than on consumption and economic interdependence, led them to fear surpluses as a sign of crisis and failure. Thus they dropped the old feudal restrictions on exports and replaced them with taxes on imports. Their greatest fear was a surplus of goods. In this respect, furthermore, mercantilism was reinforced—albeit in a back-handed and even unintentional way—by the broad ethical outlook of Puritanism (which frowned on luxury), even though mercantilism itself was a secular and almost amoral system. Likewise, the concept of a chosen people, so strong in Puritanism, also strengthened the secular and economic nationalism of mercantilism. Thus mercantilists constantly labored to build a tightly organized and protected national market and to increase their share of the world market. The key points in their program were integration at home and expansion abroad.

In the exuberant confidence of their victory over Britain, Americans tended to assume that each new state could survive and thrive as a mercantile empire unto itself. That attitude was not too surprising, for each of the new states appeared to enjoy the raw materials, labor supply, and trading facilities for a balanced economy. That estimate of the situation was supported and reinforced by the conviction, itself part of traditional theory, that a state could remain democratic in political and social life only if it were small and integrated, and by the experiences of the colonies in dealing with Great Britain's imperial policy after 1763. Yet the political outlook and faith contradicted certain basic tenets of mercantilism, which Americans also entertained, or assumed.

The first attempt to reconcile the conflict produced the Articles of Confederation. That instrument of government stressed the independence of the states as self-contained units of mercantilism and democratic republicanism, yet also established a central government for the purposes of war and, as in the case of Canada, future expansion. But specific postwar developments, such as the serious recession, the expansionist conflicts between the states, and the difficulties in dealing with other countries in economic affairs, combined to disillusion many Americans with their experiment in particularistic mercantilism.

Broadly speaking, the resulting movement toward a stronger central government grew out of internal and international economic difficulties analyzed and explained with the ideas of mercantilism. By 1785, for example, most of the states, including the agrarian ones, were switching from tariffs for revenue to tariffs for international retaliation and protection. Merchants demanded American navigation acts, artisans agitated for protection of their labor, and agricultural interests wanted help in balancing their political

economy. Various groups of Americans who concerned themselves directly
with the problem of strengthening the central government—and there were
many who were preoccupied with local and immediate difficulties or opportunities—offered several proposals for handling the problem. Centered in
New England, the smallest group favored establishing an aristocratic society
at home and rejoining the British Empire as a contractual junior partner.
Such men were not willing to return to colonial status, but they did favor
economic and social reintegration. Most Americans opposed that solution,
favoring instead either the delegation of more power to the central government under the Articles of Confederation or the substitution of an entirely
new instrument of government.

A letter from James Madison to Thomas Jefferson in the spring of 1786
not only indicates that the agrarian as well as the urban interests favored
one or the other of those last two approaches, but dramatizes the fundamental mercantilism of the entire movement. "A continuance of the present anarchy of our commerce," Madison explained, "will be a continuance of the
unfavorable balance on it, which by draining us of our metals . . . [will
bring our ruin]. In fact, most of our political evils may be traced up to our
commercial ones, and most of our moral may to our political."

Against this background, the Constitution appears as an instrument of
centralized national government framed in the classic manner by men thinking within the framework of mercantilism and blessed with the physical and
human resources for a balanced economy. It provided the foundation for a
national system of economics and politics and organized American strength
for the struggle with other mercantile empires and for the conquest of less
powerful peoples. The latter considerations were essential, for the Founding
Fathers resolved the contradiction between the stress on expansion in mercantilism and the emphasis on a small state in existing democratic political
theory by developing a theory of their own which held that democratic republicanism could be sustained by just such expansion. James Madison, often called the Father of the Constitution, provided the most striking formulation of this proposition, but Thomas Jefferson, John Adams, and other
early leaders either shared or adopted it in one form or another within a
reasonably short time.

Taking his cue from David Hume, the Englishman who attacked Montesquieu's argument that democracy was a system that could work only in
small states, Madison asserted that a large state offered a much better foundation for republicanism. Institutional checks and balances could help, and
were therefore necessary, but they were not enough in and of themselves.
"Extend the sphere," he argued, "and you take in a greater variety of parties and interests; you make it less probable that a majority of the whole will
have a common motive to invade the rights of other citizens; or if such a

common motive exists, it will be more difficult for all who feel it to discover their own strength, and to act in unison with each other. . . ."

While it is possible to conclude from Madison's remarks that he had in mind a static conception of such a large state, three considerations would appear to weaken that reading of his thesis. First, Madison used the verb "extend" in its active, unlimited sense. Second, he was stating a general theory, not making an argument in behalf of a given territorial settlement. And third, he advocated and vigorously supported the continued expansion of the United States. It seems more probable, therefore, that Madison was proposing, *as a guide to policy and action in his own time,* the same kind of an argument that Frederick Jackson Turner formulated a century later, when he advanced his frontier thesis which explained America's democracy and prosperity as the result of such expansion.

Madison's theory became the key to an American mercantilism. Merchants and manufacturers who wanted their own empire found it convincing and convenient. And Jefferson's thesis that democracy and prosperity depended upon a society of landholding freemen was a drastically simplified version of the same idea. Edward Everett of Massachusetts captured the essence of the interpretation in his judgment that expansion was the *"principle of our institutions."* Additional support for this interpretation is offered by Madison's later prophecy (in 1828–29) that a major crisis would occur in about a century, when the continent was filled up and an industrial system had deprived most people of any truly productive property. In the event, Madison's fears proved true sooner than he anticipated. For in the crisis of the 1890's, when Americans *thought* that the frontier was gone, they advanced and accepted the argument that new expansion was the best—if not the only—way to sustain their freedom and prosperity.

Madison's original statement of the expansionist thesis was important for two reasons. First, it provided the theoretical basis for an American mercantilism combining commercial and territorial expansion with political democracy. Second, by thus re-emphasizing the idea of empire, and proposing expansion as the key to national welfare, Madison opened the way for a discussion of the basic questions facing American mercantilism. Those issues concerned domestic economic affairs, the kind of expansion that was necessary and desirable, and the means to accomplish such gains while the nation was young and weak.

Washington's Farewell Address formulated a bipartisan answer to the problem of basic strategy. The solution was to build a commercial empire (which included markets for agricultural surpluses) by avoiding political involvement in the European system, meanwhile retaining complete freedom of action to secure and develop a continental empire in the Western Hemisphere. Washington's proposition was classically simple: play from the strength provided by America's basic economic wealth and geographic location in order to survive immediate weakness and emerge as *the* world power. "If we remain one people, under an efficient government," he promised, "the period is not far off when we may defy material injury from external annoyance . . . when we may choose peace or war, as our interest, guided by justice, shall counsel." Sharing that objective, and quite in agreement with the strategy, Thomas Jefferson summed it all up a bit later in one famous axiom: "entangling alliances with none." And with the enunciation of the Monroe Doctrine, freedom of action became the avowed and central bipartisan theme of American foreign policy.

As a condition of that persuasive agreement, however, several serious conflicts had to be resolved. Perhaps they can be discussed most clearly by defining and considering them within the framework of the gradual defeat and amalgamation of the pro-British and pro-French minorities by a growing consensus in favor of an American mercantilism. Such an approach has the additional value of making it possible to organize the analysis around familiar personalities as symbols of certain ideas, functional groups, and special interests. Let it be posited, therefore, that the following men are key figures in the evolution of an American mercantilism: Timothy Pickering, John Adams, and John Quincy Adams of Massachusetts; Alexander Hamilton of New York; and James Madison, Thomas Jefferson, and John Taylor of Virginia.

In many respects, at any rate, Pickering and Taylor represented the nether fringes of American mercantilism. Pickering trod the trail from reluctant revolutionary to threatening secessionist in the name of a domestic merchant aristocracy functioning as a quasi-independent contractual member of the British Empire. His ideal was a central government charged with the responsibility (and armed with the power and authority) to establish and sustain a politically and socially stratified society and to provide the economic assistance (especially funded credit) that was necessary for the rationalized operations of overseas correspondents of British mercantilism and for domestic speculative ventures. Though Pickering and his supporters fit the traditional stereotype of mercantilists, they were in fact and function no more than the agents of British mercantilism. They were very successful agents, to be sure, but they did not view or define America in terms of its own mercantilism. Rather did they visualize it as a self-governing commonwealth of the British Empire. Hence it was only very late and with great reluctance, if at all, that they supported the measures necessary for a mercantilist state in America.

At the other extreme, John Taylor developed his program as a variation on a theme first stated by the French physiocrats. He emphasized the primacy of agriculture as narrowly as Pickering stressed the virtue and necessity of the merchant-trader-speculator. Taylor's tirades against funded debts and bank stock, and his soliloquies in praise of the noble farmer, seem alike in their total opposition to the principles of mercantilism. But in other respects his ideas were not so untainted by mercantilism as his rhetoric indicated. As with most other planters, for example, his theory of labor coincided at all essential points with the view held by British mercantilists. So, too, did his conception of the role of western lands in the economy of the seaboard "mother country."

With respect to foreign trade, moreover, Taylor was trapped by the weakness of the physiocrats in that area of economics. Ostensibly free traders, the physiocrats did not favor the navy essential to such a program. Taylor and other American imbibers of the physiocratic elixir awoke to discover that their vision did not correspond to reality. Taylor himself was not very adaptive, and ended his career in attacks on Jefferson and other agrarians who did develop an American mercantilism. But Taylor's position does dramatize the dilemma faced by the agrarians. The contradiction between theory and actuality confronted them with a rather apparent choice: either they could content themselves with slow economic stagnation or they could build an American maritime system, accept dependence upon a foreign naval power, or support an American industry. In that choice lies a key aspect of the rise of a mature American mercantilism; for it developed most consciously and was ultimately practiced most rigorously by the southern agrarians who are often assumed to have been most rabidly antimercantilist. If nothing else, the weakness of their ideal program drove them into mercantilism.

It is particularly important to keep that fact in mind when considering Hamilton, about whom the discussion of American mercantilism has billowed for so long. Joseph Charles was essentially correct in his view that "the standard works on Hamilton evade the main issues which his career raises," and his judgment remains relevant despite the plethora of centennial essays and biographies. The entire question of Hamilton's mercantilism has to be decided with reference to three points: the meaning and significance of the *Report on Manufactures,* his role in the Jay Treaty episode, and his plans to join in the further expansion of the British Empire in the Western Hemisphere. However difficult it may be to pin him down with an alternate characterization, Hamilton simply cannot be considered the fountainhead of American mercantilism unless those aspects of his career can be interpreted within the framework of mercantilist thought and action.

Since the *Report on Manufactures* is often accepted as proof, as well as evidence, of Hamilton's mercantilism, it is convenient to give first consideration to that document. In doing so, it seems wise to recall the chronology of his three state papers on economic affairs. Hamilton was commissioned as

Secretary of the Treasury on September 11, 1789; and there followed the manifesto on public credit in January 1790, the report on a central bank in December 1790, and the paper on manufacturing in December 1791. Even the most cursory review of those dates catches the two-year delay between the reports on credit and manufacturers. That interval becomes even more striking when viewed in the context of other events.

It was Madison rather than Hamilton, for example, who gave more attention to protective duties on manufactures during the Constitutional Convention. That is still more illuminating since associations for the promotion of American manufactures had appeared in New York, Boston, Providence, and Baltimore as early as 1785; and resolutions for domestic goods had followed the next year from such additional and widely separated localities as Hartford, Germantown, Richmond, and Halifax (South Carolina). By 1789, furthermore, not only had the anti-Federalists picked up political support from such groups in New England, New York, and Pennsylvania, but the special session of Congress received numerous requests and petitions from various manufacturing societies.

Having passed an emergency revenue bill in the form of tariff legislation, the Congress then *ordered* Hamilton, on January 15, 1790, to prepare a specific report on manufactures. That makes his delay even more noticeable, whatever allowances may be granted for his other duties and the thoroughness of his research. As late as October 1791, moreover, the administration saw no need to increase the tariff of 1789. In matters of chronology, urgency, and emphasis, therefore, it seems clear that Hamilton gave priority to funding the debt and establishing the bank. Those operations represented precisely the needs and objectives of the merchants who were semiautonomous correspondents of British mercantilism, and who were fundamentally opposed to a strong American industry. Their economic, political, and social position would be threatened by a vigorous program of industrialization; for at the very least they would have to make drastic changes in their outlook and actions. Since Hamilton's personal and political position was based on his rapport with that group, it seems relevant to consider whether Hamilton's mercantilism was as thoroughgoing as historians have assumed it was.

In Hamilton's behalf, it can be argued with considerable validity that domestic industry had to have a sound credit system as a cornerstone. But that approach only raises the question of why Hamilton did not present his funding and bank programs as the means to achieve an independent balanced economy. Since he did not, the most relevant explanation would seem to be that Hamilton was in fact a mercantilist who was hamstrung by his political dependence upon the Federalists around Pickering. His association with Tench Coxe would serve to strengthen that analysis. The same argument could then be used to explain why Hamilton delayed his paper on manufactures for almost two years after the Congress had asked for it in January 1790.

The weakest point in that interpretation concerns Hamilton's response to Madison's resolution of January 3, 1794, that "the interests of the United States would be promoted by further restrictions and higher duties in certain cases on the manufactures and navigation of foreign nations employed in the commerce of the United States." Working through William Smith of South Carolina, Hamilton killed Madison's entire program which was designed to promote commercial and industrial independence. Instead, Hamilton's committee in the House reported in favor of more borrowing and further domestic taxes. For that matter, neither Hamilton nor the Federalist party acted to increase protection after 1792.

The explanation of Hamilton's action which does the most to sustain his reputation as an American mercantilist is not as generous to his standing as a reformed monarchist. For given the broad and vigorous agitation from manufacturing societies for greater protection, Madison's resolutions offered Hamilton a striking opportunity to widen the base of the Federalist party. That would have strengthened his hand against the pro-British group within the party and have enabled him to give substance to the *Report on Manufactures*. If it be said that Hamilton favored domestic excise taxes in preference to domestic manufacturing, then his mercantilism appears even more questionable. A stronger argument could be made by reference to Hamilton's known reservations about democracy, which would account for his refusal to court the manufacturers as a counterweight to the merchants around Pickering.

It may be, however, that Hamilton's vigorous opposition to Madison's resolutions of 1794 derived in considerable part from the fact that Madison's program was aimed at Great Britain. Not only was that true in the immediate, particular sense, but it also was the case in that Madison's proposals pointed toward general economic independence. That approach to the question of Hamilton's mercantilism has the virtue of having considerable relevance to his role in Jay's Treaty. An American mercantilist could explain and defend Hamilton's basic attitude and maneuvers behind Jay's back by one or both of two arguments. First, England had to be courted while the United States built a navy. Second, Hamilton stressed the political side of mercantilism.

Neither of those explanations is very convincing: Hamilton always favored the Army over the Navy, and political mercantilism is such a contradiction in terms that it begs the entire issue. That interpretation becomes even less convincing when asked to account for the fact that at the end of his career Hamilton turned not toward manufacturing but in the direction of becoming a partner in Britain's imperial adventures in Latin America. Indeed, Hamilton's foreign policy does less to settle the question of his mercantilism than to recall the report in 1793 that "the English considered Hamilton, [Rufus] King, and [William] Smith, of South Carolina, as main supports of British interest in America. Hamilton, not Hammond, was their effective minister." Perhaps the most to be said of Hamilton's mercantilism is that it was latent and limited, for his actions belied his rhetoric.

As in many other contexts, it is Madison who emerges as the central figure in the development of an American mercantilism. While there are many illustrations, perhaps his resolutions of January 1794 provide the most illuminating evidence. Once again Charles points the way: "The program with which Madison began the first strategic moves against the Federalists was not one which could be called anti-Federalist, particularist, or States' rights." His plan was to combine landed expansion to the west with support for domestic manufacturing and an independent American commercial policy. Considered at the practical political level, it represented a bid to the growing numbers of dissident Federalists who opposed a one-way relationship with Britain. Some of those men eyed a bull market for domestic manufactures. Others thought of an expansionist foreign policy with the established states cast in the role of "mother country." Madison saw such groups as allies for the anti-Federalists, as well as the building blocks of an American mercantilism.

Madison's conception of an American mercantilism was possibly too comprehensive as well as too premature politically to be adopted by Congress in 1794, though it was extensively debated before being sidetracked by Hamilton and Smith. But it did serve as a keen analysis and program for the growing consensus among anti-Federalists. That drive toward economic independence manifested itself in the Non-Intercourse Bill introduced in the summer of 1794, a move which was defeated only by the vote of Vice-President John Adams. Equally significant is the fact that it was backed by congressmen from Pennsylvania and Delaware as well as by those from southern states. Madison's mercantilism picked up new allies very rapidly, and two subsequent events served as catalysts in the process. Considered in the order of their importance, they were Jay's Treaty and the last stage in the defection of John Adams from High Federalism.

Following so closely upon the narrow defeat of the Non-Intercourse Bill, Jay's Treaty added injury to frustration. The great majority of Americans reacted bitterly and vigorously. Already weakened by deep fissures, the Federalist party cracked open under the ensuing attack. It cost them key leaders in such states as New Hampshire and Pennsylvania and alienated unknown numbers of voters south of the Potomac. As one who had cast the deciding vote against the Non-Intercourse Bill only with great reluctance, John Adams provided temporary leadership for such Federalist dissidents.

Adams strengthened his position even more by refusing to go quietly along to war with France at the bidding of the High Federalists. The differences between Hamilton and Adams were numerous, but perhaps none is so important to an appreciation of the maturing American mercantilism as the contrast between Hamilton's passion for a large army and Adams' emphasis on an American navy. Hamilton's military policy was that of the British nabob in North America, while that of Adams represented American mercantilism. Against that background, and in the context of his deciding vote on the Non-Intercourse Bill of 1794, it is possible to appreciate the full impact of Jay's Treaty on Adams. He made peace with France and forced Pickering out of the cabinet.

Little wonder, then, that Jefferson was willing to give way in favor of Adams. But thanks to Madison, who had been organizing a party as well as projecting a theory and a program, Jefferson became President. Once in power, Jefferson and his supporters were prodded by necessity and spurred by their own visions of empire toward the full development of an American mercantilism. There are several explanations for this phenomenon. Among the most important, one might list the following: the foreign-trade dilemma inherent in physiocratic theory (which was intensified by the wars stemming from the French Revolution); the creative leadership provided by such men as Madison and Albert Gallatin (who made his own *Report on Manufactures* in 1810); the political necessities and expediences of unifying and sustaining a national party; and the maturing thought of Jefferson himself. But wherever one chooses to place the emphasis, the fact remains that the Jeffersonians in action were far more mercantilistic than the Federalists had been—even in theory and rhetoric.

As early as 1791, for that matter, Jefferson began to shift away from the physiocratic dogma of free trade. And by 1793 he concluded his *Report on Commercial Policy* with a series of retaliatory proposals that were as mercantilistic as any he criticized. Perhaps even more significant was his early ambivalence toward manufacturing, which he never condemned outright once and for all. Jefferson disliked cities and the factory system for what he judged their negative impact on politics and morals, and for the conditions and style of life they imposed upon human beings, but he never discounted the importance of home manufacturing and commerce. He could not afford to, either as the leader of agrarians beginning to produce surpluses for sale, or as one who sought and accepted support from the increasing number of urban groups of all classes who preferred an empire of their own to rejoining the British system. Even if Jefferson had not caught the intellectual flaw in physiocratic trade theory, its practical consequences were something he could not avoid. In substance, therefore, the Jeffersonians based their strength and their policies on the mercantilistic program of a balanced economy at home and a foreign policy of expansion.

Their strategy was to exploit the policy of neutrality initiated by Washington and continued by John Adams. To do so, Jefferson ultimately resorted to the intensely mercantilistic policies of the embargo and nonimportation against Britain and France. It was with obvious pride that he remarked, in 1809, that those policies "hastened the day when an equilibrium between the occupations of agriculture, manufactures, and commerce, shall simplify our foreign concerns to the exchange only of that surplus which we cannot consume [in return] for those articles of reasonable comfort or convenience which we cannot produce." Not even Madison ever provided a more classic statement of American mercantilism.

Quite in line with Jefferson's recommendations of the 1790's, and his actions between 1800 and 1809, his successors acted vigorously against such weaker opponents as the Barbary Pirates who threatened American trade. On a more general level, Jefferson's argument that American democracy depended upon a surplus of land was but another, even more overtly formulated, version of Madison's theory that extending the sphere was the key to controlling factions. Hence he and his followers initiated and encouraged such expansion wherever they could, as in Florida and to the West; and it was precisely Jefferson's general expansionist outlook which overrode his concern that the Louisiana Purchase was unconstitutional.

The Louisiana Purchase opened the way to apply the tenets of American mercantilism to the entire hemisphere. It also encouraged an explicit American formulation of the expansionist philosophy of history that was implicit in mercantilism. Americans began to call openly and militantly for further expansion whenever and wherever they encountered domestic or foreign difficulties. Indians and Spaniards had to be pushed out of the way or destroyed. Interference with exports had to be stopped, by war if necessary. Canada offered the solution to other domestic economic problems, and should be taken forthwith.

After 1807, when economic troubles appeared at home, that expansionist outlook and program focused on Great Britain as the chief offender against the American Empire. Growing out of an alliance of business and agrarian interests which favored war to relieve immediate difficulties and forestall future crises, the War of 1812 was a classic mercantilist conflict for trade and colonies. The Jeffersonians' earlier economic and maritime warfare, which almost secured the immediate objectives, and which had appeared capable of clearing the way for a general advance, was just as mercantilistic in nature. Though in many ways it failed to attain its avowed objectives, the War of 1812 was in no sense a strategic defeat for American mercantilism. If only in turning Americans to the west and the south, it focused the general spirit of expansion in a new and powerful manner. Perhaps even more significant, the stalemate strengthened the idea of an American System as opposed to the rest of the world. It was in the wake of the War of 1812, after all, that the vapors of Manifest Destiny gathered themselves for an explosion westward to the Pacific.

John Quincy Adams formulated his own concept of Manifest Destiny as early as 1796, when he assured President Washington that the American System would "infallibly triumph over the European system. . . ." Fifteen years later he defined America as "a nation, coextensive with the North American Continent, destined by God and nature to be the most populous and most powerful people ever combined under one social compact." He pushed overseas economic expansion just as vigorously. Even his harshest critics, the High Federalists of New England who wanted to re-enter the British Empire in some form or another, recognized his mercantilism. They called him one of the species of "amphibious politicians, who live on both land and water. . . ."

Both before and after he served as Secretary of State under President James Monroe, Adams devoted his energies to building such an American Empire. His rational program for a dynamic balanced economy at home was too demanding for his countrymen. They grew ever more enamored of a philosophy that assured them that expansion was the way to ease their dilemmas and realize their dreams. Hence they paid little heed to his proposals for domestic development or to his warning that America should go "not abroad in search of monsters to destroy." But to the extent that Adams wanted an empire big enough to sustain such a balanced economy, and to the degree that he partook of the expansionist elixir, he won support and influence. And, indeed, his very presence in the cabinet of Monroe was a symbol of the maturity of American mercantilism. Having broken with the old pro-British party to vote for the Louisiana Purchase and the measures of economic warfare against Europe, Adams became the leader of those business interests which supported territorial as well as commercial expansion.

In timing, authorship, and content, the Monroe Doctrine was the classic statement of mature American mercantilism. Seizing the opportunity presented by the decay of the Spanish Empire, Monroe and Adams moved quickly, decisively, and independently to give substance to Henry Clay's fervent exhortation to "become real and true Americans and place ourselves at the head of the American System." Adams caught the tone and meaning of the doctrine in his famous remark that it was time for America to stop bobbing along as a cock-boat in the wake of the British Empire. Acting in that spirit, he spurned Secretary George Canning's not-so-subtle suggestion that America join England in a joint guarantee of Latin American independence and a pledge against their own expansion in the region. Canning claimed high honors for having brought in the New World to redress the balance of the Old, but one would like to think that Adams enjoyed a hearty chuckle over such ability to put a rhetorical gloss on a policy defeat. For what Canning had done was to block the old empires only to be confronted by the challenge of a mature American mercantilism.

In the negative sense, the Monroe Doctrine was designed to check further European colonization in the Western Hemisphere. But Americans were quite aware of the positive implications of the strategy: it left the United States as the most powerful nation on the scene. America's ultimate territorial and commercial expansion in the New World would be limited only by its energies and its preferences—just as Washington had argued. The negative side of the Monroe Doctrine is the least significant feature about it: the crucial point is that it was, in the minds of its authors, in its language, and in its reception by Americans, the manifesto of an American Empire.

The Monroe Doctrine was the capstone of a system destined to succumb to its own success. For in broad historical perspective, the classic function of mercantilism was to build a system strong enough to survive the application of the principles of Adam Smith. Without an American mercantilism there could have been no Age of Jacksonian Laissez Moi Faire. Perhaps, indeed, the greatest tribute to the leaders of American mercantilism lies in the fact that their handiwork withstood the trauma of a civil war and the sustained shock of unrestrained and irrational exploitation for some seventy years— until it became necessary in the Crisis of the 1890's to undertake the building of a new corporate system.

CHAPTER 19

THE DEVELOPMENT OF THE TWO-PARTY SYSTEM

During the first half of the twentieth century most students of American history assumed that the political parties that arose under Hamilton and Jefferson had their origins in the struggle over the ratification of the Constitution; some even assumed that parties derived from the loyalist-revolutionary disputes of the early 1770's. Thus, Hamilton and his followers were the reluctant revolutionaries who supported the Constitution. Jefferson and his supporters led in the revolutionary struggle but opposed the Constitution.

The basis for this belief was more than just a repetition of the name "Federalist," and more than a general knowledge of the political philosophies of the men involved. It was firmly rooted in a major work, *The Economic Origins of Jeffersonian Democracy** (1915), by one of America's greatest historians, Charles A. Beard. In the 1950's, this view came under strong attack with the posthumous publication in book form of a series of articles, *The Origins of the American Party System** (1956), by a very promising historian, Joseph Charles. The battle was shortly joined by a number of other scholars, including political scientists and sociologists as well as historians.

It is now well established that the political issues that gave rise to the new factions or parties were of an immediate nature rather than of historical origin. However, the importance of the nature of American political institutions in this development is not well established. Could our constitutional system function without parties? What historical and personality factors were responsible for the emergence of parties?

In addition to the works cited above, the student should also examine Manning Dauer, *The Adams Federalists** (1953), and such general studies of the development of American political parties as Herbert Agar, *The Price of Union** (1950), Roy Nichols, *The Invention of the American Political Parties* (1967), Seymour M. Lipset, *The First New Nation** (1963), and William N. Chambers, *Political Parties in a New Nation** (1963).

* Available in a paperback edition.

THE GENESIS OF MODERN PARTIES
WILLIAM N. CHAMBERS

In 1790 Alexander Hamilton, as Secretary of the Treasury in the new government of the United States, proposed to Congress the first in a long series of measures aimed at the economic development of the new nation. Before he was finished he had brought into being a powerful political engine to advance his program, to support his determined effort to shape the destiny of the infant republic. In effect, he had founded the Federalist party. He began this task fourteen years after the declaration of American independence, seven years after the treaty of peace which followed the Revolutionary War.

In 1797 Thomas Jefferson boarded a coach at Monticello, the gracious home he had built on a Virginia hilltop. After three years of retirement devoted mainly to agricultural experiments and to country life, he was on his way to the nation's capital to assume fresh duties as Vice-President. Yet the trip of a week or so was more than just a return to the chores of office. It was a crucial stage in a political odyssey which was to bring him at last to full acceptance of active leadership in the opposition Republican party, a political force which was unique for its time.

The two events symbolize the genesis and ultimate establishment of national political parties on the American scene. These political engines were not only the first parties to adventure on the precarious ground of politics in an emerging nation but also the first true parties of modern times, appearing well before such formations developed in England or other European countries. They were shaped slowly and painstakingly, as part of a general progress in which the American states moved from colonial dependence and revolutionary uncertainties to become a stable democratic, modern republic. Like the nation itself, parties were the work not only of Hamilton and Jefferson, and of other great leaders like George Washington, the industrious James Madison, and the conscientious John Adams, but of nameless lesser workers as well. The final result was not

SOURCE. Abridged from *Political Parties in a New Nation: The American Experience, 1776–1809,* by William N. Chambers, New York, 1963, pp. 1–2, 36–44, 53–67, and 106–107. Copyright 1963 by Oxford University Press, Inc. Reprinted by permission of Oxford University Press and the author.

only parties but a system of competing parties in interaction. Yet no man could have said in advance just what the outcome would be.

Indeed, the whole national and party progress was beset by the difficulties and hesitations of exploration. It was fortunate that most of the new nation's leaders were men not only of high public faith and national vision, but of a profoundly pragmatic ability to learn and invent as they went along. . . .

II

In his advocacy, political management, and nation building, Hamilton brought together the elements that came to constitute the Federalist party. He did not consciously set out to do so, but such was the ultimate result.

It took some time to set the government going, first briefly in New York and then after 1790 in Philadelphia as temporary capitals. The first session of Congress was devoted mainly to establishing the executive departments and the judicial branch, and to other housewarming chores. It was not until 1790 and 1791 that Hamilton presented his proposals, and a new political era opened. . . .

In this effort, he was favored by an unusual political context. Not only did he move in the protective shadow of Washington's prestige. He was also able to "produce the event" so brilliantly at the outset—only in the tariff did he fall much short of his goals—largely because he could "march at the head of affairs" along comparatively open ways. In a new governmental system still being formed and in an unstructured national politics, he found ready opportunity for his purposes.

At the outset, the legislative branch Hamilton addressed was a leaderless herd. Composed almost entirely of "Federalists," in the sense of men who had supported the Constitution of 1787, Congress set no direction of its own for the new government. During the first session of April-September 1789, in a nearly free flow of legislative individualism, members had agreed or disagreed as issues came and went. There was sharp cleavage over proposals by Vice-President Adams to establish a "hightoned" government by giving grandiose titles to the president and other such devices, but alignments on the issue disappeared with the defeat of Adams's proposals. The choleric "Billy" Maclay of Pennsylvania, an Ishmael in the Senate who smelled conspiracy in any alliance however temporary, noted periodic instances of "caballing and meeting of members in knots." Yet even he could find little consistency beyond certain joint exertions by the "mercantile interest," or the support that Pennsylvania, New Jersey, Maryland, and Delaware members gave proposals for imports to encourage manufactures, or the tendency of "the New England men" to join together in opposing molasses duties. The ramblings of individual views and shifting relationships were only occasionally joined into blocs representing particular interests or sections. Otherwise, there were not even clear factional divisions. A summary comment by Maclay on early Congressional behavior was not far from the mark: "The mariner's compass has thirty-two points; the political one, perhaps as many hundreds."

The sessions of 1790 and 1791, however, revealed the stamp of Hamilton's firm leadership. The law creating the Treasury Department had sketched unusual ties between the head of that department and Congress in the reports and interchange of information it required. Beginning with the debt-assumption issue, Hamilton elaborated these formal ties into the bonds of informal executive-legislative leadership, utilizing, in Maclay's phrase, "every kind of management." His "reports" were calls to action, and he and his assistants provided arguments and statistics for Congressional debates. He followed legislative affairs with the utmost care, keeping a sharp eye on timing, favorable committee appointments, and chances for maneuver. He met privately with members, and discreetly arranged informal conferences to draw his followers together. Everything "is prearranged by Hamilton and his group," Maclay cried in the anguish of opposition.

Although Maclay exaggerated, he was right in perceiving that the debt and bank issues, with the prestige of Washington's "name," had produced a "court faction." Its genesis in Hamilton's executive or "ministerial" leadership marked the beginnings of coherence and order in politics in the new nation's capital.

III

The emergence of management at the capital brought strong responses across the country. In the process, what began as a capital faction soon became a national faction and then, finally, the new Federalist party.

From the national center, ties of common interest and action were extended into the states, counties, and towns. Again Hamilton played a prominent role, weaving a web of correspondents out of his wartime associates, his business connections and friends, and the many individuals whom, as Secretary, he was able to oblige. His personal contacts and personal influence were used to draw together a new political formation, which eventually became less personal. The Federalists also drew on the first American veteran's association, the Society of the Cincinnati, a strongly knit organization of Revolutionary War officers and their descendants. Such notable figures as Fisher Ames and Theodore Sedgwick in Massachusetts, John Jay and Rufus King in New York, John Marshall in Virginia, or Robert Goodloe Harper in South Carolina joined the cause, along with many others. Thus Hamilton's original faction reached out into the countryside and developed into a national political structure which could support its capital leadership by undertaking the labors of propaganda, electioneering, and other political tasks. Its key local leaders were men of position and high respectability in their communities: former military officers everywhere, or mercantile magnates in New York; the Congregational divines in Massachusetts and Connecticut, or Episcopalian ministers in the Middle Atlantic region and in the coastal plains of the South; captains of finance in Philadelphia, or great planters in Maryland or South Carolina. From the Federalists' center at the capital to their periphery in the counties and towns, relationships among established notables provided the strong strands of the emerging Federalist structure. Such notables drew in other participants, and together they soon formed the ranks of the active workers or "cadre" of the emerging party.

Yet the party-in-the-making also rested on a broad combination of interests and opinions. Like any open major party in a pluralistic society, it came to include in its following a substantial range and significant density of groups and individuals. Domestic merchants, men in the shipping trade and shipbuilders, holders of public debt securities, bankers, investors and financiers generally, owners of struggling manufactories, great Tidewater planters, dependent business and professional men—all could look happily to Hamilton's promotion of enterprise under the protection of government action. Furthermore, most of these groups had already enjoyed sufficient economic development to enable them to support their interests with significant political power. Yet the Federalist appeal was not limited to capitalist or proprietary interests. Many wage earners, particularly in shipbuilding along the coastal rivers, where a man might farm part of the time and work in the shipyards another part, could see employment and higher wages in Hamilton's proposals. Modest farmers who looked to the export market could also anticipate prosperity and higher prices as a result of Federalist policy, although ultimately the great weakness in the Federalist fabric proved to be an insensitivity to the concerns of agriculture as a whole. The assumption scheme had a strong appeal in states that had incurred heavy Revolutionary debts and failed to pay them off. This special issue operated in Hamilton's favor in debt-ridden South Carolina as well as in mercantile New England. Indeed, Massachusetts and South Carolina became the early Northern and Southern foundations of Federalist strength.

Their emerging structure and broad base gave the Federalists a position of effective influence in the electoral arena. Working through their network of notables and lesser leaders, and through Hamilton's web of correspondents, beneficiaries, and officeholders, the Federalists were able to put forward candidates and mobilize voters for them. Though they tended to look upon elections largely as opportunities for the public to ratify their policies, Federalist managers knew that co-ordinated action in election contests was essential to maintaining power.

The Federalists also drew support from an imposing propaganda array. In 1789 Hamilton and Senator Rufus King of New York raised funds to enable John Fenno to establish the *Gazette of the United States,* which became the semi-official national Federalist organ, published first in New York and then in Philadelphia. In 1790 the *Columbian Centinel* in Boston, under the editorship of Benjamin Russell, began a long career as polemical spokesman for New England partisans. In 1793 gifts from Federalist merchants in New York launched the *American Minerva,* under the great grammarian and lexicographer Noah Webster, as the city's first daily. These and other major presses gave the lead to lesser sheets, and the Federalists could soon count a majority of the nation's editors on their side. Early newspapers were overwhelmingly political in character; and taken together they constituted a major force for factional or party cohesion, communicating partisan information and views from the centers of power to the outlying communities. Thus the Federalists undertook another key function of parties: influencing or polarizing national opinion, on particular issues as they arose or around their program as a whole. In the process, they brought additional measures of order into national politics.

The Federalists' achievement of full party status came with the development of emotional attachment to the party as such. The concerns of interest, economic as in Hamilton's proposals or otherwise, provided critical strands for party formation; but something more was also necessary. This was the emergence of unifying faiths and loyalties, of exclusive and distinctive "in-group" attitudes, of emotional commitments, of at least the beginnings of an ideology. Here again the charisma of Washington, his aura as a providential agent of national independence and national identity, supplied "an *Aegis very essential"* to Federalist party development. At the outset of his Administration the President gave an ear to the divergent views of a cabinet which included Jefferson as well as Hamilton and played a chairman-of-the board role, deliberating and deciding among alternative policy suggestions. As time passed, however, Washington himself and his Administration as a whole became more and more partisan; and by 1793 he was seeking advice almost entirely from a limited number of Federalist-minded leaders. Meanwhile, his portentous name was increasingly used as a distinctively Federalist symbol. Thus the Father of His Country became also the father figure of Federalist propaganda, a focus for partisan faiths, sentiments, and loyalties.

Reactions to new issues furthered the development of ideological ties. The French Revolution, at first widely hailed in America, ran its course toward regicide, radical republicanism, and (in February 1793) war with Great Britain. Determined to avoid involvement, Washington proclaimed a policy of official neutrality, a course Jefferson at the State Department accepted reluctantly in the face of treaties of commerce and alliance with France which had been signed in America's own hour of revolutionary trial. Yet to most Federalists the issue had become one of sanity against madness, stability against chaos, and their sentiments lay with the established order they thought England represented. The whole controversy prompted a war of words in which, as it intensified over the years, Federalist "Anglomen" came to stigmatize opponents with the cry of "Jacobin!" while opposition "Gallomen" responded with "Monocrat!" Though group or economic interests were not absent from the French-British issue in America, the controversy once again brought an emotion-alized, philosophical, or symbolic cleavage of deeper faiths, convictions, and loyalties. In the ideological controversy the Federalists could perceive their party as a knightly band of saviors, the true champions of society, stability, and the nation. Irrational as attachment to Washington as father figure may have been, exaggerated as the logomachy over the French-British question was, these symbolic reactions and emotional ties completed the great transition from a Federalist faction to a Federalist party, as part of a general transition from old-style faction politics to modern party politics. They did so by reinforcing the seams of structure with crucial threads of emotional *élan,* of Federalist party spirit.

Throughout the long shaping of the Federalist formation, Hamilton played a curious though commanding role. In effect he had initiated the whole effort with his vision and advocacy, and throughout its early years he stood forth as the party's unquestioned spokesman and leader. Yet at no time, apparently, despite his energy and brilliance, did he see himself in full consciousness as a man who was building a party. Like his colleagues, he had no pattern of party in mind to go by, and had to devise what amounted to party practices as party structure took form. His purposes, as he saw them, were to point the new nation in the "right" direction, place its new government on firm foundations, mobilize support for his management in that government, and thwart such political foes as might appear. Furthermore, even while these goals brought him to act as a bold party leader, he could condemn the very idea of party. To be sure, what he usually had in mind by the term was a "factious opposition"; it was as much the idea of a co-ordinated opposition as the idea of party that he feared, and he and other Federalists tended to use the terms "party" and "party spirit" more and more as stigmas to damage their opponents. Nonetheless, the labors of Hamilton and his allies did make a party also—the first modern party of Western history, and a remarkably effective one at that.

Indeed, its early achievements in structure, following, and ideology make the Federalist formation a powerful political phalanx, and marked it for initial success. Yet certain characteristics that grew out of its origins also marked it for ultimate failure in the American context. It began as, and remained, a "party of notables," in Max Weber's phrase, despite its wide early following. It was such because it was led by and found its center among men of established property, position, and power; and the attitudes of such men gave the Federalist outlook a particular cast. Hamilton himself had remarked, "The mass of the people are turbulent and changing—they seldom judge or determine right." Such attitudes of elitist condescension, which became typical of the Federalists, ultimately offended the mass of voters. These attitudes also led the Federalists themselves to resist the development of broad, public organization as a means to mobilize mass support. Such organization as the Federalists did achieve was largely oligarchic and more than half clandestine.

Thus, to their chronic weakness of appeal to the bulk of the nation's small farmers, the Federalists added an elitist structure, corresponding attitudes of condescension, and disdain of popular organization. As time strengthened the new democratic impulse in American society, such characteristics were to prove fatal flaws. For some years, however, their party remained dominant.

Viewed in historical analysis and against the retrospect of American faction politics in the 1770's and 1780's, the emergence of the Federalists reveals a transition from the older "connexions" of fluid factions, family cliques, or juntos to the newer, modern connection of party. . . .

IV

As the Federalist party originated with action by Hamilton at the Treasury, so the first clear impetus of opposition came in reactions led by James Madison in Congress. The opposition, however, began not only as a self-styled "Republican" group at the capital, but as a popular Republican movement in the states and communities. . . .

It was the junction of Madison's Republican faction at the capital with this indigenous opposition that ultimately made the Republican party. Yet the formation of that party was a slow process of discovery and invention for the men who came to lead it, and it was some years before its shape was fully apparent.

No bold innovative protagonist, Madison nonetheless was a dogged antagonist to "Belcour."* He was a Virginia planter's son and scholarly graduate of the College of New Jersey, which was later renamed Princeton. Barely five feet, four inches tall, soft-spoken and a bit fussy, he lacked commanding flair, and his leadership depended on the fact that he was shrewd, ready to meet the challenge Hamilton presented, and immensely industrious. He took the floor in the House of Representatives more frequently than any other member; and he was also busy behind the scenes, trying to persuade other members, carrying on a substantial political correspondence, and devising strategy. As early as the second session of Congress in 1790, the philosopher of the Constitution had established himself as the chief spokesman against what Hamilton wanted to make of the national character.

V

It was a circumspect, slow-forming sort of opposition. Like Jefferson, for example, Madison was willing to compromise on the debt assumption question if he could, even without the bait of establishing the capital on Virginia's border which had been offered by Hamilton to get assumption through. Furthermore, despite Madison's activity in Congress, opposition remained for some time fluid, undisciplined, and scattered. Only by late 1791 and early 1792 were lines discernible between Hamilton's "court faction" on the one hand and a reasonably consistent anti-Administration bloc on the other. Even so, as late as 1794 a fifth or more of the members in the House showed no consistent attachment to any faction or bloc. . . .

Generally, the Republicans took a negative stand on Hamilton's program for positive action to promote economic development. To the Republicans, the gains from Hamilton's policies for capitalist enterprisers were more than counterbalanced by their cost to agriculturists. On the whole, the opposition in addition saw no pressing need for rapid industrial advances. In their view planters, plain farmers, and many other elements

---

* A polemical reference, made in 1790, to Alexander Hamilton. (Eds.)

in the population could be happy and prosperous if they were provided the elementary protections of government, not overburdened by taxes, and then left alone. Republican economic policy thus became a policy of "equal rights for all, special privileges for none," as Jefferson put it—of opposition to Hamilton's measures as a panoply of "special privileges," and insistence on a political economy that amounted to "hands off." They were aware that, to succeed, a government must be effective and must provide satisfaction to important interests in the society; but they were convinced that a policy of *laissez faire* could best serve both agricultural interests and the principle of equality, and could also "succeed." Ultimately the forces of industrialization, economic development, and capitalism were to triumph in the sweep of modernization; and the process was to bring new outpourings of goods and services which soon raised American living standards above those of contemporaneous European nations. In the 1790's, however, the ordinary American was already relatively comfortable in comparison with his European counterpart; and thus Americans were not swept so strongly into the current of rising economic expectations which was to characterize later emerging peoples, as they looked to their own contemporaries, the modern industrial nations. In this situation, the new American nation as a whole did not find itself so pressed for the payoff of forced economic development as other new nations have been. In this situation also, the Republican economic outlook could win broad popular support from groups who could see Hamilton's measures as a threat to agrarian ways and to equality.

As the years passed, meanwhile, the Congressional opposition broadened its scope and found increased co-ordination. In 1790 Maclay in the Senate, who could see only "caballing" in Hamilton's "management," was somewhat naïvely startled to discover the peculiar role a Virginian-turned-Pennsylvanian was playing behind the scenes. This was the discreet go-between John Beckley, former mayor of Richmond and now Clerk of the House, who was intimate both with Speaker Frederick Augustus Muhlenberg of Pennsylvania and with Madison, as well as with other members. Thus Billy Maclay found that he could, "through this channel, communicate what I please to Madison." After 1791, Madison was also flanked by other leaders such as, in the Senate, his former opponent Monroe of Virginia and Burr of New York, and, in the House, the bold polemicist William Branch Giles of Virginia and the gentle, simple-republican Nathaniel Macon of North Carolina. Again and again, Giles in particular was effective as a critic of Federalist policies, from the national bank to lesser measures such as the "favoritism" of bounties to aid cod fisheries. Early in 1793 he offered a set of nine resolutions censuring virtually all of Hamilton's official conduct, and aimed at forcing him out of office. For the moment, Federalist fire was directed less against Madison and his faction than against "Giles and his junto."

The bitter Federalist orator of the House, Fisher Ames (of Massachusetts and Harvard) cried out against the new force of opposition. Writing at the beginning of 1793 to a fellow ultra-Federalist, Timothy Dwight (of Connecticut, and President of Yale), he protested: "Virginia moves in a solid column, and the discipline of party is as severe as the Prussian. Deserters are not spared. Madison is become a desperate party leader." Intolerant of any opposition, particularly opposition tinged with democratic "evil," he was exaggerating. But an anti-Administration Congressional faction existed by 1792 and 1793, and Virginia men composed its core.

Changes in relationships between major figures in the national government also exacerbated political cleavage. Quite early Madison had concluded that Adams was hopelessly embroiled in an "anti-republican" (meaning Federalist) course and had written him off. More important, as Washington himself was drawn ever more deeply into the Federalist cause, his trust in Hamilton was strengthened and his ties with Madison and Jefferson were weakened. Late in 1791 Madison's role in establishing Philip Freneau—"that rascal Freneau," Washington called him—as an anti-Hamilton editor had caused a severe chill in relations between the President and the Congressman. Finally, when by 1793 Madison's opposition role became fixed, confidential exchanges with Washington came to an end. At the same time Jefferson, slow to oppose as he was, found it increasingly difficult to get along with Hamilton; and the years brought cankers of difference which even Washington's continued tactful efforts could not heal. In 1791 both men gave the President opinions on the national bank proposal, Hamilton defending his brain child, Jefferson raising doubts on strict-constructionist constitutional grounds. Other questions sharpened the animosity: patronage contentions; differences on financial policy, with Jefferson listing for Washington in 1792 a bill of twenty-one objections to Hamilton's views; and a personal condemnation of Jefferson by Hamilton in 1792. When Jefferson left the cabinet at the end of 1793, rupture at the executive as well as the legislative centers of government was complete.

Meanwhile, events brought increasing collaboration between Jefferson and Madison. In 1791 Jefferson was inadvertently drawn into a press-and-pamphlet controversy in which John Adams was accused of being the author of an anonymous attack on Thomas Paine's pamphlet defending the French Revolution, *The Rights of Man*. Having written a letter praising the pamphlet, Jefferson could condemn (as did Paine) "the doctrine of king, lords & commons," and see Adams as its sponsor. Yet he also regretted that he had been brought into the controversy with his old friend of Revolutionary days, and proclaimed "my love of silence & quiet, & my abhorrence of dispute." By mid-1793, however, Jefferson was aghast at the pro-British, anti-French, executive-prerogative doctrines Hamilton, as "Pacificus," was expounding in a series of articles defending Washington's neutrality proclamation. He urged Madison: "For God's sake, my dear Sir, take up your pen, select the most striking heresies and cut him to pieces in the face of the public." As "Helvidius," Madison did so, urging the role of Congress in the treaty and war powers against Hamilton's penchant for executive authority. In a dramatic Congressional debate on a report Jefferson had submitted at a propitious moment concerning commercial relations with Great Britain and France, Madison directly echoed Jefferson's views. On the other side William Loughton Smith of South Carolina, working from a document Hamilton had put into his hands, took the floor as the Federalist voice. The emergence of Madison as Jefferson's spokesman, balancing Smith as Hamilton's agent, represented a significant crystallization of factional ties between executive and legislative leaders. Although the actual debate had to wait until 1794, just after Jefferson's retirement, the Madisonian Congressional faction was becoming a general capital faction—and turning to foreign as well as domestic issues. . . .

This characteristic,* plus what Jefferson had come to stand for as chief author of the Declaration of Independence, as a moderate liberal-reform governor in Virginia, and as the informal philosopher of democratic-republican convictions, inevitably made him a reference point and symbol for the opposition to Hamilton's doctrines. Even in his retirement to his Monticello home in Virginia he was, willy-nilly, the focus of the republican cause and its potential gentle hero. As factional lines drew tighter, he necessarily began to assume a qualified role of leadership, although the main direction of affairs remained with men like Madison or Beckley.

Another landmark in the emergence of resistance at the capital was the establishment of an opposition press. It began with "that rascal Freneau" in October 1791. A poet, a Princeton man also who was friendly there with such future Republicans as Madison and Burr, Philip Freneau was also an effective journalist. Largely at Madison's instigation, but with Jefferson's approval and aid, he was brought to Philadelphia to establish the *National Gazette*. He also served as printer for official

* Jefferson's charm and strong personal appeal.

State Department papers, just as John Fenno of the earlier *Gazette of the United States* acted as printer for Treasury papers. The *National Gazette* joined the bank fray with a series of essays by Madison. On the issues of world politics and ideology it was strongly pro-French, full of praises for Paine and brickbats for Burke, as champion and critic respectively of the French Revolution. Generally more "radical" and inclined to ideological blacks and whites than either Jefferson or Madison, Freneau was a vigorous catalyst for opposition reactions. He was also an early example of the use of patronage for political purposes, serving not only as printer for Jefferson's State Department but also as a clerk-translator with almost a sinecure in the department itself.

Politically, the *National Gazette* was an instrument of Republican cohesion. It communicated the words and deeds of factional leaders at the center of government to emerging local leaders and followers across the country, thus promoting a national tone. It did this in part directly, in part by playing oracle to local editors, who clipped generously from it. Never so blessed with presses as the Federalists, the inchoate Republican impulse could count on only a few large papers like the *American Advertizer* in Philadelphia and the *Independent Chronicle* in Boston, but numerous country weeklies followed Freneau's lead. The *National Gazette* remained a factional rather than a party organ, however; and it was short-lived, yielding in 1793 to the Philadelphia *Aurora* under Benjamin Franklin Bache. When Jefferson withdrew from the cabinet cockpit, Freneau withdrew from national prominence to lesser journalism in New Jersey and to composing nature lyrics.

VI

In the states, counties, and towns, meanwhile, forces of interest and opinion that could be combined into a complex political entity were beginning to gather.

In Virginia, for example, wily old Patrick Henry, during the movement for a new Constitution, had "smelled a rat." Near the end of 1790, convinced that his fears had been confirmed, he carried a series of strong resolutions through the Virginia legislature at Richmond. They condemned Federalist policies for spawning a "moneyed interest" inimical to agriculture and proper commerce, and as an excessive exercise of national power at the expense of the states. Privately, Hamilton grumbled, "This is the first symptom of a spirit which must either be killed, or it will kill the Constitution." The Federalists might act and assemble for their purposes, but it was presumably not fitting for an opposition to do so.

Again, at Pittsburgh, in western Pennsylvania: "The cause of France is the cause of man, and neutrality is desertion." These stirring words appeared in a public letter sent to President Washington by H. H. Brackenridge in May 1793, after the manifesto of neutrality between warring England and France.

Such expressions revealed a humus of national sentiment that promoted the growth of a popular Republican opposition, a ferment not only of immediate issues but also of larger moral and political questions.

Before long, the opposition had achieved some organization which revealed a strong ideological bent. In 1793 eleven popular political associations calling themselves Democratic Societies or Republican Societies were formed, and by 1794 another two dozen were established. Ten flourished in Pennsylvania, seventeen grew up in the hospitable soil of the South, and in every state but one the Societies flowered. Their political hue was vibrantly anti-Federalist. Though other interests were also intertwined in the movement—merchants looking to the French trade, or some speculators in western lands who saw Hamilton's exise tax as an obstacle to settlement, or dissident sugar or tobacco planters— the appeal of the Democratic or Republican clubs was particularly directed to the mass of "farmers" in the countryside and to "mechanics" in the towns. The latter term included such diverse callings as self-employed craftsmen, ship-carpenters, and mariners. Indeed, one ultra-populist outburst was a printed "Feast of Merriment," in which hearty mariners were heroized in pornographic anecdote while figures of Federalist respectability were subjected to salacious jibes. Yet the Societies had respectable leaders of their own, particularly urban and urbane doctors, editor-"printers," and teachers—intellectuals who gave the Society movement much of its ideological coloration. Several, like James Hutchinson and Benjamin Rush (founder of the Philadelphia Dispensary) in medicine, or Freneau and Benjamin Franklin Bache in letters or journalism, were eminent in their fields. Few lawyers, however, and only a negligible number of ministers joined the movement. Its broad liberal character was less appealing than Federalism to traditionalist-oriented men. . . .

From the Societies or insurrection to philosophical flowerings, the humus of popular antagonism was producing a lusty growth, despite bitter counterattacks evoking the magic of Washington's name. A new movement was at hand.

The whole development brought to the fore the difficult question of an opposition faction or party. Under Hamilton's leadership, the Federalists were building a "government" party, a party of stability, dedicated to the idea that the first imperative for government in a new nation was that it must govern and sustain itself. By contrast, the rising Republican movement was maintaining, in effect, that the new polity should also provide room for counteraction, for effective representation of interests and opinions that were slighted or discountenanced in the government party. In addition, the emerging Republicans were "going to the people," in a virtually unprecedented attempt not only to represent popular interests and concerns but also to mobilize popular opposition to those who held power. If they had their way, if their appeal to planters, farmers, and "mechanics" was broadened sufficiently to succeed, it would end by displacing the Federalists in power and substituting a new set of governors. It would do so, however, not by intrigue or violence but by peaceful means, by the weight of votes in elections, by popular choice or decision. In its notion of opposition and the possibility of a peaceful transfer of power, effected by peaceful democratic action, the emerging Republican movement represented a radically new outlook in political history.

Despite its commitment to peaceful means, opposition brought strains in national unity. It was perhaps fortunate as well as inevitable that the Federalists, with their emphasis on stability and consolidation, came first on the scene and held power first; that the Republicans appeared later and were slower to gain the strength that made them contenders for public power; and that both formations still reached only limited numbers of voters, instead of achieving immediately the full mobilization of popular masses in party competition. If the new polity had begun its political life with two full-blown parties, both stirring broad mass action in their behalf, the frictions of party combat might have proved unmanageable. It was also certainly fortunate that the opposition which looked to Madison or Jefferson was moderate rather than extreme, able to work within a developing national tradition rather than bound to deep social cleavages or to intransigent positions. In fact, the views of Republicans and Federalists were not "wide as the poles asunder." If they had been, or if the methods of the Whiskey Rebellion had been commonly employed, the nation might have been disrupted or opposition might have been snuffed out long before a two-party system could develop. Even as it was, it was years before the nation as a whole came to full acceptance of the idea of a governing party on the one hand and an opposition on the other.

At the outset, meanwhile, the opposition did not yet constitute a party. The Republicans were at most a capital faction that was beginning to find sympathy and support in the countryside in a congeries of dissenting elements, bodies of opinion, associations, and groups. Even more than with Hamilton and the Federalists, the ultimate Republican formation was the end result of a long and halting process of searching and of experimentation in workable ways to meet immediate problems. Although

Madison and others spoke of a "Republican party" from time to time in the early years of opposition, the term at first meant little to them beyond sympathy and some co-ordination among like-minded men; and Jefferson remained unconvinced of the wisdom or necessity of party. What the Republican leaders wanted to do at the beginning was to oppose what they took to be wrong measures and win sufficient support to block them. It was some time before they advanced to the point where they arrived at some conception of a popularly-based party in a full sense and began to fill the new roles it called for. When they did so, they brought about a new kind of political formation or institution—but it was not to spring forth in a day. . . .

It is in terms of relationships between structure and following that the Republicans may be thought of as a new kind of political institution. The Federalists achieved party structure earlier and found a substantial popular power base; and yet they never quite transcended their ministerial, English-oriented, elitist origins. They represented interests, shaped opinion, and offered choices to the electorate; but they were not given to encouraging intraparty popular participation. They always depended on a comparatively close nucleus of leaders in government, and their attitude toward the public and electorate was always an uncertain mixture of condescension and fear. The Republicans on the other hand, although slower to form, finally established a close rapport between leaders and followers.

The difference is manifest in various facets of the Republican formation. Like the Federalists, the Republicans built out from a nucleus at the center of government, many of their early leaders also were notables, and Jefferson frequently showed at least a trace of condescension in his attitude toward the people, despite his republican philosophy. Yet the coruscations of republican sentiment in currents of opinion, in the Democratic and Republican Societies, and in the furor over foreign policy, before there was a Republican party, gave the party a broad potential power base in advance. Furthermore, from the outset the Republican leaders, cadres, and actives included a large number of "politicians," of men who made their careers and achieved prominence in politics, as contrasted with notables; and the Republicans were very nearly a "party of politicians," in Max Weber's term. In this situation, the party's leaders came to look to public opinion and to the electorate as vital powers to which the party should be responsive or responsible. Thus the Republican outlook developed in terms of leaders not only acting on their following but also interacting with it. The Republican founders were the first modern party-builders to conceive of a party in a distinctively democratic role, and thus the first to create a genuinely "popular" party.

CHAPTER 20

THOMAS JEFFERSON:
HIS HERITAGE TO AMERICA

All American political figures on all sides of all questions customarily have appealed to the authority of Thomas Jefferson. His words were used by Southerners in support of secession, but they were also used by Abraham Lincoln in support of human freedom. Today, he is much quoted by states' righters, but the ringing phrases of the Declaration of Independence are used repeatedly by those in the Civil Rights Movement. His words and sentiments have been adopted by anti-Communist right-wingers and by left-leaning liberals; by Democrats and Republicans; and by traditionalists and progressives. Different generations of Americans have viewed Thomas Jefferson in a variety of ways, as the historian, Merrill D. Peterson, shows in his study, *The Jefferson Image in the American Mind** (1960).

Dumas Malone attempts to bring clarity to this confused picture by using a "common sense" approach to determine the meaning that Thomas Jefferson has for us today. Professor Malone examines Jefferson's acts, policies, and words in the area of world affairs, his presidential administrations, his views of the functions of government and, finally, the words and deeds that Jefferson himself believed had the "quality of timelessness": the items included on his tombstone. Malone specifically argues that we cannot find the relevance of Jefferson by taking him out of his

313

times and by directly applying his policies to today's problems. We must consider him in his own setting of time, place, and circumstance.

This selection raises and answers important questions about the nature and uses of history. What does Malone say about the widespread use of Jefferson's name in direct support of politicians and causes? In view of the prevalent misuse of history in the direct application of Jefferson's words and policies to modern circumstances, what more valid approach and criteria does Malone use to determine Jefferson's relevance for the modern world? Do you agree that this is the "common sense" approach to the relevance of Jefferson? What are the constant factors in history that Malone considers of major significance in the process by which historical personalities speak to subsequent generations across the years and centuries? Finally, what relevance does Thomas Jefferson have for us in the last half of the twentieth century?

Students wishing to explore this topic further should read (in addition to the Peterson volume cited above) two brilliant essays: Carl Becker, "What is Still Living in the Political Philosophy of Thomas Jefferson?," *American Historical Review,* XLVIII (July, 1943), and Dumas Malone, "Mr. Jefferson to Mr. Roosevelt; An Imaginary Letter," *Virginia Quarterly Review,* XIX (Spring, 1943). D. J. Boorstin, *The Lost World of Thomas Jefferson** (1948), is an outstanding study of Jefferson's thought.

* Available in a paperback edition.

THE RELEVANCE OF MR. JEFFERSON
DUMAS MALONE

In almost the last year of his long life, replying to a query about the Declaration of Independence, Thomas Jefferson wrote a letter which is worth recalling. Certain people, especially people who did not care for his politics, had suggested that in fact that famous document was not original. When he was eighty-two years old he made a statement about its objects—that is, his own objects in writing it—which I quote in part:

Not to find out new principles, or new arguments, never before thought of, not merely to say things which had never been said before; but to place before mankind the common sense of the subject. . . .

The present utterance can hardly be compared to the immortal Declaration, and I do not presume to address it to all mankind, but, without pretense of originality, I hope to set forth the common sense of the matter in dealing with Mr. Jefferson himself. While many true and wonderful things have been said about this inexhaustible man since his death, a considerable number of things have been said that should really be described as nonsense. Perhaps it would be fairer to say of many of these that they are partial truths which have been paraded as whole truths, deriving from the law and gospel. At all events, confusion is confounded when an historic personage is quoted on opposite sides in a contemporary controversy, as Mr. Jefferson repeatedly has been. Instances will quickly come to mind in connection with the presidential campaign of 1960, when it was solemnly announced that he would have voted for both candidates; or in connection with the New Deal, which he is said both to have opposed and favored.

It is not my purpose to declare which side he was on, since I really have no way of knowing. Also, I recognize the likelihood that I should arrive at the pleasant conclusion that he always agreed with me. The proneness of the human mind to rationalize can hardly be exaggerated. In view, however, of the well-authenticated fact that contradictory state-

SOURCE: Dumas Malone, "The Relevance of Mr. Jefferson," *The Virginia Quarterly Review* (Summer, 1961), XXXVII, pp. 332–349. Originally delivered as The Founder's Day Address at the University of Virginia in the spring of 1961. Reprinted by permission of *The Virginia Quarterly Review* and the author.

ments have been made about him ever since his death I am disposed to ask certain questions. What meaning does he really have for *us* in our present situation? Are his words and actions relevant to *our* circumstances, or irrelevant? If he is relevant in certain respects and irrelevant in others, what is the ground of distinction? How is anyone to know? On this confused situation I should like to turn what the late William S. Gilbert called "The hose of common sense." Surely the common sense of the matter is to try to distinguish between those words and actions which related solely or primarily to his own time, and those which have the quality of timelessness. That is, we need to separate what is or may be properly regarded as dateless from what is necessarily dated.

In this connection, I do not need to focus attention on him as a human being. Human nature seems to have changed little in the course of recorded history, and human personality defies barriers of space and time. In spirit we can live intimately with persons from the past whenever their words and deeds are sufficiently recorded for us to know them. We soon forget that their clothes were unlike ours and that they wore their hair quite differently. We have to allow for changes in manners and morals, and even when they employ our own language we may detect a certain quaintness in their speech. But the common denominator of human nature and individual experience is so large that great personalities can speak to us across the generations, even across the centuries, in language that is understandable since it is the language of life itself.

By precept and example the father of the University of Virginia can still teach anyone who will take the trouble to listen to him and observe him. Many things can we learn from him about the fine art of living. Not the least of these is that once an apostle of equality lived a notably elevated life, an extraordinarily rich, perennially interesting, endlessly generous, and ceaselessly useful life, in a society which he himself had made more democratic. He exemplified excellence, not the dull level of mediocrity; individuality, not unthinking conformity. He dared to build his house upon a mountain and to be himself, surveying the universe in personal independence. As a human being he has real meaning for our time: in his own person he reminds us what man can do with freedom.

Though human nature and human personality seem to be the most constant factors in history except the earth and the waters round it, along with the seasons and the tides, they manifest themselves in widely varying circumstances, of course, and no human being of either the past or the present can be fully understood apart from his particular environment. We should be foolish to assume that Mr. Jefferson would make precisely the same domestic arrangements at Monticello if he were living there now as he made a hundred and fifty years ago; or that, if one of his grandchildren became ill today, he would be as dubious as he was then about the value of medical services; presumably he would not now suggest that doctors may do more harm than good. We can appreciate the realism which enabled him to appraise them so well in his day, but we should be unwise to seek his *specific* advice in the conduct of our personal affairs, medical or otherwise.

Anything that may be said about considering a human being, in his personal life, on the background of his own environment has to be heavily underlined when we speak of him as a public man. We *have* to view statesmen, past and present, in their own settings of time, place, and circumstance. To do otherwise would be to render them a grave injustice. For forty years, with only a few interruptions, Mr. Jefferson was a public official—burgess, delegate, governor, minister to a foreign country, secretary of state, vice president, and president. During all these years he was dealing with current public affairs and day-to-day problems. More than most statesmen, he tried to take the long view and to guide his steps by enduring principles, and if he had not done so better than most men his fame would have been less enduring. Nonetheless, he could not escape the necessity, and no statesman ever can, of adjusting policies to the existing situation. Public affairs are not conducted in a vacuum. It is of the utmost importance, therefore, to seek a fair understanding of the public situation he had to face.

Since he devoted a very large part of his time and labors to foreign relations, and world affairs are of such vital concern to us today, we can profitably take a quick look at the general world situation in his era. Even in his slow-moving age that situation changed, to be sure, but certain of its features were relatively constant during most of his public life. Some of these features were so similar to what we ourselves have faced that his age seems positively familiar. Most of his career was set on a background of general war. The conflict which broke out in Europe when he was secretary of state and lasted, with only slight interruption, considerably beyond his presidency, if not world war in our sense, came nearer being that than any that our planet was to know until the twentieth century. In his day this planet was a less dangerous place than it has been in our era of world war, total war, cold war, and threat of nuclear destruction. Furthermore, because of the slowness of movement and communication, peril was less imminent. There was not the same sense of desperate urgency, and statesmen could be less hurried. That is one thing the statesmen of this day can deeply envy them. Nonetheless, the dangers faced in the two eras were strikingly similar, even if in our time they have been greatly intensified.

His age was one of revolution which touched virtually all parts of the globe that our country was concerned with. Indeed, it was commonly regarded as *the* age of revolution until our generation pre-empted the title. In our day the revolutionary spirit has spread to continents which were still slumbering in his time. It has taken on social and economic forms which were little dreamed of by our forefathers when they proclaimed revolution in the name of political independence, and which were not approached even in revolutionary France. But his time was also one of great political and considerable social convulsion. Thus one can say that, in its international aspects, no other period in American history can so fitly be compared to ours as the age of Washington and Jefferson. I have been particularly struck with what may be called the psychological parallels. Human nature being much the same, personal and social reactions to war and revolution show a great deal of similarity. This is frequently reflected in language: many of the things that were said in manifestos and resolutions, in newspapers and in private letters, sound like utterances of our time if you change the names and places.

There were numerous differences, however, and we can readily recognize the paramount importance of one of them. The position from which Mr. Jefferson and others charged with the national interest and security viewed a warring and revolutionary world was virtually the reverse of the one our leaders now occupy. The potential giant of the West was then only a stripling, a weakling among the Powers, while today our Republic is in all respects gigantic. They had to lead from weakness, where we can lead from strength. The policy which will always be associated with the names of Washington and Jefferson was to keep out of the raging power struggle in so far as possible, regardless of personal predilections one way or the other, regardless of ideology. Thus was born the classic American doctrine of neutrality or non-involvement, which, despite occasional aberrations, endured for generations. It arose from the necessities of national security, and its wisdom at that time cannot be doubted. Everybody knows that the policy has been completely reversed in our century, also because of the necessities of national security.

What does this signify about the bearing of the acts, the policies, the words of Mr. Jefferson on the world problems of our day? Can we really learn anything from him? In my opinion, we can learn much. As an example I will cite the year 1793, when the European war broadened so as to threaten us, when the French Revolution passed into its greatest excesses, when this young Republic entered upon its historic policy of neutrality. To consider the activities of Mr. Jefferson, the Secretary of State, in one of the most momentous years in modern history, observing his incessant labors, his extraordinary patience amid frustrations, his unflagging patriotism, and his basic wisdom, is to share a tremendous experience. Regarding the controversy into which he, a friend of France, was drawn in 1793 with the insolent envoy of the French revolutionary government, one of the greatest of his successors in the office of Secretary of State, John Quincy Adams, said that his papers on that controversy "present the most perfect model of diplomatic discussion and expostulation of modern times." This was American diplomacy at one of its highest points, revealing rare skill and a realistic appraisal of the existing situation which should command the admiration of anyone dealing with international problems in any age.

Yet the policy at which President Washington and Secretary Jefferson arrived has had to be repudiated in our century, when at length we reluctantly assumed the rôle of world leadership which destiny imposed upon us. Conceivably it might have been reversed sooner, to the advantage of mankind, but for the sad human proclivity to learn the wrong lessons from history and miss the right ones. As an exemplar of the skillful and realistic conduct of foreign affairs, which he generally was, Mr. Jefferson is very relevant. So far as specific policies go, however, time has rendered him quite irrelevant. To be sure, some people in our century have sought specific answers to the problems of contemporary foreign policy in the Neutrality Proclamation of 1793, Washington's Farewell Address of 1796, and Jefferson's First Inaugural of 1801. In a world that has been turned upside down, that sort of reliance on sharply dated pronouncements, wonderful as they were when written, hardly seems the common sense of the matter. Indeed, one is inclined to ask, as Elmer Davis used to: "How silly can you be?"

II

Now let us turn from the world situation to the home scene. When we fly on the wings of the spirit back into Mr. Jefferson's America, of course we can recognize many landmarks--the configuration of the coasts, the rivers flowing to the sea, the mountains on the western horizon. We can quickly perceive that he and his contemporaries were persons of like passions and vanities with ourselves. In his day political organization —party organization, for example—was rudimentary from our point of view, but the minds of politicians worked very much as they do right now and they used the same sort of wiles—slogans, name-calling, and various devices designed to show that they were more honest and more patriotic than their rivals. All of this is very familiar and should make us feel at home. But it is difficult for us to realize how few people there were or how scattered, and how slowly they got around. When Jefferson became President the population of New York did not greatly exceed that of present-day Charlottesville. If he could see the national metropolis today he would no doubt regard it as an incredible monstrosity. It took him ten days to come home to Albemarle from Philadelphia; and the post rider from Richmond was so erratic that he sometimes didn't get to Charlottesville with the mail for three weeks, although Mr. Jefferson insisted that the roads were generally passable to a carriage and always, he believed, to a man on horseback. Getting out of one's locality and keeping in touch with the outside world was an exceedingly difficult thing, and it is no wonder that so much government devolved upon the county court in Virginia, or that the town meeting was so important in New England. To a degree which is hard for us to conceive, emphasis *had* to be laid on the locality and the self-reliance of individuals. By our standards that society was amazingly simple, delightfully simple, though by the same standards life was extraordinarily inconvenient and must often have been extremely dull.

The fact is that the series of non-political revolutions which have so profoundly affected the physical conditions of existence and have transformed our economy and society occurred *after* Mr. Jefferson's public career was over. The industrial revolution had begun in Europe by his time, but it did not really get started in this country until the very end of his presidency, and even then our industries were only infants. The successive revolutions in transportation and communication all came later. Fulton's steamboat, the *Clermont,* plied the Hudson in his second term, but it has been aptly said that Jefferson, like Nebuchadnezzar, never saw anything faster than a horse.

It would be rather absurd for me to attempt to describe the various revolutions in science and technology which have followed one upon another with ever-increasing speed. I have had difficulty in adjusting my mind to the ones that have occurred in my own lifetime, finding some of them utterly bewildering. Indeed, I escape from them nearly every day into the age of Mr. Jefferson. The air seems clearer there, and the unhurried pace leaves more time for thought. In the uncrowded country there were no huge factories—scarcely any at all, in fact; there were no immense aggregations of capital and formidable organizations of labor. There were sailing vessels in the harbors and merchants in the ports and inland centers, but nearly all the workers in this farflung country were tillers of the soil. This was no Golden Age of health, comfort, and convenience, but perhaps it may be regarded as a sort of heyday of individualism. Human beings may have been dwarfed by the vastness of the land, though relatively few had traveled over much of it; they were *not* dwarfed by any of the works of man.

Almost exactly one hundred and sixty years ago the rawboned country gentleman who had been chosen head of this predominantly agricultural republic delivered his first inaugural address in the Senate chamber, the only part of the capitol that was yet finished in the straggling wilderness village that went by the name of Washington. It is said that few in the audience could hear him, he spoke so low; but his speech could be read afterwards in the newspapers, and it proved to be one of the few to which historians recur. Does it have any present bearing on *our* problems?

It was admirably suited to its particular circumstances. One of the important conflicts in the previous campaign had been over the right to oppose, to criticize the existing government—a thing the group in power had sought to prevent by means of the notorious Sedition Act. Historians often say that, whatever else Jefferson's election signified, it vindicated the legitimacy of political opposition. But terrible things had been predicted if this man should be elected; Bibles might be confiscated. Accordingly, he felt impelled to speak words of reassurance, and some of these are still fresh after more than a century and a half. He announced one principle which he called sacred and which may be regarded as timeless, I think, in any self-governing society: "that though the will of the majority is in all cases to prevail, that will, to be rightful, must be reasonable; that the minority possess their equal rights, which equal laws must protect, and to violate which would be oppression." It is a great pity that Abraham Lincoln did not quote those words in *his* first inaugural. They would have been eminently appropriate then, as they would have been on January 20, 1961.

There are other nuggets of abiding wisdom in Mr. Jefferson's address, and there is some deeply moving language. I am most concerned here, however, with what he said in the year 1801 about the way he meant to conduct the government. Since he never wrote anything like a systematic treatise on government but scattered his ideas throughout his profuse writings, the things he said here have been regarded by many as a handy summary of his working political philosophy. Judging from this address, he believed that the federal government should devote itself

largely to the conduct of foreign affairs, which were always important in
his era. With special reference to domestic matters he summed up federal
functions in a passage which has been quoted for more than a century and
a half:

Still one thing more, fellow citizens—a wise and frugal government, which
shall restrain men from injuring one another, which shall leave them otherwise free to regulate their own pursuits of industry and improvement, and
shall not take from the mouth of labor the bread it has earned. This is the
sum of good government. . . .

That is, the federal government, outside the conduct of foreign relations,
was to be little more than a policeman and an umpire. It was to grant
special privileges to none and secure equal and exact justice for all—an
obligation requiring diligence as well as forebearance—but if we take
these words at their face value its functions were to be essentially negative.
From the vantage point of today, the "sum of good government" as thus
described is very small.

Even at that time some intelligent people thought it dangerously small.
Midway in his first term his ancient antagonist, Alexander Hamilton,
lamented that the Constitution was a "frail and worthless fabric," despite
all his own efforts to prop it up. He believed that under Jefferson's
interpretation the government could withstand no serious strain; and he
had little hope that it would further the economic development of the
country in the directions he himself had pointed. Hamilton wanted to
stimulate that part of the economic society now described as "business,"
which by modern standards was then little more than rudimentary. He
was particularly interested in banks, the facilitation of trade, the creation
of fluid capital; and if anyone deserves to be described as the father of
American capitalism surely it is Hamilton. He wanted to use the government, and when in office he did use it, for the development of business.
He thought Jefferson uninformed in these matters—indifferent, even
hostile to this development. In my opinion, he did not fully understand
his great rival; it seems to me that the bitter feeling of the Eastern
merchants and emerging financiers of that time toward Jefferson went
beyond the point of reason. He certainly knew little about banks and
deplored speculation in securities; to him property pre-eminently was
real property, that is, land; but he unquestionably knew a great deal
about foreign commerce, and he was an economic nationalist in his own
way. Nonetheless, I think I can understand why to the Hamiltonians he
often seemed an old-fashioned farmer who was blind to the wave of the
future. It can be argued that John Marshall did not sufficiently recognize

the flexibility of his distant kinsman in the face of actual circumstances. Yet it is not hard to see why the Chief Justice sought to counter the centrifugal tendencies he perceived in the Jeffersonian philosophy by asserting through a long generation the scope of national authority.

How well adjusted the policies of President Jefferson really were to the conditions of his own time is a matter of historical judgment. In his own person he was certainly not negative or lethargic; this incessantly active and extraordinarily dynamic man cannot be rightly regarded as the historical prototype of Calvin Coolidge. Actually, his administration was more economical than Coolidge's, but if anybody should be disposed to think that his main service was that of counting pennies in the Executive Mansion, or that his rôle was primarily that of a caretaker, that person should take a look at the map. There was a large element of luck in the Louisiana Purchase, as well as some theoretical inconsistency on Jefferson's part—or at least this has been alleged; but no one can properly deny to him the credit for doubling the area of his country. The domestic consequences of his actions were to prove momentous. He left to his successor a different country from the one he had begun to govern at the age of fifty-eight; and as soon as new states began to emerge from this huge domain the Union began to be a different sort of Union. The balance of power within it was bound to shift, and in the long run it shifted decisively against his own Virginia. There was no little irony in the course of later events, but this majestic achievement, this creation of what he happily termed an "empire for liberty," makes it impossible to think of him as the caretaker of an old order, or as one whose main function was to put brakes on the wheels of progress.

One of his undoubted purposes, as expressed in his own words, was to "lead things into the channel of harmony between the governors and governed," and in this he was conspicuously successful. He gave his countrymen what most of them wanted, and I think he gave his country what it then needed most—which was mainly a chance to grow without either aid or interference. The immediate task and the dominant desire was to possess the land. He handed out no subsidies to farmers or anybody else, but to his land-hungry generation he pointed the door of unparalleled opportunity, seeking to maintain approximate equality of opportunity but otherwise largely leaving human nature to take its course. He hoped that the vast preponderance of his countrymen would be self-supporting farmers, whom he regarded as the best citizens and the freest and happiest men on earth. His countrymen liked the idea; indeed, they embroidered it into the legend which long survived the circumstances which gave it birth. It became a myth which invested agricultural problems of later generations with nostalgia.

What present reality is there in his pronouncement of one hundred and sixty years ago about limiting the functions of government? Does this mean today that the federal government ought to be small even though everything else has become gigantic—that the best way to solve our national political and economic problems is to set down a pigmy among the giants? And all this in a time of world crisis to which we can see no end? It would hardly be fair to Mr. Jefferson to claim that he would favor that degree of impotence. This is not to say that he would like all of our huge organizations, or any of them. The processes of consolidation in all departments of life have been greatly accelerated in our time by the series of wars and crises we have gone through. Mr. Jefferson would certainly not rejoice that we have had to adjust all our institutions to the needs of these, and he might not like the way we have done it. Very likely he would approve of Lord Acton's well-known dictum: "Power tends to corrupt; absolute power corrupts absolutely." His entire career reflects his distrust of power as well as his undying concern for freedom, and it is just as true now as it ever was that the price of liberty is eternal vigilance. But when speaking of the threat of tyranny, he kept on talking about kings, who are not much of a menace now. Tyranny changes its face from age to age, and every era has to decide for itself where the greatest and most imminent danger to the freedom of the individual really lies. The contradiction which we face arises from the dreadful circumstance that the very survival of liberty at home and abroad depends on the employment of power such as Mr. Jefferson never dreamed of and which inevitably carries within itself a threat to personal freedom. We can't expect him to resolve this contradiction. He would be bewildered by this strange new world, this wonderful and terrible new world. In his day he was an alert sentinel and generally, though not always, a sagacious guide. But he is well beyond the age of retirement and we can't expect him to chart our course for us.

He himself summed things up sufficiently in one of the most important of his sayings: "The earth belongs always to the living generation." Whatever opinions he may have held at one time or another about specific problems, he held tenaciously to the conviction that the present need not and should not be guided by the dead hand of the past. We can learn greatly from past experience, but we must not ask too much of history. It often provides suggestive analogies, but rarely if ever can we find in it an answer to a specific question, a precise solution for a contemporary problem. It offers us no detailed road map to guide the traffic of today. The common sense of the matter is that the particular policies or methods Mr. Jefferson announced one hundred and sixty years ago are now essentially irrelevant, if not wholly so. The same can be said, of course, of the historic policies of George Washington and Abraham Lincoln. And the saying goes for Queen Elizabeth I, Julius Caesar, Alexander the Great, and Pericles, though the careers of all of them are well worth studying.

III

The undiscriminating use of the past has had unfortunate consequences on Mr. Jefferson's reputation. This incessant builder, who was ceaselessly striving to advance knowledge and improve society, has often been cast in the rôle of perpetual obstructionist. One of the signers of the Declaration of Independence was known as "the great objector"; that was not Mr. Jefferson, though no one more than he insisted on the right of any man to object to anything on the merits of the case. There is an even greater danger than that of judging him unfairly: in stressing what is actually irrelevant, people tend to overlook or disregard acts and words of his which do have the ring of timelessness and are applicable to our age or any other. He left us no road map, but, more than any public man in our history, he pointed us to the star by which our course should be guided. It would be a pity if, while following some ancient and long-abandoned trail, we should fail to see what is shining overhead.

He has left us in no doubt whatever about the way to separate the temporary from the enduring elements in his heritage to posterity. He explicitly stated that he wanted no public offices listed on his tombstone— not even the Presidency of the United States. He knew that his official actions were necessarily dated, that policies could not be expected to last forever. He wanted to be remembered for words and deeds which had the quality of timelessness about them, and there can be no possible doubt that he made a wise selection.

The Declaration of Independence, which he listed first, has a date, to be sure—our most famous date since it marks the birthday of our Republic; and this was identified with him all the more irrevocably when he died fifty years later on July 4, as though by Divine Providence. Part of the document itself is unmistakably dated: historians do not accept all those charges against King George III as eternal truth. But the part of the Declaration we know best and prize most was undoubtedly regarded by its author as timeless and universal. How can you date truths which you regard as eternal and self-evident? By virtue of their birth into the world as human beings, all men are equal—not in status certainly, and surely not in ability, but in rights. The implications of the assertion that everybody is a human being and should be treated as one were not fully perceived by all who approved the historic pronouncement of our national faith, but these words have gone ringing down the generations. They were still vibrant words when we answered the mad ravings of Adolf Hitler and countered the arrogant cruelty of the German Nazis. (At the time many historians must have reflected, as I surely did, that history offers no more striking antithesis than that between Adolf Hitler and Thomas Jefferson.) No ways and means are specified in the great Declaration; these must be determined by every living generation for itself in the light of its own circumstances. But those phrases, which we have heard a hundred times, have in them the perennial freshness of the spring; today as in 1776 they breathe undying faith in human beings. Many people, many high-minded people, find it hard to extend that faith to groups they have long regarded as "lesser breeds without the law"; and it is difficult indeed to uphold the freedom and dignity of all men when so many are unworthy and so many abuse their freedom. But we need not look to our historic Declaration for soothing words, for words that condone complacency or excuse any form of arrogance. We can find there no specific solution for any of our immediate problems, but we can find an eternal summons to proceed upon unfinished tasks.

To this timeless document we can also turn for a sense of values—for an everlasting criterion by which to judge all human institutions. So far as my knowledge and judgment go, history provides none better. Man was not made for government, but government was made for man; and the final criterion of its actions or its inaction is the degree to which it supports the freedom, upholds the dignity, and promotes the happiness of individual human beings. This is our answer to Communism and to any form of totalitarianism, whether of the right or left. Man was not made for organization—business, labor, professional, or any other; these were made for man, and the only proper test of them is what they do for him. We should think of this when we consider these giants of government, of business, of labor which our society has nurtured, and which so often seem to dwarf human beings. Surely the purpose of government should never be to augment power for its own sake, of business to produce profits solely for themselves, of labor to increase wages merely for the sake of wages. What is the product worth in terms of human happiness? When change is not productive of human happiness, surely it is not progress. This is no mere matter of material things, though no one can question their importance. "Man shall not live by bread alone," was said by a greater teacher than Mr. Jefferson. The challenge of our times and of all times is to humanize institutions—*all* institutions.

The Virginia act establishing religious freedom was adopted by the General Assembly on a particular date, but the date is unimportant. Actually, Jefferson drew his bill some years before it was passed, and it is just as fresh in the twentieth century as it was on the day he drew it. Here, even more clearly than in the Declaration, perhaps, can one perceive the essence of his philosophy. Above all things, he was a champion of the freedom of the human spirit, and by this he meant even more than the right to worship God in any way one likes—supremely important as that is. He meant the entire freedom of the mind, the sacred right of any man to his own opinions, whether these be popular or not, whether they be moderate or radical or conservative. There was no mistake in choosing the key quotation for the Jefferson Memorial and in putting it as a motto on a postage stamp. He was eternally hostile to all tyrannies but most of all to tyranny over the human mind. I sometimes wonder if some of the people who take his name on their lips really like this, the most typical of all Jefferson quotations. I doubt if the Communists even begin to comprehend it, but surely it is in his insistence on the freedom of men to think that he becomes most dangerous to the monolithic state and the philosophy of complete conformity.

The University of Virginia, with which he ended his select list of memorable achievements, was chartered on a particular date, and we are not yet warranted in describing it as immortal. But in the Western world universities have been exceedingly long-lived; they flow on like so many streams, and this one may be expected to flow as long as our civilization shall endure. Besides being virtually timeless, any university, to be worthy of its name, must in spirit be universal. In his own lovely county, amid its eternal hills, this lifelong student institutionalized his undying faith in intelligence and knowledge. Nothing that he ever did was more characteristic of this inveterate builder—of this ardent farmer who prized the harvest of the mind beyond all others. If I understand him aright, he would not expect his academic heirs to pay much heed to specific things he once said about courses and regulations, but he would want them to apply to their life and learning the final tests of value. Not only does learning languish in the air of conformity and complacency; not only does it fail if it does not liberate the spirit; learning becomes a sterile thing when it loses its humanity.

Nothing is immutable but "the inherent and inalienable rights of man," he said. "The earth belongs always to the living generation." Times change, needs change, policies and methods change with them. But human beings remain, always. And the star of liberty still shines over Monticello. That star and the people it shines on are what he would most want us to see.

CHAPTER 21

THE SEARCH FOR
AMERICAN IDENTITY

Many American history texts suggest that the United States went to war in 1812 to sever the apron strings that still bound the new nation to the "Mother Country"; the War of 1812, then, was a second war for American independence, in part brought about by American nationalistic feeling. But most texts are unable to devote much attention to the theme that a developing sense of nationhood was a significant force in American history in the early nineteenth century. Thus, students are left with unanswered questions whose answers are fundamental to a better understanding of American history. To what extent was the young nation really a nation at key points in its early history—in 1789, or in 1812, or even in the 1820's? To what extent did countervailing forces, particularly those of sectionalism and state sovereignty, prevent the full development of American nationalism?

The next selection, from *The Nation Takes Shape: 1789–1837,** helps students come to grips with these questions and their implications. Marcus Cunliffe, in this fresh and provocative essay, concentrates on the search for American identity. Cunliffe discusses the symbols of the national spirit—"Liberty," the flag, the American eagle, the memory of Washington, and many others—employed by American patriots; comments on the outward manifestations of the American national consciousness; and outlines the forces opposing the development of nationalism.

Today, there are new nations in which nationalism is a self-conscious creation, in which rejection of former mother countries leads to distorted images and the imposition of a narrow, compulsory loyalty, and in which forces in opposition to nationalism create tensions and even warfare. In reading this selection students should reassess contemporary American nationalism. To what extent do large groups of Americans still identify with localities, states, or regions, thereby creating strong forces operating against the establishment of a nationalism rooted in the "affections of the people?"

For further reading on this subject, students should consult Hans Kohn, *American Nationalism: An Interpretive Essay** (1957), Merle Curti, *The Roots of American Loyalty** (1946), and P. C. Nagel *One Nation Indivisible: The Union in American Thought, 1776–1861* (1964). Invaluable for students wishing to examine the concept of nationalism from a broad perspective is Seymour M. Lipset, *The First New Nation: The United States in Historical and Comparative Perspective** (1963).

* Available in a paperback edition.

NATIONALISM AND SECTIONALISM
MARCUS CUNLIFFE

In the view of Henry Adams, whose study of the administrations of Jefferson and Madison led him to publish a nine-volume survey of that sixteen-year epoch, "the scientific interest of American history centred in national character, and in the workings of a society destined to become vast, in which individuals were important chiefly as types." Since he wrote, seventy years ago, we have become less impressed by "scientific" theories of history. However, his massive analysis is still unsurpassed as a guide to the early years of the nineteenth century. The reasons seem to be that, coupled with a polished, ironical style and a capacity for sustained research, Adams had a tireless curiosity about larger themes, and that two of the themes on which he dwelt with special persistence—nationality and democracy—were indeed as fundamental as he thought. The making of the American nation is accordingly the subject of the present chapter, and the next, chapter vii, is concerned with American democracy.

The evolution of American national feeling is nicely illustrated in a small, unofficial ceremony that took place at Göttingen in Germany. The date was July 4, 1820, and the participants were two American students, of whom one was the Boston historian-to-be George Bancroft. John Adams wrote to his wife in 1776 that July 2, when independence was actually agreed upon by Congress, was the *"Day of Deliverance"* that ought to be celebrated by succeeding generations as "the great anniversary festival." However, within a few years July 4 was singled out as *the* great day on which to commemorate America's national origins. By 1789 it was already a sacred point in the American calendar, to be marked with firecrackers, militia parades, dinners, recitals of the Declaration of Independence, and formal speechmaking.

In their German exile Bancroft and his companion were therefore very much in tradition. No American was more fervently and consciously patriotic than Bancroft, who was to narrate the story of his country's birth

SOURCE. Marcus Cunliffe, *The Nation Takes Shape: 1780–1837*, Chicago: The University of Chicago Press, 1959, pp. 122–137. Copyright 1959 by the University of Chicago. Reprinted by permission of the University of Chicago Press and the author.

in ten proudly lyrical volumes. He more than any other American scholar during the first half of the nineteenth century strove to impress upon his readers the meaning and mission of the United States as a phenomenon without parallel in history.

Several of the symbols of the national spirit he later labored to inculcate are displayed in Bancroft's Göttingen "banquet." They are enumerated for us in the toasts to which the young men raised their glasses. The list included "the sweet nymph Liberty," the heroes of the Revolution, the flag, the American eagle, the Constitution, "the memory of Washington," and "the literary prospects of America." Each is worthy of comment.

"Liberty" is one of those words that have become faceless through overuse, like a coin handled and handled until its insignia are worn away. But to Bancroft and his fellow Americans it was still in 1820 one of the strongly emotive words in the American tongue, which together with "freedom," "union," and others quickened the pulse when they were spoken. Crowded with association, incantatory, they conveyed more in the first thirty years of American independence than, say, "democracy." They struck deep, so deep that when Daniel Webster employed them in a famous speech of 1830, his "LIBERTY AND UNION— NOW AND FOREVER—ONE AND INSEPARABLE" was treated not just as compelling oratory but as great literature, as holy writ.

The practical accomplishment of liberty was the work of the "heroes of the Revolution." Washington, naturally, was foremost. Yet there was no lack of other figures and of moving incidents to awaken the pride of Americans and to fill out the pages of their children's textbooks. A Revolutionary veteran, a little more wrinkled and a little more vague and grandiloquent in his recollections as each year went by, was an indispensable exhibit in Independence Day processions. On one such occasion at Indianapolis in 1822 it turned out that the old soldier in question, though he had undoubtedly fought in the Revolution, had done so as a Hessian on the British side. The embarrassing discovery was overlooked in the mellowness of the moment and in consideration of the fact that he had after all remained behind at the end of the war to become a good American. This story may be apocryphal, since the incident has also been ascribed to other dates and places. However, it has an element of poetic truth. The authentic veteran could tell stirring anecdotes of the discomfiture of the British redcoats at Lexington and Concord, of the audacious descent on Quebec by Montgomery and Benedict Arnold, the exploits of Ethan Allen at Ticonderoga and of George Rogers Clark at Vincennes, the misery at Valley Forge, the bloody onslaught of Mad Anthony Wayne at Stony Point, the British surrenders at Saratoga and Yorktown.

Cherished slogans entered the national heritage from the war—Israel Putnam's "Don't fire until you see the whites of their eyes," John Paul Jones's "I have not yet begun to fight." Articles of national faith were consecrated by the war. One was that Americans, having defeated the strongest nation in the world, were therefore by tournament rules the champions in valor and military ability. As the British minister to the United States, Robert Liston, wrote home in 1799, Americans had such an "overweening idea of American Prowess and American Talents that they do not scruple to talk of the United States as an overmatch for any nation in Europe." Another article of faith concerned the superiority of the American volunteer fighting man to the professional. If the Massachusetts minutemen and militia could give so good an account of themselves against trained European troops at Concord and Bunker Hill, or the farmers of Vermont against Burgoyne's men at Bennington, or the southerners under Morgan against Tarleton at Cowpens, then America possessed an invincible civilian army which she could summon from the plow at a few days' notice and disband with equal simplicity.

The flag that Bancroft toasted was the Stars and Stripes. Fifty years later, in irreverent chophouse slang, the expression signified a plate of ham and beans. In 1820 such levity would probably have been unthinkable. The flag's origin was complicated; though chosen by Congress as the national flag in 1777, it was devised in the first place as a naval ensign during the Revolutionary War and not adopted by the American army until 1834. Francis Scott Key's "Star Spangled Banner" was written in 1814, under the stimulus of a British bombardment near Baltimore, but it did not become accepted as an (unofficial) national anthem until the Civil War. The composition of the flag and the idea of adding a star for each new state while restricting the quantity of stripes to thirteen (in honor of the founding states) was not finally decided upon until 1818. However, the flag was one of the emblems of nationhood that the young United States venerated.

To a lesser extent, the American eagle was also a familiar emblem. It was the American bald eagle, a different species from the heraldic birds embodied in so many European crests. The difference was not very striking at a casual glance, and Benjamin Franklin—himself among the monuments of early American patriotism—suggested half-humorously that the turkey would have been a better choice, being "a much more respectable bird, and withal a true original native of America." However, the eagle was the preferred creature. Clutching arrows in one talon and olive branches in the other, the eagle appeared on the official seal of the United States, together with the official motto "E Pluribus Unum"; on some of the coins produced by the United States mint; and in all sorts of unofficial places as a decorative device.

Slogans, flag, eagle—though all had their importance in contributing to the image of American nationhood, none bulked as large as the Constitution. In a Fourth of July oration at New Haven in 1788 Simeon Baldwin invited his audience to

turn your attention to that venerable body [the Philadelphia Convention of 1787]—examine the characters of those illustrious sages . . . see them *unfolding* the volumes of antiquity, and carefully examining the various systems of government, which different nations have experienced, and judiciously extracting the excellence of each . . . hear the mutual concessions of private interests to the general good, while they keep steadily in view the great object . . . and then glory, Americans, in the singular unanimity of that illustrious assembly of patriots in the most finished form of government that ever blessed a nation.

In his address Baldwin, like most other eulogists of the Constitution, emphasized its recency in order to maintain that it drew upon all previous forms of government and was therefore, as the most sophisticated model, better than all others. He also, in typical fashion, managed to speak of the Constitution as though it were an ancient affair. Less than twelve months after the Constitution had been drawn up, he talked of its makers as if they were all Methuselahs, whereas Hamilton, Madison, Edmund Randolph, and several other prominent delegates were well under forty years of age. Poetically, Baldwin's description was correct. In the American time scale, logarithmic in range at the formative stages, the Declaration of 1776 and the Constitution of 1787 tended to be represented as closer to, say, the Magna Carta of 1215 than to the actual events of the decade after 1787. The documents, being of eternal significance, were in a sense out of time altogether.

Something of this holy aura also enveloped George Washington, whose memory Bancroft invoked. His leading part in the War for Independence, his presence in the chair at the Philadelphia Convention, his imposing demeanor, and his integrity while President combined to elevate him after his death—and even during his own lifetime, though not so unanimously—to a status not far short of deification. His birthday, February 22, came second to July 4 as a national holiday. "Boston with every other considerable town in this state," wrote one of its citizens in 1796, "has marked . . . the last birthday with uncommon demonstrations of glee. It appears that our beloved President still reigns in every breast where genius, virtue, and patriotism are implanted." (Thanksgiving, which Washington ordained in 1789, was maintained as a special day by John Adams and James Madison also, but on widely varying dates; not until the Civil War did President Lincoln firmly institute the custom of an annual national Thanksgiving.) His Farewell Address of 1796, which is still read aloud in Congress every year on February 22, at once became a part of the sacred literature of American nationalism. It embodied the commandments enjoined on those who would keep the faith. Without embarrassment or thought of blasphemy, one or two writers even hinted that Washington had certain of the attributes of Jesus Christ: thus, the mother of each was named Mary, and Washington had led a singularly blameless life.

As for Bancroft's salute to "the literary prospects of America," part of what he had in mind is forcibly expressed in the words of Noah Webster. Webster, a Connecticut scholar, declared in his *Dissertations on the English Language* (1789): "A *national language* is a band of *national union*. Every engine should be employed to render the people of this country national; to call their attachments home to their own country; and to inspire them with the pride of national character. . . . Let us then seize the present moment, and establish a national language, as well as a national government." Webster felt that "Great Britain, whose children we are, and whose language we speak, should no longer be *our* standard." He did not contend that the United States should invent some entirely new tongue for herself, but rather that she should, while introducing local expressions, go back to the pure English which the mother country had corrupted. "I do not innovate but *reject innovation,*" he told a correspondent in 1809. "When I write *fether, lether,* and *mold,* I do nothing more than reduce the words to their original orthography, no other being used in our earliest English books." It is a characteristic assertion in the story of American nationalism; the new land claims to be the rightful heir to an immemorial heritage; not revolution but conservation is its aim. Being mainly a lexicographer, Webster was less concerned than some authors with the wider problem of what Americans were to write about. Ardently patriotic men of letters such as Philip Freneau insisted that the national character and destiny would not be complete until there was an independent American literature. They did not necessarily mean literature devoted to the United States, but rather authorship *by* Americans, whether the field be poetry, history, philosophy, or scientific investigation.

There was similar intense concern in some circles for the development of painting, sculpture, and architecture. As with literature, the discussion involved a double argument: first, that America should have a culture respectable enough to set beside that of other nations and, second, that her culture should be unmistakably *American*—in idiom, theme, and so on. It seemed fitting that in the new "Federal City" (Washington, D.C.) an attempt was made in the Capitol building at sculptural innovation. Some of the columns in the Supreme Court wing, though based on the Corinthian principle, illustrated the leaf and blossom of the American tobacco plant, while other columns in the Senate wing rotunda were fluted like American cornstalks, with corncob capitals.

Bancroft's toast list of national symbols could be added to. There was, for instance, the cartoon symbol of "Brother Jonathan," who seems to have originated as a contemptuous British nickname for Americans as early as 1776. The character of that name in Royall Tyler's *The Contrast* (1787)—which deserves to be regarded as the first play written by an American and staged successfully in the United States—is still a rather crudely comical person, in fact, a servant. But he is at heart honest and shrewd, like his master "Colonel Manly," and the "contrast" of the title is between them and an absurdly Anglophile master and manservant. Accepting the British taunt, the patriotic American shaped it to his own satisfaction, so that Brother Jonathan—lean, gawky, laconic, unpretentious—emerged as the caricaturist's counterpart to the fat, ruddy, blustering, conceited figure of the British "John Bull." He was a useful conception for others than writers and artists. Oddly for a nationalistic people, the Americans had no precise, convenient name for their country. "The United States" was cumbersome and sounded temporary; "America" was not a country but a continent. The obvious choice was "Columbia," which Freneau recommended and to which Joseph Hopkinson addressed his patriotic song "Hail Columbia" in 1798. But though "Columbia" sufficed eventually for the name of the federal district, of a river, of a college (in place of the old designation of "King's College"), and of another sovereign state (Colombia) on the American continent, it never lost its faintly literary taint for inhabitants of what remained, awkwardly yet permanently, the United States.

So designations like "Brother Jonathan" formed convenient synonyms as well as symbols. "Uncle Sam" was an acceptable addition. Its sense was not quite the same. Brother Jonathan represented either the whole United States or the typical individual American. Uncle Sam represented only the government of the United States. Though there are other suggested derivations, it seems to have been an extension of the initials U.S. The earliest known reference comes in a Troy, New York, newspaper in 1813: "This cant name for our government has got almost as common as 'John Bull.' The letters U.S. on the government waggons, &c are supposed to have given rise to it."

"Uncle Sam" was born in the War of 1812. The conflict made various contributions to the folklore of American nationalism. It provided some vivid fresh slogans. Young Oliver Hazard Perry, the American naval commander who defeated the British on Lake Erie in 1813, announced his victory in the famous message, "We have met the enemy and they are ours." His flagship *Lawrence* was named after an American captain who in another engagement of the war uttered as his dying words, "Don't give up the ship." These words were inscribed on Commodore Perry's flag.

Perry's and Lawrence's mottoes, like John Paul Jones's, redounded to the credit of the American navy, not the army. The regular army had its academy at West Point, whose name awoke echoes of the Revolutionary War, and there was no naval academy until the 1840's (when Bancroft, then Navy Secretary, conjured it into being). But the United States Military Academy, founded in 1802, was subject to some sharp criticism as an outpost of "aristocracy" and was not able to make an effective reply to its critics until the Mexican War. Up to 1837, neither it nor the regular army had as high a place as the navy in patriotic legend.

A special place was, however, accorded to the spectacular victory of Andrew Jackson over the British at New Orleans in 1815. Even more conclusively than Bunker Hill or Cowpens, the contest at New Orleans was held to prove that the American militiaman, the civilian warrior, was invincible. Moreover, the "Kentucky riflemen" of New Orleans were *western* heroes, a new national type whose spontaneous, rough-and-ready virtues were thought to be epitomized in their leader Jackson. He in his own right became a prime American hero—second only to Washington in éclat—who according to Bancroft "by intuitive conception . . . shared and possessed all the creative ideas of his country and his time."

The battle itself was a source of enormous pride to Americans. It set the seal on a war which, said Albert Gallatin, "has renewed . . . the national feelings and character which the Revolution had given. . . .The people have now more general objects of attachment. . . .They are more Americans; they feel and act more as a nation." The September, 1815, issue of *Niles' Register,* the first to be "printed on beautiful new type of *American* manufacture," also felt that "the people begin to assume, more and more, a NATIONAL CHARACTER; and to look at home for the only means, under divine goodness, of preserving their religion and liberty."

Some outward evidences of the American national consciousness have been indicated. To a dedicated patriot like Bancroft the United States held deeper significance. Richard Hofstadter remarks that "it has been our fate as a nation, not to have ideologies but to be one." For Bancroft, as for many of his countrymen, the American ideology had to do not only with words such as "liberty, union and democracy," but also with "providence, asylum, posterity, nature." They discerned unmistakable signs—of which one was the complete triumph at New Orleans, with shattering losses for the British and at negligible cost to Jackson's men—that the United States was under the special care of God. She had a special mission to perform, that of setting an object lesson to the rest of the world in tolerance, order, equality, and prosperity. She must therefore provide an "asylum for the oppressed"; the phrase recurs often in American speeches of the period, though not necessarily as an invitation to unlimited numbers of immigrants. The story was still being told; so its climax was invariably left to the imagination, to be disclosed fifty, a hundred, two hundred years hence, to a grateful posterity. This appeal to the future applied alike to the development of culture, commerce, population, in unlimited vistas of conjectural extrapolation.

By way of national sentiment, then, it could be said that Americans had a simultaneous attachment to yesterday and to tomorrow, the one invested with all the glamor of antiquity though its events belonged to recent history, the other with all the mysterious promise of futurity though Americans expected, so to speak, to live to see the future. However, if challenged to produce some present sign of American greatness, they could always (and did frequently) expatriate on nature in the United States. Nature meant many things—the sheer bigness of the country, the novelty of its fauna and flora, the abundance of life, the sense of room to spare, the conviction that the outdoors would be the domain of American art and letters, the definition of American character in terms of what was large, generous, informal, self-taught, non-European.

The vision was in some aspects raw and xenophobic: witness the naval officer Stephen Decatur's toast of 1816, "Our country! In her intercourse with foreign nations may she be always right; but our country, right or wrong." Thomas Low Nichols wrote of his schooling in New Hampshire in the 1820's:

The education we got was solid enough in some respects, and superficial in others. In arithmetic, geometry, surveying, mechanics, and such solid and practical matters, we were earnest students; but our geography was chiefly American, and the United States was larger than all the universe beside. In the same way our history was American history, brief but glorious. . . . We were taught every day and in every way that ours was the freest, the happiest, and soon to be the greatest and most powerful country in the world. This is the religious faith of every American. He learns it in his infancy, and he can never forget it. For all other countries he entertains sentiments varying from pity to hatred; they are the downtrodden despotisms of the old world.

One wonders whether Nichols was exposed in the classroom to a bizarre *Historical Reader* of the War of 1812 written by Gilbert J. Hunt (1817). Hunt, whose book was designed for use in schools and went into several editions, couched it in biblical style, even breaking the chapters up into numbered verses. Thus, the President figures as "James, whose sir-name was MADISON," and Congress as "the GREAT SANHEDRIM"; Satan abets the wicked British; and, according to this latter-day American version of the holy scriptures, Jackson at New Orleans (chapter liv, verse 13)

> . . . spake, and said unto his captains of fifties, and his captains of hundreds, Fear not; we defend our lives and our liberty, and in that thing the Lord will not forsake us:
>
> 14. Therefore, let every man be upon his watch. . . .
> 15. And ye cunning back-woodsmen, who have known only to hunt the squirrel, the wolf, and the deer, now pour forth your strength upon the mighty lion, that we may not be overcome.
> 16. And as the black dust cast upon a burning coal instantly mounteth into a flame, so was the spirit of the husbandmen of the backwoods of Columbia.

No doubt it was essential to reject Europe in order to form a national character; yet the rejection was accomplished by setting up a distorted image of Europe. Out of rawness, too, American patriotism was sometimes given a narrow, compulsory definition. What did not conform was denounced as un-American and therefore as verging on treason. Washington, himself, while President, came near to asserting that the political opponents of Federalism were traitorous. A generation later, efforts at the promotion of trade unions were castigated as subversive, "foreign" activities.

American nationalism was a self-conscious creation. Other nations had grown slowly; the United States had swiftly and deliberately to invent her own symbols of nationhood. The necessity was clearly understood. Note, for instance, the charge to a jury by Judge Addison of Pennsylvania, during Washington's first administration: "The laws and Constitution of our government ought to be regarded with reverence. Man must have an idol. And our political idol ought to be our Constitution and laws. They, like the ark of the covenant among the Jews, ought to be sacred from all profane touch." Robert Liston said of the nationwide memorial ceremonies held on February 22, 1800, only two months after Washington's death:

> The leading men in the United States appear to be of the opinion that these ceremonies . . . elevate the spirit of the people, and contribute to the formation of a *national* character, which they consider as much wanting in this

country. And assuredly, if self-opinion is . . . an essential ingredient in that *character* which promotes the prosperity and dignity of a nation, the Americans will be gainers by the periodical recital of the feats of their Revolutionary war, and the repetition of the praises of Washington.

American nationalism was more than merely self-conscious: it was a counterstatement, a plea, a continuing debate with hostile forces. Some factors in the situation strengthened the Union; others threatened to throw it apart by centrifugal action, or at least to prevent it from becoming a fully independent nation.

To deal with the last of these groups of factors first, America's cultural nationalism suffered painful setbacks. The confidently awaited American authors and artists did not arrive on the scene as promptly as had been foretold, and when they did arrive they complained of a cool reception from their countrymen. In order to gain a hearing in the United States, they had to win a previous reputation in Europe. As poets and novelists, most of them struggled in vain to compete with Walter Scott, Byron, and a multitude of other gifted and famous Europeans. Washington Irving seemed to achieve international renown only at a price—that of becoming half-European. Fenimore Cooper, while he sturdily defended America in Europe, lived there for a prolonged interval and on returning home behaved—so his enemies thought—like one corrupted by European notions of aristocracy. These men wrote in an "English" idiom; there was hardly a sign, except in comic writing of a subliterary sort, of an "American" language. Webster's *Dictionary* and *Spelling-Book* were widely used, but his American contemporaries hesitated to adopt either the local American terms he recommended or the traditional spellings he had rediscovered. Culturally, they were alarmed by his radical *and* his conservative boldness. Some believed that America was bound to reflect her recent cultural inheritance and to reveal her cultural immaturity.

Whatever their attitudes, they were vulnerable to British jibes in the quarterly reviews and elsewhere. Seen unsympathetically, American cultural pretensions were absurd; to appreciate the full overtones of the American predicament called for more detachment than either side could usually muster. One of the ironies, for example, was that the corncob capital, symbol of native genius, was carved by an Italian craftsman imported by Jefferson to work on the embellishments to the new Capitol. For that matter, most of the early patriotic statuary, from Houdon's figure of George Washington to the productions of Causici or Canova, was commissioned from foreigners. Another irony was that despite outbursts of belligerent nationalism, the United States was surprisingly reluctant to commemorate her heroes or heroic episodes. In part her caution arose from a feeling that it was dangerous to the cause of republicanism to pay too much tribute to individuals, in part from low aesthetic standards among congressmen, and in part from the erratic ways of American government. Though the Continental Congress voted an equestrian statue to George Washington some years before he became President, it was not finished until fifty years after he was dead; and the Washington Monument, projected in 1800, took even longer to complete. Jefferson did not get his memorial in Washington, D.C.—admittedly a lavish one when it came—until he had been in the grave a full century. John Browere, an American who took life masks in plaster of Jefferson and others in order to compile a national portrait gallery, exhausted his savings in the task and could not persuade President Madison to provide money for casting the likeness in bronze. Browere's collection was not rescued from oblivion until the very end of the nineteenth century, when it was found tucked away in a New York farmhouse.

But such slights were trivial in comparison with the immediate dangers to the Union. During the administrations of Washington, Adams, Jefferson, and Madison there were successive moves to dismember some portion or other of the Union, and the menace returned, after a crisis weathered by Monroe, to darken the presidency of Andrew Jackson. . . .

How can all this be reconciled with enthusiastic nationalism? Certainly there was a major contradiction within American society, this "piebald polity," in Thomas Moore's phrase, "of slaving blacks and democratic whites." The situation is accurately expressed by Tocqueville's image of nationalism and sectionalism as two separate currents "flowing in contrary directions in the same channel." Both were strong currents. Both were, in a way, artificial currents. If it was comforting to reflect that sectionalism might prove merely a temporary phase, it was disturbing to realize that the same might be said of American nationalism. Most Americans contrived to believe in both *ism's,* simultaneously or in rapid succession, as the situation dictated.

The Union had gained enormously in strength and coherence during the half-century. Washington referred to it as an "experiment." When Jackson claimed that the experiment had succeeded, he was correct by every index of material well-being. The affection for the Union shown by the new states and the nationwide enthusiasm aroused by Lafayette's visit in 1825 were heartening signs of solidarity. We should not exaggerate the extent of sectional feeling—or of its somewhat incompatible companion, desire for state sovereignty—before 1837. The states that lifted their voices in support of South Carolina did so only in a ragged, wavering, and quickly silenced chorus. Even Calhoun's own South Carolina was far from unanimous in its defiance of the federal government. The many Americans who, on one occasion or another, raised the specter of secession were fully aware of the awfulness of the threat. They could be compared to men in the Middle Ages who achieved a similar effect by invoking the devil.

More compelling than all the symbols of Americanism, however, were the physical evidences of the nation's prosperity. It was an unequal prosperity; the West and South were less well provided than the North with schools, colleges, hospitals, jails, and other signs of high civilization. But they too were growing, active regions. The United States, clearly, was a going concern, whose inhabitants' noisy verbal warfare with one another testified to an essential vigor. Nor should we overlook the relative unconcern of many Americans. They were a busy people, engrossed in local and day-to-day problems. Often they remained indifferent to what was being fought over by their legislators. They could be aroused to fury, but their emotions died away rapidly.

It was also true, as Jackson admitted, that the foundations of union "must be laid in the affections of the people." American nationalism had still to be expressed as an imperative; yet he knew that in the last analysis unity could not be enforced. Washington failed to appreciate this fully, so concerned was he to deny that any significant diversities ought to exist in the United States. By Jackson's day Americans were accustomed to the inescapable reality. The country *was* divided; behind the formal niceties of constitutional theory were shifting coalitions of interests. The task of American politics was to reach acceptable compromises. The prayer of American patriots was that the American "national character"—in the ambiguous terminology they employed—would also be a nationalist character. In any case, the search for American identity—national, sectional, individual—would no doubt be protracted. Mercifully, perhaps, the average American remained unaware that he was living in a quandary. There was much to be said for simply ignoring problems in the hope that they would eventually go away. Of no other country could it be so plausibly maintained that matter-of-factness was on occasion more valuable than intellectual discourse.

CHAPTER 22

THE DEVELOPING
AMERICAN ECONOMY

The international situation at the end of the War of 1812 and at the end of the Napoleonic Wars caused the American people to look inward for their economic growth and development. The result was a period of almost unbelievable economic growth coupled with a remarkable increase in population, and the participation of an increasing number of Americans in a great migration westward. In the following selection, Professor Jones describes this growth in its many forms.

This phenomenal and multifaceted growth leads to some important questions. What was the role of the federal government in this growth? Was this period the golden age of *laissez faire* economics in the United States? Impressive as this period of development was, could it have been more impressive if the government had exercised more positive control on the economy? What was the role of the railroad boom in the growth of the entire economy? In view of the prominence of cotton in the American economy, was the South justified in thinking that it could parlay this all-important staple into an independent Confederacy? Which region was actually becoming stronger and more stable—the North with its diversifying industrial economy, or the South with its single crop dependent on the world market?

The literature covering this economic history is rich and varied. For general economic histories of this period see, especially, Douglass C. North,

Economic Growth in the United States, 1790–1860* (1961), and Stuart Bruchey, *The Roots of American Economic Growth** (1965). For a description of the growth of transportation and its importance during this period, see George R. Taylor, *The Transportation Revolution, 1815–1860** (1951). A Pulitizer Prize-winning study is Bray Hammond, *Banks and Politics in America from the Revolution to the Civil War** (1957). Thomas Govan's *Nicholas Biddle* (1959), is an important biography of one of the shakers and movers of the economy during this period.

* Available in a paperback edition.

THE PRE-CIVIL WAR MARKET
PETER D'A. JONES

The War of 1812

That Anglo-American war, sometimes called the 'Second War of Independence,' had profound effects on the United States economy, and
marked the end of America's international role as a neutral leader. The
British Navy blockaded the Atlantic ports south of New London, and very
effectively reduced United States imports, causing severe depression and
hardship in the West. Smuggling from Canada was probably extensive,
but the only genuine hope was for Americans to be free of dependence
on foreign imports, to develop their own manufacturing industries. War
did help to overcome many of the old agrarian and seafaring prejudices
against investment in native industry. There was some surplus capital
too, lying idle for want of investment opportunities—Yankee merchant
capital, denied its normal outlet in foreign trade by the naval blockade.
Industrial development was a long-term affair, however, and in the meantime New Englanders stood to lose a great deal. They tried to prevent
the outbreak of war with Britain. It is true that much fuss had been
made by the seaboard states about 'maritime rights' and a series of cold-
war incidents between British and American sailors. It is also true that
the Royal Navy thought nothing of violating the three-mile limit, and
'arresting' American sailors on the high seas, practically in full view of
the United States coast. But northeastern merchants had strong British
connections and were highly suspicious of the French, whether in Canada
or in Europe. . . . Was not the Anglo-American disagreement a product
of Napoleon's machinations? What is more, trade was New England's
lifeblood: war with Britain could prove even more crippling than the
disastrous Embargo of 1807. . . .

A great psychic victory for the frontier nationalists, the War of 1812
also saw a temporary growth of native industry. Two years of blockade
and warfare, with imports closed off again, threw Americans onto their

SOURCE. Peter d'A. Jones, *The Consumer Society; A History of American Capitalism*, London: Penguin Books Ltd., 1964, pp. 45–57, 64–68. Copyright 1964 by
Penguin Books Ltd. Reprinted by permission of Penguin Books Ltd., and the author.

own resources. Capital, released from shipping and foreign trade, was set to work drawing native raw materials into the market economy to be processed for home demand—iron and nonferrous metals, cottons and woolens. But America's wealth was not yet to be in manufacturing. The war impetus was something of a false start, because domestic industrialists were well-nigh ruined altogether after the Treaty of Ghent: an enormous inflood occurred of imported European goods, made with cheaper labor and a more advanced British technology. United States imports multiplied overnight as British manufacturers, starved of markets during the long war and the Continental System, exploited their comparative advantage with heavy exports of finished goods (especially textiles from Lancashire) to American ports. Thriving import houses in New York, Philadelphia, and Baltimore handled about $113 million worth of products in 1815—twice the prewar figure of 1811, and many times the wartime low of 1814 ($13 million). The exports of 1815 ($53 million) were somewhat lower in value than those of 1811, but were greatly in excess of the wartime low of 1814 ($7 million). This great and rapid expansion of American trade, although it set back the emergence of native industry, was nevertheless the chief source of American wealth in the first half of the nineteenth century.

Cotton Exports and the Atlantic Economy

The main component of United States exports from the War of 1812 to the Civil War was cotton. The southern crop represented over a third of total exports in value down to the crash of 1819, rose to two-thirds in the late 1830's, and remained well over half the total until the outbreak of hostilities in 1861. In contrast, America's traditional exports—tobacco, rice, naval goods, lumber, and fish—declined as a percentage of total exports. The sale of American manufactures abroad remained very small and even declined in the 1830's before beginning a gradual rise. Wheat and flour were exported by the middle Atlantic states and made up an unsteady one-tenth of total exports down to 1820, declining afterward. It was rising cotton prices in foreign markets that underlay the economic expansion of the immediate postwar years and of the 1830's, and even in the boom of the 1850's in which many other factors are to be seen—the westward push of the frontier, the Industrial Revolution in the Northeast, gold discoveries in California, waves of immigration—the rising figures of cotton production and cotton exports are still a good guide to the general health of the economy.

Almost half of America's total exports before the Civil War went to help sustain the economy of Britain during its first and greatest period of revolutionary change. France, being slower to industrialize, took on average up to one-sixth of United States exports; the West Indies, no longer a major American customer, bought a steadily declining percentage. Since the export trade was dominated by southern cotton, the chief American consumer was the North of England textile industry. In fact, Eli Whitney's cotton gin, patented in 1794, became available to increase the productivity of southern plantations at a time when the demand for cotton in Britain was increasing voraciously. Of all the economic changes that made up the classical Industrial Revolution in Britain in the late eighteenth and early nineteenth centuries, none were swifter or more powerful than those in the cotton textile trades of Lancashire. The key industry of the British economic revolution and the key export staple in United States economic growth were very heavily interdependent. Justifiably, economists have called the international system that emerged the 'Atlantic Economy.'

There was more to the Atlantic Economy than the cotton trade, as we shall see later. But that trade itself is comprehensible only in an international setting. After the boom of the 1830's, conditions were changing, and with the coming of a more permanent native American industrialism, internal improvements such as canals and railroads, and an extension of the home market, the United States economy would in time become less dependent. After the Civil War the source of American wealth was a vast and growing domestic demand for industrial products. However, even in that stage of its economic history, in the last quarter of the nineteenth century and long after its 'take-off' into self-sustaining growth, the American economy remained a functional part of the wider Atlantic Economy, with the export of foodstuffs (grain and meat) and the 'new immigration' from eastern and southern Europe playing rather similar roles (on a larger scale) to those played previously by cotton and the northwest European immigration.

America's Merchant Navy

In the 1820's transatlantic trade was cut into very heavily by the post-1819 depression. America's chief wealth-producing changes took place internally rather than externally. The river steamboat was perfected, for instance, and in 1825 the magnificent Erie Canal was completed—boosting the growth of the two great ports, New Orleans and New York. External recovery was very slow up to about 1830. Then came a seven-year foreign trade boom, the result of a fundamental general increase in population and productivity, as well as of such specific factors as tariff reductions, international trading agreements, a growing American domestic surplus of foodstuffs, and innovations in ocean transportation.

This new expansive surge of the 1830's was brought to an end by the panic of 1837, which was international in scope, a faltering of the Atlantic Economy. But just before news of the crash broke upon the market, United States imports were worth $129 million and United States exports $190 million. Only three years later, America was already on the road to recovery, though trade fluctuated continually down to 1846. In that year American foodstuffs were urgently demanded by the British government to save the unhappy Irish peasant population from total famine and death through disastrous failure of the potato crop. The Prime Minister, Sir Robert Peel, climaxed his great series of free-trade budgets by abolishing at last the import duty on imported foreign grain, the infamous 'Corn Law' (originally imposed in 1815 by a Parliament of landlords). Britain was now free to import American grain to help ease the Irish situation. Events in other parts of the world gave American commerce a further fillip—gold discoveries in Australia, Colorado, and California coinciding with falling United States tariffs.

So the 1840's witnessed an abnormal production of American shipping to meet trade demands. Regular oceangoing steamship services brought New York nearer to Liverpool and northern Europe. But the most dramatic development was the brief flowering of the beautiful three-masted Yankee 'clipper ship'—narrow-beamed, six times as long as it was broad, with concave sides, a prodigious height and spread of canvas and a sharp, streamlined prow—the most graceful and the fastest sailing ship afloat. Donald McKay's *Flying Cloud* plowed through the ocean from Boston to San Francisco in 89 days and 8 hours—a speed not equaled even by steamships for many years to come. This speeding up of economic transfers between the east and west coasts of the continent was by far the most significant service the Yankee clipper made to United States economic growth.

But it was trade with the Orient that first stimulated the building of clipper ships before 1848. Americans had long taken the lead in opening up the Far East to Western trade and culture, and as early as 1784 the United States *Empress of China* had sailed from New York to Canton. In 1836 Siam gave special trading rights to Yankee merchants; in the forties and fifties Anglo-Chinese wars threw part of the China trade out of British and into American hands, especially since China's ports were more open to all comers after 1844. In addition, in 1849 Britain relaxed her Navigation Laws, and fast New England clippers were allowed to compete in carrying tea to the London market, where the first delivery of the season's tea crop brought a fabulous price. Five years later (1854) Commodore Perry broke through the self-spun cocoon of Japanese cultural isolation and dragged that nation out into world trade.

The mid-nineteenth-century shipbuilding boom gave the United States a merchant-marine gross tonnage not much below that of Britain herself, the high point of 1861 (5½ million tons) not being equaled again until 1901. A cost advantage in cheap timber underlay the extraordinary growth of the American shipbuilding industry, but as forests near the Atlantic seaboard were steadily depleted of pine and oak, timber prices rose and formerly marginal timber was drawn into use. Yankee builders turned to the less suitable chestnut and birch, and British consumers turned toward Scandinavian and Russian suppliers as the advantageous price differential between the United States and Europe fell drastically. The clipper ship in any case was always expensive to build, and with limited hold space was profitable only for cargo of low bulk and high value or perishability. Circumstances had favored the ship: gold discoveries in California (1849) and in Australia (1851), war (in the Crimea as well as in China), and the European revolutions in 1848. But its days were numbered. Circumstances would soon destroy it—the decline of old trade routes (Brazilian coffee capturing the United States market at the expense of Oriental tea, for instance); the perfection of the steamship in the bulky transatlantic trade markets and the cheap mass-migration passenger field; the Civil War and the preceding Panic of 1857 which was a foretaste of general decline in a shipbuilding industry that lost the initiative and was unprepared for the changeover to steel ship production. Americans lost out to better British clipper designers even before the Civil War, and Britain, since it possessed the world's most highly developed iron industry, used its cost advantage to take the lead in the increasing use of metal ships. United States capital sought new outlets in manufacturing industry and in railroad construction. America turned away from her merchant marine and foreign commerce to the subjugation and internal development of her native wealth.

GROWTH OF THE HOME MARKET

Although United States foreign trade increased noticeably down to 1860 and the export sector played a strategic role in general economic growth, the home market expanded enormously and far more dramatically. The 'extent' of the market depends on density of population (absolute size and degree of urbanization) and on the efficiency of economic transfer (movement of the factors of production: resources, men, and capital). Both these forces were at work in the United States during the first sixty years of the nineteenth century. Population grew by natural increase and by immigration, with greater urbanization; a network of trails, turnpike highways, canals, and railroads linked the sections and facilitated factor mobility. Moreover, by 1853 United States territorial expansion on the North American continent was almost complete. The purchase of Alaska from Russia after the Civil War (1867) brought the continental United States up to well over three million square miles in area —three or four times the size of the young Republic of 1790. Population was nine times greater: 36 million when the war ended (1865) as opposed to under 4 million in 1790. As the federal Constitution guaranteed there were to be no internal tariffs or artificial barriers to trade among the states, the United States became a huge free-trade domestic market.

The Web of Sectionalism: Interregional Economic Flows

The size and geographical variety of this market, and its three great sections (Northeast, South, and West) with their differences in 'comparative advantage,' led to area specialization based on the clearly patterned though changing interregional flow of economic activity. The South devoted itself to plantation staples for the export trade and for the growing textile manufacturing industry of New England, buying much of its food supply from western farmers by way of that great river artery the Mississippi, and obtaining its manufactured goods from the Northeast by sea. The West came to specialize in grain and cattle production to feed the South and the Northeast. The Northeast (New England and the middle Atlantic states) performed a function similar to that of Britain a hundred years earlier for the thirteen colonies: it supplied finished goods, tools and equipment, commercial and building know-how, foreign imports and capital.

It was after the 1812–1814 War that a regional pattern of mutual interdependency became clear. The river steamboat, by accelerating and making rather more certain the tricky passage of the Mississippi River both downstream and upstream, had much to do with this. The flow of domestic trading established before the 1830's depended heavily on the great river flowing north-south from the interior of the continent to the Gulf, which bound the West to the South with the umbilical cord of economic need. Western products floated down the wide, muddy stream through Arkansas, Tennessee, Mississippi, and Louisiana, and very often never reached the port of New Orleans, being landed informally and sold on the way. Cotton, sugar, rice, tobacco—the southern staples— were shipped from New Orleans by coastal vessels to the northern states. In turn the latter provided for southern farmers banking, insurance, transportation, and brokerage services, and manufactured articles. As for the West before 1830, the most valuable eastern manufactured goods could afford to be sent there by the expensive wagon routes, but bulkier products of necessity went first by sea to New Orleans and then by river upstream.

Drastic changes took place after 1830 or so when this web of economic relationships was struck sideways by the 'transportation revolution.' Internal improvements like the Cumberland Turnpike, the Erie and Ohio canals, and the great railroad systems such as the New York Central, the Erie, the Baltimore and Ohio, and the Pennsylvania linked the industrial, commercial Northeast with the agrarian and frontier West. Major economic flows changed direction; the alliance between West and South was badly weakened at a crucial period in the history of American sectionalism.

After about 1835 western lumber, cattle, and grain reached Buffalo and was transshipped to eastern consumers and exporters. Since 1825 the Erie Canal had served mainly to bring the output of western New York State to the tables of eastern families. Now the completion of the Ohio canal (1832) brought products from much farther west, and the railway networks of the early fifties completed this transition.

Western trade with the South continued to rise absolutely. Indeed, the antebellum decade was a bouyant era in the economic history of the Mississippi Valley. New Orleans remained America's principal export center as late as 1860, with the port of New York running second, followed by three southern ports—Mobile, Charleston, and Savannah— involved in the heavy coastal traffic, shipping raw staples from Dixie to the eastern states. But New Orleans was increasingly dependent on these regional staples of its immediate hinterland. In 1843 Buffalo had the very first grain elevator, and three years later was transshipping more wheat and flour from western states to eastern markets by way of the Erie and canals farther west than New Orleans could receive from upstream. The river was simply inadequate for ever-growing western needs. In the fifties Ohio's farmers sent the vast bulk of their grain eastward by way of canals, using the southern route only for whiskey and meat products. Buffalo's receipts tell a forceful story, with a moral for the South: in 1836 she received from the West 139,000 barrels of flour and 500,000 bushels of grain; in 1860, well over 1,000,000 barrels of flour and over 31,000,000 bushels of grain. Consequently the volume of trade at St Louis (destined for New Orleans) declined steadily after the boom of the 1850's. The transportation revolution had assured the future of New York and sealed the fate of New Orleans.

The Mechanism of Trade and the Growth of Cities

American domestic trade, like manufacturing industry in later years, was not only subject to sudden and revolutionary change but also revealed a wide variety of conditions. Sharply contrasting marketing systems existed simultaneously, from frontier barter in, say, the southern Appalachians, to the complexities of international transfers in Philadelphia or New York. Well-nigh self-sufficient backwoodsmen could transport low bulk and high value products (furs, whiskey, potash) to market by horse; in areas of more settled agriculture the sale of bulk farm surpluses was dependent on river and lake navigations before the canal and railroad era. At the local level in all parts of the country the essential mechanism of trade was the ubiquitous 'country store' with its useful extension of 'book credit' to individual farmers. From the 1830's onward, manufacturers and wholesalers in the cities began a great American tradition by sending out traveling salesmen. And of course the 'Yankee peddler' was encountered everywhere, in the North, the East, the South, and the West, bearing his load of clocks, 'notions', and Connecticut hardware.

Large-scale grain, cattle, and cotton marketing on a national and international basis called for more sophisticated and elaborate sales organization, with a hierarchy of middlemen and specialists—all of which usually implied some ultimate degree of control from New York. That city developed the greatest amount of marketing specialization: brokers, jobbers, commission houses, wholesalers, public auctioneers, and even embryo department stores. A. T. Stewart helped to introduce departmental organization into the retail dry-goods business, using the so-called 'one price system' that eliminated the haggling of the marketplace—all prices being plainly marked on goods. (Macy's, opened in the city in 1858, followed the same policy, and such famous firms as Arnold Constable and Lord & Taylor were already established, with buyers combing Europe and their stores offering a wide variety of dry goods to the fortunate city dweller.) New Yorkers controlled the export of southern raw cotton and the distribution of New England cotton textiles alike, as Boston directed in no more seemly fashion the wool trade and boots and shoes.

Meanwhile the Ohio Valley economy gave birth to Cincinnati, Pittsburgh, and Louisville, and the commerce of Lake Erie nurtured Detroit, Toledo, and Cleveland. All these growing communities were strategically located on nodal points in the western river and lake navigation systems. Farther west, St Louis sprang into being where the Missouri, still untamed after flowing hundreds of miles east and south from the Rockies across the Great Plains, pours into the Mississippi. St Louis commanded the very heart of a 4,000-mile-long river system and was the natural place of transshipment where cargo from the major steamboats serving New Orleans and Memphis was transferred to smaller vessels for distribution up far-distant streams. But the coming of the railroad gave Chicago greater advantage. Much better located for control of westward railway traffic, and enjoying a wonderful stretch of navigable lakes and canals eastward, Chicago after mid-century rapidly outrivaled both St Louis and New Orleans. To about 1850, however, western trade was dominated in fact by Cincinnati, the great meat-packing center on the Ohio, linked in 1845 to Lake Erie (Toledo) by many miles of state-owned canal.

The Transportation Revolution

The great cities that fought for control of America's growing wealth in the early century owed their existence, many of them, to the transportation revolution. For in United States history transportation innovation was not only a 'linking factor' that articulated the whole process of economic development, but very often the essential precondition of the opening up and subjugation of the continental interior. Turnpike highways reached their greatest growth period between about 1790 and the 1812–1814 War. Meanwhile, from about 1807, the river steamboat came on the national scene; its hey-day was the 1850's. Canal building was most significant between 1817 and 1850, and railroad construction from the 1830's onward.

Revolutionary changes such as these were not accepted with complete approval by Americans. When internal improvements were encouraged and aided by federal and state authorities at public expense, they became the object of heated sectional and group politics; rarely were they considered as necessary 'social overhead capital,' except when private and public interest combined. Generally western farmers in dire need of communication with eastern markets supported the enterprises, as did northeastern coastal communities with growing industrial populations demanding cheaper foodstuffs. Land speculation was mixed up with transport history through the federal and state land-grant policy and the soaring land values in turnpike, canal, and railway development areas. But leaving aside politics and finance, the creative force of the transportation revolution is undeniable, not merely supporting but locating and creating human settlements and drawing human and natural resources into the growing market economy. Railway construction in particular often preceded settlement; after about 1850 the companies themselves organized migration from the East and from Europe to the areas flanking their lines. And the political benefits of economic integration were equally obvious, especially with the advent of the transcontinentals and increased use of the telegraph once the Civil War was over. Never was Adam Smith's dictum on the extent of the market illustrated so spectacularly. . . .

Coming of the Railroad

If the United States was rather slow to take the British example in the matter of canal construction, she certainly made it up in the adoption of railroads. T. P. Kettell, the southern publicist, said of these years:

The excitement in relation to canals and steamboats was yet at its zenith, when the air began to be filled with rumour of the new application of steam to land carriages and to railroads. . . . In 1825 descriptions came across the water of the great success of the Darlington railroad, which was opened to supply London with coal, and which had passenger cars moved by steam at the rate of seven miles per hour.

Before the Stockton-Darlington line was built in Britain, there had been several native American experiments, but this foreign achievement and the later Rainhill Trials of 1829 were an enormous stimulus to Americans. 'The most animated controversy sprang up,' wrote Kettell, '. . . [and] with the national energy of character, the idea had no sooner become disseminated than it was acted upon.'

A British engine, the *Stourbridge Lion,* was the first locomotive to operate on a commercial track in the United States, but like most British engines imported in this early period it was, strange as it may seem, too heavy for American needs. So the Baltimore and Ohio used on its thirteen miles of track in 1830 a much lighter United States engine, Peter Cooper's *Tom Thumb,* while still experimenting with horse traction and sails. The second commercial railroad in the United States was built in 'the agrarian South'—the Charleston and Hamburg, connecting the major port of South Carolina with the Savannah River in the hope of diverting some of the rich cotton trade from the Georgia port of Savannah at that river's mouth. The Charleston and Hamburg had a regular passenger service from 1831, and claimed in 1833 to be the longest existing railroad in the world (136 miles).

In the Northeast the seaboard states followed a pattern of rivalry similar to that of canals. The Massachusetts legislature chartered three railroad companies to build outward from Boston in 1831, and ten years later had a through connection to the Hudson—making good its failure to do the same by canal. Pennsylvania rapidly gained ground with four lines in the 1830's going out in all directions from Philadelphia to nearby towns like Columbia, Trenton, Reading, and, farther out, to Baltimore. In fact, by 1840 all the larger eastern states except Maine had significant mileage. Though the Appalachian barrier remained to be conquered, total United States railroad mileage in 1840 equaled that of canals. Ten years later it was almost three times greater (9,000 miles), and the problems were of a different order. The question now was: How soon to the Pacific coast? A through connection to the Great Lakes was made by the New York Central in 1850. In 1853 Chicago and in 1855 St Louis were joined to New York city, and a year thereafter a railroad bridged the Mississippi. The same decade saw New Orleans linked to Chicago and Memphis, Tennessee with a through connection to the Atlantic coast of Virginia.

No transcontinental railroad could be built until Congress was able to agree. The idea had been in the air since the twenties, but politicians split on sectional lines, and the cities of Chicago, St Louis, and Memphis were keen rivals in the congressional struggle, each claiming prior right to a transcontinental connection. A line was built across Nicaragua in 1855, but nothing more. Southern secession and Civil War resolved the issue a few years later. By that time several lines stretched to the very cutting edge of the western frontier, and total United States mileage of road actually being operated was well over 30,000 miles.

Public Aid to America's Railroads

This immense network was built within the space of three decades, 1830–1860. How was such an immense program financed? Obviously, private enterprise capital alone could not handle such a feat of economic development. It is true that in the thirties private funds were used and foreign loans at high rates were much supported in London by British capitalists and investors. But however locally important this foreign investment was, it proved ultimately inadequate, especially after the debt-repudiation fiascoes of 1837; its function was to help initiate economic developments that would eventually have occurred in any case, if somewhat more slowly. Government stepped into the breach—first state and local authorities and, later on, more massively, federal authority.

Almost all the initial state charters gave wide privileges to the railroad companies, and few, if any, placed restrictions on fares or securities. Professor Milton Heath, a most distinguished student of the South, has shown that the bulk of railroad investment in that section came from government agencies and not from private enterprise. Yet some states went so far as to grant monopoly rights to railroad companies—as did Georgia, South Carolina, Kentucky, Louisiana, New Jersey, and Massachusetts—sweeping aside normal American fears of monopolistic privilege in the scramble for riches. Between New York and Philadelphia the Camden and Amboy Railroad was given the exclusive rights to provide rail transportation. Such relaxations, spurred on by city and state rivalries, were accomplished by tax exemptions, free grants of rights-of-way and permission to establish railroad banks.

This was not all. Huge amounts of outright financial aid were given by state and local governments to private railroad companies. Counties, towns, cities, and states bought railroad securities directly with public money. State debts attributable to railroads totaled $43 million in 1838, and local aid probably exceeded this figure. In the East and West, as well as in the South, tax money was lavished on railroad loans and investments. In the antebellum South this amounted to $144 million by 1861, over 95 per cent of which came from local and state governments; the state of Virginia had supplied $21 million, Missouri over $25 million. State authorities did not stint in doling out public land either; Texas alone gave away five million acres to stimulate railroad construction.

Meanwhile, the federal government was not exactly idle in this field. Army engineers surveyed and even directed the building of some lines, free of charge. Tariffs on imported British rails and other necessities were canceled (1830–1843) by a thoughtful Congress. But it was from 1850 onward that federal aid became massive, and took the form of Gallatin's proposal of 1808: land grants. A temporary alliance of southern and western states pushed through Congress a demand for land to support a north-south railroad from northern Illinois to Mobile, Alabama. The Act of 1850 gave the states of Illinois, Alabama, and Mississippi alternate sections of land in a strip six miles wide on each side of the proposed line. The states were then to give the land to the railroad companies, who either sold it or sold bonds secured by a mortgage on it. In this way constitutional difficulties over the role of the federal government were neatly sidestepped. The land—almost four million acres—eventually made up parts of the Illinois Central and the Mobile and Ohio railroads. In return the companies promised to convey federal troops and property without charge, and Congress was to fix the rates for mail. Having established a precedent, Congress acted upon it in the years that followed, and by 1857 had handed out to 45 railroad companies (through the intermediary of 10 states) about 18 million acres of the public domain. And this was nothing compared with the enormous land grants to the transcontinental lines after the Civil War. One could perhaps twist an old phrase around and call the American system of railroad financing one of 'public enterprise for private profit,' without being too far from the truth.

The Railroad and the United States Market

The railroads did everything to extend the American market that the turnpikes and canals did, only more so. The *Preliminary Report* of the Eighth Census (1860) declared that

. . . our railroals transport in the aggregate at least 850 tons of merchandise per annum to the mile of road in operation. Such a rate would give 26,000,000 tons as the total annual tonnage. . . . At $150 per ton, the aggregate value of the whole would be $3,900 million. Vast as this commerce is, more than three-quarters of it has been created since 1850.

A mere decade of growth! Railroads in the United States had much more to give, and their impetus was not exhausted so soon as in Britain, for the westward movement brought various repeat performances of the original impact, with the lateral extension and sequential growth of the economy. The roads that became part of the northwestern empire of James J. Hill did for Minnesota, North Dakota, and Montana in the eighties and nineties what the Chicago, Burlington and Quincy consolidation (1855) did earlier for the Midwest, and what the pioneer lines did for the Atlantic seaboard in the thirties.

More than any other single factor, the rate of public and private investment in the railroads drew unused natural resources into the market economy on a large scale, and within the physical framework of a favorable land-man ratio, created high living standards for the American worker. As a geographically widespread form of social capital, the railroads created jobs all over the nation and even found the labor to fill them. By deliberate 'colonizing' and by building in anticipation of traffic, the companies drew into the productive process human as well as physical resources. In any case the very building and maintenance of the network was in itself a major industry with insatiable demands for iron rails, timber, coal (eventually), engines and rolling stock, bridge and tunneling materials, and a wide range of human skills, to say nothing of huge aggregations of mobile capital. A large part of all foreign investment in nineteenth century America was tied up in railroads. New financial techniques and institutions had to be evolved, and in the process agriculture became commercialized, growing urbanization became a structural factor in American social history, the domestic market and foreign trade were metamorphosed. Externally, United States exports were cheapened and latent foreign demand for foodstuffs allowed its full expression; internally, division of labor on a continental scale became a reality—the regional specialization that has already been discussed.

In sum, the railroad created unprecedented demands for all the factors of production, and the economic, political, and psychological disturbance it caused brought successive waves of social change for years to come.

CHAPTER 23

THE NEW WEST

Frederick Jackson Turner, in his famous essay of 1893, suggested that Americans should look to the West for their heritage. In the preceding selection, Peter Jones suggested that the settlement of the West was one of the important factors in the rapid growth of the American economy. In the study that follows, George Dangerfield describes the area and its people.

The American West, which then included Ohio, Indiana, Illinois, and points South, has been blamed and praised for a number of influences on the American way of life. It has been credited with being the cradle of the unique qualities of American life. It has been praised as the birthplace of our democratic institutions and has been damned as the source of our propensity for violence. In this essay little praise or blame of this nature is assigned. Professor Dangerfield seeks rather to analyze the Western mind and to explore the influence of the West upon American life in the years immediately after 1812. How does Dangerfield define the West? What characterized Western thought (or instinct)? How does Dangerfield explain the great migration to the West? What major impact did the West have on American political development in this period?

In the 75 years following Turner's essay, the old and the new West have been studied by many historians. The West has been the subject of some of the finest history written in the United States. The non-specialist in this area needs a guide through this mountain of material. Ray Allen Billington provides such a guide to the latter part of the period in *The Far Western Frontier, 1830–1860** (1956). The eastern and older aspects of the area and period are discussed in Francis S. Philbrick, *The Rise of the West, 1754–1830** (1965). The Billington volume contains a complete and annotated bibliography, and the Philbrick work includes (as an appendix) a critical commentary on the Turner thesis.

* Available in a paperback edition.

THE WEST
GEORGE DANGERFIELD

The Peace of Ghent was a victory for the West. No Eastern demand was satisfied by it; but once the British had withdrawn their claim to the sources of the Mississippi and the control of the Northwest, the triumph of expansionism was complete. All serious territorial disputes were now confined to the northeast frontier, about which the West cared little, and the Oregon country, about which it cared much, but knew less. At the same time, the Peace of Ghent marked the beginning of a release from Europe. The time was gone when the thunders of a Trafalgar or an Austerlitz, a Jena or a Wagram, stealing across the Atlantic, could rattle the windows of American merchants and legislators; when the fortunes of an Administration seemed to rise and fall with the fluctuations of a campaign in the Spanish Peninsula; and when some obscure and secret change in the policies of Whitehall was sooner or later translated into extravagant uneasiness along the Wabash. The connection was still intricate and sensitive, as the events of the next few years were to show, and it was never for one instant severed; but it was evidently loosened, by the pull of the Pacific Ocean and by the influence of that star which marked the center of population as it ascended from the coastal plain and climbed toward the summit of the Alleghenies.

What the deliberations of Ghent had proved—and they had done so with all the elaborate arguments that commonly attend the proving of the truth of an axiom—was that the United States of America must not be considered a European appendage. American axioms, to be sure, were not always very clear to European minds; but if further arguments were needed, one was immediately supplied by the increase in the velocity of the westward movement.

SOURCE. George Dangerfield, *The Era of Good Feelings,* New York: Harcourt, Brace & World, 1952, pp. 105–112, and 115–121. Copyright 1952 by Harcourt, Brace & World, Inc. Reprinted by permission of Harcourt, Brace & World, Inc. and the author.

I

This movement had been checked to some extent by the War of 1812. Rumors of Indian uprisings halted the pioneer upon his frontiers and even pressed him back; but by 1814 the more potent influence of taxation and commercial depression had reasserted itself. Farmers, mechanics, artisans, and tradesmen, fleeing the ogres of monopoly and debt, turned their faces westward; and the frontier resumed its irregular advance. With the coming of peace, the advance became a migration. It was one of the greatest migrations in history and in its early stages was one of the most imaginative, for its impulse was centrifugal, and a centrifugal impulse favors the imaginative mind. Competition, of course, was the essence of the frontier, and there was probably no place in the Mississippi and Ohio valleys where industry, thrift, and luck were stronger than callousness, cunning, and scoundrelism. The frontier offered many awful examples of what a highly acquisitive mentality can do when it is permitted to change its environment by any means that come to hand. But the means were still crude in the 1820's; and though the implementing of ideals by practices that negated them was an exercise the frontier always performed with a certain adroitness, it cannot be denied that in the 1820's the high ideals were as noticeable as the low practices. The frontier uttered with conviction the language of the great American dream. This dream was essentially the adaptation of political ideals to territorial opportunities; and it was not called into question so long as environment took the shape, or seemed to take the shape, of vast spaces of unoccupied land. It was a dream that foresaw the simultaneous achievement of two dissimilar objectives: a maximum of political liberty and a maximum of material well-being; and those who were possessed by it were always a little impatient of the innumerable adjustments necessary to bring these two great objectives into some kind of focus. Nowadays we have learned through painful experience that the two objectives are on different planes; but in 1817, and for many years after, this fact was more inconvenient than apparent.

The tutelary geniuses of the westward movement were Necessity and Hope, which have always provided the motive force for human beings. It would be wrong to underestimate the importance of the latter. Hope is an instinctive apprehension of the fact that everything is in the process of becoming, that all things change, that nothing can be undone; and it is natural enough that this fact, admitted into the drama of human affairs, should take on some extravagant forms. The westering migrant, for example, was drawn across the Alleghenies by a strand of rumors. Some of these rumors were obviously put out by the land-speculating fraternity;

some were old and magical. In very early days, the American West was said to be full of "savannas"—Hesperian meadows of rich grass, bosom-high, and perfumed by exotic flowers and trees. The early Spanish explorer, with his lean and fantastic vision, had looked for them; but no man had ever found them. They retreated as mankind advanced; and when the news came from Lewis and Clark, and from Zebulon Pike, that beyond the Missouri lay a treeless desert, it was generally conceded that the savanna had passed beyond the reach of the pioneer farmer. In the 1820's the mythical "desert" was like the dragon of the Hesperides, all dry rustling scales and fiery breath, guarding the approaches to the promised land. None the less, the savanna, like a memory or a spell, still haunted the westward movement as it spilled into the Mississippi Valley. Men still cherished the belief that at the end of the journey lay the incomparably good life; and they continued to cherish this belief even after they had arrived at their destination.

Oddly enough, the pioneer farmer avoided the real savanna whenever he encountered it. The prairie was found in Illinois, in Indiana, even among the forests of Ohio; but the westward movement into the Ohio and the Mississippi valleys was still in the grip of seventeenth- and eighteenth-century agriculture. For two centuries, or thereabouts, the forebears of the nineteenth-century pioneer had themselves been pioneering in the forest. Girdling, grubbing, log-rolling, burning, and the building of log houses were inherited techniques. William Cobbett has testified to the extraordinary proficiency of Americans with the ax: he said that they could do ten times more work with that tool than any Englishman he ever saw, and they were very active and hardy—"they will catch you a pig in an open field by *racing* him down; and they are afraid of nothing." But he added that they knew little of such delicate skills as hedging or the use of the bill-hook; it was in forest farming that the Americans excelled. They put great faith in their ability to select a soil by the character of its forest cover; hardwood, for example—a heavy growth of it—was certain evidence of a "strong" soil. But at the prairies and treeless savannas they looked askance. They suspected a soil where no timber had ever grown; they feared the open solitude, the exposure to winds and storms. The game they coveted lived in the forests; from the forests they obtained the walls of their houses, their fuel, their fences, the wooden pins they used for nails, the wooden hinges and door latch, the wooden chimney, the hollow log that curbed their wells. The immense difficulty involved in digging a deep well with picks and shovels made the prairie hateful; and the expense of breaking up the prairie sod, which required three or four yoke of oxen and a heavy plow, was prohibitive, and the return was slow. Prairie soil had to lie fallow for a whole season until the grass roots had thoroughly rotted; whereas in the forest the pioneer, armed only with an ax and a hoe, could girdle the trees, grub out the undergrowth, plant his corn, and have a good crop the first year.

A well-found emigrant would go into the wilderness with an ax, a gun, a few household goods, a cow, a yoke of oxen or a horse, a few sheep, and some pigs. Or he might have acquired the characteristic small wagon, with its blanket "tilt," which Birkbeck noted on his westward journey in 1817, and which was the sure sign of a man with some farming experience and a little capital. Such travelers were the sober realists of the movement. Others, less prosperous, trudged westward with a single pack-horse, carrying all their household effects, while the barefoot wives followed behind with the babies. Or the family cow may have been the beast of burden. More often than not, the migrant was a man with no farming experience—a mechanic, or artisan, or merchant's clerk. A handcart on four plank wheels carried his smaller children and the family clothes, skillet, bed-quilt, and bag of corn meal; or a wheelbarrow would serve this purpose; or in cases of extreme destitution a man would carry all his property on his back. Was he driven by necessity, or drawn by hope?

Early in the spring, in the season of courage and of dreams, the rude pilgrims from the seaboard turned their faces west, and, as soon as they struck the great highways, melted into an almost continuous stream of wagons, carts, and foot parties. The journey that lay ahead was immense and terrible. William Cobbett, who never ventured out of the East, recoiled from it with the instinctive horror of a Surrey yeoman. "The rugged roads, the dirty hovels, the fire in the woods to sleep by, the pathless ways through the wilderness, the dangerous crossings of the rivers." And as for the destination! "To boil their pot in the gipsy-fashion, to have a mere board to eat on, to drink whiskey or pure water, to sit and sleep under a shed far inferior to . . . English cowpens, to have a mill at twenty miles' distance, an apothecary's shop at a hundred, and a doctor nowhere." Few English families, he thought, could put up with such conditions or could even cope with them. Did not an American farmer mend his plow, his tackle of all sorts, his household goods, his shoes? Did he not, if need be, *make* them? Could an Englishman do this? Could he live without bread and, worse, without beer, for months at a time? The whole business horrified him; it was a "transalleganian romance," he said bitterly; and he hoped his countrymen would have nothing to do with it. Let them settle in the Atlantic

states, near the great cities on the coast. Many settlers, no doubt, would
have agreed with Cobbett. "It was on the 6 of May we came here," an
anonymous woman wrote to President Monroe, from Barnsville, Ohio;
"we had no other food for our horses nor cows but what they could
procure in the woods. It took nearly all the time of one of our grown
sons to hunt the cattle (the little ones are of no use for this purpose).
Your patience sir will not hold out while I would describe swarms of
large flies which inhabit these uncultivated lands and which stinging the
cattle nearly drive them to madness. Unsound corn, sick wheat and
mills seven miles off and then only going in times of great moisture.
Indeed last summer the whole settlement were supported by one hand
mill for several months. You will conclude we did not eat much bread—
and neither we did." But the Americans had a saying that the cowards
never started, and the weak died by the way. Few of them, once they had
set out, turned back again. Thomas Jefferson told Adam Hodgson that
he never knew a person to leave the coast for the Western country and
then return to the seaboard. . . .

<h2 style="text-align:center">II</h2>

The words "West" and "frontier" are almost interchangeable for the
1820's. The West was the lurch of Christendom along the shortest route
between western Europe and eastern Asia, and it was led by the fur-
trade—conducted by men of extreme daring and organized by men of
extreme cupidity—the produce of which was still the most likely medium
of exchange between China and the United States. The frontier was
anywhere across the Alleghenies where subsistence farming predominated: thus in the 1820's the frontier was moving out of Ohio, but could
still be found in western Pennsylvania. Or again the frontier could be
the barrier—as in western Georgia, eastern Alabama, and the northern
two thirds of Mississippi—that Indian lands opposed to the advance of
cotton. It was extremely fluid; but it also settled into stagnant pools
along the mountain ridges in eastern Tennessee and Kentucky, and away
from the rivers and the coast it lingered in the lower South like a state of
mind—abandoned, primitive, and obstinate.

In 1817, the frontier was advancing along the lines of least resistance,
following the rivers, and thrusting out slender fingers towards the West.
If the pioneer had a processional, it was choired by rivers. The great
movement hastened up the Wabash and the Kaskaskia; up the Mississippi
towards the mouth of the Des Moines; up the Missouri, the Arkansas, the
Washita, the Red; and down the Pearl, the Pascagoula, the Alabama,

and the Chattahoochee. Behind it, like unsubmerged islands, lay the rough mountain regions of the Adirondacks and the Alleghenies of northwest Pennsylvania; it swerved aside from the swamps of northwest Ohio, western Indiana, and southern Georgia; it recoiled a little from the malarial flood plains along the lower course of the Mississippi. It was a ragged affair, but formidable, inspired, and inspiring. Only where the Missouri crossed the boundary of the present state did it suddenly stop; for here began the arid region, or so the readers of Zebulon Pike believed, where a treeless and waterless prairie swept away into some fearful Sahara that heaved its sands to the feet of the Shining Mountains.

The trapper, the elemental spirit of expansionism, already knew that the stories of the great American "desert" were false. But he did not write books. Although, in 1840, the westward movement had at last completely emerged from the forest into daylight, and had reached and reconciled itself to the prairie region, it waited even then upon the line of the ninety-seventh meridian until the railroad pushed on forward in the decade 1850–60. In the 1830's pioneers had begun to settle in savannas of Ohio and Indiana, and the large prairies of Illinois, Michigan, Wisconsin, and Missouri; but in the 1820's it is safe to say that pioneer farming was, with but few exceptions, forest farming. In the shade of the forest men grew sallow and sickened, but ideals flourished; and it was not until it left the forest that the frontier lost its innocence. . . .

III

In any case, the majority of settlers, upon reaching a destination, began by hewing out a clearing in the midst of the forest. It may be taken for granted that from the beginnings of settlement until after 1850 the great proportion of farms were cleared out of forest land. After this, if a settler were fortunate enough to have accessible neighbors, which was by no means always the case, he summoned them to a "raising," with whisky and a frolic, and the log cabin was built by a communal effort. He then proceeded to "girdle" or deaden an additional tract, by cutting a ring through the bark around the lower portion of the tree-trunks to prevent the sap from rising. The branches then withered and, after they had been burned, the first crop of corn and vegetables was planted. The new clearing, with its gaunt and menacing trees, wore a dismal look, as if it had been blasted by cannon or withered by fire and disease. Generally, five acres were cleared in this way, half an acre being given to the vegetable garden, half an acre to wheat, and the rest to the corn patch. Corn was the chief support of the settlers, and was almost always the first crop on newly cleared land. Such livestock as there was ran loose in the woods, each owner recognizing his animals by their earmarks; and although careful farmers made up winter feed out of Indian corn and pumpkins, in most cases the animals shifted for themselves. That image of hunger, the "wind-splitter," the fabulous hog of the Western forest, was the product of this treatment.

The pioneer farmer raised his own wool, cotton, and flax for his summer and winter clothing, which his women spun and wove and made into garments; his cap was fashioned out of raccoon fur; he was shod from the skins of deer or cattle. His household furniture, his farming utensils, his harness, were all homemade; and his wooden cart, without tires or boxes, and run without tar, would be heard creaking a mile or more away. The valiant women helped with the planting, the hoeing, and the raking at harvest time; and if there was milking to be done, they did that too—for except in Yankee families no settler, man or boy, could be persuaded to milk a cow.

Such was the Western Arcadia, and had it not been for the fever that flitted through the woods, the ague distilled by the swamps and river mists and the desecrated leaf-mold, the malaria and milk sickness, the loneliness, the corroding poverty, and the inevitable squalor, such an Arcadia might have justified even the optimistic rumors that traveled back from it towards the Eastern seaboard. But the forest left its mark. Where the primitive frontier reigned, as in Indiana, the traveler noticed that the cleared land was rich and valuable, but the people pale and deathly looking. An Englishwoman, traveling up the lower Mississippi in 1827, shrank in horror from the bluish-white complexions of the people who crept from their squalid settlements at every landing.

And yet, unless the sickness seized them with too fierce a grip, the pioneers often impressed the passerby in quite another way. The most shiftless of them—it was odd, but it was true—seemed to be the most buoyant. "Everyone in the West walks erect and easy," said one traveler; "impudent and lazy," said another. Both remarks reflect the independence of the frontier, its belief that no man was its master. As for its imagination, the expression of that was naturally crude and *farouche*. The backwoodsman who dragged his wife and children on and on into the forest, and away from the face of civilization, was a highly imaginative type—"half wild and wholly free"—a curious variant of the classical cenobite. The "generals, colonels, majors" who infested land-office towns like Kaskaskia were not obsessed with some idea of social distinction; while they probably used these self-bestowed titles as a screen for some very sharp practices, they were just as probably expressing their belief in the uncommonness of the common man. For it was the common man who, like a giant, subdued the wilderness, and the frontier never forgot it. . . .

V

Thus a fear of centralization must be considered as one of the instincts of the frontier: but it was an instinct only—a fear that is felt by individualists, not a fear that is formulated by doctrinaires. Just as the good people of Maria Creek smelled aristocracy in the Baptist Board of Foreign Missions, so the West in general saw in the Administration of James Monroe the sign of a social elite, of a dynasty of Virginians, with the inevitable entourage of professional office-holders and heirs-apparent. When depression settled upon the West after the panic of 1819 this instinct found its voice in "a general impression that there was something radically wrong in the administration of the Government." But the early West never went farther than that. It had its own brand of militant nationalism, a potent influence in the 1820's, which was oddly compounded of Jeffersonian phrases, expansionist sentiments, and a sure conviction that there was nothing wrong with centralization when it favored the debtor and the farmer, and everything wrong with it when it did not. When centralizing energy appeared in the form of a contraction of credit, as in 1819, the West was enraged; when it showed itself as a protective tariff, or a national scheme of internal improvements, the Westerner was hard put to make up his mind. There was, he believed, centralization and centralization; and he could say no more.

VI

"Old America," said the English speculator, Morris Birkbeck, in 1817, "seems to be breaking up and moving westward." His statement, on the face of it, is a trifle glib—he had acquired over 26,000 acres in Illinois and was anxious to dispose of them to likely purchasers in England—he had, indeed, written a book for that purpose. But the break-up of Old America—an idea Mr. Birkbeck advanced as a useful and legitimate piece of salesmanship—was, in a limited but extremely important sense, actually taking place. The westward migration represented, if anything, the diaspora of the American Enlightenment; for the westward migrant, trudging along his terrible roads towards his improbable wilderness, carried with him the great principles of Liberty and Equality, the twin torches that had flared and smoked through the eighteenth century and now lighted him fitfully along his way.

The pioneer and the migrant saw themselves not as wage-earners but as property owners; and surely the conflicting philosophies of the Enlightenment agreed at least upon one thing—that the property owner must be free to follow his own self-interest. As an agrarian property owner, the pioneer naturally carried farther and farther into the West some fragments of the enlightened nationalism of Thomas Jefferson, which was essentially an agrarian nationalism, and which believed that an evangelizing nation was fully as important as a self-contained one.

"We feel that we are acting under obligations not confined to the limits of our own society," Jefferson wrote. "It is impossible not to be sensible that we are acting for all mankind." An old gentleman, writing to his Congressman son in 1819, expressed this ideal with equal force. "You must not loose sight," he wrote, "that you are ligislating for a great Nation whose Decisions may be a president for ages to come." All Americans believed that they were setting precedents for ages to come, and none held this belief more firmly than did the Western pioneer. Necessity drove him, it is true: the trails he blazed through the forest were trails that led away from exhausted soils, discriminating laws, limited suffrage, unlimited slavery; but the vitalizing notion that he was the standard-bearer of a new freedom accompanied him all the way. He was convinced that somewhere in the wilderness lay the solution for the ills of the Old World. And so, while the party of Thomas Jefferson slowly disintegrated along the Eastern seaboard, or aligned itself more and more with the interests of the Southern slave-holder, the ideals of Thomas Jefferson were being carried into the wilderness.

The old nationalism of the Enlightenment, however, had already reached its apogee in 1807 with the announcement of the Embargo doctrine—the very gospel of enlightened self-interest. It was never to appear again in so concentrated a form. It was the victim of a lamentable, but oddly enough almost universal, unwillingness of self-interest to be enlightened. Thereafter, dispersed along the roads and streams leading to the Ohio and Mississippi valleys, it lost in power what it gained in mobility; for dispersal is never strength.

The pioneer, after all, was a civilizing influence only to the extent that he modified his environment as quickly as he could. For this essential purpose the Jeffersonian notion that all men are created equal was extremely useful; indeed, the pioneer could hardly have got along without it. It was a very complex notion—it may have originated in John Locke's curious misunderstanding of the nature of perception—but the society the pioneer evolved construed it into an equalitarian democracy that Jefferson himself must have thought alarming. All the new states in the West and Southwest showed a fondness for manhood suffrage which exercised a disturbing but salutary influence on the rest of the country. None the less, there is much peril in the equalitarian doctrine; for its devotees are often lulled into forgetting that political equality does not mean economic equality; and the early West was frequently woken from its social trance by sharp reminders of this simple fact. One might almost go as far as to say that this fact—which is the bug-bear of all political democracies—bewildered and provoked the pioneer at every turn.

The pioneer's solution was not a Jeffersonian one. He did not condemn central government—which in those days was taken to be the purveyor of economic inequality—but he sought to dominate it wherever he could. He represented a centrifugal energy, and central government represented a gravitational one. It was there to see that pioneer society did not fly off into space. The laws relating to the public lands are very instructive in this respect. In 1817, when a settler wished to purchase public lands, the minimum purchase allowed him by law was a quarter section (160 acres), and the minimum price per acre was $2.00, one fourth to be paid down, and the rest payable in four annual installments. This was a scheme to raise revenue, rather than a plan to assist the settler, for the credit system encouraged speculation, and the debt on the public lands rose from $3,042,613.89 in 1815 to $16,794,795.14 in 1818. The great land boom collapsed in 1819, and the settler was in a fair way of being ruined when a Senate Committee on Public Lands, all of whose members but one were from the West, brought in a thoughtful report recommending the abolition of the credit system. This was accomplished by the famous Act of April 2, 1820, which also reduced the minimum purchasable tract to 80 acres, and set the minimum cash payment at $1.25. A farm of 80 acres could now be purchased for $100. This was the first effort to legislate for the settler rather than for the Treasury; and on September 30, 1822, the debt on public lands had sunk to $10,544,454.16.

By the apportionment of 1822, the Western representation was increased to forty-seven members in the House of Representatives, which, with a delegation of eighteen in the Senate, made a formidable group: and legislation favoring the settler continued all through the 1820's, culminating in the pre-emption laws of 1830. These laws officially changed the status of the squatter from one of public pest to one of public benefactor. The squatter, supreme individualist who ranged far ahead of the government surveyors, and occupied the best of the unsurveyed lands without going through the formality of paying for them, had always been protected by frontier opinion and to some extent by Congressional sentiment. The pre-emption laws made him free of the whole public domain in the sense that he was given the right to purchase his lands, no matter how valuable they might be, at the minimum price and before anyone else could bid for them in the public auction.

Thus there was a close relationship between pioneer society and the bounty of the general government, which lasted long after the debt on public lands was extinguished in 1832. Yet the relationship was never a comfortable one. The West, considered as a centrifugal force, longed for complete control of the public land system, while the general government, as a gravitational pull, yielded this control with the utmost reluctance. Eastern capitalists, Western speculators, and Southern planters were all opposed to a liberalization of the land laws; and although the movement of American history was towards the Pacific, it was not until 1862 that a Homestead Act finally committed this movement into the hands of the common man. And by then it was too late. No society of free pioneering farmers could survive the attack of the railroad interests or disentangle itself from the nets of price-fixing monopolists.

VII

Meanwhile, in the 1820's, the West maintained an ambivalent attitude towards the general government, and expressed a nationalism that was all its own. The addition of six new states between 1816 and 1821, all but one of them in the West or Southwest, was a visible triumph for the expanding frontier, and indicates, even more than do population figures or ratios of increase, the great velocity of the westward movement. Both those who believed in a strict adherence to State Rights, and those who favored a stronger central government, professed themselves satisfied with this new development. The former welcomed to the fold six new sovereigns who would resist the pretensions of consolidation, while the latter believed that economic nationalism would, as a consolidating force, be increased rather than diminished by the addition of new states with neither the strength nor the traditions to resist it. The issues involved were not academic. Agrarian philosophy contended that if the general government grew too strong, it would inevitably align itself with the financial and investing interests; and had its professors lived until the 1870's, they would have been amply justified in all their predictions. Even centralizing opinion feared the West. The conservative financier, for example, thought that the new states were a constitutional sanction of the procreative instinct, an instinct which he was inclined to discourage on economic grounds, for he believed that "the creation of capital is retarded, rather than accelerated, by the diffusion of a thin population over a great surface of soil. The West itself oscillated in a most confusing way between the two points of view. Its several states were the creatures of the national government, deriving their very existence from an Act of Congress. It was not likely that they would have such a delicate sense of States Rights as did the more doctrinaire of their elder sisters; that they would always resist the rough advances of consolidation; or that when they did resist them they would invariably do so from the highest motives. On the other hand, they were all agrarian and debtor states; and in moments of crises or depression it was their instinct to suspect that there was some connection between the central government and the creditor interest. This confusion of sympathies was increased by the great drama of the Missouri Compromise, which began to divide the West on the free soil question.

When the Western mind was actually confronted, in the 1820's, with a program of national consolidation, its response was an odd mixture of enthusiasm and fear. Between 1816 and 1832, Henry Clay was engaged in developing his American System; and by 1824 its main features were evident for all to see. It was composed of protective tariffs; a national system of internal improvements financed by the sale of public lands; and the centralizing influence of the United States Bank. Henry Clay was a Westerner, and a man notably possessed by the great American dream: might not this system be called an answer to the needs and aspirations of the West? So Mr. Clay argued. He contended that a protective tariff, by fostering the country's industries, would provide a domestic market for the country's produce; that the internal market thus provided for could not be organized without a complex of roads and canals efficient enough to reduce the cost of transportation; and that domestic exchanges could never be regulated without a stable currency. Did not his system provide for all these things? He advanced this system with all the warmth and magic of his oratory, which have not, alas, survived the touch of cold print, and the answer to this question, as it congeals upon the cold page, would seem to be that Mr. Clay's system was an adroit commingling of the less precise formulations of the Enlightenment with some of the more exacting demands of the business community. No man touched the chords of Liberty and Prosperity with a defter, indeed with a more sincere, finger than did Mr. Clay; but somehow or other they did not harmonize with the rest of his music. He was a great man and a generous man, and he never ceased to fascinate his countrymen; but his American System was consolidation at its brassiest. Certainly, as the 1820's advanced, the country became more and more aware of the need for internal improvements; and the Western farmer, whose progress depended upon the production and marketing of an agricultural surplus, was more aware of it than anyone else. None the less, Western farming in the 1820's was still largely subsistence farming. The agricultural market was roughly organizing itself through the increased demand from Southern slave-holders for Western produce, and a program of economic nationalism with a strong financial emphasis could not be expected to find complete favor after the panic of 1819, when the agrarian West was continuously striving, by some piece of frenzied legislation, some stay law or replevin law, to gain a brief respite from the waters of debt. Might it not be said that, if Mr. Clay dreamed the great American dream, he did so with one eye open, and that the open eye was in rapt contemplation of the interests of Eastern monopoly? In any case, the Western instinct against centralization seems to have been aroused, and though Mr. Clay never ceased to command the affection of the West, as was only right and proper, it is safe to assume that after 1824 he began gradually to lose its confidence.

VIII

The West—the flow of human beings from the Alleghenies at one end to the prairies and the Gulf at the other—was a great and wonderful influence upon American life in the 1820's. It was perhaps the last time in all history when mankind discovered that one of its deepest needs— the need to own—could be satisfied by the simple process of walking towards it. Harsh as the journey was, and cruel as the wilderness could be, this movement could not help but be a hopeful one. In the 1820's, the West sank into debt; but still its inhabitants professed, in the midst of their discontents, to see some evidence of promise in the individual human being, and to look for a human being, rather than a set of principles, who should constellate this evidence for them. The Westerner was a Rousseauesque figure. While on the one hand he offered the world an inspiring picture of courage, simplicity, and ingenuity, on the other hand he became the very symbol and representative of the con-gregated discontents of a nation. He spoke for the Eastern mechanic; for the debtor in his cell; for the rural democrat of New England and New York; for any man who considered himself abused, cheated, or misunderstood. His nationalism, therefore, though exuberant, was a vis-ionary nationalism, speaking with many tongues and little clarity.

The dreams of Mr. Clay were too capitalistic to satisfy this kind of na-tionalism; the Jeffersonian philosophy, though highly quotable, was held to be too impractical to cope with the imperatives of the practical life;

the Virginia Dynasty, lingering on in Washington in the person of Mr. Monroe, was considered too narrowly professional to provide a leadership. To whom could the hopeful and the discontented turn? In the early twenties, Andrew Jackson began to emerge as just such a man. It was true that little was known about him; and that his political beliefs and economic habits, had they been carefully examined at the time, would not have satisfied either the debtor, or the antislavery man, or any of the more exacting of his followers. But the materials for a careful examination were not readily accessible; and what was known against him was always glossed over. The outline was clear, the details were mysterious; and the mystery carried its enchantment. Only one thing was certain about General Jackson—in moments of crisis he invariably behaved as the imaginative man, of the extreme martial type. This type was a Western ideal; and because it was a Western ideal it summoned, like a magnet, all sorts of aspirations that were not Western at all.

When the Monroe Administration, in 1818, turned the General loose upon the Seminoles and Spaniards of Florida, it could not possibly have foreseen all the consequences of this action. The General was a powerful weapon in 1818, and did all that was required of him. It was only later that the weapon turned upon Monroe's heir and dealt him a mortal wound.

CHAPTER 24

THE RENEWAL OF
AMERICAN NATIONALISM

Although nationalism was one of the causes of the War of 1812, the war itself renewed the sense of national self-consciousness that first found clear expression in the Revolutionary era and that had been so consciously promoted by the patriots of the early national period. The end of the War of 1812 marked a turning point in the history of the United States. Now the young nation could turn its back on the Old World and the kind of history that it represented and could devote its energies to the development of the New World. As the historian, George Dangerfield, points out in the following selection from *The Awakening of American Nationalism,** the Peace Treaty of Ghent significantly altered American relations with the one nation—Great Britain—that might have prevented this change of direction. This treaty, and the negotiations preceding it, caused the decay of British mercantilist concepts and paved the way for American expansion.

The decade following the War of 1812 is confusing and contradictory to the student of history. It was an "Era of Good Feelings," but it produced the first full-fledged sectional controversy—the Missouri controversy of 1819–1820. It was a period dominated by Jefferson's Republican party (the party that had championed limited government), but now the party's leaders advocated a uniform national currency, a

375

national bank, a protective tariff, and a national system of roads and canals. It was a period in which South Carolina's John C. Calhoun, later a great defender of states' rights, was a nationalist, and Massachusetts' Daniel Webster, the great Unionist, voted for purely sectional interests.

Professor Dangerfield, author of *The Era of Good Feelings** (from which the preceding reading is taken), seeks to put this period in its proper perspective. To what extent was the era one of good feelings? Was the program of the new Republican party really neo-Federalist or Hamiltonian in spirit? What was the nature of postwar nationalism, and what were its limits?

Indispensable to further work in this area are the two Dangerfield volumes. Also *The Twilight of Federalism* (1962) by Shaw Livermore, Jr. should be consulted.

* Available in a paperback edition.

MADISON, CONGRESS, AND AMERICAN NATIONALISM

GEORGE DANGERFIELD

Peace with Great Britain was proclaimed in Washington on February 18, 1815; and with the passing of the War of 1812, the shadow of political Europe withdrew from the scene which it had darkened and confused for many years, and a new light seemed to fall upon the map of the United States. As Henry Adams put it, with pardonable hyperbole: "The continent lay before [the American people] like an uncovered ore-bed." The continent, it is true, or all that part of it which lay west of the Mississippi and east of the Perdido, was still claimed by the King of Spain, and much of this was then believed to be a waterless desert. But "ore-bed" admirably describes the objective of a forward-looking state of mind. The American people, in 1815, endeavored to turn their backs upon Europe, insofar as Europe represented the kind of world history they most detested. For if the Napoleonic Wars constituted (as surely they did) a world war, then the War of 1812, their penultimate phase, could not be entirely freed from this character. It was now over for the Americans, and they naturally preferred to see it as nothing more than a quarrel between themselves and Great Britain. Whether this quarrel was or was not (as to its American origins) an expansionist adventure is still debated; but if there was an element of expansionism in it, then the Peace of Ghent was an ample fulfillment of this healthy impulse. Superficially, to be sure, the peace treaty which the Senate ratified on February 14 left everything much as it had been before the war began: time alone was to be the arbiter of Anglo-American relations, and the expression "not one inch ceded or lost" would be a more than adequate summary of the treaty's achievements. To the modern student of the negotiations which preceded the treaty, however, a very different idea presents itself; the treaty has become an eloquent register of historical process, because

SOURCE. George Dangerfield, *The Awakening of American Nationalism, 1815–1828,* New York: Harper & Row Publishers, Inc., 1965, pp. 1–16. Copyright 1965 by George Dangerfield. Reprinted by permission of Harper & Row Publishers, Inc. and the author.

one can observe, in the negotiations themselves, the decay of British mercantilist concepts. If the treaty meant anything at all, beyond a mere end of hostilities, or (as some Anglophobes thought) at best an armistice, it meant that in the future Britain would cease to regard the United States as a colony which paid its own expenses, and that she would look upon American expansion with a favorable eye, so long as it provided an enlargement of British industrial opportunity. In this sense, a whole new world had come into being, and for the Americans the first task was to describe the terms upon which, in America, it was to be organized.

The bonfires, the cannon, the church bells which celebrated the Peace of Ghent constituted less a shout of triumph than a sigh of relief. The American character had not so far been of a militarist nature: no militarists could have endured the mismanagement, the lukewarmness, the disaffection which marred almost every feature of the late war. As a nonmilitarist nation in 1812–15, the Americans put forth just enough energy to get the work done, and when all was over they showed no disposition to make themselves more formidable in a military sense. Efficiency and, soon enough, economy became their goals.

Moreover, the United States was, for a brief while, genuinely at peace with itself. As for the Old World, on the other hand, one has only to contemplate the Final Act of the Congress of Vienna to see that, although it had all the finality of a completed jigsaw puzzle, it was actually an instrument full of chinks and crannies, through every one of which there glared and squinted the Argus eyes of revolution. The effort to avert this dire inspection by filling these gaps with repressive laws varied widely from state to state in Europe, but it served to show that there was no longer a common tradition between the rulers and the ruled. In a community like the United States, now ready and anxious to make new experiments in self-government, it was precisely the emergence of a common tradition that counted most. The very Congress which, in 1815, took up the task of postwar readjustment was composed, as to more than one-third of its membership in both houses, of Federalists; and some of these were not a little tainted with wartime disloyalty. They sat down with their Republican opposites to discuss and to organize the peace; and since their opposition was neither very mischievous nor very resolute, they presumably acquiesced in what was done.

The Federalists, of course, remained a suspect group throughout the period of one-party rule which now began; and although their diminishing numbers and influence, and their accommodating behavior on the federal level, scarcely justified their reputation for persistent conspiracy, their efforts to inflame Republican faction in the several states did something to keep it alive. But they were not very skilled at party warfare; and even in those States where they had a real chance of survival, they were manifestly on the defensive and betrayed every anxious symptom of decline. It might be said that in the brief "Era of Good Feelings," which really ended with the Panic of 1819, the United States was free from those political and social fears which, in one form or another, haunted the Old World. The fact that the only suspect groups in America were those connected with wealthy men merely serves to emphasize the difference.

In short, as Albert Gallatin put it in 1816, "the War," and one ventures to presume that he also meant the peace, "has renewed and reinstated the national feelings which the Revolution had given and which were daily lessened. The people have now more general objects of attachment with which their pride and political opinions are connected. They are more American; they feel and act more like a nation; and I hope that the permanency of the Union is thereby better secured." In the Old World the concept of nationalism was either imperialistic or subversive of the counterrevolution, or could be accepted only in the terms—even truer for 1815 than for 1845—of Disraeli's "Two Nations."

Albert Gallatin was a most acute observer of the American scene, and he may have confined his ideas on American nationality to his own recollection: he did not arrive on these shores until 1780. Or he may have taken it for granted that national feelings and character were not actually "given" until 1776 or 1775. Like many historical axioms, this is open to technical reproach; but what Gallatin does suggest, and very forcibly, is that the postwar American had a renewed sense of a common national experience, real or imagined, with which he could face the future.

The Peace of Ghent undoubtedly bestowed upon the American nation a status among the family of nations which it had not hitherto enjoyed, but it was a status with a difference. "The mere existence of such a nation," it has been well said, "was a threat to the continuance of class government and special privilege in other countries." To the conservative and reactionary rulers of Europe the United States was little more than a grimy republican thumbprint upon the far margin of that page of history which, at Vienna, they were so ingeniously writing backward. The Tsar of Russia was possibly a friend; the British Tories were soon obliged to regulate their political behavior in terms of an American market they could not afford to antagonize; the others had simply come to accept the fact that if the thumbprint was grimy, it was also ineffaceable. That was the point in 1815.

The problem of readjustment to peace did not, at first, present the Americans with many difficulties: the Jeffersonian establishment, which had been so shaken by the Embargo of 1807 and had almost dissolved by the end of 1814, was now, all of a sudden, both strong enough and flexible enough to restate its old positions and to adopt a new one. The era of the "new Republicans" had begun. One need look no further for this than the Seventh Annual Message of President Madison, submitted to the Fourteenth Congress on December 5, 1815.

Some fourteen months before, in circumstances of great indignity, Madison had left his capital and fled like a partridge into the Virginia hills, pursued by a British army whose leaders jested that they proposed to catch him and take him back to London "for a curiosity." His prestige, already dim, had thereupon become totally invisible to all but the most friendly eyes. He was now addressing the Congress, in the language of a victor, and in terms which must have occasioned some surprise to the more doctrinaire members of his party.

Throughout his long career, from the early days when he had been a delegate to the Second Continental Congress, Madison had displayed a certain predilection—one might use a stronger term—for nationalist expedients. Had he not told Thomas Jefferson in 1787 that the Constitution "will neither effectually answer its *national object,* nor prevent the local mischiefs which everywhere excite disgust against the State Governments"? It is true that he had never gone so far along the road to centralization as Robert Yates suggested in his *Secret Proceedings and Debates,* or as he himself seems to have proposed in his Number 44 of *The Federalist;* and in his subsequent battles with Hamilton and with Adams he had often discarded his nationalist weapons for the outrageous slings and arrows of particularist dispute. Between the coauthor of *The Federalist* and the writer of the Virginia Resolutions there certainly exists a wide gulf, yet during his later years of executive power he was able to straddle it without too much discomfort. His was a subtle and athletic mind, which only became baffling in his later years. In 1815, much as he may have suffered in reputation from his handling of the War of 1812, he was a victorious statesman; and his Seventh-Annual Message is remarkable, not merely for being statesmanlike, but for its candid acceptance of the likelihood that it would sooner or later be called something else.

The Message, in its three more significant passages, is not exactly a ringing document: under the circumstances, it could hardly have been that. But it is an admirable mixture of constitutional prudence and enlightened common sense.

It is [he wrote] essential to every modification of the finances that the benefits of an uniform national currency should be restored to the community. . . . If the operation of the State banks can not produce this result, the probable operation of a national bank will merit consideration; and if neither of these expedients be deemed effectual it may become necessary to ascertain the terms upon which the notes of the Government (no longer required as an instrument of credit) shall be issued upon motives of general policy as a common medium of circulation.

[And again:] In adjusting the duties on imports to the object of revenue the influence of the tariff on manufactures will necessarily present itself for consideration. However wise the theory may be which leaves to the sagacity of individuals the application of their industry and resources, there are in this as in other cases exceptions to the general rule. . . . Under circumstances giving a powerful impulse to manufacturing industry it has made among us a progress and exhibited an efficiency which justify the belief that with a protection not more than is due to the enterprising citizens whose interests are now at stake it will become at an early day not only safe against occasional competitions from abroad, but a source of domestic wealth and even of external commerce.

[And finally:] Among the means of advancing the public interest the occasion is a proper one for recalling the attention of Congress to the great importance of establishing throughout our country the roads and canals which can best be executed under national authority . . . requiring national jurisdiction and national means . . . and it is a happy reflection that any defect of constitutional authority which may be encountered can be supplied in a mode which the Constitution itself has providently pointed out.

It has often been said that this tripartite scheme was more Hamiltonian than anything else, or, at best, that it endeavored to employ Hamiltonian means for Jeffersonian ends. But, in truth, the national bank was the only Hamiltonian feature in it—a feature, to be sure, of a startling prominence; and even here it should be remembered that the rechartering of the First Bank of the United States in 1811 had not met with Madison's disapproval or that of Gallatin, and that it failed for other reasons. Aside from the national bank, which (together with its alternative solution of a national currency in terms of treasury notes) required no little boldness in its advocate, there was nothing especially Hamiltonian in the rest of Madison's program. Did not the great *Report on Manufactures* show that Hamilton really preferred bounties to tariffs; but did not Jefferson, in his Second Inaugural, propose a scheme of internal improvements to be financed by tariff receipts? Would Gallatin's superb *Report* on internal improvements have been relegated to a dusty shelf if the government and the nation had not been bemused and divided by the war fever of 1807 and its aftermath? And in his suggestion that no national system of internal improvements would be valid without a constitutional amendment Madison—like his great predecessor—sounded a note of caution: his nationalism retained a distinctly Jeffersonian bias.

A vast and varied experience, needless to say, had interposed itself between Jefferson's Second Inaugural and Madison's Seventh Annual Message. The Message was a document which had been created by the Napoleonic Wars: it was what an unmilitary nation required if it was to profit from all that it had so recently and so painfully learned. For example, the Treasury had become bankrupt in 1814 because the national currency had fallen into such disorder that revenues could not be moved from one place to another. This immobility had been repeated in another realm, by a difficulty in moving and subsisting the nation's troops: bad currency, with only a local circulation, had found its counterpart in bad roads, with only a local usefulness. As for manufactures, they had been nourished by embargo and war into an infancy so vigorous that to expose them to free trade might well have seemed a cruelly Spartan measure. Thus a national bank and a system of internal improvements might be seen as an effort to remedy those weaknesses which the War of 1812 had revealed, and a plan for protective tariffs as an effort to preserve what the war had fostered.

The Fourteenth Congress, having been elected in the final autumn of the war, and in the shadow of disaster, was fortunately well qualified to act upon this program: the people had submitted their affairs to their ablest men, of whatever persuasion. The best of the war party were back in the House: Henry Clay, William Lowndes, John Forsyth, Peter B. Porter, Richard M. Johnson, Samuel Ingham, John Caldwell Calhoun. Only Felix Grundy and Langdon Cheves were missing; neither had cared to stand for re-election. The stalwarts of the peace party were also present: Timothy Pickering, Daniel Webster, Thomas P. Grosvenor, John Randolph. In the Senate the old obstructionists, Michael Leib, Samuel Smith, David Stone, Joseph Anderson had all vanished; the President would hardly recognize it for the same body which, since 1808, had practiced so successfully upon his peace of mind.

Once it had swallowed the hard morsel of a continuance of the direct tax, Congress turned its attention to the question of a central bank. The President's carefully qualified proposals in the Annual Message had been implemented by a more direct plea from his Secretary of the Treasury, A. J. Dallas. In a letter to John Caldwell Calhoun, of South Carolina, chairman of the House Committee on National Currency, Dallas outlined a plan for a national bank and, like the President, refrained from discussing the constitutionality of such a measure.

Certainly, if the government were to regain some control of the national currency—which not everyone thought a necessity—it would have been quixotic indeed if it had set constitutional traps for itself in its own messages. Nor was Dallas the man to have thought them necessary. Born in Jamaica of Scots parentage, a graduate of Edinburgh University, married to the daughter of a British general, he had reached British-occupied New York, by way of the West Indies, in June, 1783. He had then found his way to Philadelphia, and in Pennsylvania, after some preliminary difficulties, he had founded a legal career of mingled brilliance and unpopularity. He was an odd kind of Jeffersonian. A tall and courtly personage, with powdered hair and exquisitely oldfashioned clothes, he never overindulged his courtliness: he never concealed his belief that he was in every respect superior to the usual run of politicians. As a member of the Republican party, he was for ordinary purposes a liability. It was only in a season of despair, when Secretary Campbell had resigned from the Treasury after confessing his own incompetence, that the Thirteenth Congress—then meeting at the Patent Office, the solitary public building which the British had spared—could bring itself to accept the Pennsylvanian as Campbell's successor. In a mordant report upon the difficulties of the Treasury's situation, which was one of virtual bankruptcy, Dallas could only suggest the creation of a national bank; but as Daniel Webster put it all too truly, he founded his bank upon the discredit of the government and then hoped to enrich the government out of the insolvency of the bank. Dallas' best support, in this preposterous dilemma, was the fact that behind him there loomed the figures of John Jacob Astor, Stephen Girard, and David Parish. In April, 1813, Parish and Girard had taken $7,055,800 of Government 6 per cent stock at 88, and Astor had taken $2,056,000 at the same figure. Jacob Barker had also contracted for a huge sum, $5 million, but could find no one to join him: in the March 16, 1814, issue of the *National Intelligencer* he had called for a national bank. One need not impugn the patriotism of these capitalists, who were, after all, willing to venture large sums to maintain the nation's credit; but it would be flouting the long annals of financial behavior to suppose that they would not endeavor to protect themselves against the consequences of patriotism, should these prove to be unfortunate. They proposed, in short, to appreciate the price of government bonds by making them exchangeable for stock in a national bank; their plans had been maturing since early 1814; and it is reasonably certain that the influence of Astor and Girard upon the President, and upon certain members of Congress, had been in some measure responsible for Dallas' appointment.

The energetic Calhoun had of course been privy to their plans, and although he had not seen eye to eye with Dallas in matters of detail, in principle they were agreed. When the war came to an end, Dallas was still Secretary of the Treasury and Calhoun was one of the most prominent nationalists in the House of Representatives. Thus, in support of Madison's modest proposal, there existed an alliance between the Treasury, on the one hand, and the Committee on National Currency, on the other. In a very real sense, this was the surviving monument to the efforts of Astor, Girard, and Parish; for while these three were still influential among capitalists, the initiative now lay with Madison, Dallas, and Calhoun, and with a phenomenon which defies exact analysis—the political climate itself.

It was a warm, beneficent climate, eminently suited to the shedding of inconvenient creeds. Now that the war had been, somehow or other, won, now that the Republican party was, somehow or other, still in the saddle and likely to stay there—it was useless to insist upon constitutional quibbles. The Republicans were now administering a state of affairs in which, Albert Gallatin wrote in December, 1815, "we are guilty of a continued breach of faith towards our creditors, our soldiers, our seamen, our civil officers. Public credit, heretofore supported simply by common honesty, declines at home and abroad; private capital placed on a still more uncertain basis; the value of property and the nature of every person's engagements equally uncertain; a baseless currency varying every fifty miles and fluctuating everywhere."

The obvious remedy for this, if the banks could not be persuaded to resume specie payments, was a national institution with regulatory powers, and James Madison, who had fought the chartering of the First Bank of the United States on constitutional principles in 1791, was now ready, on expedient ones, to consent to the chartering of a second.

Very few men possessed Albert Gallatin's sensitive financial conscience, but Madison's broadmindedness was quite in keeping with the new mood of the times. On January 8, 1816, Calhoun introduced a bill to incorporate the subscribers of a Bank of the United States; Henry Clay, descending from the Speaker's chair, reminded the House that in 1811 he had sternly opposed the rechartering of the First Bank on the grounds that Congress had no right to incorporate such an institution. "The force of circumstance and the lights of experience," he now said, had convinced him that Congress actually did have this "constructive power." A penitential garb of some kind the Speaker had to wear on such a painful occasion; one cannot say that loose construction was ill-chosen or unbecoming.

The Federalist opposition, at any rate, was purely formal; and that of the unreconstructed Jeffersonians was led by John Randolph of Roanoke, who happened to be more suspicious of the state banks than he was of the projected national one, and who contented himself with insinuations.

The bill passed the House, 80 to 71, on March 14 and, after certain Senate amendments had been concurred in, received the President's signature on April 10, 1816.

When the First Bank was incorporated in 1791, it was the North which had supported it and the South which had opposed it. Now their positions were reversed. Combining the votes of both houses, the New England and middle states gave 44 votes for the Bank and 53 against it; the southern and western states gave 58 for it and 30 against. In other words, "Jeffersonian policy had got itself into a position where a national bank was as essential to it as it had been to the Federalists twenty-five years before." To judge from the temper of the debates in House and Senate, and from the regional distribution of the votes, nobody was really eager to call this position into strict account.

As for the Bank which now emerged, it had a capital of $35,000,000, of which the government owned $7,500,000, and the government was to receive a bonus of $1,500,000 payable in three installments during the first years of operation. The head office was to be in Philadelphia; its directors were authorized to establish branches where they saw fit; and its charter was to run for twenty years. It was to be the principal depository of the United States Treasury, was to report to the Treasury, and was to be subject to Treasury inspection. There were to be twenty-five directors, of whom five were to be appointed by the President, with the approval of the Senate. Finally, in order to fix a day for the resumption of specie payments, a resolution was adopted requiring payment of all government revenues in legal tender after February 20, 1817. Here one may leave the Bank, for the moment a symbol of financial chastity and nationalist order; its relapses will be examined later on.

Having agreed to this substantial and statesmanlike reform, the Fourteenth Congress was not likely to make heavy weather out of protective tariffs. A demand for protection had been more or less coeval with constitutional government itself, and never did it appear more justified than after the Peace of Ghent. The metaphor of a peaceful nation which now turned its face toward the West is historically sound, but only if one concedes that this nation was constantly looking over its shoulder. In fact, the United States was now exposed to the mercies of a world market, as Americans began to contemplate the strange phenomenon of a Europe at peace, "a Europe that had the whole world in which to buy supplies, a Europe that was able to do much of its own ocean carrying, and an England that had new and well-developed manufactures."

To the planters, the farmers, and the land speculators of America this change in world relations had, for the time being, a hopeful aspect. Europe, already blighted by the marching and countermarching of its locust armies, was now subjected to the calamity of poor harvests, and the demand thus created for American staples was further enhanced by a European propensity to gamble in tobacco and cotton. The American manufacturer, on the other hand, the latest child of the Industrial Revolution, was now in danger, through British dumping, of being smothered by his own parent. Madison's call for protective tariffs was statesmanlike, since it recognized the difficulties of adjusting from a state of war to a state of peace, but he did not expect the adjustment to be a lengthy one; he assumed that some equilibrium would soon be established between the forces of American and of British industry. Dallas' report, less mechanistic, was more forthright. He proposed, for example, a duty of 33⅓ per cent on cotton products and 28 per cent on woolens; the Committee of Ways and Means, which had not blenched at adopting a duty of 56 per cent on sugar, reduced both cotton and woolen duties to 20 per cent; and it was only after some striking scenes in the committee that the 20 per cent was raised to 25 per cent.

The debates in the House were acrimonious, as is the nature of tariff debates, but they were not divisive. There was an underlying agreement which could be expressed in three ways. In the first place, a tariff *did* answer the needs of a wide variety of interests.

War industries, suffering from the dumping of British manufactures, were crying for protection, from which almost every section of the country expected to benefit. In New England few cotton manufacturers managed to survive the fall in prices unless they adopted improved spinning machinery and the power loom. The few experimental mills in the Carolinas were staggering. Pittsburgh, already a flourishing smelter for iron deposits of the northern Appalachians, was eager to push its iron pigs and bars into the coastal region, in place of British and Swedish iron. In Kentucky there was a new industry of weaving local hemp into cotton bagging, which was menaced by the Scottish bagging industry. . . . The shepherds of Vermont and Ohio needed protection against English wool; the granaries of central New York, shut out of England by the corn laws, were attracted by the home market argument. Even Jefferson, outgrowing his old prejudice against factories, wrote, "We must now place the manufacturer by the side of the agriculturalist."

In the second place, the tariff as enacted on April 27, 1816, was a very temperate piece of legislation. The duty of 25 per cent on cottons and woolens was to continue until June 30, 1819, after which, it was assumed, a duty of 20 per cent would be sufficient to repel the competition of British manufacturers. A duty of 30 per cent was imposed upon rolled bar, leather, hats, writing paper, and cabinetware, and a specific duty of 3 cents a pound on sugar. But the only protective feature in the whole act was the principle of minimum valuation on coarse cottons: all cotton goods whose value was less than 25 cents a square yard should be considered as having cost that sum. (Its object was to exclude all low-grade prints and East Indian fabrics; and, since the price of these imported cottons tended to fall with the price of raw cotton and the use of the power loom, this importation gradually ceased.)

In the third place, the voting in the House was not exactly partisan: 63 Republicans voted for the tariff and 31 against; 25 Federalists were for it, 23 against; and the state divisions themselves were more perplexing than factious. It might seem ironical that maritime New England voted against a principle from which, in due time, it would be the first to benefit, and that congressmen from states that would later prefer secession to protection were disposed to support the protection of 1816. But here the real meaning of Madison's nationalistic program begins to reveal itself. The South considered that it alone had given the War of 1812 a substantial and decisive support; it identified itself in spirit with the successful outcome of the war; and it observed the nation's readjustment to peace with a benevolent eye. If the Tariff of 1816 had, as its chief beneficiary, the northern manufacturer, did he not deserve to be protected against the dumping practices of the late enemy? It could only have been on patriotic considerations such as these that representatives from southern districts which had no interest whatsoever in manufacturers gave, as many of them did, their votes for protection. Moreover, the southern leaders still believed that they controlled the triumphant Republican party, and with it the machinery of the central government: their nationalism rose and fell with this sense of control, so that one could say, without risking a paradox, that in the last two years of James Madison's Presidency the congressional South was most nationalistic when it was most sectional.

A Utopian element in the mild Tariff of 1816 can be detected, not only in the peculiar character of southern nationalism at this point, but more specifically in a speech which John Caldwell Calhoun delivered on April 4. He believed that the South would soon participate in New England's industrial development, and he argued that in the event of another war with England—which he did not consider unlikely—the interests of the army and navy imperatively required a balanced domestic economy. Should there be no war, however, into what channels could the vast accumulations of capital, themselves derived from a state of war, be peacefully directed? Obviously into manufactures. At this point any doctrinaire Jefferson might have protested that a system of manufactures would return America precisely to that kind of history from which, since the beginning of her national existence, his party had sought to divorce her. But Calhoun maintained that despotism and pauperism in England were due, not to England's industrial system, but to bad laws and excessive taxes. He foresaw a national state, in which commerce, navigation, agriculture, and manufacturing would be mutually, indeed serenely, dependent. The most trenchant criticism of Calhoun's quasi-corporate state was uttered by a man who was preternaturally quick to detect, though not to correct, an error. "On whom bears the duty on coarse woolens and linens, and blankets, upon salt and all the necessaries of life?" said John Randolph. "On poor men and on slaveholders." From this question and its answer there was never to be an escape, but Randolph was a kind of male Cassandra, more feared than honored; and in spite of his predictions or maledictions, the Tariff of 1816 was the symbol of consensus not conflict.

Into this happy state of affairs there intruded itself one incongruous but most significant event. Since the First Congress itself, surely nobody had been more able or more energetic than the Fourteenth. It seems to have decided that its labors should be rewarded in some fitting way. It therefore proposed and passed a Compensation Bill, which changed the emolument of Congressmen from $6 per diem to $1,500 per annum. There were sound reasons for this change; but the open nerve in the bill was soon touched by Calhoun, a statesman to whom intelligence and tact were not granted in equal measure, and who said that its real purpose was "to attract and secure ability and integrity to the public service . . . and any people, as they use or neglect them, flourish or decay."

The people, strange to say, did not agree. What they perceived in the Compensation Bill was an effort on the part of Congress to turn itself into an elite. The result was that in the fall elections, two-thirds of the representatives were replaced. "That this remarkable body of men should have incurred almost instantly the severest popular rebuke ever visited on a House of Representatives, could not have been mere accident." Nor was it. The people evidently wished their House of Representatives to represent them as they were, not as they ought to be; a strain of democratic or egalitarian nationalism was beginning to show itself, and legislators who distinguished themselves even with such modest laurels as a stipend of $1,500 simply did not conform to this.

CHAPTER 25

THE MARSHALL COURT
AND AMERICAN
NATIONALISM

Robert McCloskey demonstrates, in *The American Supreme Court**
(1960), that Chief Justice Hughes' statement that the Constitution "is
what the Supreme Court says it is" is certainly true when it is applied
to the Marshall Court. Under the leadership of John Marshall (one of
the most remarkable of a remarkable generation of Virginians), the
Supreme Court created for itself a position in the power structure of
American government that it occasionally has mislaid but never has
permanently lost.

John Marshall had no blueprints and few tools when he constructed
this position for the Court. The Court's broad duties are vaguely stated
in the Constitution, but its more specific duties are left to the discretion
of Congress—the Court's potential rival. Moreover, the Court has no
institutional means of enforcing its decisions, particularly in a conflict with
one of the states (for example, *Fletcher* v. *Peck)* or with the national
government *(Marbury* v. *Madison).* The Court must use sound reasoning, solid logic, majestic language and, on occasion, must "row to its objective with muffled oars." McCloskey shows that John Marshall and his
associates were masters of these techniques. But this selection also indi-

389

cates that Marshall—with all his understanding of the nuances of political power—was too fine a jurist to forget that "it is a Constitution we are expounding."

However, in spite of Marshall's judicial genius, significant questions arise when we study the record of his Court. Was the Court actually fulfilling the function that the founding fathers intended for it in the framework of the national government? Did its decisions, with their emphasis on increasing the national power, conflict with the framers' view of the nature of state-federal relations? Did the nation and the economy change sufficiently by 1815 to make the new interpretations imperative?

There are a number of good, general constitutional histories available. Among them are Alfred H. Kelly and Winfred A. Harbison, *The American Constitution: Its Origins and Development* (third edition, 1963). For a detailed study of Marshall, both as man and as a judge, see Albert J. Beveridge's classic, *The Life of John Marshall,* 4 vols. (1916–1919). Edward S. Corwin, one of this century's greatest constitutional historians, wrote a briefer, but excellent study, *John Marshall and the Constitution* (1919).

* Available in a paperback edition.

THE MARSHALL COURT AND THE SHAPING OF THE NATION

ROBERT McCLOSKEY

So far the story of the Supreme Court has been largely prelude. The judges have been deviled by uncertainties about their own status in the young American polity and about the power and malevolence of the forces that might imperil that status. Since the constitutional agreement of 1789 was inexplicit about the nature and scope of judicial authority, the Court has inherited the responsibility for drawing up its own commission, one line at a time, and the task has been delicate. Only gradually has it become apparent that the Court is being accepted as a symbol of constitutionalism and can therefore count on a solid measure of public support. Only with experience has it become clear to Marshall and his judicial brethren that the Republicans are not after all savage revolutionaries, that their bark is worse than their bite, and that the rule of law can therefore survive even though the Federalist party may not. In such a prelude, amid such uncertainties, the Court has been able to lay the argumentative bases for future accomplishments; it has fashioned some of the tools which may later be used to help govern America. But it has not yet been in a position to exert much real influence on the course of affairs. It has built its own fences with some cunning, but has not so far done much to build the nation.

However, with the War of 1812 and its immediate aftermath a new stage in the Court's history was inaugurated. We have seen that the slow accretion of precedents and confidence culminated in 1810, when the judges at last felt secure enough to hold a state law unconstitutional. Logically, the Court was then ready to begin to make its weight felt in the political order, to defend and foster in a concrete way the principle of national union. Now this logical development was stimulated and strengthened by the war's impact on American attitudes and political alignments.

SOURCE. Robert McCloskey, *The American Supreme Court,* Chicago: University of Chicago Press, 1960, pp. 54–71, 77–80. Copyright 1960 by the University of Chicago. Reprinted by permission of the University of Chicago Press and the author.

Many of the old Federalists, especially in New England, had fiercely opposed "Mr. Madison's war," had talked darkly of seceding from the Union, and had espoused a states' rights position strangely reminiscent of the extreme Republicanism of the Virginia and Kentucky resolutions. The politically dominant Republicans, on the other hand, were forced, in defending their war, to embrace the idea of nationalism, and to abjure in part their own localist tradition. Since they were in the ascendancy, this meant that the creed of nationalism enjoyed an unprecedented, if temporary, popularity and—the other side of the coin—that localism was for the moment bereft of really powerful defenders. To be sure localist sentiment soon revived and its exponents were as vocal as ever. But the nationalist spirit, once awakened, could not be dismissed at will. These events had intruded a cross-current in the Republican ideology; leaders like Madison and Monroe though by no means unqualified nationalists were not consistent localists either; the tradition they spoke for was now ambivalent on the great question of the nature of the Union.

This ambivalence persisted for some years and gave John Marshall his opportunity to use the judicial instruments he had been preparing. But his way, though now passable, was still far from easy. The Court after all was in the process of attaining a position more exalted than any attained by a judicial tribunal in modern world history; great tasks were impending. For one thing it was necessary both to confirm and to extend the Court's claim to authority, to transmute "judicial review" into "judicial sovereignty." Granted that it was proper for the Court to adjudge questions of constitutionality, did this imply that the Court's judgment was final? Did it imply that the judges could call the other branches to account even when the question of constitutionality was doubtful? Did it imply that the Court would exercise a general supervision over some governmental affairs that fell outside the traditional judicial orbit?

To Marshall it implied all this, for he was firmly convinced that the more America was guided by judges the happier and more just its system would be. But others, in politics and out, were not ready to bear the Chief Justice's mild yoke, and there was always a threat that overweening judicial power would encounter resistance or counterattack more formidable than its recently established independence could withstand. Though moving onward and upward, then, the Court must still tread carefully.

Secondly and simultaneously, the Court of Marshall's remaining years was engaged in using its still nascent authority to establish the substantive constitutional principles on which the American polity should rest. It was interpreting the document of 1789 so as to provide maximum protection to property rights and maximum support for the idea of nationalism.

Usually these two objectives were conjoined, so that a pro-nationalist constitutional doctrine best served the cause of property rights and vice versa. The national government was not at this time much inclined to interfere in commercial affairs, whereas the states, one or the other, presented a constant threat to the stability of currency, the sanctity of debts, or the freedom of business enterprise. Thus Marshall, happily for his peace of mind, was able to assure himself that he made property rights more secure when he deprived the states of power by enhancing the power of the nation. If these two primary values of his had conflicted, his soul-search would have been agonizing. But they seldom did conflict, and his historic achievements in the cause of union were therefore not clouded by confusion of motives.

He had troubles enough without adding internal uncertainty to them. The antinationalist front of the Republicans (soon to be called Democrats) had indeed been impaired, but specific and bitter centers of opposition still developed when specific provocations aroused them, and almost every major decision was met by a storm of intemperate denunciation from some politically potent quarter. Even worse, as the 1820's neared their end, it became increasingly apparent that the tide of states' rights sentiment was rising if not in volume at any rate in intensity. From time to time he was compellingly reminded of a fact that all Supreme Court justices must learn to live with: that the Court's decrees are backed only by its own prestige and ultimately by the willingness of the President to help enforce them. Over and over he was reminded that Congress could destroy in a day the judicial independence that had been building for decades.

In this context Marshall faced his great task of augmenting the judicial power and shaping the Constitution into a charter for nationalism. These two interwoven themes run through nearly all his decisions; each case raises the question of the Court's authority together with that of nation-state relationship, and the Court must always decide one question in the light of the other, taking care that its nationalist zeal does not compromise its own status or that claims for judicial power are never so extreme as to vitiate the crusade for nationalism. And little by little, in spite of the delicacy of this balancing feat, in spite of the deep antagonism of affected litigants, in spite of the rising wave of states' rights sentiment, the job is done. The Court's empire of decision is extended and stabilized as firmly as it ever can be in a governmental arrangement that rests on inference and acquiescence rather than on final definition. The great operative phrases of the Constitution—the supremacy clause, the contract clause, the necessary and proper clause, the commerce clause—are impregnated with the nationalist meanings so dear to Marshall's heart. And most important of all, these judicially contrived mutations in the character of American constitutionalism are generally accepted by the nation they are designed to guide.

How were these remarkable results achieved? How was the Court able, in the face of these adversities, to have its way? Partly the answer goes back to factors mentioned in previous chapters—the American attachment to the idea of fundamental law and the gradual identification of the Supreme Court with that idea. Partly the answer is to be found in the judges themselves and most of all of course in Marshall—the judicial sense of strategy and timing, the rhetorical virtuosity which should never be undervalued, the capacity to engender respect even among those who disagreed. Partly, as has been said, the difficulties were eased by the temporary ambivalence of Republican opinion on the nature of the Union.

But the Court's progress was also aided by a basic disability of the localist movement—its very lack of unity. The states were so individualistic that they defeated themselves, for it was (and is) a peculiarity of the states' rights doctrine that its partisans were devoted to it only when their own oxen were being gored, when nationalism presented a specific threat to a concrete interest. If states' rights could be associated with a common and long-term economic issue like slavery or the tariff, then the affected states would stand long and firm against their mutual adversary. But if Virginia had a problem today that Maryland did not share, Virginia's outraged protest in the name of states' rights would attract little support from Maryland any more than Maryland's similar protest tomorrow would bring Virginia rushing to her standard. Both states were being true to the fractional principle that lay at the heart of states' rights doctrine. But, because of their adherence to that principle, the Supreme Court, with its eye steadily on a single target, was spared the calamity of confronting a united opposition. The Court left such potentially unifying issues as the tariff and slavery pretty much alone, and it was not even necessary, then, to divide to conquer, for the opposition had thoughtfully divided itself.

THE COURT OVER THE STATES

One of the Court's great problems was presented either by direct or by implied challenge in nearly every significant case of the era: the problem of its right to review decisions of state courts involving the validity of acts undertaken by the state governments. Such a right was granted to the Court under Section 25 of the Judiciary Act of 1789; state court decisions that denied a claim made in the name of the federal Constitution, laws, or treaties could be reviewed by the Supreme Court by a "writ of error." And of course if the state court was thought to have erred, its judgment could be reversed and any state law it rested on invalidated.

That was the Supreme Court's nominal statutory authority, but it was one thing for Congress to pass such an empowering act and another thing to persuade the states to yield to it. From the first, localists had contended that Section 25 involved an unconstitutional encroachment on state sovereignty, and although the Court had several times exercised this supposedly unwarranted power with comparative impunity, the rumbles of protest had never quite been stilled. The case of *Martin* v. *Hunter's Lessee* in 1816 compelled the Court, which had so far tried to ignore arguments against Section 25, finally to meet them head on.

The case involved the title to some 300,000 acres of Virginia land which had once belonged to Lord Fairfax but which had been confiscated by the state in Revolutionary times partly on the ground that Fairfax and his heirs were enemy aliens. Virginia had proceeded to grant a section of the land, which it now claimed as its own, to David Hunter, who later sought in the courts of Virginia to eject the Fairfax heirs. But in the meantime of course the Revolution had ended, the Treaty of Peace with Great Britain had been signed, the national Constitution had come into being, and the new national government had been endowed with the power to make treaties. It was argued that both the Treaty of Peace and Jay's Treaty of 1795 confirmed the titles of British subjects to land in America and that the Fairfax title was therefore still valid.

In spite of this, the Virginia Court of Appeals held against the Fairfax heirs, and the Supreme Court of the United States, having granted review of this holding on a writ of error, ordered it reversed. The Virginia court, which was headed by Spencer Roane, an ardent states' righter and bitter foe of Marshall, pondered this order for a while and then decided to ignore it, arguing that Section 25 was itself unconstitutional. The Virginia judges conceded of course that they were bound to observe the federal Constitution, but they insisted that the meaning of the Constitution was for them to decide and that the Supreme Court had no power to impose its own interpretation upon them. It was this contention, so fatal to the prospects for both judicial supervision and centralism, that faced the Court in *Martin* v. *Hunter's Lessee*. If the Constitution was to mean whatever the various states wanted it to mean, the cause of national union was lost at the outset.

Justice Story spoke for the Court, Marshall having disqualified himself because he had been financially involved with the Fairfax interests. Story had been appointed by Madison in 1811 as a New England Republican, but now, after five years on the Court, he was as nationalistic in his views as Marshall himself. Indeed the supreme bench consisted of two Federalists and five nominal Republicans, and yet Marshall was seldom to have much difficulty enlisting his fellows in the nationalist crusade. His success in doing so has often been attributed to the witch-craft of his strong and charming personality; Jefferson had once predicted that "it will be difficult to find a character with firmness enough to preserve his independence on the same bench with Marshall." There can be no doubt that Marshall was an immensely attractive and convincing colleague, but it seems reasonable to suppose that the judges who came to share his nationalist views were beguiled not only by him but by a growing aware-ness that the Court's status and their own depended on the strength of the Union. It is hardly surprising that the Supreme Court, an intrinsically national institution, should be drawn to the doctrine of nationalism.

Story's powerful opinion in this case followed a pattern which can be traced through most of the great nationalistic decisions of the era. In the first place, he felt called upon to argue, or rather to assert, that the Constitution was the creation of "the people of the United States" as the Preamble says, and not of the several states. This contention, which may seem merely abstract, was essential to his purpose. Since at least 1776, most Americans had conceded that the people were the ultimate source of sovereignty and that the people could therefore, as Story says, "invest the general government with all powers which they might deem proper and necessary." If the Constitution was the work of the people, the powers it granted the national government *could* be as extensive as sovereignty itself. But if, on the other hand, the states had created the Constitution, it was arguable that the powers of the national government must stop at the point where they encroached on state sovereignty, and this very argument had been insisted upon by the embattled Virginians. The assertion that the Constitution represented the higher sovereignty of the people enabled Story to controvert the argument that state sovereignty is inviolable; if the people, in enacting the Constitution, wanted to modify state sovereignty, they had an incontestable right to do so.

The second great step in the opinion was to contend that the people *did* want to modify state sovereignty and had given evidence of that desire in the language of the Constitution. Article III extends the judicial power to all *cases* arising under the Constitution, laws, or treaties. There is no suggestion that the judicial power must stop short if a case originates in a state court rather than a federal. Since the language is general and is not restricted by the context or by necessary implication, it must be assumed that any case presenting a federal question is within reach of the judicial power, whatever may be the tribunal in which it arises.

This opinion contains, in more or less explicit statement, practically all the major items in the bag of tricks the Marshall Court was to use in future years against the minions of disunion. It invokes the doctrine of popular sovereignty to accomplish traditionally Federalist ends, a gambit that was particularly frustrating to the Court's Republican opponents, who were accustomed to think of themselves as the champions of that doctrine. The doctrine is then used by Story to deprecate the idea that state sovereignty was left intact at the time the Union was formed. Next he sets forth the proposition that national powers should be construed generously, a notion disastrous to states' rights when its implications are developed. From these principles "in respect to which no difference of opinion ought to be indulged," as Story says, he is able to infer a super-visory power for the Supreme Court so broad that it embraces all state tribunals. And finally this panoply of authority is used to defend property rights against spoliation by a capricious public. Each of these themes will be echoed over and over in the decisions of the future; each of them serves a vital purpose in the judges' struggle to make America the nation they believed it ought to be.

The specific problem of the *Martin* case—whether the Court's power under Section 25 could be maintained—was not of course entirely settled by Story's argumentative dexterities. In the years that followed, when-ever a state felt aggrieved by a Court decision, the familiar cry against Section 25 was again heard. In 1821, in *Cohens* v. *Virginia,* Marshall not only reiterated Story's basic points but interpreted the Eleventh Amendment, that supposed warranty of states' rights, so as to permit individuals to appeal to the Supreme Court even though a state was the other party in the litigation. The Amendment, said Marshall, prevents individual suits against states only if the action is "commenced" by the individual; if the state has initiated the action (for instance, by arresting a person), the person can still bring the state into the Supreme Court to defend itself against an appeal.

At this point, the Virginian defenders of states' rights felt that judicial sophistry has surpassed itself, since not even a constitutional amendment had arrested its course. They urged that the Court's authority be curbed by statute or by more carefully drawn amendment, and hereafter through-out the 1820's hardly a session of Congress went by without a proposal to modify, in one way or another, the doctrine of judicial control. These threats were serious enough to alarm the Court and its friends, but in truth none of them ever came very close to succeeding. As John Taylor of Caroline complained, the apathy of the "sister states," when one of their number was assailed, for a long time made a united front of states' rights sentiment impossible to assemble. Meanwhile, decision after decision accustomed the nation to accept the Court's view of its own function; each year that passed, each holding that was submitted to, made it a little harder to question that view. When South Carolina radically assailed the whole principle of nationalism in the Nullification Ordinance of 1832, its formidable adversaries included not only Andrew Jackson but a federal judiciary which had become a focus of public respect and a symbol of Union.

THE ENHANCEMENT OF NATIONAL POWER

One handicap of the Supreme Court during these early years and indeed throughout its history was its divorce from the sources of political power. Seven men in Washington, armed with nothing save their robes and their intellects, seem pitiful rivals to state legislatures, congresses, and presidents who command the machinery of government and are backed by the mighty force of the electoral process. But the Court's apparent weakness was also, as we have seen, a kind of opportunity. Because it was an independent, small, cohesive body, it could maintain a long-term view that gave it a decided advantage over opponents divided between a variety of special, temporary concerns and often confused in the basic premises of their opposition.

This advantage is further illustrated by the great Marshallian decisions involving the question of national legislative authority. Story's argument in the *Martin* case that national powers should be liberally construed enabled him to contend that Congress had a right to pass Section 25 and thus to make the Court the dominant tribunal of the nation. But his interest and Marshall's in the doctrine of liberal construction went far beyond its use to bolster judicial status. They wanted to enhance national power in all respects, partly because this would simultaneously restrict the power of the states, but partly too because they anticipated awesome tasks for the nation and wanted to insure that it was constitutionally equipped to deal with them. And the Court's success in accomplishing this aim must be attributed in no small degree to self-contradiction among the forces that opposed it.

McCulloch v. *Maryland* in 1821 is by almost any reckoning the greatest decision John Marshall ever handed down—the one most important to the future of America, most influential in the Court's own doctrinal history, and most revealing of Marshall's unique talent for stately argument. It involved a state tax on note issues of the Bank of the United States, which had been incorporated by act of Congress in 1816. The government argued that such a tax on a federal instrumentality was invalid and need not be paid. The state replied that the incorporation of the Bank exceeded Congress' constitutional powers and that in any event the states could tax as they willed within their own borders. These contentions raised vast and difficult questions both for the present and the future. The Bank was viewed with special loathing by the states' rights advocates; any decision upholding its claim to exist and denying the state's claim to tax could be counted on to infuriate them. And not the least of their heated objections would be the familiar one that the Court had no power in spite of Section 25 to entertain the cause. On the other hand, it was clear to Marshall, as it has been to posterity, that a national government restricted in its powers by Maryland's narrow interpretation would be incapable of the great tasks that might lie before it.

Speaking for a unanimous Court, Marshall therefore upheld the constitutionality of the Bank's incorporation, and in doing so set down the classic statement of the doctrine of national authority. The argument he advanced was not new; its main outlines had been endlessly debated since the first Congress and Hamilton's famous paper urging the Bank's establishment; and much of it had been given judicial expression by Story in 1816. But Marshall deserves the credit for stamping it with the die of his memorable rhetoric and converting it from a political theory into the master doctrine of American constitutional law.

Because the argument is logical it lends itself to summary, falling into three major phases. The first is concerned with the problem of the nature of the Constitution itself. Two crucial premises are laid down: First, the Constitution emanates from the hand of the sovereign people and speaks in broad language so that it can "be adapted to the various crises of human affairs." We must never forget that "it is a *constitution* we are expounding." These premises infuse the second phase, which concerns the nature of the national government the Constitution created. The people made that government supreme over all rivals within the sphere of its powers (Art. VI), and those powers must be construed generously if they are to be sufficient for the "various crises" of the ages to come.

The third phase is simply the application of these weighty principles. The power to incorporate the Bank is upheld under the clause endowing Congress with the power to make all laws "necessary and proper" for carrying into execution the other powers (Art. I, sec. 8); the words "necessary and proper" are interpreted generously, in accord with the principles advanced, to mean "appropriate" and "plainly adapted." The Maryland tax is invalidated, because since "the power to tax involves the power to destroy," to uphold the tax would grant the state the power to defeat the national government's supremacy; an inferior (in these matters) would be empowered to destroy a superior. But no summary can convey the air of high seriousness that pervades the opinion, the magisterial dignity with which it marches to its conclusions, the sense of righteous certitude with which it announces them. It was such qualities as these that made it persuasive to contemporaries and to the generations to come; and to appreciate these qualities the reader must go to the opinion itself.

The reaction was what might have been expected. In the North and the East the decision was praised; in the South and West, where the Bank was especially unpopular, the Court was roundly condemned. But even in Virginia, the fastness of such philosophers of Republicanism as Jefferson, Roane, and Taylor, the assailants curiously compromised their own position by putting the immediate issue of the Bank ahead of the broader issue of principle. Most of them denounced the Court for *not* holding the incorporation statute unconstitutional, thus of course tacitly conceding that the Court had the power to do so. Yet surely if the Court had the exalted power of overthrowing an act of Congress, it was not unreasonable to suppose that it also had the right to disapprove state laws. And if it did have these high prerogatives the Court must have some discretion in exercising them, that is, it could not be condemned merely because Spencer Roane, wielding the same power, would have decided the case differently.

In short most of the critics conceded too much for the good of their own criticisms. Their proper course would have been to deny that the Court had any business judging the validity of either national or state laws. But as usual they were more concerned about the immediate, concrete issue than they were about such a general doctrine as judicial sovereignty or even states' rights; and once again the Court profited from the fact that it alone seemed to understand the value of consistency and generality.

Much the same lesson can be drawn from the "Steamboat Monopoly Case," *Gibbons* v. *Ogden* in 1824, in which the Court was confronted for the first time by the problem of interpreting the commerce clause. A quarter-century before, the New York legislature had granted Robert R. Livingston and Robert Fulton the exclusive right to steamboat navigation in the waters of New York, and in the course of time the monopoly had extracted a similar privilege from Louisiana. The value of this controlling position in the two great port states of the nation was of course enormous, and rival states were deeply resentful of the arrangement. The *Gibbons* case involved an action for encroachment on the monopoly, and the defendant contented that the state had no right to grant it in the first place, because navigation is "commerce among the several states," which is the business of Congress.

This contention raised a series of questions that were destined for long and checkered careers in the development of constitutional law. First, what *is* interstate commerce? Does the term cover only buying and selling, or does it apply to such activities as navigation? Second, once we have determined what interstate commerce is, what is the extent of the power to regulate it? Third, what is the effect on the states of this grant of power to Congress? Must they stay out of the field altogether, or do they have a concurrent right to control it? It is not too much to say that the future of America as a nation depended on the answers that were given to these questions.

And Marshall, with his usual foresight, was well aware that he stood at another major constitutional crossroad. The opinion, like so many of his great ones, is a deft blend of boldness and restraint. In answer to the first two questions, he advanced the kind of broad, nationalistic definitions that the Hamiltonian tradition approved. Commerce, he said, is not merely buying and selling; it includes "every species of commercial intercourse," and this is true whether we are talking of either interstate or foreign commerce. Nor does interstate commerce stop at state boundaries; a journey that begins in Boston and ends in Philadelphia is subject to congressional power from start to finish. Of course, so inclusive a definition amply covers navigation. As for the extent of Congress' power to regulate a subject, once it is found to be in interstate commerce, that power is "complete in itself, may be exercised to its utmost extent, and acknowledges no limitations other than are prescribed in the Constitution." It is no less than the power "to prescribe the rule by which commerce is to be governed."

Perhaps only in the perspective of the future can it be understood how much these words meant; a twentieth-century observer looking back on them is impressed because he knows that the definitions have proved elastic enough to justify all the extensive commercial enterprises in which the national government has since engaged. But to contemporaries the most urgent question was yet to come: are the states precluded from acting in the commercial area thus defined? And at this point Marshall grew curiously evasive. He stated sympathetically the argument that the commerce power is exclusive, remarked that it had "great force" and said: ". . . the court is not satisfied that it has been refuted." He came as close to formally approving the doctrine as he could without quite doing so. But, he went on, it is not now necessary to decide this issue, because the New York monopoly law conflicts with a federal coasting license statute. Whether or not the commerce clause alone would invalidate the state law, surely it must be admitted that the federal coasting license law does, for the Constitution makes congressional enactments "the supreme law of the land." The lucrative but controversial monopoly was thus at last brought to an end.

Once again, as so often in the past, Marshall had managed to achieve imperishable results while side-stepping the area of greatest controversy. In other commerce clause cases he refined the notion of interstate (and foreign) commerce somewhat further by holding that goods were still subject to national control so long as they remained in their original shipping packages (the "original package doctrine"); and confused the question of state regulatory power still more by allowing a state to maintain a dam that blocked a navigable stream. No watchful guardian of states' rights could contend that Marshall had erected constitutional barriers to all state commercial regulation. Surely he had implied that some such regulation might be prohibited by the commerce clause alone, and surely his dicta about the extent of the commerce power had opened up the possibility of prodigious congressional regulation in this field. But it was present actualities, not implications and possibilities, that most concerned his contemporaries, and they found it hard to condemn a judicial stroke that slew the hated monopoly, whatever the flourishes that accompanied it. Jefferson and a few like him were horrified by *Gibbons,* but in general the decision was welcomed; the fact that it did after all overthrow a state law and hammer a few more nails in the coffin of state sovereignty was easy to minimize in the face of its immediately popular conclusion. . . .

THE ACHIEVEMENT OF JOHN MARSHALL

Few intellectual feats are more difficult than the assessment of history while we are living it, and perhaps the problem is all the greater for those who are themselves playing the leading roles. In his last years, Marshall was beset with misgivings about America's future, full of gloomy convictions that he had failed in his campaign to establish judicial sovereignty and to cement the bonds of national union. The states' rights movement was waxing ever stronger and more vocal under the ministrations of John C. Calhoun; the Court had recently been defied in two spectacular cases by Georgia, and President Jackson's unwillingness to back the judges had underlined the Court's ultimate dependency on external support. The old Federalist dream of rule by "the wise, the rich, and the good" seemed more chimerical than ever, as the spirit of Jacksonian democracy swept the nation.

But, ominous though these developments appeared, Marshall was wrong to think that they spelled the failure of his programs. Not even he, the architect-in-chief, realized how securely the cornerstones of American constitutionalism had been laid. His error probably was that he hoped for absolute certitude in a system that had been dedicated by its framers to the principle of relativism. We cannot say that the doctrine of judicial sovereignty was established beyond the shadow of doubt by *Cohens* v. *Virginia* in 1821, or that the broad construction of national powers was settled once and for all by *McCulloch* v. *Maryland* and *Gibbons* v. *Ogden,* or that the *Dartmouth* case stilled all uncertainties about the contract clause. We cannot say that at one moment the constitutional basis for union was an aspiration and at the next a firm reality, for constitutional history does not move in this way. The vagueness of the Constitution on these issues gave the Court its chance to be creative, but by the same token it was decreed that the creations would never be final and perfect. The Court's title to power, being inferred rather than explicitly stated, must always be somewhat tentative; interpretations of the Constitution, being fashioned by the historical context rather than by the fiat of 1789, must submit to the verdict of later history, as well as the past. With all this subtlety and shrewdness, Marshall's mind was attracted by absolutes, and the contingency of the constitutional universe never ceased to trouble him.

But if we can tolerate, as Marshall could not, a world of half-certainty (and if we enjoy, as he did not, the perspective of the future), we can see that his forebodings were excessive, and his accomplishments greater than he knew. The doctrine of judicial sovereignty was still subject to occasional challenge in moments of stress; men like Jackson and Calhoun were unwilling to admit that the Supreme Court was the *only* authority on the Constitution's meaning. But surely the judicial monopoly, though imperfect, was very impressive. The nation in general thought of the Court as the principal authority and conceded its right to supervise the states in most matters. When the Court impinged on the great primary interest of a state or region, a line might be drawn; but in the considerable distance before that line was reached judicial sovereignty held its sway. The Supreme Court was now far more serene and formidable than the precariously balanced institution Marshall had taken over in 1801. America's devotion to the idea of fundamental law and the Court's ability to capitalize on opponents' errors had made sure of that.

This establishment of judicial hegemony was itself a highly important victory in the struggle to promote the principle of national union, for it meant (with the qualifications already mentioned) that the Constitution spoke with one voice throughout America. But the other substantive principles Marshall had laid down also served that purpose and were also more solidly fixed than Marshall, in his somber old age, imagined. The national-power doctrines of *McCulloch* and *Gibbons* were to have their great day in a more remote future when the national government felt inclined to use the constitutional sinews Marshall's court had provided; until then their significance was more moral than practical. But the corollary doctrine—that the states may not encroach on these federally reserved realms—was well accepted and immediately relevant. These limitations on state power based on the doctrine of national supremacy, plus such specific limitations as those derived from the contract clause, helped open the way to the development of commercial enterprise on a national scale in the next half-century.

Marshall was right in thinking that he had failed to resolve for America the great problem of nation-state relationships. No court could finally settle an issue of such dimensions, an issue that had already brought the nation near the brink of civil war. But he might justifiably have felt that he and his Court had made a priceless contribution to its settlement, had fashioned out of judicial materials an ideology of seasoned strength to which those who cared for the Union could repair, had established a pattern of control that would help to shore up the Union even though nothing but bloodshed could ultimately save it. He could have comforted himself with the thought that no court in world history had every done so much to affect the destiny of a great nation.

CHAPTER 26

JOHN QUINCY ADAMS AND AMERICAN EXPANSIONISM

In the introductory chapter of *When the Eagle Screamed,** William Goetzmann of the University of Texas covers the expansionist foreign policy of John Quincy Adams in order to set the stage for his interpretation of United States expansionism in the 1830's, 1840's, and 1850's. Adams' historical reputation has not been based primarily on his performance as President. Before 1824 he was the country's brightest diplomat and, following his term in the White House, he began a career in the House of Representatives where he acquired the title "Old Man Eloquent." However, it is his diplomatic career that concerns us here.

As Secretary of State under James Monroe, Adams certainly must be ranked as one of America's outstanding diplomats. His handling of the English during the period when he formulated the Monroe Doctrine places him among the outstanding Secretaries of State. Yet, as Goetzmann demonstrates, the Adams-Onis Treaty is probably Adams' greatest achievement. During these negotiations, he performed a series of diplomatic bluffs that must have pleased Henry Clay—one of this country's finest political poker players. Adams simultaneously and judiciously threatened the Spanish with (1) the forcible acquisition of both East and West Florida, (2) the recognition of the independence of the rebellious republics of South America, and (3) the pressing of our Louisiana

Purchase claims to Texas. Moreover, Adams constantly encouraged Monroe not to lose faith or to show signs of backing down. As a result of Adams' bargaining, the United States received a peaceful and cheap title to the Floridas and strengthened its claims to the Oregon country. Shortly after the Spanish accepted this treaty, the United States became the first power to recognize the independence of the former Spanish colonies in the New World. Thus, all that the nation gave up for this grant of territory and claims was a very dubious claim to the Texas country and, within twenty-five years, this area, as well as the Oregon country, had become United States territory. In the long run, the nation gave up nothing and gained much. Although Adams did not negotiate the later territorial acquisitions, there is little doubt that his expansionist policies stood his successors in good stead—serving not only as examples but also, in the case of the Oregon country, giving his successors strong diplomatic grounds on which to stand.

In reading this account, the student should seek to determine the relationship between Adams' diplomacy and the developing American nationalism discussed in previous selections. To what extent did Adams' chief policies, expressed in the Adams-Onis Treaty and the Monroe Doctrine, reflect the mood and temper of the nation? Were these two policies connected? If so, how? Finally, what can be learned from this essay about the nature of nineteenth-century diplomacy?

Adams has an outstanding biographer in Samuel Flagg Bemis, whose *John Quincy Adams and the Foundations of American Foreign Policy* (1949), is a study of Adams both as a man and a diplomat. The basic study of the Monroe Doctrine is Dexter Perkins, *The Monroe Doctrine** (1927). For additional insights on the Adams-Onis Treaty see R. W. Van Alstyne, *The Rising American Empire** (1960), and Henry Nash Smith, *Virgin Land** (1950).

* Available in a paperback edition.

CLEAR-EYED MEN OF DESTINY

WILLIAM H. GOETZMANN

The foundations of American expansionism were laid by two very different men, who nevertheless had much in common—Thomas Jefferson and John Quincy Adams. Jefferson, the Virginian, stood for the agrarian way of life. As a farmer and local politician he believed that "those who till the earth are the chosen people of God." And as a young surveyor, he had traveled in the backcountry enough to learn something of the needs, indeed the demands, of the sturdy Scotch-Irish pioneers who were pushing westward regardless of the dangers and the niceties of national jurisdiction. But the image of Jefferson the simple agrarian can be misleading. He was also a cosmopolite—a romantic child of the eighteenth-century Enlightenment, who had been to France, who had absorbed much of the science and learning of the day, and whose imagination was therefore global. Even in his Revolutionary days his instinct, and that of many of his associates, was to address himself to "a candid world." His friends were veterans of the world's political battlefields—Joseph Priestly, the Marquis de Lafayette, and Tom Paine. Later, following Franklin, he became president of one of the most important world organizations of the time, the American Philosophical Society—modeled successfully on its more famous English counterpart, the Royal Society of London. His house, built atop a mountain in the Virginia wilds, was a Palladian villa with a simulated Roman ruin in the garden. It was the height of fashion and sophistication, but it stood on the edge of a wilderness facing West. Jefferson, therefore, combined the values of the republican and agrarian democrat with the instinct, taste, and knowledge of a man of the world.

John Quincy Adams of Braintree, Massachusetts, has always seemed the more provincial of the two. Adams was almost a caricature of the staunch, introspective New England puritan. He arose before dawn to

SOURCE. William H. Goetzmann, *When the Eagle Screamed: The Romantic Horizon in American Diplomacy, 1800–1860*, New York: John Wiley & Sons, Inc, 1966, pp. 1–3, 9–20. Copyright 1966 by John Wiley & Sons, Inc. Reprinted by permission of John Wiley & Sons and the author.

read his Bible and study his Latin classics, and was dyspeptic throughout the day if, on a rare occasion, he failed to beat the sun. However, he was also a man of the world. From the beginning, thanks to the advantage of being a child of the Revolution and having a presidential, one might say "founding," father, John Quincy Adams was keenly aware of the intricacies and perils of world diplomacy. He was among the first, for example, to note the dangers of prolonging the Revolutionary alliance with France, and at an early age expressed his sentiments in speeches and letters to the editors of various Boston papers, a gesture more effective then than now. In 1794, at the age of 31, he was appointed by Washington as an envoy to the Hague and thus began his long career in the foreign service. He went to Holland, then London, then Prussia, and then to Russia where he secured the friendship and allegiance of the Czar to the American cause. He was one of the negotiators of the Treaty of Ghent ending the War of 1812, and just before becoming Secretary of State under President Monroe, he was Minister to the Court of St. James, the premier position in the American diplomatic service. Therefore, although Adams loved New England—loved it enough to place the plight of codfishermen and poor impressed seamen, and the fortunes of sea otter hunters and whalers uppermost in his mind, he was also a man of the world. He was no stranger to continental and intercontinental strategy. He, too, was a devotee of European science and learning and, like Jefferson, he worked to advance these enterprises in America. He was not an agrarian, however. He represented the maritime interests of New England; but he was enough of a strategist to realize that America's maritime interests could best be served by a policy of continentalism that looked westward to the Pacific. And so, along with Jefferson, he became one of the architects of American westward expansion.

The vision of these two men of the world—the one looking toward development of an inland and democratic empire, the other looking toward eventual command of the sea—became the cornerstone of American expansionism. They set the pattern, and a daring pattern it was, for the fledgling American empire that flung itself brashly and boldly across the romantic world horizon, and from which to this day there has been no retreat. . . .

Although the acquisition of Louisiana was a master stroke for American continental diplomacy, it nevertheless raised serious problems which remained to be solved in the future. It forecast the dispersion of people and energies over a vast territory which, through lack of communications, would be but loosely held. "We rush like a comet into infinite space" wailed the Federalist Fisher Ames with this very danger in mind.

In addition to the dispersion and disunity that might result, possession of Louisiana inevitably brought the United States once again into direct confrontation with Spain and, more importantly, with England, the most powerful nation on earth. These twin confrontations drew the perilous lines of continental diplomacy virtually until mid-century.

II

The burden of these later anxieties was assumed by the gentleman from Braintree, John Quincy Adams. In the course of his career he was to extend American continental commitments even farther, and although he was successful, he did nothing to lessen the tensions between the United States and its two powerful rivals. When Adams assumed his post as Secretary of State he faced several severe problems which related to the question of expansion. To begin with, according to the agreement signed at Ghent, all territories seized by the British or the Americans were to revert back to their *status quo ante bellum*. In the Northwest this presented a particularly acute problem for during the war Canada had moved south. British agents and traders controlled virtually the entire near Northwest, and it was only through the valiant efforts of Manuel Lisa, the St. Louis fur trader, who mobilized the Sioux against them on the Upper Missouri, that the British were not able to move south as far as St. Louis. In the far Northwest, Astoria had fallen to a ragtag and bobtail brigade of Northwest Company men who came out of the woods and down the Columbia to demand its surrender. Fearing British military conquest, the Astoria partners had sold Astoria to the Northwest Company. But since this was a private commercial venture they had no right to bargain away American political claims to the Columbia region and they did not do so. Sometime later when the British Man-of-War H.M.S. *Raccoon* put in at Astoria, its commander found to his dismay that the fort was already in British hands and he could not have the "glory" of capturing it. So he contented himself with raising the Union Jack and sailing away. However, by the Treaty of Ghent, Astoria should properly have been returned to the United States, and the near Northwest cleared of British officials. Adams helped to accomplish these two things.

Albert Gallatin and Richard Rush, the two men sent in 1818 to negotiate with England concerning these and numerous other postwar difficulties, such as impressment of sailors and the Newfoundland fishing rights, under Adams' orders also held fast to the northern boundary line of the 49th parallel from the Lake of the Woods to the crest of the Rockies, thus denying British traders the easy access to the Missouri and the Mississippi which they once enjoyed. A short while before this, out in St. Louis, William Clark, the Governor of Louisiana, began the practice of licensing would-be fur traders, which was an on-the-spot means of excluding Canadian competition. Earlier, in 1795, the federal government had established a group of government-owned trading posts in the region to assert federal control over the Indian trade—a measure that proved somewhat ineffective. In addition, however, after Major Stephen Long surveyed a series of frontier defense posts, John C. Calhoun, the Secretary of War, began planning what came to be called the Yellowstone Expedition. It was to be an expedition in force up the Missouri River which would establish a strategic military outpost at the mouth of the Yellowstone River on the upper Missouri. Although this expedition ultimately proved to be a dismal failure, rumors of an American show of strength in the North Country undoubtedly helped to expedite the agreements of 1818.

On the political front the enthusiasm of the American, if not the British, negotiators was also spurred by the series of articles published by the young western politician, Thomas Hart Benton, in the St. Louis *Enquirer*. Benton, speaking for the St. Louis fur trade interests, for John Floyd of Virginia, and for a number of western-minded men, demanded that the United States government do something about the upper-Missouri situation, and also take steps to acquire Oregon. Following Jefferson, as he did most of his life, Benton felt that the United States could probably not extend its sovereignty to Oregon—indeed he pictured the "fabled god Terminus" astride the Rocky Mountains preventing future mass migrations in that direction—but he saw Oregon and the Columbia as a strategic trading outpost on the road to India: hence of supreme importance to American interests. A settlement of republican-minded emigrants from the United States at the mouth of the Columbia would give the new nation a window on the Pacific, keep the British out, and make the Columbia, and what came to be the Oregon Trail (discovered by Robert Stuart in 1813) a vital path of inland commerce between the Mississippi Valley and the Pacific with its sea otter and China trade. Benton's grandiose rhetoric in defense of this aggressive plan more than matched the audacity of the plan itself, which had once been the dream of John Jacob Astor and of Thomas Jefferson.

Given these pressures, the results of the negotiations of 1818 were at least satisfactory. No boundary west of the Rocky Mountains was agreed upon. In August, 1818, Astoria was returned to American sovereignty and an official American claim was established north of the Columbia River, although it took a warship, the U.S.S. *Ontario,* to do it. And finally the negotiators agreed to a joint occupation treaty to extend for ten years which left both the British and Americans free to trade in the Oregon country, but which did not prejudice the claims of either nation to political sovereignty over the region. Spanish interests in the Northwest were for the time being ignored.

Adams was not, however, unmindful of Spain. The object of his immediate attention was Florida, both East Florida, "the pistol pointed at the heart of the United States," and West Florida, the region extending from the Mississippi to the present-day Florida line. The latter, Spain claimed, was not properly part of the Louisiana Purchase, and the former, though she held it loosely under tolerance from the Indians, she regarded as having great strategic if not sentimental value. Both of these areas were troublesome to the United States because from them, spurred on by British and Spanish soldiers of fortune and agents of the Panton-Leslie Company, bands of brigands, red men and white, terrorized settlements on the American southwestern frontier. It fell to Adams to extinguish these conflagrations by acquiring the Floridas by any peaceful means possible. In performing this task he had powerful aid from his future lifelong political antagonist, General Andrew Jackson.

Under Monroe's orders Jackson employed the doctrine of "hot pursuit" and invaded Florida, capturing Pensacola and St. Mark's. There, with 3,000 men he chastised the Indians, humiliated the Spanish officials, and precipitated a serious international crisis by executing two British filibusters, Armbrister and Arbuthnot—one by hanging and the other by the firing squad. Weak-minded, vindictive or politically opportunistic members of Monroe's cabinet wished to disavow or publicly condemn Jackson's actions. But Adams persuaded Monroe against this action, despite the possibility of war with England and Spain. This course proved to be an expedient one. Lord Castlereagh and the British negotiators in London acknowledged the justice of Jackson's actions and proceeded in good spirits to negotiate the other issues of the treaty of 1818. Spain, on the other hand, although she protested vehemently, saw clearly that the Floridas were beyond her practical control. This increased her willingness to trade them for some more secure piece of property, in point of fact Texas, and if possible the entire Trans-Mississippi West, as far north as the upper Missouri.

Adams' negotiation of the transcontinental boundary treaty of 1819 thus began as a swap: Texas (whatever that was) for the Floridas. As a student of history, Adams could not help being aware of Spain's insecurity over Texas and New Mexico. In 1806, Zebulon Pike was captured on the upper Rio Grande and held prisoner, his papers and maps were confiscated, and he was summarily sent back to the United States by the quickest possible route. Shortly afterward, in 1807, Captains Freeman and Sparks were turned back on the Red River. That same year the fur trader Anthony Glass was repeatedly threatened by Spanish authorities as he intruded on what they regarded as their territory. An 1812 trading expedition by Robert McKnight to Santa Fe landed him in a Chihuahua prison for nine years. The Gutierrez-Magee filibustering expedition into Texas in 1813 was put down and its leaders executed. In 1818 the fur trader Auguste Chouteau and his partner Jules De Mun were captured on the upper Arkansas. Their furs were confiscated; they were forced to kneel and kiss the document sentencing them; and then they were sent home with a bare minimum of equipment. These were convincing demonstrations of Spanish insecurities regarding Texas, but what made them seem outrageous to the United States was the fact that, if the limits of the Louisiana Purchase included the watershed of the Mississippi, then the territory to the headwaters of the Arkansas and Red Rivers belonged to the United States. Indeed, certain enthusiasts with a poor knowledge of geography claimed even the Rio Grande on this basis.

Needless to say, faced by a threatened American penetration of its territories, Spain, by 1819, was ready to negotiate a boundary that would give her a buffer against American invasion. Though Adams never knew it, she was willing to retreat all the way to the Rio Grande.

The negotiations with the Spanish minister Onis, a harried but tenacious diplomat, who awoke one morning to find a dead chicken tied to his doorbell rope, began with Adams offering a Texas boundary and indemnity for the Floridas. The Spanish sought a larger buffer to the West, however, and attempted to extend the Texas border from the high point of land between two creeks near Natchitoches, Louisiana, north to the Missouri River. In this way they could acquire most of Louisiana in exchange for the Floridas, which they could not hold in any case. This strategy, however, caused Adams to revise his own thinking. Previously he had been concerned with southern and southwestern problems; now the vision of a continental empire arose, and he shifted ground. If in exchange for Texas he could acquire the Floridas and also an extension of Louisiana in a wide swath to the Pacific, he would have opened the way to an American empire on the Pacific and gained the key to the continent.

Thus began a series of new negotiations, with the implied threat of an American invasion of the Floridas and Texas hanging in the background. On July 16 Adams, using Melish's inaccurate map of 1818, offered a line up the Colorado River of Texas to the Red River, and then across from the Red River to the crest of the Rocky Mountains, thence along the 41st parallel to the Pacific. Onis countered with a line northward from Natchitoches to the Missouri, then along the Missouri to its headwaters at the Three Forks, the line west from there not specified. And so the negotiations went throughout the fall and winter of 1818-1819, with Onis trying ultimately to get a Missouri-Columbia line to the Pacific with rights of trade on these rivers, and Adams stumping for the Colorado River of Texas or the Sabine River and the 41st parallel. Even an ultimatum offer of October 31, 1818, made at the behest of President Monroe, who had grown impatient, failed to impress Onis. Then Monroe began to give ground and seemed almost inclined to accept Onis' proposal of February 1, 1819, which was a line up the Arkansas River to the mythical San Clemente River, to the 43rd parallel and along it to the sea. But Adams held firm, and eventually on February 22, 1819, he had his transcontinental boundary treaty. The major provisions of the treaty included the Spanish cession of the Floridas, East and West, to the United States, the assumption by the United States of American claims against Spain up to $5 million, and a western boundary line which began at the mouth of the Sabine River, continued north along the western bank of that river to the 32nd parallel of latitude, thence by a line due north to the Red River, thence westward up the south bank of the Red River to the 100th meridian of longitude, thence across the Red River due north on the 100th meridian to the south bank of the Arkansas River, thence up that river to its source in latitude 42° north, and westward from that point along the 42nd parallel to the Pacific, as laid down in Melish's map of 1818.

Adams had thus bartered away Texas, but he had gained the Floridas and, equally important, he had gained his coveted transcontinental corridor to the Pacific. In accomplishing this he had served the New England sea traders well. But, in addition, despite much western opposition, he had served the West equally well since the acquisition of the Spanish claims to the Northwest opened the way for the development of the Rocky Mountain fur trade. However, Westerners fretted that he had given up Texas and the potential riches of the Southwest. Present-day knowledge of Spanish documents indicates that he had indeed done so.

But Adams could not have known this at the time, and thus he did the best he could. As his biographer remarks,

Even without Texas the Transcontinental Treaty with Spain was the greatest diplomatic victory won by any single individual in the history of the United States.

III

One further course of diplomatic events that took place while Adams was Secretary of State continued—indeed exaggerated—the emergence of America on the horizon of world diplomacy. This involved the development or formulation of an American policy for the entire western hemisphere that culminated in the Monroe Doctrine.

During the time Adams was negotiating with Spain, the countries of Latin America, encouraged by tradesmen from England and the United States, revolted against Spain, and in a long series of civil wars succeeded in establishing a de facto independence. Since the delicate negotiations with Spain were in progress, Adams was reluctant to recognize the new revolutionary nations although, like Jefferson, he sympathized with their desire for independence. As a New Englander, however, Adams also deplored the outfitting by the new countries of privateers which preyed on world shipping, including that of neutrals. He stood for the principle of freedom of the seas, and the violation of that principle by any power, however just its cause, threatened the principle itself. At least during the Spanish treaty negotiations the canny Braintree moralist used this as an agrument to counter the enthusiastic trumpetings of Henry Clay, who was demanding immediate recognition of the new republics, partly out of sincerity and partly because of a desire to embarrass the Monroe administration.

Eventually the new Latin republics ceased their privateering. American business representatives were established in the major ports. And, in 1821, Spain ratified the transcontinental treaty. Between 1822 and 1826 the United States recognized the independence of the seven new Latin American countries, although not all of them were republics patterned after the Jeffersonian democratic model. The United States was the first major nation to recognize formally the independence of the Latin states, and she did so at the risk of offending the major powers of Europe.

After the defeat of Napoleon, the chief continental powers led by the Czar of Russia formed the Holy Alliance with the avowed purpose of keeping peace in Europe through pacts of mutual assistance. Although we now know that there was little chance of a continental nation coming to the aid of Spain in her attempt to regain her lost New World colonies, this did not necessarily appear to be the case when the United States extended its recognition. Rather than a feat of diplomatic daring, however, the recognition of the Latin states appears to have been a response to demands by American trading and maritime interests for official government support in their competition with Britain for the trade of South and Central America.

While these events were occurring, Adams faced still another challenge to his dream of a continental empire. In 1816 the Russians had landed at Bodega Bay north of San Francisco and established a colony, Fort Ross. Subsequently Russia claimed all of the Pacific coast from Alaska to the latitude of Fort Ross, which of course encompassed the newly won Spanish claims above the 42nd parallel. Adams sternly rebuked the Russian expansionists in a note which was later to become the model for the Monroe Doctrine. He wrote to the Russian minister in Washington that the United States contested the right of Russia to her coastal claims, and furthermore he declared, "We should assume distinctly the principle that the American continents are no longer subjects for any new European colonial establishments." Russia retreated from her untenable and unprofitable position in the face of opposition not only from the United States but also from Britain, and in 1824 concluded a treaty with the United States limiting her territorial aspirations to 54° 40', the present Alaskan boundary. In 1825 a similar treaty with Britain was consummated. Adams had forestalled still another threat by a major power, although the United States had no way of defending her position by anything like the force of arms.

The Monroe Doctrine grew out of this anti-European position. Interested in maintaining good trade relations with South America, the British Minister, George Canning, proposed in 1823 that the United States join with England in making a declaration against any further attempts by the continental powers to colonize the New World. At Adams' insistence Monroe refused to join the British plan. Instead he issued an independent American statement, since known as the Monroe Doctrine, although Adams claimed to be its primary author. The Monroe Doctrine declared:

(1) That the United States did not wish to take part in the politics or wars of Europe.

(2) That the United States would regard as manifestations of an unfriendly disposition to itself the effort of any European power to interfere with the political system of the American continents, or to acquire any new territory on these continents.

The Monroe Doctrine, at first hailed by the new countries of Latin America, now much maligned by the same countries and transgressed by Soviet intrusions into the Caribbean, was something more and something less than tradition has made it seem. Enforcement of the doctrine depended, of course, in the main, on the British fleet, and in this sense many have considered it a hollow gesture although it was a true commitment. Later generations have seen it as a weapon or facade behind which the United States was able to interfere unduly in the internal affairs of its neighbors, and it has also on occasion served this purpose. Still others regard it as one more inflexible American principle that by its unyielding quality has limited American maneuverability in Latin American affairs, and this is certainly correct. But understood in the context of its own day, the Monroe Doctrine would appear to have several other legitimate purposes. First, it was a refusal to allow Latin America to become exclusively a British protectorate. Second, it reinforced American trading interests in the hemisphere. Third, it announced America's emergence as a power among nations that had to be reckoned with. Fourth, it was a gesture of genuine goodwill and concern for the new Latin republics. Fifth, it was a continual renunciation of European political alliances and a strategic refusal to play the balance-of-power game on Britain's terms. And finally, it was a rallying cry, a nationalistic symbol for Americans at home, that drew the nation together in terms of its ultimate ideals of republican democracy for all. Only the fact of slavery beclouded the lofty pretensions of such a democratic mission.

By the time Adams became president, the United States had acquired a continental empire of its own that looked both inward and outward, south toward the Caribbean, and west toward China and the Pacific. It had, moreover, taken an important place in the world family of nations and, following Jefferson's prophecy, it had spawned sister republics based on the American model as far as Cape Horn. The French had been ousted from North America, and the British, Spanish, and Russians severely circumscribed. This was not the work of a nation that sought or needed a comfortable security. It was the missionary impulse of individuals who had fought their way to freedom and independence, and therefore appreciated their virtues, an impulse making itself felt for the first time around the world.

CHAPTER 27

THE DISINTEGRATION AND REESTABLISHMENT OF THE AMERICAN PARTY SYSTEM

Wilfred Binkley's *American Political Parties: Their Natural History* is one of those rare books to which the student constantly returns, not only for its detail but also for its many insights. The following excerpt is not an exception. In the scope of a single chapter, Binkley discusses the election of James Monroe, the demise of the once powerful Federalist party, the congressional caucus and its decline, the election of 1824 (in which four men campaigned), and, finally, the election of Andrew Jackson in 1828 and the rebirth of two party politics.

In covering this mass of material, Binkley raises a number of intriguing questions concerning the nature of the political process in the United States—questions that apply both to the period under discussion and to the political process in general. Why did the Federalist party vanish by the 1820's? Of course the party was damaged by its opposition to the War of 1812, but the Democratic party did not dissolve following the Civil War (certainly a more cataclysmic event than the War of 1812). How were the Jacksonians able to "canalize mass movements" during this period, considering the primitive nature of their communication facilities? If the Jacksonians had not used the tactics that Binkley views with disfavor in 1825 to 1828, could they have won in 1828? Or, more important, could they have developed their organization without using public antipathy toward John Quincy Adams and without amplifying the "moral outrage" of his "corrupt bargain" with Henry Clay? This leads to the question of how a political organization is created down to "even the rural school district."

There is a growing library devoted to such questions. An excellent study of the period is Robert Remini, *The Election of Andrew Jackson** (1963). For a first-rate discussion of the problems inherent in the building of a national political party, see Richard P. McCormick, *The Second American Party System: Party Formation in the Jacksonian Era** (1966). Arthur M. Schlesinger, Jr., *The Age of Jackson** (1946), is very readable.

* Available in a paperback edition.

ONE-PARTY GOVERNMENT
WILFRED E. BINKLEY

We are about to behold an administration of the Jeffersonian Republicans, who after conducting the War of 1812 with incredible ineptitude, emerged from the conflict covered with glory at the very moment when their Federalist opponents experienced irreparable ruin. Left unchallenged masters of the political field after 1816, the Republicans were to discover presently the disintegrating effect on a multi-group party of the disappearance of a common enemy, a vigorous political opposition. The "War Hawks" of 1811-12 evolved in the post-war period into supernationalists, literally contemptuous of the prescriptions of the Constitution and irrepressible in their determination to convert the Federal government into a paternalistic institution providing a powerful standing army, a great navy, a new Bank of the United States, government-built roads and canals, and protective tariffs. Here, however, was a program that stirred in the hearts of the older Jeffersonians memories of the Virginia and Kentucky Resolutions—the bible of the original Republicans, which had proclaimed the anti-national dogma of state rights. In little more than a decade this ideological clash was to produce two distinct factions of the Jeffersonian party, the National Republicans and the Democratic Republicans, from which were to evolve in due time the Whig and Democratic parties of the thirties.

Eventually, then, the Federalists were to behold their ideal of a partyless or one-party government achieved not, as they had so fondly hoped, by eradicating the opposition, but instead by the gradual dispersal of their own forces and their leaving the field to the triumphant Republicans. The pre-war policy of non-intercourse and embargoes had baffled the party of mercantile capitalism, but war against their chief customers induced a madness that led to their ruin.

Possessing the bulk of the nation's financial resources, these New England Federalists deliberately refused to finance the war and presently

SOURCE. From Wilfred E. Binkley, *American Political Parties: Their Natural History,* New York: Alfred A. Knopf, Inc., 1943, pp. 94–115. Copyright 1943, 1958 by A. A. Knopf, Inc. Reprinted by permission of the publisher.

placed the government in a desperate financial predicament. Nor would the New England states contribute their militia for the conquest of Canada and the consequent creation of new agrarian states, with increased congressional delegations and votes in the electoral college certain to reduce their own section to a still more hopeless minority. So disaffected, indeed, did New Englanders become that the British navy refrained from blockading their coast until almost the end of the war, and news of allied—that is to say, British—victories across the sea were celebrated by the fatuous Federalists. Commodore Stephen Decatur even complained that blue-light signals, set on dark nights to warn British war vessels, had prevented his running the blockade and putting out to sea from New London in 1813. Never were these luckless partisans to hear the last of the opprobrious epithet, the "Blue Light" Federalists. In the fall of 1814 their discontent culminated in the convention of delegates at Hartford, assembled to air their grievances and to seek means of redress. Fortunately the extremists among them, the Essex Junto, stark disunionists, were in the minority and the resolutions adopted, consisting of the proposal of some amendments to the Constitution, sound moderate enough today. Collectively they constitute the swan song of the Federalist Party. . . .

During Monroe's first term all but the irreconcilable Federalists moved over into the Republican column and were presently modifying that party's agrarianism by the pressures of once Federalist interests. Indeed, the Republican Party, in time, "became almost as much a party of business groups as the old Federalist party had been," thus confirming John Taylor's dictum that the business interests were devoid of principle and would combine with any party. It was an outstanding Federalist leader, Josiah Quincy, who gave utterance to the poignant lament that the Republicans had "out-Federalized Federalism." Even that staunch Federalist, John Marshall, had been tempted to vote for Madison, but he repressed the impulse and cast no vote for President from 1800 to 1824, when he voted for John Quincy Adams.

In the absence of an opposition the Republicans gradually lost their party discipline and their organization on a national scale. There is no better evidence of the disappearance of the old party alignments than the fact that Republican newspapers in 1816 reprinted in support of the second Bank of the United States Hamilton's argument for the first bank. This was simply using, in support of a Republican measure in 1816, the identical Federalist reasoning of 1791 that had aroused the opposition then and even contributed to the origin of the Republican Party. Thus cavalierly was Jefferson's historic opinion against the chartering of the first bank, including his classic statement of the dogma of strict construction, given the *coup de grâce* by his own disciples. And to make the topsy-turviness of politics complete, Webster and other Federalists opposed the chartering of the new bank.

When the time came to nominate presidential candidates in the spring of 1820, there were invited to the congressional caucus not only Republicans but all Congressmen who saw fit to attend. Even the old New England Federalists were satisfied with Monroe, and the incorporation of Federalists within the Republican fold seemed to be practically complete. The Massachusetts presidential electors in 1820 consisted of seven old-line Republicans and eight former Federalists, among whom were ex-President John Adams and Daniel Webster; and all, of course, voted for the re-election of Monroe.

It had now become as fashionable for Republicans as it once was for Federalists to disparage political parties as such. Paradoxical as it may seem, it was that later prince of partisans Andrew Jackson who was to give authentic expression to this prevailing sentiment in a letter of advice to President-elect Monroe in 1816. Concerning the choice of cabinet members he advised: "In every selection party and party feeling should be avoided. Now is the time to exterminate the monster called party spirit. By selecting characters most conspicuous for their probity, virtue, capacity and firmness, without any regard to party, you will go far to, if not entirely, eradicate those feelings which, on former occasions, threw so many obstacles in the way of government; and perhaps have the pleasure of uniting a people heretofore politically divided. The chief magistrate of a great and powerful nation should never engage in party feelings. His conduct should be liberal and disinterested, always bearing in mind that he acts for the whole and not a part of the community. By this course you will exalt the national character and acquire for yourself a name as imperishable as monumental marble. Consult no party in your choice."

Monroe reciprocated the sentiment in a letter to Jackson, writing: "We have hitherto been divided into two great parties. That some of the leaders of the Federalist party entertained principles unfriendly to our system of government, I have been thoroughly convinced; and that they meant to work a change in it, by taking advantage of favorable circumstances, I am equally satisfied."

Intimately related to the disappearance of political parties was the concurrent decline in the significance of the presidential office. Since the President is the focus of American party conflicts, under the circumstances then obtaining the office sank to comparative insignificance. It was no snap judgment of R. V. Harlow's that "Madison could scarcely have played a less significant part during those eight uncomfortable years if he had remained in Virginia." Had the office then possessed its present pre-eminent importance, Monroe could not have been re-elected without opposition in the midst of the nation-rocking controversy over the admission of Missouri to the Union and just as the economic depression starting in 1819 was spreading disaster throughout the length and breadth of the land. Since then no President has been re-elected following a term of his in which a depression began. During this quarter of a century not only had Congress overshadowed the President, but it had, in every case, determined the choice, either directly through election by the House of Representatives or through nomination by the congressional caucus, which in the absence of any significant opposition was tantamount to an election.

The revival of a two-party alignment was involved in the fact that the Virginia dynasty had now run its course. The tobacco plantation of the Old Dominion had produced its last outstanding statesman-President. Powerful interests in other sections were ready to bid for the stakes of power inherent in the presidential office. Their particular candidates were about to engage in a severe competition for the presidency. Universal manhood suffrage had swept the frontier, forcing the older settlements to consider its adoption in the hope of discouraging somewhat the tide of western migration. The aspirant to the presidency was now compelled to adapt his appeal to a rapidly expanding electorate in which the common man was becoming a distinct force. No longer would the congressional caucus that had so long maintained the Virginia dynasty by mechanically promoting the Secretary of State to the presidency be complacently accepted. Nor could the legislatures of half the states hope to continue much longer to choose presidential electors instead of permitting the people to elect them.

With the restoration of a free competition for the presidency in the middle twenties, aspirants were being compelled to search for issues or combinations of them with a nationwide popular appeal. The most ingenious of these was the so-called "American System" of Henry Clay, which he began to formulate soon after the Peace of Ghent in 1815. The end of the war marked the beginning of a new era, in which Americans stopped calling each other "Anglomen" and "Gallomaniacs." The colonial psychology had given way to a conviction of genuine American independence. Public opinion found its focus on the domestic issues of currency, banking, tariff, transportation, public lands, and western migration. The dogma of state rights proved unsuitable for dealing with these problems, and national needs now induced the resurgence of nationalism, already noted.

The war and its aftermath had demonstrated so convincingly the vulnerability of American prosperity that Henry Clay believed his fellow countrymen were ready for a planned national economy based on a protective tariff. Nor should it be assumed that this plan was merely the revival of an old Federalist dream. The center of gravity in that party combination had been the merchant shipowners of the Atlantic ports from Boston to Charleston. These men certainly wanted no artificial restrictions placed on either incoming or outgoing cargoes. As shipowners they did not relish the early protection of hemp, cordage, flax for sail duck, and iron, all used in shipbuilding. Nor did they welcome the establishment of industries here that could not fail to reduce their import trade. When Henry Clay presented his American System he found himself in controversy with the champion of the New England shipping interests, the Federalist Daniel Webster, who could see nothing "American" about it. . . .

A native of Virginia, young Henry Clay had migrated to frontier Kentucky, grown up with the community, and, like Lincoln later, whose exemplar he was to be, deliberately cultivated an inherent talent for politics. Law was then the high-road to political preferment, and Clay so fascinated his juries that it was said no person ever hanged where he spoke for the defense. Perused in cold print today, his speeches seem tame, but so magnetic was the personality of this master of men that for five decades he led Kentucky emotions and reason captive. "In his understanding of human nature, in his ability to appeal to the common reason, and in his absolute fearlessness in stating his convictions, he was unexcelled by any of his contemporaries." Having served his legislative apprenticeship in the Kentucky lower house, he came in 1811 to the national House of Representatives, there to be elected at once to the speakership, where his mastery was to be impressed no less on the incorrigible John Randolph than on the complaisant President Madison, whom we have seen obliged to come out for war with England as virtually the price of a second term.

Clay's well-matured exposition of the American System, set forth in the House of Representatives as the presidential competition of 1824 developed, resembled that of the "Open Door at Home" revived by Charles A. Beard more than a century later. "Now our people," declared Clay, "present the spectacle of a vast assemblage of jealous rivals, all eagerly rushing to the seaboard, jostling each other on their way, to hurry off to glutted foreign markets the perishable produce of their labor. The tendency of that policy, in conformity with which this bill is prepared, is to transform these competitors into friends and mutual customers, and, by reciprocal exchange of their respective productions, to place the confederacy upon the most solid of all foundations, the basis of common interest." The presidential aspirant counted on attaching to himself practically every section and interest in the nation. Through adequate protection there might be created the home market for farm products on the one hand and for manufactured products on the other. Reduced prices of the output of factories, once they were firmly established, was held forth. Revenues from tariff duties would finance the network of canals and highways required for this internal traffic.

The Middle and Ohio Valley states, realizing that the European market was now gone beyond recall, had developed an almost childlike faith in the protection of wool, hemp, flax, wheat, and corn. The frustration of Ohio Valley farmers at seeing their marketable surpluses rot for lack of transportation united them on internal improvements as on no other issue. Already there were, according to McMaster's estimate, 2,000,000 factory workers becoming impressed by the argument for protection as a maintainer of wages and a means of keeping the mills running. If only Clay could manage to convince the farmers, shepherds, road and canal contractors, factory-owners, mill hands, and handicraftsmen of a common interest in his American System, the grand prize of the presidency might be his reward.

Unfortunately for Clay, the post-war nationalist enthusiasm had already spent its force when he presented his formula, and the South never found it acceptable. The cotton-planters wanted no restrictions on the free flow of foreign trade in and out. Moreover, nature had provided their states with magnificent systems of river transportation. Not only would protection favor particular industries, but the planter was convinced that he would, as John Randolph put it, "only get much worse things at a much higher price," and the funds extracted from him at the detested custom house would be used to construct Northern canals and highways. In short, it was, to the planters, a system of vicious class legislation. Nor was the West swept off its feet by the Clay formula. After all, its appeal was to the intellect and not to the feelings. "Its acceptance carried no intoxication" and "could not be adapted to the western style of exhortation." Confronted by the dynamic personality of Old Hickory, then emerging as a presidential possibility, the emotion-starved pioneer lost interest in Clay's elaborate argument.

The West had taken, in the early twenties, a keen interest in discussing the relative strength of the followings of Clay and Jackson. The section was ready for a leader who could sense, phrase, and symbolize the needs of the depression-vexed West as well as those of the Eastern urban masses now beginning to stir uneasily under their social subordination. Clay's essay at this was his American System. What had others to offer in this first free-for-all competition for the American presidency? In 1822 *Niles' Register* found sixteen or seventeen candidates, but a year later only half a dozen remained in the field. Easily first among these was William H. Crawford, Secretary of the Treasury, whose candidacy enjoyed the blessing of no less a notable than the aged Jefferson himself. Macon, Madison, Randolph, Van Buren, and Marcy also backed him and he was given the formal nomination of the congressional caucus which made him the official party nominee, the candidate of the regular Republican politicians. Regionally regarded, he was the candidate of the cotton-planters, who were insisting upon the removal of the Indians from the fertile black belts. Ideologically he was the legatee of the Jeffersonian tradition, standing on the extreme ground of the Kentucky Resolutions with their "rightful remedy" of "nullification." The wide appeal of these Resolutions was evident from the fact that the legislature of Ohio was just then using them in its protest against the Supreme Court decision that it could not tax the branches of the Bank of the United States located in Ohio.

Crawford revealed the regional candidate's typical reaching out for a nation-wide union of interests in his support of moderate tariffs and the maintenance of the Bank of the United States. Presently it was Crawford against the field, which "ganged up" on him and proceeded to "smear" him as the candidate of the "undemocratic" congressional caucus, while other candidates were nominated instead by state legislatures presumed to be more immediate agents of the popular will. In any case Crawford was eliminated by a paralytic stroke in the midst of his campaign.

That Andrew Jackson should even be considered for the chair so long occupied by a line of distinguished Virginia statesmen seemed at first thought utterly preposterous to most men, not even excepting General Jackson himself. "Do they think I am such a damned fool as to think myself fit for the presidency?" he asked in 1821 when for the first time he saw his name mentioned in that connection in a newspaper. "No, sir," he continued, "I know what I am good for. I can command a body of men in a rough way, but I am not fit to be president." Yet the smoke of the Battle of New Orleans had scarcely more than cleared away when his availability had been perceived by one of the keenest practical politicians of that day. In 1815 Aaron Burr, eager to find a candidate around whom might be rallied the forces to overthrow the Virginia "oligarchy," had suggested Jackson in a letter to his own son-in-law, Joseph Alston.

It was the depression of the twenties that had provided the seed-bed of what has since come to be known as the Jacksonian movement. Keen political observers perceived deep-seated stirrings of both the rural and the urban masses accentuated by the prevailing hard times. A profound conviction that the ruling class had betrayed the people's interests was taking possession of the common man. A new species of politicians expert in canalizing mass movements began to emerge and sweep the horizon in search of a national leader. That a man of Jackson's background should be called upon for this purpose would have seemed preposterous to any but these new politicians. This Nashville ex-judge, sound-money man, and creditor distinctly distrusted the turbulent masses and had habitually sided with the haves and against the have-nots. Nevertheless the "Nashville Junto" of designing politicians decided to ignore the party machinery, on which, in any case, the Crawford men had an iron grip, and boldly proclaim their fellow citizen as the hope of the underdogs, the champion of the masses then groping for leadership.

Ever since his victory at New Orleans there had not been a more widely known celebrity in the United States than General Jackson. To the depression-frustrated ordinary citizen, whether urban worker, yeoman, or frontiersman, he was a veritable miracle-worker, invincible in battle against Indians, British, or "hard times." Even the illiteracy of voters worked to his advantage, because, as one of his supporters wrote in a letter, "they are illy acquainted with the character and qualifications of the other candidates" and need no education to know of "the glorious exploits which have crowned the career of Jackson."

Nor was Andrew Jackson in 1824 by any means a mere novice in politics. The general, passing down the tense lines in the pitch darkness of one o'clock in the morning before the Battle of New Orleans and picking out by voice and calling by name the soldiers who spoke to him, whether he realized it or not was already practicing the great art. Called upon to give his opinion of the tariff measure pending in the campaign year of 1824, he wrote with an eye keenly alert to all the interests concerned: "So far as the Tariff before us embraces the design of fostering, protecting, and preserving within ourselves the means of national defense, I support it . . . Providence has filled our mountains and our plains with . . . lead, iron, and copper, and given us a climate and soil for growing hemp and wool. These being the grand materials of our national defense, they ought to have extended to them . . . protection, that our manufacturers and laborers . . . may produce within our own borders a supply . . . essential to war. . . ." What candidate in any decade could, with such verbal economy, make a neater bid for the support of seven different interests and, at the same time, base his argument on the universal and fundamentally sound argument of national defense?

Measured by experience, learning, intelligence, and sheer devotion to the public interest, John Quincy Adams was best fitted of all the competitors for the presidency in 1824. Moreover, according to established precedent he was the heir apparent to the high office. As Secretary of State he occupied the position from which every President for almost a quarter of a century had been promoted. "I am a man of reserved, cold, austere and forbidding manners," confessed this unbending Puritan; "my political adversaries say, a gloomy misanthrope; and my personal enemies an unsocial savage." Despite these handicaps here is the candidate who in the end captured the grand prize. Nor was this capable stateman utterly innocent of the game of practical politics. He gave dinners, owned a newspaper, found loans for its editor and public printing for its support.

Since Adams's views corresponded closely with Clay's American System, their candidacies tended to split the vote of the interests soon to form the National Republican Party. When the results of the balloting in the fall of 1824 were available, it was seen that Adams had captured all the counties in New England and those in New York and Ohio wherever the New England stock predominated. Some scattered counties in New York and Missouri gave Clay majorities, but his strength, though far from uniform, lay largely in the Ohio Valley. . . .

Jackson's astonishing showing was due to the support of his fanatically devoted fellow Scotch-Irish scattered throughout Pennsylvania, the upland South, and the entire West south of the Mississippi and St. Lawrence divide, the Germans of Pennsylvania and Ohio, and everywhere the underdog marshaled by Jacksonian politicians who knew how to utilize the popular ferment of the twenties. Jackson's vote in the electoral college was 99 to 84 for Adams, while Crawford received 41.

In case of the failure of any candidate to obtain a majority in the electoral college, one of the highest three would be elected by the House of Representatives, with each state casting one vote as the Constitution prescribed. Clay was, of course, disappointed at his exclusion, for he must have considered his chances good in an election by the House, of which he was the Speaker and in which, of course, he possessed an enormous influence. As it now turned out, he and his following in Congress consciously held a balance of power between Jackson and Adams and were thus in a position to determine the next President. For weeks Clay seemed undecided whether to express his loyalty to the West by supporting Jackson or, for his own future advantage, to endeavor to eliminate his Western rival by supporting Adams. Whatever his motives, his influence ultimately made Adams President, and since the views of the men were so similar on the American System, the action might be regarded as logical and indeed the fulfillment of what amounted to practically a referendum on the paramount issue of the campaign of 1824.

To the Jackson men there was nothing at all logical about the election of Adams. None of them doubted that the House had been morally bound to elect the one who ranked first in the electoral college. Then, too, it was argued that the popular vote carried a like mandate. Even though the legislatures and not the voters had chosen the presidential electors in half the states and despite the fact that in only four states had the electorate voted on all four candidates, nevertheless, for the first time in our history, estimates of the total popular vote for each candidate were published. These seemed to indicate that Jackson had received a plurality of forty-two percent of the votes. The reaction of the masses to the publication of these data betokened the new force in American politics. Jackson's followers, among whom the Scotch-Irish were most partisan, maintained that the House had flouted their cherished doctrine of popular sovereignty. It was as their peculiar spokesman that Jackson eventually was to recommend the popular election of the President in every one of his eight annual messages to Congress. We have here in fact a germinal dogma of emerging Jacksonian Democracy and it was to be dinned into the ears of the public daily during the four years of Adams's presidency.

Thurlow Weed has given us the opinion of a contemporary expert in party politics that the new President was no practical politician. "Mr. Adams," said he, "during his administration failed to cherish, strengthen, or even recognize the party to which he owed his election; nor as far as I am informed, with the great power he possessed did he make a single influential friend." Adams had indicated a willingness to have Andrew Jackson considered the vice-presidential candidate with him "on correct principle—his fitness for the place, the fitness of the place for him and the peculiar advantages of the geographical situation." Utterly oblivious of the incipient renaissance of political parties, he offered cabinet appointments to all his rivals for the presidency, only to be repulsed by all except Clay, whom he made Secretary of State. This appointment proved to be a fatal error since it served only to confirm the conviction of the Jacksonians that Clay had made a "corrupt bargain" whereby he would make Adams President in return for his own appointment to the office of Secretary of State. The significance attached to this appointment was due to the fact that the office had become the established stepping-stone to the presidency, so the cry at once arose: "Clay is in the succession."

The Jacksonians stubbornly insisted that Adams was thereby dictating the choice of his successor to the "sovereign" people—or, at any rate, assuming to do so.

Ill fortune dogged every move of President Adams during his four miserable years in the White House. His first annual message seems commonplace today, but it rent the country asunder. The President's grandson, Brooks Adams, saw in it a revival of Washington's dream of tying the West to the East with a system of canals, thereby checking the growing sectionalism of the North and South by diversifying the industries of Virginia and Maryland. Adams's message proposed canals, highways, harbor improvements, a stronger navy, military schools, a strengthened militia, a national university, and an observatory, all at Federal expense. This terrifying program, in the opinion of W.B. Giles, published in the Richmond *Enquirer,* created "a crisis involving the liberty and happiness of all future ages." Nor did the President's message catch the popular favor even of the North, where it was only reminiscent of a post-war nationalism that had already subsided, and prophetic of an enthusiasm for the Union yet to develop and find classic expression in Webster's sonorous periods.

A "minority" President who would remove no enemy from office, not even his Postmaster General, busy employing patronage against him, who prevented his supporters from copying the public record of the court-martial decision on the six militiamen Jackson had executed, for fear it "would be construed as a measure of hostility against General Jackson," but who persisted with inflexible Puritan sternness in the performance of his duty, simply played into the hands of the anti-Adams men. These had no scruples against arousing the pioneer's prejudice against the administration's unprecedented expenditures of $14,000,000 in four years of peace. The absurd rumor that part of this money had been spent on a billiard table installed in the White House for the amusement of the President's son set Western tongues wagging. The Scotch Presbyterians scarcely knew whether to be more incensed over the waste of taxpayers' money or the sin of the game, but thrifty Pennsylvania Dutch puzzled over no such alternative. It was in fact a four-year "smear" campaign in which the Jacksonians converted "a personal prejudice into a political force that was positive, aggressive and effective." So contemptible, in fact, was the propaganda employed that one distinguished recent historian wondered whether it would not have been more honorable for Jackson to have lost than won in 1828.

John Quincy Adams was the first of our Presidents to be confronted by a Congress deliberately organized against the administration. Clay's alleged "corrupt bargain" was aired *ad nauseam,* and filibustering against the President's measures was unblushingly carried on. The crowning device intended to overwhelm Adams was the Tariff Act of 1828. It was an over-clever politician's intrigue for snaring votes, which, as crabbed John Randolph averred, "referred to manufactures of no sort or kind except the manufacture of a President of the United States." The stake was the protectionist vote of Pennsylvania and the West. Jacksonian politicians, with diabolical ingenuity, framed a high-protection bill so loaded with provisos damaging to New England's interests as to invite the Adams men to vote it down. If they did so, the Pennsylvania protectionists would be turned against Adams, while if the measure passed, the Democrats were the champions of protection anyhow. If the tossed coin came up tails, Adams lost; if it turned up heads, Jackson won. To the discomfiture of the Jacksonian politicians, the New England Congressmen accepted the measure, and when passed, Adams signed it.

The transformation of these anti-Adams men into Jacksonian Democrats constitutes a landmark in the history of American party politics. The traditional revolutionary machinery of the committees of correspondence was utilized in order to overthrow the ruling class. The Jacksonian politicians organized the now enfranchised masses through conventions, caucuses, and committees down into the county, the township, and even the rural school districts. National politicians were learning to weave the local sectional and class interests into intricate national patterns. "Their cross sections instead of displaying a few simple colors, were a jig-saw puzzle of radicalism and conservatism, national and state rights, personal loyalties and local issues. Party strategy was directed toward accumulating as many bundles as possible; and statesmanship was the art of finding some person or principle common to all the bundles that would make them forget their differences and in union find strength."

On a national scale the politician *par excellence* of his generation was Martin Van Buren, who perfected his art in the severe competition of the factions in New York politics. "Few men in American life," wrote Turner, "so united the ability to make political combinations and the power of critical analysis of underlying principles. Suave and conciliatory, Van Buren was perhaps the highest type of New York politician. He rose to national greatness and achieved a reputation as a statesman by his ability to think in national terms, to formulate Democratic party principles that remained substantially unchanged down to recent years and at times to make decisions hazardous to his career and to abide by them."

CHAPTER 28

THE TRIUMPH OF DEMOCRACY

A traditional American legend assumes that democracy, like religious freedom, sprang up full-grown when European colonists set foot on the soil of the New World. But we have learned from previous readings that colonial and revolutionary America were far from being democratic. Property and other qualifications limited the suffrage and office-holding. A fairly well-defined privileged class, composed of those with a "stake in society," dominated American government, society, and the economy. Yet from its beginning, America was significantly different from Europe. Economic opportunity was more widespread, more people owned property and thus could vote, the American ruling class lacked the traditional and legal roots of European aristocracy, and a degree of class mobility existed even during the colonial period. Some of these seeds of democracy developed fully during the first half of the nineteenth century.

In this selection from *Out of Our Past: The Forces that Shaped Modern America**, the historian, Carl Degler, concentrates on the extension of American democracy. His emphasis is on the democratization of politics and government—the expansion of suffrage and office-holding, new attitudes toward majority rule, acceptance of the principle of rotation in office, and the strengthening of the office of President. Professor Degler also comments on the increased commitment to the ideal of the equality of man and to a more equalitarian and a more open society. He not only describes the growth of democracy but also explores the factors that made this growth possible.

In this, the latter half of the twentieth century, we might well try to evaluate America as a democratic society in light of Degler's treatment of Jacksonian America. To what extent is the nation more or less democratic than it was over a hundred years ago? What are the forces operating to expand or curtail democracy? Are we still shielded from the reality of American society by the myth of democracy?

For a brief critical summary of recent scholarship on this topic, see Marcus Cunliffe, *The Nation Takes Shape: 1789–1837** (1959). Another good, general treatment is Gilman Ostrander, *The Rights of Man in America, 1606–1861** (1960). Also, read Alice Felt Tyler, *Freedom's Ferment: Phases of American Social History to 1860** (1940).

* Available in a paperback edition.

THE GREAT EXPERIMENT
CARL N. DEGLER

Even before the first settlers had arrived, America was an object of curiosity to Europeans; but in the thirties, forties, and fifties of the nineteenth century the United States was as interesting to Europeans as Soviet Russia was to the world a hundred years later. Scores of foreign travelers made the Grand Tour of America in those years, dutifully recording their impressions for the edification of their less fortunate, but no less curious, fellow Europeans. This was the era of Tocqueville, Mrs. Trollope, Charles Dickens, Harriet Martineau, Charles Lyell, Fredrika Bremer, and Captain Hall. And whatever else America may have been in the writings of visitors, all seemed agreed that the United States was the great experiment in democracy. To English Chartists, struggling to democratize English government, the United States appeared as "the bright luminary of the western hemisphere whose radiance will extend across the Atlantic's broad expanse and light the whole world to freedom and happiness."

It was in the course of these years that the Democratic Dogma, as Brooks Adams was to call it later, was pushed to its outer limits. The common people came into their own as political arbiters and participants; majority rule was invested with a kind of sanctity. By the time the era was over, new, popular colors had been added to the bare outline of American politics inherited from the Revolutionary Fathers. The modern party system was in being, the Presidency bore the indelible marks of Andrew Jackson and James K. Polk, and the principle of a people's administration of government had been permanently implanted in American political thought.

"LET THE PEOPLE RULE"

Even during the eighteenth century, as we have noticed, more people could vote, proportionately, in the United States than in England and

SOURCE. Carl N. Degler, *Out of Our Past: The Forces that shaped Modern America,* New York: Harper & Row Publishers, Inc., 1959, pp. 136–146. Copyright 1959 by Carl N. Degler. Reprinted by permission of Harper & Row Publishers, Inc. and the author.

other European countries. But in the years after 1815, Americans deliberately expanded the suffrage in order to rest their governments upon
the consent of all the governed.

By the decades of the 1830's and 1840's this movement reached flood
tide, as the states altered their constitutions in conformity with the principle
that manhood, not property, was the most just basis for political rights.
This was a new view, one which constituted a sharp departure from
colonial and early republican theory and practice. "The pretense has
been that none but the rich have a stake in society," James Fenimore
Cooper wrote. But this is wrong, he insisted. "Every man who has wants,
feelings, affections and character, has a stake in society." Hence he is
entitled to vote. It was precisely this abandonment of the traditional
assumptions regarding the suffrage which renders this period significant;
goodly numbers of people had always voted in America, where property
was widely distributed. Now, however, even property was removed as a
limitation. Once it was conceded that the basis for the suffrage was mere
citizenship, then it was possible for any group or class to advance a
claim to participation in government. The floodgates of democracy were
open. In due time, on this basis, women, Negroes, and eighteen-year-old
youths would be accepted as voters.

The shift away from the stake-in-society conception of politics was
dramatic because it was accomplished so rapidly. In 1800, only three of
the fifteen states of the Union granted the vote to all white men, regardless of property; by 1860, in a Union of thirty states, all but seven
states extended the ballot to all white men, rich and poor alike. Property
holding as a test of fitness to hold office was also discarded. Most of the
new states in the early years of the century entered the Union without
such requirements, while the original states gradually dropped theirs:
Maryland began in 1810, Pennsylvania followed in 1838, then New
Jersey in 1844, and so on.

The suffrage was only one of the several governmental innovations
which embodied the upsurge in democratic ideals. Governors, for example, were now popularly elected instead of being chosen by the legislature. Maryland in 1837, North Carolina in 1835, New Jersy in 1844,
and Virginia in 1850 all made changes in this direction. A large number
of other offices were also made elective; indeed, it might be said that
during this period the "long ballot" came into being, for a host of minor
and middling offices were newly opened to election on the state and local
level.

Most striking as a measure of the belief in the validity and value
of a wide suffrage was the subjection of the judiciary to popular election.

Between 1846 and 1853, thirteen states made various of their judges subject to the direct pleasure of the people—an extension of the democratic ideal which probably none of the Founding Fathers would have sanctioned.

The democratic faith was also extended to the making of the state constitutions. At the time of the Revolution only two states had found it necessary to submit their constitutions to the people for ratification; by the Age of Jackson, however, such a procedure was the usual practice; only an occasional state failed to seek the people's judgment on a constitution. The principle that just government derives from the consent of the governed was taken literally in this democratic age.

Faith in the infallibility of the people's judgment was the sun around which American political thought now revolved. Andrew Jackson, for example, upon retiring from the Presidency in 1837, told the people in his Farewell Address that they should "Never for a moment believe that the great body of the citizens of any State can deliberately intend to do wrong." It is true, he confessed, that they may be misled, "but in a community so enlightened and patriotic as the people of the United States, argument will soon make them sensible of their errors" and they will therefore rectify them. Martin Van Buren, Jackson's successor, was widely known for his dictum that "the sober second thought of the people is never wrong." And George Bancroft, Democratic theoretician, historian, and politician, contended that "true political science does indeed venerate the masses. . . . Individuals are of limited sagacity; the common mind is infinite in its experience. . . . Individuals are time-serving; the masses are fearless." To Bancroft the new democratic upsurge meant that "the day of the multitude is now dawned." "Democracy is the cause of Humanity," proclaimed the first number of the radical Democratic organ *The United States Magazine and Democratic Review*. "It has faith in human nature. It believes in its essential equality and fundamental goodness. It respects, with a solemn reverence to which the proudest artificial institutions and distinctions of society have no claim, the human soul. It is the cause of philanthropy." The virtues of the common man as a class were often said to be superior. At the New York Constitutional Convention of 1821, for example, it was asserted that "more integrity and more patriotism are generally found in the labouring class of the community than in the higher orders."

Such a deeply held belief in the people's wisdom was something new in conservative America; neither Thomas Jefferson nor even Tom Paine would have gone to such extremes, for both these advocates of the people saw the flaws as well as the beauty in humankind. To be sure, there still were many who would not accept the new-found democratic oracle; the Whig party in general for a while stood against such doctrine. But by the election of 1840 even the Whigs, at least publicly, were throwing their money and their oratory in the same direction as the Jacksonians—that is, in outright flattery of the people. After 1840 no political party would again dare to doubt the wisdom of the people as the Federalists and even some of the Whigs had done in earlier years. Charles Francis Adams, for example, while editing his grandfather's works in 1851, bemoaned the fact that candid political criticism was no longer possible in America. ". . . The fact is certain," he wrote, "that no leading political man" since John Adams' day "has been known to express a serious doubt of the immaculate nature of the government established by the majority." America was now committed to the dubious dogma that wisdom in politics was in direct proportion to the participation of the people.

The people did not need politicians to bolster their self-esteem; they demanded not only the ballot but access to appointive office as well. Even before Jackson's administration there was popular demand for a rotation of officers among the people. Jackson, however, gave the movement intellectual footing when, in his first annual message to Congress, he justified the removal of many old civil servants. "I cannot but believe," the new President wrote, "that more is lost by the long continuance of men in office than is generally gained from their experience." And it was true that many officeholders were superannuated in both mind and body. (Not insignificant in Jackson's motivation was the patent fact that a good number of the officeholders thought "the wild man from the West" a real danger in the White House after the incumbency of cultivated John Quincy Adams.) Moreover, many of them had come to think of their offices as a species of personal property—as Englishmen were wont to do in the eighteenth century. "In a country where offices are created solely for the benefit of the people," Jackson argued in lofty democratic tones, "no one man has any more intrinsic right to official station than another. Offices were not established to give support to particular men at the public expense."

Though the rotation of public office among the people opened the gates for an increasingly vicious spoils system, it also faithfully mirrored the American democratic philosophy that any citizen could adequately perform the work of government. Nor was this rather naïve conception of governmental work without truth. While today the tasks of government bureaus are infinitely complex and technical, in the early years of the Republic the bulk of the employees were little more than clerks, postmasters, and the like. The vast proportion of the jobs of the government could be effectively and efficiently carried on by the average citizen.

Jackson's deliberate removal of the old and the partisan from the offices of his administration brought forth a flood of aspirants for the vacancies. Thus was initiated the burden of the patronage system, the weight of which, in the course of subsequent years, has almost borne down the Presidency. Whig Daniel Webster said in 1835: "No one can deny that office of every kind is now sought with extraordinary avidity. . . ." Convinced that theirs was a people's government, the people were not hesitant in demanding their places. The policy initiated under the Democrats was continued by the Whigs in 1841, the faithful rushing "pell-mell to Washington, every man with a raccoon's tail in his hat" to identify himself as a supporter of William Henry Harrison. Such men, John Quincy Adams wrote with distate in 1842, were "wolves of the antechamber, prowling for offices." President after President struggled hopelessly and unendingly with the "wolves" until the murder of a Chief Executive in 1881 by a disappointed office-seeker startled the American people from their unconcern. It was only then that civil service reform got an opportunity to lighten the crushing burden of the patronage.

Though the rotation system unquestionably wasted much of the Presidents' time and threatened to reduce officeholding to the work of party hacks, something of value, nevertheless, came out of it. Principally this was democratization of administration on both the federal and state levels. There would never grow up in America any remote civil service which was divorced from the people or which conceived of itself as a superior caste or class, outside or above the main body of the citizenry, as, for example, occurred in Germany to the detriment of the democratic Weimar Republic. Americans made sure, in this period, that their government, like the society at large, reflected their firm belief in the equality of men. Undoubtedly, a democratic administrative structure has been a prop and a succor to the whole democratic way of life in America.

At first glance it appears incongruous that in this very period when popular control of government was at its height, the office of the President, occupied as it is by a single person, should also attain new strength and prestige. This consequence is largely the result of two men's influence upon the people and upon the office. It is true that George Washington, as the first President, did more than any other incumbent to create the mold from which the Chief Magistracy of the Republic would thereafter be cast. But if the austere and essentially aristocratic Washington bequeathed dignity, independence, and high prestige to the Presidency, it remained for Andrew Jackson and James K. Polk to make it also an expression of the democratic spirit of the American people.

It was Jackson, for instance, who first declared that "the President is the direct representative of the people" and no less capable of speaking for the people than the Congress. In practice, Jackson did not hesitate to appeal to the people to sustain policies which the Congress opposed, as, for example, when he vetoed the Bank recharter bill in 1832. Polk, who with reason was often called "Young Hickory," made no secret of following Jackson's conception of the President as the Tribune of the People. "The President," Polk wrote, "represents in the executive department the whole people of the United States, as each member of the legislative department represents portions of them." As early as 1824, ardently democratic Senator Thomas Hart Benton advocated changes which would bring the President closer to the people than the cautious Founding Fathers had intended. Stigmatizing indirect election through the Electoral College as a "favorite institution of aristocratic republics," Benton urged that the people be able to vote directly for the Chief Magistrate. Jackson himself, in his first annual message, also urged the amending of the Constitution in order to permit the people to elect the President directly. Though nothing came of either Benton's or Jackson's proposals regarding election, the nomination of the President was democratized in the early 1830's. The Anti-Masonic party held the first Presidential nominating convention in the United States in 1831; within a few years the two major parties abandoned the old caucus system in favor of the more popular convention.

It was Jackson who conclusively established the right of a President to control his Cabinet, even though the Congress may have legislated otherwise. At the time of his war against the Bank of the United States in 1832–33, Jackson, despite Congress' deliberate effort to make the Secretary of the Treasury responsible to the legislature, successfully compelled two Secretaries of the Treasury to resign because they would not implement his policies. Congress protested vehemently and the Senate, in an extraordinary procedure, formally censured the President. But Jackson was vindicated and the President's power enhanced when a more friendly Senate later, in a dramatic ceremony, expunged the censure from its records. Since that time all Presidents, with the exception of the befuddled Grant, have been encouraged by the example of Jackson to fight vigorously against any congressional efforts to control the Cabinet.

It was left to James Polk to explore the immense reservoir of power inherent in the President as Commander in Chief of the armed forces. The Mexican War, as Leonard White has pointed out, was really fought from the White House: Polk named the generals, set forth the grand strategy which won the war, cajoled and bullied the Congress into granting the necessary credits and support, and finally drew up the peace terms. All this was achieved with a minimum of consultation with or dependence upon the Congress. When faced with a much greater military challenge, Abraham Lincoln would find encouraging precedent in Polk's use of the Presidential power.

Under imaginative handling by Jackson and Polk, even an essentially negative power like the veto was made to strengthen the authority and prestige of the Presidency. For the first forty years of the Republic it was more or less assumed, from the precedent set by Washington, that the veto was merely a check on unconstitutional legislation and not a weapon which the President could use to enforce his own views. All the Presidents prior to 1829 used their negatives so sparingly that Jackson's vetoes numbered more than all those of his predecessors combined. More important, Jackson made no effort to conceal the fact that the motives behind his vetoes were at best a compound of constitutional scruple and expediency. It is true that he said he doubted the constitutionality of the Bank when he vetoed the recharter bill. But a perusal of his veto message made it clear to everyone that his opposition stemmed from his distrust of the Bank as such and not from any questions of constitutional niceties concerning an institution which, after all, had functioned for almost forty years.

The new Democratic view of the veto power was not discarded by John Tyler, the first Whig President. And even though Tyler was threatened with impeachment for daring to veto legislation which the Congress considered constitutional, the Jacksonian conception of the veto prevailed then and later. In vetoing a river and harbors bill Polk did not find it necessary to offer any justification for his act other than his mere disapproval. The power and prestige which the Jacksonian veto added to the arsenal of the President is best appreciated when it is realized that no veto was overridden by Congress until 1866.

Such an accretion of Presidential power was possible only after the President had been transformed into the Tribune of the People. Prior to that time, the unlimited exercise of the veto smacked of the royal prerogative and of the flouting of the will of the people's representatives. But once the President was accepted as a representative of the people, then the augmentation of his power, even during a period of expanding popular participation in politics, was quite possible and in conformity with democratic ideals.

Indeed, it might be said that the expansion of Presidential power during these years, as well as the increasingly popular character of the office, bear testimony to the realistic political judgment of the American people. Rather than being jealous of the power of the executive, the people seemed to recognize the vital role which strong executive leadership must occupy in any democratic polity which seeks to avoid the deadly paralysis of factionalism. As a result, twentieth-century Americans enjoy an executive unparalleled in its independence and power, yet one responsive to the people's will.

"ALL MEN ARE CREATED EQUAL"

The democratization of politics and government was only one of the signs spelling out the Rise of the Common Man; the new democratic spirit was apparent throughout society. Dixon Ryan Fox went so far as to entitle his history of these years *The Decline of Aristocracy*. But that is a phrase which almost sacrifices accuracy to neatness. For as we have seen, it is doubtful that an aristocracy, as the term has meaning in European history, ever existed in America, much less declined. Any ruling class which may have existed in this country has always been tempered by the fact that it could lay no claim to a long tradition of wealth and power such as European aristocracies enjoyed and which is the true soil of an aristocracy.

But even if Fox's phrase somewhat overstates the situation, it does serve to accentuate the fact that in the years between 1820 and 1860, Americans made it quite clear that theirs was to be an equalitarian and open society. Earlier expressions of this sentiment had been sporadic and moderate; in the Age of Jackson it was blatantly and continuously proclaimed. "The equality of Man is, to this moment," wrote British traveler Alexander Mackay in 1842, the "cornerstone" of American society. Earlier Alexis de Tocqueville concluded that democratic societies like America were "ardent, insatiable, incessant and invincible" in their passion for equality. "They will endure poverty, servitude, barbarism, but they will not endure aristocracy."

A symptomatic expression of this strong distaste for privilege was evident in the attacks upon West Point during the mid-1830's. Tennessee, for example, in a resolution of the legislature, stigmatized the Military Academy as "this aristocratical institution." And the Ohio legislature declared that West Point was "wholly inconsistent with the spirit and genius of our liberal institutions." And so sure were Americans of their "liberal institutions," wrote Mrs. Trollope, that she "once got so heartily scolded for saying that I did not think all American citizens were equally eligible" for the Presidency "that I shall never again venture to doubt it."

The source from which the reservoir of American faith in equality was constantly being replenished was opportunity. "The United States are certainly the land of promise for the labouring class," wrote Michel Chevalier in 1834. "After landing in New York, I thought every day was Sunday, for the whole population that throngs Broadway seemed to be arrayed in their Sunday's best." Even prickly Mrs. Trollope bore witness to the opportunities of the new country. "Any man's son may become the equal of any other Man's son," she admitted, "and the consciousness of this is certainly a spur to exertion." Harriet Martineau thought she saw unlimited horizons for the lowly in America: "an artisan may attain to be governor of the state, member of Congress, even President," she said. "It is extremely seldom," Englishman Alexander Mackay observed, "that the willing hand in America is in want of employment."

The opportunities open to Americans were reflected in how well the average citizen lived. "I saw no table spread, in the lowest order of houses," Harriet Martineau recalled, "that had not meat and bread on it. Every factory child carried its umbrella; and pig-drivers wear spectacles." Michel Chevalier related the story of a newly arrived Irishman who showed his employer a letter he wrote to his family in the old country. " 'But Patrick,' said his master, 'why do you say that you have meat three times a week, when you have it three times a day?' 'Why is it?' replied Pat; 'it is because they wouldn't believe me, if I told them so.' " Other observers remarked on the notable absence of beggars. There were poor in America, to be sure, for while some men prospered others slipped and fell. And already the tenements of the burgeoning cities were open for inspection and the slum was no longer a European monopoly. But even with such qualifications, and especially when compared with European social conditions, this country opened new economic vistas for Everyman. As Emerson said, "America is another word for opportunity."

One immediate consequence of the breadth of opportunity was the looseness of class lines. We have noticed already a tendency in this direction all through American history; during the first half of the nineteenth century, however, this blurring of classes was a fact and a boast. "We have no different estates," Erastus Root told the New York Constitutional Convention of 1821, "having different interests, necessary to be guarded from encroachment by the watchful eye of jealousy. We are all of the same estate—commoners. . . ." New citizen Achille Murat said that "the lines which divide" Americans "are so delicate that they melt into each other; and that . . . there are neither castes nor ranks." European social patterns do not fit in the United States, German immigrant Francis Lieber wrote home. "In America there is no peasant. . . . He is a farmer, and may be rich or poor; that is all the difference."

In a country in which most men possessed "a competence," as Alexander Mackay put it, property was in no danger. Where acquisition of property

is relatively easy, as it was in America, the demand for equality of holdings is rarely heard. It is significant that at no time, insofar as the great
majority of Americans was concerned, did "equality" signify an equal
division of wealth; too many men owned wealth, or soon expected to, to
become involved in schemes or theories which might someday be fashioned
into weapons with which to wrest from them their tangible goods. "There
will be no attack on property in the United States," Harriet Martineau
correctly prophesied. Because property was distributed throughout the
various levels of society, no philosophy or organization fundamentally opposed to private property, be it Brook Farm or "agrarianism," was able
to win the support of the American people.

CHAPTER 29

JACKSONIAN DEMOCRACY

Few men in American history have been more controversial during their lifetimes and afterward than Andrew Jackson. He was both despised and idolized by Americans living in the 1820's and 1830's, and historians differ sharply in their interpretations of him. Some historians have viewed Jackson as the democratic champion of the common man; others have considered him as a conservative and wealthy demagogue. Some historians attribute his political success to his appeal to Western frontiersmen and Southern farmers; others attribute it to the support he received from Eastern and urban workers. Some writers argue that Jackson was an anticapitalist; others argue that his aim was to open doors for the emerging capitalists and entrepreneurs.

If Jackson is controversial, so is the meaning of Jacksonian Democracy. This term is illusive and difficult to define because historians have used it to mean many different things. For our purposes it will be used to designate the aims, the approach, the style, and the program of Jackson and his administration. Gilman Ostrander devotes a chapter of *The Rights of Man In America, 1606–1861** to Jacksonian Democracy. He seeks to answer questions that must be answered if we are to achieve a better understanding of the Jacksonian era and of the man who dominated and symbolized that vigorous period of American History.

As you read this selection, keep these questions in mind. What kind of man was Andrew Jackson, and what was he really trying to do? Was his primary concern personal political power or the welfare of the nation?

Or both? Were Jackson's actions based on firm commitment to principles, or were they determined by expediency and opportunism? Was Jacksonian Democracy a broad reform movement with Jackson as its symbolic and actual leader, or was it something else? Finally, how do you explain the general agreement of historians that Jackson was an outstanding President? Do you agree?

The literature on Jackson is voluminous. The interested student should begin with one of Charles Grier Sellers' essays on Jacksonian historiography, *Jacksonian Democracy** (Service Center for Teachers of History, 1958), and "Andrew Jackson versus the Historians," *Mississippi Valley Historical Review*, XLIV (March 1958). James L. Bugg has compiled an excellent collection of readings on the subject entitled *Jacksonian Democracy: Myth or Reality?** (1962). Arthur M. Schlesinger, Jr., *The Age of Jackson** (1945) is a work of major significance. Marvin Meyers, author of *The Jacksonian Persuasion** (1960), approaches his subject from the vantage point of intellectual and social history.

* Available in a paperback edition.

JACKSONIAN DEMOCRACY
GILMAN OSTRANDER

The election [of 1828] brought to the Presidency a man who, at the age of sixty-two, was broken in health. It was doubted that he would live out his term of office. If he did, it was generally assumed in political circles, he would remain merely titular President, to be manipulated by the professionals who had conducted his campaign. Jackson's campaign, from the first, had been managed by others with little more than his passive consent. He had been willing clay, as James Parton wrote, in the hands of a few friendly potters. Until his defeat in 1824, by what he was convinced had been a corrupt bargain, Jackson had seemed almost indifferent to his own candidacy. After Adams' election by Congress, Jackson's heightened interest appeared to be little more than a personal desire for vengeance against Adams and Clay. Once in the Presidency, however, Jackson gathered into his hands the authority of the office, augmented by his own popularity. The first President to be elected by the people, he became in his own eyes the special guardian of the people by the divine right of majority assent. In the view of conservatives he became the dreaded demagogue, that fearful threat to republican institutions which the founding fathers, through the contrivance of the electoral college, had so carefully defended against.

James Parton concluded his biography of Andrew Jackson with an equivocal reflection.

Respecting the character of Andrew Jackson and his influence, there will still be differences of opinion. One fact, however, has been established: during the last thirty years of his life, he was the idol of the American people. His faults, whatever they were, were such as a majority of the American citizens of the last generation could easily forgive. His virtues, whatever they were, were such as a majority of American citizens of the last generation could warmly admire. It is this fact which renders him historically interesting. Columbus had sailed; Raleigh and the Puritans had planted; Franklin had lived; Washington

SOURCE. Gilman Ostrander, *The Rights of Man in America, 1606–1861*, Columbia, Missouri: The University of Missouri Press, 1960, pp. 183–198. Copyright 1960 by the Curators of the University of Missouri. Reprinted by permission of the University of Missouri Press and the author.

fought; Jefferson written; fifty years of democratic government had passed; free schools, a free press, a voluntary church had done what they could to instruct the people; the population of the country had been quadrupled and its resources increased ten fold; and the result of all was, that the people of the United States had arrived at the capacity of honoring Andrew Jackson before all other living men.

That, as Parton said, is the fact that renders Jackson historically interesting. He personified the American idea to the American people as no other President until General Eisenhower. "Other men are lenses through which we read our own minds," Ralph Waldo Emerson wrote in *Representative Men.* Among all of America's Presidents these two generals emerge as Emerson's "representative men."

Jackson was the visible sign of the people's triumph. His inauguration is remembered, not for what he said, which was very little and to no clear point, but for the motley crowd of farmers and mechanics who obtruded themselves upon a ceremony which formerly had been reserved for gentle folk. Traveling by horse and by foot over roads made all but impassable by spring rains, these common people converged on Washington by the thousands, some of them coming as far as five hundred miles for the occasion. Muddy and unmannerly, they crowded their way, uninvited, into the post-inauguration reception, threatening to reduce the White House to shambles, until they were diverted by tubs of punch hastily carried out to the White House lawn. They announced their sovereignty to the world.

There were hostile observers who found this inauguration of democracy disgraceful and fittingly so. As Alexis de Tocqueville noted, many Americans of wealth, position, and education privately despised democracy. Publicly, however, these men were compelled to accept the prevailing democratic shibboleths. Privately they might be guided by sensible and decorous religious conventions; publicly they were obliged to conduct themselves in such a way as to give no offense to the prevailing mores of the evangelical religions. They might profess to despise a society which made money the naked measure of social position, but the southern gentleman who disdained the counting house sometimes found his place in society pre-empted by his overseer. And however much certain rich men might despise the democratic process, the age of Jackson taught them the hard lesson that if they desired the political power to which they felt their position entitled them, they would have to go to the people to get it. As a class the aristocracy had become separated from the national character, which was democratic.

I

What followed Jackson's White House reception was anticlimax. The nation, awaiting the outcome of the Jacksonian revolution, waited in vain for any startling political changes. It turned out that Thomas Jefferson had disturbed himself unnecessarily over the possibility of a Jacksonian *coup d'etat* against the republic. The new President and his chief lieutenants thought of themselves, not as political innovators, but as good, safe Jeffersonians, whose duty it was to safeguard the people against dangerous centralizing tendencies in the national government.

The Jacksonians pledged themselves to reduce government personnel and introduce other economies to the end that the national debt be paid off, the government freed from the grasp of the money power, and the burden of taxation be lifted from the people. The Constitution should be strictly construed to the end that the states be protected in their rights from the encroachments of Federal power. The Federal government should always act in the general interest; never in the interest of a special group.

Where Jackson departed from the Jeffersonian tradition, the difference was often largely a matter of style. Where Jefferson believed that a good government was one which operated so quietly as to go almost unnoticed, Jackson acted on the principle that a good democratic government ought to trumpet forth in the name of the people now and then. Where Jefferson, fearing the city mobs, placed his reliance upon those "who labor in the earth," Jackson presented himself as the spokesman for the workingman as well as the farmer. In practice, however, the two followed very similar policies toward those who labored in the shops and mills. The Jeffersonians had eagerly made common cause, both with the urban radicalism of the Democratic-Republican societies, and with the urban political machinery of the Tammany Society. Jackson, on the other hand, while drawing political strength from these same elements, showed no marked interest in the problems which were peculiarly those of the city worker. It was his successor, Van Buren, who set out to secure the workingman's vote by adopting measures, notably the ten-hour working day, which were demanded by urban workers particularly, rather than by laboring classes as a whole. Most Americans were still farmers in Jackson's day, and most of the laborers in whose name Jackson spoke were those who labored in the earth.

The most startling novelty to occur during Jackson's first year in office, his defense of the spoils system, was, at the time, largely academic. Concerning the inevitable redistribution of political offices which accompanied the change in administrations, Jackson presented an aggressive defense on democratic grounds. Rotation in office, he said, freed the nation's government from control by an entrenched bureaucracy. To argue that public offices should remain in the hands of those trained by experience to perform them was to call democracy itself into question. "The duties of all public offices are, or at least admit of being made, so plain and simple that men of intelligence may readily qualify themselves for their performance." Jackson's defense of the spoils system shocked those who were prepared to be shocked by anything that this plebian President said, and certainly it was a world apart from Jefferson's idea of a natural aristocracy. In practice, however, Jackson showed considerable restraint in his redistribution of the patronage. The turnover in personnel was roughly comparable to that which had taken place under Jefferson. After Jackson, President Van Buren, who, of course, inherited an administration he himself had helped to staff, made only eighty removals. It was not until the forties that the spoils system really came into its own.

No part of the Jackson administration has been so widely and uncompromisingly denounced by historians as Jackson's defense of the spoils system; yet, as Carl Russell Fish pointed out, the system was essential to the very existence of democracy. Some citizens there no doubt were who would exert themselves politically with no thought of patronage, but they would be exceptional. The people as a whole could be expected to play an active and effective role in the maintenance of their governments only through political parties which could keep discipline based upon expectations of future rewards. In the Old South, Fish noted, democracy, in terms of a broad suffrage, existed everywhere by the eve of the Civil War, but it existed without elaborate party organization and without the spoils system, and the aristocracy did not find it difficult to control the state governments.

There remained a further basic difference between Jeffersonian republicanism and Jacksonian democracy: Jackson rejected the Jeffersonian idea that government was a necessary evil and by its very nature an abridgement of liberty. "There are no necessary evils in government," he declared. "Its evils exist only in its abuses. If it would confine itself to equal protection, and, as Heaven does its rains, shower its favors alike on the high and the low, the rich and the poor, it would be an unqualified blessing." Jefferson, with his generation, feared the tyranny of the majority. Jackson supposed that the nation was secure against tyranny so long as it was under majority rule. As the first President literally to represent the popular will, Jackson conceived of himself as the embodiment of the majority, and in its name the special guardian of the Constitution.

It was in his emphasis upon the sovereign will of the majority that Jackson departed farthest from Jeffersonian republicanism. While Jefferson, with John Locke, had viewed sovereignty as residing in the will of the majority, those two political philosophers of the enlightenment had proceeded from the original assumption that men were endowed by their Creator with inalienable rights, and that the purpose of governments was to secure them in these rights. What was to be done if the majority asserted its sovereignty for the purpose of depriving individuals of their inalienable rights? Locke did not meet this problem, but there can be no doubt as to how he would have resolved it. For Locke and for Jefferson the whole purpose of society was to secure the liberty of the individual. For Jackson this was not the case. The individual already was sufficiently secure in his rights, protected by common law, by the first nine amendments to the Constitution, by the balance of powers within the Federal government, and by the balance of powers between the Federal and the state governments. These arrangements, devised by America's "sages and patriots," were accepted by Jackson as "sacred." At the same time, all of these arrangements together did not entitle the individual to flaunt the will of the majority. For Jackson, and for Jacksonian democracy, those citizens who opposed the will of the majority were the enemies of democracy, and, the sacred principles of the Constitution aside, they should be treated accordingly.

Jacksonian democracy demanded social as well as political conformity to the will of the majority. The man who differed from his neighbors publicly in matters of dress, speech, morals, or religion risked a tarring and feathering, and rightly so. The history of Joseph Palmer is a case in point, though no doubt an extreme one. Palmer, an eccentric Massachusetts farmer, was "Persecuted for Wearing the Beard," as his gravestone testifies. Palmer wore a full beard during the Age of Jackson, at a time when it was customary to go about cleanshaven. This defiance of accepted convention was more than the democratic community of Fitchburg, Massachusetts, could tolerate. Palmer's physician told him to shave; that he was spreading disease. Ministers labored to bring him out of his waywardness, and the minister of his own church attempted to prohibit him from receiving communion. When argument did not suffice, Palmer was set upon by men of the town, who attempted to shave him forcibly.

When some of his assailants were injured in the struggle, Palmer was jailed on charges of unprovoked assault. Refusing to pay his fine, he

remained in jail, where the jailer and the prisoners attempted unsuccessfully in their turn to force him to shave. He remained in jail for a
year, until unfavorable publicity resulted in his release. A temperance
man, abolitionist and advocate of a wide number of reforms, he moved
on to help Bronson Alcott found a utopian community, Fruitlands. To
Alcott and the Transcendentalists, Palmer's brand of crusty individualism
was a vital part of American democracy. That was not the view of the
democratic majority, however. To the majority, the ideals of democracy
called for identification with the community and conformity to the accepted social and moral code.

Amid the fierce sectarian struggles of the period, Jacksonian democracy
demanded at least an outward show of conformity to Christian belief.
Jefferson, a religious liberal, understood religious liberty as including the
right to be a professing atheist. Jacksonian democracy did not join him
in this view. The nation accepted the doctrine of separation of church
and state necessarily, in the face of the fact that no sect was sufficiently
dominant to establish itself against the competition of rival sects. But
the view that an atheist could be a good American was not widely held.
Jackson personally accepted the principle of religious liberty as part of
the sacred order of things. That was not to say that he was ever quite
easy with it. On Sunday mornings, Parton relates, Jackson would say to
his guests, "Gentlemen, do what you please in my house; *I* am going
to church." Among Jackson's advisers there were religious liberals and
outright materialists, but the religious views of these men were suffered,
rather than gladly tolerated, by Jackson and by Jacksonian democracy.

II

Jackson's first administration was a democratic pageant; his second
was a democratic crusade. Until the veto of the bank bill late in his
first term, Jackson led a party without a political program of its own,
and it was no doubt the deep desire of his political lieutenants that he
avoid ever arriving at a program. Jackson had been elected by high-
tariff and low-tariff men, by broad nationalists and states-rights men, by
inflationists and hard-money men, and by friends and foes of internal
improvements. Under such circumstances the interests of the party
seemed best served by doing as little as possible about anything.

Jackson, himself, seemed to think that he possessed a political program
and, furthermore, that he had presented it to the public in his first
annual message to Congress. The message contained no specific recommendations concerning domestic legislation, however, and it led to the

passage of no bill. The Peggy Eaton episode was by far the most important event of Jackson's first three presidential years, when the chivalrous President used the full weight of his office to defend the wife of his friend the Secretary of War, John Eaton, against the snobbery and aspersions of Washington society. The event was important because it contributed to the political break between Jackson and Vice-President Calhoun, the husband of Washington's leading socialite. As the most important event to follow the democratic revolution of 1828, however, the Eaton episode was significantly lacking in ideological import.

Second in importance to the Eaton episode during those years was the Maysville Road bill veto, which placed Jackson in opposition to Federally financed intrastate internal improvements, on grounds of both economy and constitutionality. Jackson broke no new political ground with the veto, however. He merely reaffirmed a principle established by several of his predecessors. Nor did the veto commit Jackson to any very clear policy in the field of internal improvements, for subsequently he signed other very similar measures, on the grounds that they were national rather than local in scope, and the Federal internal improvements program did not diminish during his administration. Not even his chief Whig opponent Henry Clay could find in Jackson's vigorously worded veto a campaign issue for 1832. Jackson's treatment of the tariff question was similarly vague, cautious, and middle-of-the-road. He signed both the tariff of 1832 and the compromise tariff of 1833, but neither of them was passed as an administration measure. They were associated rather with his presidential rival Clay. They hardly could serve to separate the Jacksonians from their political opponents.

Had Jackson not been presented by Congress with a bill rechartering the United States Bank in 1832, he would have entered the campaign for re-election as little involved in any real political issues as he had been four years earlier. As it happened, Nicholas Biddle, director of the bank, called for a new charter four years before the expiration of the existing one. Biddle and Congressional leaders, knowing Jackson's hostility to the bank, reasoned that political considerations would force Jackson to sign the bill, if it were presented to him before the election. Jackson returned the bill to Congress with what has remained the most famous veto in American history, and he launched an attack which continued throughout his second term, serving, more than any other circumstance, to crystallize the national political forces at last into two separate organized political parties of Whig and Democrat.

In vetoing the bill Jackson followed his own private convictions. Typically, the veto for him was as much a private matter between himself and Biddle as it was a matter of political principle. "The bank is trying to kill me," Jackson told Van Buren, "but I will kill it." As Richard Hofstadter writes, the challenge aroused the dueling instinct in Jackson. The glove was thrown down, and Jackson picked it up—and instinctively in the name of the people and against the forces of wealth and privilege. The bank war made Jackson the hero of radical democrats, many of whom had shown little previous enthusiasm for the old hero of Horseshoe Bend. In American financial history the bank bill veto was a disastrous error which committed the nation for a century to the least serviceable banking system of any major industrial nation in the world. In the history of American democracy it was a heroic attack by the people's President against the bastion of wealth and privilege. With the bank bill veto, Jacksonian democracy at last went into action on a national scale.

Jackson's veto was vigorously forthright in style, and electric with ideology.

It is to be regretted that the rich and powerful too often bend the acts of government to their selfish purposes. Distinctions in society will always exist under every just government. Equality of talents, of education, or of wealth can not be produced by human institutions. In the full enjoyment of the gifts of Heaven and the fruits of superior industry, economy, and virtue, every man is equally entitled to protection by law; but when the laws undertake to add to these natural and just advantages artificial distinctions, to grant titles, gratuities, and exclusive privileges, to make the rich richer and the potent more powerful, the humble members of society—the farmers, mechanics, and laborers—who have neither the time nor the means of securing like favors to themselves, have a right to complain of the injustice of their Government.

This line of argument, although it represented the dominant economic radicalism of democratic America, was neither novel nor peculiar to American democratic thought, except in its aversion to titles and its pointed concern for the farmers, mechanics, and laborers. With those exceptions, the statement might well have been presented more than two centuries earlier amid loud cheers to that Elizabethan House of Commons which in 1601 successfully forced the Queen to rescind certain chartered monopolies.

Considering the strength of the anti-monopoly spirit in English tradition, the wonder is that the spirit emerged so late in American history and remained relatively so impotent. Part of the reason no doubt lies in the fact that almost all of the American colonies came into existence as state or private monopolies, and that colonial and frontier conditions necessitated a large measure of government supervision. Then, once independence was won, the American people tended to the view that they controlled their own governments and therefore had little to fear from the monopoly-creating power. The United States began life with a long-established tradition of government economic regulation to the minutest detail, including government-chartered local monopolies over a wide variety of economic activities.

The Bible of economic liberalism, Adam Smith's *Wealth of Nations* was published in the same year that Jefferson wrote the *Declaration of Independence*. The *Wealth of Nations* was the economic declaration of independence for the British businessman, who went on to win England to free trade over the opposition of the landed interests during the second quarter of the nineteenth century. Jacksonian America, meanwhile, experienced a somewhat similar struggle with the sides roughly reversed. The landed interests of the Cotton Kingdom won a partial victory for free trade over the opposition of the tariff-minded business community. Economic liberalism, in the sense of free trade, was never accepted by the American businessman, and, if it was accepted privately by Jackson, he did not advocate it as President.

Jackson did place himself at the forefront of the anti-monopoly fight with his bank bill veto, but he did so in a highly qualified manner. The veto lashed out at the principle of monopoly itself, but specifically it was an attack upon a national, as opposed to a state, monopoly. Indeed one of Jackson's arguments against the bank was that it infringed upon the rights of the less powerful banks which had been chartered by the states. The monopolistic state banking interests fully appreciated this argument, as their strong support of Jackson indicated in 1832.

The truth is that even in the heyday of Jacksonian democracy the anti-monopoly spirit, although it dominated one wing of the Democratic party, did not triumph in the nation. As the industrial revolution progressed, the scope of government regulation widened, and the chartering of government monopolies of banks as well as of bridges, canals, turnpikes, and then railroads, continued. These monopolies brought criticism, but they were nevertheless accepted as the most expeditious means of exploiting the resources of the nation. The nearest approach to the triumph of liberal capitalism in the age of Jackson was the passage of uniform laws of incorporation in various states, giving any group an equal chance to enter a field of economic activity—banking for instance —providing it fulfilled the general requirements of the law. In the pre-Civil War period, however, most corporations continued to operate under special charters.

In the meantime, the Jacksonian Supreme Court handed down a series of decisions, most notably the Charles River Bridge case, attacking the vested interest of old chartered companies, where their assertion of monopoly rights interfered with the rights of the community, in a country "free, active, and enterprising, continually advancing in numbers and wealth." To spokesmen for vested interest, the Charles River Bridge case was a Jacobinical attack upon the rights of private property. Actually it was a sensible decision which, as Charles Warren has written, encouraged "all business men who contemplated investments of capital in new corporate enterprise and who were relieved against claims of monopoly concealed in ambiguous clauses of old charters."

The notion that economic liberalism emerged hand in hand with political liberalism in America outside the planting states is absurdly false, as recent studies of Massachusetts, Pennsylvania, Georgia, and Missouri make abundantly clear. In each of these states down to the Civil War the governments engaged themselves vigorously and un-self-consciously in regulating, financing, and even administering, a bewildering variety of economic activities. "Massachusetts observers," wrote Oscar and Mary Handlin, "conceived of the beneficent hand of the state as reaching out to touch every part of the economy." The Locofoco movement in attacking monopolies was not proposing *laissez faire*. The Locofocos accepted government control, and they did not oppose government support for private enterprise. They simply wished, as Jackson said, to live under a government which would "shower its favors alike on the high and the low, the rich and poor." Jefferson the Physiocrat was an advocate of *laissez faire,* and he was joined in this doctrine by other southern planters, who wished to be let alone on their lordly plantations. The doctrine did not fail altogether to win its converts in the North as well, especially in academic circles, but it was no significant part of Jacksonian democracy. Its strength remained with the broadcloth party of southern Whig planters.

In one respect, however, Jackson was curiously Jeffersonian in his economic views. A successful career as lawyer, land speculator, and merchant had failed to win him away from the ascetic policy of hard money. To the enterprising America of Jacksonian democracy banking institutions were absolute necessities. The railroad age was unthinkable without the existence of extensive credit; yet Jackson, with the left wing Locofoco Democrats, was opposed to all banks. Metallic currency was the only honest currency. Bank notes were means by which the wealth produced by labor was syphoned off to the financial manipulators—the monocrats. Jackson favored the entire elimination of banking institutions, and he was joined in this wish by certain of his leading advisers and supporters, including Thomas Hart Benton, Roger B. Taney, and Van Buren. Their views, as Bray Hammond has written, "belonged with an idealism in which America was still a land of refuge and freedom rather than a place to make money," the land of Jefferson's golden dream, where commerce and industry would remain the handmaidens of agriculture, in a nation of self-sufficient farmers.

Upon this subject Jacksonian democracy was divided, however, and so were Jackson's lieutenants. Among his closest advisers Jackson counted men who had been closely connected with state banks and who represented the more enterprising wing of the party. These easy money Democrats, especially the state banking interests, disliked the United States Bank, not on hard money grounds, but on grounds that the bank imposed a restraint upon their own lending activities. They wished to destroy the bank to free themselves from all central control. Facing the election of 1832, Jackson worded his veto in such a way as to commit himself to neither wing of his party. The veto made no criticism of the state banks or of banks as such, and it suggested no alternative to the United States Bank. It straddled the issue so successfully that Jackson entered the campaign with the enthusiastic support of both the hard money men and the state banking interests.

Jackson's policy toward the bank during his second administration reflected the ambivalent character of his political following. Upon his reelection Jackson struck at the bank by removing Federal funds and distributing them among "pet" state banks. The banks were requested not to use the funds for speculative purposes, but nothing was done to enforce the request. The banks naturally followed their inclinations, and a rapid extension of credit ensued. At the same time, the national debt was paid off, and Congress enacted the Jacksonian policy of distributing the surplus revenue among the states, thus further accelerating the inflationary tendency. Then, during his last year in office, Jackson reverted to his hard-money principles with the Specie Circular, requiring specie payments for public lands, and helping to trigger the panic of 1837. The panic broke upon the country several months after Jackson went into retirement in the Hermitage.

Inheriting the panic as well as the concerted animosity of the dominant economic interests of the nation, Jackson's successor, Van Buren, moved unsuccessfully to settle the crisis according to hard-money principles. An independent treasury would be established to hold government funds where they could not be used for speculative purposes. Against the hard-money program of Van Buren the business interests struggled without final success until the Civil War, when southern secession gave them the opportunity to pass new laws authorizing the establishment of banks under a uniform national charter.

Within the Jacksonian ranks the bank war revealed the fundamental conflict between the Jeffersonian ideal of the simple, virtuous, agrarian society and the democratic reality of an acquisitive society which could call upon its government to assist in the exploitation of a continent. Senator Benton indignantly declared that he "did not join in putting down the Bank of the United States to put up a wilderness of local banks." It did not matter. His old-fashioned intentions were powerless to alter the fact. In attempting to make democratic practice conform to Jeffersonian theory he was attempting the impossible. Democratic America believed with Abraham Lincoln that "it is best for all to leave each man free to acquire property as fast as he can," and the motto for democratic government was, "boost; don't knock."

CHAPTER 30

AMERICAN CULTURE IN
THE NINETEENTH CENTURY

Historians have traditionally paid their respects to certain aspects of the culture of the people about whom they are writing. They have dutifully commented on the great literature, music, and artwork of various nations or areas of the world, and have measured the extent to which artists and men of letters have been supported in their own countries. But in the past two decades American historians in particular have turned more and more to a consideration of cultural history more broadly conceived. Now attention is given not only to what might be termed "high culture" but also, increasingly, to the activities, the attitudes, the values, and the mores of the thousands or millions of ordinary persons who make up a particular society. Considered in this sense, the term "culture" refers to the life-style or patterns of living of the people concerned.

History of this type is difficult to write. Political figures, military leaders, writers, and the like generally leave records that allow an assessment of their activities and thought. But, as Ruth Miller Elson points out in this selection, determining what the ordinary person of the past thought and did is a much more difficult task. Contrary to much opinion, however, the task is not impossible. There are historical sources that give us insights into the attitudes and ideals that influenced the lives of the common people of the past. In the essay that follows, Professor Elson uses American schoolbooks of the nineteenth century for this purpose. She seeks specifically to determine what the ordinary American in the young nation thought and felt about the necessity of encouraging activity in scholarship and the fine arts. Her study also tells us much about the attitudes, beliefs, and values that helped to shape the American character and history during the nineteenth century.

Professor Elson's essay is based on the premise that the schoolbooks of the nineteenth century provide a valid reflection of the values and thought of that day, but she also suggests that these widely read works had a tremendous influence on the creation of American traditions and character traits. To what extent do you agree with the latter assumption? What were the major ideas and concepts that the schoolbooks presented as constituting the ideal American character configuration? According to Professor Elson, what were the criteria set forth in the schoolbooks for determining what was good art or scholarship in the nineteenth century? Finally, to what extent does the concept of utility still influence American attitudes toward artistic and scholarly activity?

The literature in the subject area of this topic is extensive. An older work, Alice Felt Tyler, *Freedom's Ferment: Phases of American Social History to 1860** (1944), is still valuable. Vernon Louis Parrington, *Main Currents in American Thought:* Volume II, *The Romantic Revolution in America, 1800–1860** (1930), is dated but it is useful despite its biases. Two newer surveys are C. S. Griffin, *The Ferment of Reform, 1830–1860** (1967), and Charles A. Baker, *American Convictions: Cycles of Public Thought, 1600–1950* (1970). Professor Elson has expanded her treatment of the subject matter of this essay in *Guardians of Tradition: American Schoolbooks of the 19th Century* (1964).

* Available in a paperback edition.

AMERICAN SCHOOLBOOKS AND "CULTURE" IN THE NINETEENTH CENTURY
RUTH MILLER ELSON

Does America have a culture of its own? Has America contributed to that concept of culture which Noah Webster and the nineteenth century defined as "the enlightenment and refinement of taste acquired by intellectual and aesthetic training"? This issue has been lightly and hotly debated across the Atlantic for a century and a half, and European criticisms of our contributions to scholarship and the fine arts made Americans painfully sensitive to any trans-Atlantic discussions in these areas. But the discussion in the United States was continuous; it reached points of egocentric frenzy at times when Americans were particularly proud of themselves in other respects vis-à-vis Europe, as in the periods after the American Revolution, the War of 1812, and World War II. The discussion has generally revolved around two questions: Has the United States produced art and scholarship of a quality comparable to that of Europe? Has the United States a literary and aesthetic culture of its own?

After the Revolution these issues were posed by American writers and intellectuals when they called for the development of a distinctively American culture. Immediately after the achievement of American political independence, Noah Webster hoped to separate America from Britain culturally by the creation of a distinctive American system of spelling. Charles Brockden Brown called on American literary men to use the resources of the American scene and, in his novel *Wieland,* illustrated his point by transposing the Gothic novel from the ruined castle of Europe to the American forest. In 1837 Ralph Waldo Emerson issued his famous declaration of independence for American scholars in an address at Harvard. The activities of James Fenimore Cooper, William Cullen Bryant, and others in calling for an American art as well as in creating one are well known.

That the American intellectual in the first part of our national existence wished to encourage American creativity in the fine arts and in scholarship cannot be questioned. But was the ordinary American aware of this? Was he encouraged to consider these fields worth cultivating in America? Was the

SOURCE. Elson, Ruth Miller, "American Schoolbooks and 'Culture' in the Nineteenth Century," *Mississippi Valley Historical Review, XLVI* (December 1959), 411–434. Reprinted by permission of *The Journal of American History* (formerly *The Mississippi Valley Historical Review*) and the Author.

intellectual climate in which the American lived favorable to the development of American scholars, or were potential scholars generally turned into the more useful field of schoolteaching? Was the American public encouraged to consider the fine arts an important element in national development?

What the a-verbal man of the past thought about anything is probably forever lost to historical research. But by examining the books that most Americans read one can at least discover those ideas to which they were exposed. In the nineteenth century, apart from the Bible, the books most widely read were not those written by intellectuals, but schoolbooks written by printers, journalists, future lawyers earning their way through college, teachers, and ministers. However ill-qualified to do so, the authors of schoolbooks both created and solidified American traditions. The selective process by which they decided what political, economic, social, cultural, and moral concepts should be presented to American youth undoubtedly helped to form the average American's view of the past, the present, and the possible future of man. Their choice of what was to be admired in the past and present and preserved for the future was likely to be the first formal evaluation of man and his works to which the child was exposed, and it came to him from authority. The schoolbooks also delineated for the American child an idealized image of himself and of the history that had produced the much-admired American type. These books, then, were a kind of compendium of ideas popularly approved at the time, and they are an excellent index of concepts considered proper for the nineteenth-century American. And while their nationalism demanded pride in American productions of any sort, they were far from encouraging to the potential artist or scholar. In these schoolbooks, scholarship and the fine arts were considered fields unfit for the American.

The primary intellectual value embodied in these books is that the only important knowledge is that which is "useful." The word "knowledge" is so often preceded by the word "useful" that it is clear only such knowledge is approved, and it is this kind of knowledge that is provided by a sound education. Useful knowledge is presumed to be uniquely characteristic of American education. . . .

And because of our special preparation in this kind of knowledge, the useful arts have become the peculiar province of the American. A reader of the 1850's notes: "In the arts which contribute to domestic culture and national aggrandizement, the American states will sustain no unfavorable comparison with Europe." By the latter part of the century American achievements in this area have been recognized by all: "The ingenuity of the people of the United States has passed into a proverb. To them are due many of the inventions which have contributed most to the comfort and improvement of the race." Thus useful knowledge is interpreted in a narrow sense; those arts that are functional to a more comfortable material life are equated to republicanism and to Americanism. Talents in these fields are inherent in the Americans and unique to them: "While many other nations are wasting the brilliant efforts of genius in monuments of ingenious folly, to perpetuate their pride, the Americans, according to the true spirit of republicanism, are employed almost entirely in works of public and private utility."

In all of these books the fact that we have not produced scholars is noted with pride as a sign that knowledge is democratically diffused instead of being concentrated in the hands of an upper class. . . . Our institutions of higher learning are not designed to produce scholars; they are institutions

> Where homebred freemen seize the solid prize;
> Fixt in small spheres with safer beams to shine.
> They reach the useful and refuse the fine,
> Found on its proper base, the social plan,
> The broad plain truths, the common sense of man.

. . . Instead of an isolated group of scholars toiling away in useless labor we produce educated men whose minds are bent to the improvement of society. "The greatest scholars of the country . . . have not deemed the latter [schoolbooks] an unworthy labor." Most of our learned men "are so devoted to the instruction of youth, or the active employments of life, as to leave little opportunity for the prosecution of literary research, or scientific discovery." And indeed the actual situation described here was sometimes elevated and abstracted into a principle of virtuous behavior for scholars: "It is not in literary production only, or chiefly, that the educated mind finds fit expression, and fulfills its mission in honor and beneficence. In the great theatre of the world's affairs there is a worthy and sufficient sphere." Even on an elementary level scholarship was associated with Europe rather than with America. A delightful illustration of this occurs in an 1828 reader. Next to a picture entitled "German with Book" is the sentence: "The Germans read, write, and think a great deal." Such activities were evidently not to be regarded by the child as part of the ordinary life of man, but were worthy of note as functions of a particular foreign culture.

Besides reserving education for the elite and sponsoring useless knowledge, the European universities have another serious disadvantage which is corrected in American institutions of higher learning. "The colleges and universities of Europe differ materially from those of the United States. They are rather places of study for such as wish to acquire knowledge. Scarcely any control or care is exercised over the character and conduct of the students, and their efforts are purely voluntary." As a result, although the European university produced serious scholars it also produced men learned in the ways of drink, gambling, dissipation, and vice—activities that aroused transports of horror in the schoolbooks.

The picture of the American college in these schoolbooks is one of an institution designed to inculcate moral values rather than intellectual ones; it should instill useful knowledge in the sense of principles useful to the maintenance of Christianity (Protestant, except in those books written for the parochial schools), the American form of government, and the American society. The colleges were firmly founded on the principle stated by Webster in a most popular 1805 reader: "How little of our peace and security depends on REASON and how much on *religion* and *government.*" The function of the American college was to produce men who were prepared to uphold the values already dominant in society rather than to examine them critically. It was the formation of character and sound principles rather than the pursuit of truth that was to engage the university student. This conception of the function of higher education in America has interesting implications for the principle of academic freedom. If the primary duty of the professor is to train the student in principles accepted as good by American society, then it is logical to contend that American society has the right to investigate the beliefs held by college teachers.

It was not the university, however, that was regarded in American schoolbooks as the most effective carrier of civilization; it was rather the common school that was to perpetuate what the authors considered most important in American civilization. Every author pointed with pride to the public school system as one of the most distinctive features of American civilization. A typical statement, emphasizing spread rather than depth, is the following: "Education is more widely diffused in this than in any other country in the world." And America's devotion to universal education is old: "The idea of popular education was brought to the new world by our forefathers. Even in the wilderness, while the wolf prowled about the log-house, and the cry of the wild-cat was still heard, the school and even the college, were established."

But it is clear from the books used in these schools that the purpose of the common school as well as of the university was to train the heart rather than the head. Emma Willard's preface to her 1868 history was quite explicit: "We have, indeed, been desirous to cultivate the memory, the intellect and the taste. But much more anxious have we been to sow the seeds of virtue by showing the good in such amicable lights that the youthful heart shall kindle into desires of imitation." That virtue is superior to knowledge or even to wisdom was stressed, as in this admonition by Alice Cary: "Little children, you must seek Rather to be good than wise"; or, on a more advanced level, "Man's intellect is not man's sole nor best adorning." It has often been stated in histories of American education that the American public school system was instituted to train citizens, native and immigrant, and to equalize classes, but the evidence of the schoolbooks would seem to indicate that this was to be accomplished by training character as well as by imparting knowledge. The "useful knowledge" offered in the school was useful to success in the material world, but it was also aimed to produce those qualities of character that we associate both with Puritanism and with the self-made man: thrift, hard work, and the rejection of frivolity.

In the early readers and spellers most of the literary excerpts are taken from *The Tatler* and *The Spectator,* from the writings of Franklin, Pope, Sterne, Dryden, Swift, and from various religious tracts. From the 1820's on the contemporary literature of Romanticism became dominant, and remained so throughout the century, disregarding newer trends in literature. Bryant, Longfellow, Whittier, Emerson, and watered down versions of these were fed to the child in a steady diet. Heroism, death, illness, decay, a mystical nationalism, a transcendental approach to nature, and the process of winning success against great odds were the popular subjects. But underlying all of these was the premise that the heart was more important than the head. The nearest approach to realism in the late nineteenth century was in the very large literature of the self-made man; here, although the head was important in achieving success, yet success came only to the pure in heart.

In the schoolbook characterizations of the great men of America some of the same attitudes are evident. All assumed that the function of American society was to produce men great in character as well as in achievements. And all were confident that America was peculiarly distinguished by these virtuous heroes; the United States "has already produced some of the greatest and best men who have ever lived." . . . The distinction between the great men of Europe and those of America was a sharp one in the schoolbooks. American heroes were distinguished for their virtue; European heroes were remembered for their vices as soldiers, or as "great scholars who were pensioned flatterers of power, and poets, who profaned the high gift of genius, to pamper the vices of a corrupted court."

The two men who appeared most often and most emphatically as heroes were George Washington and Benjamin Franklin. In words attributed to John Quincy Adams: "What other two men, whose lives belong to the eighteenth century of Christendom, have left a deeper impression of themselves upon the age in which they lived, and upon all after time?" The heroic stature of Washington was unique; he appeared rather as divinity than as man. As a Christlike liberator the contrast between Washington and European heroes was sharp indeed. That this greatest of all men appeared in the United States is sufficient justification for American civilization. . . . The same idea is contained in an excerpt from Daniel Webster's oration at

Bunker Hill in 1843, which appears in many books: "America has furnished to the world the character of Washington! And if our American institutions had done nothing else, that alone would have entitled them to the respect of mankind."

As they did with all hero-figures, the textbook authors attach to Washington's prestige-giving figure the virtues that they expect the child to emulate, whether these bear any resemblance to the hero's life or not. He is brave, charitable, industrious, religious, courteous, and a paragon of the domestic virtues. The best qualities of the self-made man are his, and from the 1840's on he is exalted as such in many books. But in no instance are intelligence, learning, or disinterested inquiry associated with Washington. Indeed, in some of the later books he is specifically shown as a practical man who rejected the intellectual life. It is said that "He was more solid than brilliant, and had more judgment than genius. He had great dread of public life, cared little for books, and possessed no library." As a child Washington "was fonder of playing out of doors than study in school, for he was a strong, manly boy, who could best all his school-mates in their sports." This would seem to imply an unbridgeable abyss between the physically active boy and the student, between the successful man of affairs and the scholar. Manliness and scholarship would seem to be antithetical. And manliness was for the American, scholarship for the effete European.

Nor are intellectual qualities attached, as in this case they might logically be, to the second hero-figure of these books—Benjamin Franklin. It is not Franklin the scientist, cosmopolite, and democrat who appears here; it is rather Franklin the Apotheosis of the self-made man. His temperance, industry, and thrift are praised to the highest degree as ends in themselves rather than as the conveniences that they seemed to be to Franklin himself. His biography appears many times, and almost every schoolbook contains some of his adages with or without acknowledgment of their source. Washington is the hero of great actions and virtue; Franklin is the typical American writ large. But in both cases it is moral and patriotic rather than intellectual stature that elevates these Americans.

The only public figure to whom scholarship is ever a sign of distinction is Thomas Jefferson, but he is a quite minor figure in these books, only occasionally noted as a scholar. He is more than offset by Daniel Boone, a figure with obvious appeal to schoolchildren, and one who was "ignorant of books, but versed in the forest and forest life." The American hero-figure was stereotyped, then, as a practical, moral, hard-working man who needs "useful knowledge" to get ahead in the world, but finds scholarship unnecessary and even demeaning.

Was the child specifically encouraged to read on his own? He was exhorted to apply the Franklin virtues to his school work and to the acquisition of "useful knowledge" as a part of his struggle for success in the world. But doubts were frequently expressed as to both the quantity and the quality of books that he should read. He must be careful not to read too much: "She is a strange child. She will take a book and read it while the boys and girls run and play near her. I fear she reads and thinks too much. The brain must have rest." Furthermore the frequent appearance of excerpts from the writings of Emerson and Wordsworth, shorn in this context of transcendental qualities, seems to recommend the achievement of the good life only by the rejection of the intellectual life in favor of direct experience. . . . Taken out of context in this way, Wordsworth (more popular in the first half of the century) and Emerson (popular in the second half of the century) seem to stand for anti-intellectualism rather than awareness of the insufficiency of reason. There are countless tales of the value of direct experience over the value of book experience. A typical case is the tale of a boy forced by family difficulties to go to work rather than to go on with school. A merchant about to hire him gives him this advice: "Manhood is better than Greek. Self-reliance is worth more to a man than Latin." Here, obviously, it is the self-reliance of self-support in a financial, not a spiritual sense that is considered desirable. Emerson has been adapted to the market place.

Apart from the question of quantity, it was thought that reading must be carefully limited in quality to those books that impart "useful knowledge" and that strengthen character. William H. McGuffey, for example, believed that only "good" books are to be used—books that will inspire the reader with "love of what is right and useful." He continued: "Next to the fear of God, implanted in the heart nothing is a better safeguard to character, than the love of good books. They are the handmaids of virtue and religion." Conversely: "Bad books are the public fountains of vice." The reading of novels (and few distinctions are made among them) was almost always condemned in the first half of the century, and frequently in the latter half. An 1868 reader, in seeking the cause of the complete deterioration of a character under discussion, asks: "Is it the bottle or the betting book? Is it the billiard table or the theatre? Is it smoking? Is it laziness? Is it novel-reading?" So the child was cautioned to read with great selectivity—a selectivity based not on training one's taste by wide reading but by canons laid down by authority. He was not only warned not to read too much, but his purpose in reading was to be censored. To read for pleasure was frowned upon: "A book which is torn and mutilated is abused, but one which is merely read for enjoyment is misused."

It is clear from this evidence that anti-intellectualism is not only not new in American civilization, but that it is thoroughly embedded in the schoolbooks that have been read by generations of pupils since the beginning of the republic. The rejection of the intellectual required the rejection of an intellectual past—that of the Puritans and of the founders of the republic—as part of the American tradition. The frontier did not need scholarship, whereas "useful knowledge" was essential to survival. And the needs of the frontier were probably reinforced by the needs of expanding business. Thus an 1875 speller records current attitudes in saying: "We do not blame a man who is proud of his success, so much as one who is vain of his learning."

To these schoolbook writers the concept of "usefulness" was perhaps even more important for the fine arts than for the intellectual elements of American culture. Historically, the arts occupied a quite different position from that of scholarship in American development. In undertaking to determine what was to be considered the American tradition it was possible to draw upon an actual scholarly heritage; but the arts had always been held in a distinctly subservient position in America. In the colonial period literary labors were made to serve theology and politics, but the visual and auditory arts were regarded with suspicion by New Englanders as being inconsistent with Puritan precautions against the seductiveness of the senses. It was also true that in a frontier environment relatively few had the leisure or the opportunity to participate, either as creator or as audience, in the fine arts and belles-lettres. Yet by the nineteenth century America had produced many creative artists whose art was not designed to serve some other cause; and the fact that their work was too important to be ignored raises questions as to how the schoolbooks evaluated their contributions. Was the American child in this period, for example, taught to regard the arts as worthy of serious attention? To what extent were they considered to be essential or, at the least, important to national development?

Music and the fine arts appeared in these schoolbooks primarily in discussions of three subjects: the self-made artist, national monuments, and evaluations of American art. Those paintings and sculptures that glorified American heroes and the American past were frequently noted. For example, the statues of Washington in Richmond, Baltimore, and Raleigh were almost always mentioned in the sections of the geographies devoted to those cities. But discussions of the aesthetic qualities of such works are absent; they are to be observed for nationalistic rather than for aesthetic reasons.

Discussions of the fine arts appear mainly in the examples of self-made men in the field of the arts, and it is evident that in these tales their self-achieved success is more important than their art. The career of the Italian sculptor, Antonio Canova, for example, is described in the same terms as those used to describe the career of a successful businessman of the nineteenth century. The story of his boyhood act of carving a lion out of butter to provide a substitute for a centerpiece which had not been delivered was frequently told. He was praised, however, not as a man of artistic achievement but as one who "was diligent and regular in his habits," and who saw an opportunity for success and used it. A similar tale that appeared more often in the schoolbooks was that the American painter, Benjamin West, too poor as a boy to buy paint brushes, made them of hairs plucked from his cat's tail and taught himself to paint. "Thus we see," runs the moral, "that, by industry, ingenuity, and perseverance, a little American boy became the most distinguished painter of his day in England." Obviously, these are not discussions of talented artists but of self-made men who happened to be artists. Their success was accomplished by diligence combined with the ability to recognize opportunity.

The aesthetic theories held in these books necessarily settled the fine arts into a position inferior to that of literature. The statement that "Statues and pictures are pleasing representations of nature" expressed their attitude throughout the century, and Longfellow's aphorism, "Nature is a revelation of God, art is a revelation of man," was quoted to show that as imitations of nature works of art could never approach nature itself. According to this theory a landscape is of necessity more beautiful than a pleasing representation of it, and God, who is manifest through nature itself, can be discerned but dimly, if at all, through an imperfect imitation. Consequently in the schoolbooks painting and sculpture acquire importance only for extra-artistic qualities. Sculpture was useful to commemorate the dead, and the schoolbooks were not alone in the nineteenth century in recommending tours of the cemeteries of Philadelphia and Boston. But more important than this, the fine arts were useful in engendering nationalism by portraying American heroes and historical events. This is made quite clear in what purports to be an aesthetic judgment of the field of painting: "Q. What are the most esteemed paintings? A. Those representing historical events."

The most curious argument in favor of encouraging the fine arts in the United States, and indeed the only argument for encouraging them on any grounds, was presented in an 1826 reader under the heading "Usefulness of the Fine Arts." In this article the fine arts are recommended partly because they would produce a new class of people to be fed and, in the case of sculpture, would stimulate the marble and granite industries. Furthermore, those artists who did not succeed in the fine arts would then turn their talents to the useful arts in the clay, glass, and cotton industries. This process of failure in the fine arts had given England her lead in manufacturing. So, concluded this ingenious author, America should encourage the fine arts not for their own sakes, but that they may be transmuted into the useful arts and so stimulate American industry.

When the arts serve no useful project, however, they are often looked on with suspicion. In statement and by implication the schoolbooks fear that too much concentration on the arts is unhealthy and indeed dangerous to civilization. An excerpt from the writings of Hannah More as quoted in an 1876 text specifically warns of the possibility of such subversion: "It will be prudent to reflect, that in all polished countries an entire devotedness to the fine arts has been one grand source of the corruption of women. . . . And while corruption brought on by an excessive cultivation of the arts has contributed its full share to the decline of states, it has always furnished an infallible symptom of their impending fall." Art and the decadence of the individual and society are regarded as natural companions in many of these books. . . .

In the geographies which survey the state of civilization in every country, Europe is always introduced as the seat of the arts and sciences. But the Europe that has produced great art is also the Europe of rigid class distinctions, vice, and degeneracy. In particular, "The Italians are celebrated for their musical skill and perfection in the fine arts"; but the descriptions of Italian national character and Italian morals would hardly be a recommendation for accomplishments in the arts. Italy is generally described as a land of beggars, filth, and poverty, and the Italians as a degenerate, superstitious, revengeful, effeminate, and immoral people. This unfavorable view of the Italians was undoubtedly the result of a strong anti-Catholic bias in American schoolbooks, but the conjunction of such a national character with the greatest talents in the fine arts of any country in the world would hardly persuade the Americans that the cultivation of the fine arts was necessary for national development.

On the other hand, in the view of these schoolbooks art can and should have a moral purpose. It should show that virtue inevitably leads to beauty, and that the only true beauty is that which is equated to goodness. . . . But it was to literature rather than to painting and sculpture that the schoolbooks turned for their discussion of the relationship between beauty and goodness. The literary man, according to one of them, "thinks beautiful thoughts, and tells them in beautiful words, and he helps to make people better by showing how beautiful goodness is." Even here, however, it was content, not artistic form, that determined the merit of a literary production. The same piece (a comment on Henry Wadsworth Longfellow) goes on to say: "But it is not the way it is written that makes a poem, but rather the beautiful thought in it." Indeed it is clear from the literary excerpts in the spellers and readers (most of these, beyond the primer, are anthologies) that style was considered in the nature of a clever trick and was of very little importance to the authors and editors of these books. Wordsworth, Emerson, Irving, and Dickens are there, but they are outspaced by Alcott, Longfellow, Mrs. Hemans, Mrs. Sigourney, and Lydia Maria Child. Longfellow's poem "The Day Is Done" was taken to heart by these authors and editors, especially the passage in which the poet asks to have poetry read to him:

> Not from the grand old masters,
> Not from the bards sublime. . . .
>
> Read from some humbler poet,
>   Whose songs gushed from his heart,
> As showers from the clouds of summer
> Or tears from the eyelids start.

That good literature is thought to be moral, and to engender morality in its readers is evident in the following samples of the adjectives used in literary criticism in the schoolbooks: Bryant—"Lofty moral tone"; Alcott—"Healthy tone"; Whittier—"His verse is distinguished by vigor and a certain moral sweetness"; Scott—"Healthfulness of tone." And because moral qualities should be paramount in his writings, it was considered entirely proper to inquire into the author's moral behavior in life. Scott comes out very well in this respect. More attention is given in several books to his labors to pay back creditors than to his writings: "The sterling integrity of the man shown forth in this dark hour." This portrayal of an honest and industrious man was used as an introduction to and an evaluation of his writings. Byron, on the other hand, is to be read with caution. His poems are of "startling power on new and original themes. The principles inculcated in some of these shocked his countrymen, and still offend the moral sense of readers." Coleridge's use of opium and the dissipation of Burns interfered with and marred the work of these two writers. And ironically, Poe, the American writer of whom they could have been the most proud because of his European reputation, also falls into this category. Although his writings showed "marked ability, [they] are marred by their morbid subjects and their absence of moral feeling." "He was intemperate, quarrelsome and without business ability. . . . Nothing that he has written can fairly be called of a high class. His chief fame rests on his cleverness in constructing plots, and his use of the grotesque and weird." Only one book admits that although he led a dissipated life and died young in consequence, still "He left behind him some of the choicest treasures of American Literature." Frequently the introduction to a literary excerpt, and its moral evaluation of the author, is more extensive than the piece of literature itself. Literature was to be interpreted according to its moral tone; should it lack moral qualities or embody the wrong ones it was not good literature.

It should be noted that the selectivity used in discarding improper pieces from the schoolbooks did not operate as effectively in some of the books published before 1820. Excerpts from Shakespeare and Moliere used in that period did not always embody the "lofty moral tone" that later became standard in the schoolbooks. On the other hand, these pieces were often taken out of context in such peculiar ways that they made no sense, moral or otherwise. Pedagogical improvement changed the books in the latter respect, but also eliminated some subjects that had heretofore appeared.

From the 1820's on, all gambling, drinking, and laziness are condemned. All women are virtuous, or wish they had been as they sink into a miserable death; all widows are poor and honest; all married women are mothers with the virtues thereof; all self-respecting men try for financial success; there are no physical relations between the sexes even if hallowed by marriage. Yet this does not indicate a general denial of the material world, for the acquisition of goods by the individual and the nation is regarded as a national blessing. But just as Whitman is conspicuously absent from the anthologies, so the physical nature of man is a subject to be subdued if mentioned at all.

Throughout the century all of the schoolbooks were sensitive to such European criticisms as those of the Abbé Raynal, who had taken America to task for producing no important artists. Those published before 1830 responded by a simple rejection of Raynal's evaluation and by catalogues of the artists America had produced, such as Trumbull, Copley, West, Barlowe, and others. Many of the lists of American artists culminated with the name of George Washington! This would seem to indicate that the textbook authors were not arguing that America had produced better artists than those of Europe, but that she had produced greater men; and one Washington would obviously outweigh any number of artists or scholars. A typical early evaluation of American arts asserted that "Printing, engraving and architecture among the fine arts, as well as the mechanic arts, exhibit as much native genius in the United States as in any part of the world. This genius has been cultivated for the last few years to such a degree as, in some instances, to rival the most splendid and useful exhibitions of art in Europe." A few of the authors at the beginning of the century complained, however, that the American artist found it hard to make a living by his art. They ascribed this situation to the snobbish attitude of some Americans who believed that the only good art was European and refused to give any attention to art produced by an American.

After 1830 the textbook writers changed the grounds for their defense of American art. Abandoning their simple refusal to accept the low evaluation of our arts by European critics, they admitted our inferiority in the arts with an explanation. This inferiority, they said proudly, came from the fact that we had deliberately neglected the fine arts in favor of the arts that produce a comfortable and happy life for everyone. If the founders of America produced no great music, painting, sculpture, architecture, or literature, "It was enough for them to lay the foundation of that noble fabric of civil liberty."

McGuffey in 1858 lists freedom, useful knowledge, and patriotism as American gifts to the world which more than make up for our lack of artistic contributions. Our monuments are not Gothic cathedrals, said another commentary, but "an active, vigorous, intelligent, moral population." Thus the American answer to European critics from 1830 through the Civil War held that although American artists might not be equal to those of Europe, America had been engaged in producing something of far greater significance to the world—a superior society.

After the Civil War, however, American schoolbooks aggressively placed American artists and writers on a level with those of Europe. Bolstered by a newly proved nationalism and backed by solid accomplishments in American literature they were ready to refute European criticisms. "It is not long," one of them said, "since it was asked 'Who reads an American book?' Now the question is, who does not cherish as household words the names of our charming fiction writers, Irving, Cooper and Hawthorne—our historians, Bancroft, Prescott and Motley—our poets, Bryant and Longfellow, Halleck and Whittier, Lowell and Holmes?" The same author, however, evidently had some slight doubt about the status of American belles-lettres, because he added: "In magazines and school-books especially, the United States has nothing to fear from a comparison with the most cultivated of the older nations." By the 1870's there was general and confident agreement that America had her own literary culture. America has produced many authors, "some of whom have acquired a reputation even in the Old World, and whose works have now become sufficiently numerous and important to form an American literature." Two late-nineteenth-century authors admit that in the past "The greatest triumphs achieved in the United States have been in the direction of mechanical ingenuity; and American literature, science, and art have not yet won the applause of the world quite so thoroughly as have American sewing machines and agricultural implements." But both say that this is much less true in their day, and they are confident that it will be even less so in the future.

In rating American artists, the major criterion used in the schoolbooks is whether they compare favorably to European artists and whether they have been accepted abroad. Gilbert Stuart is proudly put into the first category: "Some critics think he is the best portrait painter of the age except for Joshua Reynolds." And American historiography comes out well by comparison to that of Europe: "Bancroft, Hildreth, Prescott and Motley stand among the best writers of history the world has ever produced." The great landmark in American literature came with its first recognition abroad. The distinction of being the first to achieve this is variously accorded to Irving and Cooper. The author who has brought greatest acclaim to American literature in the eyes of Europe is Emerson, and he is placed even above European writers. McGuffey records Matthew Arnold's opinion that Emerson's work was "the most important work done in prose" in the nineteenth century. At the end of the century this was reaffirmed: "Abroad, Emerson was recognized as a master-mind."

What made American literature American in the eyes of schoolbook writers? Was it part of American literature because it was produced by American citizens, or did it have characteristics of its own? Most of the schoolbooks echo the opinion of Noah Webster in 1783 that America must be culturally independent of Europe. . . .

To implement his desire for cultural reform Webster himself engaged in a famous attempt to differentiate American from English spelling. Other authors of schoolbooks suggest that the American artist should find his inspiration in American landscape rather than in the Alps or Westminster Abbey. The American literary man should use American scenes and situations to illustrate American virtues. In this way he will improve on European literature by teaching self-control, initiative, honesty, industry, and other characteristics that differentiate the American from the European. Just as European literature reflects the vices and crimes of Europe, so American literature should reflect the virtues of America, and should then be supported for moral as well as nationalistic reasons. Bryant is frequently used as the ideal American man of letters: "We find in his pages all the most obvious and all the most retiring graces of our native landscapes, but nothing borrowed from books—nothing transplanted from a foreign soil." A lofty moral tone is regarded as characteristic of American authors; it is this that makes American literature unique. Lacking this quality an American author is not considered to be a part of American literature. The most obvious case in point is Edgar Allan Poe. According to the major canon of literary eminence used in these books, European recognition, Poe should have replaced Emerson as our greatest writer by the end of the century. He was not only seriously read abroad, but he influenced the development of French literature. This accolade could not be transferred from the virtuous Emerson to the immoral Poe. Although Poe lived in America, it was said, he did not write American literature.

Whatever might be said of the past, American nationalism demanded that the future of American art be assured. With the establishment of our political and social foundations, our intellectual and artistic prospects were seen to be boundless and unprecedented. To achieve this one need not sponsor or even encourage the arts; in fact, this is to be avoided. But it is our manifest destiny, when the time comes, to reach such eminence naturally. America is "ordained, we believe, to be the chosen seat of intelligence, of literature, of arts, and of science." It shall be "The first in letters, as the first in arms." Furthermore, American efforts, freed from class limitations, will provide a larger audience for the arts than Europe can afford: "The universal diffusion of knowledge, which distinguishes the United States from the rest of the world, by exciting a literary thirst among the people in general, must also render the patrons of ingenuity and taste infinitely more numerous than they can possibly be in those nations, where the means, the pleasures, and the advantages of information are confined within the limited circles of nobility and wealth." This confidence in the future of America was apparently based on nationalistic optimism, but also on the assumption that a superior political and social system will inevitably breed great art. Since America has the former she will inevitably develop the latter in time. . . .

Thus, although the future of American art was to be as glorious as were all things American, yet no preparation whatever was made in the schoolbooks to encourage the development either of future artists or of a public for art. The American was not expected to accept art, let alone sponsor it for its own sake. This was the attitude of an effete and declining Europe whose civilization the schoolbooks specifically and carefully reject. Only when art becomes propaganda for good morals, or nationalism, or when it is in the service of the useful arts is it worthy of serious attention. According to the schoolbooks it is this kind of art that Americans have produced and will continue to produce.

The child was of course influenced by things other than schoolbooks. But the latter came from authority, and laid a careful foundation particularly important in those areas of thought in which the child might have little personal experience. The nineteenth-century schoolbook, as compared to that of the twentieth century, had relatively little competition from outside sources of information, and poorly trained teachers were often entirely dependent on the text adopted for use in their schools. The method of the classroom in most schools consisted primarily in memorizing the schoolbook.

And the child who accepted the meaning of the words that he memorized would consider scholarship and the fine arts mere embellishments identified with Europe and therefore with a civilization that he was taught to reject as inferior to his own. He would expect men of talent in the arts to serve their nationality consciously in their art. He would think it a waste of time to engage himself in these fields; American creativity was and should be directed to the immediately practical. Only when the artist or the scholar used his talents for the extension of good morals, for the development of a comfortable material existence, or for the propagation of nationalism was his work to be respected as good art or scholarship. Guided by his schoolbooks the nineteenth-century American child would grow up to be honest, industrious, religious, and moral. He would be a useful citizen untouched by the effeminate and perhaps even dangerous influence of the arts or scholarship. The concept of American culture presented in these schoolbooks, therefore, had prepared him for a life devoted to the pursuit of material success and a perfected character, but a life in which intellectual and artistic achievements would seem important only when they could be made to subserve some useful purpose.

CHAPTER 31

THE AMERICAN WOMAN IN
THE NINETEENTH CENTURY

Spokesmen for various minorities, the poor, and women often complain that these groups have been systematically ignored in the writing of United States history. They contend that the history of this nation has been made to appear to be the almost exclusive work of white males of the middle and upper classes. When minorities, the poor, or women have appeared in history books, their roles have almost never been those of active participants; they have almost invariably been acted upon. According to their spokesmen, the roles of these groups have been ignored or have been presented as being essentially passive. Unfortunately, these charges are well-founded.

There is, however, a reason for some of this neglect. Traditionally history has been the study of past wars, diplomacy, and politics. Military history has usually been written from the top down; that is, most of the historian's attention has been directed toward the nature of command, the movement of troops, and the major decisions that determined the battle. Little if any attention has been devoted to the daily life of troops except as local color to enliven these traditional accounts. The situation is much the same in political history. Until the New Deal, politics was the almost exclusive domain of the adult, white male. The poor white male could vote, but the nature of the electoral process made it extremely difficult for a poor man to run for office. Thus political history necessarily has been the study of the white male officeholder or decision maker and those who supported him. The latter are usually merely voting statistics. Because of the close relationship of diplomacy to politics, the same group has dominated foreign policy making.

In the period after World War II, however, scholars began to develop an interest in new topics such as social and cultural history. Particularly during the 1960's historians began to recognize the significance in American History of minority groups (such as the poor, Indians, blacks, Chicanos, and women) and also of the majority of ordinary persons who make up the citizenry of this nation. Professor Barbara Welter's essay is one of the best examples of the blending of social history with cultural history. Her emphasis is not so much on the real women of the pre-Civil War period as on the idealized concept of womanhood created by the society of the day. Utilizing magazines and other popular literature of the period, Professor Welter describes the attempts of antebellum Americans to place women on a pedestal while simultaneously making it very clear that they were to stay in their alloted place. This paradoxical conception of the role of the American woman has been challenged in the years since the Civil War, but the recent work of the women's liberation movement has demonstrated dramatically the continued persistence of the attitudes and ideas associated with the nineteenth-century cult of True Womanhood.

As you read this selection, keep in mind the following questions. First, to what degree was male chauvinism important in the creation of the cult of True Womanhood? Remember that Professor Welter is describing an idealized role for women, and a series of questions arises regarding the actual success of the model presented. To what extent did the women of the period live up to the ideal? Did the women of every social and economic class share the same conception of women's role in society? If the cult of True Womanhood was shared only by women of means and education, how did the rest of society perceive the role of the woman?

Some of the preceding questions are not answered by this essay. For additional explorations of the subject, see Andrew Sinclair, *The Emancipation of the American Woman** (1961), Eleanor Flexnor *Century of Struggle** (1968); William O'Neill, *Everyone Was Brave; The Rise And Fall of Feminism in America** (1969); and Page Smith, *Daughters of the Promised Land** (1970). Gerda Lerner, "The Lady and the Mill Girl: Changes in the Status of Women in the Age of Jackson," *American Studies Journal, XV, Vol. no. 1,* 1969, pp. 5–15, is an excellent discussion of how class differences affected the role of women in society.

* Available in a paperback edition.

THE CULT OF TRUE WOMANHOOD: 1820–1860
BARBARA WELTER

The nineteenth-century American man was a busy builder of bridges and railroads, at work long hours in a materialistic society. The religious values of his forebears were neglected in practice if not in intent, and he occasionally felt some guilt that he had turned this new land, this temple of the chosen people, into one vast countinghouse. But he could salve his conscience by reflecting that he had left behind a hostage, not only to fortune, but to all the values which he held so dear and treated so lightly. Woman, in the cult of True Womanhood[1] presented by the women's magazines, gift annuals and religious literature of the nineteenth century, was the hostage in the home. In a society where values changed frequently, where fortunes rose and fell with frightening rapidity, where social and economic mobility provided instability as well as hope, one thing at least remained the same—a true woman was a true woman, wherever she was found. If anyone, male or female, dared to tamper with the complex of virtues which made up True Womanhood, he was damned immediately as an enemy of God, of civilization and of the Republic. It was a fearful obligation, a solemn responsibility, which the nineteenth-century American woman had—to uphold the pillars of the temple with her frail white hand.

The attributes of True Womanhood, by which a woman judged herself and was judged by her husband, her neighbors and society could be divided into four cardinal virtues—piety, purity, submissiveness and domesticity. Put them all together and they spelled mother, daughter, sister, wife—woman. Without them, no matter whether there was fame, achievement or wealth, all was ashes. With them she was promised happiness and power.

---

[1] Authors who addressed themselves to the subject of women in the mid-nineteenth century used this phrase as frequently as writers on religion mentioned God. Neither group felt it necessary to define their favorite terms; they simply assumed—with some justification—that readers would intuitively understand exactly what they meant. Frequently what people of one era take for granted is most striking and revealing to the student from another. In a sense this analysis of the ideal woman of the mid-nineteenth century is an examination of what writers of that period actually meant when they used so confidently the vague phrase True Womanhood.

SOURCE.   Welter, Barbara, "The Cult of True Womanhood: 1820–1860," *American Quarterly,* (Summer, 1966), XVIII, No. 2, Part 1, pp. 151–174 Copyright 1966 by Trustees of the University of Pennsylvania. Reprinted by permission.

Religion or piety was the core of woman's virtue, the source of her strength. Young men looking for a mate were cautioned to search first for piety, for if that were there, all else would follow. Religion belonged to woman by divine right, a gift of God and nature. This "peculiar susceptibility" to religion was given her for a reason: "the vestal flame of piety, lighted up by Heaven in the breast of woman" would throw its beams into the naughty world of men. So far would its candle power reach that the "Universe might be Enlightened, Improved, and Harmonized by WOMAN!!" She would be another, better Eve, working in cooperation with the Redeemer, bringing the world back "from its revolt and sin." The world would be reclaimed for God through her suffering, for "God increased the cares and sorrows of woman, that she might be sooner constrained to accept the terms of salvation." A popular poem by Mrs. Frances Osgood, "The Triumph of the Spiritual Over the Sensual" expressed just this sentiment, woman's purifying passionless love bringing an erring man back to Christ.

Dr. Charles Meigs, explaining to a graduating class of medical students why women were naturally religious, said that "hers is a pious mind. Her confiding nature leads her more readily than men to accept the proffered grace of the Gospel." Caleb Atwater, Esq., writing in *The Ladies' Repository,* saw the hand of the Lord in female piety: "Religion is exactly what a woman needs, for it gives her that dignity that best suits her dependence." And Mrs. John Sandford, who had no very high opinion of her sex, agreed thoroughly: "Religion is just what woman needs. Without it she is ever restless or unhappy. . . ." Mrs. Sandford and the others did not speak only of that restlessness of the human heart, which St. Augustine notes, that can only find its peace in God. They spoke rather of religion as a kind of tranquilizer for the many undefined longings which swept even the most pious young girl, and about which it was better to pray than to think.

One reason religion was valued was that it did not take a woman away from her "proper sphere," her home. Unlike participation in other societies or movements, church work would not make her less domestic or submissive, less a True Woman. In religious vineyards, said the *Young Ladies' Literary and Missionary Report,* "you may labor without the apprehension of detracting from the charms of feminine delicacy." Mrs. S. L. Dagg, writing from her chapter of the Society in Tuscaloosa, Alabama, was equally reassuring: "As no sensible woman will suffer her intellectual pursuits to clash with her domestic duties" she should concentrate on religious work "which promotes these very duties."

The women's seminaries aimed at aiding women to be religious, as well as accomplished. Mt. Holyoke's catalogue promised to make female education "a handmaid to the Gospel and an efficient auxiliary in the great task of renovating the world." The Young Ladies' Seminary at Bordentown, New Jersey, declared its most important function to be "the forming of a sound and virtuous character." In Keene, New Hampshire, the Seminary tried to instill a "consistent and useful character" in its students, to enable them in this life to be "a good friend, wife and mother" but more important, to qualify them for "the enjoyment of Celestial Happiness in the life to come." And Joseph M' D. Mathews, Principal of Oakland Female Seminary in Hillsborough, Ohio, believed that "female education should be preeminently religious."

If religion was so vital to a woman, irreligion was almost too awful to contemplate. Women were warned not to let their literary or intellectual pursuits take them away from God. Sarah Josepha Hale spoke darkly of those who, like Margaret Fuller, threw away the "One True Book" for others, open to error. Mrs. Hale used the unfortunate Miss Fuller as fateful proof that "the greater the intellectual force, the greater and more fatal the errors into which women fall who wander from the Rock of Salvation, Christ the Saviour. . . ."

One gentleman, writing on "Female Irreligion" reminded his readers that "Man may make himself a brute, and does so very often, but can woman brutify herself to his level—the lowest level of human nature—without exerting special wonder?" Fanny Wright, because she was godless, "was no woman, mother though she be." A few years ago, he recalls, such women would have been whipped. In any case, "woman never looks lovelier than in her reverence for religion" and, conversely, "female irreligion is the most revolting feature in human character."

Purity was as essential as piety to a young woman, its absence as unnatural and unfeminine. Without it she was, in fact, no woman at all, but a member of some lower order. A "fallen woman" was a "fallen angel," unworthy of the celestial company of her sex. To contemplate the loss of purity brought tears; to be guilty of such a crime, in the women's magazines at least, brought madness or death. Even the language of the flowers had bitter words for it: a dried white rose symbolized "Death Preferable to Loss of Innocence." The marriage night was the single great event of a woman's life, when she bestowed her greatest treasure upon her husband, and from that time on was completely dependent upon him, an empty vessel, without legal or emotional existence of her own.

Therefore all True Women were urged, in the strongest possible terms, to maintain their virtue, although men, being by nature more sensual than they, would try to assault it. Thomas Branagan admitted in *The Excellency of the Female Character Vindicated* that his sex would sin and sin again, they could not help it, but woman, stronger and purer, must not give in and let man "take liberties incompatible with her delicacy." "If you do," Branagan addressed his gentle reader, "You will be left in silent sadness to bewail your credulity, imbecility, duplicity, and premature prostitution."

Mrs. Eliza Farrar, in *The Young Lady's Friend,* gave practical logistics to avoid trouble: "Sit not with another in a place that is too narrow; read not out of the same book; let not your eagerness to see anything induce you to place your head close to another person's."

If such good advice was ignored the consequences were terrible and inexorable. In *Girlhood and Womanhood: Or Sketches of My Schoolmates,* by Mrs. A. J. Graves (a kind of mid-nineteenth-century *The Group),* the bad ends of a boarding school class of girls are scrupulously recorded. The worst end of all is reserved for "Amelia Dorrington: The Lost One." Amelia died in the almshouse "the wretched victim of depravity and intemperance" and all because her mother had let her be "high-spirited not prudent." These girlish high spirits had been misinterpreted by a young man, with disastrous results. Amelia's "thoughtless levity" was "followed by a total loss of virtuous principle" and Mrs. Graves editorializes that "the coldest reserve is more admirable in a woman a man wishes to make his wife, than the least approach to undue familiarity."

A popular and often-reprinted story by Fanny Forester told the sad tale of "Lucy Dutton." Lucy "with the seal of innocence upon her heart, and a rose-leaf on her cheek" came out of her vine-covered cottage and ran into a city slicker. "And Lucy was beautiful and trusting, and thoughtless: and he was gay, selfish and profligate. Needs the story to be told? . . . Nay, censor, Lucy was a child—consider how young, how very untaught—oh! her innocence was no match for the sophistry of a gay, city youth! Spring came and shame was stamped upon the cottage at the foot of the hill." The baby died; Lucy went mad at the funeral and finally died herself. "Poor, poor Lucy Dutton! The grave is a blessed couch and pillow to the wretched. Rest thee there, poor Lucy!" The frequency with which derangement follows loss of virtue suggests the exquisite sensibility of woman, and the possibility that, in the women's magazines at least, her intellect was geared to her hymen, not her brain.

If, however, a woman managed to withstand man's assaults on her virtue, she demonstrated her superiority and her power over him. Eliza Farnham, trying to prove this female superiority, concluded smugly that "the purity of women is the everlasting barrier against which the tides of man's sensual nature surge."

A story in *The Lady's Amaranth* illustrates this dominance. It is set, improbably, in Sicily, where two lovers, Bianca and Tebaldo, have been separated because her family insisted she marry a rich old man. By some strange circumstance the two are in a shipwreck and cast on a desert island, the only survivors. Even here, however, the rigid standards of True Womanhood prevail. Tebaldo unfortunately forgets himself slightly, so that Bianca must warn him: "We may not indeed gratify our fondness by caresses, but it is still something to bestow our kindest language, and looks and prayers, and all lawful and honest attentions on each other." Something, perhaps, but not enough, and Bianca must further remonstrate: "It is true that another man is my husband, but you are my guardian angel." When even that does not work she says in a voice of sweet reason, passive and proper to the end, that she wishes he wouldn't but "still, if you insist, I will become what you wish; but I beseech you to consider, ere that decision, that debasement which I must suffer in your esteem." This appeal to his own double standards holds the beast in him at bay. They are rescued, discover that the old husband is dead, and after "mourning a decent season" Bianca finally gives in, legally.

Men could be counted on to be grateful when women thus saved them from themselves. William Alcott, guiding young men in their relations with the opposite sex, told them that "Nothing is better calculated to preserve a young man from contamination of low pleasures and pursuits than frequent intercourse with the more refined and virtuous of the other sex." And he added, one assumes in equal innocence, that youths should "observe and learn to admire, that purity and ignorance of evil which is the characteristic of well-educated young ladies, and which, when we are near them, raises us above those sordid and sensual considerations which hold such sway over men in their intercourse with each other."

The Rev. Jonathan F. Stearns was also impressed by female chastity in the face of male passion, and warned woman never to compromise the source of her power: "Let her lay aside delicacy, and her influence over our sex is gone."

Women themselves accepted, with pride but suitable modesty, this priceless virtue. *The Ladies' Wreath,* in "Woman the Creature of God and the Manufacturer of Society" saw purity as her greatest gift and chief means of discharging her duty to save the world: "Purity is the highest beauty—the true pole-star which is to guide humanity aright in its long, varied, and perilous voyage."

Sometimes, however, a woman did not see the dangers to her treasure. In that case, they must be pointed out to her, usually by a male. In the nineteenth century any form of social change was tantamount to an attack on woman's virtue, if only it was correctly understood. For example, dress reform seemed innocuous enough and the bloomers worn by the lady of that name and her followers were certainly modest attire. Such was the reasoning only of the ignorant. In another issue of *The Ladies' Wreath* a young lady is represented in dialogue with her "Professor." The girl expresses admiration for the bloomer costume—it gives freedom of motion, is healthful and attractive. The "Professor" sets her straight. Trousers, he explains, are "only one of the many manifestations of that wild spirit of socialism and agrarian radicalism which is at present so rife in our land." The young lady recants immediately: "If this dress has any connexion with Fourierism or Socialism, or fanaticism in any shape whatever, I have no disposition to wear it at all . . . no true woman would so far compromise her delicacy as to espouse, however unwittingly, such a cause."

America could boast that her daughters were particularly innocent. In a poem on "The American Girl" the author wrote proudly:

> Her eye of light is the diamond bright,
> Her innocence the pearl,
> And these are ever the bridal gems
> That are worn by the American girl.

Lydia Maria Child, giving advice to mothers, aimed at preserving that spirit of innocence. She regretted that "want of confidence between mothers and daughters on delicate subjects" and suggested a woman tell her daughter a few facts when she reached the age of twelve to "set her mind at rest." Then Mrs. Child confidently hoped that a young lady's "instinctive modesty" would "prevent her from dwelling on the information until she was called upon to use it." In the same vein, a book of advice to the newly-married was titled *Whisper to a Bride.* As far as intimate information was concerned, there was no need to whisper, since the book contained none at all.

A masculine summary of this virtue was expressed in a poem "Female Charms":

> I would have her as pure as the snow on the mount—
>   As true as the smile that to infamy's given—
> As pure as the wave of the crystalline fount,
>   Yet as warm in the heart as the sunlight of heaven.
> With a mind cultivated, not boastingly wise,
>   I could gaze on such beauty, with exquisite bliss;
> With her heart on her lips and her soul in her eyes—
>   What more could I wish in dear woman than this.

Man might, in fact, ask no more than this in woman, but she was beginning to ask more of herself, and in the asking was threatening the third powerful and necessary virtue, submission. Purity, considered as a moral imperative, set up a dilemma which was hard to resolve. Woman must preserve her virtue until marriage and marriage was necessary for her happiness. Yet marriage was, literally, an end to innocence. She was told not to question this dilemma, but simply to accept it.

Submission was perhaps the most feminine virtue expected of women. Men were supposed to be religious, although they rarely had time for it, and suppose to be pure, although it came awfully hard to them, but men were the movers, the doers, the actors. Women were the passive, submissive responders. The order of dialogue was, of course, fixed in Heaven. Man was "woman's superior by God's appointment, if not in intellectual dowry, at least by official decree." Therefore, as Charles Elliott argued in *The Ladies' Repository,* she should submit to him "for the sake of good order at least." In *The Ladies Companion* a young wife was quoted approvingly as saying that she did not think woman should "feel and act for herself" because "When, next to God, her husband is not the tribunal to which her heart and intellect appeals—the golden bowl of affection is broken." Women were warned that if they tampered with this quality they tampered with the order of the Universe.

The Young Lady's Book summarized the necessity of the passive virtues in its readers' lives: "It is, however, certain, that in whatever situation of life a woman is placed from her cradle to her grave, a spirit of obedience and submission, pliability of temper, and humility of mind, are required from her."

Woman understood her position if she was the right kind of woman, a true woman. "She feels herself weak and timid. She needs a protector," declared George Burnap, in his lectures on *The Sphere and Duties of Woman.* "She is in a measure dependent. She asks for wisdom, constancy, firmness, perseverance, and she is willing to repay it all by the surrender of the full treasure of her affections. Woman despises in man every thing like herself except a tender heart. It is enough that she is effeminate and weak; she does not want another like herself." Or put even more strongly by Mrs. Sandford: "A really sensible woman feels her dependence. She does what she can, but she is conscious of inferiority, and therefore grateful for support."

Mrs. Sigourney, however, assured young ladies that although they were separate, they were equal. This difference of the sexes did not imply inferiority, for it was part of that same order of Nature established by Him "who bids the oak brave the fury of the tempest, and the alpine flower lean its cheek on the bosom of eternal snows." Dr. Meigs had a different analogy to make the same point, contrasting the anatomy of the Apollo of the Belvedere (illustrating the male principle) with the Venus de Medici (illustrating the female principle). "Woman," said the physician, with a kind of clinical gallantry, "has a head almost too small for intellect but just big enough for love."

This love itself was to be passive and responsive. "Love, in the heart of a woman," wrote Mrs. Farrar, "should partake largely of the nature of gratitude. She should love, because she is already loved by one deserving her regard."

Woman was to work in silence, unseen, like Wordsworth's Lucy. Yet "working like nature, in secret" her love goes forth to the world "to regulate its pulsation, and send forth from its heart, in pure and temperate flow, the life-giving current." She was to work only for pure affection, without thought of money or ambition. A poem, "Woman and Fame," by Felicia Hemans, widely quoted in many of the gift books, concludes with a spirited renunciation of the gift of fame:

> Away! to me, a woman, bring
> Sweet flowers from affection's spring.

"True feminine genius," said Grace Greenwood (Sara Jane Clarke) "is ever timid, doubtful, and clingingly dependent; a perpetual childhood." And she advised literary ladies in an essay on "The Intellectual Woman"— "Don't trample on the flowers while longing for the stars." A wife who submerged her own talents to work for her husband was extolled as an example of a true woman. In *Women of Worth: A Book for Girls,* Mrs. Ann Flaxman, an artist of promise herself, was praised because she "devoted herself to sustain her husband's genius and aid him in his arduous career."

Caroline Gilman's advice to the bride aimed at establishing this proper order from the beginning of a marriage: "Oh, young and lovely bride, watch well the first moments when your will conflicts with his to whom God and society have given the control. Reverence his *wishes* even when you do not his *opinions.*"

Mrs. Gilman's perfect wife in *Recollections of a Southern Matron* realizes that "the three golden threads with which domestic happiness is woven" are "to repress a harsh answer, to confess a fault, and to stop (right or wrong) in the midst of self-defense, in gentle submission." Woman could do this, hard though it was, because in her heart she knew she was right and so could afford to be forgiving, even a trifle condescending. "Men are not unreasonable," averred Mrs. Gilman. "Their difficulties lie in not understanding the moral and physical nature of our sex. They often wound through ignorance, and are surprised at having offended." Wives were advised to do their best to reform men, but if they couldn't, to give up gracefully. "If any habit of his annoyed me, I spoke of it once or twice, calmly, then bore it quietly."

A wife should occupy herself "only with domestic affairs—wait till your husband confides to you those of a high importance—and do not give your advice until he asks for it," advised the *Lady's Token.* At all times she should behave in a manner becoming a woman, who had "no arms other than gentleness." Thus "if he is abusive, never retort." *A Young Lady's Guide to the Harmonious Development of a Christian Character* suggested that females should "become as little children" and "avoid a controversial spirit." *The Mother's Assistant and Young Lady's Friend* listed "Always Conciliate" as its first commandment in "Rules for Conjugal and Domestic Happiness." Small wonder that these same rules ended with the succinct maxim: "Do not expect too much."

As mother, as well as wife, woman was required to submit to fortune. In *Letters to Mothers* Mrs. Sigourney sighed: "To bear the evils and sorrows which may be appointed us, with a patient mind, should be the continual effort of our sex. . . . It seems, indeed, to be expected of us; since the passive and enduring virtues are more immediately within our province." Of these trials "the hardest was to bear the loss of children with submission" but the indomitable Mrs. Sigourney found strength to murmur to the bereaved mother: "The Lord loveth a cheerful giver." *The Ladies' Parlor Companion* agreed thoroughly in "A Submissive Mother," in which a mother who had already buried two children and was nursing a dying baby saw her sole remaining child "probably scalded to death. Handing over the infant to die in the arms of a friend, she bowed in sweet submission to the double stroke." But the child "through the goodness of God survived, and the mother learned to say 'Thy will be done.' "

Woman then, in all her roles, accepted submission as her lot. It was a lot she had not chosen or deserved. As *Godey's* said, "the lesson of submission is forced upon woman." Without comment or criticism the writer affirms that "To suffer and to be silent under suffering seems the great command she has to obey." George Burnap referred to a woman's life as "a series of suppressed emotions." She was, as Emerson said, "more vulnerable, more infirm, more mortal than man." The death of a beautiful woman, cherished in fiction, represented woman as the innocent victim, suffering without sin, too pure and good for this world but too weak and passive to resist its evil forces. The best refuge for such a delicate creature was the warmth and safety of her home.

The true woman's place was unquestionably by her own fireside—as daughter, sister, but most of all as wife and mother. Therefore domesticity was among the virtues most prized by the women's magazines. "As society is constituted," wrote Mrs. S. E. Farley, on the "Domestic and Social Claims on Woman," "the true dignity and beauty of the female character seem to consist in a right understanding and faithful and cheerful performance of social and family duties." Sacred Scripture re-enforced social pressure: "St. Paul knew what was best for women when he advised them to be domestic," said Mrs. Sandford. "There is composure at home; there is something sedative in the duties which home involves. It affords security not only from the world, but from delusions and errors of every kind."

From her home woman performed her great task of bringing men back to God. *The Young Ladies' Class Book* was sure that "the domestic fireside is the great guardian of society against the excesses of human passions." *The Lady at Home* expressed its convictions in its very title and concluded that "even if we cannot reform the world in a moment, we can begin the work by reforming ourselves and our households—It is woman's mission. Let her not look away from her own little family circle for the means of producing moral and social reforms, but begin at home."

Home was supposed to be a cheerful place, so that brothers, husbands and sons would not go elsewhere in search of a good time. Woman was expected to dispense comfort and cheer. In writing the biography of Margaret Mercer (every inch a true woman) her biographer (male) notes: "She never forgot that it is the peculiar province of woman to minister to the comfort, and promote the happiness, first, of those most nearly allied to her, and then of those, who by the Providence of God are placed in a state of dependence upon her." Many other essays in the women's journals showed woman as comforter: "Woman, Man's Best Friend," "Woman, the Greatest Social Benefit," "Woman, A Being to Come Home To," "The Wife: Source of Comfort and the Spring of Joy."

One of the most important functions of woman as comforter was her role as nurse. Her own health was probably, although regrettably, delicate. Many homes had "little sufferers," those pale children who wasted away to saintly deaths. And there were enough other illnesses of youth and age, major and minor, to give the nineteenth-century American woman nursing experience. The sickroom called for the exercise of her higher qualities of patience, mercy and gentleness as well as for her housewifely arts. She could thus fulfill her dual feminine function—beauty and usefulness.

The cookbooks of the period offer formulas for gout cordials, ointment for sore nipples, hiccough and cough remedies, opening pills and refreshing drinks for fever, along with recipes for pound cake, jumbles, stewed calves head and currant wine. *The Ladies' New Book of Cookery* believed that "food prepared by the kind hand of a wife, mother, sister, friend" tasted better and had a "restorative power which money cannot purchase."

A chapter of *The Young Lady's Friend* was devoted to woman's privilege as "ministering spirit at the couch of the sick." Mrs. Farrar advised a soft voice, gentle and clean hands, and a cheerful smile. She also cautioned against an excess of female delicacy. That was all right for a young lady in the parlor, but not for bedside manners. Leeches, for example, were to be regarded as "a curious piece of mechanism . . . their ornamental stripes should recommend them even to the eye, and their valuable services to our feelings." And she went on calmly to discuss their use. Nor were women to shrink from medical terminology, since "If you cultivate right views of the wonderful structure of the body, you will be as willing to speak to a physician of the bowels as the brains of your patient."

Nursing the sick, particularly sick males, not only made a woman feel useful and accomplished, but increased her influence. In a piece of heavy-handed humor in *Godey's* a man confessed that some women were only happy when their husbands were ailing that they might have the joy of nursing him to recovery "thus gratifying their medical vanity and their love of power by making him more dependent upon them." In a similar vein a husband sometimes suspected his wife "almost wishes me dead—for the pleasure of being utterly inconsolable."

In the home women were not only the highest adornment of civilization, but they were supposed to keep busy at morally uplifting tasks. Fortunately most of housework, if looked at in true womanly fashion, could be regarded as uplifting. Mrs. Sigourney extolled its virtues: "The science of housekeeping affords exercise for the judgment and energy, ready recollection, and patient self-possession, that are the characteristics of a superior mind." According to Mrs. Farrar, making beds was good exercise, the repetitiveness of routine tasks inculcated patience and perseverance, and proper management of the home was a surprisingly complex art: "There is more to be learned about pouring out tea and coffee, than most young ladies are willing to believe." Godey's went so far as to suggest coyly, in "Learning vs. Housewifery" that the two were complementary, not opposed: chemistry could be utilized in cooking, geometry in dividing cloth, and phrenology in discovering talent in children.

Women were to master every variety of needlework, for, as Mrs. Sigourney pointed out, "Needle-work, in all its forms of use, elegance, and ornament, has ever been the appropriate occupation of woman." Embroidery improved taste; knitting promoted serenity and economy. Other forms of artsy-craftsy activity for her leisure moments included painting on glass or velvet, Poonah work, tussy-mussy frames for her own needlepoint or water colors, stands for hyacinths, hair bracelets or baskets of feathers.

She was expected to have a special affinity for flowers. To the editors of *The Lady's Token* "A Woman never appears more truly in her sphere, than when she divides her time between her domestic avocations and the culture of flowers." She could write letters, an activity particularly feminine since it had to do with the outpourings of the heart, or practice her drawingroom skills of singing and playing an instrument. She might even read.

Here she faced a bewildering array of advice. The female was dangerously addicted to novels, according to the literature of the period. She should avoid them, since they interfered with "serious piety." If she simply couldn't help herself and read them anyway, she should choose edifying ones from lists of morally acceptable authors. She should study history since it "showed the depravity of the human heart and the evil nature of sin." On the whole, "religious biography was best."

The women's magazines themselves could be read without any loss of concern for the home. *Godey's* promised the husband that he would find his wife "no less assiduous for his reception, or less sincere in welcoming his return" as a result of reading their magazine. *The Lily of the Valley* won its right to be admitted to the boudoir by confessing that it was "like its name-sake humble and unostentatious, but it is yet pure, and, we trust, free from moral imperfections."

No matter what later authorities claimed, the nineteenth century knew that girls *could* be ruined by a book. The seduction stories regard "exciting and dangerous books" as contributory causes of disaster. The man without honorable intentions always provides the innocent maiden with such books as a prelude to his assault on her virtue. Books which attacked or seemed to attack woman's accepted place in society were regarded as equally danger-ous. A reviewer of Harriet Martineau's *Society in America* wanted it kept out of the hands of American women. They were so susceptible to persua-sion, with their "gentle yielding natures" that they might listen to "the bold ravings of the hard-featured of their own sex." The frightening result: "such reading will unsettle them for their true station and pursuits, and they will throw the world back again into confusion."

The debate over women's education posed the question of whether a "finished" education detracted from the practice of housewifely arts. Again it proved to be a case of semantics, for a true woman's education was never "finished" until she was instructed in the gentle science of homemaking. Helen Irving, writing on "Literary Women," made it very clear that if women invoked the muse, it was as a genie of the household lamp. "If the necessi-ties of her position require these duties at her hands, she will perform them nonetheless cheerfully, that she knows herself capable of higher things." The literary woman must conform to the same standards as any other woman: "That her home shall be made a loving place of rest and joy and comfort for those who are dear to her, will be the first wish of every true woman's heart." Mrs. Ann Stephens told women who wrote to make sure they did not sacrifice one domestic duty. "As for genius, make it a domestic plant. Let its roots strike deep in your house. . . ."

The fear of "blue stockings" (the eighteenth-century male's term of deri-sion for educated or literary women) need not persist for nineteenth-century American men. The magazines presented spurious dialogues in which bach-elors were convinced of their fallacy in fearing educated wives. One such dialogue took place between a young man and his female cousin. Ernest dep-recates learned ladies ("A *Woman* is far more lovable than a *philosopher*") but Alice refutes him with the beautiful example of their Aunt Barbara who "although she *has* perpetrated the heinous crime of writing some half dozen folios" is still a model of "the spirit of feminine gentleness." His memory prodded, Ernest concedes that, by George, there was a woman: "When I last had a cold she not only made me a bottle of cough syrup, but when I complained of nothing new to read, set to work and wrote some twenty stan-zas on consumption."

The magazines were filled with domestic tragedies in which spoiled young girls learned that when there was a hungry man to feed French and china painting were not helpful. According to these stories many a marriage is jeopardized because the wife has not learned to keep house. Harriet Beecher Stowe wrote a sprightly piece of personal experience for *Godey's,* ridiculing her own bad housekeeping as a bride. She used the same theme in a story "The Only Daughter," in which the pampered beauty learns the facts of domestic life from a rather difficult source, her mother-in-law. Mrs. Hamilton tells Caroline in the sweetest way possible to shape up in the kitchen, reserving her rebuke for her son: "You are her husband—her guide—her protector—now see what you can do," she admonishes him. "Give her credit for every effort: treat her faults with tenderness; encourage and praise whenever you can, and depend upon it, you will see another woman in her." He is properly masterful, she properly domestic and in a few months Caroline is making lumpless gravy and keeping up with the darning. Domestic tranquillity has been restored and the young wife moralizes: "Bring up a girl to feel that she has a responsible part to bear in promoting the happiness of the family, and you make a reflecting being of her at once, and remove that lightness and frivolity of character which makes her shrink from graver studies." These stories end with the heroine drying her hands on her apron and vowing that *her* daughter will be properly educated, in piecrust as well as Poonah work.

The female seminaries were quick to defend themselves against any suspicion of interfering with the role which nature's God had assigned to women. They hoped to enlarge and deepen that role, but not to change its setting. At the Young Ladies' Seminary and Collegiate Institute in Monroe City, Michigan, the catalogue admitted few of its graduates would be likely "to fill the learned professions." Still, they were called to "other scenes of usefulness and honor." The average woman is to be "the presiding genius of love" in the home, where she is to "give a correct and elevated literary taste to her children, and to assume that influential station that she ought to possess as the companion of an educated man."

At Miss Pierce's famous school in Litchfield, the students were taught that they had "attained the perfection of their characters when they could combine their elegant accomplishments with a turn for solid domestic virtues." Mt. Holyoke paid pious tribute to domestic skills: "Let a young lady despise this branch of the duties of woman, and she despises the appointments of her existence." God, nature and the Bible "enjoin these duties on the sex, and she cannot violate them with impunity." Thus warned, the young lady would have to seek knowledge of these duties elsewhere, since it is not in the curriculum at Mt. Holyoke. "We would not take this privilege from the mother."

One reason for knowing her way around a kitchen was that America was "a land of precarious fortunes," as Lydia Maria Child pointed out in her book *The Frugal Housewife: Dedicated to Those Who Are Not Ashamed of Economy.* Mrs. Child's chapter "How To Endure Poverty" prescribed a combination of piety and knowledge—the kind of knowledge found in a true woman's education, "a thorough religious *useful* education." The woman who had servants today, might tomorrow, because of a depression or panic, be forced to do her own work. If that happened she knew how to act, for she was to be the same cheerful consoler of her husband in their cottage as in their mansion.

An essay by Washington Irving, much quoted in the gift annuals, discussed the value of a wife in case of business reverses: "I have observed that a married man falling into misfortune is more apt to achieve his situation in the world than a single one . . . it is beautifully ordained by Providence that woman, who is the ornament of man in his happier hours, should be his stay and solace when smitten with sudden calamity."

A story titled simply but eloquently "The Wife" dealt with the quiet heroism of Ellen Graham during her husband's plunge from fortune to poverty. Ned Graham said of her: "Words are too poor to tell you what I owe to that noble woman. In our darkest seasons of adversity, she has been an angel of consolation—utterly forgetful of self and anxious only to comfort and sustain me." Of course she had a little help from "faithful Dinah who absolutely refused to leave her beloved mistress," but even so Ellen did no more than would be expected of any true woman.

Most of this advice was directed to woman as wife. Marriage was the proper state for the exercise of the domestic virtues. "True Love and a Happy Home," an essay in *The Young Ladies' Oasis,* might have been carved on every girl's hope chest. But although marriage was best, it was not absolutely necessary. The women's magazines tried to remove the stigma from being an "Old Maid." They advised no marriage at all rather than an unhappy one contracted out of selfish motives. Their stories showed maiden ladies as unselfish ministers to the sick, teachers of the young, or moral preceptors with their pens, beloved of the entire village. Usually the life of single blessedness resulted from the premature death of a fiancé, or was chosen through fidelity to some high mission. For example, in "Two Sisters," Mary devotes herself to Ellen and her abandoned children, giving up her own chance for marriage. "Her devotion to her sister's happiness has met its reward in the consciousness of having fulfilled a sacred duty." Very rarely a "woman of genius" was absolved from the necessity of marriage, being so extraordinary that she did not need the security or status of being a wife. Most often, however, if girls proved "difficult," marriage and a family were regarded as a cure. The "sedative quality" of a home could be counted on to subdue even the most restless spirits.

George Burnap saw marriage as "that sphere for which woman was originally intended, and to which she is so exactly fitted to adorn and bless, as the wife, the mistress of a home, the solace, the aid, and the counsellor of that ONE, for whose sake alone the world is of any consequence to her." Samuel Miller preached a sermon on women:

> How interesting and important are the duties devolved on females as WIVES . . . the counsellor and friend of the husband; who makes it her daily study to lighten his cares, to soothe his sorrows, and to augment his joys; who, like a guardian angel, watches over his interests, warns him against dangers, comforts him under trials; and by her pious, assiduous, and attractive deportment, constantly endeavors to render him more virtuous, more useful, more honourable, and more happy.

A woman's whole interest should be focused on her husband, paying him "those numberless attentions to which the French give the title of *petits soins* and which the woman who loves knows so well how to pay . . . she should consider nothing as trivial which could win a smile of approbation from him."

Marriage was seen not only in terms of service but as an increase in authority for woman. Burnap concluded that marriage improves the female character "not only because it puts her under the best possible tuition, that of the affections, and affords scope to her active energies, but because it gives her higher aims, and a more dignified position." *The Lady's Amaranth* saw it as a balance of power: "The man bears rule over his wife's person and conduct. She bears rule over his inclinations: he governs by law; she by persuasion. . . . The empire of the woman is an empire of softness . . . her commands are caresses, her menaces are tears."

Woman should marry, but not for money. She should choose only the high road of true love and not truckle to the values of a materialistic society. A story "Marrying for Money" (subtlety was not the strong point of the ladies' magazines) depicts Gertrude, the heroine, rueing the day she made her crass choice: "It is a terrible thing to live without love. . . . A woman who dares marry for aught but the purest affection, calls down the just judgments of heaven upon her head."

The corollary to marriage, with or without true love, was motherhood, which added another dimension to her usefulness and her prestige. It also anchored her even more firmly to the home. "My Friend," wrote Mrs. Sigourney, "If in becoming a mother, you have reached the climax of your happiness, you have also taken a higher place in the scale of being . . . you have gained an increase of power." The Rev. J. N. Danforth pleaded in *The*

Ladies' Casket, "Oh, mother, acquit thyself well in thy humble sphere, for thou mayest affect the world." A true woman naturally loved her children; to suggest otherwise was monstrous.

America depended upon her mothers to raise up a whole generation of Christian statesmen who could say "all that I am I owe to my angel mother." The mothers must do the inculcating of virtue since the fathers, alas, were too busy chasing the dollar. Or as *The Ladies' Companion* put it more effusively, the father "weary with the heat and burden of life's summer day, or trampling with unwilling foot the decaying leaves of life's autumn, has forgotten the sympathies of life's joyous springtime. . . . The acquisition of wealth, the advancement of his children in worldly honor—these are his self-imposed tasks." It was his wife who formed "the infant mind as yet untainted by contact with evil . . . like wax beneath the plastic hand of the mother."

The Ladies' Wreath offered a fifty-dollar prize to the woman who submitted the most convincing essay on "How May An American Woman Best Show Her Patriotism." The winner was Miss Elizabeth Wetherell who provided herself with a husband in her answer. The wife in the essay of course asked her husband's opinion. He tried a few jokes first—"Call her eldest son George Washington," "Don't speak French, speak American"—but then got down to telling her in sober prize-winning truth what women could do for their country. Voting was no asset, since that would result only in "a vast increase of confusion and expense without in the smallest degree affecting the result." Besides, continued this oracle, "looking down at their child," if "we were to go a step further and let the children vote, their first act would be to vote their mothers at home." There is no comment on this devastating male logic and he continues: "Most women would follow the lead of their fathers and husbands," and the few who would "fly off on a tangent from the circle of home influence would cancel each other out."

The wife responds dutifully: "I see all that. I never understood so well before." Encouraged by her quick womanly perception, the master of the house resolves the question—an American woman best shows her patriotism by staying at home, where she brings her influence to bear "upon the right side for the country's weal." That woman will instinctively choose the side of right he has no doubt. Besides her "natural refinement and closeness to God" she has the "blessed advantage of a quiet life" while man is exposed to conflict and evil. She stays home with "her Bible and a well-balanced mind" and raises her sons to be good Americans. The judges rejoiced in this conclusion and paid the prize money cheerfully, remarking "they deemed it cheap at the price."

If any woman asked for greater scope for her gifts the magazines were sharply critical. Such women were tampering with society, undermining civilization. Mary Wollstonecraft, Frances Wright and Harriet Martineau were condemned in the strongest possible language—they were read out of the sex. "They are only semi-women, mental hermaphrodites." The Rev. Harrington knew the women of America could not possibly approve of such perversions and went to some wives and mothers to ask if they did want a "wider sphere of interest" as these nonwomen claimed. The answer was reassuring. " 'NO!' they cried simultaneously, 'Let the men take care of politics, *we will take care of the children!' "* Again female discontent resulted only from a lack of understanding: women were not subservient, they were rather "chosen vessels." Looked at in this light the conclusion was inescapable: "Noble, sublime is the task of the American mother."

"Women's Rights" meant one thing to reformers, but quite another to the True Woman. She knew her rights,

> The right to love whom others scorn,
> The right to comfort and to mourn,
> The right to shed new joy on earth,
> The right to feel the soul's high worth . . .
> Such women's rights, and God will bless
> And crown their champions with success.

The American woman had her choice—she could define her rights in the way of the women's magazines and insure them by the practice of the requisite virtues, or she could go outside the home, seeking other rewards than love. It was a decision on which, she was told, everything in her world depended. "Yours it is to determine," the Rev. Mr. Stearns solemnly warned from the pulpit, "whether the beautiful order of society . . . shall continue as it has been" or whether "society shall break up and become a chaos of disjointed and unsightly elements." If she chose to listen to other voices than those of her proper mentors, sought other rooms than those of her home, she lost both her happiness and her power—"that almost magic power, which, in her proper sphere, she now wields over the destinies of the world."

But even while the women's magazines and related literature encouraged this ideal of the perfect woman, forces were at work in the nineteenth century which impelled woman herself to change, to play a more creative role in society. The movements for social reform, westward migration, missionary activity, utopian communities, industrialism, the Civil War—all called forth responses from women which differed from those she was trained to believe were hers by nature and divine decree. The very perfection of True Womanhood, moreover, carried within itself the seeds of its own destruction. For if woman was so very little less than the angels, she should surely take a more active part in running the world, especially since men were making such a hash of things.

Real women often felt they did not live up to the ideal of True Woman-hood: some of them blamed themselves, some challenged the standard, some tried to keep the virtues and enlarge the scope of womanhood. Some-how through this mixture of challenge and acceptance, of change and conti-nuity, the True Woman evolved into the New Woman—a transformation as startling in its way as the abolition of slavery or the coming of the machine age. And yet the stereotype, the "mystique" if you will, of what woman was and ought to be persisted, bringing guilt and confusion in the midst of op-portunity.

The women's magazines and related literature had feared this very dislo-cation of values and blurring of roles. By careful manipulation and interpre-tation they sought to convince woman that she had the best of both worlds —power and virtue—and that a stable order of society depended upon her maintaining her traditional place in it. To that end she was identified with everything that was beautiful and holy.

"Who Can Find a Valiant Woman?" was asked frequently from the pulpit and the editorial pages. There was only one place to look for her—at home. Clearly and confidently these authorities proclaimed the True Woman of the nineteenth century to be the Valiant Woman of the Bible, in whom the heart of her husband rejoiced and whose price was above rubies.

CHAPTER 32

MANIFEST DESTINY

In this chapter from *Ideas, Ideals, and American Diplomacy** (1966), Arthur Ekirch easily demonstrates that, in the 1840's, the nation reaped the unharvested fruits of J. Q. Adams' diplomacy. During the earlier days of our nation we were expansionist but, after 1815, we avoided the risk of war. By the middle of the 1840's we were not only expansionist but were prepared to fight for additional territory, if necessary. This reading from Ekirch's work and the blunt fact of the Mexican War document this change in attitude.

Moreover, as this reading shows, we, as a nation, tend to identify our acquisitive interest with moral imperatives. In other words, any acquisition or occupation of territory and any military intervention by the United States is defended as absolutely necessary for the good of the entire world. The irony of this global moral posturing is that, generally, it has been accepted as valid only by ourselves.

This sense that the United States is doing God's work in the world did not originate in the Mexican War period. It is probably one of the least desirable heritages of our Puritan forefathers. (However, we should point out that it has also undergirded efforts to improve American society.) Neither did it vanish at the end of the era under discussion. We need only read a recent debate on American foreign policy to realize that the participants still evoke varying concepts of the national "mission." Only in the 1840's and 1850's, however, did the idea of

mission became so central to the events of the period that both contemporaries and historians have given it a specific title—"Manifest
Destiny."

It was this spirit that led to the annexation of Texas, the Mexican war,
and the war's result—the subsequent acquisition of New Mexico, Ari-
zona, California, and parts of Utah, Nevada, and Colorado. Although
there was a peaceful settlement of the Oregon question, it was preceded
by a long, bellicose period. Probably, this spirit might also have led
to the acquisition of such Caribbean islands as Cuba and Santo Domingo and, perhaps, even more of Mexico if even stronger social forces
—sectionalism and slavery—had not entered the political arena. A
quarreling North and South could not unite on further expansion. Here,
again, the irony of history enters the picture since, in part, the acquisitions of the 1840's caused the nation's growing awareness of the particular
needs of the "Peculiar Institution." The future of slavery in the territories became the fateful disruptive issue.

In reading this essay, students should consider these important questions.
First, how does Professor Ekirch define manifest destiny? Was it merely
a popular phrase of justification for American expansionism, or were the
words the outward expression of a deeply-rooted pattern of thought that
had wider ramifications? If so, what were these ramifications? What were
the basic characteristics of manifest destiny? Was it broadly idealistic
or narrowly nationalistic? Was it passive or aggressive? Finally, what
influence did it have on the subsequent course of American foreign
policy?

Several volumes stand out in the literature of this period. Of course,
essential to this topic is Albert Weinberg, *Manifest Destiny: A Study of
National Expansionism in American History** (1935), with its detailed
examination of the degree to which the concept permeated American
thinking of the period. Frederick Merk, *Manifest Destiny and Mission in
American History** (1965), is a collection of essays and articles dealing
with this period and this concept. R. W. Van Alstyne in *The Rising
American Empire** (1960), discusses expansionism as one of the central
themes of American diplomatic history. William Goetzmann, *When the
Eagle Screamed: The Romantic Horizon in American Diplomacy, 1800–
1860** (1966), covers the entire period in delightful prose.

* Available in a paperback edition.

MANIFEST DESTINY
ARTHUR EKIRCH

The concept of manifest destiny is particularly associated in American history with the aggressive diplomacy of the 1840's. In this decade the continental limits of the United States were carried westward to the shores of the Pacific and as far south as the Rio Grande. The national domain was rounded out by the accession of vast and valuable territories, and the United States could be said to have achieved its "natural boundaries." Thus, in a short span of time, the United States had already moved to fulfill the prediction of Tocqueville, when he wrote:

At a period which may be said to be near,—for we are speaking of the life of a nation,—the Anglo-Americans alone will cover the immense space contained between the polar regions and the tropics, extending from the coasts of the Atlantic to those of the Pacific Ocean.

The first widely noted use of the phrase "manifest destiny" seems to have occurred in 1845 in an editorial by John L. O'Sullivan in the *Democratic Review*. Under the title "Annexation," O'Sullivan declared that God had marked out Oregon, Texas, and the remaining continental territories for possession by the United States. Even though other reasons were not wanting, he contended that the recent United States annexation of Texas was justified by the intrusion of foreign nations into this American matter "for the avowed object of thwarting our policy and hampering our power, limiting our greatness and checking the fulfillment of our manifest destiny to overspread the continent allotted by Providence for the free development of our yearly multiplying millions." Some years earlier another O'Sullivan essay in the *Democratic Review,* depicting America as "The Great Nation of Futurity," not only foreshadowed his use of the phrase manifest destiny, but also exemplified the transition from the peaceful idea of American mission to the aggressive concept of territorial expansion.

SOURCE. From *Ideas, Ideals, and American Diplomacy: A History of Their Growth and Interaction* by Arthur Ekirch, Jr., pp. 40–45, 50–60. Copyright 1966 by Meredith Publishing Company. Reprinted by permission of Appleton-Century-Crofts and the author.

The far-reaching, the boundless future will be the era of American greatness. In its magnificent domain of space and time, the nation of many nations is destined to manifest to mankind the excellence of divine principles. . . . Its floor shall be the hemisphere—its roof the firmament of the star-studded heavens, and its congregation a Union of many Republics, comprising hundreds of happy millions, calling, owning no man master, but governed by God's natural and moral law of equality, the law of brotherhood—of "peace and good will amongst men."

O'Sullivan's 1845 editorial reflected the view that Great Britain, by its continued occupation of Oregon and recognition of the Lone Star Republic of Texas, had interfered with American territorial progress. The Democratic party in 1844 had seemed to gauge correctly the strength of this American expansionist sentiment when it picked James K. Polk as its candidate and adopted a platform which included the resolution:

That our title to the whole of the Territory of Oregon is clear and unquestionable; that no portion of the same ought to be ceded to England or any other power, and that the re-occupation of Oregon and the re-annexation of Texas at the earliest and practicable period are great American measures, which this convention recommends to the cordial support of the Democracy of the Union.

"These were the days," diplomatic historian Thomas A. Bailey has written, "when Manifest Destiny was a dynamic force—when it was widely believed that America's multiplying millions were manifestly destined to spread their republican institutions, though not necessarily by force, over at least the whole continent. These were the days when men talked of 'the universal Yankee nation' and 'an ocean-bound republic'; when the eagle was made to scream and the buffalo to bellow."

Popular support for the notion of manifest destiny received tangible encouragement from a number of factors which, for the first time in American life, seemed to come together in the 1840's. Developing railroad lines and the experimental work in electricity which culminated in the Morse telegraph and promised better communication with the Far West overcame early American fears that the Pacific Coast could not be integrated with the rest of the nation. "The magnetic telegraph," the exuberant O'Sullivan wrote in 1845, "will enable the editors of the 'San Francisco Union,' the 'Astoria Evening Post,' or the 'Nootka Morning News' to set up in type the first half of the President's Inaugural before the echoes of the latter half shall have died away. . . ." At the same time the belief that much of the plains and the mountain area within the Louisiana Purchase—the so-called "Great American Desert"—was unsuited for agricultural settlement gave rise to an uneasy feeling that additional territories might be needed to satisfy the demands of land-hungry American pioneers and planters. Meanwhile the economic problems of the frontiersmen had been heightened by the hard times following the Panic of 1837. Texas and Oregon accordingly might offer a fresh start on the way to wealth. Finally, the prospect of bringing distant regions under the American flag had a jingoistic appeal for many citizens. A young and growing population, convinced of the reality of material progress, proved an eager audience for the expansionist propaganda of the penny press—the mass media of the new democracy. Andrew Jackson himself, the hero of this democracy, was an ardent expansionist who, in his own person and career, glamorized the spirit of manifest destiny.

Although the term manifest destiny proved a popular and useful phrase of justification and rationalization for the expansionist course of American foreign policy in the 1840's, the ideas and philosophy behind the words had wider ramifications. In the first place, manifest destiny conveyed a strong impression that American expansionism was inevitable and providential. Americans were a chosen people intended by Heaven to spread across the continent. Secondly, manifest destiny transformed such broad concepts as the idea of progress into the specific terms of a law of natural territorial growth. Third, it gave a new dynamic and positive value to the older doctrines of isolationism and the American mission. Neither isolation nor missionary ideas were discarded. Instead, under the guiding hand of manifest destiny, they were imbued with greater nationalist vigor and precision. Thus the further accessions of territory in North America in the 1840's were viewed as strengthening the position of the United States and making its independence of Europe more certain. At the same time, the vague ideal of the American mission to spread democracy by example was translated into the actuality of the reach of free institutions across the continent.

In changing in this way the general into the specific, American foreign policy was, of course, also losing something of its idealistic and universal significance and appeal. While the concept of an American mission embraced a concern for the well-being of all nations and peoples, the doctrine of manifest destiny stressed the welfare of the United States. Moreover, despite the argument that expansion was the inevitable and inexorable fate decreed by Providence for the American people, there was actually a good deal of human will and effort which had to be called upon before the goals of manifest destiny could be reached. For example, much political agitation and propaganda, war, and threat of war, had to take place before the territorial aspirations of the advocates of manifest destiny were achieved.

Manifest destiny was an expression of exaggerated nationalism in American foreign policy. This expansionism of the 1840's was nationalist, not in the sense that it enjoyed the united support of all Americans, but in the way in which the nation selfishly pursued its own interests at the expense of other nations. While isolationism and the concept of an American mission were, of course, also nationalistic, neither concept was as aggressive as that of manifest destiny. Isolationism stressed the defense and security of the American Republic in a world of hostile European monarchies. And the idea of mission, though expansionist, emphasized on the whole the peaceful export of American ideology and the realization of the natural rights of man through the spread of American political institutions. In contrast, the concept of manifest destiny implied expansion in a more belligerent manner. It turned the defensive and idealistic notions of isolationism and mission toward the course of a unilateral, nationalist, political and territorial expansion. And, in so doing it also transposed broader, more universal values of genuine international importance—the natural rights philosophy, for example—into a narrower doctrine of the special rights of Americans over and against other peoples.

In pursuit of its goals the United States had the immense advantage of being able to work out its destiny without the serious opposition of other world powers. At the very birth of American expansionist designs in the first years of the Republic, Europe was absorbed in the French Revolutionary and Napoleonic struggles. Thus American foreign policy was able to profit immediately from the strife of Europe. As J. Fred Rippy points out, not only is it "doubtful indeed whether the United States would even have been born," but "A harmonious Europe would never have permitted the United States to extend its boundaries and its political dominance from the Appalachians to the Pacific Ocean and from the tropical Caribbean to the snows of Alaska."

Finally, it should be noted that the doctrine of manifest destiny not only implied inevitability, but it also indicated that the process of expansion was unlimited in time or place. Once the Pacific Coast had been reached, Americans looked outward across the waters to the islands and shores beyond. And then, as the desire for new territories and overseas dependencies eventually waned, manifest destiny was increasingly identified with the search for foreign markets and the desire to exercise a dominating military and ideological influence in world affairs.

Thus the general philosophy and outlook of manifest destiny became one of the major controlling assumptions underlying American foreign policy in both the nineteenth and twentieth centuries.

In the course of the contemporary justification of manifest destiny as distinct from the more material factors which also influenced expansionism, the American people invoked, as Albert K. Weinberg's massive scholarly study of nationalist expansion has shown, a wealth of argument and illustration, touching virtually every aspect of American foreign policy. From the natural rights philosophy of the American Revolution to the assertions of world leadership in the twentieth century, American spokesmen described at length what they understood to be the destined direction of United States expansion. Except briefly in the crisis of the Civil War, American confidence in the manifest destiny of the nation hardly wavered. For, in the words of Franklin Roosevelt, the American people quite literally always believed that they had a rendezvous with destiny. . . .

Increasingly in the 1840's arguments used to justify the progress of manifest destiny in relation to the Indians proved useful as well to support American policies with respect to Mexico and Oregon. At the expense of the Indian tribes the national domain of the United States was gradually being increased without the addition of new foreign territories, but merely through the acts and treaties by which the Indians' land claims were extinguished. Louisiana and Florida had also been acquired by treaty, but in the mid-forties the workings of American diplomacy no longer seemed so inexorable or automatic. Mexico refused to recognize the annexation of Texas, and Great Britain continued to be reluctant to yield all of Oregon. At this juncture, as the Polk Administration called upon the country to prepare for war to defend what was regarded as its true title to both Oregon and Texas, American expansionists invoked the higher sanction of an appeal to democracy. Possession of Texas and Oregon, it was said, would extend the area of freedom and further the progress of civilization.

This incantation to democracy to justify American acquisition of Texas and Oregon was a relatively new form of the expansionist argument. Jefferson, it is true, had referred to the idea of "an empire for liberty" to include Canada, Florida, and even Cuba, but democracy as a positive ideal was seldom used to support the case for American territorial expansion until the 1830's and '40's. Although Jefferson expressed the view that possession of an extensive territory would strengthen American democracy by minimizing the divisive force of selfish local interests, he also shared the widespread feeling that the growth of free institutions could be achieved best by peaceful example rather than through force. Thus there seemed to be a distinction in the American mind between the general mission to advance democracy and free institutions and the specific desire to annex new lands.

The extension of democracy had not been an important factor in the early American expansionist interest in Louisiana or Florida. And, in the case of the inhabitants of New Orleans, the United States had acted tardily in enabling them to benefit from the American practice of local self-government. But the opinion of many of the Revolutionary and Founding Fathers that a republican form of government and free institutions could not well be extended over large areas was gradually weakened as the United States gained new territories and indulged in expansionist dreams in the War of 1812. "The expansion of our Union over a vast territory can not operate unfavorably to the States individually," President Monroe declared in 1822. "With governments separate, vigorous, and efficient for all local purposes, their distance from each other can have no injurious effect upon their respective interests." By the 1830's all remaining American apprehensions of this incompatibility of democracy and territorial growth virtually disappeared in the midst of the strong desires of the country to gain Canada, Cuba, Texas, Oregon, and California.

Important additional support for the linkage of democracy and expansion was provided by American concern over European ambitions in North America. As Professor Rippy has remarked, "manifest destiny never pointed to the acquisition of a region so unmistakably as when undemocratic, conservative Europe revealed an inclination to interfere or to absorb." Although the Texas Republic already enjoyed political freedom, British commercial interests there encouraged American expansionists to call for annexation in order to preserve democracy. Some Texans, it is true, resented such a patronizing attitude on the part of their fellow Americans to the north, and abolitionists and antiexpansionists also complained vigorously that the United States wished to extend the area of freedom by enlarging the area of slavery. Once the Texas question became a part of war with Mexico, however, expansionists were able to contend that the boundaries of political freedom were being extended over regions hitherto suffering from Mexican misrule.

In the course of the Mexican War, United States interest in carrying the benefits of democracy south of the Rio Grande became intertwined with the contention that the war was necessary as a part of an American mission of regeneration for the Mexican people. Under the spell of the idea that the Anglo-Saxon countries were destined to conquer the world, American nativists considered the Mexicans an inferior people. While some expansionists, desiring only territory, warned that the United States would be corrupted by intimate contact with a non-Anglo-Saxon race, others were eager to accept responsibility for the regeneration of so-called lesser nationalities. When the results of the war left American armies of occupation in command of large areas of Mexican territory, the editors of prominent Democratic publications were quick to accept the mission of regeneration for the United States. "The latter expectation," Weinberg comments, "perhaps showed more optimism than the previous history of military occupations warranted." But the enthusiasm of the *New York Herald,* at least, was undaunted:

The universal Yankee nation can regenerate and disenthrall the people of Mexico in a few years; and we believe it is a part of our destiny to civilize that beautiful country and enable its inhabitants to appreciate some of the many advantages and blessings they enjoy.

As the appetite for expansion grew with the war, some Americans came around to the view that even all of Mexico might safely be absorbed by the United States. The *Democratic Review,* which had previously opposed such complete annexation, now declared in February, 1848:

Whatever danger there may be in blending people of different religions into one nation, where religion is established by law,—or in annexing by conquest, under arbitrary governments, which trample upon the rights of all their subjects, and conquer only to enslave,—a free nation, which shows equal toleration and protection to all religions, and conquers only to bestow freedom, has no such danger to fear.

In their acceptance of an American destiny to regenerate the Mexican people and extend the benefits of freedom to their Government, the expansionists of the 1840's were anticipating the argument, fifty years later, of the white man's burden. Meanwhile, in the midst of nativist hostility to European immigrants, the doctrine of an Anglo-Saxon civilizing mission to all lesser races became in a sense the positive aspect of American pride and prejudice. As the national feelings toward the Indians and Mexicans demonstrated, an egocentric and ethnocentric intolerance was becoming an important part of the philosophy of manifest destiny. In the 1840's and 50's the rationale of manifest destiny in all of its varied ramifications gave vital backing to the aggressive goals of American foreign policy. And, at the same time, the angry protests of those who opposed this expansionism were effectively countered by the claim that American arms and diplomacy carried in their wake the blessings of democracy and civilization.

In Oregon the pressure of the pioneers taking the westward trail in the 1840's made untenable joint occupation of the territory with Great Britain. The farmers of the Northwest associated an expanding frontier with American individualism and economic opportunity. Oregon, it was said, "must be occupied for poor men who needed homes and for the extension of free institutions," and this economic individualism "perhaps did more than anything to cement the association between democracy and expansion." To the pioneers democracy meant economic opportunity as well as a form of government. British fur trading interests in the Northwest as well as British monarchy were, therefore, a threat to American democratic expansionism. While England wanted to keep Oregon "for the benefit of the wild beasts as well as of the savage nations," John Quincy Adams, in upholding the American claims to 54° 40′, asserted that the national purpose was "To make the wilderness blossom as the rose, to establish laws, to increase, multiply, and subdue the earth. . . ."

In his denunciation of British imperialism in Oregon, Senator William Allen of Ohio declared that exclusive American occupation would give the United States "the first place in the modern system of the world, . . . leading it on to that social regeneration, which promises the delivery of mankind from the miseries of antiquated monarchy." "Expansionism, later to be depicted by anti-imperialists as a means to economic exploitation and slavery, was seen in this period as a means to economic liberty. Economic freedom had become as important as political freedom to the philosophy of democracy. . . . Freedom for the American nation; freedom for the American State; freedom for the American individual; such then were the principal elements in the fundamentally egoistic program of extending the area of freedom."

The extravagant hopes of the American pioneer in the West were illustrated in the career of a young soldier and journalist, William Gilpin. Gilpin was a personal friend of Andrew Jackson, who appointed him to West Point. Later he came into contact with such ardent Western expansionists as Thomas Hart Benton and John Charles Frémont. Returning to Washington in 1844 from an expedition to the Oregon country with Frémont, Gilpin found employment as an expert adviser to Benton, Buchanan, Polk, and other expansionist-minded Democratic statesmen.

Then, after Army service in the Mexican War and a later stint of fighting against the Pawnees and Commanches, Gilpin turned to writing and speaking about the West. In one of the first examples of his literary work Gilpin summed up in grandiloquent fashion the millenium that he foresaw if the workings of manifest destiny were fulfilled:

The *untransacted* destiny of the American people is to subdue the continent—to rush over this vast field to the Pacific Ocean—to animate the many hundred of millions of its people, and to cheer them upward . . . —to agitate these herculean masses—to establish a new order in human affairs . . . —to regenerate superannuated nations— . . . to stir up the sleep of a hundred centuries—to teach old nations a new civilization—to confirm the destiny of the human race—to carry the career of mankind to its culminating point—to cause a stagnant people to be reborn—to perfect science—to emblazon history with the conquest of peace—to shed a new and resplendent glory upon mankind—to unite the world in one social family—to dissolve the spell of tyranny and exalt charity—to absolve the curse that weighs down humanity, and to shed blessings round the world!

In language as extravagant as Gilpin's, James D. B. De Bow, the New Orleans magazine editor, in the journal that bore his name, exclaimed in 1850:

We have a destiny to perform, a 'manifest destiny' over all Mexico, over South America, over the West Indies and Canada. The Sandwich Islands are as necessary to our eastern, as the isles of the gulf to our western commerce. The gates of the Chinese empire must be thrown down by the men from the Sacramento and the Oregon, and the haughty Japanese tramplers upon the cross be enlightened in the doctrines of republicanism and the ballot box. The eagle of the republic shall poise itself over the field of Waterloo, after tracing its flight among the gorges of the Himalaya or the Ural mountains, and a successor of Washington ascend the chair of universal empire! These are the giddy dreams of the day. The martial spirit must have its employ. The people stand ready to hail tomorrow, with shouts and enthusiasm, a collision with the proudest and the mightiest empire on earth.

The territorial growth which Americans proudly rationalized in the extraordinarily elastic meanings that they assigned to the concept of manifest destiny had been accomplished with an abnormal amount of speed in the 1840's. But the winning of Texas, Oregon, and California for the American flag did not curtail the activities of American expansionists. The success of the Mexican War, instead of satiating, merely whetted their appetite for more territory. Even though the regions already acquired seemed to be in excess of any immediate national needs, Southern slaveholders, for example, were far from satisfied. Thus the early 1850's saw the climax of American efforts to annex Cuba and other lands deemed suitable for the extension of slavery.

That the sole expansionist achievement of the 1850's was the purchase of a strip of southwest territory by Gadsden's Treaty was, it has been suggested, more a matter of lack of luck than of boldness. President Pierce, as a representative of the "Young America" expansionist wing of the Democratic party, frankly favored an aggressive foreign policy. In his Inaugural Address he announced that the policies of his administration would "not be controlled by any timid forebodings of evil from expansion. . . . The apprehension of dangers from extended territory, multiplied States, accumulated wealth, and augmented population has proved to be unfounded," he declared. Pierce accordingly gave his support to the Perry expedition to Japan, initiated by his Whig predecessor, and only the renewed sectional dispute over slavery following the Kansas-Nebraska bill forestalled more ambitious expansionist projects in Cuba and the Caribbean. By antagonizing antislavery opinion the Kansas-Nebraska bill insured the opposition of the North to the longstanding American hopes of acquiring the island of Cuba, and the Pierce administration had to admit the defeat of its expansionist dreams.

Although prospects for territorial growth in specific areas were therefore dim by the mid-fifties, the overall confidence of the advocates of manifest destiny was hardly diminished. "Expansion," said President Buchanan, "is in the future the policy of our country, and only cowards fear and oppose it." Whatever their temporary disappointments, American expansionists could take refuge in their unassailable confidence that growth was the law of nature for all healthy nations. The historic extension of American territory and the ever-increasing American population were assurances that this natural growth was indeed the destined future of the Republic. To themselves, Americans felt, the famous observation of Humboldt was applied with particular force: "It is with nations as with nature which knows no pause in progress and development, and attaches her curse on all inaction."

Even those who drew back from the more extreme notions of manifest destiny were content to accept the accessions that might be expected to come from the natural growth of the American national domain. Thus Edward Everett, the scholarly Secretary of State in the anti-expansionist Fillmore Administration, in countering an Anglo-French proposal to tie American hands in regard to Cuba, adroitly suggested that in contrast to the foreign policies of the Old World, that of the United States was subject to "the law of American growth and progress." Like Everett a man of peace, Parke Godwin, in his book of political essays published in 1854, wrote:

Precisely, however, because this tendency to the assimilation of foreign ingredients, or the putting forth of new members, is an inevitable incident of our growth . . . there is no need that it should be especially fostered or stimulated. It will thrive of itself; it will supply the fuel of its own fires; and all that it requires is only a wise direction. . . . The fruit will fall into our hands when it is ripe, without an officious shaking of the tree. Cuba will be ours, and Canada and Mexico, too—if we want them—in due season, and without the wicked imperative of a war.

Less forbearing and patient than Everett or Godwin, the Democratic expansionists of the late 1850's were continually hopeful that this law of natural growth and expansion would once again receive official political encouragement. Southern annexationists and their supporters, in particular, refused to concede that the Kansas-Nebraska question had doomed all chance for the acquisition of Cuba and other potential slave territory. Sympathetic with these expectations and convinced that Mexico, and perhaps Cuba, lay within the path of American destiny, Caleb Cushing asked:

Is not the occupation of any portion of the earth by those competent to hold and till it, a providential law of national life? Can you say to the tide that it ought not to flow, or the rain to fall? I reply, *it must!* And so it is with well-constituted, and therefore, progressive and expansive nations. They cannot help advancing; it is the condition of their existence.

A Senate report, advocating the purchase of Cuba in 1859, declared: "The law of our national existence is growth. We cannot, if we would disobey it. While we should do nothing to stimulate it unnaturally, we should be careful not to impose upon ourselves a regimen so strict as to prevent its healthful development." And on the eve of the Civil War, retired Congressman J. F. H. Claiborne, in defending the American filibusters who sought to liberate Cuba, asserted:

We proceed upon the theory that the condition of a republic is repose. What an error! That is the normal condition of absolutism. The law of a republic is progress. Its nature is aggressive.

We are in the restless period of youth; the law of the age is progress; let our flag be given to the winds, and our principles go with it wherever it is unfurled. Conquest is essential to our internal repose. War sometimes becomes the best security for peace.

Not only was natural growth the manifest destiny of the American nation, but the attempt to violate this law could be the harbinger of disaster. The nations that failed to advance with the progress of civilization could not expect to enjoy the repose of stability. Instead, the alternative to progress was swift descent in a retrograde motion. In making out his case for the accession of Cuba, a writer in the *Democratic Review* for 1859 observed:

'We are governed by the laws under which the universe was created;' and therefore, in obedience to those laws, we must of necessity move forward in the paths of destiny shaped for us by the great Ruler of the Universe. Activity and progress is the law of heaven and of earth; and in the 'violation of this law there is danger.'

This same thought in connection with expansionist ambitions was expressed earlier by the magazine writers who pointed out:

Civilization is a progressive work—there is no standing still—its principle is continual advancement. The nation that ceases to go forward must certainly go back.

National glory—national greatness—the spread of political liberty on this continent, must be the thought and action by day, and the throbbing dream by night, of the whole American people, or they will sink into oblivion.

Thus the advocates of manifest destiny found support for their ambitious views in the philosophical concept of the idea of progress. The law of progress for nations, as for individuals, indicated growth and activity as the only alternative to decline and death.

As the Civil War cast its shadow over the land to disrupt the course of American manifest destiny, American expansionists were forced to postpone their conviction that Cuba, Canada, Mexico, and other regions in the New World would eventually come under the American flag. But confidence in the force of American political gravitation and in the inevitability of the American destiny was not lost. While the Civil War armies were joined in their fearful struggle, Darwinian concepts of evolution and competition emerged to provide new arguments for growth, and to create a bridge from the manifest destiny of the early nineteenth century to the imperialism of later years. At the same time the achievement of a stronger national union as a result of the Civil War reinforced American security and helped to establish thereby the foundations for the development of the United States as a major world power.

CHAPTER 33

THE FRONTIER AND THE
AMERICAN WOMAN

In her beautiful and poignant volume, *The American Country Woman* (1973), Dorothea Lange, the great American photographer, includes a portrait of an Utah woman in her eighties, one of the members of the second handcart expedition to Utah. With this magnificent portrait is a brief reminiscence of the trip from the Midwest to Utah that the woman had made on foot when she was a child of six. The woman's mother had dragged the family handcart with all the family possessions and the younger children across the American West by herself; her husband had gone ahead to prepare a house and a farm so that the family would be able to survive when they reached their destination. The old woman's most vivid memory of the journey involved the death of her younger sister. Looking back over the years, the woman remembered the child's illness and death and recalled simply that the family had buried her. As a poet later put it, they had left her "on the lone prairie where the coyotes howl and the wind blows free." It does not take much historical imagination or knowledge of human emotions to realize that the episode was not as simple as it appeared in the telling. The fact that it was recalled more than three-fourths of a century later is evidence of the emotional impact it had had on a young child. We can only imagine how the mother and the rest of the family felt. The episode was hardly unique—it was repeated in one form or another in thousands of

places by thousands of people. Such incidents were part of the cost of settling a continent, and they played their part in the development of the
American national character.

The selection that follows differs significantly from the others in this volume. It is a type of fiction. Terry Brown, having made an exhaustive study
of the guidebooks published during the antebellum period, uses her knowledge in an act of creative imagination. Mentally transplanting herself back
to the year 1850, she constructs a guidebook addressed to the daily, practical, and essential problems that women on the difficult journey along the
Oregon trail actually faced. Ms. Brown draws on manuscript sources and
the contemporary periodical literature of the period, but she relies most
heavily on the material in the guidebooks themselves.

Good historical writing has the power to develop empathy for the characters involved in the unfolding story. In reading this selection, try to put yourself in the place of the settler traveling across a roadless, signless West,
in a slowly moving wagon or even pulling a handcart across the rugged ter-
rain. Give your imagination free rein. What are the problems that you would
have had to face? What kind of drive, courage, and resourcefulness would
you have had to possess to accomplish such an arduous task? After you
have read and thought about this selection, you might reflect on the following questions: Has success spoiled America and Americans? Do Americans
still possess the strength of character that our emigrant forebears relied on
so heavily in the settling of this nation?

The history of common people and their lives is difficult to write, but
there is some excellent literature available. Francis Parkman, *The Oregon
Trail** (1849), is a vivid first-hand account of the Oregon Trail by a very
uncommon man. An excellent study of daily life on the Great Plains is Everett Dick, *The Sod House Frontier** (1937). The more colorful aspects of
the Ohio and Mississippi Valley frontiers are presented in Thomas D. Clark,
*The Rampaging Frontier** (1939). A magnificent fictional treatment of
prairie life and its effects on women is Ole E. Rolvagg, *Giants in the Earth**
(1929). The Oregon country is treated sensibly and sensitively in A. B.
Guthrie, Jr., *The Way West** (1949).

* Available in a paperback edition.

AN EMIGRANT'S GUIDE FOR WOMEN
TERRY BROWN

I venture that nothing you have ever done will give you such a clear idea of the journey of the Israelites to the Promised Land as your trip along the Oregon Trail. We, in Oregon, urge you to prepare carefully and come ahead. To suggest that the trek across the plains from Missouri is easy would be dishonest. No one knows how many emigrants have turned back in discouragement. My intention, in this pamphlet, is to impart some of the knowledge gained by women who have traveled west during the past few years. I hope that, if you are forewarned, your trip will prove safer and more pleasant for having considered the suggestions. Because so many more men than women have made the trip, particularly in the early days, most of the letters and all of the guides known to me are written by and for men. As valuable as these guides are, they leave unanswered many questions of special concern to wives and mothers.

Before launching into a discussion of your preparations, let me assure you that life here is wonderful. The weather is mild and invigorating. We are no longer burdened with the threat of floods as we were in the Midwest, for the rains here are gentle. We need not fear cyclones or tornadoes. Best of all, when thinking of day-to-day life, the plague of fever and ague is only a memory. We find the land fertile as well as beautiful. And now that the question of whether this territory belongs to Great Britain or the United States is resolved, we look forward to the time when we will achieve statehood.

HOW TO PREPARE FOR THE JOURNEY

Careful planning for the trip is essential. Bear in mind that you will be about five months on the trail, and few supplies can be purchased between your place of embarkation and your ultimate destination. Not only are prices high at trading posts, but many items are not available. Take what you need, but do not overload your wagon. You must anticipate the needs of your family for the long trip ahead.

SOURCE. Reprinted by permission of the publisher. "An Emigrants' Guide for Women," by Terry Brown. *The American West,* September 1970. American West Publishing Company, Palo Alto, California.

There is a great variety of wagons and conveyances available. From all reports, the most popular is a modified Conestoga version. As there are frequent drenching rains and rivers to ford during the first quarter of your drive, the more waterproof you can make your wagon and supplies, the better. You should have two covers for each wagon; well-oiled or painted canvas, linen, or osnaburg are best. Some families choose bright colors and write slogans or place names on the top. Any note of gaiety will be welcome, but never sacrifice utility. An extra cloth awning hooked from the top at the rear of the wagon and stretched to the ground provides welcome shade for the hasty noon meal.

The bow of the top should be as low as reasonable comfort and convenience dictate. You will be living and working in the wagon, but the higher the top the more problems you will have with wind. The sides should be high enough to prevent the little ones from falling out. Some ruts on the trail are kingpin deep; a lurch into such a hole can easily topple a child off a seat or over a low front board. A swayback floor may prove awkward for neat stacking of belongings, but the advantage of less shifting of gear on steep hills is worth the inconvenience.

In packing your wagon, plan storage arrangements wisely. Be guided by the knowledge that often the gear must be removed from the wagon to lighten the load during difficult travel and through mountains. Before leaving home, practice loading and unloading your conveyance to establish a routine; each member of the family should learn his assigned tasks.

Here are some suggestions for practicality and prudence in choosing and packing your supplies. Use the front box under the driver's seat to stow cooking materials you may need for the next meal. It is easily accessible when you stop the train and the team is put out to graze. It is also heartily recommended that you bring a small sheet iron stove. Cooking meals over a fire in poor weather is hard on the back and the disposition of the cook. A folding table to serve as work space and a place to eat is also worth taking. If you bring a cow, you will want to put a hook on the side of the wagon to hold a tightly covered churn; after a day's ride you will have butter for the family. This is also a good place to dangle all types of sundries for the trip —lanterns, fry pans, clotheslines, and water keg, to name a few. In the past, even coops of chickens have been lashed to the backs of wagons. Certainly, eggs will provide a desirable variety in your family's diet.

In odd corners of the wagon you can tuck books, soap, a clock, boxes of plant cuttings, and perhaps a collapsible rocking chair. One family even brought an entire wagon of apple seedlings and now have an established orchard.

The complete openness of the prairie, with its attendant lack of privacy, surprises many people raised in forested areas. We suggest that you plan for a chamber pot in the rear of the wagon.

The matter of proper clothing for the trip is important. Trail life is harder on apparel than you would expect. Men should take five or six rough shirts, a buckskin coat, and two pairs of buckskin pantaloons. Broad-brimmed hats will be essential under the hot sun. The women would be wise to overcome their scruples and wear loose pantaloons with long coat or hunting frock, along with stout, rugged shoes, and sunbonnets. Do be sure to take the minimum number of comfortable, sturdy garments to protect your family from the sun, wind, and rain.

Consider buying sun goggles for every member of your party. The gritty dust in the alkali springs area and in windstorms irritates the eyes. Inflammation can be serious enough to distort vision temporarily. The investment of thirty-seven and one-half cents a pair is money well spent.

If space does not permit all members of the family to sleep in the wagon, purchase a good tent. With oilcloth floor, and careful pitching and proper trenching, it will provide privacy and protection from the wind and rain.

For food supplies, consider the following essentials: flour, corn meal, parched cracked corn, hard bread, crackers, smoked fish, ham, bacon, dried beef and venison, dried fruits, rice, dried beans and peas, sugar, molasses, coffee, tea, saleratus [baking soda], cheese, lard, and butter. Rolls of solid butter should be wrapped in salted cloths and buried in flour, and eggs can be stored in corn meal. Occasionally the men will find fresh game along the route, but the bulk of your meals will be prepared from what you carry with you. Knowing your family habits and food preferences, use your own good judgment and bear in mind that life in the open enlarges appetites.

MEDICAL PROVISIONS

Because sickness can jeopardize your journey and possibly the lives of many in your party, be sure to take a well-stocked medicine chest.

Fever and ague are probably well known to you. Emigrants from Missouri support the theory of treatment recently advanced by Dr. John Sappington of Arrowrock, Missouri. He recommends his "anti-fever" pills made from Peruvian bark [quinine], which can be found in Westport, Independence, or St. Joseph, if not available in your community. Dr. Sappington also differs with his medical colleagues in another major area of treatment. He deplores bloodletting as debilitating to the patient's health. For the dread disease cholera, the cause of which is unknown, some train captains advise burning or otherwise disinfecting the wagon and effects of cholera patients. Some people hold the radically different idea that cholera is transmitted by bad water. Surely, some of the water is poor, not only for the mineral taste and hardness, but also for the muddiness. However, it's doubtful that it actually causes cholera. A handful of corn meal will settle most of the dirt, but only straining clears out the little wiggling animals.

Perhaps you will be fortunate to have a doctor on your train. If not, it is always wise to inquire, when passing or being passed by other travelers, whether they have a physician with them. Setting simple broken bones may be common practice for many fathers, but with the complications that can arise with accidents, expert help is important. This is also an opportunity to have a doctor examine any babies born while traveling on the train, as to their general health and strength for the journey.

Include among your medical supplies: calomel and castor oil for purgatives, paregoric, laudanum, morphine for pain, anti-fever pills, anodyne for sedation, and essence of peppermint for digestive problems.

Lest you be alarmed by all of this, I must tell you that some persons have been sent west to recover their health. Also, I believe the following to be confirmed by others: there is no more disease among those on the trail than among those at home. Nevertheless, preparation for anything that may befall you is essential.

MAJOR DIFFICULTIES YOU MAY ENCOUNTER EN ROUTE

Will there be difficulties on the trail? Certainly. It is expected that difficulties will be part of a great westward migration over desert and mountain areas. However, anticipation can be worse than the actual experience, on this trip as well as in other dealings with life. You'll see common insects, but sometimes in uncommon numbers: mosquitoes, crickets, grasshoppers, and beetles. To be on the safe side, warn children to be alert for rattlesnakes, although previous trains have reported seeing such snakes infrequently.

Wild animals seem to avoid humans most of the time, although occasionally wolves, coyotes, and bears will attack the stock at night. The most interesting and dangerous of all the wild beasts you will encounter are the buffalo. One cannot escape hearing the dreadful tales of stampedes. It is comforting to know that their sound precedes them, and they can usually be diverted by gunfire from the men. Sometimes the buffalo become confused and join the train's cows for grazing at night. Older children tending cattle should be cautioned not to try to solve this problem themselves.

As mentioned, the weather will give you some discomfort; the wind, rain, and dust can be fierce. In duststorms, a dampened cloth over the face is some relief, but rain is the only real cure. In rainy times, you may go for days without dry clothing or beds, and hot meals are a blessing if you can manage a fire. Hail can bruise people badly and rip a wagon cover to shreds. If you can, you must keep going forward; in times like these, remind yourself that you are coming ever closer to Oregon.

Most trains get through to Oregon without serious trouble and very little contact with Indians. If Indians do come into your camp, treat them with courtesy and share your meals. They are curious because we seem so foreign. Try not to be annoyed at this curiosity. Many women in the trains carry extra needles as gifts for Indian women. Other small gifts or trade items may appeal to them, but above all, never give them alcohol. Apparently, Indians are easily addicted to spirits.

You can save yourself and others grief if you plan and practice a safety program for firearms. Scarcely a train arrives in Oregon without a report of some hideous gun accident owing to carelessness. Guns in the hands of the inexperienced offer far greater dangers than all the Indians between Missouri and the Rockies.

WHAT YOU WILL SEE ON THE TRIP

Much natural wildlife abounds in the West. Great flights of birds will pass over your train, many unknown to you. For a quick test to differentiate between vultures and hawks, look at the wings when the birds soar. If the position of the wings is a flattened V, it is a vulture. In noting the avian variety, your family may enjoy keeping a record of what they see.

Beautiful wildflowers grow in profusion along some parts of the trail. Animals such as wild horses, elk, deer, and occasionally a herd of grazing buffalo will be visible from your train. When you arrive at the area of bluffs, buttes, and mesas, there are many fossils on the ground. Searching for them always proves a diverting activity for travelers.

Most of all, the beautiful scenery of this western country will captivate you in its richness of color, variety, and naturalness.

CODE OF CONDUCT ON THE JOURNEY

It is important that your group understands the organization of the train and the code of conduct. Failure to select a good leader and abide by the accepted rules is borrowing trouble. The pressures of trail life can strain relationships, and the quality of the elected leaders affects the success of the journey. Choose wisely. If you travel in a large group, you will need officers such as lieutenants, sergeants, and record keepers. The captain will appoint a master wagonmaker to supervise repairs, a master blacksmith, and road- and bridge-builder. The captain chooses the route, schedules the guards, and represents the party if you should meet Indians. With no government beyond Missouri, some rules must be established. And these usually comprise, basically, the prohibitions of the Ten Commandments. Punishments include reprimands, fines, and, as last resort, banishment. It is imperative that the travelers recognize the authority of their leader and respect his authority.

A TYPICAL DAY ON THE OREGON TRAIL

What happens on an average day? As soon as the first streaks of light appear, the night guard arouses the camp. Sleepers tumble out, and everyone begins his morning task. The boys assigned to the cattle circle around the herd looking for tracks of strays. Within the corral, tents must be struck, gear stowed in wagons, and breakfast prepared. Water for the dishes heats while the family eats. Of course you will prefer a seated breakfast with the entire family, but time is so critical that you are more likely to eat in shifts around the extended back board of the wagon. The teams for the day are located, brought in, yoked, and hitched to the wagon. The train guards move out to ride parallel and in sight of the wagons, and everyone gets himself and his belongings in place in the train. "Ready to roll" means precisely that, and as the trumpet sounds, the drivers start the teams, the wagons creak forward and you are under way. It is seven o'clock.

As the train rambles along, the children play much as they would at home. The older boys may be privileged to measure the distance covered with a surveyor's chain and help keep the record. You way visit with friends, give the children spelling drill, or observe the passing countryside.

As the morning progresses, thoughts turn to "nooning." About eleven o'clock the captain signals a halt, and all scurry around to their assigned tasks for the noon meal. If there is a need, a council is called to deal with any problems. It is hoped that any necessary repairs can be completed before one o'clock when the train continues, or they will have to be delayed until the end of the day. Aside from naps for small children, the afternoon repeats the morning, with life carrying on as normally as possible on the trail.

By four o'clock the captain has selected the night campground. Drivers circle the wagons to form the corral, the teams are released for grazing, and dinner is prepared. After the hot meal, the travelers relax and enjoy such diversions as dancing, music, or storytelling. The night guards take their posts at eight o'clock, and gradually the corral sounds give way to silence. The children are put to bed, and the journals are brought out for recording the day.

By all means, do plan to keep a family record of the trip. After you have settled in your new home in Oregon, you will be thankful that you have kept the experiences and memories of the trek across this country for posterity.

CHAPTER 34

AFRO-AMERICANS AND THE PECULIAR INSTITUTION

Historians have long been keenly interested in slavery in the United States, but until recently they paid surprisingly little attention to the Afro-American slave himself. With very few exceptions, studies about slavery dealt with slave masters and the treatment accorded slaves, the management and discipline of slaves, the economics of slavery, and various aspects of the institutional side of slavery. In these studies the emphasis was invariably on whites and their attitudes and actions relative to slavery and to the slaves. Never was the slave the focus of attention, and slave life and culture were consistently ignored. In recent years, however, with the dramatically increasing interest in Afro-American or black history, historians have begun to present blacks as active forces in the history of this nation, and in their studies of slavery they have begun to utilize neglected sources and new techniques and approaches to view the Peculiar Institution from the perspective of the slaves themselves. Through their efforts these scholars have greatly broadened our understanding of slavery and have deepened our sensitivity to contemporary problems involving black and white relationships.

The pioneering effort in this new approach was Stanley Elkins, *Slavery: A Problem in American Institutional and Intellectual Life** (1959). Professor Elkins suggested that the time had come to employ fresh approaches and to ask new questions in exploring the problem of slavery. He argued that

517

historians—including the authors of the two classic studies of American slavery, U. B. Phillips, *American Negro Slavery** (1918), and Kenneth Stampp, *The Peculiar Institution** (1956), had engaged, for too long a time, in the same type of debate as had the abolitionists and proslavery proponents of the antebellum years. The rhythm of "right" and "wrong," "benign" and "malignant," and "profitable" or "nonprofitable" had dominated the discourse to the point of diminishing returns. Elkins shifted the area of debate. Borrowing a technique from Frank Tannebaum, *Slave and Citizen** (1948), he compared the institutions that influenced slavery, the church, law, custom, and the like, in the United States and Latin America. In addition, he attempted to study the effect of slavery on the personality of the slave by examining the responses of victims in another stressful dehumanizing situation—confinement in Nazi concentration camps. This was a daring, perhaps even exciting, method of dealing with the past. It produced results as controversial as they were different; as stimulating as they were hard to gauge. They also produced a number of new studies of slavery and of Elkins' conclusions. The following selection is from such a study.

In this selection the black slave occupies center stage. Professors James H. Dormon and Robert R. Jones are concerned with the routine, daily lives of the millions of slaves who were held in bondage, particularly in the Southern states in the middle to late antebellum period. The authors have drawn on slave songs, slave folklore, accounts written by the slaves themselves, and other contemporary sources to discuss slave family life, slave religion, slave self-conceptions, the development among the slaves of a sense of community and, finally, slave resistance to the institution of bondage. In their treatment, Professors Dormon and Jones effectively counter many commonly held misconceptions about slaves and slave life. Their central argument is that over the years Afro-American slaves developed life patterns that were quite different from those of white Americans; in short, the slaves created a distinct Afro-American culture. It was this cultural development, the authors contend, that allowed slaves to resist the brutalizing effects of bondage and to maintain, in the fullest sense, their humanity.

In reading this essay, students should consider the following questions. Was the African past of significance in slave life? If so, how? To what extent were the life patterns of slaves dictated by the dominant whites, and to what degree were blacks themselves responsible for the development of an Afro-American culture? Do you think this essay presents some idea of how slaves thought and felt about slavery? Is there any evidence that the distinct Afro-American culture that originated during the slavery period continues to exist today? What assumptions which you have held about Afro-American life, past or present, are brought into question by this essay?

The literature on slavery is enormous and greatly varied. An excellent beginning is the collection of readings edited by Allen Weinstein and Frank O. Gatell, *American Negro Slavery: A Modern Reader** (1973), and by Ann J. Lane, *The Debate over SLAVERY: Stanley Elkins and His Critics** (1971). In addition to the works cited in this introduction, the student might also wish to consult John W. Blassingame, *The Slave Community: Plantation Life in the Old South** (1972); George P. Rawick, *The American Slave: A Composite Autobiography,* Vol. I, *From Sundown to Sunup: The Making of the Black Community* (1972); David B. Davis, *The Problem of Slavery in Western Culture** (1968); Eugene Genovese, *In Red and Black: Marxian Explorations in Southern and Afro-American History** (1971), and Winthrop D. Jordan, *White Over Black: American Attitudes Toward the Negro, 1550–1812** (1968). Carl Degler, *Neither Black Nor White: Slavery and Race Relations in Brazil and the United States** (1971), is an excellent study in comparative history. Contemporary accounts of slavery are to be found in Eugene R. Berwanger (ed.), *As They Saw Slavery** (1973); Solomon Northup, *Twelve Years A Slave** edited by Sue Eakin and Joseph Logsdon (1968), and Gilbert Osofsky (ed.), *Puttin' on Ole Massa** (1969).

* Available in a paperback edition.

THE AFRO-AMERICAN SLAVE: LIFE AND CULTURE

JAMES H. DORMON AND ROBERT R. JONES

Scholars can discuss the institutional aspects of slavery with considerable confidence. We know a great deal about the laws and regulations that governed the system and about the practices of slave management that prevailed in the cities and on the plantations. We are learning more about the customs and traditions that influenced slave treatment and control. But the most informed treatments of institutional slavery tell little about the lives of slaves, in particular about such important matters as slave consciousness and self-expression, slave behavior, and slave personality. What was the impact of slavery on its subjects? How did slavery influence the character and personality development, mating and childbearing patterns, the family structure, and the overall cultural condition of slaves? This chapter seeks to investigate these questions, to explore, in other words, the psycho-cultural dynamics of slavery. . . .

First, it is obvious that African culture was not applicable in the new circumstances in which enslaved Africans found themselves. Hence, if they were to survive, the slaves had to make profound cultural adjustments. The consensus of most historians of slavery has been that the cultural adaptation required by the systems of slavery in North America was so thorough that Africans lost essentially all their traditional culture. Under close scrutiny this view simply does not hold up. Culture is tenacious and persistent, and tends to maintain powerful continuity. One cannot shed his culture easily even when subjugated in an oppressive institution. Hence, the cultural heritage of the slaves was not only relevant but was highly significant in shaping the Afro-American experience. Scholars have too often overlooked the process of cultural adjustment . . . by which the African heritage was adapted by Afro-Americans to meet the conditions they encountered in their new environment. African culture could not simply be transferred to the New World and planted in new soil. African institutions and forms, customs, and cultural patterns were inapplicable in the new environment, and African slaves were forbidden to take any material

SOURCE.   James H. Dormon and Robert R. Jones, *The Afro-American Experience: A Cultural History Through Emancipation.* New York: John Wiley & Sons, 1974, pp. 169, 171–175, 187–207, 215–216. Copyright © 1974 by John Wiley & Sons. Reprinted by permission of John Wiley & Sons and the authors.

possessions with them. But Africa culture was not lost. Historian George P. Rawick argues cogently that the Afro-American slave could not lose or give up the essence of his culture because "he brought with him his past":

He brought with him the content of his mind, his memory; he recognized as socially significant that which he had been taught from childhood to see and comprehend as significant; he gestured, laughed, cried, and used his facial muscles in ways that he had learned as a child. He valued that which his previous life had taught him to value; he feared that which he had feared in Africa; his very motions were those of his people and he passed all of this on to his children.

As numerous scholars point out, Afro-Americans did retain in their life patterns a few cultural elements that were clearly African. But the influence of Africa on Afro-American life and culture was not limited to these specific retentions. Much more significant was what individual blacks retained of their African heritage in their innermost beings: retentions that were reflected in Afro-American thought patterns, beliefs, emotions, and mental attitudes and images. The most important Africanism by far was the continued use of African philosophical concepts by Afro-Americans, in their outlook on the world and life itself, and in the ways they thought, acted, and spoke in various life situations.

Afro-American religion, for example, while not African in institutional aspects, was profoundly influenced by the retention of African thought and outlook. As with Africans, religion permeated the lives of Afro-Americans to an extent that modern man has difficulty comprehending. Religion was a part of everyday life, and black slaves, like their African forebears, made no sharp distinction between the worldly and the sacred. Hence, the sacred songs of the slaves, the spirituals, were commonly sung not only during religious ceremonies but while the singers were rowing boats, milling grain, walking home from the fields, or relaxing and socializing in the quarters. Just as African gods and spirits were an immediate and intimate part of the world of man, so, too, were God and the other chief figures in Afro-American religion. Thus in their spirituals blacks spoke on extraordinarily intimate and personal terms with God, and with Jesus, Mary, and the mythic Old Testament heroes. In numerous songs Afro-Americans casually indicated how with redemption they would walk with, talk with, and live with God and Jesus; the extent of the intimacy they assumed is well expressed in the spiritual "Hold the Wind":

When I get to heaven, gwine be at ease,
Me and my God gonna do as we please.

Gonna chatter with the Father, argue with the Son,
Tell um 'bout the world I just come from.

In its underlying purposes and approaches, Afro-American religion was essentially an adaptation of traditional African religion to meet the needs of African descendants in the New World. Culture historian Lawrence W. Levine contends that Afro-Americans, denied meaningful participation in the temporal world of the slaveholders, fashioned their own special world, incorporating African conceptions of existence and being and fusing the secular and spiritual sides of life:

> They extended the boundaries of their restrictive universe backward until it fused with the world of the Old Testament, and upward until it became one with the world beyond. The spirituals are the record of a people who found the status, the harmony, the values, the order they needed to survive by internally creating an expanded universe, by literally willing themselves reborn.

The self-generated world of the slaves, reflected in their religious music, was characterized by a sense of affirmation and ultimate justice, and it held out to every man the certain prospect of spiritual rebirth within his lifetime. In Afro-American religion, past time and future time were telescoped into the present. Blacks sang of events of the distant past, such as the crucifixion or the battle of Jericho, as if they themselves had been present and the events had just occurred. Likewise, salvation was always seen as imminent, and the Kingdom of Heaven was described as vividly as if it were right around the corner. Salvation, for all practical purposes, was not in the future, but in the present-to-come. Afro-American religion, like its traditional African counterpart, was strongly oriented to the present or, in other words, to the here and now. Writers who have viewed black religion as fundamentally otherworldly and escapist have simply failed to realize how the worlds of the slave—temporal and spiritual—were integrated in his mind, and how the "New Jerusalem" was to be attained not in some distant future but within his lifetime. . . .

· · ·

It is now becoming evident to scholars that Afro-Americans, uprooted from their African homeland and denied access to much of the dominant white culture, found neither African nor Euro-American culture adequate for their needs. Consequently, they were compelled to develop their own life-styles, their own life patterns, their own Afro-American subculture, utilizing elements of both the African and white American cultural traditions. The resultant subculture was more than simply a mixture or amalgam of the two older cultural patterns; it was essentially a new cultural system especially adapted to the needs of Afro-Americans and to the peculiar circumstances in which they lived in the United States.

All blacks shared in the black subculture. White racism prevented the escape of recognizable blacks, with extremely few exceptions, into the dominant society, and guaranteed that all blacks would be influenced, to a great-er or lesser degree, by the sanctions operating toward the development of a distinct subculture. Thus free blacks in the North as well as the South, slaves on small farms, and urban slaves, however much they made adjust-ments to Euro-American culture, were products of the black subculture and participated, at least partially, therein. But the strongest impetus for the de-velopment of a unique Afro-American cultural system came on the great plantations where the slave population was large; consequently, the black subculture was shaped predominantly by the way of life of plantation slaves. In the following pages we will examine the nature and dimensions of the black subculture that developed in the plantation South.

In examining slave culture, it is essential to apply the concept of cultural relativity and to avoid ethnocentrism. Students of slavery have generally given little attention to slave life, and when they have, they have often made clearly ethnocentric judgments. Thus, historian David B. Davis has made the sweeping suggestion that it is "doubtful . . . whether the mass of slaves in any country ever enjoyed a meaningful religious life." Scholars generally have argued that the slave family, lacking stability, cohesiveness, and legal standing, served little economic or social purpose in slave life. Historian Kenneth M. Stampp went so far in a 1956 publication as to maintain that "only incidentally" was the slave woman "a wife, mother, and home-mak-er," and he concluded that "the male slave's only crucial function within the family was that of siring offspring." In the past most students of slavery have agreed, at least tacitly, with Stampp's conclusion that the "average bondsman . . . lived more or less aimlessly in a bleak and narrow world."

Writers who have made such statements have taken white Euro-American institutions, behavior, and values as normal and desirable. The impossibility of a fair evaluation of slave life from this perspective is pointedly demon-strated by the gratuitous assertion of sociologist Jessie Bernard that because slave marriages of any kind were "so uncommon," most slave children "were born out of wedlock"! Slave culture must be judged on its own mer-its. Neither weddings nor legal sanctions make marriages, and familial insti-tutions and practices among the slaves must not be judged as ineffective and substandard simply because they differed from those in white culture. Nor may one conclude that because slaves did not enjoy various benefits and ad-vantages of the larger society they necessarily lived pointless and miserable lives. Lastly, it is highly presumptuous and somewhat arrogant to denigrate the various life roles of slaves on the assumption that slaves *must be* what their masters wanted them to be. Afro-American slaves were not made in the image and likeness of their masters.

Although the attitudes and actions of white Americans operated to force blacks to develop an alternative cultural system, the Afro-American subculture was basically the creation of blacks. Whites, for all their authority and power, did not determine the development of black culture. For example, the absence of Euro-American legal sanctions for slave marriages did not determine the structure and role of the slave family. Similarly, the fact that slaveowners permitted or encouraged conversion to Christianity did not give slave religion its central meaning or major characteristics. Afro-American slaves lived, in effect, in two worlds. One world was the white man's world, where slaves lived in close contact with whites, as on small farms, or when they worked under the relatively close scrutiny of whites, in the fields or in plantation households. Here white influence on slave behavior was most pronounced, but even here it was not deterministic. Theoretically slaves were under the control of their masters at all times, but on the large plantations and, to some extent, on the small farms there were often opportunities for slaves to escape into their own black world, beyond the effective exercise of close scrutiny. In the slave quarters and black settlements, the Northern journalist Frederick Law Olmsted reported, slave life was "relatively unconstrained." Here slaves related to other slaves on their own terms; here other sanctions besides the slave codes and the overwhelming power of the whites influenced slave consciousness, slave behavior, and slave patterns of life. The slave quarters were the crucible in which slave culture was forged.

It was largely in the slave quarters, for instance, that the Afro-American slaves created the slave family, a familial system developed to meet the human desires and needs of the slaves themselves as well as the demands of the system of chattel slavery. Contrary to common opinion, the family did exist as a viable institution among slaves. As indicated in the previous chapter, slaveholders promoted pair-bond mating and childbearing by slave couples. With this encouragement, the decided trend in slave family organization was in the direction of the Euro-American standard, the single family unit, with modifications produced by the exigencies of slave life. Historian Willie Lee Rose has suggested that "the most *typical* domestic picture [of slaves] is of a father and mother living together in a humble cabin with their children."

Moreover, the sense of family was strong. The trauma of family separation is a pervasive theme running through the slave narratives, indicating the extensiveness and strength of family ties. As fugitive slave Alexander Hemsley put it, "the unwillingness to separate of husbands and wives, parents and children was so great, that to part them seemed to me a sin higher than the heavens,—it was dreadful to hear their outcries, as they were forced into the wagons of the drivers." The depth of a slave mother's love for her children is evident in the painfully touching remarks of ex-slave Mary Younger. "It almost kills me," she said, "that . . . . [my children] are there [in slavery], and that I can do them no good." The slaves' strong sense of family was expressed frequently and in various ways. Slave mothers hid children, suffered severe punishment, and pleaded with sellers and buyers alike in attempts to prevent the breakup of their families. Mothers and fathers risked punishment and sale in trying to protect their children from mistreatment, and many a runaway slave virtually sacrificed his freedom in fulfilling his desire to be near loved ones. Much of the resistance to "being sold South," which included self-mutilation and suicide, resulted from the reluctance of slaves to be separated from their families and their kinsmen.

The evidence for a viable family life among slaves comes from both slave and planter sources. Although slaveholders referred not infrequently to slave promiscuity and inconstancy, their attitudes and actions relative to the internal slave trade and to slave management indicate that they clearly understood that family attachments were very important to slaves. If slave families were frequently broken up, it was not usually through the action of the slaves, but through the operation of forces beyond their control; and with the demise of slavery thousands of blacks traveled across the South seeking reunion with loved ones and relatives. The recent research of historian Herbert Gutman shows that a very large majority of rural blacks, including adult men, lived in single family units during the Reconstruction period, and studies by other scholars suggest that this situation was a continuation of family patterns established during slavery. The evidence clearly points to a greater stability and cohesiveness in the slave family than students of slavery have traditionally recognized.

The relatively high degree of family stability and cohesiveness achieved by slaves was possible only because both slave men and slave women carved out viable familial roles and worked together to accomplish the goals that they set for their families. Too much has been made of the emasculation of the male slave and the dominance of women in slave society. Once again, evidence from both white and black sources, but particularly from the slave narratives, contradicts the traditional view. The slave husband and father generally performed important functions in the family. Although not the breadwinner in the usual sense of that term, he often played an important economic role by hunting and fishing to supplement the family diet, by constructing and repairing furniture and household items, by organizing the family garden if one were allowed or, in some instances, earning cash to be spent for his family's benefit. But more important, the male slave also participated actively in the most significant task of slave parents, the preparation of their offspring for adult life in the world they knew. Slave fathers shared with slave mothers in disciplining and teaching their children, and in laying down rules and customs for family behavior. Former slave Jacob Stroyer noted that he was whipped by both his father and his mother, and ex-slave Joseph Sanford indicated that both parents took part in the teaching process: "My father always advised me to be tractable, and get along with the white people in the best manner I could, and not be saucy. My mother always taught me to serve the Lord—which has ever been my aim. . . ."

Slave men sometimes exercised dominant authority in the home, and apparently they frequently used physical coercion on both wives and children. But it is not necessary to prove that slave husbands generally were the primary source of family authority, or that they were highly successful in protecting their families. What should be established is that the male slave was not generally emasculated nor relegated to a position of secondary importance in the family. There is little indication from slave sources that slavery destroyed the manliness of slave men or undermined their status and prestige in slave society. There is little evidence that the slaves themselves considered women the primary source of authority in the family or in the larger society. The slave family was a tenacious and vital institution because of the strength and energy infused into it by both slave men and women. The slave family survived because, in their own minds, slave men and slave women were first husbands and wives, fathers and mothers, providers and homemakers and members of the black community, and only incidentally laborers for and the property of the master class.

Although the tendency in slave society was toward the establishment of family units similar to those in white society, the circumstances of slavery forced significant modifications. The slave family developed and existed in the face of continual, varied, and severe difficulties. Families were often disrupted through sale, separation, or divorce, oftentimes despite vigorous objection by the family members. Sometimes the slave father or another member of the family was absent much of the time because he did not live or work where his family resided. And when all members of the family lived in the same household, both parents were normally away from the family for a large part of each working day. Even under optimum conditions, slaves were limited in their ability to perform the familial roles customary in the autonomous white family. Consequently, the slave family system developed a flexibility that contributed not only to the complexity of the system's structure but also to its strength and vitality. Because the single family unit was unable to carry out fully the functions required of an effective family system, Afro-American slaves created an extended family system in which the responsibilities of rearing children and caring for family members were shared to some extent by the larger community.

In the slave family the biological parents might well exercise duties and prerogatives similar to those exercised by parents in an autonomous white family, but slave society did not delineate sharply the roles of "father" and "mother" nor insist on the rigid fulfillment of these roles by slave fathers and mothers. George P. Rawick is essentially correct in suggesting that the "slave community acted like a generalized extended kinship system" in which there was community concern for the well-being of all individuals, especially children, in each slave family. In slave families, children generally had considerable family responsibilities; older children, for instance, were frequently assigned the task of caring for younger children. Relatives of the immediate family, including grandparents, uncles, aunts, step and half siblings, and close and distant cousins, sometimes lived with the family and performed important familial functions. In addition, other members of the slave community, especially older men and women who were highly respected or who had had wide experience in family affairs, were called on to help fulfill family purposes. In some instances, such as in the punishment of misbehaving children, the slave community as a whole exercised a collective responsibility. The extended family system operated effectively both on a day-to-day basis and in times of crisis, supporting in the one instance the work of the actual slave parents and providing in the second parent surrogates or other family members. In short, the system provided a degree of security and stability by its insurance that complete deprival of kin and family was highly unlikely. Whatever the dispersal of the immediate family, it was almost certain that someone would be available to care for the members of the family wherever they came to live in the realm of slavery. Clearly the flexible and improvisational extended family system fulfilled the deepest needs of Afro-American slaves far more adequately than a rigid nuclear family system could have.

The operation of the extended family system in slave society suggests that the role of community was more significant than most students have believed. Historians have generally assumed that the slaveholders were largely successful in their attempts to forestall the development of a sense of unity and common purpose among their bondsmen. And in recent decades, some black writers and leaders, frustrated in their attempts to achieve black solidarity, have echoed this interpretation, at least to the point of emphasizing the presence on the plantations of a minority of slaves who identified with the ruling whites and served their purposes, even to the extent of betraying their fellow slaves. Yet the evidence is clear that despite the genius, the strong purpose, and the manipulative power of the slaveholders, the slaves came to view themselves as a people quite distinct from whites, a people with common-problems, common interests, and a common destiny. In short, there developed among blacks on the plantations of the South a strong sense of community, a form of incipient black nationalism. Professor Rawick argues that the "reality of community was the major adaptive process for the black man in America."

The slave sense of community, however, was far from perfect. By deftly playing on the desire of their slaves for recognition, prestige, and special favors, slaveholders deliberately fostered class consciousness and divisiveness in slave society. House servants, said the former slave Austin Steward, "are ever regarded as a privileged class; and are sometimes greatly envied, while others are bitterly hated." Some slave drivers were considered "vicious" by their fellow slaves; fugitive slave Jacob Stroyer even expressed pleasure at the death of a cruel driver, "Uncle Esan." Henry Bibb noted that there were marked distinctions in slave society, with some slaves "refusing to associate with others whom they deem beneath them in point of character, color, [or] condition. . . ." There was considerable distrust of house servants by other slaves, but the numbers of "despicable talebearers and mischiefmakers" who would betray fellow slaves were swelled by bondsmen from every rank. The escape or resistance plans of numerous slaves were revealed by black brothers who hoped thereby to earn special favors from the whites. John Little, a runaway slave, was betrayed by a free black in return for a reward of $10, and another fugitive, Leonard Black, was turned in by his own closest friend. There is little wonder, then, that slaves often distrusted fellow slaves, or that those who were planning escape or resistance moved with extreme caution. Some slaves did not even keep their brothers, wives, or parents informed of their plans.

There were numerous conflicts of a more petty nature in slave society. Field slaves as well as artisans and domestics vied among themselves for assignments that were thought to carry high prestige, and bondsmen from different plantations quarreled and fought over the relative merits of their masters. One ex-slave noted that he had heard slaves object to working in the field in small groups, lest "some passer-by should think that they belonged to a poor man, who was unable to keep a large gang." Ex-slaves Austin Steward, Josiah Henson, and Frederick Douglass all commented that slaves frequently exhibited a "foolish pride" which prompted them to go to inordinate lengths to please their masters and, ultimately, to identify at least in part with their oppressors. "Often," wrote Josiah Henson, "was the encomium of 'smart nigger' bestowed upon me, to my immense gratification." It is Henson who offers the extreme example of slave identification with the system of bondage in the almost incredible story of how, in accordance with his master's wishes, he led a group of 21 slaves, including his wife and two children, from Maryland through a portion of the free state of Ohio to Kentucky.

But despite the betrayals, the class divisions, and the partial identification with the master class, the central loyalty of slaves was generally to the slave community. Slaves sought to define and to enforce what was best for the slave community, and the value system that operated in slave society was oriented toward the promotion of black solidarity and mutual concern.

Hence, tattling and informing were taboo in slave society, and slaves who betrayed fellow bondsmen risked ostracism or perhaps severe physical punishment. As Austin Steward noted, masters sometimes had to send their informants away, "for fear of the vengeance of the betrayed slaves." The attitude of the slave community was apparently well understood by whites; in commenting on a slave who had betrayed another, a Tennessee judge observed that the fact that a slave "should abandon the interests of his caste, and betray black folks to the white people, rendered him an object of general aversion."

The operation of the slaves' self-generated value system tended to encourage resistance to slavery and made the task of slaveholders infinitely more difficult. It made possible a situation in which thousands of slaves all over the South were able to escape temporarily from their plantations for periods varying from a few hours up to several years. The commitment of slaves to the common cause provided the protection of silence for those who stole from whites, for those who resisted work, sabotaged plantation operations, or simply engaged in "putting on" "ole' massa," and for those who sought to disrupt the system through violence. The sense of community also helped to make it possible for a relatively small number of slaves to make it to the North or to Canada and to escape altogether from slavery. The slave narratives are replete with examples of blacks, free and slave, who lent helping hands to fellow blacks, whatever the nature of their need. These black Good Samaritans were acting on the premise that they and their fellow sufferers were a different people from whites, a people unto themselves. The actions of these thousands of blacks speak louder than any words as proof that a real and tenacious sense of community bound together the black slaves of the plantation South.

In no other area of slave life was the role of community more significant than in the creation and development of black religion. Only a people with a strong sense of togetherness and a firm belief in their own destiny could have carved out a religious experience that reflected such a positive world view and that came so close to fulfilling satisfactorily their deepest temporal and spiritual needs. The clearest expression of slave religion, of course, are the sacred songs, the slave spirituals. Despite disagreements over the origins of the spirituals, almost all students of slavery and slave life have been profoundly impressed by these religious songs and have viewed them as creative expressions of great beauty and sensitivity. Musicologist Newman I. White has referred to them as "the most impressive religious folk songs in our language," and historian Vincent Harding has described them as "the most profound verbal expression of Afro-American religious experience." As early as the 1920s White suggested that the spirituals represented "the greatest single outlet for the expression of the Negro folkmind."

Yet scholars have generally failed to appreciate the significance of the spirituals and of slave religion to an understanding of slave life and culture. They have not perceived that creations as beautiful and powerful as the spirituals could not have been the product of a hand-me-down Christianity that the slaves had accepted from their masters as they would have a bundle of old clothes. Students of slavery have usually exaggerated the role of whites in shaping the religious beliefs and practices of the slaves, suggesting that the mass of slaves accepted meekly the propagandistic preachings of white ministers on submission and obedience. The traditional view of slave religion all but denies the slaves any meaningful religious experience. Slave religion was, as the traditional myth has it, a distorted, degraded version of Christianity fashioned to meet the needs of ignorant and superstitious slaves. It was characterized by a primitive fundamentalism in belief and an unrestrained emotionalism in practice. It served primarily to provide release from the cares of this world and the promise of a better life to come, and its escapist orientation and focus on the hereafter prompted its adherents to accept unquestioningly their condition in this world. In the traditional view slave religion was truly the opium of the oppressed.

Actually, as we have noted previously, Afro-Americans did not adopt as their own a bastard Christianity; instead, they combined aspects of traditional African religions and Christianity to produce a new black faith, a functioning, integrated religion especially suited to sustaining their religious needs. Religion cannot be dismissed lightly in any discussion of a people's life and culture, and this is particularly true of North American slaves. The slaves were profoundly religious; their very existence and every department of their lives were intimately associated with religion. Moreover, in their sacred songs, the slaves have left a record of their religious experience that is remarkably useful for an inquiry into slave life and culture.

The single most important fact about slave religion is that it was largely created and controlled by the slave community. Slaveholders had made little attempt to convert slaves to Christianity before 1750, and intensive and systematic efforts at conversion were not made until the last three and one-half decades of slavery. As a result, Afro-American slaves had been able to retain important aspects of traditional African religions and to adapt Christianity to the imperatives of their peculiar condition. Uprooted from his African past, the North American slave needed what anthropologist Paul Radin calls a "fixed point," and he found that stability in the Christian God. But, Radin adds, "The ante-bellum Negro was not converted to God. He converted God to himself." Afro-Americans transformed Christianity to meet their needs, adding new practices and ceremonies, expanding the galaxy of supernatural beings, infusing new sensibilities, emphasizing different aspects of God's revelation, and even altering the traditional image of Christ the Savior.

The slaves clearly recognized the differences between their religion and their masters', between their God and the white man's God. "White folks can't pray to the black man's God," noted Henrietta Perry, a Virginia slave. The persistent efforts of white ministers and masters to induce slaves in the name of religion to submit and obey, to accept their status as one ordained by God, and not to lie or steal simply "turned off" many slaves. Moreover, most of the white churches did not sanction the shouting, the moaning, the hand-clapping, the dancing, the exuberant singing—in short, the freedom of expression—that blacks felt were essential in the exercise of a fulfilling religion. Throughout the antebellum period, slaves continued to participate outwardly in the religion of their masters, sometimes attending the same services as the whites or, more often, meeting as a special group to hear a white minister or a slave preacher under white supervision. But white religion did not neet the needs of Afro-Americans, and the slaves turned to their own community to order their religious lives and to seek spiritual fulfillment.

Of all the areas of plantation life, slave religion was the one least influenced by white example. It was the slaves themselves who determined the nature and types of expression, the content, the orientation, the tone and character of slave religion. It was for this reason that black religion differed so much from traditional Western Christianity. The slaves picked and chose, omitted and altered to fashion their own religion. They related very closely with the oppressed "Hebrew children," seeing themselves as God's special chosen people in eighteenth- and nineteenth-century America. The spirituals make repeated reference to the slaves as the people of God, and contain innumerable allusions to the deliverance of the Israelites and their leaders from situations of distress. It is little wonder, then, that black religion had a strong Old Testament flavor, and that the slaves found their religious heroes among its great figures—Noah, Jonah, Samson, Daniel, David, Joshua, Moses, and the archangel Gabriel. Their God was a mighty God, their Jesus a powerful and protective warrior king.

Slave religion was essentially a communal, not a private affair. Individual religiosity was not curtailed, but the primary outlet for religious expression was through the community of slaves. In speaking of their religious experiences, slaves and ex-slaves almost always used the plural "we" and they invariably spoke of communal functions such as praise meetings, funerals, sings, ring shouts, and prayer-and-experience meetings. The very structure of the spirituals, based on a call and response pattern, demanded communal participation. It is most significant that the sacred songs of the blacks made almost no positive references to whites but posited a black world peopled by parents, relatives, and friends, living and dead. Leadership in this world of the slaves was apparently dominated by those who were believed to possess special religious powers. The leadership roles of the black preachers, mystics, and oracles depended on their special relationships with their black brothers and sisters; their power resulted, Professor Rawick writes, from "their deep contact with the soul of the congregation and the community." The "amen" and "hallelujah" responses in black religious services were a means through which the congregation could verify the leader's mystic communion with his people.

In concentrating on the language of the spirituals as evidence of the travails of those held in bondage, scholars have generally failed to recognize that slave religion was emphatically a religion not only of hope but of *promise*. It is true that a man so sensitive to the nuances of the Afro-American experience as the great black leader, W. E. B. DuBois, called the spirituals the "sorrow songs," and that Frederick Douglass spoke of the "deep melancholy" and bitter "anguish" expressed in slave songs. The slaves, of course, did sing in their spirituals of their problems, their sorrows, and their sufferings. The emphasis of the spirituals, however, was not on the tribulations of the slaves, but on their deliverance from their troubles. Persistently the sacred songs emphasized transformation, triumph, and salvation. The spirituals are filled with references to "Canaan," the "Kingdom," the "Holy City," the "mansions above" or, most significantly, simply "home." The slaves were certain that deliverance would come and that they would be going "home"; it was only a matter of time before they "would walk the golden streets of the New Jerusalem." Slave religion was characterized by the supreme confidence so evident in the spirituals.

In their sacred songs, the slaves expressed almost no sense of unworthiness and projected a decidedly positive self-image. They were God's people, a troubled but struggling, persevering, and righteous people, wholly worthy of salvation if only they followed the Lord. Indeed, many slaves felt morally superior to their white slaveowners. After seeing his sister whipped and her persecutor shortly afterward attend religious services, Austin Steward could hardly help feeling that whites were hypocrites: "Can any one wonder that I, and other slaves, often doubted the sincerity of every white man's religion?" Ex-slave David West noted that he loved his former master, since deceased, but he continued, ". . . I can read the Bible, and I do not see any thing there by which he could be justified in holding slaves: and I know not where he has gone to." Fugitive slave Henry Brant thought it would be "a hard case" for a man to "continue to do as the slaveholders do" and then to "obtain heaven." Henry Atkinson, another fugitive slave, was even more certain: "It appears to me that God cannot receive into the kingdom of heaven, those who deal in slaves." There seems little question that the slaves were alluding symbolically to a retributive justice for whites when they referred in the spirituals to events such as the drowning of Pharaoh's army or to Goliath's downfall. Ultimately God's justice would prevail, and the slaves would wear crowns of glory while the slaveholders suffered punishment. In the words of abolitionist Moncure D. Conway, the slaves, ignorant and un-lettered as they were, "had conceived a symbolism of their own, and bur-dens of prophecy, and had changed the fields on which they toiled into the pavements of the New Jerusalem, glorified with spirits arrayed in white."

But the slaves were not concerned only with salvation after death. Their whole religious experience is a testament to their desire for and belief in de-liverance in this world. It is significant that all of the Old Testament heroes of Afro-American slave religion faced difficulties and troubles that were an-alogous, in the minds of the slaves, to their own trials and tribulations; it is more significant that each of these great religious figures achieved deliver-ance in this world. If God had delivered Daniel "from de lion's den," Jonah "from de belly ob de whale," and the Hebrew children "from de fiery fur-nace," then, the slaves asked, "why not every man?" In speaking of the sa-cred songs Frederick Douglass observed that "Every tone was a testimony against slavery, and a prayer to God for deliverance from chains." And Charles Ball, another ex-slave, observed that the religious faith of the slaves was premised on the firm belief that they would be delivered from their earthly bondage: "The idea of a revolution in the conditions of the whites and the blacks is the cornerstone of the religion of the latter." In essence Afro-American slaves, who neither separated the sacred from the secular nor envisioned heaven as being far off in time or space, simply fused the ideas of worldly and of spiritual deliverance.

Slave religion was inherently subversive of the institution of slavery. It not only held out the hope of radical improvement in the earthly condition of slaves, but it also fostered the development of slave communal autonomy and individual self-esteem. Moreover, the very fact that slaves adhered to and practiced a religion that was considered by whites pernicious and dan-gerous and that was usually prohibited tended to undermine a system of so-cial control based on the existence of absolute power and authority. In the practice of their religion, slaves generally had to defy their masters, covert-ly or overtly. To be able to express themselves freely, they held their prayer meetings or sings late at night, in slave cabins, in hollows or dugouts in the fields, in selected sites or constructed "hush-harbors" in the woods or swamps. Detection meant punishment, and consequently the slaves became adept at carrying on surreptitiously their religious activities.

Because the slaveholders were unable to exercise the close supervision that would have cut off normal channels of communication in the slave community, the slaves generally had little need for an elaborate system of secret communication. Occasionally, however, they may have employed prearranged signals, including the words of sacred songs like "Steal away, steal away, steal away to Jesus." Whether or not such songs were conscious-ly composed to dupe slaveholders, they clearly came to have double meanings for some slaves. To Frederick Douglass and other slaves, for example, being "bound for the land of Canaan" connotated not only a hope of reaching heaven but also of escaping to the free states of the North. Douglass recalled that it was a spiritual, which included the line "I don't expect to stay much longer here," that first planted in his mind the idea of running for freedom, and many other fugitive slaves were sustained in their hopes of achieving freedom by their religious faith. There can be no doubt that for a large number of those in bondage, slave religion served to amplify, or even to induce, the ideas and feelings of protest. Slave protest cannot be separated from slave religion.

The discussion of slave religion brings up the question of slave morals and ethics, a subject that has been much misunderstood by whites. Whites have recognized that Afro-Americans have generally been zealously religious people, but it has also been their common opinion that blacks have usually not been very "moral." George Washington, expressing the typical views of a slaveholder, observed that his slaves stole and ruined his property, feigned illness to escape work, and were habitual liars and malingerers. Slave carpenters, Washington wrote, were notorious slackers, and he complained that he could not trust a single one of the domestic servants. It is clear from Washington's observations that the Protestant work ethic had little appeal for slaves, particularly for those like Betty Davis, who was "laid up" for two days for every one she worked.

Slave immorality, in the minds of white contemporaries, was most pronounced in the area of sexual behavior. Southern whites believed that most slaves took an easygoing attitude toward marriage, that relationships between slave mates were generally quite casual, and that marriage among slaves was actually a euphemism for sexual relations. Most whites, North and South, believed that slaves were generally and incurably promiscuous. A Mississippi planter, writing in *DeBow's Review,* knew of no means by which to regulate or restrain slave "habits of amalgamation and intercourse", and abolitionist Moncure D. Conway, born and reared in Virginia, spoke of "general licentiousness" and "wholesale prostitution" among the slaves, conditions that were often encouraged or even compelled, Conway charged, by the slaveholders. Gordon Chapman, a Northern visitor to a Southern plantation, after observing that "not one of the slaves attended church on the Sabbath," commented further on the sexual lives of the slaves: "The social relations were scarcely recognized among them, and they lived in a state of promiscuous concubinage."

Antebellum whites, of course, were judging slaves in terms of accepted white moral standards. They, as have whites in the years since, failed to understand that the activities of Afro-American slaves were governed by an in-group moral code, incorporating moral values and standards that did not conform to white conceptions of "right" and "wrong." Of course, the moral and ethical precepts of Christianity and of western culture did have some influence, but the specific and unique circumstances of black bondage were of far greater significance in the emergence of a system of slave morality. It is not surprising, given their belief in the sinfulness of slavery and in white moral hypocrisy, that black slaves did not adopt unchanged the ethics and moral standards of whites; however, it is ironic that the slaves employed a type of situational ethics, respecting Christian prohibitions such as those against lying and stealing only in their dealings with fellow slaves or other blacks.

There is overwhelming evidence in the slave narratives and in slave folklore, for example, of a black double standard in the appropriation of property belonging to another. The slaves commonly "liberated" their masters' corn, watermelons, sheep, young calves, and food of various sorts, but chickens and pigs seemed to be the most sought after prizes. Universally, the slaves justified such actions; they reasoned among themselves, ex-slave Austin Steward noted, ". . . as slaves often do, that it can not be *stealing,* because 'it belongs to massa, and so do *we,* and we only use one part of his property to benefit another. Sure, 'tis all massa's'." Mary Raines, recalling her days in slavery, took the same position: "I never call it stealin'. I just call it taking de jams, de jellies, de biscuits, de butter and de 'lasses. . . ." To whites such transgressions could only be defined as stealing and were clearly immoral; to slaves these acts simply constituted "taking" and were necessary and legitimate. Josiah Henson was so convinced of the justice of taking one of his master's chickens for a female friend that he felt "good, moral, heroic." Moreover, the slave community generally protected the transgressors against white authority; black brothers and sisters universally feigned ignorance or offered erroneous explanations, sometimes quite imaginative, of what happened to the property in question.

Standards governing relations among the slaves themselves were another matter. For instance, theft by one slave from another was *not* sanctioned or tolerated. The slave community had its own system of searching out guilty parties and of meting out justice to slaves who had violated its standards of conduct. A thief might be detected, Jacob Stroyer tells us, by any of three intriguing ways: "one with a Bible, one with a sieve, and another with graveyard dust." Once discovered, a slave who had transgressed against his fellow slaves might be ridiculed, isolated, or punished physically, even to the point of death in extreme cases. The degree to which slaves abided by their own moral standards varied widely, depending on numerous circumstances and individual personalities, but the evidence suggests that adversity strengthened the sense of community and the disposition of slaves to deal with their fellow bondsmen with sensitivity and fairness.

The conditions under which slaves lived necessarily influenced their attitudes about sexuality. Slaves were thrown together, irregardless of sex, into crowded quarters where they ate, slept, and lived with a minimum of privacy. "In a single room," Josiah Henson recalled, "were huddled, like cattle, ten or a dozen persons, men, women, and children. All ideas of refinement and decency were, of course, out of the question." Slaves were provided skimpy clothing, and mature men and women often wore only a long cotton or linen shirt or frock in the summer. Thomas Hedgebeth, a free black, observed that some of the slaves with whom he worked were "without clothing enough for decency." Under such circumstances, with slaveholders universally encouraging procreation, and in the absence of significant institutional restraints on the sexual activity of the bondsmen, there is little wonder that many a slave woman bore numerous children by different fathers, that many unmarried slaves became mothers and fathers, and that, in the words of Moncure Conway, "an old maid is utterly unknown among the women." In describing slave marriage, fugitive slave Soloman Northup felt compelled to add to his statement the qualifier, "if such an institution may be said to exist among them." "Either party can," he noted, "have as many husbands or wives as the owner will permit, and either is at liberty to discard the other at pleasure."

Clearly, sexual attitudes and practices among the slaves differed widely from those approved in white society. In general, blacks were much less inhibited than whites in sexual matters, and apparently they engaged in greater heterosexual activity, particularly in the adolescent and early adulthood years. But their nonadherence to the Victorian morality espoused (but often not practiced) by Southern whites does not justify the assumption that sexual morality was nonexistent among slaves. There were in the slave community strong cultural sanctions for a basic fidelity in marriage, once the couple involved felt they had contracted a marriage. Religious faith, concern about the care of children and relatives, and real affection and love between husband and wife operated to hold together slave marriages. The devotion of many slave wives and husbands to each other is strikingly demonstrated in historical records, both from white and black sources. Like whites, black wives do not seem to have been very understanding of transgressing husbands, and vice versa. Fidelity among slaves probably varied considerably from individual to individual and from family to family. The Reverend William Ruth of Colchester, Canada, a former slave, believed that his congregation of ex-slaves excelled whites in the observance of the "laws of chastity." However, to imply that slaves generally were more chaste than whites would not only be unwarranted but beside the point. What is important to understand is that blacks developed and generally adhered to their own standards of morality, in sexual as well as in other aspects of life. In this sense we can say of the entire slave community, as the Reverend Smith said of his small flock, ". . . as a general thing [they] are a moral people." . . .

. . .

What is implicit in the preceding pages is that slavery, for all its elaborate system of regulation and control, never developed to its logical conclusion; it never became a total institution requiring total subservience and submissiveness. Any system of absolute control requires the isolation of individuals and the denial of meaningful interpersonal relationships. But the antebellum slaveholding class was unable to exercise anything like complete authority over their bondsmen, because their system of control did not provide for the systematic and thorough physical and psychological isolation of the slaves as individuals. Consequently, slavery in the antebellum South could not and did not close off the opportunity for the generality of slaves to develop as individual beings. It follows that the institution, contrary to the claims of scholars such as Stanley Elkins, was simply not "closed" enough to produce in large numbers the infantile, irresponsible, servile, and happy-go-lucky Sambo personality so common in white folklore and literature.

In the antebellum South the developing slave community stood as a buffer for most Afro-Americans, operating to preclude their individual isolation and thus to prevent their complete degradation and dehumanization. The system of slavery did teach submissiveness and servility; it did indoctrinate the slave with a sense of deep inferiority and self-hatred. But the slave community covertly countered the message of slavery, making it extremely difficult for the slaveholders to enslave the minds of their slaves as they had their bodies. The slave community provided "significant others" that reduced slave identification with the master class, and offered an alternative cultural system geared to the everyday needs and desires of the slaves themselves. As members of the slave community Afro-American slaves developed friendships and other interpersonal relationships and also experienced, however imperfectly, an affirmation of self. Bolstered by that community, they clung tenaciously to a degree of self-pride and a sense of their worth as individuals. As members of the slave community, black bondsmen were more than chattels; they were—and they knew it—human beings with all the attributes that set men apart from the other animals. "I was black," John Little recalled, "but I had the feelings of a man as well as any man."

Without question, the growth of the black community and the creation of an essentially autonomous black subculture were the most important developments of the Afro-American experience to 1865, and these developments were to have a profound effect on the subsequent course of black history. It was because Afro-American slaves retained a positive self-image and continued to regard themselves as a "moral people" that they were able, not only to survive in slavery, but to transcend the institution that bound them, bequeathing to their posterity and to the world a unique example of survival and creativity in the face of extreme adversity. They "made it."

CHAPTER 35

ATTITUDES TOWARD
SLAVERY: PRO AND CON

As suggested in the introduction to Chapter 33, Americans have long differed on the subject of slavery. Every student of American history is aware of the opposed views of slavery held by the abolitionists and by the Southern defenders of the institution, although the proslavery argument is often less dramatically and more briefly presented than the abolitionist crusade. Students often are almost wholly unaware of the changing attitudes toward slavery in the United States during the late eighteenth and early nineteenth centuries. Little has been published regarding the Southern liberal opposition to slavery until the 1830's (and its subsequent harsh suppression thereafter); and, likewise, only slight attention is paid to Southern and Northern support of the colonization project, to the debate on whether colonization was a practical or a racist solution to the "Negro problem," to Negro participation in the growing antislavery chorus, and to the hostility in the North to an antislavery offensive both before and after the 1830's.

In this essay Professor Clement Eaton concentrates on the less familiar aspects of American (particularly Southern) attitudes toward slavery, although he outlines the major developments in the abolitionist crusade. He discusses Southern liberal views in the Revolutionary era, Southern support for emancipation and for colonization of slaves, the antislavery activities of Southern Quakers, and the continuing but ineffective opposition to slavery by a small number of Southern liberals. However, Professor Eaton's major contribution is his tracing of the development of the elaborate proslavery argument, which he tags as "one of the great rationalizations that the human mind has conceived." Today, when students demand that people "tell it like it is," the story of how a society succumbed to well-conceived and well-articulated propaganda in a classic example of self-deception is particularly pertinent and relevant.

In reading this selection, students become aware of the dangers of simplistic approaches (for instance, the abolitionist and proslavery arguments) to matters as complex and deeply rooted as American Negro slavery. Specifically, the reader should concentrate on this set of questions: How do you explain the Southern tendency to apologize for slavery and the absence in the North of a strong antislavery movement before the 1830's? What does your answer suggest about the tendency among historians and others to view the North (past and present) as, in Robert Penn Warren's words, the "Treasury of Virtue"? Do you believe that the failure of the American colonization movement and its unpopularity among Negroes have any lessons to teach today, when the relationship between blacks in Africa and in the United States is in the process of definition? Finally, what were the major tenets and the significant effects of the proslavery argument? How does Eaton explain this great victory of "mass propoganda" over the mind of a society?

For an excellent treatment of both the proslavery argument and the antislavery movement, see Alice Felt Tyler, *Freedom's Ferment: Phases of American Social History to 1860** (1944). Louis Filler, *The Crusade Against Slavery** (1960), is a recent scholarly treatment of abolitionism, and Clement Eaton, *The Freedom-of-Thought Struggle in the Old South** (1964), concentrates on the general relationship of the defense of slavery to civil liberties. Avery Craven, *The Growth of Southern Nationalism* (1953), is also especially good on the South. Eric McKitrick's *Slavery Defended** (1963), and John L. Thomas, *Slavery Attacked** (1965), are collections of proslavery and antislavery arguments that are quite valuable.

CHANGING ATTITUDES TOWARD SLAVERY
CLEMENT EATON

The argument, that Southerners evolved to justify the institution of slavery is one of the great rationalizations that the human mind has conceived. Like the philosophy of the Scholastics of the Middle Ages, it was a product of many minds, a remarkable intellectual achievement, finely articulated, and based on the far-reaching assumption that Negroes are innately inferior to whites. Before the rise of the proslavery argument large numbers of Southerners, especially in Virginia, did not subscribe to this faith in the rightfulness and permanence of slavery. There was, indeed, a time when Southerners in general apologized for the existence of human bondage in their region—a period extending from the American Revolution to the middle of the decade of the 1830's.

The development of a liberal attitude toward the emancipation of the slaves during this period was explained in part by economic considerations. The exhaustion of tobacco lands and the shift to wheat growing gave to the upper South a surplus of slaves. Slavery was becoming decidedly unprofitable in this region until the invention of the cotton gin in 1793 restored the value of slaves. Washington declared that he had twice as many working Negroes on his estate as could be profitably employed. John Randolph of Roanoke wittily described the economic burden of supporting slavery during this period by remarking that, instead of masters advertising for runaway slaves, the slaves would be advertising for the arrest of fugitive masters.

In addition to economic motives, the natural-rights philosophy of the Revolutionary period predisposed Southerners to a desire for gradual emancipation. One of the earliest persons in America to link the right of Negroes to freedom with the Declaration of Independence was the wealthy South Carolina merchant and planter Henry Laurens, who became president of the Continental Congress in 1777 and 1778. In writing to a son in England, a student of law there, on August 14, 1776, he ex-

SOURCE. Clement Eaton, *A History of the Old South,* New York: The Macmillan Company, 1966 (second edition), pp. 337–356. Copyright 1949, 1966 by The Macmillan Company. Reprinted by permission of The Macmillan Company and the author.

pressed his abhorence of slavery as an institution that was in conflict with the golden rule of Christianity. He was planning, therefore, he declared, to manumit some of slaves and cut off the entail on the remaining servants. But such a bold step, he anticipated, would encounter the opposition of the society in which he had been reared, and might cause his children to reproach him for having deprived them of so much of his estate.

A considerable number of Southerners freed their slaves by will during this period. George Washington set an example by emancipating his slaves by will, so did John Randolph of Roanoke later, and Jefferson was prevented from adopting a similar course by his financial bankruptcy. The wills of emancipation indicate that the liberal planters were disturbed by the inconsistency of holding slaves and subscribing to the equalitarian doctrines of the Declaration of Independence. Most of the prominent Virginia leaders, such as Patrick Henry, George Wythe, and James Madison, condemned slavery as an institution that should be eradicated from a free America. George Mason, the proprietor of beautiful *Gunston Hall* on the Potomac, and the master of 300 slaves, declared slavery to be an infernal school of tyranny for the future leaders of the South, which caused slaveholders to lose sight of "the Dignity of Man which the Hand of Nature had planted in us for great and useful purposes." Furthermore, the most enlightened planters, such as Jefferson, realized that slavery had a pernicious effect on the white population, degrading manual labor, encouraging pride and arrogance, and exposing children to the corrupting influence of licentious slaves.

The grave problem in emancipating slaves was what to do with the freedmen. Practically all Southerners believed that the process of liberation should be gradual and that the freedmen should be colonized. Professor St. George Tucker of William and Mary College proposed in 1796 a plan of gradual emancipation based on liberating all female slaves at birth. Several of the Southern states repealed their colonial laws forbidding the manumission of slaves except for meritorious services, adjudged by the governor and council or the county court, and now permitted emancipation of slaves provided the owner gave guarantees that the freedmen would not become public charges. The experiences of planters who emancipated their slaves, however, were frequently unfortunate. Robert Carter of *Nomini Hall* emancipated in 1791 more than 500 slaves by a plan of gradually freeing groups over a period of 20 years. He tried to rent small patches of land to them, but this practice was not an economic success. The neighbors protested that the freedmen stole and abused their freedom and corrupted the slaves. Ironically, two of Carter's sons, whom he had sent to the Baptist College in Rhode

Island (Brown Univerity) in order that they might escape the immoral influence of slavery, tried to frustrate the noble experiment of their father. When Carter liberated his slaves he was influenced by the teachings of the Baptist and Swedenborgian churches, but also, it is to be noted, the price of slaves had reached the bottom of a 20-year decline in this last decade of the eighteenth century.

The Quakers of the upper South were the principal Southern group that tried to do something practical about removing slavery. Those planters who apologized for slavery, as a rule, made no positive efforts toward eradicating the institution. Since slavery had not originated in their generation, they were willing for its removal to be left to the gradual operation of time. But the Quakers, who loathed the element of force in human relations, actively sought to dissolve the institution. One method they adopted was the use of antislavery propaganda through the press. In 1819 Elihu Embree founded *The Emancipator* at Jonesborough, Tennessee, the first antislavery newspaper in the South. Benjamin Lundy, a saddlemaker who worked in Wheeling, Virginia, established in 1821 the *Genius of Universal Emancipation* at Baltimore, Maryland. In North Carolina flourished the Quaker newspaper the *Greensborough Patriot,* which as late as 1834 championed the cause of freeing the slaves.

To agitate for the removal of slavery, the Quakers organized abolition societies. Since they were close to slavery, they were practical enough to urge the gradual rather than the immediate abolition of the peculiar institution and the amelioration of slavery by repealing the laws against the education of the slaves. Charles Osborn, a Quaker preacher born in Guilford County, North Carolina, was the pioneer organizer of manumission societies in Tennessee (1814–1816). After he had emigrated to Mount Pleasant, Ohio, he published an antislavery newspaper as early as 1817. By the year 1827 fifty antislavery societies, with a membership of 3,000, were reported in North Carolina, 25 in Tennessee, and eight in Virginia—a much greater number of antislavery societies than existed in the North. Besides this method of attacking the institution of slavery, the Quakers formed free produce societies, pledged not to use products of slave labor, and became operators in the Underground Railroad. The antislavery sentiment in the South was weakened greatly as many of the Quakers emigrated to free territory beyond the Ohio River in the first three decades of the nineteenth century. In 1834 the last meeting of the North Carolina Manumission Society was held at Marlborough, and in 1860 only about 1,500 Quakers were left in the state.

Most Southerners believed that if the slaves were freed and remained in the South a race conflict would follow and Southern civilization would be destroyed. Jefferson, Clay, Calhoun, and practically all Southern leaders believed that the removal of the freed Negro was indispensable to a scheme of emancipation. In 1817 the American Colonization Society was founded at Washington, D.C., to solve this problem by transporting freed Negroes to Africa. Liberals saw in the movement an encouragement to kindly masters to free their slaves, whereas conservatives supported the colonization society as a means of strengthening slavery by removing the objectionable free Negroes already present in the South. The society, composed largely of Southerners, elected Bushrod Washington, a nephew of the Revolutionary hero, as the first president. In 1819 agents were sent to the west coast of Africa and acquired from the native chiefs large areas for a colony, which was named Liberia, "land of freedom," and its capital, Monrovia, in honor of President Monroe. Not until 1847, however, did Liberia become a republic with a Negro as president.

The American Colonization Society failed miserably in its larger purposes. It was unable to persuade the Federal government to give financial support to its adventure. Sections of the colony were set aside for Negro groups from various Southern states, such as Mississippi in Liberia, Maryland in Liberia, and Kentucky in Liberia. Agents were sent throughout the South to obtain funds and emigrants, and a magazine, the *African Repository,* was published in Washington as a means of propaganda. In Mississippi the society raised approximately $100,000, and the legislature of Maryland pledged its credit to the amount of $200,000 to aid in the colonization of Maryland Negroes. Some benevolent planters provided in their wills for the emancipation of their slaves and transportation to Liberia. Despite the efforts of the American Colonization Society, a relatively small number of Negroes were sent to Africa, 571 from Mississippi, for example, and 1,363 from North Carolina. The Society transported a total of over 15,000 Negroes between 1821, when the first contingent was sent, and 1860. So prodigious was the Negro birth rate that this number was a pitiful fraction of the increase of black babies born in slavery during this period. Thus, colonization proved utterly impractical, not only because of the invincible birth rate of the Negro, but also because of the cost and difficulties of transportation to Africa. The American Colonization Society was branded by the abolitionists as a proslavery device to get rid of the free Negro, but after 1831 slaveholders gave it slight support.

The Southern Negroes themselves had no enthusiasm to return to their ancient home in the Dark Continent. Having become accustomed to American food, climate, and civilization, they dreaded going to a strange land. Many of those who did emigrate to Liberia died from tropical disease. The interior tribes were hostile and dangerous. Some of the Negroes who emigrated wrote discouraging reports to their masters and brethren in the United States—that the Negroes had farms usually no larger than five acres, which they tilled with the hoe without the aid of horses and mules, lived in bamboo houses in a wilderness, and "tell Uncle pleasant that we have snakes here 15 to 20 feet and can Swalow a man, Dear, or a hog with ease." Even to this day Liberia is not an attractive asylum to the American Negro. Sleeping sickness, malaria, hookworm, and dysentery make life precarious. The American Negroes and their descendants have enslaved the interior tribes until as late as 1930. Moreover, they developed the idea that manual labor was degrading and a caste system arose—the descendants of slaves were copying the patterns of the white masters.

In January, 1831, William Lloyd Garrison began the publication in Boston, Massachusetts, of *The Liberator,* the first newspaper in the United States devoted to *immediate* abolition of slavery. This New England printer and journalist was a natural agitator who espoused many other reforms besides the abolition of slavery. Always an enthusiast, Garrison reversed the life process of many men who are liberal in youth but become conservative in middle life; as a young man Garrison was a strong conservative, an ardent Federalist, a scorner of democracy, who was later to become a radical. He had worked for a short time with Benjamin Lundy on the latter's antislavery newspaper in Baltimore, but he knew practically nothing of slavery from observation or experience. Nevertheless, he and his followers indulged in the most bitter attacks against the moral character of the slaveholders in language so extreme that they injured their cause, both in the North and the South. The platform of *The Liberator* was immediate emancipation of the slaves without any compensation to slaveholders. Since the Federal Constitution sanctioned slavery, Garrison condemned it as a compact with Hell and urged his followers not to vote or have anything to do with this iniquitous government. Indeed, he made slavery a great moral issue, upon which he would neither speak with moderation nor accept compromise. In 1857 he and his followers held a Secession Convention at Worcester, Massachusetts, to advocate that the *Northern* states should secede from the union with slaveholders.

The abolition movement in the North was soon organized into very vocal and active societies. The New England Anti-Slavery Society was founded by Garrison in 1832, and during the next year the American Anti-Slavery Society was started in New York City. The New York group of abolitionists until recently has been neglected by historians, but it contained such effective agitators as the wealthy merchants Lewis and Arthur Tappan, William Jay, the son of Chief Justice John Jay, and

Gerrit Smith, the millionaire of Peterboro. The Northern abolitionists were profoundly influenced by the English antislavery crusade, which had led to the abolition of slavery in the British West Indies in 1833. From the reformers across the Atlantic were learned most of the techniques used in advancing the antislavery cause in the United States. The New England and New York societies published tons of lurid and fervid antislavery publications which they sent through the mails to leading men in the South. Although the New York group adopted as their slogan "immediate emancipation," they interpreted this term to mean that "measures looking toward ultimate emancipation be immediately begun"—which was a reasonable program that Jefferson might have approved. Southerners made the mistake of thinking of all abolitionists in terms of the extremists. But there were many type of abolitionists, some of them admirable persons. Indeed, there is a reaction today toward a much more favorable view of the abolitionists than was held before the present civil rights struggle developed.

Less spectacular than the eastern abolitionists, but tremendously influential, was the Ohio group, led by Theodore D. Weld. The publication of the correspondence of Weld, the Grimké sisters, and of James G. Birney, as well as modern studies of the abolition movement have called attention to this group. Although Garrison remained in Southern eyes the symbol of the antislavery movement, it is possible that the Midwestern band of abolitionists accomplished more effective work in converting Northerners to the cause than did the Garrisonians. This group arose out of the great religious revivals conducted in the decade of the 1820's by Charles Grandison Finney. These Western abolitionists applied the technique of religious revivals to the abolitionist crusade, emphasizing the point that Southern slavery was a moral sin. Weld compiled a terrible tract called *American Slavery As It Is,* composed of recitals of abnormal and sensational incidents of Southern slavery that he had culled from newspapers and antislavery literature. Oberlin College, Ohio, founded in 1833, became the center of Western abolitionists and also one of the first American colleges to admit Negro students.

The abolitionists started out by attacking the institution of Southern slavery, but soon they began a violent and indiscriminate denunciation of Southerners and their way of life. They built up a stereotype of slavery and of Southern society that modern historians have found difficult to dispel. Ignoring the handicaps of the Negro as a human being and the rural condition of the South, they blamed all the backwardness of the region, the illiteracy of the people, the exhaustion of the soil, and the lack of industrialization on slavery. The abolitionists painted the South as a land where masters made female slaves their concubines and enslaved their mulatto offspring. The whip never ceased to sear the flesh of their trembling bond servants, for Southerners were cruel and coarse in all the relations of life. The slave trade and the separation of families were a constant staple of their exaggeration. The existence of a substantial middle class of yeoman farmers in the South was ignored, and members of the nonslaveholding class were portrayed as debased creatures. In politics the Slave Power was envisaged as always on the aggressive, striving to pollute free soil and exclude honest laborers from the North from settling on the public domain. In short, the abolitionist propaganda was a black-and-white type of ideology. Their libels of Southern civilization naturally aroused the deepest resentment and intolerance below the Mason and Dixon line. Furthermore, with few exceptions, notably the millionaire abolitionist, Gerrit Smith, they did not advocate the only fair and practical step toward accomplishing their objective, namely, the use of Federal funds to aid in compensating the owners of slaves for their loss of property as a result of adopting the abolition program.

The abolition movement led to one of the most violent struggles in the history of the nation to suppress civil liberties. Some of the worst offenses against civil liberties occurred in the Northern border states during the decade of the 1830's. Here abolitionists were mobbed countless times and denied their constitutional rights of free speech and freedom of the press. In 1835 they discovered an effective means of advertising their cause by linking it to the cause of civil liberties. They began the strategy of presenting petitions to Congress to abolish slavery in the District of Columbia. Southern Congressmen maintained that such petitions should not be received, on the ground that Congress had no jurisdiction over domestic slavery. On the other hand, Northern Representatives, as a group, believed that the antislavery petitions should be received, for the freedom of petition, one of the sacred rights of a democracy, was involved in this issue. The chief presenter of the abolitionist petitions, which came in a flood in 1835–1837, was John Quincy Adams, the ex-President, who was now serving as a Congressman from Massachusetts. In this new role as the introducer of antislavery petitions, Adams maintained, perhaps insincerely, that he was not an abolitionist but was fighting for the freedom of petition. This bald-headed, irascible, and satirical New Englander enjoyed taunting the long-haired orators from the South, and his activities in Congress increased the atmosphere of bitter hatred between the sections. The South was not lacking in violent champions, chief of whom was

Henry A. Wise of Virginia, who replied to Adams in kind, and who led a secession of Southern Congressmen from the House of Representatives in 1836 when William Slade of Vermont caustically attacked Southern slavery.

On account of Southern pressure, the lower house of Congress in 1836 adopted the Gag Resolution. Introduced by Henry L. Pinckney of South Carolina, this resolution provided that the House of Representatives should technically receive the abolition petitions, but that such petitions should immediately be laid on the table, without referring them to a committee and without debate. The Gag Rule was continually renewed until it was repealed in December, 1844. The Gag Rule of 1840 read, "That no petition, memorial, resolution or other paper praying the abolition of slavery in the District of Columbia, or any State or Territory, or the slave trade between the States or Territories of the United States in which it now exists, shall be received by the House, or entertained in any way whatever." This rule was finally abandoned when Northern allies withdrew their support and when some Southerners realized that it was doing more harm than good to their cause. Southern chauvinists who insisted on a rigid rejection of abolitionist petitions in Congress did the South a great disservice by alienating the sympathy of many sincere lovers of democracy in the North who were indifferent to the reform of abolishing slavery.

Another flaming issue that involved civil liberties was the right of the abolitionists to use the Federal mails to forward their publications into the Southern states. In the summer of 1835 a mob in Charleston, South Carolina, supported by ex-Governor Robert Y. Hayne, entered the post office and destroyed several sacks of mail containing abolition literature. The whole South was aroused to the menace of the circulation of abolition publications below the Mason and Dixon line. It is an established fact that the abolition societies of the North had adopted a concerted plan in 1835 to flood the South with antislavery pamphlets, newspapers, and periodicals. These publications were addressed to white people to persuade them to abandon slavery, but Southerners believed that the abolitionists designed their publications to foment servile insurrections. A small minority of the slaves could read, some of whom were taught illegally by their masters. It was feared in the South that the lurid antislavery literature would fall into the hands of some brooding Nat Turner who would lead a slave revolt.

In a message to Congress, December, 1835, President Jackson recommended that Congress pass a law prohibiting the circulation through the mails in the Southern states of "incendiary publications intended to instigate the slaves to insurrection." Calhoun was opposed to such a law that would enhance the power of the Federal government. Instead, he introduced into the Senate early in 1836 a bill that would accomplish the object of erecting a *cordon sanitaire* against the entry of abolition literature into the South. His bill would have made it illegal for Northern postmasters to receive and forward abolition publications to those states whose laws prohibited the circulation of such publications. This bill failed to pass Congress, but a policy of Federal censorship of the mails, preventing the free circulation of abolition publications in the South, was adopted unofficially by the Postal Department. With impunity, individual postmasters in the South refused to deliver abolition literature. A series of Postmasters General, from the days of Amos Kendall in Jackson's cabinet to Joseph Holt in Buchanan's cabinet, permitted this extralegal censorship of the mails. No attempt was made to discriminate between literature that was a rational discussion of the evils of slavery and that which comprised incendiary appeals to violence. Thus, a genuine blockade was set up that protected the minds of Southern whites from the contagion of abolitionist arguments as well as kept the slaves from being inflamed to dissatisfaction or revolt by emotional antislavery literature.

The development of an elaborate argument justifying slavery began in the South before the rise of the abolition movement. South Carolina was the cradle of the proslavery argument, which originated as early as 1789. In the Palmetto State the economic and social humus was most suited to the growth of an intellectual defense of slavery. South Carolina had inherited its type of slavery and its attitudes toward the Negro from the rich sugar island of Barbados. Moreover, rice culture was peculiarly adapted to the use of slave labor. The Negroes who worked in the rice fields were blacker and closer to Africa than the slaves of the upper South. Many of the Gullah Negroes, indeed, had been imported during the period when the state reopened the African slave trade, and they needed stricter control than the slaves of the upper South who had been habituated to the white man's society for a considerable period of time. Also the prevalence of malaria in the swampy, coastal region of South Carolina and Georgia caused the wealthy planters to flee from the miasmic lowlands during the spring and summer seasons, leaving the blacks and the overseers to the tender mercies of disease-bearing mosquitoes. It was natural that South Carolina should have discarded the apologetic tone of defending slavery, and that, in such leaders as Senator William Smith, Whitemarsh B. Seabrook, and Doctor Thomas Cooper, president of South Carolina College during the decade of the 1820's and early 1830's, should have produced some of the early exponents of slavery as a positive good. Later, in 1852, the great classic of slavery defense, *The Pro-Slavery Argument,* containing essays by the South Carolinians, William Gilmore Simms, Chancellor William Harper, James H. Hammond, and others, was published at Charleston. Was this elaborate rationalization of a great social evil motivated by the desire to convince nonslaveholders in order to preserve planter control, or was it evoked to quiet the conscience of Southern slaveholders, or was it a recognition of the moral power of world opinion?

In the upper South a pioneer in producing an able argument in defense of slavery was Thomas Roderick Dew. He was a young professor at William and Mary College who had recently returned from study in Germany. In 1832 he published a pamphlet, *Review of the Debates in the Virginia Legislature of 1831 and 1832,* in which he refuted arguments for the emancipation of the slaves made in the Virginia legislature following the Nat Turner revolt. Dew based his polemic partly upon his study of Aristotle, who had justified Greek slavery as a recognition of the natural inequality of man. In addition to deriving a justification of slavery from the order of nature, Dew pointed out that the Bible sanctioned this ancient institution. These philosophical arguments were buttressed by the economic argument, namely, the lucrative profits obtained from the internal slave trade and the immense property loss that emancipation would entail.

One of the most powerful arguments in the proslavery dialectic was the alleged support of the Bible, for the overwhelming majority of Southern people were firmly indoctrinated in a belief in the sacredness of the literal word of the Bible. The apologists of slavery drew their arguments chiefly from the Old Testament, which described a primitive society among the Jews in which the patriarchs held slaves. They also maintained that slavery was ordained by God as a punishment of Canaan, son of Ham, from whom, they affirmed without reliable evidence, the Negroes were descended. In the New Testament the defenders of slavery pointed to the advice that the Apostle Paul had given to a fugitive slave to return to his master as well as Christ's silence in regard to this contemporary institution.

The Baptist, Methodist, and Presbyterian churches in the South, which had condemned slavery in their pioneering period, gradually became proslavery as their congregations grew wealthier and more attached to the vested interests of Negro slavery. Leading Southern ministers, such as J. H. Thornwell, B. H. Palmer, Thornton Stringfellow, H. B. Bascom, and William A. Smith, wrote books and delivered sermons showing that the institution was approved by God. In 1844 the general conference of the Methodist Episcopal Church requested Bishop James O. Andrew of Georgia to cease his episcopal duties until he had disposed of his slaves acquired by a second marriage. This incident led to the separation of the Southern churches from the national organization and the formation at Louisville in 1845 of the Methodist Episcopal Church, South. During the same year, the Southern Baptists, incensed over the refusal of the national missions board to employ a slaveholder as a missionary, organized the "Southern Baptist Convention."

A myriad of arguments were adduced to show that slavery was needed as a social discipline. If the slaves were emancipated, the proslavery argument maintained, they would be uncontrollable, refusing to work, stealing, and committing other crimes. The example of the shiftless free Negro was brought forward as a solemn warning against a wholesale freeing of the blacks. The poor whites and mechanics feared the consequences of competition with hordes of emancipated Negroes. The massacre of the whites in Santo Domingo and the great decline of agriculture in Jamaica after emancipation were cited as proofs of the dangers of emancipation. Religious apologists maintained that the Negro had benefited tremendously from slavery, for he was transported from the barbarism of Africa and was civilized and Christianized in America.

Demagogues raised the bogey of social amalgamation if the slaves were freed and allowed to remain in the country. Deeply rooted in Southern psychology was a fear that the emancipation movement would break down the barriers set up to preserve a pure white race in the South. The census of 1860 clearly indicated that racial antipathy was not enough to prevent considerable miscegenation, for approximately 13 per cent of the Negroes in the United States were mulattoes. The presence of mixed blood among the free Negroes was striking, approximately three fourths of the free Negroes having an admixture of white blood. New Orleans was notorious for the concubinage system by which Creoles maintained mulatto and quadroon mistresses.

The emphasis in the Old South on the biological inferiority of the Negroes bears some resemblance to the Nazi ideology of race. Most Southerners took it for granted that the Negroes constituted a permanently subordinate race, inferior to the white man in intellect, character, and physiology—a childlike people. Dr. Josiah C. Nott, a physician of Mobile, Alabama, strengthened the ethnological argument justifying slavery by his theory of the plural origin of the races. In 1854, with the collaboration of the archaeologist, George R. Gliddon, he published his work *Types of Mankind,* in which he maintained that mankind did not have a common progenitor but that the Negro and the white man were

separately created species. This theory, which denied the unity of mankind, did not win general acceptance in the South, because it conflicted
with the Biblical account of the origin of man. Reverend John Bachman
of Charleston, South Carolina, confuted the pluralists in his volume *The
Doctrine of the Unity of the Human Race* (1850), and Dr. John Wesley
Monette of Mississippi wrote a manuscript entitled "The Causes of the
Variety of the Complexion and Form of the Human Species," in which
he affirmed the primitive unity of the races and explained racial differences as caused by environment and climate. One of the degrading
effects of the proslavery argument that has continued into our day is the
emphasis on the basic inferiority of the Negro to the white man. Although
it is impossible at the present time to determine conclusively whether
Negroes as a group are equal in innate intelligence and personality to
Caucasians, the advances that have been made within recent years in
measuring human intelligence tend to throw doubt on the old allegation
of the inherent inferiority of the Negro.

In the last decade of the ante-bellum period the proslavery argument
acquired a militant leadership under Henry Hughes of Port Gibson,
Mississippi, William J. Grayson, collector of the port of Charleston, and
George Fitzhugh, a Virginia lawyer. Hughes wrote a defense of slavery
in 1854 entitled *A Treatise on Sociology,* in which the word *sociology*
was first used in the title of an American book. It is interesting to note
that the proslavery argument led to pioneering efforts, however preju-
diced, in developing the science of sociology. Hughes maintained that the
advance of civilization in the South had essentially changed Southern
slavery, although he produced no valid evidence for his conclusion. He
held that slavery had advanced to warranteeism, which gave to the master
a trusteeship over the slave and the ownership of the slave's labor only
and not of his body. Convinced that slavery was a positive good, he was a
strong advocate for reopening the African slave trade under an apprenticeship system. In 1856 Grayson published a vigorous poem, "The
Hireling and the Slave," defending Southern slavery as a paternal institution far more humane than the wage slavery of New England.

Fitzhugh's important contribution was to focus attention on the evils
of Northern capitalism, which the abolitionists had ignored in their zeal
to reform their Southern brethren. He proclaimed "the failure" of free
society, for the condition of the laboring class in the industrial states, he
asserted, was worse than that of the Southern slave. Slavery, he maintained, was a wholesome and natural institution for free *white* workers as
well as black slaves. He predicted that the North would experience the
diseased symptoms of competitive society prevalent in Europe, strikes, the

rise of socialism, and the degradation of the laboring class, whereas the South with its harmonious labor system would become the conservative balance wheel of the nation. In the land of plantations the slaves were cared for during sickness, old age, and in times of economic depression, whereas in the North wages were barely enough to sustain life, child labor of the worst type prevailed, and the workers were ruthlessly exploited by capitalists in a form of wage slavery. These arguments were propagated in *De Bow's Review,* in Southern newspapers, and in two paradoxical books, *Sociology for the South; or, the Failure of Free Society* (1854), and *Cannibals All! or, Slaves Without Masters* (1857). Fitzhugh was not a deep or original thinker, deriving many of his ideas from Carlyle and the English reviews, but he was primarily "a propagandist of the Old South." He did a great deal of harm by exacerbating the relations between the North and the South.

One of the significant phases of the proslavery argument was the repudiation of the philosophy of liberalism. Senator James H. Hammond of South Carolina denounced the Declaration of Independence with its doctrine of the equality of men as a fallacious and glittering generalization. On the contrary, he declared that men were naturally unequal and that Negro slavery furnished "a mudsill" for a white democracy. Calhoun supported this argument in behalf of slavery, contending that the Southern slaves freed the master class from drudgery and allowed them the leisure to cultivate the art of politics and refined living. Thus Southern society was idealized as being a Greek democracy, resting on a base of slave labor. The Whig leader, Abel P. Upshur, and later Fitzhugh, flatly rejected the romantic liberalism of Thomas Jefferson in favor of a thoroughly conservative and aristocratic caste system. But they misrepresented public opinion in the South, which was devoted to a decentralized white democracy. When Fitzhugh proclaimed an irrespressible conflict between the free form of society and the slave system, which would be resolved by the extension of slavery into the North, he represented only a distinct minority of Southerners. By his extreme editorials in the Richmond press he furnished Seward and Lincoln with the ammunition for their famous speeches on "the irrepressible conflict" and "the House Divided" doctrine that alarmed Northern workers and small farmers.

Opposing the overwhelming propaganda of the proslavery argument was a small group of Southern liberals. No one will ever know the strength of the antislavery sentiment in the South during the period 1831–1861, whose finest representatives were persons of tender conscience or critical-minded individuals who were able to free themselves from traditional views. Probably most of the antislavery people were inarticulate because of prudence. The outspoken opponents of slavery, of whom records have been preserved, were chiefly members of the professional class, preachers, college professors, lawyers, and literary men. As regards geographical distribution, they were located principally in the upper South, where Negroes were decidedly less concentrated than in the deep South. . . .

The Southern liberals of the ante-bellum period were lonely individuals, free lances, who were, in general, denied the use of the press or the right of subjecting the Southern social system to sanative criticism. Almost without exception they spurned the epithet *abolitionist,* for they advocated a gradual process of emancipating the Negroes. Some of them were belated Jeffersonians, who believed in the dignity of man even if he wore a black skin. Perhaps the two most powerful impulses that led them to urge the removal of slavery were moral considerations, as evidenced by the considerable proportion of ministers in their ranks, and economic realism. . . .

The conviction of the Southern people in 1860 that slavery was justified (whereas their forefathers had thought it to be wrong) represents a striking victory of mass propaganda—one of the greatest in human history. It may be compared to the absolute victories of the Nazi and Communist propaganda in Germany and Russia. Such conquests over the mind of a society can occur only when the economic and social conditions are ripe for the acceptance of the propaganda. Such was the case of the Old South. These conditions were: (1) a strong economic involvement with the institution of slavery, (2) the fluctuating fear of a servile insurrection incited by the Northern abolition crusade, (3) a power struggle between the sections over the expansion of slavery, and (4) the rise of a fundamentalist type of religion that provided perhaps the strongest support for the preservation of an archaic institution of labor.

CHAPTER 36

THE ANTISLAVERY
MOVEMENT: THE
BLACK ABOLITIONISTS

Although American historians have become, in recent years, extremely interested in Negro history, much of the historical writing about Negroes tells us more about what whites have done to or for the black man than about what blacks themselves have done. In the history books, Negroes have seldom been at the center of historical action. A case in point is the history of the abolitionist movement. The movement clearly concerned Negroes, but most historical treatments emphasize the activities of white abolitionists, such as William Lloyd Garrison, Theodore Dwight Weld, and the Tappan brothers, on behalf of Negroes. Usually ignored, or slighted, is the active and important role that blacks played in the antislavery cause.

In this selection, Leon F. Litwack concentrates on the activities of black antislavery workers, placing them squarely in the mainstream of the abolitionist movement. Negroes not only demonstrated an appreciation of the work of antislavery leaders, but they also provided a black critique of the movement by attacking abolitionist apathy, prejudice, and lack of concern for the Northern Negro. But most important, Negroes participated actively in the movement against slavery. Professor Litwack discusses the part played by Negroes in the post-Revolutionary emancipation movement, the use by Negroes of newspapers, tracts, orations, legislative petitions, and conventions in their antislavery activity, disagreements between white and black abolitionists, internal dissension among Negro leaders over policy and ideology and, finally, the emergence of a new militancy among Negro abolitionists.

A central theme in this selection is the prevalence of disagreement, between blacks and whites, and among Negroes themselves, over the best approach to the slavery problem. Is there a corresponding disagreement today among the leaders of the movement for the uplift of Negroes? On the other hand, despite the differences among black abolitionists, does it appear that their activities had the effect of moving the antislavery crusade toward a more militant approach—one which did not necessarily exclude the use of violence? Has the increased participation of Negroes in the modern movement tended to have the same effect? Finally, to what extent do you see parallels between the attitudes and positions of the black abolitionists and black leaders of the present day? In answering these questions, a perusal of Chapters 38 and 39 in Volume II will be helpful.

In addition to Litwack and Louis Filler, who is cited in the introduction to Chapter 34, the student will find useful Richard Bardolph, *The Negro Vanguard** (1959), Herbert Aptheker, *The Negro in the Abolitionist Movement* (1941), Carter G. Woodson, *The Mind of the Negro as Reflected in Letters Written during the Crisis, 1800-1860* (1926), and Herbert Aptheker, *A Documentary History of the Negro People in the United States** (1951). For use in comparing Negro participation in the abolition movement and in the modern Negro revolt, see Charles E. Silberman, *Crisis in Black and White** (1964).

ABOLITIONISM: WHITE AND BLACK
LEON F. LITWACK

The widely publicized activities of white antislavery workers and the commanding figures of William Lloyd Garrison, Wendell Phillips, and Theodore Weld have tended to obscure the important and active role of the Negro abolitionist. The antislavery movement was not solely a white man's movement. Through their own newspapers, conventions, tracts, orations, and legislative petitions, Negroes agitated for an end to southern bondage and northern repression. The white abolitionist encountered strong and often violent public opposition, but the Negro abolitionist risked even greater hostility, for his very presence on the antislavery platform challenged those popular notions which had stereotyped his people as passive, meek, and docile. As a common laborer, the Negro might be tolerated, even valued, for his services; as an antislavery agitator, he was frequently mobbed.

Negro abolitionism preceded by several years the appearance of Garrison and *The Liberator*. Encouraged by the post-Revolutionary emancipation movement, Negroes worked with sympathetic whites to remove the last traces of slavery in the North and to call for its abolition in the South. As early as 1797, four illegally manumitted North Carolina Negroes, who had fled to the North to escape re-enslavement, petitioned Congress to consider "our relief as a people." Three years later, a group of Philadelphia free Negroes appealed directly to Congress to revise the federal laws concerning the African trade and fugitive slaves and to adopt "such measures as shall in due course emancipate the whole of their brethren from their present situation." In addition to legislative petitions, meetings commemorating the abolition of the African slave trade or the end of slavery in a particular state afforded opportunities for such prominent Negro leaders as Peter Williams, Nathaniel Paul, William Hamilton, and Joseph Sidney to voice their sentiments on public issues. The organization of independent churches, Free African societies, Masonic lodges, and anti-

SOURCE. Leon F. Litwack, *North of Slavery: The Negro in the Free States, 1790-1860,* Chicago: University of Chicago Press, 1961, pp. 230-246. Copyright 1961 by University of Chicago Press. Reprinted by permission of University of Chicago Press and the author.

558 THE SWEEP OF AMERICAN HISTORY, VOL. I

colonialization meetings further intensified a growing race consciousness and helped to arouse the Negro community in several areas to a more vigorous defense of its civil rights.

Four years before the publication of the first issue of *The Liberator,* two Negro leaders, John Russwurm and Samuel E. Cornish, launched the first Negro newspaper—*Freedom's Journal*—in an effort to disseminate useful ideas and information and to attract public attention to the plight of those still in bondage. In the first issue, the editors announced that Negroes had to plead their own cause: "Too long have others spoken for us. Too long has the publick been deceived by misrepresentations." During its two years of publication, *Freedom's Journal* featured articles on the evils of slavery and intemperance, the importance of education and the progress of Negro schools, literary and historical selections, moral lessons, information on the various Afro-American benevolent societies, and a discussion of colonization. Cornish subsequently withdrew from the partnership and established a short-lived newspaper, *The Rights of All,* and Russwurm abandoned his editorial duties to join the colonizationists.

Negro antislavery agitation took on a more aggressive tone in 1829 as David Walker, a Boston clothing dealer and local agent for *Freedom's Journal,* contributed a powerful tract to abolitionist literature—*Walker's Appeal, in Four Articles.* Addressing his sentiments to the "coloured citizens" of the world, but particularly to those of the United States, Walker described American Negroes as "the most degraded, wretched, and abject set of beings that ever lived since the world began." Indeed, he asked, "Can our condition be any worse?—Can it be more mean and abject? If there are any changes, will they not be for the better, though they may appear for the worst at first? Can they get us any lower? Where can they get us? They are afraid to treat us worse, for they know well, the day they do it they are gone."

In Walker's estimation, four major factors accounted for this wretched state of affairs: slavery, ignorance, "the preachers of Jesus Christ," and the African colonization movement. Consequently, Negroes had to strive for economic and educational improvement and resist the encroachments of the colonizationists. ("America is as much our country, as it is yours.") The southern Negro, on the other hand, faced an even greater challenge, for he had to strike directly and perhaps violently for his freedom as a natural right. Once that thrust for liberty had been made, Walker advised, "make sure work—do not trifle, for they will not trifle with you—they want us for their slaves, and think nothing of murdering us in order to subject us to that wretched condition—therefore, if there is an *attempt* made by us, kill or be killed." To prevent the outbreak of racial war,

Walker warned the white man, recognize the legal rights of Negroes. There can be no mistaking the alternative. "Remember, Americans, that we must and shall be free and enlightened as you are, will you wait until we shall, under God, obtain our liberty by the crushing arm of power? Will it not be dreadful for you? I speak Americans for your good. We must and shall be free I say, in spite of you . . . . And wo, wo, will be to you if we have to obtain our freedom by fighting."

Within a year after its publication, the apparent popularity—or notoriety—of Walker's pamphlet warranted a third edition. The often violent reaction to its contents and the mysterious death of the author in 1830 undoubtedly assisted its circulation. Indeed, it had already caused some consternation in the North, and it understandably created outright alarm in portions of the South. Already beset by a growing fear of slave uprisings, the South could not afford to tolerate the potentially explosive appeal of a Boston clothing dealer. The governor of North Carolina denounced it as "an open appeal to their [the slaves'] natural love of liberty . . . and throughout expressing sentiments totally subversive of all subordination in our slaves"; the mayor of Savannah wrote to the mayor of Boston requesting that Walker be arrested and punished, and Richmond's mayor reported that several copies of *Walker's Appeal* had been found in the possession of local free Negroes; the governors of Georgia and North Carolina submitted the pamphlet to their state legislatures for appropriate action; and the Virginia legislature held secret sessions to consider proper measures to prevent the pamphlet's circulation. Finally, four southern states—Georgia, North Carolina, Mississippi, and Louisiana—seized upon the pamphlet to enact severe restrictions to cope with such "seditious" propaganda.

The South was not alone in its critical reaction. Walker's medicine for the ills of American Negroes was too strong for many white abolitionists. "A more bold, daring, inflammatory publication, perhaps never issued from the press of any country," antislavery publisher Benjamin Lundy declared. "I can do no less than set the broadest seal of condemnation on it." Lundy's disciple, William Lloyd Garrison, had just launched his own career as an aggressive antislavery publicist and was more equivocal in his reaction. The editor of *The Liberator* found it difficult to reconcile his belief in nonresistance with his unconcealed admiration of Walker's courage and forthrightness. While deploring the circulation of this "most injudicious publication" and "its general spirit," Garrison admitted that it contained "many valuable truths and seasonable warnings."

The appearance of *The Liberator* in 1831 and the formation of the American Anti-Slavery Society two years later thus found northern Ne-

groes already engaged in a variety of abolitionist activities. In addition
to publishing a newspaper and several antislavery tracts, Negroes had
taken steps to co-ordinate their actions through annual national conventions. On September 15, 1830, delegates gathered in Philadelphia's Bethel
Church to launch the first in a series of such conventions. Against a background of increasing repressive legislation in the North, the delegates
adopted an address to the free Negro population, pointing out that their
present "forlorn and deplorable situation" demanded immediate action.
Where Negroes were subjected to constant harassment and denied even
the right of residence, the most recent and blatant case being Ohio, such
action would have to take the form of emigration to Canada. There, the
convention advised, Negroes could establish themselves "in a land where
the laws and prejudices of society will have no effect in retarding their
advancement to the summit of civil and religious improvement." Meanwhile, those Negroes who chose to remain in the United States would have
to utilize every legal means to improve their political and economic position. Before adjourning, the delegates called upon Negroes to establish
auxiliary societies and send delegates to the next annual convention.

Convening annually up to 1835 and periodically thereafter, the national
Negro conventions regularly condemned the American Colonization Society, deprecated segregation and "oppressive, unjust and unconstitutional"
legislation, stressed the importance of organization, education, temperance,
and economy, and set aside the Fourth of July as a day of "humiliation,
fasting and prayer" when Negroes would ask for divine intervention to
break "the shackles of slavery." Meanwhile, the formation of auxiliary
state organizations, temperance groups, moral-reform societies, and educational associations created an unprecedented amount of unity and activity among northern Negroes, developed new leadership, and contributed
mightily to the strength of the newly formed white antislavery societies.

While engaged in these independent activities, Negro abolitionists also
hailed the appearance of a new militancy among their white supporters;
they not only welcomed the publication of *The Liberator* but actually
outnumbered white subscribers in the early years. "It is a remarkable
fact," William Lloyd Garrison wrote in 1834, "that, of the whole number
of subscribers to the *Liberator,* only about one-fourth are white. The
paper, then, belongs emphatically to the people of color—it is their organ."
In addition to contributing articles and letters to the antislavery press,
Negroes also attended and addressed abolitionist conventions and, notwithstanding some opposition, served as members of the executive committee and board of managers of both the American Anti-Slavery Society
and its later rival, the American and Foreign Anti-Slavery Society.

Negro abolitionists did not confine their activities to the United States. In the 1840's and 1850's, several of them toured the British Isles to promote antislavery sentiment and raise money for abolitionist enterprises. Englishmen crowded into meeting halls to see and hear leading American Negroes tell of the plight of their people and their own experiences as slaves or freemen. Frederick Douglass, for example, described his years of bondage in the South; William G. Allen told of his narrow escape from an enraged northern mob after proposing to marry a white girl; William and Ellen Craft related their flight to freedom and their subsequent exile to avoid prosecution under the Fugitive Slave Act; and Henry Highland Garnet undoubtedly mentioned the mob that ejected him from a Connecticut boys' academy. While arousing their foreign audiences with these tales of slavery and racial violence, Negroes also found much to amaze them. "Here the colored man feels himself among friends, and not among enemies," one Negro "exile" wrote from England, "among a people who, when they treat him well, do it not in the patronizing (and, of course insulting) spirit, even of hundreds of the American abolitionists, but in a spirit rightly appreciative of the doctrine of human equality." For some of these Negro abolitionists, returning home must have been difficult. After extensive travels in England and Europe, for example, William Wells Brown came back to Philadelphia, only to find himself proscribed from the Chestnut Street omnibus on his first day home. "The omnibuses of Paris, Edinburgh, Glasgow, and Liverpool, had stopped to take me up," he recollected, "but what mattered that? My face was not white, my hair was not straight; and, therefore, I must be excluded from a seat in a third-rate American omnibus."

Both Negro and white abolitionists suffered from internal dissension over fundamental questions of policy and ideology. While the white antislavery societies split over the issues of political action, nonresistance, women's rights, disunion, and the nature of the Constitution, Negroes argued the merits of moral suasion and separate conventions. By 1835, the American Moral Reform Society, dominated largely by Philadelphia Negroes, replaced the regular convention movement. Dedicated to "improving the condition of mankind," the new organization urged Negroes to abandon the use of the terms "colored" and "African," to refrain from holding separate colored conventions, to integrate as fully as possible into white society, to support the equality of women, and to adopt the principles of peace, temperance, brotherly love, and nonresistance "under all circumstances." In adopting such a program, the moral reformers obviously allied themselves with the Garrisonians in the growing factional struggle within the antislavery movement.

The American Moral Reform Society found little support outside the Garrisonian strongholds of Philadelphia and Boston. Meanwhile, New York Negro leaders launched a new weekly newspaper, the *Colored American,* which expressed dismay over the growing split in abolitionist ranks and the activities of the moral reformers. Editor Samuel Cornish noted that the delegates to a recent moral-reform convention had impressed him as "vague, wild, indefinite and confused in their views." Only drastic reorganization and the adoption of a more vigorous program of action could possibly salvage the society. As for their efforts to substitute the term "oppressed Americans" for "colored people," Cornish called this sheer nonsense. "Oppressed Americans! *who are they?"* he asked. "Nonsense brethren!! You are COLORED AMERICANS. The indians are RED AMERICANS, and the white people are WHITE AMERICANS and *you are good as they, and they are no better than you."*

While scolding the moral reformers, the *Colored American* also engaged in a controversy with the pro-Garrison *National Anti-Slavery Standard* over the advisability of colored conventions. "We oppose all exclusive action on the part of the colored people," the *Standard* announced in June, 1840, "except where the clearest necessity demands it." As long as Negroes contented themselves with separate churches, schools, and conventions, public sentiment would remain unaltered. Instead, Negroes should join with their white friends to demand equal rights as men, not as colored persons, and thus confirm the abolitionists' contention that racial distinctions had no place in American society. The moral reformers enthusiastically indorsed the position of the *Standard*. Other Negro leaders, however, immediately condemned it and upheld the need for independent action. The abolitionists had done much for the Negro, Samuel R. Ward wrote to the editor of the *Standard,* but too many of them "best love the colored man at a distance" and refuse to admit or eradicate their own prejudices. In the meantime, Negroes had to meet and act for themselves.

Although the American Moral Reform Society had a short life, the split in white abolitionist ranks continued to undermine Negro unity. By 1840, Garrisonians shared the field of agitation with the American and Foreign Anti-Slavery Society and the Liberty party. New England and Philadelphia Negroes generally supported the American Anti-Slavery Society and condemned the critics of Garrison as unworthy of confidence or support. New York Negroes, on the other hand, not only dissociated themselves from the moral reformers but generally indorsed direct political action and contributed to the leadership and campaigns of the Liberty party. At one point, the *Colored American* attempted to restore some semblance of sanity and unity to abolitionists by urging them to avoid peripheral issues and petty bickering and get back to opposing slavery. "Why . . . make governments or anti-governments—resistance or non-resistance—women's rights or men's rights—Sabbaths or anti-Sabbaths, a bone of contention?" the Negro newspaper asked. "None of these should have any thing to do with our Anti-Slavery efforts. *They are neither parts nor parcels of that great and holy cause,* nor should they be intruded into its measures." Rather than promote abolitionist harmony, however, such sentiments, coupled with the editors' indorsement of political action and their refusal to censure Garrison's critics, induced some severe attacks and threats to cut off financial support from the paper. Defending their right to differ with Garrison on any issue and to adopt an independent editorial policy, the editors of the *Colored American* warned Negroes that as long as they permitted white abolitionists to act and think for them, "so long they will outwardly treat us as men, while in their hearts they still hold us as slaves."

In a desperate effort to retain their hold on the antislavery movement, Garrison and his associates made every effort to secure Negro support. In Boston and New Bedford, Negro meetings acclaimed Garrison as a "friend and benefactor" and indorsed his antislavery position. Already abandoned by many of his white followers, Garrison expressed gratification over such reactions. The opposition knew, he wrote, "that, so long as I retain the confidence of my colored friends, all of their machinations against me will prove abortive." Had Garrison known that his most important Negro ally, Frederick Douglass, was about to desert him, he would have had much less cause for optimism.

As late as September 4, 1849, Douglass had insisted that he was a loyal Garrisonian abolitionist, and there was little reason to doubt him. According to the tenets of that faith, he had excoriated the Constitution as "a most foul and bloody conspiracy" against the rights of three million slaves, had supported disunion as the most effective means to remove federal protection from the "peculiar institution," had belittled political action as futile and necessarily compromising, and had advocated moral persuasion rather than violence in attacking slavery. Nevertheless, signs of revolt became increasingly apparent. After founding the *North Star* in 1847 against the advice of his Boston friends and moving from New England to Rochester, Douglass carefully re-evaluated his position and listened to the arguments of various New York abolitionists who had already broken with Garrison. Before long, the Negro leader reached the conclusion that disunion would only place the slaves at the complete mercy of the South, that political action constituted "a legitimate and

powerful means for abolishing slavery," that southern bondage would probably have to expire in violence, and that the Constitution made no guarantees to slavery but in fact implied its eventual extinction. In May, 1851,
Douglass utilized the annual convention of the American Anti-Slavery
Society to proclaim his heresy publicly. "There is roguery somewhere,"
Garrison reputedly declared as he moved to strike the *North Star* from
the list of approved abolitionist publications. Douglass had gone over to
the enemy.

Although he voiced his new position on the lecture platform and in the
North Star, Douglass hoped to avert a complete break with Garrison. "I
stand in relation to him something like that of a child to a parent," he
wrote to Charles Sumner. Nevertheless, Garrisonian anxiety and alarm
soon changed to vigorous denunciation and even personal defamation.
The Liberator now placed Douglass' editorials in the section usually reserved for proslavery sentiments, and it charged that the Negro leader
had betrayed his former friends for the sake of financial gain, that he
possessed ambitions to become the spokesman of the colored race, and
that he had lost much of his moral fervor and influence. When Douglass
reduced the size of his newspaper, one Garrisonian gleefully wrote to an
English friend that the Negro editor "has the confidence of very few, the
respect . . . of none. Do what he may, we shall take no notice of him,
and I think his career—on professedly anti-slavery grounds—will soon
come to an end." Although Garrison generally allowed his followers to
deal editorially with the Negro upstart, he confided to friends that he
regarded Douglass as a malignant enemy, "thoroughly base and selfish,"
"destitute of every principle of honor, ungrateful to the last degree, and
malevolent in spirit," and unworthy of "respect, confidence, or counte-
nance." Such was the thoroughness of the Garrison indictment.

Replying to his critics with equal bitterness, Douglass called them "vigilant enemies" and labeled their Negro followers as "practical enemies of
the colored people" and contemptible tools. The Garrisonians had first
attempted to silence his newspaper, he charged, and now they sought to
expel him from the antislavery fold as a dangerous heretic. "They talk
down there [Boston] just as if the Anti-Slavery Cause belonged to them
—and as if all Anti-Slavery ideas originated with them and that no man
has a right to 'peep or mutter' on the subject, who does not hold letters
patent from them." Douglass also sought to clarify his differences with
Garrison, but these appeared to be lost in the bitter editorial war. Before
long, Negroes in various parts of the country were meeting to discuss the
conflict and to choose sides. Chicago Negroes condemned Garrison's "vile
crusade" against "the voice of the colored people"; a Rhode Island convention hailed Douglass as "our acknowledged leader"; and an Ohio

gathering decisively defeated a proposal calling on Negroes to abstain from voting in those areas where they enjoyed the franchise. Meanwhile, Garrisonian Negro leaders reiterated the charges of *The Liberator* and claimed to speak for "all the true colored men in the country."

Efforts to reconcile the two antislavery leaders met with no success— only time could heal the deep wounds left by this useless and wasteful struggle. To many Negro and white abolitionists, the entire affair presented a rather sordid and dreary spectacle. "Where is this work of excommunication to end?" Harriet Beecher Stowe wrote Garrison. "Is there but one true anti-slavery church and all others infidels?—Who shall declare which it is." While the dispute helped to reduce the effectiveness of the antislavery movement, it also clearly demonstrated some of the weaknesses in Garrison's ideological and tactical position. Nonresistance, the rejection of political action, disunion, and a proslavery interpretation of the Constitution did not strike many abolitionists in the 1840's and 1850's as being either suitable or realistic weapons with which to abolish southern bondage or northern proscription. Indeed, the final triumph of Garrisonian objectives resulted almost entirely from the employment of strictly non-Garrisonian methods—political agitation and armed force.

Internal dissension hampered but did not stifle the independent activities of Negro abolitionists. Despite the Garrisonian antipathy to "complexional conventions," local and state organizations continued to meet in the 1840's, and several national conventions revived interstate co-operation. On August 15, 1843, Negroes from various states met in Buffalo to consider "their moral and political condition as American citizens." After several heated debates—which partly reflected the growing split in abolitionist ranks—the convention adopted a series of resolutions which denounced the American Colonization Society and the proslavery churches, indorsed the Liberty party, stressed the value of temperance, education, the mechanical arts, and agriculture, and attributed the plight of free Negroes—North and South—to the evils of slavery.

Henry Highland Garnet, a New York Negro leader, hoped to secure from the Buffalo delegates a more aggressive stand against slavery. Indicting the cruelties of southern bondage and praising as martyrs those Negroes who had led revolts for freedom, Garnet delivered a powerful plea to the slave population in tones reminiscent of David Walker's *Appeal*. "Brethren arise, arise!" he declared. "Strike for your lives and liberties. Now is the day and the hour. Let every slave throughout the land do this, and the days of slavery are numbered. You cannot be more oppressed than you have been—you cannot suffer greater cruelties than you have already. *Rather die freemen than live to be slaves.* Remember that you are FOUR MILLIONS! . . . Let your motto be resistance! resistance! RESISTANCE!" Although the Garrisonians had suffered a defeat on the issue of political action, they managed to steer the convention away from such a commitment to physical violence in overthrowing slavery. By a vote of nineteen to eighteen, the delegates refused to indorse Garnet's address. Instead, the convention affirmed its faith in the ultimate righteousness of human government and the abolition of slavery through its instrumentality. Relieved at this outcome, one Garrisonian intimated that Garnet, who had also been one of the first Negroes to indorse the Liberty party, had fallen under the influence of bad advisers. "If it has come to this," Garnet replied, "that I must think as you do, because you are an abolitionist, or be exterminated by your thunder, then I do not hesitate to say that your abolitionism is abject slavery."

Although the Buffalo delegates refused to indorse Garnet's address, its contents and the closeness of the convention vote indicated the emergence of a new militancy among Negro abolitionists. Six years later, Garnet's address and Walker's appeal appeared together in a published pamphlet—reportedly at the expense of an obscure New York farmer, John Brown. An Ohio Negro convention immediately ordered five hundred copies to be "gratuitously" circulated. That same year, a New York Negro editor reminded the governor and legislature of Louisiana that their recent expressions of sympathy for Hungarian rebels might be equally applicable to their own bondsmen. "Strike for your freedom now, at the suggestion of your enslavers," the editor wrote. "Make up your minds to die, rather than bequeath a state of slavery to your posterity."

By the end of the 1840's, the appeals of Garnet and Walker—once deemed too radical—received growing support in Negro conventions, newspapers, and antislavery tracts. Even Frederick Douglass, who had bitterly opposed Garnet's address, abandoned his previous conviction that moral persuasion and nonresistance alone could abolish slavery. While still a loyal Garrisonian, he created a "marked sensation" in 1849 when he told a Faneuil Hall audience that he would "welcome the intelligence to-morrow, should it come, that the slaves had risen in the South, and that the sable arms which had been engaged in beautifying and adorning the South were engaged in spreading death and devastation there." Three years later, Douglass told the national Free Soil party convention that the slaveholders had forfeited their right to live. The potential horrors of a slave insurrection should no longer be allowed to obstruct the path of freedom. "The slaveholder has been tried and sentenced," he declared in 1857. "He is training his own executioners." The following year, John Brown visited the Douglass home and remained there for several weeks, devoting most of his time to writing financial appeals for a yet unrevealed plan.

CHAPTER 37

THE ISSUE OF SLAVERY EXPANSIONISM

We have learned in previous readings that in the 1850's the debate over slavery began to dominate the political scene. Sooner or later in a debate concerning the political merits of any of the great questions of the day, someone was sure to point out the effect that a decision would have on Negro slavery. Questions relating to the acquisition and settlement of new lands were not exceptions. Eugene Genovese, in this chapter from his book, *The Political Economy of Slavery** (1965), discusses Southern attitudes toward expansion. He shows that these attitudes, notwithstanding the opinion of earlier historians, were solidly favorable, at least among the members of the slaveholding aristocracy, which was the element that dominated the South's political life.

As is obvious from this selection, Genovese's view is not the customary historical outlook on slavery. Whereas past writers considered matters such as the profitability of the institution and its relative harshness or mildness, Genovese explores other questions. He argues that one cannot understand the hold that slavery had on the South and on the slaveholder unless he views slavery as the cornerstone of the Southern planters' way of life. This approach has won much acclaim for Genovese's book but has also stirred up considerable controversy.

Genovese's approach to slavery reopens the following questions to historical speculation. Did slavery have to expand to exist? Why? What were the political consequences to the slave system of nonexpansionism? What were the social and economic consequences of nonexpansionism? What were the political, social, and economic consequences of expansionism to the North?

A traditional statement, doubting that slavery was expansionistic, may be found in Avery O. Craven's *The Coming of the Civil War** (original edition, 1942), which is somewhat updated in the same author's *Civil War in the Making** (1959). Harry Jaffa, *Crisis of the House Divided* (1959), insists, in the course of an analysis of the Lincoln-Douglas debates, that slavery was expansionistic. Allan Nevins, in *The Ordeal of the Union,* 2 vols. (1947), and *The Emergence of Lincoln,* 2 vols. (1950), gives a detailed account of events concerning slavery in the territories. Somewhat tighter in compass is J. G. Randall and David Donald, *The Civil War and Reconstruction* (1961). An even briefer treatment, synthesizing recent scholarship, is E. B. Smith, *The Death of Slavery* (1967).

* Available in a paperback edition.

THE ORIGINS OF SLAVERY EXPANSIONISM
EUGENE GENOVESE

Once upon a time in the happy and innocent days of the nineteenth century, men believed that Negro slavery had raised an expansionist slaveocracy to power in the American South. Today we know better. The revisionists have denied that slavery was expansionist and have virtually driven their opponents from the field. Their arguments, as distinct from their faith in the possibilities of resolving antagonisms peacefully, rest on two formidable essays. In 1926, Avery O. Craven published his *Soil Exhaustion As A Factor in the Agricultural History of Maryland and Virginia,* which sought to prove that the slave economy could reform itself, and three years later Charles William Ramsdell published his famous article on "The Natural Limits of Slavery Expansion," which constituted a frontal attack on the "irrepressible conflict" school.

I propose to restate the traditional view, but in such a way as to avoid the simplistic and mechanistic notions of Cairnes and his followers and to account for the data that has emerged from the conscientious and often splendid researches of the revisionist historians. Specifically, I propose to show that economics, politics, social life, ideology, and psychology converged to thrust the system outward and that beneath each factor lay the exigencies of the slaveholding class. Each dictated expansion if the men who made up the ruling class of the South were to continue to rule.

ROOTS AND TAPROOTS

Antebellum Southern economic history reinforces rather than overturns the nineteenth-century notion of an expansionist slaveocracy. That notion undoubtedly suffered from grave defects and considerable crudeness, for it insisted on the lack of versatility of slave labor and the steady deterioration of the soil without appreciating the partially effective at-

SOURCE. Eugene D. Genovese, *The Political Economy of Slavery: Studies in the Economy and Society of the Slave South,* New York: Pantheon Books, 1961, pp. 243–270. Copyright 1961, 1963, 1965 by Eugene D. Genovese. Reprinted by permission of Pantheon Books, a Division of Random House, Inc., and the author.

tempts to reform the slave economy. Yet the revisionist work of the Craven school, which has contributed so much toward an understanding of the economic complexities, has not added up to a successful refutation.

We may recapitulate briefly the main points of the preceding studies, which lead to the economic root of slavery expansionism. At the beginning we encounter the low productivity of slave labor, defined not according to some absolute or purely economic standard, but according to the political exigencies of the slaveholders. The slaves worked well enough in the cotton and sugar fields, when organized in gangs, but the old criticism of labor given grudgingly retains its force.

Slave labor lacked that degree and kind of versatility which would have permitted general agricultural diversification. Slaves could and did work in a variety of pursuits, including industrial, but under circumstances not easily created within the economy as a whole. Division of labor on the plantations and in society proceeded slowly and under great handicaps. The level of technology, especially on the plantations, was kept low by the quality and size of the labor force. Mules and oxen, for example, replaced faster horses principally because they could more easily withstand rough and perhaps vengeful handling. Negro laborers had been disciplined to sustained agricultural labor before being brought to the Americas. Their low productivity arose from the human and technological conditions under which they worked, and these arose from the slave system.

An analysis of Southern livestock and the attempts to improve it reveals the complex and debilitating interrelationships within the slave economy. The South had more than enough animals to feed its population but had to import meat. A shortage of liquid capital made acquisition of better breeds difficult, and the poor treatment of the animals by the slaves made maintenance of any reasonable standards close to impossible. As a further complication, the lack of urban markets inhibited attention to livestock by depriving planters of outlets for potential surpluses. The South boasted an enormous number of animals but suffered from their wretched quality.

Slavery provided a sufficient although not a necessary cause of soil exhaustion. It dictated one-crop production beyond the limits of commercial advantage and in opposition to the political safety of the slaveholders. Planters could not easily rotate crops under the existing credit structure, with a difficult labor force, and without those markets which could only accompany industrial and urban advance. The sheer size of the plantations discouraged fertilization. Barnyard manure was scarce, commercial fertilizers too expensive, and the care necessary for advantageous application unavailable. The shortage of good implements complicated the operation, for manures are easily wasted when not applied properly.

Craven insists that the existence of a moving frontier, north and south, brought about the same result, but as we have seen, the special force of slavery cannot so easily be brushed aside. The North confronted the devastating effects of soil exhaustion and built a diversified economy in the older areas as the frontier pushed westward. The South, faced with the debilitating effects of slavery long after the frontier had passed, had to struggle against hopeless odds.

These direct effects of slavery received enormous reinforcement from such indirect effects as the shortage of capital and entrepreneurship and the weakness of the market. Capital investments in slaves and a notable tendency toward aristocratic consumption had their economic advantages but inhibited the rise of new industries. The Southern market consisted primarily of the plantations and could not support more than a limited industrial advance. The restricted purchasing power of the rural whites, of the urban lower classes, and indirectly of the slaves hemmed in Southern manufacturers and put them at a severe competitive disadvantage relative to Northerners, who had had a head start and who had much wider markets in the free states to sustain production on an increasing scale. The barriers to industrialization also blocked urbanization and thereby undermined the market for foodstuffs.

Southern industrialization proceeded within the narrow limits set by the social milieu as well as by the market. The slaveholders controlled the state legislatures and the police power; they granted charters, set taxes, and ultimately controlled the lives of regional industries. So long as industry remained within safe limits the slaveholders offered no firm resistance, or at least no united front. Those limits included guarantees against the rise of a hostile and independent bourgeoisie and excessive concentrations of white workers of doubtful loyalty. Since the big slaveholders provided much of the capital for industry and since the plantations provided much of the regional market, the risks remained small, for even the nonslaveholding industrialists necessarily bound themselves to the rural regime and tried to do good business within the established limits. Industry made some progress; industrialization, understood as a self-propelling process, did not.

The South made one form of agricultural adjustment while slavery remained. The great agricultural revival in the Upper South overcame the most serious effects of slavery by reducing the size of slaveholdings, converting surplus slaves into cash, and investing the funds in the supervision, fertilization, and reconversion of smaller estates. This process threatened the economic and ideological solidity of the slaveholders' regime and had other drawbacks, but most important, it broke on an immanent contradiction. The sale of surplus slaves depended on markets further south, which necessarily depended on virgin lands on which to apply the old, wasteful methods of farming. Reform in one region implied exhaustive agriculture in another. Thus, the process of agricultural reform had narrow limits in a closed slave system and had to be reversed when it pressed against them. No solution emerged from within the system, but one beckoned from without. The steady acquisition of new land could alone guarantee the maintenance of that interregional slave trade which held the system together.

This economic root of slavery expansion was only one of several roots, but itself grew strong enough to produce an ugly organism. If we begin with the economic process it is because the external threat to the slaveholders mounted so clearly, objectively and in their consciousness, with each new census report on the material conditions of the contending forces. The slaveholders might, of course, have resigned themselves to Lincoln's victory, accepted the essentials of the Wilmot Proviso, faced the impending crisis of their system, and prepared to convert to some form of free labor. Anything is possible where men retain the power to reason. Such a choice would have spelled their death as a ruling class and would have constituted moral and political suicide. Many contemporaries and many historians ever since have thought that they should have agreed to do themselves in. With this view I do not wish to argue. Neither did they.

The economic process propelling the slave South along expansionist paths had its political and social parallels, the most obvious being the need to re-establish parity in the Senate or at least to guarantee enough voting strength in Washington to protect Southern interests. In an immediate political sense the demand for more slave-state Congressmen was among the important roots of expansionism, but in a deeper sense it was merely a symptom of something more fundamental. Had the South not had a distinct social system to preserve and a distinct and powerful ruling class at its helm, a decline of its political and economic power would have caused no greater alarm than it did in New England.

A second political root was the need to protect slavery where it was profitable by establishing buffer areas where it might not be. Just as the British had to spend money to secure ascendancy in Tibet so that they could make money in India, the South had to establish political control over areas with dubious potentialities as slave states in order to protect existing slave states. The success of the Texas cause removed the fear of Mexican tampering with slaves in Louisiana, much as annexation removed potential British-inspired tampering. "Texas must be a slave country," wrote Stephen F. Austin to his sister. "The interest of Louisiana requires that it should be; a population of fanatical abolitionists in Texas would have a very pernicious and dangerous influence on the overgrown population of the state." In 1835, when a large Mexican force was reported near the Brazos River, the slaves apparently did attempt to rise. One hundred Negroes were severely punished, some executed.

John A. Quitman, former governor of Mississippi, tried to organize a filibustering expedition to Cuba during 1853–1855, particularly because he feared that abolition there would present dangers to the South. Samuel R. Walker and Albert W. Ely, among others, warned that Britain and France would force a weak Spain to sacrifice Cuban slavery and thereby isolate the South as a slaveholding country. Many far-sighted Southerners understood the danger of permitting the isolation of Southern slavery. They desired Cuba in order to secure political control of the Caribbean, as well as for economic reasons.

Beyond Cuba and the Caribbean lay Brazil, the other great slave-holding country. "These two great valleys of the Amazon and the Mississippi," declared the *Richmond Enquirer* in 1854, "are now possessed by two governments of the earth most deeply interested in African slavery— Brazil and the United States . . . The whole intermediate countries between these two great valleys . . . is a region under the plastic hand of a beneficent Providence . . . How is it to be developed?" [*sic*] With black labor and white skill. Cuba and Santo Domingo, it continued, were potentially the bases for the control of the whole Caribbean. Such a political complex would cause the whole world to "fall back upon African labor."

The warning of the Louisville *Daily Courier* in 1860 that Kentucky could afford to remain in the Union but that the Lower South could not touched the central issue. Suppose, it asked, Kentucky sold its slaves south. "And then what? Antislavery will not be content to rest. . . . The war will be transferred to the Cotton States."

The need to push forward in order to ward off concentrations of hostile power arose from the anachronistic nature of the slave regime. By 1850, if not much earlier, world opinion could no longer tolerate chattel slavery, and British opposition in particular was both formidable and implacable. The transformation of the Caribbean into a slaveholders' lake and an alliance or understanding with Brazil held out the only hope of preventing a dangerous and tightening containment.

Slaveholders also sought additional territory to reduce the danger of internal convulsion. Lieutenant Matthew F. Maury, who helped bring about the American exploration of the Amazon Valley in the 1850s, discussed the eventual absorption of much of Latin America by the United States:

I cannot be blind to what I see going on here. It is becoming a matter of *faith*—I use a strong word—yes a matter of faith among leading Southern men, that the time is coming, nay that it is rapidly approaching when in order to prevent this war of the races and all its horrors, they will in self-defense be compelled to conquer parts of Mexico and Central America, and make slave territory of that—and that is now free.

Representative Thomas L. Clingman of North Carolina told the House that Northerners were "too intelligent to believe that humanity, either to the slave or the master, requires that they should be pent up within a territory which after a time will be insufficient for their subsistence, and where they must perish from want, or from collision that would occur between the races." Southerners always kept the West Indian experience in front of them when they discussed the racial proportions of the population.

Probably, steady infusions of new land were also needed to placate the nonslaveholders, but we know little about slaveholder-nonslaveholder relationships as yet and little can be said with certainty.

The psychological dimension of slavery expansionism has been the subject of various essays and has, for example, emerged from interpretations of Southern frustration and resultant aggression. We need not pursue esoteric lines of inquiry, especially with formulas so broad as to be able to encompass almost every society in any age, to appreciate that a psychological dimension did exist. As Southerners came to regard slavery as a positive good and as they came to value the civilization it made possible as the world's finest, they could hardly accept limits on its expansion. To agree to containment meant to agree that slavery constituted an evil, however necessary for the benefit of the savage Africans. That sense of mission so characteristic of the United States as a whole had its Southern manifestation in the mission of slavery. If slavery was making possible the finest society the world had ever known, the objections to its expansion were intolerable. The free-soil argument struck at the foundations of the slaveholder's pride and belief in himself.

It is difficult but unnecessary to assess the relative strength of the roots of slavery expansionism. Each supported and fed the taproot—the exigencies of slaveholder hegemony in a South that fought against comparative disadvantages in the world market and that found itself increasingly isolated morally and politically. From another point of view, each was a manifestation of those exigencies. Although some appear to be objective, or matters of social process, whereas others appear to be subjective, or matters of psychological reaction to possibly imaginary dangers, the difference becomes unimportant when each is related to the fundamental position of the slaveholders in Southern society. The existence of a threatening economic process, such as has been described, would have been enough to generate fear and suspicion, even without the undeniable hostility arising in the North on political and moral grounds. . . .

THE CONTRADICTORY NATURE OF THE "NATURAL LIMITS" THESIS

The "natural limits" thesis is self-contradictory—and, in one important sense, irrevelant—for it simultaneously asserts that slavery was nonexpansionist and that it would have perished without room to expand. The only way to avoid judging the thesis to be self-contradictory is to read it so as to state that slavery needed room to expand but that, first, it needed room only in the long run and, second, that it had no room. This reading removes the contradiction but destroys the thesis.

If the slave states would eventually need room to expand, they had to set aside new territory when they could get it or face a disaster in a few years or decades. Hence, wisdom dictated a fight for the right to take slaves into the territories, for ultimately that right would be transformed from an abstraction into a matter of life and death. W. Burwell of Virginia wrote in 1856 that the South needed no more territory at the moment and faced no immediate danger of a redundant slave population. "Yet statesmen," he concluded, "like provident farmers, look to the prospective demands of these who rely upon their forethought for protection and employment. Though, therefore, there may be no need for Southern territory for many years, yet it is important to provide for its acquisition when needed . . ."

To establish that slavery had no room to expand is not to refute the theory of slavery expansionism. If it could be firmly established that slavery needed room to expand but had none, then we should have described a society entering a period of internal convulsion. The decision of most slaveholders to stake everything on a desperate gamble for a political independence that would have freed them to push their system southward emerges as a rational, if dangerous, course of action.

THE TERRITORIAL QUESTION

One of the most puzzling features of Ramsdell's essay is the virtual equation of cotton and slavery. Only occasionally and never carefully does he glance at the prospects for using slave labor outside the cotton fields. To identify any social system with a single commodity is indefensible, and in any case, Southern slavery had much greater flexibility. Ramsdell's essay is puzzling with respect to these general considerations but even more so with respect to his specific contention that contemporary Southerners viewed the territorial question as a cotton question. They did not.

When the more intelligent and informed Southerners demanded the West for slavery they often, perhaps most often, spoke of minerals, not cotton or even hemp. Slavery, from ancient times to modern, had proved itself splendidly adaptable to mining. Mining constituted one of the more important industries of the Negroes of preconquest Africa, and slave labor had a long history there. The Berbers, for example, used Negro slaves in West Africa, where the salt mines provided one of the great impetuses to the development of commercial, as opposed to traditional and patriarchal, forms of slavery. Closer in time and place to the South, Brazil afforded an impressive example of the successful use of slave labor in mining. In the middle of the eighteenth century diamond mining supplemented gold mining in Minas Gerais and accounted for a massive transfer of masters and slaves from the northeastern sugar region. Southern leaders knew a good deal about this experience. "The mines of Brazil," reported *De Bow's Review* in 1848, "are most prolific of iron, gold, and diamonds. . . . The operation is performed by negroes . . . 30,000 negroes have been so employed." The eastern slave states had had experience with gold mining, and although the results were mixed, the potentialities of slave labor had been demonstrated. Planters in the Southwestern states expressed interest in gold mines in Arkansas and hopefully looked further west. "If mines of such temporary value should, as they may, be found in the territories, and slaves could be excluded from these," wrote A. F. Hopkins of Mobile in 1860, "it would present a case of monstrous injustice." . . .

It is one thing to note that Southerners sought to expand slavery into Mexico's mining districts or that they lamented the political barriers to the expansion of slavery into New Mexico's; it is another for us to conclude that their hopes and desires were more than wishful thinking. Allan Nevins has presented a formidable case to suggest that slavery had little room even in the mining districts of the Southwest and Mexico. He shows that even in the Gadsden Purchase the economic exigencies of mining brought about the quick suppression of the enterprising individual by the corporation. Western mining, as well as transportation, lumbering, and some forms of agriculture, required much capital and became fields for big business. High labor costs led to a rising demand for labor-saving machinery, but Nevins does not consider that this very condition might, under certain circumstances, have spurred the introduction of slave labor. . . . On economic grounds Nevins' analysis has much to offer, but his remarks on the competitive struggle in the Southwest and on the inability of Southerners to get national support for Caribbean adventures do not prove nearly so much as he thinks. At most, they suggest that the North was strong enough to block slavery expansionism into the Southwest and frustrate Southern ambitions elsewhere. If so, the case for secession, from the proslavery viewpoint, was unanswerable.

Nevins' remarks illustrate the wisdom of other Southern arguments— that the South had to secure new land politically, not by economic advance, and that the South had to have guarantees of positive federal protection for slavery in the territories. The *Charleston Mercury,* climaxing a decade of Southern complaints, insisted in 1860 that slavery would have triumphed in California's gold-mining areas if Southerners had had assurances of protection for their property. It singled out the mineral wealth of New Mexico as beckoning the South and even saw possibilities for slave-worked mining in Kansas. With fewer exaggerations De Bow, a decade earlier, had pointed to the political aspect of the problem: "Such is the strength and power of the Northern opposition that property, which is ever timid, and will seek no hazards, is excluded from the country in the person of the slave, and Southerners are forced, willingly or not, to remain at home. Emigrants, meanwhile, crowd from the North." During the bitter debate in Congress over the admission of California, Senator Jeremiah Clemens of Alabama replied heatedly to Clay in words similar to those used by De Bow. Free-soil agitation, he said, had kept slavery from the territories. "Property is proverbially timid. The slaveholder would not carry his property there with a threat hanging over him that it was to be taken away by operation of law the moment he landed."

Representative Joseph M. Root of Ohio, Whig and later Republican, commented on such charges by boasting that if the Wilmot Proviso had accomplished nothing more than to create a political climate inimical to slavery expansion, it had accomplished its purpose.

The Southern demand for federal guarantees made sense, but even that did not go far enough. Ultimately, the South needed not equal protection for slave property but complete political control. If a given territory could be organized by a proslavery party, then slaveholders would feel free to migrate. Time would be needed to allow the slave population to catch up; meanwhile, free-soil farmers had to be kept out in favor of men who looked forward to becoming slaveholders. Under such circumstances the territory's population might grow very slowly, and the exploitation of its resources might lag far behind that of the free territories. Nothing essential would be lost to the South by underdevelopment; the South as a whole was underdeveloped. In short, the question of political power necessarily had priority over the strictly economic questions. . . .

Historians like Nevins and Paul W. Gates have expressed confidence that slavery could not have triumphed in Kansas even if it had been allowed a foothold. They may be right, but only if one assumes that the South remained in the Union. Slavery expansionism required fastening proslavery regimes in such territories, but ultimately it required secession to protect the gains. Had Kansas joined a Southern Confederacy as a slave state, its wheat-growing slaveholders could have secured the same internal advantages as the sugar planters of Louisiana, and Union wheat could effectively have been placed at a competitive disadvantage in the Southern market.

Ramsdell's dismissal of Southern interest in Cuba and Central America, however necessary for his argument, does not bear examination. Southern sugar planters, who might have been expected to fear the glutting of the sugar market should Cuba enter the Union, spoke out for annexation. They seem to have been convinced that suspension of the African slave trade to Cuba would raise the cost of production there to American levels and that they would be able to buy Cuban slaves cheaply. Besides, as Basil Rauch points out, Louisiana sugar planters were moving to Cuba during the 1850s and looking forward to extending their fortunes. Southerners, like Northerners, often spoke of annexation in nationalist terms and sometimes went to great lengths to avoid the slavery question. J. J. Ampère heard that Cuba had been detached from the mainland by the Gulf Stream and rightfully belonged to the United States. He recommended that France reclaim Britain on the same grounds. He also heard that Cuba had to be annexed to provide a rest home for American consumptives. J. C. Reynolds, writing in *De Bow's Review* in 1850, described appalling losses in the illegal slave trade to Cuba and urged annexation to bring American law enforcement there and to end the terrible treatment of the Negroes. More sweepingly, some argued that without more territory the Negroes of the United States would be extinguished by overpopulation and attendant famine. All for the poor Negroes! Others, like Soulé and Albert Gallatin Brown, bluntly demanded Cuba and Central America to strengthen and defend slavery.

As for William Walker, he said enough to refute the Scroggs-Ramsdell interpretation. His *War in Nicaragua* makes clear that American politics made it necessary for him to appear to renounce annexation and that he was biding his time. No matter. His purpose there, as he boldly proclaimed, was to expand slavery as a system.

Opposition to territorial expansion by many Southerners has led some historians to deny the existence of an "aggressive slaveocracy" or to assert, with Ramsdell, that Southerners were too individualistic to be mobilized for such political adventures, which were often contrary to their private interests. No conspiracy theory is required. That there were many Southern leaders who sensed the need for more territory and fought for it is indisputable. That individual Southerners were not always willing to move when the interests of their class and system required them to merely indicates one of the ways in which slavery expansionism proved a contradictory process. Southerners opposed expansion for a variety of reasons, but mostly because they feared more free states. Expansion southward had the great advantage of not being cotton expansion, and the economic argument against it was weak. On the other hand, many feared that the annexation of Cuba would provide an excuse for the annexation of Canada or that the annexation of Mexico would repeat the experience of California. This opposition should be understood essentially as a preference for delaying expansion until secession had been effected, although there were, of course, many who opposed both. . . .

INVITATION TO A (SELF INFLICTED) BEHEADING

The South had to expand, and its leaders knew it. "There is not a slaveholder in this House or out of it," Judge Warner of Georgia declared in the House of Representatives in 1856, "but who knows perfectly well that whenever slavery is confined within certain specified limits, its future existence is doomed." The Republican party, said an editorial in *The Plantation* in 1860, denies that it wants to war on slavery, but it admits that it wants to surround it with free states. To do so would be to crush slavery where it now exists. Percy L. Rainwater's study of sentiment in Mississippi in the 1850s shows how firmly convinced slaveholders were that the system had to expand or die. Lincoln made the same point in his own way. He opposed any compromise on slavery expansion in 1860 because he feared new and bolder expansionist schemes and because he wished to contain slavery in order to guarantee its ultimate extinction.

Nevins' discussion of Lincoln's view illuminates one of the most tenacious and dubious assumptions on which many historians have based their interpretations of the origins of the war:

> In view of all the trends of nineteenth century civilization, the terrible problem of slavery could be given a final solution only upon the principle . . . of gradual emancipation. . . . The first step was to stop the expansion of slavery, and to confine the institution within the fifteen states it already possessed. Such a decision would be equivalent to a decree that slavery was marked for gradual evolution into a higher labor system. Slavery confined would be a slavery under sentence of slow death. The second step would be the termination of slavery in the border states. Missouri by 1859 stood near the verge of emancipation . . .

The assumption on which these notions rest is that the South, faced with containment, could have accepted its consequences. On the further assumption that men may agree to commit suicide, the assumption is plausible.

If instead of speaking of the South or of the system of slavery, we speak of the slaveholders who ruled both, the assumption is less plausible. The extinction of slavery would have broken the power of the slaveholders in general and the planters in particular. Ideologically, these men had committed themselves to slaveholding and the plantation regime as the proper foundations of civilization. Politically, the preservation of their power depended on the preservation of its economic base. Economically, the plantation system would have tottered under free labor conditions and would have existed under some intermediary form like sharecropping only at the expense of the old ruling class. The "higher" forms depended on the introduction of commercial relations that would have gradually undermined the planters and guaranteed the penetration of outside capital. We have the postbellum experience to cite here, although it took place at a time when the planters had suffered hard blows, but slaveholders saw the dangers before the war and before the blows. "Python," in a series of brilliant articles in *De Bow's Review* in 1860, warned that emancipation, even with some form of "apprenticeship" for the Negroes, would open the way for Northern capital to command the productive power of the South. Once Negro labor is linked to capital in the open market, he argued, rather than through the patriarchal system of plantation slavery, it will fall prey to a predatory, soulless, Northern capitalism. There will be no place left for the old master class, which will be crushed by the superior force of Northern capital and enterprise or absorbed into them. "Of what advantage is it to the South," he asked, "to be destroyed by Mr. Douglas through territorial sovereignty to the exclusion of Southern institutions, rather than by Mr. Seward through Congressional sovereignty to the same end? What difference is there to the South whether they are forcibly led to immolation by Seward, or accorded, in the alternative, the Roman privilege of selecting their own mode of death, by Douglas? Die they must in either event."

These words demonstrate that the probable effect of a "higher labor system" on the fortunes of the slaveholding class was not beyond the appreciation of its intellectual leaders. We need not try to prove that so specific an appreciation was general. The slaveholders knew their own power and could not help being suspicious of sweeping changes in their way of life, no matter how persuasively advanced. Their slaveholding psychology, habit of command, race pride, rural lordship, aristocratic pretensions, political domination, and economic strength militated in defense of the status quo. Under such circumstances an occasional voice warning that a conversion to tenantry or sharecropping carried serious dangers to their material interests sufficed to stiffen their resistance.

No demagogy or dogmatic speculation produced "Python's" fears. Even modest compensation—paid for by whom?—would have left the planters in a precarious position. At best, it would have extended their life as a class a little while longer than postbellum conditions permitted, but Northern capital could not long be kept from establishing direct relationships with tenants and sharecroppers. The planters would have steadily been reduced to middlemen of doubtful economic value or would have merged imperceptibly into a national business class. The change would have required, and eventually did require under disorderly postbellum conditions, extensive advances to laborers in the form of additional implements, fertilizer, household utensils, even food, and innumerable incidentals. This process guaranteed the disintegration of the old landowning class, however good an adjustment many of its members might have made to the new order.

Those who, like Max Weber, Ramsdell, even Phillips, and countless others, assume that the South could have accepted a peaceful transition to free labor gravely misjudge the character of its ruling class. The question of such a judgment is precisely what is at issue. As noted in the Introduction to this volume, a revisionist historian might accept the empirical findings reported here and even the specific interpretations of their economic significance and still draw different conclusions on the larger issues. The final set of conclusions, and the notion of a general crisis itself, eventually must rest on agreement that the slaveholders constituted a ruling class and that they displayed an ideology and psychology such as has merely been suggested in these studies.

The slaveholders, not the South, held the power to accede or resist. To these men slaves were a source of power, pride, and prestige, a duty and a responsibility, a privilege and a trust; slavery was the foundation of a special civilization imprinted with their own character. The defense of slavery, to them, meant the defense of their honor and dignity, which they saw as the essence of life. They could never agree to renounce the foundation of their power and moral sensibility and to undergo a metamorphosis into a class the nature and values of which were an inversion of their own. Slavery represented the cornerstone of their way of life, and life to them meant an honor and dignity associated with the power of command. When the slaveholders rose in insurrection, they knew what they were about: in the fullest sense, they were fighting for their lives.

CHAPTER 38

THE DISRUPTION OF

AMERICAN POLITICS

Perhaps the best way to describe the election of 1860 would be to say that the Democrats lost it rather than that the Republicans won it. In this essay, Roy Nichols describes how some Democrats lost faith in nominating conventions and disrupted the Democratic party, one of the most significant bonds that united the nation. Nichols also shows how relatively minor events can sometimes assume real magnitude. Such an event was the decision (reached at the 1856 Democratic convention in Cincinnati) to hold the 1860 convention in Charleston, South Carolina. In view of the incredibly disruptive issues of 1860, the Democrats would have had trouble reaching compromises anywhere. To meet in the hotbed of secession was to multiply these problems and to make compromise even more difficult. With the aid of historical hindsight, one can easily see that they should have met on neutral ground.

A significant point that Nichols makes by inference is the importance of compromise in making the American political system work. As Herbert Agar states in the preface to the 1966 edition of his great work, *The Price of Union,** "Once, unhappily, both parties failed at the same time in their assuaging mission, both offered us 'a choice instead of an echo.' The result was Civil War." Agar's judgment should be weighed in the light of two facts: (1) that the Republican party was still extremely young, so that there is no exact comparison between 1860 and the two-party contests of later years, and (2) that, actually, four parties entered the race and, therefore, the voters had the opportunity to choose variety of positions after the conventions.

The Nichols essay also raises the question of whether it was necessary for the South to secede at all. His answer would appear to be "no." Actually, the Democrats controlled the House, Senate, and the Supreme Court. Did this control mean that the voice of the South would be heard and respected? Could Southerners thus hope for a permanent deadlock on the more obnoxious proposals of Lincoln and his party? However, it is possible that, if the South had not made its bid to establish an independent slaveholding Confederacy, it would have continued to decline in economic and industrial importance until, eventually, having lost its political power, it would have been so weak in relation to the North and the West that it could not have seriously contemplated secession. In short, was it now or never for the disunionists? Perhaps it was even later than they thought. Since the South had already suffered a decline during the fifties, can it be argued that Clay and Webster, by their efforts to achieve the Compromise of 1850, delayed the Civil War in a way that ultimately added to the advantages of the North and that, in fact, they saved the Union (although not peaceably) as they had hoped?

In addition to Agar's work (cited above), the student should study two classics of modern American historical writing. They are Roy Nichols, *The Disruption of the American Democracy** (1948), and Allan Nevins, *The Ordeal of the Union,* 2 vols. (1947) and *The Emergence of Lincoln,* 2 vols. (1950). See E. B. Smith, *The Death of Slavery* (1967), for a recent, concise treatment.

* Available in a paperback edition.

WHY THE DEMOCRATIC PARTY DIVIDED
ROY F. NICHOLS

Like the causes of the Civil War, the reasons for the disintegration of
the Democratic party in 1860 can be and have been elaborated at any
desired length. Rather than repeat the varieties of exegesis involved in
the use of such terms as the morals of slavery, the economic rivalry of
diverse interests, the cultural conflict between the sections, and the ecological and demographic elements among the determinants, it is more
realistic to consider some concepts in group dynamics, in the behavior of
individuals, small groups, and the masses in political association. For the
crux of the matter lay in the fact that complex party machinery collapsed
in a context of human failure. Because the behavior involved in failure
depends on the nature of the stimulation created by individuals and
groups through the senses of sight and hearing for those others in association, an analysis of it becomes a study in communication. In other words,
the analysis involves a consideration of who meets whom, of what is said
and seen during the course of recurrent interchanges, and, what is less
obvious and therefore harder to discover, the kind of reaction countless
nervous systems produce when confronted with the presence and behavior
of other organisms.

An understanding of such complexity requires a close look at the series
of meetings which brought into one train of communication the political
operators who directed the Democratic party's conventions in several
large meeting halls and in auxiliary places of accommodation. Here was
generated the great and devastating explosion of human emotion which in
time rocked the growing nation to its foundations, for the national conventions of the Democratic party were significant bridges of communication

SOURCE. Roy F. Nichols, in George Harmon Knoles, *The Crisis of the Union, 1860–
1861*, Baton Rouge, Louisiana: Louisiana State University Press, 1965, pp. 30–50.
Copyright 1965 by the Louisiana State University Press. Reprinted by permission
of the Louisiana State University Press and the author. Professor Nichols is Professor of History Emeritus, University of Pennsylvania, sometime Vice Provost and
Dean of the Graduate School of the University of Pennsylvania, and was President
of the American Historical Association in 1966.

over which the "great forces" moved to influence the behavior of the nation's political operators.

In Charleston, Richmond, Washington, and Baltimore in April, May, and June of 1860, there were a concentration and dispersion of definable and identifiable human beings through which the forces shaping political behavior operated. It was there that the doctrinaire position of certain Southern Democrats insisting on an endorsement of an impossible idea encountered the overweaning ambitions of Douglas and his followers who were determined to maintain power by demanding a heroic bit of realism. Such a collision produced a fatal impasse. In the almost unbelievable confusion of these meetings it was demonstrated that the Democratic party after thirty years of success was not strong enough, despite its age, its experience, and the skill of its operators, to maintain itself midst the confusion into which the action and interaction of the numerous forces shaping this growing nation had plunged American politics. . . .

For a decade these Democratic national conventions functioned with a reasonable degree of efficiency. But the next ten years told another story. Calhoun's presidential ambitions were not finally completely frustrated in the 1840's and he turned his bitterness on the convention which he charged was an instrument of the spoilsmen. Upon their manipulations he blamed much of his discomfiture. He and his followers wanted to change its rules and upon occasion refused to attend its sessions. Also a new generation, tired of Van Buren and the domination of his henchmen, demanded a "new deal." They were dismayed by the defeat of 1840 and by the rising Whigs; they feared Henry Clay might beat the rather shopworn "Little Van" in 1844. A group of Southern and Western politicos with some help from New England took over the convention in 1844 from the traditional Van Buren managers; the nomination of a "dark horse" was negotiated in the person of James Knox Polk.

Polk's selection was a convention maneuver engineered by a combination of state and congressional managers which eventually was to result in the disruption and disaffection of the New York party. This split in large part occurred because Polk developed no aptitude for party leadership. He was an avowed one-term candidate and thereby abdicated as party leader as soon as he had distributed the patronage. His efforts to heal the breach within New York by distributing offices was a dismal failure; and his foreign policy in Mexico and Oregon, despite its spectacular success, served to break up the New York party for years to come.

This schism destroyed the unity of the leaderless national convention of 1848. Here for the first time a candidate from the Northwest, General Lewis Cass, received the nomination; but the Van Buren half of the New

Yorkers walked out because they were not recognized as *the* Democracy and later joined with certain antislavery groups in forming an enlarged Free-Soil party. This break rather unfairly got the credit for the party's defeat in the fall at the hands of the hero, General Zachary Taylor. The precedent of walking out of a national convention had been set, and the secessionists were given credit for a capacity to defeat which they probably did not deserve.

In the conventions of 1844 and 1848 a new device was being set up for control: the National Committee presumed to give direction to the management of the party conclaves. However, by 1852 it had not achieved full stature; and, in the wake of the defeat of 1848, the party seemed to be drifting, for a second time leaderless, toward 1852. The professionals, by and large attracted by the understandings of 1848 and their status which had been established in that campaign, seemed inclined to renominate Cass now that the schism of 1848 apparently had been healed by a tenuous reunion of the wings of the New York party and by the Compromise of 1850. But such a variety of contestants arose opposing following this ancient trail that confusion began to descend.

The convention of 1852 promised to be a symbol of impotence. It was at this junction that a self-appointed inner group emerged to take over. One of Cass's chief rivals was James Buchanan of Pennsylvania, a candidate since 1844. His Pennsylvania managers joined a Southern bloc from Virginia, North Carolina, Georgia, Alabama, and Mississippi, some of whom had been active in the 1844 coup, to produce another dark horse. A combination of New Englanders and Mexican War generals from the Aztec Club had been pushing as second choice a New Hampshire brigadier general, Franklin Pierce; and he was the one the cabal "put over." They completed the ticket with Buchanan's friend, Senator William R. King of Alabama. The nonentity of this ticket, plus the pacifying influence of the Compromise of 1850 and the absurdity of General Winfield Scott as an opposing candidate, made Pierce's electoral college majority huge although his majority of the popular vote was slim.

Pierce had even less capacity for party leadership than had Polk, and despite his deceptive victory in 1852 the party was soon in difficulties. The New England President not only made similar mistakes in handling party patronage but he had none of Polk's success in foreign policy and in congressional legislation. Most unfortunately he joined Douglas and the other Senators in engineering the castastrophic repeal of the Missouri Compromise, and almost immediately a precocious phoenix arose from the ashes of the Whig party in the form of the young Republican eagle, dedicated to furthering Northern interests. The congressional elections of 1854–55 sounded a sharp warning which at first no one seemed able to heed. Were the days of Democratic power and Southern security numbered?

The maneuverings anticipating the Democratic convention of 1860 really began in 1856. As that fateful presidential year approached, the Democrats found themselves face to face for the first time with their new foe of unknown potential, the Republican party, born in an atmosphere of moral indignation and promotional expectation. Under these circumstances they commenced another chapter in their history. During their first decade they had been led by an efficient group of Jacksonian operators, Van Buren and his Albany Regency and the Richmond Junto associates; and at first Francis P. Blair, Sr., was in charge of the propaganda. In the 1840's the management was seized by a younger group with some senatorial guidance including lower South, Southwestern and Western participation and with old Father Ritchie taking over Blair's pen.

This guidance during the second phase had produced three candidates, Polk, Cass, and Pierce, two of them dark horses and the latter two not fortunate in their leadership. None of these candidates had been of Jacksonian stature. Despite the disasters during the Pierce regime and the threat of the new Republicans, this inept management seemed about to give Pierce the usually available renomination with the blessing of almost the solid South, the popular sovereignty West, and New England Democrats who were emotionally committed to their "first success." Such an invitation to defeat appeared so disturbing that it invited new leadership.

On the eve of the convention of 1856 a few practical operators came to the conclusion that they must intervene. A self-appointed senatorial group therefore decided to try a coup something along the order of the one of 1844. It is significant of the nature of the system of party control that the move originated in the Senate. Four Senators, John Slidell and Judah P. Benjamin of Louisiana, J. D. Bright of Indiana, and James A. Bayard of Delaware, motivated not only by a determination to avert defeat but also by extreme dislike of Douglas and a combination of distrust and contempt for Pierce, set up a headquarters at the convention in the house of a railroad promoter in Cincinnati, a new location for the national conventions. The Democratic National Committee headed by a Maryland chairman had decided that perhaps they had met in Baltimore long enough and that the growth of the Western wing of the party demanded recognition. Therefore they had picked out Cincinnati, the Queen City of the West, for the point of congregation; and it was thither that the Senatorial cabal wended its way.

Its members planned to accomplish their purpose by throwning over-board Pierce, bypassing Douglas, and negotiating the nomination of the veteran James Buchanan. His great assets were his long career and expert knowledge, the fact that he had been out of the country since 1853 and thus had avoided the Kansas malaise, and finally the fact that the hardheaded Senator Slidell of Louisiana thought of him as "his man." These contrivers succeeded. They formed a scattered combination led by Pennsylvania, Virginia, and Louisiana which could and did stop Pierce and Douglas and named Old Buck.

But the nomination of Buchanan was not all that happened at Cincinnati. When the Pierce cause became hopeless his strength was transferred to Douglas. Despite the shift Buchanan soon secured a majority; and at this point instead of fighting it out further and perhaps forcing another dark horse in at the finish, Douglas retired gracefully. Whether to secure this he had been promised a clear field in 1860 or whether he merely hoped he would have it because of his action is anybody's guess. Probably Douglas took encouragement from his situation. At any rate his friend John C. Breckinridge of Kentucky was nominated for the vice-presidency. The disappointed Southern supporters of Pierce would be somewhat placated, it was hoped, by designating Charleston, South Carolina, as the place for the Convention of 1860.

The administration of James Buchanan, the veteran expert, was even more disastrous than that of the novice, Pierce. The new President suffered every disaster from dysentery to John Brown's raid. Douglas likewise had had a trying four years. Buchanan slighted him in distributing patronage. The Supreme Court declared popular sovereignty, his great principle upon which he depended to harmonize Northern and Southern support, to be unconstitutional. The practical working of this provision had blown up in Kansas and had placed him in an almost unbearable dilemma in Congress. He had beaten Lincoln, but he had been compelled to advertise his rival's political skill. His Southern colleagues had taken away his chairmanship of the Senate Committee on Territories, thus depriving him even of office space. His wife had lost their baby through a miscarriage, and he himself had been seriously ill. Despite all this he had been picking up delegates and endorsements.

The climax of calamity came in the form of John Brown's raid in October, 1859, almost on the eve of the Charleston Convention. This disaster set the stage for a third coup, and for a third time its chief operators were in the Senate. When the Congress came together in December, 1859, Brown had just been hanged, certain elements in the South were arming and drilling, and there was no party in certain control of the House though it seemed likely that the Republicans would take over. The Republican management was preparing campaign literature for 1860 which was interpreted as endorsing the idea of slave uprising, and Douglas had appealed from the Supreme Court to history and had published a magazine article proving by historical evidence that the South was without any platform. Also the census of 1860 was being projected, and its figures quite obviously would register the fact that the South was doomed politically to hopeless minority. To the Southern Democracy the prospect was desperate, and to make it unbearable Douglas was the only candidate of prominence. In fact he might easily come to Charleston with a majority of the votes, certainly enough to stop anybody else under the two-thirds rule and to secure an endorsement of the popular sovereignty platform of 1856.

While the House took another frightening two months to organize, thus repeating 1855, the wheels of government were stalled. The Senate had time on its hands and a Southern bloc, reminiscent of those of 1844 and 1856, planned again. What they did has been called a "conspiracy" —this is a somewhat hysterical term, but it is near enough the truth to warrant its use in quotation marks. Certain Senators, and here we find Slidell and his Cincinnati associates working together with Jefferson Davis and a group of other Southern solons, had arrived at a determination. Apprehension had reached such a pitch in their constituencies that their Whig-American opponents were preparing to be 100 per cent Southern and fight them on the ground that they were "soft" on squatter sovereignty which was selling the South down the river. They must have an explicit endorsement of Southern rights in the Charleston platform. Jefferson Davis, in assuming Calhoun's mantle, wrote the formula which was presented to the Senate the day the Republicans at long last organized the House. If this platform was not accepted, the South would leave the convention as the Barnburners had in 1848. As an earnest of this the Alabama state Democratic convention instructed its delegation to Charleston to take the lead in this walkout if the demand was refused.

How far the senatorial managers had gone toward making a firm decision on breaking up the convention at this time is not of record. The indications are that they had, for it should be remembered that there was a code of honor observed in certain Southern political quarters under which it was dishonorable for delegates to refuse to support the program prescribed by a convention in which they had participated. There was a possibility that the Southern platform might be defeated and Douglas nominated. As a significant number of Southern delegates had determined never to support Douglas on a squatter sovereignty platform, honor bound them if they were defeated on platform to leave before he or anyone was nominated on a platform they could not accept.

A further step was also under discussion. What should be done if a Republican were elected in 1860? Here again Alabama serves as an indicator. Her state legislature passed a law requiring her governor, in that event, to summon a state convention to determine whether Alabama should secede. The question of the formation of a confederacy was likewise discussed. How far definite plans were formulated again cannot be categorically stated. It was an age of romantic empiricism so beefed up by hyperbolic rhetoric that it is difficult to discover exactly what some of these extravagant speakers were thinking. Despite the variety of possibilities talked about, it is probable that only one firm decision had been reached. There must be an "honest platform," or the party must be judged to have outlived its usefulness and be scrapped. Such action would clear the stage for new political engineering. Congress might take over. There might be a new Constitutional Convention as Calhoun had proposed. There might be secession and the formation of a new confederacy.

Douglas was living in the midst of this planning and sharing in some of its convivial moments. The practical Eastern operators were fully aware of what was going on; and at least one Republican Senator, William H. Seward, who most observers thought might well be that party's nominee in 1860, was on intimate terms with certain of his Senatorial colleagues from the South. It must not be forgotten that the Senate was a species of social club.

With some general lines of strategy laid out, Slidell, Bright, and Bayard went to Charleston and set up headquarters at the convention city, this time behind an ice cream saloon. From the moment of the opening of the convention shock tactics were employed, an old convention technique. Douglas' strength must be discovered at once and his managers, who after all came in large part from rotten boroughs or from states which could not deliver an electoral vote, must be given unmistakable warning that if the convention didn't damn well take the Southern platform, Douglas and the party could go to hell. This notice was registered in no uncertain terms by shouting, by climbing on tables, by variegated parliamentary disorder, and by threats and certain forms of alcoholic exaggeration.

The Douglas forces were ill-prepared for such a shock. They had come down into this atmosphere, new and strange to them, under close organization and strict discipline. They had hired a hall and set up a dormitory in it where they all slept row on row and where their leaders could keep track of them. They were probably very uncomfortable in the unaccustomed heat and also conscious of their lack of status in aristocratic Charleston. Politically they were as desperate as the Southerners. If they went home with this "honest" platform of Southern rights how could they survive in even the few Northern states left to them after the near disaster of 1856? Douglas was their only chance with some platform that had at least a coincidental resemblance to squatter sovereignty, Douglas' "great brinziple" of "let the people rule." Only this could beat "no more slave states" and "let freedom ring."

But it must not be forgotten that there was a third element in the compound. New York was back in strength though with the usual contest on hand. New York's truculent mayor, Fernando Wood, had tried to capture the management of the party in New York state by strong-arm methods at the state convention. He was in Charleston working up Southern support for his contesting delegation on the ground that his New York City was the only Democratic stronghold left in New York and that he and his "shoulder-hitters," as they were called, were the only outfit which could deliver. Pennsylvania, New Jersey, and the New England states were there likewise looking for the main chance. They had no particular loyalty to Douglas though they recognized his vote-getting power. Their main interest was a negotiated peace; they wanted somehow to trade it out by prestidigious manipulations of words and candidates.

All factions were confronted by statistics. The Southern states had only 120 electoral votes. The victor in the electoral college needed 152. The required 32 votes must come from free states. Southern statisticians figured however that these 32 could probably be acquired only at a semantic price which might cost 34 votes in those Southern states that could go Whig. What a dilemma and besides the weather was hot, the hotels were expensive, bad, and hellishly crowded, and the meeting hall was atrocious. Calhoun's bones rested in a neighboring church yard; perhaps his spirit hovered disapprovingly over the convention which he had always distrusted.

Thirty years of convention experience were drawn upon to discover the way out of this statistical and emotional confusion. The Southerners, who had on occasion shared Calhoun's dislike for conventions, served their violent notice. The Douglasites with their numerical majority sought to change it into a two-thirds endorsement by controlling the committees and the crucial floor votes. The "practical operators" sought to arrange accommodations. But the forces would not budge.

When the Douglas platform, though somewhat modified, was adopted, Alabama began the projected walkout. However the exit was disappointing, only eight of the fifteen slave states responded; and these were only from the lower South. The seceders, despite their disappointment, settled down in an adjacent hall. One of the objects of this secession was to establish possible negotiations which might bring about a compromise nomination or a revised platform or both. Some of the seceders thought that under such circumstances they might still go home not only with a good chance of keeping their local strength but also with some hope of national victory. They would bet on enough support from Northerners who feared Seward's higher law and irrepressible conflict heresies to get the Northern votes necessary. They counted on Seward's enemies within his own party and the distrust of his radicalism in his own section. Let it be remembered that nobody in Charleston then dreamed of Lincoln. Also some of the leading Senators were boon companions of Seward and would have suffered him, not gladly perhaps, but as an alternative to Douglas whose guts they hated. But not only where they not joined by the majority of the South, no one even came to offer overtures for reunion. It was an anticlimax just to sit, despite the fact that they were cheered by the inability of those they called "the rump" to accomplish anything.

The only positive step achieved was the fact that a numerical majority cast their votes for Douglas. The Douglas managers had expected that when the Southerners seceded, two-thirds of the remaining quorum were all that would be necessary to nominate. This was one reason why some of them were in effect anxious to get at least a few of the Southern delegates out. But New York defeated this, holding the door open even wider for negotiation. It would have taken more skill and concession to secure 202 than 168, but since Douglas seemed able to muster only 152½, he would have to make concessions to those who were adept at manipulation.

After balloting fifty-seven times the convention decided on an unprecedented act. On the morning of the tenth day the members recessed until June 18, then to reassemble in Baltimore. Both factions would go home to sound out opinion. The Douglasites hoped that others could be found in the seceders' districts to repudiate them and less intransigent Democrats to fill their places in Baltimore. The seceders could but hope for the endorsement of their stand.

During the ensuing six weeks the hopes of the Douglas managers were in part fulfilled. New delegations were dispatched from Alabama, Arkansas, Georgia, and Louisiana. The original delegates from Mississippi and Texas returned. Those from Florida were in the city but did not attend the sessions as delegates. The controlling facts were probably certain events in the weeks between the two conventions. The Whigs and Americans together with other conservatives had organized a new party called the Constitutional Union party and had nominated John Bell of Tennessee and Edward Everett of Massachusetts on a simple platform endorsing the Constitution and the Union. This ticket would be likely to be strong in the South. Then, too, Abraham Lincoln, not Seward, had been nominated by the Republicans upon a platform offering generous subsidies. Lincoln's slate would be more formidable than any headed by Seward. Facing such developments the Southern wing felt it impossible to yield on their platform, and the Northern wing on their candidate.

Thus the experienced politicos, who had faced walkouts before and had composed differences on several occasions, and their less tutored associates found themselves without any of the familiar materials with which to work: neither faction would advance concessions on either principles or candidates. An unprecedented impasse had been reached, and no accommodation was achieved. The majority nominated Douglas as they had determined to do from the beginning while the traders from the middle states sat by helpless and of necessity acquiescent. The seceders, joined by the rest of the South and a few from Northern constituencies, chose the Vice-President, John C. Breckinridge, and a Senator, Joseph Lane of Oregon, to head the ticket on the "honest platform." This was canny. Now that there were four tickets, the contest might be thrown into Congress. The likelihood that the splintered House could muster a majority of the states for any of those who might be the three highest seemed remote. But the safely Democratic Senate would have no difficulty in choosing their colleague, Joseph Lane. The Democrats might thus save the presidency after all. Some perhaps looked ahead to another contingency. If there were to be secession, it could be convenient to have the Vice-President of the United States, Breckinridge, in a positon to help in their effort. But to most it looked as if the Democrats had elected Lincoln.

Thus the Democratic party broke up when its national convention collapsed in 1860. A bloc of Southern delegates shattered the organization deliberately. They had come to Charleston with no candidate to propose. In the convention they made much of formulae. Though the majority of the delegates were against them, they sought to control because they had a majority of the states. As they demanded full recognition of the rights of the states, they proclaimed themselves firm supporters of the Constitution which they maintained was more important than the Union. They had been suffering in power and prestige ever since 1856. Then they had failed to renominate Pierce. Twice they had lost control of the House of Representatives. Now in 1860 they had lost control of the national convention. Power meant a great deal to them as it naturally would in an aggregation in which so many were slaveholders. Particularly after the shock of John Brown's raid, power was more than ever necessary for protection and survival. They must have the autonomy with security which Calhoun had prescribed. If they could not find it in the old Union, they would create a new agency to insure it.

So they would destroy the convention and the party as instruments no longer serving their purpose. They were ready to try something new. Douglas and his associates on their part strove desperately to salvage the party mechanism. But they were not strong enough; and besides, they had nothing to take its place. The convention system latterly had been plagued by a weakness which was now proving fatal. The professionals who had invented and operated it had failed to provide real leadership. They had preferred usually to nominate their own kind. They were not favorable to superior talent, to statesmen, or to the nineteenth century equivalent of "eggheads." They chose those who spoke their language and understood their own mores. The Democrats had never in these years of convention practice nominated a man of great talent or commanding reputation. One can go far without finding a more colorless group than Van Buren, Polk, Cass, Pierce, or Buchanan. They were certaintly not much more than representatives of the average man. Van Buren and Buchanan were men of experience and craft but with no capacity to deal with the unusual. Polk had some skill and luck, but he was a man of decided limitations, a statesman incapable of foreseeing or forestalling dangers; even less can be said for Cass and Pierce.

The nation was growing fast in size, wealth, and power. It was also fragmentizing, falling apart because of its own weight. Emotions were getting out of hand, morals were deteriorating, health was bad, and the nature of republican self-government was yielding to temptation and succumbing to corruption. But the leadership necessary to recall men to their duty in maintaining the ideals of democracy could not be summoned by any of the instruments available.

It cannot be said with certainty that in 1860 and in the preceding years a consistently higher grade of leadership would have solved more of the problems and avoided more of the crises, but it can be emphasized that no leadership which could cope with the troubled times became available. Rather the current methods required the choosing of those who patently could not rouse the innate capacities of the people of the United States. A party requires leadership to be effective; one cannot carry any society through trying times by a committee or a conference. There must be a personality, a symbol which can inspire trust and confidence, a personality whom the mass will follow.

It can never be known what might have happened had the Convention of 1860 been able to agree on a platform and on a candidate. With all the confusion stirred up by four tickets, the Democrats were still able to recapture the House in 1860 which they had lost in 1858. Their hold on the Senate was not even threatened. The Supreme Court was safely Democratic. There may be probability, although there can be no certainty, that Lincoln would have been elected in a three-cornered contest. But had he been victorious, with the legislative and the judicial arms against him, could he have done more than the Whig Presidents of a decade and more ago? This is all in the realm of conjecture. But John Brown was dead and the likelihood of other forays exists only in the imagination. Had the nation held together and experienced the ineptitudes of what would have been Lincoln's helpless minority administration, the fears might have been quieted; and the South, with its control of the Congress might have continued to exercise its accustomed rule.

But no, the Democrats destroyed the instrument of accommodation they had used effectively for thirty years rather than exhaust its possibilities, and in so doing they precipitated the catastrophe which was to follow. Their invention was smashed because a large faction, mainly from the South, found it no longer useful. The party must try something else to serve their purposes.

The Douglas wing had nothing else to use so they clung desperately to it. The Southern wing had the ghost of Calhoun and set forth to make use of it. They would keep power in the states by seceding from Charleston and Baltimore. If they were defied by the North they would create a new power—just how they would use it, its engineers hardly knew—but the purpose generally was to insure for themselves, somehow, a position of power, autonomy, and security within a reorganized Union. Unfortunately Calhoun was not alive to lead them; and the steps they took were haphazard, badly planned, and undertaken under circumstances that almost insured failure. Had they been able to enlist their entire strength—fifteen states plus the city of Washington—and had they been able to resist the temptation to assault Sumter, there is a chance they might have won. But Calhoun was dead, and Lincoln very much alive. They had not realized their potential—only seven of the fifteen slave states had seceded. The ratio of manpower and resources was very much against them. They had no navy. They must bear the onus of slavery, and they had fired on the flag. The odds, physical and psychological, were just too heavy. From John Brown's raid to Sumter the course of Southern leadership included an unhappy series of unfortunate decisions. In the name of seeking security and their rights they had temporarily destroyed their own creation. Neither they nor anybody else after this long convention experience of shrinking leadership could have foreseen that the prairie galoot from distant Illinois could in any sense prove to be a messiah.

Had the nation followed its original intent and had no President, the republic would have been governed by the legislative arm in which factions of lawmakers, representing state organizations rather than any nationally organized parties, would have operated. Had these factions been unable to agree and had they developed severe group hostility, if their constituencies had withdrawn from the confederation, there might have been no resistance to this secession as there was no executive to make decisions. However this eventuality might well have destroyed the great republic and put in its place a Balkanized society or something like present-day Africa.

As the turbulent year of 1859 had drawn to its close the New York socialite diarist George Templeton Strong recorded in his voluminous daily commentary: "It's a sick nation, and I fear it must be worse before it's better. The growing, vigorous North must sooner or later assert its right to equality with the stagnant, semi-barbarous South, and that assertion must bring on a struggle and convulsion. It must come. Pity it could not be postponed some twenty years, when Northern preponderance would be overwhelming. If Northern abolitionism precipitate the crisis and force the battle on us *now,* it will be a fearful and doubtful contest."

Had a Southern diarist been commenting at this time he might have written a paraphrase of the above. "This republic has been corrupted and it must be purged of its corruption. The civilized South, cultured in its rural felicity, must maintain its equality with the growing, rapacious North, and that exertion must bring on a struggle and convulsion. It must come. It must come soon before Northern preponderance becomes overwhelming. Northern abolitionism may precipitate the crisis and force the battle on us now; it will be a fearful and doubtful contest."

The Democrats at Charleston and Baltimore had realized that changing conditions were in fact pointing to the emergence of a new establishment governed by a new power based on a new consensus. Despite the demonstration of experience from 1776 to 1860 that Americans possessed the capacity to rule and shape the United States, through the instrumentation of Congress and partisan conventions, in 1860 that capacity failed. It failed because its operators lost faith in its efficiency. Instead of using the convention as an instrument of adjustment and the creation of consensus, they destroyed it. They destroyed it because they did not trust it any longer. They had lost their faith because of fear, conscience, a

sense of honor, bad health, and a complicated series of personal antagonisms built up over years of association in Congress, conventions, and
the peculiar environment of Washington. The Democratic party broke
up because of a complex series of personal failures where, in an intricate
system of group dynamics, people entrusted with responsibility for leadership could not measure up to the demands of the perilous times. The
most spectacular evidence of this failure was the destruction of the
Democratic party by its own managers. Calhoun had always disliked
and distrusted the device employed to destroy him. It was his following
who thirty years later scrapped it.

CHAPTER 39

LINCOLN: THE MAN, THE PRESIDENT, THE MYTH

Almost no one, especially if he is a student of history, doubts Abraham Lincoln's claim to greatness. Literally hundreds of books and articles have been written about Lincoln, the man, and Lincoln, the President, and multivolume collections of his writings, including his personal letters, are readily available to all. Down through the years Lincoln has remained one of our most revered, honored, quoted, and respected Presidents. Part of the aura of awe in which we hold him is a direct result of the dramatic times in which he lived and died so tragically.

He saved the Union, but was slain within a week after the end of the Civil War. Thus he is credited with winning the war but is spared blame for the failures—however defined—of Reconstruction. But there are other factors that are responsible for the awe and the reverence. There is the man himself. Tall, gaunt, homely, humorous, and melancholy, Lincoln is the embodiment of the American Dream. From humble beginnings to the White House. That is what we want America to be about and that is what the Abraham Lincoln that everybody knows is about.

And yet, there is a Lincoln that nobody knows. In some respects, Lincoln remains to this day a mystery to us. We can know with certainty what Lincoln did, but we can only speculate as to why he did certain things. We can only answer partially and tentatively questions about the great man's thoughts and feelings. But these are the matters to which Professor Richard N. Current addresses himself in the following essay. In particular, Professor Current seeks to explore Lincoln's attitudes on slavery and race and to explain his positions on slavery and expansion, on slavery as a cause of the war, and on the role of blacks in the war and in the postwar period. Professor Current's most difficult task, of course, is trying to come to grips with the motivations that ultimately governed Lincoln's thoughts and actions.

In reading this essay, students should consider the following questions. How did Lincoln really feel about slavery? Would he and could he have stopped the spread of slavery if the South had not seceded? Was he a confirmed racist or did he merely drift with the "conventional wisdom" of the day with regard to race? In statements about blacks and slavery made for public consumption, did Lincoln always say what he meant and mean what he said? Was Lincoln a man of his times in his racial attitudes, or was he well ahead of his times but, as a political figure, forced to camouflage his feelings? Finally, do you think that Lincoln could have avoided the problems that Andrew Johnson faced during Reconstruction?

As we mentioned earlier, the literature on Lincoln is immense and varied. Carl Sandburg, *Abraham Lincoln,* 6 vols. (1926–1939), is readable, poetic, and often imaginative. James G. Randall, *Lincoln The President,* 4 vols. (1945–1955), and *Lincoln the Liberal Statesman* (1947), are indispensable. The best single-volume biography remains B. P. Thomas, *Abraham Lincoln** (1952).

* Available in a paperback edition.

THE FRIEND OF FREEDOM
RICHARD CURRENT

His hand trembled as he held the gold pen, ready to sign. He hesitated. Before him lay the broad sheet of paper on which was written the proclamation, complete except for his signature.

"Now, therefore I, Abraham Lincoln . . . on this first day of January, in the year of our Lord one thousand eight hundred and sixty-three . . . do order and declare that all persons held as slaves . . . are, and henceforward shall be free. . . ."

Finally, with several men about him in his office witnessing the act, he signed, writing out his full name (rather than the usual *A. Lincoln*). For all the care he took, his signature was noticeably uneven and infirm.

This, he insisted, was due to no hesitation or uncertainty about the policy he was proclaiming. For three hours he had been shaking hands with the visitors who trooped into the White House from the mud and slush of a dismal, overcast New Year's Day. His hand was tired, swollen, hard to control.

Though, as he said, *he* had no doubt about the policy he was confirming, others since have disagreed as to what that policy actually was. Supposedly, of course, it was emancipation. Supposedly, with the trembling movement of his pen, he prepared the way for universal freedom even if he did not strike the shackles from the millions of bondsmen all at once. But possibly he was doing the opposite of what he seemed to do. Possibly he had adopted the idea of an Emancipation Proclamation as a stratagem to delay rather than to hasten the freeing of the slaves.

II

Some of the admirers of Lincoln, viewing the Emancipation Proclamation as the grand climax of his career, have thought of him as at heart an abolitionist, one who from early manhood had been awaiting his chance to put an end to slavery. This notion can be made to seem plausible enough if only a part of the record is revealed.

There is, for instance, the story of his second flatboat voyage down the Mississippi. He was then twenty-two. In New Orleans (the story goes) he with his companions attended a slave auction at which a "vigorous and

SOURCE. From *The Lincoln Nobody Knows* by Richard Current. Copyright © 1958 pp. 214–236 by Richard N. Current. Used with permission of McGraw-Hill Book Company.

comely" mulatto girl was being offered for sale. She was treated like a mare, the prospective bidders inspecting her up and down, pinching and feeling, and then watching while she was made to trot back and forth. To Lincoln the spectacle was so shameful it aroused in him at once an "unconquerable hate" toward the whole institution of slavery. "If I ever get a chance to hit that thing," he swore as he walked away, "I'll hit it hard."

Lincoln perhaps took a stand for freedom as a member of the Illinois Legislature in 1837, when resolutions were introduced in response to the mob murder of Elijah Lovejoy, the antislavery newspaperman of Alton. These resolutions, instead of denouncing lynch law, condemned abolitionist societies and upheld slavery within the Southern states as "sacred" by virtue of the Federal Constitution. Lincoln refused to vote for the resolutions. Not only that. Together with a fellow member he drew up a protest against them, declaring that slavery was "founded on both injustice and bad policy."

Interesting also are his reflections on his experience of 1841, when with his friend Joshua Speed he was returning from a Kentucky visit. He made part of the trip by steamboat down the Ohio. "You may remember, as I well do," he wrote to Speed fourteen years later, in 1855, "that from Louisville to the mouth of the Ohio there were, on board, ten or a dozen slaves, shackled together with irons. That sight was a continual torment to me; and I see something like it every time I touch the Ohio, or any other slave-border." Speed, having resettled in Kentucky, had come to differ with Lincoln on the slavery question, and Lincoln now was defending his own point of view. "It is hardly fair for you to assume," he wrote, "that I have no interest in a thing which has, and continually exercises, the power of making me miserable."

As a member of Congress, in 1850, Lincoln drafted and introduced a bill for the abolition of slavery in the District of Columbia.

During the 1850s, in his arguments with Stephen A. Douglas, Lincoln spoke often and with eloquence against slavery. On one occasion, in 1854, he said he hated Douglas's attitude of indifference toward the spread of slavery to new areas. "I hate it because of the monstrous injustice of slavery itself," he declared. "I hate it because it deprives our republican example of its just influence in the world—enables the enemies of free institutions, with plausibility, to taunt us as hypocrites. . . ." On another occasion Lincoln made his oft-quoted remark that the nation could not long endure half slave and half free. No wonder many Southerners considered him "all broke out" with abolitionism at the time he was elected President.

After he was in the White House, Lincoln continued to express himself eloquently for freedom. In a published reply to Horace Greeley, who was demanding action against slavery, he said (1862) it was his "oft-expressed *personal* wish that all men every where could be free." He confided in a private letter (1864): "I am naturally anti-slavery. If slavery is not wrong, nothing is wrong. I can not remember when I did not so think, and feel." And in a talk to Indiana soldiers (1865) he remarked: "Whenever I hear anyone arguing for slavery I feel a strong impulse to see it tried on him personally." . . .

It is not even clear whether in fact Lincoln ever underwent the New Orleans experience which was supposed to have made him an eternal foe of slavery. John Hanks told the anecdote to Herndon in 1865. Hanks had been one of Lincoln's fellow voyagers on the flatboat, but did not go all the way with the others to New Orleans. So he could not have seen with his own eyes what happened at the slave auction he later described. Herndon said he also heard the story from Lincoln himself. In the account of the journey he gave in his autobiography of 1860, however, Lincoln made no mention of slaves or the slave trade (though of course he intended the autobiography for campaign purposes and could not have been so indiscreet as to emphasize any abolitionist convictions). In the autobiography he also spoke of a previous trip to New Orleans. With regard to this trip, he said nothing about slaves but did refer to Negroes, recalling that he and his one companion "were attacked by seven Negroes with intent to kill and rob them" and were "hurt some in the melee, but succeeded in driving the Negroes from the boat."

As for his stand against the 1837 resolutions of the Illinois Legislature, it is enough to point out that he actually took a position against *both sides* of the controversy. Slavery was bad, he held, but he also contended that "the promulgation of abolition doctrines tends rather to increase than to abate its evils."

Regarding the shackled slaves on the Ohio river boat, he gave at the time, in 1841, an account very different from the one he gave fourteen years afterward to Joshua Speed. Writing to Speed's sister Mary (September 27, 1841) he described the scene on board the boat quite philosophically as exemplifying "the effect of *condition* upon human happiness." Here were a dozen slaves, "strung together like so many fish upon a trotline," who were being taken from their old Kentucky homes to be sold down the river, who were being separated from families and friends and carried off where slavery was reputed to be at its harshest. Yet, as Lincoln saw them, "they were the most cheerful and apparently happy creatures on board." He concluded that God "renders the worst of human conditions tolerable, while He permits the best, to be nothing better than tolerable."

The point is not that Lincoln was falsifying his emotions when, in the much later account to Speed, he wrote of the sight of those slaves in chains as having been a "continual torment" to him. Certainly he had not forgotten

the scene, and very likely he had come to view it in retrospect with heightened feeling. His attitude toward slaves and slavery might well have changed
with the passing years—especially the years after 1850, when the issue of
slavery extension engrossed national politics.

As late as 1847 his torment apparently was not troublesome enough to
deter him from accepting a slaveholder as a law client and arguing against a
slave's claim to freedom. Though Illinois presumably was a free state, its
laws still provided for Negro servitude of a sort. Under the laws slave labor
could be used, provided the slaves were not kept permanently in the state.
Slaves worked the Coles County farm of Robert Matson, who brought his
blacks from Kentucky every spring and took them back to Kentucky every
fall. One of them, Jane Bryant, aroused the ire of Matson's housekeeper and
mistress, who demanded that she be sold and sent to the Deep South. Jane
fled, enlisted the aid of antislavery people, was taken from them, and, lacking the required certificate of freedom, was held in accordance with the Illinois laws. Matson, claiming her as his property, appealed to Lincoln for legal aid. Lincoln took the case and lost.

In Congress, despite his bill for abolition in the District of Columbia, he
took a yes-and-no attitude toward slavery. His bill was carefully hedged
about, so as to offend no slaveholder. It provided for gradual emancipation,
with payment to owners, and it was not to go into effect unless approved by
the "free white citizens" of the District, in a referendum. The bill did not
please abolitionists. One of them, Wendell Phillips, called Lincoln "the slave
hound of Illinois."

As for his remarks on slavery during the 1850s, it should be borne in
mind that Lincoln always was opposing the spread of the institution into the
territories. He was not advocating its destruction in the Southern states.
When he said the nation could not long remain half slave and half free, but
must eventually become all one or the other, he doubtless was thinking of
the real danger that the country might become *all slave*—if slavery were allowed to spread. He resisted the aggressive pro-slavery forces not only because of his concern for the sufferings of the black man, but also because of
his concern for the welfare of the white man. Again and again he indicated
that the civil liberties of every American, white as well as black, were at
stake. He insisted upon "keeping the territories free for the settlement of
free laborers." He was a free-soil man.

"You enquire where I now stand," he wrote in his letter of 1854 to Joshua Speed. "That is a disputed point. I think I am a Whig; but others say
there are no Whigs, and that I am an abolitionist." And then he stated the
limits of his antislavery zeal as precisely as he could: "I now do no more
than oppose the *extension* of slavery." That was where he stood in 1854,
and there is no convincing evidence that he had moved beyond that position
by 1860 or 1861.

In fact, in the most widely read of his pre-nomination speeches, the one at Cooper Union in New York on Feburary 27, 1860, Lincoln said he agreed with Thomas Jefferson and other founding fathers that slavery should be merely contained, not directly attacked. *"This is all Republicans ask—all Republicans desire—in relation to slavery,"* he emphasized, underlining the words. *"As those fathers marked it, so let it be again marked, as an evil not to be extended, but to be tolerated and protected only because of and so far as its actual presence among us makes that toleration and protection a necessity."* Lincoln further said that emancipation should be most gradual and should be accompanied by deportation of the freed slaves. "In the language of Mr. Jefferson, uttered many years ago, 'It is still in our power to direct the process of emancipation, and deportation, peaceably, and in such slow degrees, as that the evil will wear off insensibly; and their places be, *pari passu,* filled up by free white laborers. If, on the contrary, it is left to force itself on, human nature must shudder at the prospect held up.' "

III

As President, even if he personally had desired immediate emancipation, Lincoln had reasons of policy for going slow with regard to slavery. At the outset of the war the border slave states—Maryland, Delaware, Missouri, and above all Kentucky—hung in the balance. It seemed to Lincoln essential that these states be kept loyal to the Union, and it also seemed to him that a forthright antislavery program might incline them toward the Confederacy.

Whatever the reasons, Lincoln in the beginning was most reluctant to use his Presidential powers against slavery. During his first year and more in office he lagged well behind the majority of his party in the cause of freedom. If, as he said, General McCellan had "the slows" when it came to advancing against the Confederate army, he himself had the same affliction when it was a matter of attacking the institution which Alexander H. Stephens called the cornerstone of the Confederacy.

. . . In the summer of 1861 Congress passed a confiscation act which freed such slaves as the foe put to military use. The next summer Congress passed a second confiscation act, which declared "forever free" all slaves whose owners were in rebellion, whether or not the slaves were being used for military purposes. Lincoln did not veto these laws, but neither did he see that they faithfully were carried out. He considered vetoing the second one, because in his judgment it amounted to an unconstitutional bill of attainder. He did not sign it until it had been amended, and even then he expressed to Congress his dissatisfaction with it.

While hesitating to enforce these laws, Lincoln responded in his own way to the rising sentiment in favor of emancipation. He came forth with a characteristically Lincolnian solution to the slavery problem. His plan contained five elements. First, the states themselves must emancipate the slaves, for in his opinion slavery was a "domestic" institution, the concern of the states alone. Second, slaveowners must be paid for the chattels of which they were to be deprived. Third, the Federal government must share the financial burden by providing Federal bonds as grants-in-aid to the states. Fourth, the actual freeing of the slaves must not be hurried; the states must be given plenty of time, delaying final freedom until as late as 1900 if they wished. Fifth, the freed Negroes must be shipped out of the country and colonized abroad, but they must be persuaded to go willingly. State action, compensation, Federal aid, gradual emancipation, and voluntary colonization—these were the indispensable features of the Lincoln plan.

To carry out this plan he had to gain the approval of Congress, the border slave states, and the leaders of the Negro race. Congress responded affirmatively but without enthusiasm, indicating its willingness to vote the necessary funds. None of the border politicians were won over to the scheme, however, and very few Negroes could be persuaded to leave their native land, the United States.

. . .

Meanwhile he did not let up in his efforts to talk the free Negroes into leaving the country. Some of their own leaders advocated starting life anew in the Negro republic of Liberia or Haiti. Lincoln preferred Central America as their new home. In his eagerness he was taken in by a group of land speculators who offered to sell the Chiriqui territory on the Isthmus of Panama. . . .

He was nevertheless loath to give up the colonization idea itself. He invited to the White House a group of five prominent Negroes—the first of their race a President ever so honored—and he honored them further by saying frankly that there was no place for them and their people in the United States. Though they might be treated better in the North than in the South, they would suffer discrimination everywhere so long as they remained in this country. "The ban," he said, "is still upon you." From Negroes who heard of this interview, the response was most unfavorable. One wrote to Lincoln: "Pray tell us is our right to a home in this country less than your own?"

If, in the summer of 1862, Lincoln had had his way, the later history of this country would have been radically changed. For instance, if the states had adopted his plan, there would probably be few Negroes left in the country, North or South. By 1900 the slaves of the border states would have been set free and sent abroad. The slaves of the Confederate states, if these states too had chosen to adopt the Lincoln plan, would have enjoyed the same fortune or suffered the same fate.

If, on the other hand, the war had come to an early end, as Lincoln hoped, the slaves of the Confederate states could have been left in bondage indefinitely, or at least until they were freed by some hand other than his. Even in the border states, after emancipation, slavery might have been reestablished by action of the states. What these states had done, they could undo, according to Lincoln's conception of State rights. Indeed, in order to discourage this contingency, he drafted an emancipation bill containing the proviso that, if any state should abolish and then reintroduce the institution, it would have to return to the Federal government the Federal funds it had received as a grant-in-aid!

IV

President Lincoln did not behave like a great emancipator during the first year-and-a-half of his term of office. The question is, did he change his mind and his policy after that? More particularly, did he intend—with the preliminary proclamation of September 21, 1862, and the final one of January 1, 1863—to free the slaves?

According to most accounts, he did. Despite his campaign pledges and the constraints of the Constitution, argue supporters of this position, he decided that he must strike at slavery for reasons of military necessity. He came to this conclusion, and drafted a fitting proclamation, in July of 1862. When he read this draft to his Cabinet, Seward advised him to withhold the announcement till the Union armies had won a victory on the battlefield. Otherwise, Seward cautioned, the proclamation might sound like a confession of military failure, like "the last *shriek* on our retreat." So Lincoln stalled, awaiting the hoped-for victory. When a delegation of Chicago churchmen appealed to him, he asked them whether a proclamation would do any good, whether it would not be as futile as the Pope's legendary bull against the comet. Before they left, he assured them that he had not decided against a proclamation, but held the matter under advisement. When Horace Greeley in the *New York Tribune* called upon him to make freedom a reality, he patiently replied (August 22, 1862): "My paramount object in this struggle *is* to save the Union, and is *not* either to save or to destroy slavery. If I could save the Union without freeing *any* slave I would do it, and if I could save it by freeing *all* the slaves I would do it; and if I could do it by freeing some and leaving others alone I would also do that." At last McClellan's checking of Lee at Antietam gave Lincoln at least a substitute for victory, and a few days later he accordingly issued the document he long since had decided upon.

This is a familiar story, and there is a certain amount of evidence to give it historical substance. There is, for example, the record Welles made of a conversation Lincoln had with him and Seward on Sunday, July 13, while on a carriage ride to a funeral. "It was on this occasion and on this ride that he first mentioned to Mr. Seward and myself the subject of emancipating the slaves by proclamation in case the Rebels did not cease to persist in their war on the Government and the Union, of which he saw no evidence," Welles wrote afterward. "He dwelt earnestly on the gravity, importance, and delicacy of the movement, said he had given it much thought and had about come to the conclusion that it was a military necessity absolutely essential for the salvation of the Union, that we must free the slaves or be ourselves subdued, etc., etc." Welles added this comment: "It was a new departure for the President, for until this time, in all our previous interviews, whenever the question of emancipation or the mitigation of slavery had been in any way alluded to, he had been prompt and emphatic in denouncing any interference by the General Government with the subject."

Welles may have remembered accurately what the President said on that Sunday, though the record of the conversation is not a regular diary entry but a reminiscence that the diarist put down after the lapse of considerable time. And Lincoln, if Welles summarized his sentiments accurately, may have meant what he said. . . .

These inconsistencies of his have led to the suspicion that, till after the battle of Antietam, he made no irrevocable commitment, even to himself. Here and there he dropped hints that he might issue the proclamation—and then again might not. Apparently his purpose was to prepare his hearers for the possibility that he might call the whole thing off. He was waiting for a decisive victory, but if that kind of victory had come, he might have forgotten about the proclamation. Some historians claim that he dusted it off and gave it to the world only when he learned the true proportions of Antietam. McClellan, though he turned Lee back, had let him get away. If McClellan had administered a crushing defeat, the proclamation might have stayed in its pigeonhole.

This theory depends on the supposition that Lincoln at the time was not so much concerned about military necessity as about political necessity. He had to contend with a strong bloc of Republicans in Congress, headed by Thaddeus Stevens in the House and Charles Sumner and Henry Wilson in the Senate, backed by a majority of the party, who had become Radicals on the slave question. They were demanding that the President carry out the laws, the confiscation acts, the act for the enrollment of Negro troops. They held the firm conviction that, to win the war, the government must free the slaves and use them against their former masters. As their strongest argument, the Radicals cited the succession of Union defeats on the Virginia front. The way the war was being fought, it was not being won, and it therefore must be fought another way. There was even the possibility that they might try to stop the flow of money and supplies if Lincoln did not give in. Only a conclusive victory, only a dramatic refutation of the Radical argument, would restore his freedom of action. He prayed for such a victory, and then came the disappointing news of Antietam.

To pursue this argument to its logical conclusion, Lincoln then pulled out the proclamation as his trump. In issuing it he did not really yield to the Radicals. Rather, he outfoxed them. At first they hailed the document as a triumph for them and their cause, but soon they were disillusioned, since the proclamation had as its purpose and effect the checking of the Radical program. Having announced in September that he would make a final proclamation the first of the following year, Lincoln had an excuse for disregarding the laws about confiscation and Negro troops throughout the intervening months. He also had a policy with which to frustrate Stevens's drive for legislation to make soldiers and freemen out of slaves from the border states. During the months of delay he hoped at last to gain approval for his own plan, the familiar plan of gradual emancipation by the states themselves, with Federal funds to pay to slaveowners and to rid the country of the freed slaves.

There is testimony, from some of the men who knew Lincoln, to give credence to this view. There is, for instance, the testimony of Edward Stanly, a proslavery, State-rights, Unionist North Carolinian whom Lincoln had appointed as military governor of the occupied North Carolina coast. Stanly had taken the job with the understanding that Lincoln would not interfere with slavery in the states. Once the proclamation had been issued, Stanly went to Washington intending to resign. After several talks with Lincoln, however, Stanly was satisfied. He returned to his job, but first he called at the office of James C. Welling, editor of the *National Intelligencer*. Welling wrote in his diary: "Mr. Stanly said that the President had stated to him that the proclamation had become a civil necessity to prevent the Radicals from openly embarrassing the government in the conduct of the war."

Quite apart from testimony such as this, a fairly strong inference of Lincoln's delaying tactics can be drawn from the text of the proclamation. The preliminary announcement said that after January 1, 1863, the slaves in states then still in rebellion would be considered free. The final proclamation excluded from the area of freedom not only the loyal border states but all the Confederate states and parts of states that the Union forces had occupied. As cynics pointed out at the time, Lincoln was leaving the slaves untouched in places where he had the ability to free them, and he was offering liberty only to those he had no power to reach. Congress already had enabled him to do more than this. . . .

Lincoln himself gave indisputable proof that, after the preliminary proclamation, he remained as passionately devoted as ever to his own gradual-emancipation scheme. In his message to Congress of December 1, 1862, just one month before the final proclamation, he had little to say about that forthcoming pronouncement and much to say about his favored plan. He proposed a constitutional amendment to put the plan into effect. On this subject he reached one of the peaks of his eloquence. "Fellow-citizens, *we* cannot escape history," he said. "We of this Congress and this administration, will be remembered in spite of ourselves. The fiery trial through which we pass, will light us down, in honor or dishonor, to the latest generation." These words are justly famous. What is often forgotten is the fact that they were conceived as part of a plea for deporting American-born Negroes from America. . . .

No inspired phrases were to be found in the paper that Lincoln signed with the gold pen, in the quavering hand, on January 1, 1863. In itself this proclamation was a dull and prosaic document—no ringing call to freedom. . . .

All this does not necessarily disprove the commonly accepted story of what Lincoln did or tried to do in signing his famous proclamation. Maybe he meant to hasten freedom, maybe to delay it. Nobody knows.

V

Actual freedom for the Negroes—or at least the end of chattel slavery—came in consequence of the Thirteenth Amendment. President Lincoln played a part in bringing about this constitutional change, yet he was slow to take an out-and-out antislavery stand, and indeed he gave some indications that his conversion never was complete.

He did not claim to have originated the idea of such an amendment, though the abolitionists did. At Cleveland in May 1864 a group of these extreme Republicans nominated John C. Frémont for the Presidency and adopted a platform with a Thirteenth Amendment as the key plank.

When the regular Republicans met in convention the following month, Lincoln was aware of the need for winning the dissidents back to the party fold. He called to the White House the chairman of the Republican National Committee, Senator E. D. Morgan, and gave him instructions for his speech opening the convention. "Senator Morgan," he is reported to have said, "I want you to mention in your speech when you call the convention to order, as its keynote, and to put into the platform as the keystone, the amendment of the Constitution abolishing and prohibiting slavery forever." Senator Morgan did as the President wished. That platform included a plank stating that slavery was the cause of the rebellion, that the President's proclamations had aimed "a death blow at this gigantic evil," and that a constitutional amendment was necessary to "terminate and forever prohibit" it. Undoubtedly the delegates would have adopted such a plank whether or not Lincoln, through Senator Morgan, had urged it.

When Lincoln was reelected on this platform, and the Republican majority in Congress was increased, he was justified in feeling, as he apparently did, that he had a mandate from the people for the Thirteenth Amendment. The newly chosen Congress, with its overwhelming Republican majority, would not meet until after the Lame Duck Session of the old Congress during the winter of 1864–1865. But Lincoln did not wait. Using all his resources of patronage and persuasion on certain of the Democrats, he managed to get the necessary two-thirds vote before the session's end. He rejoiced as the amendment went out to the states for ratification, and he rejoiced again and again as his own Illinois led off and other states followed one by one in acting favorably upon it. He did not live to rejoice in its ultimate adoption.

VI

Lincoln is a paradoxical hero. His name has been lighted down from generation to generation as a synonym for liberty and equality. His name also has been made to symbolize the opposite doctrine of white supremacy and black oppression.

Lincoln the friend of freedom is well and widely known. For most liberals, he occupies a place beside that of Thomas Jefferson. For many Negroes, he long has held a lone position as a kind of folk god.

His exaltation dates back to January 1, 1863, when throughout the North and the conquered areas of the South the colored people held proclamation meetings to celebrate his deed in their behalf. At a Washington meeting, which began on New Year's Eve, a pastor told each member of his flock to "get down on *both knees* to thank Almighty God for his freedom and President Lincoln too." To people such as these the proclamation, whatever its inward meaning, was the outward sign of an answer to their prayers.

Most of the abolitionists joined in honoring Lincoln at the time of his emancipation edict, but some of them qualified their praise, still doubting his sincerity. At last, when he had won Congressional approval for the Thirteenth Amendment, almost all the lingering doubts were dispelled and almost all the doubters satisfied. Even William Lloyd Garrison no longer could contain himself. To a Boston meeting of celebrators Garrison said: "And to whom is the country more immediately indebted for this vital and saving amendment of the Constitution than, perhaps, to any other man? I believe I may confidently answer—to the humble rail splitter of Illinois—to the Presidential chainbreaker for millions of the oppressed—to Abraham Lincoln!"

Less well known than Lincoln the slaves' chainbreaker is Lincoln the hero of Negro-baiters and white supremacists. Yet he has been that kind of image also. Few Negroes or friends of the Negro ever admired him more or praised him oftener than did a certain Mississippi advocate of white supremacy, James K. Vardaman.

In the early 1900s this long-haired, dramatic Great White Chief of Mississippi stood out as the most rabid racialist in the most racist-dominated Southern state. When Theodore Roosevelt dined with the Negro educator Booker T. Washington in the White House, Vardaman sneered at the President as a "wild broncho buster and coon-flavored miscegenationist." . . .

This Mississippian once made a pilgrimage to his hero's home town, to Springfield, Illinois. The year was 1909, the centennial of Lincoln's birth. The previous year had been a disgraceful one for Springfield. Municipal leaders were looking ahead to anniversary celebrations when, on a summer night, thousands of the townspeople suddenly went wild with hate. They set out to lynch a Negro who (though innocent) was being held on the charge of raping a white woman, and when the sheriff frustrated them by spiriting the man away, they turned their vengeance upon the whole colored community. It took four thousand state troopers all of a week to quiet the city and end the so-called "race riot." (This incident, by the way, and not some crisis in the South, gave rise to the National Association for the Advancement of Colored People.) When Vardaman visited Springfield the feeling among local Negrophobes still ran high, and a huge crowd came out to applaud his lecture on the inherent virtue of the white race.

Vardaman never tired of praising "the immortal Lincoln," never tired of quoting "the wise words of this wondrous man." He insisted that he and Lincoln saw eye to eye. "I have made a very careful study of Mr. Lincoln's ideas on this question," he declared in a Senate speech, "and I have said often, and I repeat here, that my views and his on the race question are substantially identical." Next to Thomas Jefferson, he thought, Lincoln understood the Negro problem better than anyone else of former days. To prove his point, Vardaman cited Lincoln's advocacy of Negro colonization. He explained the Lincoln policy thus:

"Up to the very time of Mr. Lincoln's death he told the Negroes who came to see him here in Washington, 'You will not be permitted to share in the government of this country, and I am not prepared to say that you ought to be, if I had the power to give you that right.'

"He said further: 'The shackles of slavery will be stricken from your arms. You, the educated and more fortunate members of your race, take the others and go to some country'—his idea was the same that Jefferson's was —'and there work out your own salvation.' I do not pretend to quote Mr. Lincoln literally. The great desire of his patriotic heart was that the friction might be avoided by deportation."

The words of Lincoln that Vardaman repeated oftenest, the words he knew almost by heart, came from the debate with Douglas at Charleston, Illinois, on September 18, 1858. These words formed for Vardaman a sort of golden text. . . .

VII

Yet, despite these contradictions, Lincoln does deserve his reputation as emancipator. True, his claim to the honor is supported very uncertainly, if at all, by the proclamation itself. The honor has a better basis in the support he gave to the Thirteenth Amendment. It is well founded also in his greatness as the war leader, who carried the nation safely through the four-year struggle that brought freedom in its train. But the best reason for his reputation is, perhaps, to be discovered in something else. Consider the example he set his fellow Americans by treating all men as human beings, regardless of the pigment of their skin.

The real and final emancipation of the Negro may depend more upon attitudes than upon laws. The laws, the constitutional amendments, are important, even indispensable. But, as the abolitionist Henry Wilson observed, many of those who voted for the Thirteenth Amendment and other antislavery measures did so without conversion or conviction. Many acted from a desire to hurt the slaveholder rather than to help the slave. Within their hearts still lurked the "foul spirit of caste," the spirit of race prejudice. Until this prejudice was overcome, the Negroes, though no longer the slaves of individual masters, would continue to be in a sense the slaves of the community as a whole.

Now, Lincoln himself was one of those who veered to an actively antislavery line for reasons of wartime expediency. He did not pretend to do otherwise. And he was well aware of race prejudice as an existing fact in the United States. Hence his pathetic eagerness to find new homes for freedmen in foreign lands. Yet he had the capacity to rise above prejudice, and he grandly rose above it. Again and again, during the last two years of his life, he made the White House a scene of practical demonstrations of respect for human worth and dignity. He proved that whites and Negroes, without the master-servant tie, could get along together happily in his own official home, no matter what the antagonisms that might trouble the nation at large. A kindly, unself-conscious host, he greeted Negro visitors as no President had done before.

The distinguished former slave Frederick Douglass called upon Lincoln several times at his summer cottage at the Soldiers' Home. Douglass made at least three visits to the White House. On the final occasion, when he tried to enter as an invited guest at the inaugural reception in 1865, policemen man-handled him and forced him out. Making his way in again, he managed to catch Lincoln's eye. "Here comes my friend Douglass," the President exclaimed, and, leaving the circle of guests he had been conversing with, he took Douglass by the hand and began to chat with him. Years later Douglass wrote:

> In all my interviews with Mr. Lincoln I was impressed with his entire freedom from popular prejudice against the colored race. He was the first great man that I talked with in the United States freely, who in no single instance reminded me of the difference between himself and myself, of the difference of color, and I thought that all the more remarkable because he came from a state where there were black laws.

There were black laws in Illinois indeed—laws that denied the Negro the vote and deprived him of other rights. Illinois in those days was a Jim Crow state. That was where Lincoln had spent most of the years of his manhood, among people who had migrated from slave country farther south, as he himself had done. Naturally he had shared some of the Negrophobic feeling of his neighbors in Kentucky, in southern Indiana, in central Illinois. That was where, in geography and in sentiment, he came from.

But he did not stay there. The most remarkable thing about him was his tremendous power of growth. He grew in sympathy, in the breadth of his humaneness, as he grew in other aspects of the mind and spirit. In more ways than one he succeeded in breaking through the narrow bounds of his early environment.

This helps to explain and to reconcile those conflicting images of Lincoln —on the one hand, the racist; on the other, the champion of the common man, black as well as white. The one view reflects the position he started from, the other the position he was moving toward. There is confusion regarding particular phases of his Presidential career because nobody knows for sure just what point he had reached at any given moment. But there should be little question as to which way he was going.

To see Lincoln in this light is to make him more than ever relevant, more than ever inspiring, for us in the stormy present, in the fiery trial through which we too must pass. Lincoln, as a symbol of man's ability to outgrow his prejudices, still serves the cause of human freedom. He will go on serving so long as boundaries of color hem in and hinder any man, any woman, any child.

CHAPTER 40

THE FIRST MODERN WAR

Too often military history is ignored or passed over lightly in American history courses. Too often historians and teachers denigrate military history as fit material for history buffs, genealogists, hero-worshipers, and antiquarians, failing to consider that military history (like other fields of history) can be as meaningless or as significant as historians choose to make it. The following selection is military history—not narrowly conceived, but broadly conceived. Such history can not only tell us a great deal about our past but, in a day of international strife and warfare, can also tell us much about ourselves that will be of value as we confront the problems of today and the future.

In this selection, T. Harry Williams, one of America's foremost military historians, examines the military systems of North and South during the Civil War. Professor Williams views that struggle as basically different from previous wars, and he suggests that the military leadership of both North and South were generally inexperienced in modern warfare and failed to understand the essential nature of the contest. From this point of view Williams discusses the military leadership of the two sections, the development of Northern and Southern strategy, the leadership of the two war presidents, Lincoln and Davis, and the ultimate creation by Lincoln, Halleck, and Grant of a modern command system for the North.

Central to this essay is Professor Williams' view of the Civil War as the first modern war. How does he define modern warfare, and what were the two characteristic features of the Civil War which justify its definition as a modern war? How did the Civil War differ from previous wars, and how did the differences affect demands upon the military leadership of North and South? How does Professor Williams compare Southern and Northern military strategy; how does he compare the war leadership of the two presidents, Lincoln and Davis? Granted the brilliance of Southern tactical maneuvers and battlefield strategy, how does one explain, essentially, the failure of the South to achieve military victory? On the other hand, what role did the 1864 Northern command system play in bringing military victory to the North? Was the development of that command system of importance to Americans of the last half of the twentieth century?

Perhaps more books have been written on the Civil War than any other topic in American history. Of major importance for the specific topic of this selection is Walter Millis' study of the development of the American military system, *Arms and Men** (1956). The writings of Bruce Catton, particularly *This Hallowed Ground** (1956), and *U. S. Grant and the American Military Tradition** (1954), are very valuable. Clement Eaton, *A History of the Southern Confederacy** (1954), is an excellent account of the Confederacy. Charles P. Roland, *The Confederacy** (1960), goes over the same ground and uses more recent material. Frank Vandiver, *Rebel Brass* (1956), touches more directly on Southern martial leadership. T. Harry Williams deals at length with the Northern command system in *Lincoln and His Generals** (1952).

* Available in a paperback edition.

THE MILITARY SYSTEMS OF NORTH AND SOUTH

T. HARRY WILLIAMS

I

Trite it may be to say that the Civil War was the first of the modern wars, but this is a truth that needs to be repeated. If the Civil War was not quite total, it missed totality by only a narrow margin. Instead of ending a military cycle as historians once thought, the war began a new one that has not yet been completed. In two ways the Civil War differed from previous conflicts of the modern era in both America and Europe. First, as a war of ideas on the part of both participants, it was a struggle of unlimited objectives. The policy of the North was to restore the Union by force; the policy of the South was to establish its independence by force. Between these two purposes there could be no compromise, no halfway triumph for either side. One or the other had to achieve a complete and decisive victory.[1] Second, the Civil War was a war of matériel, bringing into full play for the first time the great transforming forces of the Industrial Revolution. Among the techniques and weapons employed—either used for the first time or given their first prominent use—were conscription and mass armies, mass production of weapons, railroads, armored ships, submarines, the telegraph, breech-loading and repeating rifles, various precursors of the machine gun, and an incipient air force in the form of signal balloons. Because of these distinguishing qualities the Civil War was, compared with earlier conflicts, a ruthless, lethal, no-holds-barred war. In the high command arrangements, especially in the North, it witnessed an unprecedented measure of civilian participation in strategic planning and of civilian direction of the war.

[1] The North's objectives could be obtained only by a total military victory. The South, on the other hand, could attain its objectives by preventing the North from winning such a victory. But the South's policy objectives were total; it could accept no result except independence.

SOURCE. T. Harry Williams, *Americans at War: The Development of the American Military System,* Baton Rouge, Louisiana: Louisiana State University Press, 1960, pp. 47-61, 77-81. Copyright 1960 by the Louisiana State University Press. Reprinted by permission of the Louisiana State University Press and the author.

II

At the beginning of the war there were only two officers in the service who had ever commanded troops in numbers large enough to be called an army. One was Winfield Scott, who was seventy-five years of age, and the other was John E. Wool, who was two years older, and both of them had had their active experience in the Mexican War, when the largest field armies numbered about 14,000. Besides Scott and Wool, not an officer on either side had directed as large a unit as a brigade; only a few had commanded a regiment. The largest single army that the younger officers, the men who would become the generals of the war, had ever seen, except for the handful who had visited Europe, was Scott's or Taylor's force in the Mexican War. The 30,000 troops collected by the Federal government at Washington in the spring of 1861 were the largest single American army yet assembled. The photographs of Civil War generals tend to mislead us. We look at those fierce, bearded faces and think of the subjects as being old and hardened warriors. But despite the hirsute adornments, most of them were young men, and none of them, regardless of age, had ever handled troops in numbers before the war. This explains many of the mistakes made by both Northern and Southern generals in the early stages of the conflict. They were simply not prepared to direct the huge armies that were suddenly called into being and thrust upon them. The West Pointers, with the advantage of their technical training, were able to learn their jobs, but sometimes the educational process was painful—for them and their troops.

Both sides at first attempted to raise their armies by the traditional American method of calling for volunteers, and in the first year of the war, when both sections were moved by emotional outbursts of patriotism and optimistic estimates that the war would be of short duration, volunteering served to fill up the armies. But after the initial flush of enthusiasm had flickered out, enlistments dwindled away, and it became evident that the volunteer system would not supply enough men to constitute the huge armies the war was going to require. Both combatants had to resort to conscription, the Confederate States in 1862 and the United States a year later—the first time in the American military experience that national conscription was employed. Because of faulty methods of keeping statistics the total number of men raised by either side can only be estimated. In the Confederacy 1,300,000 enlistments were counted, but this figure includes many short-term enlistments and duplicates. The same qualification must be made of the North's enlistment total of 2,900,000. The best estimates are that 1,500,000 men served in Federal armies for three years and 900,000 in Southern armies for the same period.

The field armies that appeared in the war dwarfed in size any force in previous American wars. Disregarding the many small army units that operated in various theaters, we will concern ourselves here with the maximum forces employed by North and South. In the Eastern theater the Federal Army of the Potomac varied from a minimum of 90,000 to a maximum of 130,000. The highest number attained by its opponent, the Army of Northern Virignia, was 85,000, but the average size of this force was smaller, ranging between 55,000 and 70,000. The largest Federal army in the West comprised 90,000 troops, while the biggest army which the Confederacy placed in the field in this theater numbered 70,000, a total far above average, which ranged between 40,000 and 60,000.

The generals who commanded the large field armies were without exception professional soldiers, graduates of West Point. A large number of citizen soldiers in both armies proved themselves capable of directing divisions and corps, but the few amateurs who were given command of even small independent armies—as Benjamin F. Butler and N. P. Banks —were unequal to the task; N. B. Forrest on the Confederate side was a natural genius who probably could have led an army, but in actual experience he commanded only a cavalry force. It was the professionals, then, who in the area of battle operations fought the war and, for the North, won it. But it would be highly inaccurate to conclude from this that the trained experts demonstrated a consistent level of competence or manifested an immediate and perceptive awareness of the nature of modern war.

On the contrary, most of the Northern generals who came to prominence in the first half of the war were sorry field leaders—were, in fact, unfit for high level command. They exhibited a number of excellent qualities: they knew how—or, more accurately, they readily learned how—to prepare, train, and administer armies. There was only one quality that they lacked, but it was a fatal inadequacy: they did not want to fight their armies. In the first of the modern wars, in a war that both sides were playing for keeps, they were ruled by the military concepts of the eighteenth century. They thought of war as an exercise in bloodless strategy, as a series of maneuvers to checkmate an enemy on a gigantic chessboard. Above all—and here George B. McClellan is the supreme example of the type—they envisioned a leisurely, gentlemanly kind of war; in short, a war of limited objectives: if you don't accomplish your objective this time, all right, try it again later, next month, next year. McClellan always saw the war as a kind of game practiced by himself and other experts off in a private sphere of action that had no connection with the political community. If the public demanded action, if the government might fall because there was no action, such considerations impressed McClellan not at all. Ignorant politicians and other people should not be interfering with the specialists, who would move when the conditions of the game were exactly right and not one minute before.

Generals like McClellan were simply not competent to command in a conflict like the Civil War—a rough, mean war and one in which, whether the military liked it or not, civilians were going to have their say. Instead of recognizing the reality of civilian interference and accommodating himself to it, McClellan wasted his energies by wailing that it should not exist—the same kind of futile protest that his supporters have advanced ever since. Not until 1864 did the North succeed in bringing into the important command posts, in the persons of U. S. Grant, William T. Sherman, Philip H. Sheridan, and George H. Thomas, men who possessed the hard, driving qualities required in modern war and who understood the political nature of the war. Although the South owned its share of fumbling generals, it can be said of most Confederate commanders that, from the beginning, they were at least willing to fight their armies. Doubtless the inferior human and material resources of the South, which compelled her generals to act when they could with what they had, explains their greater aggressiveness.

III

At the outbreak of war neither side had ready at hand a plan of general strategy. The newly formed Confederate government could hardly have been expected to possess a previously devised design, but such a measure of preparation was well within the capacities of the Federal military organization. That no plan existed is, of course, not surprising. Nobody had thought, until the crisis suddenly broke, that the difficulties between the sections would come to war, and—here is the crux of the matter—nobody or any agency in the military system, neither Scott nor the General Staff, was charged with the function of studying strategy or of preparing plans for a possible war. The strategy of the war, then, had to be worked out as the conflict developed in the light of what the planners on each side could learn about the strategic situation. So far as prior preparations were concerned, neither government approached the standards of President Polk and his cabinet, who had outlined a general plan of operations a year before the war with Mexico started.[2]

The policy of the North, or the United States, was to restore the Union by force; hence, Northern strategy had to be offensive. But the strategic objectives of the North were complicated by the fact that this was a civil instead of a foreign war. If it was to win, the North had to do more than occupy the enemy capital or defeat enemy armies. It had to do these things and, in addition, convince the Southern people that their cause was hopeless. In short, to conquer a peace the North had to subdue a population. Northern armies would have to invade the South, seize key points and areas, and occupy large regions of the enemy country—all of which would require a vast expenditure of human and military resources. Northern strategy, as it was finally formulated, set up three principal objectives to be attained: (1) in the Eastern theater to capture Richmond and defeat the defending Confederate army; (2) to seize the line of the Mississippi River, thereby splitting the Confederacy into two parts; and (3) after the second objective had been achieved, to occupy Chattanooga and the Tennessee River line, thereby gaining a base from which an offensive could be launched to divide the South, east of the Mississippi.

The policy of the Confederacy was to establish its independence by force, and to accomplish this purpose the government decided on a defensive strategy. In part, the South had no choice in the matter; its decision was a forced reaction to Northern strategy. But the adoption of a defensive strategy was also in part a deliberate determination by its leaders, particularly by President Davis. For a power that wanted only to be let alone and that harbored no aggressive designs against anybody, a strategy of defense seemed so beautifully logical—and Confederates were always beguiled by logic. But because the South's only purpose was to resist conquest was not sufficient reason to rely on such an inert strategy. With equal logic, and probably with more effect, the South might have achieved its policy of independence by taking the offensive early in the war when its resources were greatest, by demonstrating that it was too strong to be conquered through victories on Northern soil.

---

[2] The several statements in these essays calling attention to the absence of plans at the beginning of wars are not to be taken as a belief in the necessity or feasibility of having a previously drawn up and detailed scheme of operations. Indeed, the possession of a rigid design may handicap a nation, as the experience of Germany with the Schlieffen plan attests. Especially today, when the nature of war is so fluid, it may be advantageous to be able to choose among a number of plans after war begins. What I am saying here is that in some of our wars *no thinking* about what might happen had been done before the advent of hostilities.

Confederate strategy was pervasively and, in a sense, passively defensive. The high command decided to defend every part of the Confederacy, to meet every threatened attack, to hold every threatened point—a policy which dispersed its resources, inferior to those of the North, over a wide strategic circumference and yielded the strategic initiative to the enemy.[3] If the South chose to await attack, it might have adopted an alternative defensive strategy; it could have shortened its lines to inclose the most defensible areas or those containing important resources or possessing a symbolic value. It did not do this, partly for valid reasons. For the new Southern government to abandon any of its territory would have seemed an admission of weakness and would certainly have lost it a measure of popular support. But even without these practical political considerations, President Davis and other civil leaders seemed to think almost instinctively in terms of defending places for their own sake, of holding territory simply because it was their territory.

In general, at the highest command levels the North displayed a greater degree of efficiency and originality than did the South. The Confederates, so brilliant in tactical maneuvers and in battlefield strategy, never succeeded in creating a competent command system or in setting up a unified plan of strategy. The Northern strategy of offense was basically sound; the Southern strategy of defense was fundamentally defective. But it would be inaccurate and unfair to ascribe the differences between the strategic systems to the human beings who operated them, to say that one side had wise leaders and the other had not, to dismiss Davis and his advisers as inept and unintelligent men (as a matter of fact, they were very intelligent) who did not rise to their opportunities. Warfare should always be considered a social institution. As Clausewitz said, a nation's social system or culture will determine the kind of war it will fight. Davis and Lee and other Confederates were the products of their culture, and their culture decided and limited their military thinking. Whereas, the North was a nation of the nineteenth century and looked to the future, the South was a confederation of sovereignties that refused to accept the nineteenth century and looked to the past. The Confederacy was founded on state rights—localism was imbedded in every segment of its system—and it fought a state-rights war and, on the strategic level, a

---

[3] It is recognized, of course, that on occasion the Confederacy did go over to the offensive, as in Bragg's invasion of Kentucky in 1862 and, most notably, in Lee's thrusts into the North in 1862 and 1863. But these operations were exceptions to the rule. Also, in every case where an offensive was attempted, the size of the Confederate army could have been significantly augmented by adding to it forces that were guarding places at home.

traditional, eighteenth-century type of war. Just as it was difficult for Southern political leaders to envision centralism in government, so it was hard for Confederate military directors to see the war as a whole or to install centralism in its direction.

IV

At the head of the military systems of both countries and of their command organizations were the two presidents, Abraham Lincoln and Jefferson Davis. They form an interesting contrast and offer the materials for an instructive and fascinating study in civil-military relationships and in the higher direction of war. Judging them solely by their backgrounds, one would expect that the Confederate President would be a great war leader, that he would far eclipse his rival. Few civilian war directors have come to their office with Davis' technical advantages. He was a graduate of West Point, he had served in the regular army, he had had battle experience in the Mexican War, and he had been Secretary of War. Lincoln had been a civilian all his life, he had received no military education, and he had had no military experience except briefly as a militia soldier in the Black Hawk War, when, as he liked to recall, he had made some ferocious charges on the wild onions and engaged in bloody struggles with the mosquitoes. And yet the truth is that Lincoln was a great war president and Davis was a mediocre one. The command careers of the two men illustrate perfectly the truth of Clausewitz' dictum that an acquaintance with military affairs is not the principal qualification for a director of war but that "a remarkable, superior mind and strength of character" are more important.

We cannot pause here to measure Davis' defects as a political leader of his people, intriguing though such an analysis of this sincere and tormented man would be. But certainly the weaknesses that he displayed—his excessive pride, his sensitivity to criticism, his impatience of contradiction, his lack of passion for anything, even for the South— detracted from his effectiveness as President and contributed to the final defeat of the Southern cause. We are concerned with his qualities as a war director, and we are obliged to note that in this area he failed as surely as he did in the political sphere.

He failed because he did not seem to realize what his task was or what his proper functions were. He could not grasp the vital fact that the Confederacy was not a going, recognized government but a revolution and that, in order to win, it would have to act with remorseless revolutionary vigor. Always he proceeded on the theory that the Confederacy was a permanent government and could act like older established governments, and always he observed every nicety of legal punctilio and tied himself up in every possible piece of red tape. Because of his military background, he fancied himself a military expert; he would rather have been a general than the head of state. Somebody in our own times has quipped that Davis learned enough about war in a few minutes at Buena Vista in the Mexican War to defeat the South; and during the war Richmond wags, referring to Davis' boasting about a formation he had led at Buena Vista, said that the Confederacy was dying of an inverted V. His image of himself being what it was, he concerned himself overly much with military affairs. The criticism here is not that he interfered with his generals—this point will be discussed later—but that he spent too much time on unimportant routine items, on matters that he should have left to subordinates. Once he even proposed to go through 1,500 documents bearing on promotions high and low. He could not delegate authority to people he knew were not as competent as he. Because he was a capable administrator, he loved to do the administrating himself. He has been an outstanding Secretary of War, but as President he rarely rose above the secretarial level.

Nor can we take time to analyze the qualities that made Lincoln a great war President. They are so well known, perhaps, that they do not need repetition. We may note two factors, however, that reveal something of his concept of the role of commander-in-chief and that help to explain his success as a war director. First, Lincoln was, in a technical sense, a poor administrator. Unlike Davis, who spent much time in his office, Lincoln was rarely in his office. He was often to be found in the offices of other people, generals and secretaries, ostensibly visiting around and telling stories, but really sizing up subordinates and deciding whether he could delegate authority to them. When he found a man whom he could trust to do a job, Lincoln was quite willing to let him handle the details of his office. In short, he was interested in the big administrative picture, and he did not, if he could avoid it, burden himself with petty routine—all of which means that he understood perfectly his function and the proper function of administration (or if he did not understand good administration, he intuitively practiced it). Second, Lincoln realized immediately that the war was a revolution, and he dealt with it on that basis. Whenever he felt that revolutionary methods were necessary to attain the objectives of Union policy, he used them, even to the length of violating law or the Constitution. He was not, he explained, going to see the government and the nation go to smash because of a squeamish regard for legal niceties. It is a curious fact that Lincoln, who headed an established government, acted with more revolutionary zeal than Davis, who led an experimental government.

As a director of war Lincoln displayed, almost from the beginning, a fine strategic sense. He was a better natural strategist than were most of his generals who were trained soldiers. Grasping the importance of economic warfare, he proclaimed a naval blockade of the South. Realizing that numbers were on his side, he called for 400,000 volunteers in 1861. Almost immediately he understood one of the great all-time strategic maxims, which his first generals seem never to have heard of, and applied it to his war: the proper objective of Union armies, he insisted, was the destruction of Confederate armies and not the occupation of Southern territory. Knowing the advantage that superior forces gave the North, he disregarded the traditional Jomini doctrine of concentrating at one point, and showing a startling originality in his strategic thinking, he urged his commanders to keep up a constant pressure on the whole strategic line of the Confederacy until a weak spot was found and a breakthrough could be made. Always, always, he prodded the generals to move, to execute an offensive strategy.

Both Lincoln and Davis have been criticized by historians and military writers for "interfering" with generals and military affairs. Most of these strictures seem misinformed. Judged by modern standards both presidents did some things that a civil director of war should not do. But it must be emphasized that they were operating without benefit of a formal command system, that they executed functions which, in the organization then existing, could have been performed by no other agency. Moreover, if the caliber of many of the generals, the so-called trained experts, is carefully measured, it is evident that the presidents were often justified in the supervision they exerted. Particularly for the Union cause, as will be demonstrated later, it was fortunate that Lincoln called his generals to account. But the vital point about such "interfering" is the purpose for which the war director intervenes—the strategic objective he is trying to accomplish. If the strategy is sound and if the director of war is a man of "a remarkable, superior mind," the results of his intervention will be generally good. Lincoln interfered to make a sound offensive strategy stronger, and Davis interfered to make a defective defensive strategy more defensive. One acted from a valid theory and the other from a faulty one. . . .

VII

Although Lincoln wielded his great powers as war director with a certainty that came from ever growing confidence, he was willing, as he had always indicated, to yield those powers to a general who was competent and willing to exercise them. By 1864 he had found his man—and Congress and the nation ratified the choice—in U. S. Grant, who in the

West had emerged as the greatest Union general of the war. In February Congress created the rank of lieutenant general, expressing a wish that Grant would receive the grade and the position of General-in-Chief, and Lincoln unhesitatingly named Grant to both. At last the United States was about to get a modern command system.

In the system arrived at in 1864, which was the joint product of Lincoln, Grant, and maybe of Halleck, Grant as general-in-chief was charged with the functions of framing over-all Union strategy and directing the movements of all Federal armies. As commanding general, Grant might have been expected to establish his command post in Washington, where he would be near the President and in quick contact with Federal field generals all over the country. But Grant disliked the political atmosphere of the capital, and he set up his headquarters with the Army of the Potomac in the field. He was always close to Washington, which he could reach in a short train trip, and he was in almost instant telegraphic communication with the President. Technically, Grant did not become commander of the Eastern field army—Meade continued to hold that position—but since he traveled with that army, it was subject to his close supervision.

Under the new arrangement Halleck received a new command office, the Chief of Staff. Again, as when we dealt with the nature of the General Staff, we must avoid confusion between nineteenth-century and contemporary usages of the same term. Halleck was not a chief of staff in the modern sense. In the present command system his position would correspond perhaps to the Secretary of the General Staff. Primarily he was a channel of communication between Lincoln and Grant and between Grant and the seventeen departmental commanders under the general-in-chief. Grant sent most of his dispatches for the President to Halleck, who, when necessary, briefed or explained them for Lincoln. Similarly, Halleck transmitted to Grant many of Lincoln's directives or inquiries concerning strategic matters. Because of Halleck's facility in the languages of both soldier and civilian, Lincoln and Grant never misunderstood each other, as Lincoln and McClellan so often had.

Halleck also served as a liaison between Grant and the department and field commanders. If Grant had had to read all the reports from these officers and frame detailed instructions for them, he would not have had much time for strategic planning. At Grant's direction, the subordinate commanders sent their dispatches for Grant to Halleck, who either transmitted them to the general-in-chief or summarized their contents for him. Grant sent most of his orders to subordinates through Halleck. Often he would tell the chief of staff in general terms what he wanted done and ask him to put the objective in a written directive, or he would delegate authority to Halleck to handle a particular situation. Although Halleck professed to think that his role in the command system was insignificant, it was really vitally important. Without such a coordinator of information the system would not have worked as brilliantly as it did.

But the key military man in the system was Grant. As general-in-chief, he proved to be the general for whom Lincoln had been searching. And because the President came to realize Grant's capacities, he gave him more latitude in determining strategy than he had permitted McClellan or Halleck. To a man who asked whether Grant did not have too much freedom of decision, Lincoln said, "Do you hire a man to do your work and then do it yourself?" Grant possessed the rare ability to see the war as a total picture and to devise what in later wars would be called "global" strategy. In fact, he was probably the only general on either side who could envision the war as a whole, the only one who was qualified to act as general-in-chief in a modern war. This is not the place to discuss his plan of grand operations for 1864, but it was a brilliant demonstration of strategic thinking and would do credit to the most finished student of a series of modern staff and command schools. Un-hampered by traditional military doctrine Grant was boldly original in innovating new strategic concepts. A young officer once asked him what he thought of Jomini. Grant said he had never read the French-Swiss master, the guiding authority for so many other Civil War generals. He then expressed his own theory of war: "The art of war is simple enough. Find out where your enemy is. Get at him as soon as you can. Strike at him hard as you can, and keep moving on."

It is not true, however, as Grant stated in his memoirs and as many historians have repeated since, that Lincoln gave him an absolutely free hand in deciding strategy and directing operations. According to Grant's account, the President was a military innocent who greeted him with relief when he came to Washington and said, in effect: General, I am not a military man, I don't understand war and don't want to know your plans—go ahead and do exactly as you please. Grant wrote under the influence of his own postwar myth, which cast him in the image of the great soldier who was the architect of victory. Actually, as the evidence in contemporary war documents amply demonstrates, Lincoln, while per-mitting his general-in-chief wide latitude of action, watched him closely and never hesitated to check him when the need arose. On at least two occasions, as when he forced Grant to come to Washington to supervise personally the launching of the campaign against Jubal Early in the Shenandoah Valley and when he restrained him from removing General George H. Thomas before the battle of Nashville, he saved the general from serious mistakes.

Moreover, as the documents again show, the victorious strategy of the North was the joint product of consultations between Lincoln and Grant. The general submitted to Lincoln the broad outlines of his plans, and the President, approving the objectives and trusting Grant, did not seek to learn the details. Indeed, Grant made his strategy conform to the strategy Lincoln had been advocating since 1862: make enemy armies the objective and move all Federal forces against the enemy line simultaneously so as to bring into play the Federal advantage of superior numbers. An offensive all along the line, violating the Jomini maxim of concentration, was the essence of Grant's strategy. When Grant explained to Lincoln this plan, so eminently sensible for the side with the greater numbers and the superior transportation, he remarked that those forces not fighting could still help the fighting by advancing. Grasping the point and recognizing the application of his own ideas, the President uttered a maxim of his own, one that for modern war was more valid than most of Jomini's dictums: "Those not skinning can hold a leg."

The 1864 command system was a major factor in the final victory of the North. By providing a sound basis for participation by the civil and military branches in the formulating of strategy, it gave the United States a modern command organization for a modern war. With a commander-in-chief to state policy and the general objectives of strategy, a general-in-chief to put the strategy in specific form, and a chief of staff to coordinate information, the United States possessed a model system of civil and military relationships and the finest command arrangements of any country in the world. Created in the strain of war, it expressed the national genius to improvise an arrangement to fit the requirements of the moment. The American system was superior to most command organizations then existing in Europe and was at least as good as the Prussian general staff machine. Indeed, it was probably the most efficient system that we have ever had.

CHAPTER 41

THE AMERICAN CHARACTER

The very title of the next reading—"What then is the American, this new man?"—is significant in a discussion of the American character. From colonial times to the present, both Americans and Europeans have been intrigued about the nature of Americans, but on one thing nearly all commentators have agreed—the American was a new man. He was not a European; neither was he fundamentally a person with regional or local identification. Despite real and persistent differences among themselves Americans were more similar to each other than dissimilar and possessed a distinctive national character.

In this selection, Arthur M. Schlesinger, Sr., suggests that the American character was produced by the interplay of Old World influences and New World conditions. Professor Schlesinger discusses the development of the American character in light of the specific European heritage that was transplanted to America and the ways in which that heritage underwent change. Schlesinger identifies four basic elements, about which are clustered numerous additional attributes, as the bases of American character. It should be noted that in this excerpt the author focuses upon pre-Civil War America; in an omitted section he discusses the changes in the national pattern produced by the rise of urbanization and industrialization after 1860.

In reading this essay the student should concentrate on defining the American character and on identifying the factors most important in shaping this "new man." Do you agree with Schlesinger's suggestion that Americans can explore the American character more deeply and meaningfully than "outsiders" generally can? In view of the unrest and dislocation in American society in recent history, does there still exist a national character? If so, is the national character still distinctive? How does the character of Americans today differ from the American character as defined by Schlesinger? Finally, do the enduring qualities of the national character pinpointed by the author in the last paragraph of this selection still endure?

A great deal of work has been done in this area. A good place to begin is Michael McGiffert, *The Character of Americans: A Book of Readings** (1964). Two indispensable monographs are David M. Potter, *People of Plenty: Economic Abundance and the American Character** (1954), and David Riesman (in collaboration with Reuel Denney and Nathan Glazer), *The Lonely Crowd: A Study of the Changing American Character** (1950). The two volumes of Daniel J. Boorstin's study of the national "personality," *The Americans: The Colonial Experience** (1958), and *The Americans: The National Experience** (1964), are extraordinarily provocative and valuable.

* Available in a paperback edition.

"WHAT THEN IS THE AMERICAN, THIS NEW MAN?"

ARTHUR M. SCHLESINGER, SR.

THE question which forms the title of this essay has never ceased to arouse interest since Crèvecœur posed it in the last years of the Revolution. If we can learn why the American has come to be what he is, how he reacts instinctively to life, wherein he differs from other peoples, we shall have gained a deep insight into the springs of national behavior. Crèvecœur's own answer, the considered opinion of a Frenchman long resident in the New World, may still be read with profit. The American, he said, "is either an European, or the descendant of an European, hence that strange mixture of blood which you will find in no other country. . . . *He* is an American, who leaving behind him all his ancient prejudices and manners, receives new ones from the new mode of life he has embraced, the new government he obeys, and the new rank he holds. . . . From involuntary idleness, servile dependence, penury, and useless labour, he has passed to toils of a very different nature. — This is an American."

I

Crèvecœur, of course, was one of a long procession of Europeans who have tried to describe and appraise the American. Their writings, though of varying merit, possess the common advantage of presenting an outsider's point of view, free from the predilections and prepossessions which blur the American's vision of himself. Viewing the scene from a different background, they are also sensitive to national divergences of which the nativeborn are usually unaware. Though bias may influence the individual observer's judgment, the total number of visitors has been so great as to render far more significant their points of agreement.

The composite portrait that emerges deserves thoughtful consideration. The attributes most frequently noted have been a belief in the universal obligation to work; the urge to move from place to place; a high standard

SOURCE. Arthur M. Schlesinger, Sr., *Paths to the Present,* New York: The Macmillan Company, 1949, pp. 1–21. Copyright 1949 by The Macmillan Company. Reprinted by permission of The Macmillan Company.

of average comfort; faith in progress; the eternal pursuit of material gain; an absence of permanent class barriers; the neglect of abstract thinking and of the aesthetic side of life; boastfulness; a deference for women; the prevalence of spoiled children; the general restlessness and hurry of life, always illustrated by the practice of fast eating; and certain miscellaneous traits such as overheated houses, the vice of spitting and the passion for rocking chairs and ice water.

This inventory, so far as it goes, reveals qualities and attitudes recognizably American. Moreover, the travelers express no doubt as to the existence of a distinctive national character. The native-born looking at their fellow countrymen readily identify them as New Englanders or Middle Westerners or Southerners, as products of old American stock or newcomers of immigrant origin; and they remember that at one period of their history the differences between Northerner and Southerner sharpened into a tragic war. But the detached observer from Europe has always been less impressed by these regional deviations than by the evidences of fundamental kinship, even in slavery times.

James Bryce, most perspicacious of the commentators, goes so far as to say, "Scotchmen and Irishmen are more unlike Englishmen, the native of Normandy more unlike the native of Provence, the Pomeranian more unlike the Wurtemberger, the Piedmontese more unlike the Neapolitan, the Basque more unlike the Andalusian, than the American from any part of the country is to the American from any other part." His conclusion is that "it is rather more difficult to take any assemblage of attributes in any of these European countries and call it the national type than it is to do the like in the United States." The preoccupation of American historians with local and sectional diversities has tended to obscure this underlying reality.

But the particular "assemblage of attributes" recorded by the travelers leaves much to be desired. Not only is the list incomplete, but it carelessly lumps the significant with the trivial. Since the typical European tried to cover as much ground as possible in a short time, his attention was caught by externals, with the result that annoying traits and ways assumed undue importance, much as dust in the eye of a wayfarer distorts the appearance of the landscape. The gospel of work, for example, hardly deserves to be equated with the addiction to spitting. Though the more thoughtful sought to correlate what they noticed with the avowed ideals of the people, they usually lacked sufficient knowledge of the deeper historical trends to grasp either the true import of the ideals or how they manifested themselves in action. Finally, the traveler gave little attention to the crucial problem of why the special combination of qualities and attitudes had become endemic within the borders of the United States.

Hence the judgment of these onlookers, though often clearsighted and frequently valuable as a corrective, leaves ample room for the student of United States history to venture an answer to Crèvecœur's question. If the native-born historian be suspect as a party in interest, he may at least strive to observe that counsel of objectivity which his professional conscience reveres.

II

What then is the American from a historian's point of view? The answer, briefly expressed, is so simple as to be a platitude. This "new man" is the product of the interplay of Old World influences and New World conditions. But just what heritage did the colonists bring with them from Europe, and why and how was it changed? Predominantly it involved that part of Europe's social experience in which they themselves had shared. The great bulk of the settlers, like the immigrants of later times, belonged to the poorer classes. They and their ancestors, whether in England or on the Continent, had been artisans, small tradesmen, farmers, day laborers—the broad foundation which supported the fine super-structure of European civilization. Shut out from a life of wealth, leisure and aesthetic enjoyment, they had tended to regard the ways of their social superiors with misgiving, if not resentment, and by the same token they magnified their own qualities of sobriety, diligence and thrift. Even when many of them, as notably in England, improved their economic position in the sixteenth and seventeenth centuries as a result of the great growth of commerce and industry, they continued to exalt the ancient proprieties.

This attitude found its classic spiritual expression in Calvinism. As Professor Tawney has said, Calvinism was "perhaps the first systematic body of religious teaching which can be said to recognize and applaud the economic virtues." It neatly fitted the glove of divine sanction to the hand of prudential conduct, thereby giving a sense of personal rectitude to the business of getting ahead in the world. But whether in Britain or elsewhere, whether in the religious groups directly concerned or those more remotely affected, Calvinism merely intensified a pre-existing bent. It is similarly true that the stringent code of morals often attributed to Calvinism, and more particularly to the Puritans, represented a lower-middle-class mentality long antedating the Geneva teachings.

This, then, was the type of humanity upon which the untamed New World wielded its influence. It has often been observed that plants and animals undergo modification when removed to America. These mutations arise from differences in climate and geography. But other factors as well affected transplanted people. One was the temperament of the settler, the fact that he was more adventurous, more ambitious or more rebellious against conditions at home than his fellows. It is not necessary to believe with William Stoughton in 1670 that "God sifted a whole Nation that he might send Choice Grain over into this Wilderness," but undoubtedly the act of quitting a familiar existence for a strange and perilous one demanded uncommon attributes of hardihood, self-reliance and imagination. Once the ocean was crossed, sheer distance from the old country and the challenge of new experiences further weakened the bonds of custom, evoked latent capacities and awakened the settler to possibilities of improvement hitherto unsuspected.

The undeveloped continent prescribed the conditions of living the new life, the mold within which the American character took shape. Farming was the primary occupation. At first resorted to to keep from starvation, it quickly became the mainstay of existence. The Revolution was fought by a people of whom nineteen out of twenty tilled the soil. With good land obtainable for more than a century after Independence, agriculture continued, though with gradually diminishing effect, to provide the pervasive atmosphere of American life and thought. "The vast majority of the people of this country live by the land, and carry its quality in their manners and opinions," wrote Ralph Waldo Emerson in 1844. Even when the hosts from Continental Europe began to swell the population after the middle of the nineteenth century, the rural temper of the nation remained pretty much unaltered, for many of the immigrants also turned to farming. This long apprenticeship to the soil made an indelible impress on the developing American character, with results which the modern age of the city has not wholly effaced.

Agriculture in the New World, however, differed from agriculture in the Old. This was the initial lesson which the colonists were compelled to learn. Those who had been farmers in their homelands found many of the traditional methods unsuitable. Those who had worked at urban occupations suffered an even greater handicap. Densely forested land must be cleared; the wildness taken out of the soil; a knowledge gained of indigenous plants and of the best means of growing them. The settlers of Jamestown were barely able to struggle through the early years. "There were never Englishmen left in a forreigne Country in such miserie as wee," wrote one of them. "Unsufferable hunger" caused them to eat horses, dogs, rats and snakes, and instances even of cannibalism are recorded. As is well known, the Plymouth colonists experienced similar trials. Yet in both cases the woods abounded with native fruits, berries, roots and nuts, game was plentiful, and near-by waters teemed with fish.

Had these courageous men been more readily adaptable, they could have enjoyed a gastronomic abundance beyond the dreams of the wealthiest classes at home. But they had never faced such an experience before, and reversion to a stage of civilization which the white man had long since outgrown was not easy. At the very first, all the early settlements actually imported food supplies; the Swedish colony on the Delaware did so for twenty years. A knowledge of self-sufficient farming came slowly and painfully, with untold numbers of men, women and children perishing in the process. In the long run, however, the settlers learned how to master their environment. Utilizing native crops and Indian methods of tillage, they abandoned the intensive cultivation required by the limited land resources of the Old World. It was simpler to move on to new fields when the fertility of the old was exhausted. The typical farm was a small one, worked by the owner and his family. Even when the system of staple production developed in the South, the small independent farmers considerably outnumbered the great slaveholding planters.

Though the colonial agriculturalist owed much to the savage, he had no wish to live like one. Accustomed in the old country to simple comforts and mechanical devices in the home and about the farm, he duplicated them in the wilderness. Every husbandman became a manufacturer and every farmhouse a small factory, producing flour, soap and candles, tanning skins, preparing the winter's meat supply, making nails, harness, hats, shoes and rugs, contriving tools, churns, casks, beds, chairs and tables. Such activities he supplemented with trapping, hunting and fishing. As cold weather closed in, he used his spare time getting out rough timber products, such as shingles and planks, or spent the long evenings before the open fireplace carving gunstocks or making brooms while his womenfolk knitted, spun or wove.

Under pressure of circumstances the farmer thus became a Jack-of-all-trades. As Chancellor Livingston wrote, "being habituated from early life to rely upon himself he acquires a skill in every branch of his profession, which is unknown in countries where labour is more divided." Take the case of a typical New Englander, John Marshall of Braintree, early in the eighteenth century. Besides tending his farm, he bought and sold hogs, was a painter, brickmaker and carpenter, turning out as many as three hundred laths in a day, and served as a precinct constable. The primitive state of society fostered a similar omnicompetence in other walks of life, as the career of Benjamin Franklin so well exemplifies. Lord Cornbury, the governor of New York, characterized Francis Makemie as "a Preacher, a Doctor of Physick, a Merchant, an Attorney, or Counsellor at Law, and," he ruefully added, "which is worse of all, a Disturber of Governments."

The pioneer farmer of later times was the colonial farmer reborn. Up and down the Mississippi Valley he faced the same difficulties and opportunities as his forefathers, and he dealt with them in much the same way. As time went on, to be sure, he managed to buy more and more of his tools and household conveniences. He also took advantage of new inventions like the iron plow and the reaper, while increasingly he raised crops for sale in a general market. Meanwhile along the Atlantic Seaboard similar changes occurred. But whether in the older or newer communities these innovations affected the surface rather than the substance of the traditional mode of life. Nor did the advent of cities at first do much to alter the situation. Mere islands in a sea of forests and farms, they long retained marked rural characteristics and depended for a large part of their growth on continued accessions from the countryside.

III

What elements of the national character are attributable to this long-time agrarian environment? First and foremost is the habit of work. For the colonial farmer ceaseless striving constituted the price of survival; every member of the community must be up and doing. When anyone failed to do his part, the authorities, whether Puritan, Anglican or otherwise, laid a heavy hand upon the culprit. The Virginia Assembly in 1619 ordered the slothful to be bound over to compulsory labor. A few years later the Massachusetts Bay Company instructed Governor John Endecott that "noe idle drone bee permitted to live amongst us," and the General Court followed this up in 1633 with a decree that "noe prson, howse houlder or othr, shall spend his time idlely or unproffitably, under paine of such punishmt as the Court shall thinke meete to inflicte." Such regulations had long existed in England, where it was hoped, vainly, they might combat the unemployment and vagrancy of a surplus laboring class; in America the object was to overcome a labor shortage—that exigent problem of every new country. Of course, most of the settlers, having been inured to toil in the homeland, needed no official prodding.

They were the hardest-working people on earth, their only respite being afforded by strict observance of the Sabbath as demanded by both church and state.

The tradition of toil so begun found new sustenance as settlers opened up the boundless stretches of the interior. "In the free States," wrote Harriet Martineau in 1837, "labour is more really and heartily honoured than, perhaps, in any other part of the civilised world." Alonzo Potter voiced the general opinion of the American people when he asserted a few years later, "Without a definite pursuit, a man is an excrescence on society. . . . In isolating himself from the cares and employments of other men, he forfeits much of their sympathy, and can neither give nor receive great benefit." Even when the usual motives for work did not exist, the social compulsion remained. As William Ellery Channing put it, "The rich man has no more right to repose than the poor," for nobody should so live as to "throw all toil on another class of society."

One source of Northern antagonism to the system of human bondage was the fear that it was jeopardizing this basic tenet of the American creed. "Wherever labor is mainly performed by slaves," Daniel Webster told the United States Senate, "it is regarded as degrading to freemen"; and Kentucky abolitionist David Rice pointed out that in the South "To labour, is to *slave;* to work, is *to work like a Negroe.*" After the Civil War, General W. T. Sherman found public occasion to thank God that now at long last Southern whites would have "to earn an honest living."

Probably no legacy from our farmer forebears has entered more deeply into the national psychology. If an American has no purposeful work on hand, the fever in his blood impels him nevertheless to some visible form of activity. When seated he keeps moving in a rocking chair. A European visitor in the 1890's saw more fact than fancy in a magazine caricature which pictured a foreigner as saying to his American hostess, "It's a defect in your country, that you have no leisured classes." "But we have them," she replied, "only we call them tramps." The traveler's own comment was: "America is the only country in the world, where one is ashamed of having nothing to do."

This worship of work has made it difficult for Americans to learn how to play. As Poor Richard saw it, "Leisure is the Time for doing something useful"; and James Russell Lowell confessed,

> Pleasure doos make us Yankees kind o'winch,
> Ez though 't wuz sunthin' paid for by the inch;
> But yit we du contrive to worry thru,
> Ef Dooty tells us thet the thing's to du.

The first mitigations of the daily grind took the form of hunting, fishing, barn-raisings and logrollings—activities that had no social stigma because they contributed to the basic needs of living. As the years went on, the great Southern planters, imitating the landed gentry in England, developed rural diversions of elaborate sort; but their example, like that of the fashionable circles in the Northern cities, merely made the common man all the more self-conscious when he turned to recreation. Nor did the mid-nineteenth-century German and Irish immigrants, who indulged in spontaneous enjoyments when the day was over, have any other effect upon the native stock than to reinforce suspicions of the newcomers formed on other grounds. "The American," wrote the New Yorker, Henry T. Tuckerman, in 1857, "enters into festivity as if it were a serious business." And a serious business it has in considerable degree continued to be ever since.

Into it goes all the fierce energy that once felled the forests and broke the prairies. Americans play games not for fun but to win. They attend social gatherings grimly determined to have a "good time." Maxim Gorky said of Coney Island, "What an unhappy people it must be that turns for happiness here." The "rich gift of extemporizing pleasures," of taking leisure leisurely, seems alien to the national temper. It is significant that the English *Who's Who* includes the recreations of the notables listed, while the American does not.

The importance attached to useful work had the further effect of helping to make "this new man" indifferent to aesthetic considerations. To the farmer a tree was not a thing of beauty and a joy forever, but an obstacle to be replaced as quickly as possible with a patch of corn. In the words of an eighteenth-century American, "The Plow-man that raiseth Grain is more serviceable to Mankind, than the Painter who draws only to please the Eye. The Carpenter who builds a good House to defend us from the Wind and Weather, is more serviceable than the curious Carver, who employs his Art to please the Fancy." The cult of beauty, in other words, had nothing to contribute to the stern business of living; it wasn't "practical." The bias thus given to the national mentality lasted well into America's urban age. One result has been the architectural monotony and ugliness which have invariably offended travelers used to the picturesque charm of Old World cities.

IV

On the other hand, the complicated nature of the farmer's job, especially during the first two and a half centuries, afforded an unexcelled training in mechanical ingenuity. These ex-Europeans and their descendants became a race of whittlers and tinkers, daily engaged in devising, improving and repairing tools and other utensils until, as Emerson said, they had "the power and habit of invention in their brain." "Would any one but an American," asked one of Emerson's contemporaries, "have ever invented a milking machine? or a machine to beat eggs? or machines to black boots, scour knives, pare apples, and do a hundred things that all other peoples have done with their ten fingers from time immemorial?"

As population increased and manufacturing developed on a commercial scale, men merely turned to new purposes the skills and aptitudes that had become second nature to them. Thus Eli Whitney, who as a Massachusetts farm youth had made nails and hatpins for sale to his neighbors, later contrived the cotton gin and successfully applied the principle of interchangeable parts to the production of muskets; and Theodore T. Woodruff, a New York farm boy, won subsequent fame as the inventor of a sleeping car, a coffee-hulling machine and a steam plow. In this manner another trait became imbedded in the American character.

The farmer's success in coping with his multitudinous tasks aroused a pride of accomplishment that made him scorn the specialist or expert. As a Jack-of-all-trades he was content to be master of none, choosing to do many things well enough rather than anything supremely well. Accordingly, versatility became another outstanding American attribute. In public affairs the common man agreed with President Jackson that any intelligent citizen could discharge the duties of any governmental office. He had an abiding suspicion of the theorist or the "scholar in politics," preferring to trust his own quick perceptions and to deal from day to day with matters as they arose. In his breadwinning pursuits the American flitted freely from job to job in marked contrast to the European custom of following occupations which often descended from father to son.

The most casual scrutiny of the *Dictionary of American Biography* discloses countless instances reminiscent of John Marshall and Francis Makemie in colonial times. Thomas Buchanan Read, born on a Pennsylvania farm, was in turn a tailor's apprentice, grocer's assistant, cigar maker, tombstone carver, sign painter and actor before he became a portrait painter, novelist and poet. Another personage is listed as "ornithologist and wholesale druggist"; another as "preacher, railway president, author"; and still another as "physician, merchant, political leader, magazine editor, poet, and critic." The wonder is that, despite such a squandering of energies, they could yet gain sufficient distinction in any phase of their activities to be recalled by posterity.

Even in his principal occupation of growing food, the farmer encountered harsh criticism from foreign observers because of the way he wore out the land, neglected livestock and destroyed forest resources. But Old World agriculture rested on a ratio of man to land which in the New World was the reverse. It was as logical for the American farmer to "mine" the soil and move on to a virgin tract as it was for the European peasant to husband his few acres in the interest of generations unborn. Not till the opening years of the twentieth century, when the pressure of population dramatized the evils of past misuse, did the conservation of natural resources become a set national policy.

Meanwhile the tradition of wasteful living, bred by an environment of plenty, had fastened itself upon the American character, disposing men to condone extravagance in public as well as in private life. Even governmental corruption could be winked at on the ground that a wealthy country like the United States could afford it. In their daily living, Americans were improvident of riches that another people would have carefully preserved. One newcomer from England in the early nineteenth century wrote that the apples and peaches rotting in Ohio orchards were more "than would sink the British fleet." Another said of her neighbors that she wished "the poor people of England had the leavings of their tables, that goes to their dogs and hogs." A great national emergency like that of the Axis war reveals the extent to which the practice still prevails. People learned that, by responding to the government's appeal to salvage kitchen fats, old iron and other materials usually discarded, they could make a substantial contribution to the war effort.

Toward women the American male early acquired an attitude which sharply distinguished him from his brother in the Old World. As in every new country, women had a high scarcity value, both in the colonies and later in the pioneer West. They were in demand not only as sweethearts and wives, but also because of their economic importance, for they performed the endless work about the house and helped with the heavy farm labor. "The cry is everywhere for girls; girls, and more girls!" wrote a traveler in 1866. He noted that men outnumbered women in thirty-eight of the forty-five states and territories. In California the proportion was three to one; in Colorado, twenty to one. "Guess my husband's got to look after me, and make himself agreeable to me, if he can," a pretty Western girl remarked—"if he don't, there's plenty will." In the circumstances men paid women a deference and accorded them a status unknown in older societies. European observers attributed the high standard of sex morals largely to this fact, and it is significant that the most rapid strides toward equal suffrage took place in those commonwealths whose rural characteristics were strongest.

V

Since the agriculturalist regarded his farm as only a temporary abode —an investment rather than a home—he soon contracted the habit of being "permanently transitory." Distances that would have daunted the stoutest-hearted European deterred "this new man" not at all. Many an Atlantic Coast family migrated from place to place across the continent until the second or third generation reached the rim of the Pacific, then the next one began the journey back. "In no State of the Union," wrote James Bryce in 1888, "is the bulk of the population so fixed in its residence as everywhere in Europe; in many it is almost nomadic."

But for this constant mingling of people and ideas the spirit of sectionalism would have opened far deeper fissures in American society than it did, for the breadth of the land, the regional diversification of economic interests and the concentration of European immigrants in certain areas were all factors conducive to disaffection and disunity. Apart from the crisis of 1861, however, it has always been possible to adjust sectional differences peaceably. The war between North and South might itself have been avoided if the system of slave labor had not increasingly stopped the inflow of persons from other parts of the country as well as from Europe. Denied such infusions of new blood, the Southerners lived more and more to themselves, came to exalt their peculiarities over the traits they had in common with their fellow countrymen and, in the end, determined to establish an independent state.

As the nation grew older and its institutions took on a more settled aspect, the locomotive tendencies of the Americans showed no signs of abatement. . . .

Geographic or horizontal mobility, however, was a less fundamental aspect of American life than social or vertical mobility, though the two were not unrelated. The European conception of a graded society, with each class everlastingly performing its allotted function, vanished quickly amidst primitive surroundings that invited the humblest to move upward as well as outward. Instead of everybody being nobody, they found that anybody might become somebody. In the language of James Russell Lowell, "Here, on the edge of the forest, where civilized man was brought face to face again with nature and taught mainly to rely on himself, mere manhood became a fact of prime importance." This emancipation from hoary custom was "no bantling of theory, no fruit of forethought," but "a gift of the sky and of the forest."

Accordingly, there arose the ingrained belief in equality of opportunity, the right of all men to a free and fair start—a view which in one of its most significant ramifications led to the establishment of free tax-supported schools. This was far from being a dogma of enforced equality. To benefit from equality of opportunity a man must be equal to his opportunities, with the government serving principally as an umpire to supervise the game with a minimum of rules. The upshot was a conception of democracy rigorously qualified by individualism.

This individualistic bias sometimes assumed forms that defied government. The colonists in their relations with the mother country evaded unwelcome regulations and, prompted by their theologians and lawyers, insisted that acts of Parliament contrary to their "unalienable rights" were void. Within the colonies those who dwelt remote from centers of law and order adopted a like attitude toward the provincial authorities. The Scotch-Irish who illegally occupied Pennsylvania soil in the early eighteenth century contended "it was against the laws of God and nature, that so much land should be idle while so many Christians wanted it to labor on and to raise their bread." As a substitute for constituted authority the settlers sometimes created their own unofficial tribunals, which adjudicated property titles and punished offenders against the public peace. In other instances they resorted to the swifter retribution of individual gunplay, or of mob action and lynch law, for from taking the law into one's hands when it could not function it was but a step to taking the law into one's hands when it did not function as one wanted it to.

The tendency to violence so generated has continued to condition the national mentality to the present time. Thoreau, the great philosopher of individualism, knew of no reason why a citizen should "ever for a moment, or in the least degree, resign his conscience to the legislator," declaring that "we should be men first, and subjects afterward." A similar conviction undoubtedly inspired William H. Seward's flaming declaration to the proslavery Senators in 1850 that "there is a higher law than the Constitution," just as it actuated the thousands of churchgoing Northerners who secretly banded together to violate the Fugitive Slave Act. But generally it has been self-interest or convenience, rather than conscience, that has provided the incentive to lawbreaking, as in the case of the businessman chafing against legislative restrictions or of the motorist disobeying traffic regulations. Sometimes the attitude has paraded under such high-sounding names as states' rights and nullification. This lawless streak in the American character has often been directed to wrong purposes, but it has also served as a check on the abuse of governmental powers and as a safeguard of minority rights.

In still another aspect, the individualism of the pioneer farmer does much to explain the intense cultivation of the acquisitive spirit. In the absence of hereditary distinctions of birth and rank the piling up of wealth constituted the most obvious badge of social superiority, and once the process was begun, the inbred urge to keep on working made it difficult to stop. "The poor struggle to be rich, the rich to be richer," remarked an onlooker in the mid-nineteenth century. Thanks to equality of opportunity with plenty for all, the class struggle in America has consisted in the struggle to climb out of one class into a higher one. The zest of competition frequently led to sharp trading, fraud and chicanery, but in the popular mind guilt attached less to the practices than to being caught at them. Financial success was accepted as the highest success, and not till the twentieth century did a religious leader venture to advance the un-American doctrine that ill-gotten wealth was "tainted money," even when devoted to benevolent uses.

VI

It would be a mistake, however, to think of the American simply as a mechanism set in motion by dropping a coin in the slot. When President Coolidge made his famous remark, "The business of America is business," he quite properly added, "The chief ideal of the American people is idealism. I cannot repeat too often that America is a nation of idealists." This ambivalence puzzled foreign commentators, who found it difficult, for example, to reconcile worship of the Almighty Dollar with the equally universal tendency to spend freely and give money away. In contrast to Europe, America has had practically no misers, and one consequence of the winning of Independence was the abolition of primogeniture and entail. Harriet Martineau was among those who concluded that "the eager pursuit of wealth does not necessarily indicate a love of wealth for its own sake."

The fact is that, for a people who recalled how hungry and oppressed their ancestors had been through long centuries in the Old World, the chance to make money was like the sunlight at the end of a tunnel. It was the means of living a life of human dignity. It was a symbol of idealism rather than materialism. Hence "this new man" had an instinctive sympathy for the underdog, and even persons of moderate substance freely shared it with the less fortunate, helping to endow charities, schools, hospitals and art galleries and to nourish humanitarian undertakings which might otherwise have died a-borning.

The energy that entered into many of these causes was heightened by another national attitude: optimism. It was this quality that sustained the European men and women who with heavy hearts left ancestral homes to try their fortunes in a wild and faroff continent. The same trait animated the pioneer farmers confronted by the hardships, loneliness and terrors of the primeval forest, and served also to spur their successors who, though facing less dire conditions, were constantly pitted against both the uncertainties of the weather and the unpredictable demands of the market. When Thomas Jefferson remarked, "I steer my bark with Hope in the head, leaving Fear astern," he spoke for his compatriots. To doubt the future was to confess oneself a failure since the life history of almost any American documented the opposite view. A belief in progress blossomed spontaneously in such a soil.

If this belief made some men tolerant of present abuses in the confident expectation that time would provide the cure, it fired others with an apostolic zeal to hasten the happy day. As a keen observer in the middle of the last century said of his countrymen, "Americans are sanguine enough to believe that no evil is without a remedy, if they could only find it, and they see no good reason why they should not try to find remedies for all the evils of life." Not even fatalism in religion could long withstand the bracing atmosphere of the New World. This quality of optimism sometimes soared to dizzy heights, impelling men to strive for earthly perfection in communistic societies or to prepare to greet the imminent return of Christ.

It attained its most blatant expression, however, in the national addiction to bragging. At bottom, this habit sprang from pride in a country of vast distances and huge elevations plus an illimitable faith in its possibilities of being great as well as big. The American glorified the future in much the same spirit as the European glorified the past, both tending to exalt what they had the most of. And by a simple transition the American went on to speak of expected events as though they had already happened, being prompted perhaps by an urge to compensate for an inner sense of inferiority. This frame of mind led statesmen to cultivate spread-eagle oratory—a style which the *North American Review* in 1858 defined as "a compound of exaggeration, effrontery, bombast, and extravagance, mixed metaphors, platitudes, defiant threats thrown at the world, and irreverent appeals flung at the Supreme Being."

For the same reason the ordinary citizen resorted to hyperbole. In the thinly settled sections this manner of speech went by the name of tall talk, causing the backwoods to be known as a "paradise of puffers." A Frenchman, however, referred to a national, not a regional, trait when he said Americans seemed loath to admit that Christopher Columbus himself had not been an American, and it was an Easterner writing in an Eastern magazine who soberly averred, "It is easier, say the midwives, to come into this world of America . . . than in any other world extant." In business life this indulgent attitude toward truth lent itself to deliberate attempts to defraud, and made the land speculator with his "lithographed mendacity" the natural forerunner of the dishonest stock promoter of later times. Boastfulness is an attribute of youth which greater national maturity has helped to temper. Still the War Department in its manual of behavior for Yankee soldiers in England during the Axis war thought it prudent to admonish them: "Don't show off or brag or bluster."

This facility for overstatement has lent a distinctive quality to American humor. In the United States humor has never been part of a general gaiety of spirit. It has had to break through a crust of life thick with serious purpose. Hence it has had to be boisterous and bold, delighting in exaggeration, incongruities and farcical effects and reaching a grand climax in the practical joke. Out of a comic mood so induced arose such folk heroes as Mike Fink, Paul Bunyan, Pecos Bill and the myth-embroidered Davy Crockett, whose fabulous exploits flourished in oral tradition long before they were reduced to print. In deference to the national sobriety of temperament the most succesful professional humorists have been those who told their yarns while preserving a decorous gravity of expression. . . .

VIII

Just as the American character has undergone modification in the past, so it will doubtless undergo modincation in the future. Nevertheless, certain of its elements seem so deeply rooted as to withstand the erosion of time and circumstance. Of this order are the qualities that made possible the development of the continent, the building of a democratic society and the continuing concern for the welfare of the underprivileged. These are attributes better suited to peace than to war, yet every great crisis has found the people ready to die for their conception of life so that their children might live it. The American character, whatever its shortcomings, abounds in courage, creative energy and resourcefulness, and is bottomed upon the profound conviction that nothing in the world is beyond its power to accomplish.